APR 1995

Overcoming Law

RICHARD A. POSNER

Overcoming Law

HARVARD UNIVERSITY PRESS

CAMBRIDGE, MASSACHUSETTS, AND LONDON, ENGLAND 1995

Copyright © 1995 by the President and Fellows
  of Harvard College
All rights reserved
Printed in the United States of America

This book is printed on acid-free paper, and its binding
materials have been chosen for strength and durability.

Library of Congress Cataloging-in-Publication Data

Posner, Richard A.
Overcoming law / Richard A. Posner.
  p. cm.
Includes index.
ISBN 0-674-64925-7 (acid-free paper)
1. Jurisprudence. 2. Law—Methodology. I. Title.
K230.P665095 1995
340'.1—dc20   94-12753
CIP

Contents

Preface

"LEGAL THEORY" is the body of systematic thinking about (or bearing closely on) law to which nonlawyers can and do make important contributions, and which lawyers ignore at their peril. My conception of legal theory is broad, sweeping within it matters that might be thought to belong to political or social theory rather than to legal theory. This breadth reflects the broadening of interests that is characteristic of contemporary legal scholarship. We live at a time when economists, like Ronald Coase and Gary Becker, philosophers, like John Rawls and Richard Rorty, and literary critics, like Stanley Fish, are real presences in legal scholarship. So the reader of this book will find, along with chapters on judges, the legal profession, legal scholarship, the Constitution, and the regulation of employment contracts, chapters that deal with sexuality, social constructionism, feminism, rhetoric, institutional economics, political theory, and the depiction of law in literature. Even my forays into topics as remote from the conventional domain of legal theory as the ancestry of Beethoven, feuds in medieval Iceland, child care in ancient Greece, and the education of deaf children have grown out of my professional interests as a judge and legal scholar.

This is a book both *of* and *about* legal theory; the prepositions denote the constructive and the critical aspects of the book, respectively. The Introduction and the chapters in Part One and Part Six are primarily constructive. Through an examination of such topics as the behavior of judges, the effect of the structure of the legal profession on legal thought, the interrelation of law and literature, the economic and philosophical character of legal advocacy and reasoning, the protection of privacy, and the social response to homosexual behavior, these chapters illustrate how I think legal theory should be done. The intermediate parts of the book are primarily critical. Examining representative figures drawn from all points of the ideological and methodological compass—Coase, Rorty, and Rawls, but also Patricia Williams, James Fitzjames Stephen, Robert Bork, John Hart Ely, Morton Horwitz, Catharine MacKinnon, Walter Berns, Martha Minow, and others— these chapters illustrate how I think legal theory, including some forms of pragmatic legal theory, should not be done. Law is rather lacking in a critical tradition, so I offer no apology for devoting so much attention to the criticism of other theorists; and readers of the manuscript of the book have told me (and I believe them) that the critical chapters are the liveliest. It is easier to find the holes in other people's work than to build a durable structure of one's own. But a merely critical approach lacks staying power; and even devastating criticisms fail to devastate when the critic has nothing to offer in the place of the ruins that he wishes to make. I do not attempt a complete work of reconstruction; but even in areas such as constitutional law that are not the subject of a "constructive" chapter, my criticisms have a constructive aspect: they point the way to an alternative approach.

That approach, which I claim has both critical and constructive power, is not, as the reader may be primed to expect, an exclusively economic one. I do not believe that the economist holds all the keys to legal theory. Rather I believe that economics is one of three keys. The others are pragmatism, shorn however of postmodernist excesses, and liberalism, especially that of the classical tradition, of which John Stuart Mill remains the preeminent spokesman. Pragmatism and liberalism, so understood, make a comfortable fit with economics, the three approaches joining to form a powerful beam with which to illuminate theoretical issues in law. My argument is that a taste for fact, a respect for social science, an eclectic curiosity, a desire to be practical, a belief in individualism, and an openness to new perspectives—all interrelated characteristics of a certain kind of pragmatism, alternatively of a certain kind of economics and a certain kind of liberalism—can make legal theory an effective instrument for understanding and improving law, and social institutions generally; for demonstrating the inadequacies of existing legal thought and for putting something better in its place.

Although most of the chapters originated in articles or book reviews, five are published here for the first time (Chapter 18 plus the four chapters in Part Six), as well as the Introduction, which contains the fullest articulation to date of my overall theoretical stance; these six new essays account for more than a quarter of the length of the book. And all the chapters that did begin life in journals have been revised, many of them very extensively, for this book. There is not only much new material in most of them but also much rearranging, rewording, and pruning of old material, and several chapters combine materials from separately published papers. The book is not a potpourri or an encyclopedia. It is meant to be read consecutively.

I have received a great deal of help. For excellent research assistance I thank Benjamin Aller, John Fee, Wesley Kelman, Harry Lind, Richard Madris, Jeffrey Richards, Susan Steinthal, John Wright, and Douglas Y'Barbo. I am indebted to Andrew Abbott, Terence Halliday, and Donald Levine for a stimulating discussion of the sociology of the professions that helped me formulate the thesis of Chapter 1. For major comments on one or more of the chapters in their original form as essays or reviews, I thank Gary Becker, Harold Demsetz, Frank Easterbrook, David Friedman, Donald Gjerdingen, Henry Hansmann, Lynne Henderson, Stephen Holmes, Daniel Klerman, William Landes, Lawrence Lessig, Geoffrey Miller, Martha Nussbaum, Eric Rasmusen, Eva Saks, Pierre Schlag, Jeffrey Stake, and Cass Sunstein. Lessig, Nussbaum, and Sunstein, along with Michael Aronson, Neil Duxbury, William Eskridge, Mary Ann Glendon, Thomas Grey, Sanford Levinson, Frank Michelman, Charlene Posner, and Eric Posner, read the entire manuscript and made many helpful suggestions. Friedman, as well as Paul Campos, Gerhard Casper, David Cohen, Drucilla Cornell, Donald Davidson, Markus Dubber, Ronald Dworkin, Eldon Eisenach, Daniel Farber, Henry Louis Gates Jr., Julius Kirschner, Jane Larson, Donald McCloskey, Bernard Meltzer, Thomas Nagel, Richard Rorty, Brian Simpson, and David Strauss, read and made helpful comments on parts of the manuscript.

Earlier versions of Chapter 1 were given as the 1993 Addison C. Harris Lecture at Indiana University School of Law and at the faculty workshop of Chicago-Kent College of Law. A part of Chapter 2 began as a contribution to a symposium on Civic and Legal Education at Stanford Law School, and other parts as talks at an annual meeting of the Association of American Law Schools. Earlier versions of Chapter 3 were given at a conference at George Mason University School of Law, at an annual meeting of the American Law and Economics Association, and as a Political Economy Lecture at Harvard University.

A version of Chapter 5 was delivered as a talk at the Bill of Rights Bicentennial Conference at the University of Chicago Law School. Chapter 13 originated as a paper delivered at a conference on Hegel and the Law at Cardozo Law School, Chapter 19 as a paper for a symposium on Pragmatism in Law and Society at the University of Southern California Law School, Chapter 21 as a paper for a conference on the new institutional economics held at the Universität des Saarlandes, and Chapter 26 as a paper for a conference at Brown University on Law and Nature. Several chapters, finally, were subjected to the intensive critical scrutiny of the Colloquium in Law, Philosophy, and Political Theory at New York University Law School, organized by Ronald Dworkin and Thomas Nagel. I am indebted to participants in all these sessions for many helpful comments.

Introduction: Pragmatism, Economics, Liberalism

THERE is a story about law, told mainly but not only by adherents of the critical legal studies movement, that goes as follows. Legal thinking in the late nineteenth century in England and the United States was formalistic: law, like mathematics, was understood to be about the relations among concepts rather than about the relations between concepts and reality. The student of geometry does not establish the relation between the square of the hypotenuse of a right-angle triangle and the squares of the two sides by measuring triangular objects. Similarly, to the legal formalist the issue in a contract case involving a reward offered for the return of lost property and claimed by a finder who hadn't known about the offer was not whether enforcing an entitlement to the reward would advance some social goal at an acceptable cost; it was whether unconscious acceptance of an offer was consistent with the concept of a legally enforceable contract. This reifying approach (as distinct from an instrumental one) to legal concepts was, the story continues, overthrown in the 1920s and 1930s by legal realism, the first antiformalist school of academic legal thought. The formalists fought back, in the 1950s with the jurisprudence of "legal process" and, in the following decade and continuing right up to the present, with "law and economics," that is, the application of economics to law. According to the story that I am recounting, law and economics replaces legal conceptualism with economic conceptualism, evaluating legal outcomes by their conformity to economic theory but still keeping well away from facts. The antidote to this conceptualism is pragmatism, the theory (or antitheory) that debunks all pretenses to having constructed a pipeline to the truth and that, along with its twin, postmodernism, underwrites (thus illustrating the antifoundational as foundational) the radical critique of law by feminist jurisprudence, critical legal studies, and critical race theory.

I like the beginning of this story, although I think it exaggerates the formalism of late nineteenth century law. But it jumps the tracks when it reaches legal realism, a much-overblown movement. What is true is that ever since Socrates there have been influential thinkers who were skeptical about the capacity of legal reasoning to deliver something that could reasonably be called "truth." The leading American figure is Oliver Wendell Holmes. Almost everything of merit that the realists said can be found in essays by Holmes or books by Benjamin Cardozo, only more elegantly and incisively expressed than by any of the realists.[1] What the realists added, and bequeathed to the critical legal studies movement, were for the most part crude extensions of Holmes's and Cardozo's thought. To legal realism we owe the worst book ever written by a professor at a major law school—*Woe Unto You, Lawyers!*—in which Fred Rodell of the Yale Law School proposed to make the practice of law a crime and to replace courts by commissions of technical experts whose decisions would be final, including a "Killing Com-

---

1. Holmes's most important essay is "The Path of the Law," 10 *Harvard Law Review* 457 (1897), reprinted in (among other places) *The Essential Holmes: Selections from the Letters, Speeches, Judicial Opinions, and Other Writings of Oliver Wendell Holmes, Jr.* 160 (Richard A. Posner ed. 1992). Cardozo's most important book is *The Nature of the Judicial Process* (1921). "The Path of the Law" is one of several works cited again and again in this book, so to save some space I give the full citations to these frequently cited works in this note only. Besides "The Path of the Law," these works are: Holmes's book *The Common Law* (1881); several of my books—*Law and Literature: A Misunderstood Relation* (1988), *The Problems of Jurisprudence* (1990), *Economic Analysis of Law* (4th ed. 1992), and *Sex and Reason* (1992); and the following judicial decisions: Lochner v. New York, 198 U.S. 45 (1905); Brown v. Board of Education, 347 U.S. 483 (1954); Griswold v. Connecticut, 381 U.S. 479 (1965); Roe v. Wade, 410 U.S. 113 (1973); Bowers v. Hardwick, 478 U.S. 186 (1986). To minimize footnotes—that bane of legal writing—I place page references in the text whenever I am making frequent reference to a particular book or article.

mission to apply its laws about what are now called murder and man-slaughter."[2]

The "crits" worry that the practitioners of law and economics will contest with them the mantle of legal realism. They needn't worry. We economic types have no desire to be pronounced the intellectual heirs of Fred Rodell, or for that matter of William Douglas, Jerome Frank, or Karl Llewellyn. The law and economics movement owes little to legal realism—perhaps nothing beyond the fact that Donald Turner and Guido Calabresi, pioneering figures in the application of economics to law, graduated from the Yale Law School and may have been influenced by the school's legal-realist tradition to examine law from the perspective of another discipline.[3] Although the legal realist Robert Hale anticipated some of the discoveries (inventions?) of law and economics, most modern law and economics scholars were unaware of his work until recently. It is difficult to measure and therefore treacherous to disclaim influence, but, speaking as one who received his legal education at the Harvard Law School between 1959 and 1962, I can attest that to a student the school seemed untouched by legal realism. And none of the legal and economic thinkers who since law school have most shaped my own academic and judicial thinking—Holmes, Coase, Stigler, Becker, Director, and others—was himself a product in whole or part of legal realism.

While disclaiming the bequest of realism, economic analysts of law refuse to go to the other extreme and anoint law and economics the new formalism. Formalism and realism do not divide up the jurisprudential universe between them. One can be skeptical about the claims of traditional lawyers that law is an autonomous discipline deploying cogent tools of inquiry without concluding that law is just politics, that legal rules and doctrines are just smokescreens, that lawyers should be got rid of and legal justice replaced by popular justice. The idea that

2. Rodell, *Woe Unto You, Lawyers!* 176, 182 (1939). The book was reissued in 1957 with a "Foreword to New Edition" in which Rodell stated that he stood by every word in the first edition.

3. Another linkage is conjectured in "The Fire of Truth: A Remembrance of Law and Economics at Chicago, 1932–1970" (Edmund W. Kitch ed.), 26 *Journal of Law and Economics* 163, 166–167 (1983) (introductory remarks by Professor Kitch). The fullest study of the relation between legal realism and modern law and economics is Neil Duxbury, "Law and Economics in America" (unpublished, University of Manchester Faculty of Law, n.d.). His conclusion about the relation coincides with mine.

law stands or falls by its proximity to mathematics is the fallacy shared by Langdellians and many crits. The middle way is pragmatism.

The Pragmatic Approach

I will discuss the relation of pragmatism to legal realism and other movements in legal scholarship later in the book (Chapter 19). For now the important thing is that the reader understand what I mean by the term—which is not what everyone means by it; there is no canonical concept of pragmatism. I mean, to begin with, an approach that is practical and instrumental rather than essentialist—interested in what works and what is useful rather than in what "really" is. It is therefore *forward-looking*, valuing continuity with the past only so far as such continuity can help us cope with the problems of the present and of the future. "We create the past from a sense of what can be done in the present."[4] The pragmatist remembers Santayana's dictum that those who forget the past are condemned to repeat it; but he also remembers T. S. Eliot's admonition (in "The Dry Salvages") "Not fare well, / But fare forward, voyagers," and Ezra Pound's slogan, "Make it new!" and Talleyrand's quip about the Bourbon kings—that they had learned nothing and forgotten nothing. The pragmatist is not afraid to say that a little forgetting is a good thing. Forgetting emancipates us from the sense, which can be paralyzing, of belatedness.[5] Conservative pragmatists must not be confused with reactionary nostalgists.

Applied to law, pragmatism would treat decision according to precedent (the doctrine known as "stare decisis") as a policy rather than as a duty. But an anterior question is whether pragmatism should be applied to law in the sense of being used as a guide for legal decision-making. Stanley Fish would say not, would say that pragmatism is a part of theory talk, not of practice—including legal and judicial practice—talk.[6] That question is examined later.

The pragmatic attitude is *activist*—progressive, "can do"—rejecting both the conservative counsel that whatever is is best and the fatalist

---

4. John Casey, "The Comprehensive Ideal," in *The Modern Movement: A TLS Companion* 93, 95 (John Gross ed. 1993), describing T. S. Eliot's antihistorical view of tradition.

5. Friedrich Nietzsche, "On the Uses and Disadvantage of History for Life," in Nietzsche, *Untimely Meditations* 57, 120–122 (R. J. Hollingdale trans. 1983).

6. Fish, "Almost Pragmatism: Richard Posner's Jurisprudence," 57 *University of Chicago Law Review* 1447 (1990).

counsel that all consequences are unintended. The pragmatist believes in progress without pretending to be able to define it, and believes that it can be effected by deliberate human action. These beliefs are connected with the instrumental character of pragmatism. It is a philosophy of action and of betterment—which is not to say that the pragmatist *judge* is necessarily an activist. Judicial activism properly so-called is a view of the capacity and responsibility of courts relative to other agencies of government. A pragmatist might have good pragmatic reasons for thinking that courts should maintain a low profile.

Emphasizing the practical, the forward-looking, and the consequential, the pragmatist, or at least my kind of pragmatist (for we shall see that pragmatism comes in an anti-empirical, antiscientific version), is *empirical*. The pragmatist is interested in "the facts," and thus wants to be well informed about the operation, properties, and probable effects of alternative courses of action. At the same time he is *skeptical* about claims that we can have justified confidence in having arrived at the final truth about anything. Most of our certitudes are simply the beliefs current in whatever community we happen to belong to, beliefs that may be the uncritical reflection of our upbringing, education, professional training, or social milieu. Even our most tenaciously held "truths" are not those that can be proved, probed, discussed, investigated, but those so integral to our frame of reference that to doubt them would, by undermining our other deeply held beliefs, throw us into a state of hopeless disorientation. A proof is no stronger than its premises, and at the bottom of a chain of premises are unshakable intuitions, our indubitables, Holmes's "can't helps." That we are of a certain age, that we have a body, that no human being born in the eighteenth century is alive today, that objects do not cease to exist when they are out of our sight, that other people besides ourself have conscious mental states, and that the earth preexisted us are all beliefs of this character. Imagine, if we doubted any of these things, what else we would be forced to doubt.

These things are "common sense," the lay term for what I am calling the frame of reference. Pragmatism is both for and against common sense. The pragmatist knows that the frame of reference in which certain propositions have the status of common sense can change, sometimes rapidly, as happened in recent decades with regard to views of women's preferences and capabilities. But if he is sensible he also knows that the fact that something cannot be proved doesn't mean that it can be dislodged. The first point is overlooked by many conservatives, the second by many social constructionists (see Chapter 26).

The beliefs that are universally shared within a culture—the dictates of common sense—do not exhaust the contents of an individual's frame of reference in a complex and heterogeneous society such as that of the United States. Americans do not share an overarching frame of reference with which to resolve disputes between individuals whose personal frames of reference do not overlap completely. A claim that every human being has had a human father except Jesus Christ belongs to one frame of reference, the Christian; the denial of the claim to another, the scientific; both are found in our society. Conversion from one to another is common enough but it is not brought about by proof, by deduction and induction and other logical or scientific methods. Canons of logic and proof are elements of a frame of reference rather than means of dislodging one frame in favor of another.

While skeptical and relativistic, the pragmatist rejects skepticism and relativism when embraced as dogmas, as "philosophical" positions. Belief that the world exists independently of ourselves (the belief challenged by skepticism) and belief that some propositions are sounder than others (the belief self-contradictorily challenged by relativism) are part of the frame of reference shared by all readers of this book. One can only pretend to doubt them. Yet while unable to doubt them in the sense of being willing to act on our doubts, we can accept intellectually the possibility that they will someday be supplanted by fundamental beliefs equally unshakable—and transient.

Doubting that we will ever know that we have arrived at the ultimate truth(s), the pragmatist is *antidogmatic*. He wants to keep debate going and inquiry open. Recognizing that progress comes not merely through the patient accretion of knowledge within a given frame of reference but also through changes in the frame of reference—the replacement of one perspective or world view by another—that open new paths to knowledge and insight, the pragmatist values freedom of inquiry, a diversity of inquirers, and experimentation. He sees the scientist not as the discoverer of the ultimate truths about the universe—truths that once discovered by the experts should be forced on the rest of us—but as the exposer of falsehoods, who seeks to narrow the area of human uncertainty by generating falsifiable hypotheses and confronting them with data. From this standpoint what is most distinctive about science is that it epitomizes a rare and valuable human quality: the courage to risk being wrong. Pragmatists don't think that scientists have characters superior to those of other people, only that science has institutional characteristics which create a high probability that errors will be detected.

Being antimetaphysical and antidogmatic, the pragmatist views scientific theories as tools for helping human beings to explain and predict and, through explanation, prediction, and technology, to understand and control our physical and social environment. Theories of great beauty but little power leave him cold. He is drawn to the *experimental* scientist, whom he urges us to emulate by asking, whenever a disagreement arises: What practical, palpable, observable difference does it make to us? What, for example, are the stakes when lawyers debate whether some theory of judicial action comports with "democratic legitimacy"? How do we recognize "democracy" anyway? What difference does it make whether one thinks that judges found the current doctrines of constitutional law in the Constitution or put them there? These questions, all examined in this book, differ from those asked by traditional jurisprudential thinkers. They illustrate the possibility of thinking scientifically outside the domain of science as ordinarily understood.

Pragmatism emphasizes the *primacy of the social over the natural.* When Cardinal Bellarmine refused to look through Galileo's telescope at the moons of Jupiter, whose existence seemed to refute the orthodox view that the planets were fixed to the surface of crystalline spheres, he was not being irrational. He was just refusing to play the science game, in which theories are required to conform to observations, to "the facts," rather than the other way around. Bellarmine's game was faith. It is a common game in our society as well, taking many forms, the cosmological one being astrology. Another game of faith today is "political correctness." If you show a player in that game a sheaf of scientific reports purporting to show that the races or the sexes differ in their potential for doing mathematics, the player will refuse to read them; the empirical investigation of racial and sexual differences is rejected in that game, just as the empirical investigation of planetary motion was rejected by Bellarmine. (We shall encounter the p.c. game in Chapters 16 and 18.) A similar game on the other side of the ideological divide is the monocultural Western civ game, the players in which, if you show them a brilliant novel written by a Nigerian or a Jamaican, will refuse to read it.

I use the metaphor of game frequently in this book. Not in the sense in which the umpire's role in a game can be compared or contrasted with that of a judge, a sense common in conventional jurisprudence. Or the sense in which game theory models social interactions. Rather the sense in which Wittgenstein spoke of "language games," that is, of human activities constituted by a set of rules. There is a judicial game in this sense; and a major goal of this book is to nudge the judicial game a little closer to the science game. This is a feasible aspiration because the rules of the judicial game are fluid in comparison to those of chess, for example. But not even the rules of chess are immutable; a point the game metaphor brings out is that rules, unlike metaphysical foundations, can be changed by people, though not always easily.

Societies that refuse to play the science game suffer various consequences, including high levels of poverty and illness and an acute risk of being dominated or destroyed by other societies. Those consequences are important to the pragmatist, and a society that ignores them may be inflicting great suffering on its people, but in doing so the society is not necessarily making a mistake about what is "real." It is making a mistake if it thinks that through prayer, faith, or magic it can avert the consequences that I have mentioned. That is an example of the crossing of the scientific with the religious game. But if the society is prepared to pay the price for forgoing science, the pragmatist will doubt that the scientist has any purchase for criticism.

With his emphasis on the practical and the useful, the pragmatist philosopher undercuts his own activity, that of philosophizing. He is not comfortable being told that the value of philosophy is inverse to its utility and that a proper qualifying examination for graduate study in philosophy would consist entirely of jokes.[7] His doubts about the pragmatic worth of philosophy even touch analytic philosophy, though many heroes of analytic philosophy, such as Hume, Wittgenstein, Quine, and Davidson, are also heroes of pragmatism. The use of analytic methods as by Hume and Quine to knock down metaphysical entities such as free will[8] must be distinguished from the use of those

7. Ronald de Sousa, *The Rationality of Emotion* 292 n., 297 (1987). Cf. Norman Malcolm, *Ludwig Wittgenstein: A Memoir* 29 (1958).
8. *The Problems of Jurisprudence* 171–174; and see Chapter 19 of the present book.

methods to construct theories designed to guide action. The distinction corresponds to the use of legal reasoning to show up the weaknesses in an opponent's position and its use to construct one's own position. In fact the methods of analytic philosophy and of legal reasoning—the making of careful distinctions and definitions, the determination of logical consistency through the construction and examination of hypothetical cases, the bringing of buried assumptions to the surface, the breaking up of a problem into manageable components, the meticulous exploration of the implications of an opponent's arguments—are mainly the same. The pragmatist thinks the analytic philosopher and the legal reasoner alike too prone to equate disagreement with error by exaggerating the domain of logic[9] and thus prematurely dismissing opposing views, and, what is related, insufficiently interested in the empirical support for those views. The pragmatist is especially dubious that the methods of analytic philosophy and its twin, legal reasoning, can be used to establish moral duties or legal rights.

Pragmatism is not, however, logical positivism, though there is an affinity. Logical positivists believe that all propositions can be sorted into one of three bins: tautological, empirically verifiable, and nonsensical. Pragmatists think this too simple an epistemology, because it leaves no room for nontautological propositions that can be neither verified nor disbelieved, such as that no human being has ever eaten a full-grown hippopotamus at one sitting. But the pragmatist shares the logical positivist's suspicion of propositions that cannot be tested by observation, propositions that run the gamut from the maxims of common sense to the claims of metaphysics and theology.

Another thing that pragmatism is not is philosophical idealism. Like the idealist, the pragmatist is skeptical of the possibility of uninterpreted knowledge of reality. But he does not think that the only reality is mental. He merely doubts that there is such a nice correspondence between our minds and the structure of the universe that we are capable of making complete and conclusive descriptions of the way things are. That is why he thinks of theories, including scientific theories, as tools rather than as visions of reality. This type of skepticism has nothing to do with being puzzled by such statements as, "The witness did not tell

9. For a good discussion, see Dale Jacquette, "Contradiction," 25 *Philosophy and Rhetoric* 365 (1992).

the truth"; "Some scientific theories have been proved false"; "Scientists are seekers after truth." To be puzzled by such statements is just not to understand English well. They are not claims of apodictic certainty. The first recognizes that there are correct and incorrect reports of events; the second, that some scientific theories are rejected because they make predictions that turn out to be false; the third that scientists are committed to following practices that enable errors to be caught. The pragmatist may be more alert than the scientific realist, committed as the latter is to a correspondence theory of truth, to the possibility that erroneous theories may actually help science by stimulating promising lines of inquiry. Or that metaphor—which, properly understood, has no truth value (see Chapter 24)—can be productive of knowledge by altering an inquirer's frame of reference. Or that rhetoric or even "hotter" speech can have a cognitive payoff, again by jarring people out of their accustomed, and limited, perspectives—and all perspectives are, the pragmatist believes, partial.

But to acknowledge that mistakes, emotive utterances, and literal falsehoods (which may be imaginative or emotional "truths") can have social utility is not to deny that truth and falsity can and ordinarily must be distinguished. It is not to endorse sloppy or tendentious scholarship, an "anything goes" attitude toward claims and assertions, or, what is closely related, the belief that, like everything else, science and mathematics are "just rhetoric." Emerson and Whitman to one side, the pragmatist recognizes the importance of logic and clear thinking. He admires the critical triumphs of the analytic tradition and employs the tools of that tradition. He believes in being systematic, even if he does not believe in ambitious "systems" of moral or metaphysical speculation. Pragmatism is not—at least it does not have to be—postmodernism, though there is an affinity. And I have already pointed out that it is not epistemological or moral skepticism, or scientific or moral relativism.

The real antithesis to pragmatism is the kind of rationalism, fairly termed Platonic, that claims to use purely analytic methods to reason to the truth about contested metaphysical and ethical claims.[10] The rationalist style is common in the law; legal formalism is rationalistic.

10. For an illustration, see Brand Blanshard, "'Good,' 'Right,' 'Ought,' 'Bad,'" in *Readings in Ethical Theory* 222, 233 (Wilfrid Sellars and John Hospers eds., 2d ed. 1970).

The Pragmatic Approach in Law

Because "pragmatism" has no precise meaning, one is not always sure what is at stake in debates over it. Friends of pragmatism often define it in a way that makes it seem synonymous with being sensible, while enemies make it a synonym for irrationality and self-contradiction.[11] There is something at stake, though. The adjectives that I have used to characterize the pragmatic outlook—practical, instrumental, forward-looking, activist, empirical, skeptical, antidogmatic, experimental—are not the ones that leap to mind when one considers the work of, say, Ronald Dworkin. Not that his work does not have many virtues, but they are not those picked out by my list. He describes law as interpretive, compares the task of the judge to that of the writer of a chapter in a chain novel, requires that new decisions fit in with the earlier ones, speaks reverently of the living past, denies that judges should adjust rights to changed views of policy, is revolted at the thought of law as a policy science, is not much interested in facts or in the social or natural sciences, insists even that judges have a *moral* obligation to keep faith with their predecessors, that adherence to prior decisions conceived of as commitments is an essential element of justice.[12] A pragmatist is unlikely to view the judicial function in the same light. He is apt to think it as odd to suppose that a judge has an obligation to maintain a "fit" between what he does and what his predecessors did as to suppose that a modern scientist has an obligation to maintain a fit between what he does and what Archimedes and Aristotle did. There are practical reasons of both an epistemological and political character why judges should usually follow precedent and should usually adhere to the immanent values of their legal tradition, but no question of *obligation* is involved, and if there are good reasons to break with the past for the sake of the present and the future the judge should not hesitate to do so, just as mature sciences do not

11. Compare the essays by Rorty and Dworkin in *Pragmatism in Law and Society* (Michael Brint and William Weaver eds. 1991). Rorty, in "The Banality of Pragmatism and the Poetry of Justice," in id. at 89, defines pragmatism broadly and says that Dworkin is a pragmatist. (See also Steven D. Smith, "The Pursuit of Pragmatism," 100 *Yale Law Journal* 409, 410–424 [1990].) Dworkin defines pragmatism narrowly and calls it "philosophically a dog's dinner." "Pragmatism, Right Answers, and True Banality," in *Pragmatism in Law and Society,* above, at 359, 360.

12. Dworkin, *Law's Empire* (1986). "The past must be allowed some special power of its own in court, contrary to the pragmatist's claim that it must not." Id. at 169.

hesitate to forget their founders. Richard Rorty can classify Dworkin as a pragmatist in a perfectly good sense of the term (see note 11), but there is a more useful sense in which Dworkin can be said to stand for the rejection of pragmatism in legal theory. It is the sense captured by Cornel West's description of the "common denominator" of pragmatism as "a future-oriented instrumentalism that tries to deploy thought as a weapon to enable more effective action."[13] That is not how a Dworkinian conceives of law.

But might I be confusing different *senses* of pragmatism with different *levels* of pragmatism? A pragmatic philosopher might without inconsistency think that judges should be formalists rather than pragmatists, in much the same way that a utilitarian philosopher of law might think without inconsistency that judges should be Kantians rather than utilitarians. There might be pragmatic reasons why it would be good for judges to consider themselves morally bound to follow precedent rather than free to make a pragmatic judgment in each case whether to follow precedent,[14] just as there are pragmatic reasons (very similar ones, indeed) why bureaucrats normally should follow rules rather than always doing what they think is best in the circumstances, or why scientists normally should worry about the accuracy rather than the social consequences of their theories. Dworkin, however, while emphatic in rejecting legal pragmatism,[15] does not attempt to justify this rejection pragmatically, or to justify his own jurisprudence, a jurisprudence broadly Kantian in insisting that rights can never be sacrificed on the altar of policy, as a pragmatic construct. His archenemy, Stanley Fish, goes him one better by arguing that pragmatism can have no bite at the practical level, because it is part of the game of describing or theorizing about action rather than of acting. I don't agree with that, but I do agree that pragmatism like everything else must be prepared to defend itself on pragmatic grounds, and later in this Introduction I note a pragmatic limitation on pragmatic judging.

The decisive objection to trying to embed a formalist approach to judging within a pragmatic or for that matter any other philosophical framework is that in our legal system formalism is an unworkable response to difficult cases. The multi-layered character of American law

13. West, *The American Evasion of Philosophy: A Genealogy of Pragmatism* 5 (1989).

14. See, for example, Frederick Schauer, *Playing by the Rules: A Philosophical Examination of Rule-Based Decision-Making in Law and in Life* 145–149 (1991).

15. Dworkin, note 12 above, ch. 5.

(legislation superimposed on common law, federal law superimposed on state law, and federal constitutional law superimposed on state and federal statutory and common law), the undisciplined character of our legislatures, the intricacy and complexity of our society, and the moral heterogeneity of our population combine to thrust on the courts a responsibility for creative lawmaking that cannot be discharged either by applying existing rules to the letter or by reasoning by analogy—the standard judicial technique for dealing with novelty—from existing cases. We know this because a true-blue formalist like Robert Bork cannot find a single consistent judicial exemplar of the technique on the Supreme Court, past or present (see Chapter 9).

Granted, not everything that is not legal pragmatism is legal formalism; to oppose the latter is not to be compelled to embrace the former. My skepticism about constitutional theory has an affinity with that of Mark Tushnet,[16] a prominent "crit," because we are looking at the same phenomenon from a skeptical perspective. But he is not a pragmatic economics-minded Millian liberal and I am not a crit. Dworkin does not call himself a formalist, though others still march under that tattered banner (see note 28). Yet as antimetaphysical, antidogmatic, anticasuistic, even (as Rorty argues) "pragmatic" as Dworkin's jurisprudence could be thought to be, we shall see in Chapter 5 that its rhetorical strengths and substantive weaknesses track those of formalism.

Law's greatest pragmatist remains Holmes—admirer of Emerson (a family friend), admired by Dewey, friend of William James and at one time of Charles Sanders Peirce and Nicholas St. John Green, the cofounders of pragmatism. Holmes's pragmatism has been discussed at length elsewhere.[17] I want to illustrate it here with a brief address that Holmes gave commemorating the one hundredth anniversary of John Marshall's becoming Chief Justice of the United States.[18] It begins: "As we walk down Court Street in the midst of a jostling crowd, intent like us upon today and its affairs, our eyes are like to fall upon the small, dark building that stands at the head of State Street, and, like an

16. Compare his book-length attack on constitutional theory, *Red, White, and Blue: A Critical Analysis of Constitutional Law* (1988), esp. pt. 1, with Part Two of this book.

17. See, for example, Thomas C. Grey, "Holmes, Pragmatism, and Democracy," 71 *Oregon Law Review* 521 (1992); Grey, "Holmes and Legal Pragmatism," 41 *Stanford Law Review* 787 (1989); Patrick J. Kelley, "Was Holmes a Pragmatist? Reflections on a New Twist to an Old Argument," 14 *Southern Illinois University Law Journal* 427 (1990).

18. Holmes, "John Marshall" (1901), in *The Essential Holmes,* note 1 above, at 206–209.

ominous reef, divides the stream of business in its course to the gray cliffs that tower beyond." The building is the Massachusetts State House, and Holmes explains that "the first waves that foretold the coming storm of the Revolution broke around that reef." The building is dwarfed by the newer, larger buildings around it. No matter; it "is not diminished, but rather is enhanced and glorified, by the vast structures which somehow it turns into a background." In just the same way, "the beginnings of our national life, whether in battle or in law, lose none of their greatness by contrast with all the mighty things of later date, beside which, by every law of number and measure, they ought to seem so small." Holmes points out how small the greatest battles of the Revolution seem to those like himself who fought in the Civil War. "If I were to think of John Marshall simply by number and measure in the abstract, I might hesitate in my superlatives, just as I should hesitate over the battle of the Brandywine if I thought of it apart from its place in the line of historic cause. But such thinking is empty in the same proportion that it is abstract. It is most idle to take a man apart from the circumstances which, in fact, were his."

Here Holmes seems to digress—it is not really a disgression, as we shall see—to remark that his own "keenest interest is excited, not by what are called great questions and great cases, but by little decisions which . . . yet have in them the germ of some wider theory . . . The men I should be tempted to commemorate would be the originators of transforming thought," who "often are half obscure." But he does not therefore "join in this celebration . . . in any half-hearted way . . . I do fully believe that if American law were to be represented by a single figure, sceptic and worshipper alike would agree without dispute that the figure could be but one alone, and that one John Marshall . . . What shall be symbolized by any image of the sight depends upon the mind of him who sees it . . . The setting aside of this day in honor of a great judge" will thus stand for different things to different people— "to a patriot for the fact that time has been on Marshall's side . . . This day marks the fact that all thought is social, is on its way to action . . . It is all a symbol, if you like, but so is the flag. The flag is but a bit of bunting to one who insists on prose. Yet, thanks to Marshall and to the men of his generation . . . its red is our life-blood, its stars our world, its blue our heaven. It owns our land. At will it throws away our lives."

To interpret this address as just a rather grudging tribute to Marshall would be to miss a lot. Holmes is saying in good pragmatist fashion that personal achievement is relative to circumstances and evaluated by consequences and (a closely related point) that meaning is social rather than immanent. The Massachusetts State House is nothing in itself, a little old building dwarfed by much larger modern buildings. It gains significance from its connection to the life of the present. The battles of the Revolution were nothing much in themselves either. Their significance, too, lies in their consequences for the present. A man happily fitted to his historical circumstances, Marshall had the good luck to play a shaping role in an institution that has helped to make the country what it is. His luck was even better than this. Though he was executor rather than inventor—even the Constitution was designed by others, and American law at large is the creation of half-obscure originators—it is he, not they, who symbolizes American law. A symbol need be nothing great in itself; a flag is just a piece of bunting. The thing or person made symbolic is only a receptacle of meaning. We invest it or him with meaning for our own purposes. In brief, "all thought is social," its purpose action in the present or future. We are not the slaves of our history, traditions, and precursors; they are our instruments.

Economic Analysis of Law

When a pragmatic approach is taken to law, as I tried to do in *The Problems of Jurisprudence* and try to do in this book as well, the results are damaging to the *amour propre* of the legal profession. The organization of the profession, the conception of the judge, the interpretation of the Constitution, "the law" as an entity that guides interpretation and decision, legal theoreticians Left and Right, the premises of hotly contested judicial decisions (premises such as "equality," "democracy," "original meaning," and "judicial self-restraint"), even jurisprudence itself, do not escape serious damage. A certain conception of economics withers as well.[19] But the enterprise of "law and economics" does not. Not because it is my enterprise but because it epitomizes the operation in law of the ethic of scientific inquiry, pragmatically understood. Far from being reductionist, as its detractors believe, economics is the instrumental science par excellence. Its project is not to reduce human behavior to some biological propensity, some faculty of reason, let alone

---

19. See Chapter 20, "Ronald Coase and Methodology."

to prove that deep within us, pulling the strings, is a nasty little "economic man." It is to construct and test models of human behavior for the purpose of predicting and (where appropriate) controlling that behavior. Economics imagines the individual not as "economic man," but as—a pragmatist. As one who bases decisions not on sunk costs— these he treats as bygones ("Don't cry over spilt milk")—but on the costs to be incurred and the benefits to be reaped from alternative courses of action that remain open. The individual imagined by economics is not committed to any narrow, selfish goal such as pecuniary wealth maximization. Nothing in economics prescribes an individual's goals. But whatever his goal or goals, some or for that matter all of which may be altruistic, he is assumed to pursue them in forward-looking fashion by comparing the opportunities open to him at the moment when he must choose.[20]

Realistic about means as well as ends, economics does not depend on the idea that human beings are effortless and infallible calculators. A market may behave rationally, and hence the economic model of human behavior apply to it, even if most of the individual buyers (or buys) are irrational.[21] Irrational purchase decisions are likely to be random and hence cancel each other out, leaving the average behavior of the market to be determined by the minority of rational buyers (or purchases).[22] Similarly, a model of criminals as rational maximizers may

20. Gary S. Becker, "Nobel Lecture: The Economic Way of Looking at Behavior," 101 *Journal of Political Economy* 395 (1993).

21. Jack Hirshleifer, "The Expanding Domain of Economics," 75 *American Economic Review* 53, 59 n. 24 (Dec. 1985, special anniversary issue). It is true that several of the standard results of the rational-choice model, notably but not only the downward-sloping market demand curve, can be shown to be consistent with irrational behavior by all market participants. Gary S. Becker, "Irrational Behavior and Economic Theory," 70 *Journal of Political Economy* 1 (1962), reprinted in Becker, *The Economic Approach to Human Behavior*, ch. 5 (1976). See also Dhananjay K. Gode and Shyam Sunder, "Allocative Efficiency of Markets with Zero-Intelligence Traders," 101 *Journal of Political Economy* 119 (1993). The significance of this point is easily misunderstood, however, as I point out in Chapter 21.

22. Let there be a good that is sold under conditions of competition, which is to say at a single price equal to the value of the marginal purchase of the good to the marginal purchaser. Let there be two types of buyer, a high-value buyer and a low-value buyer. High-value buyers value the first purchase of the good at $10 and the second at $7, and low-value buyers value the first purchase of the good at $7 and the second at $5. At an output of 100 units, half to each type of buyer (and let there be five buyers of each type), the marginal cost of producing the good, which let us say is independent of the quantity produced, is $5, and therefore the competitive price is $5. (So, should either type of buyer value additional units at less than $5, the market will not provide them.) Suppose that, because of an increase in the marginal cost of the good, the sellers raise their price to $5.25. High-value buyers are unaffected. Rational low-value buyers would reduce their purchases by one-half, since $5.25

correctly predict that an increase in the severity of punishment or in the probability of its imposition will reduce the crime rate[23] even if most criminals have serious cognitive or emotional deficits. They are sufficiently rational to respond, though perhaps only moderately, to changes in incentives. Although the assumption that human beings (in some models all beings) are rational is important to the construction of mathematically tractable models of economic behavior, the models hold as useful approximations even when the assumption is false.

The economic and pragmatic approaches to law might seem incompatible on the ground that the former wants to replace one formal theory (the jurisprudence of Cicero, Coke, Blackstone, Langdell, and Frankfurter) with another (economic theory with all its normative as well as positive baggage, such as efficiency and wealth maximization), while the latter insists on the inadequacy of theory to capture what it means to do law. Evaluation of this claim requires distinguishing among "autonomy," "impersonality," and "objectivity" as formalist criteria of law. "Autonomy" refers to law's self-sufficiency, and has two aspects. The first is law's autonomy from society—the idea that law has its own internal logic and therefore that when it changes it does so in response to the promptings of its inner nature, like a caterpillar turning into a moth, rather than in response to political and economic pressures. Thus conventional legal history tells the story of how modern legal doctrines evolved from ancient ones, rather than how, at every stage of history, legal doctrines have been shaped by the needs of society or the pressures of powerful groups within it.[24] The second aspect of "autonomy" is the independence of legal thought from other disciplines, such as economics. If autonomy in either or both senses is deemed an essential

---

> \$5.00, the value they attach to half the units they bought at the previous price. Suppose, however, that only one of the five low-value buyers is rational. The others do not respond to the price increase at all. He does. He reduces his purchases by one-half, that is, from 10 to 5. As a result, the quantity demanded by the market will fall by 5 percent, from 100 to 95, in response to the 5 percent price increase, from \$5.00 to \$5.25. The economist's prediction that a rise in price will cause a fall in quantity demanded will thus be fulfilled, even though one of the assumptions that generates it—that buyers are rational—is more false than true.

23. As found, for example, in Isaac Ehrlich, "Participation in Illegitimate Activities: An Economic Analysis," in *Essays in the Economics of Crime and Punishment* 68 (Gary S. Becker and William M. Landes eds. 1974). See also Daryl A. Hellman and Neil O. Alper, *Economics of Crime: Theory and Practice* (2d ed. 1990); William N. Trumbull, "Estimation of the Economic Model of Crime Using Aggregate and Individual Level Data," 56 *Southern Economic Journal* 423 (1989).

24. Robert W. Gordon, "Introduction: J. Willard Hurst and the Common Law Tradition in American Legal Historiography," 10 *Law and Society Review* 9, 16–25 (1975).

ingredient of legal formalism, economic analysis of law cannot be considered formalistic. It could, however, be an "impersonal" mode of analysis in the sense of generating results that would command agreement among persons having different values and preferences. It could even be "objective." To the pragmatist, "objective" does not mean corresponding to the way things really are; no one *knows* the way things *really* are. It means capable of commanding agreement among all members of a group subscribing to common principles. In the community of chess players, moving a rook diagonally is objectively wrong, while in the community of scientists, disbelieving certain kinds of data is objectively wrong.[25]

To those like myself who think of the basic claim of the jurisprudential traditionalist as the claim to autonomy, because the autonomy of law and legal reasoning is fundamental to the legal profession's self-interest in repelling the competition of nonlawyers for the provision of legal services (see Chapter 1), the frequent suggestion that economics is the "new Langdellism"[26] is hard to understand. Economic analysis of law almost by definition denies law's autonomy. But if the emphasis is laid instead on the traditionalist's desire for impersonality and objectivity, for a government of laws and not men, for methods of inquiry and analysis that can generate reasonable though not always compelling answers to even the most difficult legal questions, for finding principles of order in the luxuriant efflorescence of legal doctrine, the suggestion has greater merit. On this plane, the antithesis of formalism is not the economic approach to law; it is the deep skepticism about the desirability or even the existence of legal rules that is characteristic of some versions of legal realism and critical legal studies.

I can imagine, if barely, the legal profession and the judiciary buying into the idea that economics ought to guide legal decisions in all cases in which the Constitution or statutes do not speak unequivocally to the contrary. In effect, the legal community would accept the methods of inquiry that define the economics community. But the decision to make economics the logic of the law could not itself be derived from economics any more than the decision to be scientific can be derived from science. And even if such a decision were made, the resulting regime

25. Cf. Sabina Lovibond, *Realism and Imagination in Ethics* (1983), esp. pp. 41–45, 67–68; also J. Huizinga, *Homo Ludens: A Study of the Play-Element in Culture* 11, 152–153 (1950).

26. See references in Duxbury, note 3 above, at 3–4.

would not much resemble Langdell's. Both Langdellian legal theory and economic theory are deductive systems, but Langdell wanted to stop with deduction—with comparing the facts of a case to a rule derived from a priori concepts, such as that of contract. The economist is committed to testing his theories empirically and discarding them if they are falsified by data.

But if science (including social science, and thus economics) can be thought formalistic because of the deductive structure of scientific theories, and pragmatism is taken to be antiscientific and antitheoretical, the fusion of pragmatic rejection of legal formalism with economic analysis of law will seem oxymoronic; and perhaps the "oxy" should be dropped.[27] Some pragmatists *are* hostile to science, and more broadly to theory; we shall meet a number of them in this book. They are heirs of Emerson and Whitman, famous mockers of consistency. And some construals of science do make it seem highly formalistic. But nothing "in" pragmatism, if one can speak so, justifies a hostile attitude toward science. When science is viewed as delivering ultimate truths, and thus as a secular restatement of Platonism or monotheism, the pragmatist's hackles rise; but that is not the only light in which to view science. Another is as a collection of proven methods of enlarging the stock of useful and accurate human knowledge.

Pragmatists want the law to be more empirical, more realistic, more attuned to the real needs of real people. But it would be a mistake to draw the corollary that legal scholars should eschew theory. Fact and theory are not opposed; science, including good social science, unites them. Legal scholars should eschew bad theory and bad empirical research alike. The empirical projects of the legal realists, which not only failed but in failing gave empirical research rather a bad name among legal academics, illustrate the futility of empirical investigation severed from a theoretical framework. (We shall encounter another example of this severance in Chapter 21, that of the "old" institutional economics.) Modern economics can furnish the indispensable theoretical framework for the empirical research that law so badly needs.

If science isn't formalistic in an illuminating sense, maybe traditional legal reasoning isn't either. Maybe "legal formalism" is a straw man.

27. Smith, note 11 above, at 425–429. "Despite his avowed pragmatism, it seems that Judge Posner is not of a pragmatic disposition; his economic analysis, in particular, evinces a powerful need to reduce the disparate materials of law to a coherent system." Id. at 438 n. 144.

Writers on law do tend to use "formalistic" as an all-purpose term of legal abuse (like "activist" or "result-oriented") and to exaggerate the degree to which mainstream legal thought is formalistic. No modern formalist believes that legal reasoning even "at its best" has the axiomatic-deductive structure of geometry. Yet most lawyers, judges, and law professors still believe that demonstrably correct rather than merely plausible or reasonable answers to most legal questions, even very difficult and contentious ones, can be found—and it is imperative that they be found[28]—by reasoning from authoritative texts, either legislative enactments (including constitutions) or judicial decisions, and therefore without recourse to the theories, data, insights, or empirical methods of the social sciences, or to personal or political values: without, in other words, an encounter, necessarily messy, with the worlds of fact and feeling.

But I would not like the reader to infer either from the title of this book or from my disparagement of legal formalism that, like Fred Rodell, I want to replace the rule of law by the rule of economic or other experts. The rule of law, in the sense of a system of social control operated in accordance with norms of disinterestedness and predictability, is a public good of immense value. Along with a market economy and a democratic political system, which in fact it undergirds, it is a presupposition of modern liberalism. This is well understood in the ex-communist nations. It is bad-boy legal realists like Jerome Frank and Fred Rodell and their crit epigones who deny that law has any principles. Nevertheless a realistic (not legal-realist) concept of the rule of law, one that (in the words of the federal judicial oath)[29] requires the judge to decide cases "without respect to persons"—that is, without respect to a litigant's wealth, social position, political influence, racial or ethnic identity, or relation to the judge—is remote from the legal profession's dream of law so impersonal that the values, personal experiences, and social and political opinions of the judge do not affect

---

28. "If no uniquely correct resolution exists to a particular legal dispute, judges must decide as their personal convictions or political preferences dictate rather than as authoritative legal materials prescribe." Eric Rakowski, "Posner's Pragmatism," 104 *Harvard Law Review* 1681, 1682 (1991). For recent academic defenses of formalism, see Michael Corrado, "The Place of Formalism in Legal Theory," 70 *North Carolina Law Review* 1545 (1992); Frederick Schauer, "Formalism," 97 *Yale Law Journal* 509 (1988); Ernest J. Weinrib, "Corrective Justice," 77 *Iowa Law Review* 403 (1992); Weinrib, "Legal Formalism: On the Immanent Rationality of Law," 97 *Yale Law Journal* 949 (1988).

29. 28 U.S.C. § 453.

judicial outcomes. The "law" to which my title refers is a professional totem signifying all that is pretentious, uninformed, prejudiced, and spurious in the legal tradition. A pragmatic approach can help to demolish the totem. Economic analysis of law can help put better things in its place even when we are dealing with the most emotional, politicized, and taboo subjects that law regulates, such as sexuality.

But there is more, even on a pragmatic construal, to the rule of law than deciding cases without respect to persons, and it circumscribes the role of pragmatic and economic thinking in giving shape to legal doctrines. The rule of law connotes an institutional structure that the idea of impersonal judging, by itself, does not. The latter one could get in a system of ad hoc arbitration by nonlawyers, which is in fact a common method of resolving contract disputes but not one that can be generalized to the entire spectrum of legal disputes. We need professional adjudicators who will not only avoid the most palpable forms of bias but also play the judicial game, described in Chapter 3, which includes at least a qualified adherence to rules laid down in legislation and in previous cases. The game can be justified in pragmatic and economic terms, but it cannot be played in a purely pragmatic or economic spirit. The judge is not to change the rules and doctrines that he is applying whenever he thinks that a change would improve the substantive rationality of the rules, for example by bringing them closer to the dictates of microeconomic theory. So there is something after all to Dworkin's belief that the judicial game is nonpragmatic and noneconomic, even if that game is embedded in a larger system of values and institutions of a pragmatic and economic character and can be justified by reference to those values and institutions. Something, but perhaps not much. Dworkin is interested in precisely those difficult cases, those cases of genuine novelty, where the methods that he espouses for deciding cases don't work; where only pragmatic methods will.

Liberalism and Democracy

Whenever a case cannot be decided by reference to precedent or some clear statutory text, the judicial task is inescapably normative. But the use of economics to guide decision in the open areas of law ought to be discussable without immersion in the deep waters of political and moral philosophy. It is true that some people insist on treating quite narrow and technical legal questions as microcosms of the vastest social issues. They see antitrust cases as raising issues of political liberty rather than merely of efficient allocation of resources, contract cases as raising issues of human autonomy rather than merely of transaction costs, corporate cases as raising issues of democracy rather than issues concerning optimal investment, criminal cases as raising deep issues of free will and autonomy rather than the issue of how to minimize the social costs of crime. From time to time I shall be glancing at efforts to philosophize about such matters.[30] But I think the economist can easily hold his own in these debates by showing that the most fruitful framework for analyzing this range of legal questions is an economic one.

  Not all questions that come up in law, however, can be effortlessly recast as economic questions. Cases involving the regulation of sexuality and reproduction furnish endless illustrations. The economist has great difficulty getting a clear "fix" on such questions. The costs of forcing a woman to bear an unwanted child are readily analyzed within an economic framework, but what of the costs to the fetus of being aborted? Whether those costs (as distinct from the costs to persons who may value the fetus's life) shall be counted at all depends on whether fetuses are deemed part of the community whose welfare is to be maximized. That question, which is connected to whether utilitarians should be concerned with average or total utility (the latter being more likely to be increased by a policy of saving fetuses and thus increasing the population), cannot be answered within economics. And it cannot be elided by replacing utility maximization with wealth maximization, in which the criterion of value is how much you would be willing to pay for something (or if you own it already, how much you would charge to give it up) rather than the amount of utility that having the thing would (or does) confer.[31] For whether allowing abortion is wealth-maximizing depends on whether the right over the fetus's life is assigned to the fetus or to the mother; and that determination—the locating of the boundaries of the community whose wealth is to be maximized—cannot be made within economics any more than the economist can decide whether the goal of our society should be to maximize the wealth of the United States or the wealth of the entire world.

30. See, for example, Chapter 13 ("Hegel and Employment at Will").
31. See *The Problems of Jurisprudence* 356–357.

Many people of conservative bent are distressed by the thought that some people are committing homosexual acts, even adults, even in private. That distress could be thought an external cost of homosexuality—a cost that homosexuals impose on other people, akin to the cost of pollution—and hence a ground for limiting the freedom of homosexuals. But once purely mental externalities are brought into economic analysis, economics becomes a potential menace to basic liberties. Mental externalities could furnish economic justification for every manner of discrimination against despised minorities. Bentham thought beggars should be locked up because of the distress that their appearance and importunings caused passersby.

The illiberal implications of typical utilitarian and economic thinking, implications that seem to include condoning torture and gruesome punishments, enforcing contracts of self-enslavement, permitting gladiatorial contests in which the contestants fight to the death, enforcing Shylock's pound-of-flesh bond, and abolishing all welfare programs and other forms of social insurance, cannot be brushed aside on the ground that we ought to give efficiency priority over liberty. Why should we? Our liberal intuitions are as deep as our utilitarian ones, and there is no intellectual procedure that will or should force us to abandon them.

We cannot make these illiberal implications disappear by judicious assignment of rights, by saying for example that if beggars have the right to use the streets the affluent will have to pay them to desist from begging. There is no basis in economics for assigning rights over begging to the beggars rather than to the begged-from. At some point even one strongly committed to the economic approach to law will have to take a stand on issues of political and moral philosophy. I take my stand with the John Stuart Mill of *On Liberty* (1859), the classic statement of classical liberalism.[32] *On Liberty* argues that every person is entitled to the maximum liberty—both personal and economic—consistent with the liberty of every other person in the society.[33] Neither

32. Not that Mill was a completely orthodox exponent of classical liberalism. His flirtation with socialism (for example in the *Principles of Political Economy*) presaged the modern welfare liberal's severing of personal from economic liberty and disparaging of the latter. Nevertheless, Mill's final view of socialism was a skeptical one. See "Chapters on Socialism," in Mill, *On Liberty, with The Subjection of Women and Chapters on Socialism* 221, 260–279 (Stefan Collini ed. 1989).

33. For an earlier statement, see Immanuel Kant, *The Metaphysical Elements of Justice* 35 (John Ladd trans. 1965). The germ of "classical" liberalism—making the adjective particularly apt—appears to be the ancient Greek idea, famously articulated in the funeral oration by

government nor public opinion should seek to repress "self-regarding" behavior, that is, behavior that does not palpably harm other people. The qualification in "palpably" is necessary in order to exclude what I have called mental externalities. To Mill, the fact that most Americans were horrified at the thought that the Mormons in far-off Utah were practicing polygamy was not an adequate basis for the U.S. government's forbidding the practice. The exclusion of mental externalities separates liberalism from utilitarianism and economics, although not completely. Liberalism is related to one version of normative economics, the Pareto principle, which defines an efficient change as one that makes at least one person better off and no one worse off, or in other words that does no harm. The problem with this as a *liberal* principle is that once mental and pecuniary externalities are allowed for, few transactions do not make someone, somewhere, worse off, and in circumstances in which compensating the someone would be impossible. The problem becomes insoluble when people's preferences include the desire to deny some form of liberty (for example, to watch pornographic movies) to other people, so that the exercise of that liberty, although self-regarding in Mill's sense, harms others.[34]

Liberalism also has an intimate *practical* relation to economics. Competitive markets, being arenas of self-regarding behavior, are in classical liberal theory off limits to government interference. Even purely voluntary market transactions can nevertheless affect prices and wages paid and received by nonparties (so they are not truly voluntary). But these pecuniary externalities,[35] along with the mental ones, the classical liberal is inclined (whether rightly or wrongly) to exclude from his definition of harm, although the Paretian would not.

By creating a large sphere of inviolate private activity and by facilitating the operation of free markets, liberalism creates the conditions that experience teaches are necessary for personal liberty and economic prosperity. And although these goods depend on controlling domestic

---

Pericles as reported by Thucydides, that there is a private sphere of beliefs and activities with which the state has no business. See David Cohen, *Law, Sexuality and Society: The Enforcement of Morals in Classical Athens* (1991).

34. Amartya Sen, "The Impossibility of a Paretian Liberal," 78 *Journal of Political Economy* 152 (1970).

35. Pecuniary rather than real, as the economist uses these terms, because perfectly offset elsewhere in the economic system. A higher price is a cost to the consumer but an equal benefit to the producer; the aggregate value of the society's output is unaffected. In contrast, a real externality, such as pollution, reduces aggregate value.

violence and holding foreign enemies at bay, in modern times the strongest states, domestically and internationally, have been liberal states,[36] Great Britain in the nineteenth century and the United States in the twentieth. Liberalism fosters the exchanges of information that are necessary to scientific and technological progress, enlists uncoerced citizen support, maximizes productive output, encourages and rewards competence, prevents excessive centralization of decision-making, weakens competing loyalties to family or clan, and defuses sectarian strife. The case for liberalism is pragmatic.

Liberalism is not a complete philosophy of government and law. Vital details, such as optimal taxation (to pay for the limited but not negligible government activities that liberalism approves), are omitted. The legitimacy of "buying off" clamorous interest groups for the sake of social peace is unclear. And the deep commitment of liberal polities to certain paternalistic, hence prima facie illiberal, policies, such as the prohibition of torture, of gruesome punishments, and of lethal sports, is a puzzle. Maybe, as Nietzsche thought, such policies can be explained in liberal terms by the idea that squeamish people are better citizens of a liberal polity than people inured to violence, suffering, and death. But the causation may run the other way: nations become liberal when people who fear and despise the pursuit of honor and glory, a pursuit associated with a taste for violence, gain the ascendancy and express their distaste in law.

Liberalism is in tension with democracy. Democracy is a means not only of dispersing political power and thus of protecting the private sphere against invasion by the public sphere, but also of enabling people to enforce their dislike of other people's self-regarding behavior. Liberalism implies the limited state, but democracy implies majority rule—and majorities are often willing to coerce minorities. Yet democracy and liberalism support as well as oppose each other. By placing government under popular control, democracy reduces the power of the state to infringe liberty; and liberty is a precondition of informed and uncoerced, and hence authentic, democratic choice. But liberty in period t can lead to a popular government at period $t + 1$ that may decide to immiserate an unpopular minority. Some defenders of democracy try to bridge the gap between it and liberalism by arguing that voters

36. As emphasized by Stephen Holmes in *The Paradox of Democracy* (forthcoming from University of Chicago Press).

should never allow themselves to vote selfishly or emotionally, or in a word illiberally. Their votes should always be the result of informed and disinterested deliberation, and, if they are, democracy will (these defenders argue) produce wise and just solutions to social problems.[37] There is such a thing as disinterested voting, as we shall see in Chapter 3; and public opinion, which voting registers, is not wholly uninformed. So there is something to the idea of deliberative democracy. But how much? Joshua Cohen tips his hand when he speaks of "consensus" as the goal of deliberative democracy, voting as a last resort when deliberation threatens to become interminable.[38] He is thinking of political democracy on the model of a faculty meeting, where homogeneous and highly educated people deliberate in leisurely fashion over matters of which they have first-hand knowledge. Democracy doesn't work that way in polities of millions. It is nonparticipatory: except in the occasional referendum, people vote for representatives rather than for policies. In its practical operation ignorance is pervasive, selfishness is salient, and at times a disinterested malevolence is at work. Our statute books overflow with vicious, exploitive, inane, ineffectual, and extravagantly costly laws, and there would be more rather than fewer if our democracy were more populist. Recognizing the tension between liberalism and democracy, liberals want to limit the scope of democratic politics through separation of powers and judicial review of executive and legislative actions.

Another difficult question for the liberal theorist is whether liberty should be thought of in purely negative terms, as merely freedom from coercion by government, or in positive terms as well, as human autonomy, capability, or self-realization (see Chapter 6). On the latter construal a government policy such as redistributing wealth from rich to poor might be thought liberal; and this shows the ease of sliding, as did Mill himself, from classical to welfare liberalism. Liberalism thus is

---

37. See, for example, Cass R. Sunstein, *Democracy and the Problem of Free Speech*, ch. 8 (1993); Joshua Cohen, "Deliberation and Democratic Legitimacy," in *The Good Polity: Normative Analysis of the State* 17 (Alan Hamlin and Philip Pettit eds. 1989); David Estlund, "Making Truth Safe for Democracy," in *The Idea of Democracy* 71 (David Copp, Jean Hampton, and John E. Roemer eds. 1993) ("epistemic democracy"). I am speaking here of *political* democracy. In a broader sense familiar from the works of John Dewey and Richard Rorty, democracy is the name of the characteristic pragmatist belief that truth is the agreement of the relevant community, and is thus in a sense arrived at "democratically," rather than the preserve of experts, descendants of Plato's philosopher kings.

38. Cohen, note 37 above, at 23.

fuzzy at the edges—and speaking of edges, it is no more successful than economics in dealing with boundary issues, such as abortion, where the question whether behavior is "self-regarding" depends on whether someone (the fetus, for example) is a member of the community. Liberalism does well with the issue of homosexual rights, however, where the issue of self-regarding versus other-regarding is relatively clear-cut; and it does better than economics in dealing with some fine-grained legal issues, as I will illustrate with the rationale for the legal doctrine of entrapment. If a criminal defendant would not have committed a particular type of crime unless the government had induced him to do so, he is said to have been "entrapped," and must be acquitted. The economist can explain this result by noting that the expenditure of resources to punish a person who is not a threat to society is wasteful, and is to be distinguished from merely arranging for a criminal to commit his next crime at a time and place of the government's choosing so that he can be apprehended and convicted at least cost.[39] But the explanation is not entirely convincing, because courts do not usually concern themselves with the efficient allocation of law enforcement resources; that is the business of the executive branch. Liberal theory can plug the gap. Liberalism commands government to leave harmless people alone. A person who will not commit a crime unless the government entices him to do so is harmless. The punishment of harmless people is wrong even if they have weak characters or harbor evil thoughts.

Mill painted an attractive picture of the liberal society but offered few *reasons* why it should be preferred to a more communal one. The history of the twentieth century is rich with evidence that communal alternatives to liberalism, whether fascistic or socialistic, are monstrous, nonviable, or both. But the history lesson is blurred by the fact that modern "liberal" states are suffused with socialist elements.

George Kateb defends liberalism on the basis of the desirability, as he sees it, of encouraging "sentiments of democratic self-assertion or self-reliance," the Emersonian ideal that Kateb charmingly summarizes as:

(1) the wish to be different; the wish to be unique; the wish to go off in one's own direction; the wish to experiment, to wander, to float;

(2) the wish to be let alone; the wish to be uninvolved in somebody

---

39. *Economic Analysis of Law* 217–218.

else's game; the wish to be unobserved; the wish to be mysterious, to have secrets, to be thought undefined;

(3) the wish to be unbeholden; the wish to own oneself;

(4) the wish to think, judge, and interpret for oneself;

(5) the wish to feel real, not dazed; the wish to live, not play just one lifelong role or perform just one lifelong function;

(6) the wish to go to one's limit; the wish to score, to accumulate heterogeneous experiences;

(7) the wish to shape one's life, but not into a well-shaped story, or a well-made work of art; the wish to be fluid, not substantial;

(8) the wish to find oneself, to find the "real me"; to be oneself rather than somebody else's idea of that self; the wish to be reborn as oneself.[40]

It is easy to see that *if* this is the sort of personality we want to encourage, we had better, as a minimum principle of government, adopt the Millian principle that "your rights end where my nose begins," in order to head off a fight to the death among all these aggressive egoists. But why should we want to encourage self-assertiveness to begin with, in a population with an average IQ of only 100? And if we do, why stop with the harm principle? (And who is this "we"?) Well-off people tend to be more self-assertive, though less violent, than the poor, so a more egalitarian redistribution of wealth might maximize the number of self-assertive people; once again we find liberalism modulating into state coercion via egalitarianism. And why stop there? If liberty means capability rather than legal autonomy, modern transportation may have made the inhabitants of modern dictatorships freer than the inhabitants of nineteenth-century democracies. On this view, liberty dissolves into wealth, and we are back to economics.[41] Mill thought it made no difference whether constraints on personal freedom came from law or from public opinion; why should it make a difference if they come from technology instead? And what can "self-assertiveness" even *mean*, if one happens not to believe in free will? Why is it better for human behavior to be determined by technol-

---

40. Kateb, "Democratic Individuality and the Meaning of Rights," in *Liberalism and the Moral Life* 183, 191 (Nancy L. Rosenblum ed. 1989). Notice the resemblance to Mill's principle of individuality, on which see Alan Ryan, *The Philosophy of John Stuart Mill*, ch. 13 (2d ed. 1990). Kateb's last clause ("the wish to be reborn as oneself") puts one in mind of Nietzsche's idea of eternal recurrence.

41. George J. Stigler, "Wealth, and Possibly Liberty," 7 *Journal of Legal Studies* 213 (1978).

ogy, advertising, and popular culture than by religion, ethnicity, and tradition?

Kateb's conception of man as self-fashioner equates the ordinary individual to the scientist—an explorer, a maker, a freethinker, an active inquirer, an experimenter, a person who dares to be wrong: types I like. As the questions in the preceding paragraph should make clear, I do not suggest that this ideal has a solid grounding in pragmatism or anything else—and anyway pragmatism is not in the business of supplying foundations. But I shall try throughout this book to show that liberal individualism can be defended pragmatically by comparing its consequences with those likely to be produced by such alternatives as social democracy and moral conservatism.

Emerson is not the only link between pragmatism and liberalism. Both doctrines reject—pragmatism at the level of general philosophy, liberalism at the level of political philosophy—the idea of using some comprehensive doctrine (whether Aquinas's, or Mohammed's, or Calvin's, or Kant's, or Marx's) to supply the answers to questions about either reality or personal conduct. Liberalism (though not necessarily in Mill's or Emerson's form) is the political philosophy best suited for societies in which people don't agree on the foundations of morality,[42] and pragmatism is the philosophy of living without foundations.[43]

So liberalism and pragmatism fit well with each other and, as we saw earlier, with economics. The fusion can transform legal theory. That at least is the thesis of this book.

42. As emphasized in John Rawls, *Political Liberalism* (1993).

43. The connection between liberalism, or at least a version of liberalism, and pragmatism is brought out in some remarks by Rawls: "Different conceptions of the world can reasonably be elaborated from different standpoints and diversity arises in part from our distinct perspectives. It is unrealistic—or worse, it arouses mutual suspicion and hostility—to suppose that all our differences are rooted solely in ignorance and perversity, or else in the rivalries for power, status or economic gain . . . Many of our most important judgments are made under conditions where it is not to be expected that conscientious persons with full powers of reason, even after free discussion, will all arrive at the same conclusion." Id. at 58. But we shall see in Chapter 5 that it would be a mistake to think *Political Liberalism* a work of pragmatism.

PART ONE

The Profession

chapter 1

The Material Basis of Jurisprudence

T H E history of the legal profession is to a great extent, and despite noisy and incessant protestation and apologetics, the history of efforts by all branches of the profession, including the professoriat and the judiciary, to secure a lustrous place in the financial and social-status sun. Until recently, the legal profession in the United States as in most other wealthy countries was succeeding triumphantly in this endeavor. The profession was an intricately and ingeniously reticulated though imperfect cartel, held together against the dangers that beset and ordinarily would destroy a cartel of many members by governmental regulations designed to secure it against competition and new entry from without and centrifugal, disintegrative competitive pressures from within. The profession's cartel structure produced as a by-product a certain view of "law"—that it is an enigmatic but "real" and ultimately knowable entity that by constraining the behavior of lawyers and judges justifies the independence of the profession from political and market controls.

The cartel has weakened since the 1960s. (I shall analogize this decline to the decline of medieval craft production—also organized in cartels—and the rise of modern mass-production industry.) Symptoms include changes in the size and organization of law firms, changes in the relative compensation of junior and senior lawyers, an increase in the hours of work of lawyers, and a diminution in the satisfactions that practitioners, judges, and law professors derive from their jobs. Because mainstream legal thought is to a significant degree a by-product of cartelization, the weakening of the cartel has altered that thought—altered it in the direction of disintegration and of a search, so far unavailing, for methods of reintegration. Should the cartel collapse entirely and law become largely an unregulated service like business management or retail selling, we can expect a profound change in the reigning conception of law: a change from the idea of law as an autonomous realm of thought to an idea of law as a heterogeneous medley of rhetorical thrusts and parries, of advice and mediation by wise elders, of policy analyses and investigations, of miscellaneous clerical and bureaucratic tasks. Such a change would kill "jurisprudence" in the special sense of the legal profession's flattering self-conception of what it means to do, to be, to live in, "the law."[1]

Only thirty years ago the legal profession was secure in the belief that it had cogent tools of inquiry—primarily deduction, analogy, precedent, interpretation, rule application, the identification and balancing of competing social policies, the formulation and application of neutral principles, and judicial restraint—which added up to a methodology that could generate objectively correct answers to even the most difficult legal questions. The Supreme Court was said by the highest of academic authorities to be "predestined . . . to be a voice of reason," for "reason is the life of the law."[2] Today, in contrast, it is fast becoming a commonplace, though one stubbornly resisted in some quarters, that the idea of the law's "objectivity" and all that the term connotes have been exploded, that "we are all pragmatists now."[3] Pragmatists do not deny objectivity. But by predicating objectivity on agreement, they deny

---

1. My definition of "jurisprudence" is not canonical, but neither is it entirely unprecedented. See Thurman W. Arnold, "Apologia for Jurisprudence," 44 *Yale Law Journal* 729 (1935).

2. Henry M. Hart, Jr., "The Supreme Court 1958 Term: Foreword: The Time Chart of the Justices," 73 *Harvard Law Review* 84, 99, 125 (1959). Hart's mentor, Felix Frankfurter, had spoken in even more extravagant terms, of "reason called law." Frankfurter, "Chief Justices I Have Known," 39 *Virginia Law Review* 883, 905 (1953). Holmes, in contrast, had thought the "life of the law" was "experience." *The Common Law* 1. The shift in terms is portentous, as we shall see.

3. The theme, not the words, of Richard Rorty, "The Banality of Pragmatism and the Poetry of Justice," 63 *University of Southern California Law Review* 1811 (1990), reprinted in *Pragmatism in Law and Society* 89 (Michael Brint and William Weaver eds. 1991).

that law (or any other practice) can be objective once agreement on premises has shattered. It has been shattered.

A professional ideology is a result of the way in which the members of the profession work, the form and content of their careers, the activities that constitute their daily rounds, in short the economic and social structure of the profession. So at least I shall argue, drawing on the scholarly literature on the effect of work on consciousness[4] and a distinct scholarly literature on the history of the medieval craft guilds.

I ask the reader not to dismiss out of hand, merely because Marxism is a discredited political philosophy, the suggestion that a profession's characteristic modes of thought might have economic causes. Medicine is rich in examples.[5] Why has preventive medicine always been such an orphan of the medical profession? Because some of its most effective methods, such as simple hygiene and water purification, do not require or depend on medical training and their benefits to health are not easily appropriated in the form of fees. Why did medieval physicians place such emphasis on prognosis? Because, given the paucity of knowledge about how to cure disease, the skill essential to professional success was the ability to determine whether a prospective patient was likely to recover on his own; if not, the case would be declined, to protect the profession's reputation. And why did those same physicians consider surgery not to be the practice of medicine and leave it to barbers? Because the surgical skills of the time were almost entirely mechanical, having no tincture of abstract knowledge and hence inconsistent with the medical profession's self-advertisement as a learned profession. Should we be surprised to find that self-interest has played as big a role in legal thought as in medical thought?

Realism and Materialism

Even the most committed scientific realist would admit that the rate and direction of scientific research are influenced by factors of a political, ideological, or self-interested character extraneous to the truth of

4. A literature well illustrated by Joseph Bensman and Robert Lilienfeld, *Craft and Consciousness: Occupational Technique and the Development of World Images* (1973). See also Arthur L. Stinchcombe, "Reason and Rationality," in *The Limits of Rationality* 285 (Karen Schweers Cook and Margaret Levi eds. 1990), and Andrew Abbott's comment thereon, in id. at 317; and Robert Blauner, *Alienation and Freedom* (1964).

5. The following examples are drawn from Erwin H. Ackerknecht, *A Short History of Medicine* 54, 82, 195 (1955).

scientific ideas.[6] But almost everyone, including the committed pragmatist, would also admit that the experimental, statistical, predictive, and observational procedures of modern science, together with the technical capability of embodying and thereby testing scientific theories in technology (such as atomic theory, embodied in nuclear weapons and reactors), enable many scientific ideas to be reasonably held with a degree of confidence (never a hundred percent of course) that enables them to be called "true" without a sense of strain, rather than merely convenient to believe.

It is otherwise in law. Not because the law is different in different places, whereas mathematical and scientific propositions hold everywhere. A proposition about the law of X might be as demonstrable in Y as in X even though the law of Y on the point was different. Nor is the problem that lawyers and judges make little use of scientific methods. Many propositions, not all of them of a purely formal character (for example, that a chess pawn cannot move backwards), that we hold as unshakably as we hold core scientific propositions are not scientific. The statement that it is wrong to torture children is as true a statement of contemporary morality as the statement—itself merely an approximation, and impossible to verify by means comprehensible to the ordinary person—that the earth revolves around the sun is a true statement of contemporary science. And it is a statement that the inhabitants of a culture that had no concept of child abuse could be brought to agree with, for it is merely a descriptive statement about our morality, not a normative statement.

The problem with law (with ethics too) as a system of reasoning is that in a pluralistic society it lacks cogent techniques for resolving disagreement. If everyone in our society just happened to agree that laws which forbid abortion infringe constitutional liberty (just as everyone in the relevant community believes that moving a rook diagonally is a violation of the rules of chess), this would be a true proposition of contemporary American law. But if enough rational persons disagree—

6. As emphasized in recent sociological studies of scientific knowledge. For a review, see H. M. Collins, "The Sociology of Scientific Knowledge: Studies of Contemporary Science," 9 *Annual Review of Sociology* 265 (1983). I reject the extreme position (the so-called "strong programme" in the sociology of science, well illustrated by Bruno Latour and Steve Woolgar, *Laboratory Life: The Construction of Scientific Facts* [1986]) that the acceptance of scientific beliefs is unrelated to their truth.

and disagreement with this proposition cannot itself be deemed a sign of irrationality, as might disagreement with the proposition that it is considered wrong in our society to torture children or that the earth revolves around the sun[7]—there is no method of resolving their disagreement other than by force or some equivalently nonanalytic method of dispute resolution, such as voting. There are no tests, procedures, protocols, algorithms, experiments, computations, or observations for determining which side in the dispute is right. Some arguments can be rejected as bad, but enough good arguments remain on both sides to leave the issue suspended in indeterminacy (see Chapter 5). One can expect, therefore, that political, self-interested, traditional, habitual, or other truth-independent considerations will play a far larger role in explaining the content, character, and acceptance of legal ideas than they play in the case of modern science, where the relevant community agrees on the criteria for verification.

Professionalism

A profession is an occupation thought to require not merely know-how, experience, and general "smarts" but also mastery of a body of specialized but relatively (sometimes highly) abstract knowledge—of a science or some other field believed to have an intellectual structure and system such as theology, or the law, or military science (the study of the general laws, in the scientific sense of the word, of military tactics and strategy). With the growth of universities in their modern form—institutions that specialize in imparting as well as enlarging abstract knowledge—the training for the professions has increasingly assumed, especially in the United States, the form of postgraduate study, although the older system of professional training—apprenticeship—remains influential in such professions as journalism and the military, and for that matter in medicine. So economics is a profession but business is not, because you can be a successful businessman without having mastered a body of abstract knowledge but not a successful economist. Carpentry is not a profession either; although it involves more specialized training than

---

7. It would take me too far afield to consider how people are adjudged to be rational or irrational.

business does, it does not require a high degree of intellectual training or competence.[8]

I am interested in *restricted* professions, such as law and medicine. Anyone can call himself an economist, can be hired as an economist, can (if he is able to) do the work of an economist. But one cannot practice law or medicine, or call oneself a physician or a lawyer, or for that matter teach in a public school, without a license. Many occupations that are not professions are also restricted, such as barbering or driving a taxi. But precisely because they are not professions the restrictions take a different form. The most characteristic though not only professional restriction today is a requirement of protracted formal education, including some, and sometimes a great deal of, specialized university-type education, plus proof of intellectual competence demonstrated by passing a demanding written examination. It was not always thus. Until this century, the formal educational prerequisites for lawyers in this country and England were modest, and often nil. But law was always understood to be a "learned" activity in both senses of the word, and entry into it was almost always restricted in one way or another.

Professional restrictions can be governmental or private, but the latter will rarely be effective for long unless they have some backing from government. Accreditation, for example, may be private; but unless the licensing authorities, which are public, refuse to license the graduates of nonaccredited schools, accreditation may not do much to limit entry into the profession. A few states, notably California, allow persons who have not graduated from an accredited law school to be admitted to the bar if they pass the state bar exam; one consequence is that unaccredited law schools have a significant foothold in California. The California bar exam is uncommonly difficult, however, so the superior training available at the accredited schools is of real value to the student and enables such schools to charge higher tuition than unaccredited schools do (and few try to pass the bar exam without having attended any law school). Still, in California the brunt of limit-

---

8. The vast literature, mainly sociological, on the professions is well represented by Eliot Freidson, *Professional Powers: A Study of the Institutionalization of Formal Knowledge* (1986); Andrew Abbott, *The System of Professions: An Essay on the Division of Expert Labor* (1988); and JoAnne Brown, *The Definition of a Profession: The Authority of Metaphor in the History of Intelligence Testing, 1890–1930* (1992).

ing entry is shifted from the accrediting authorities and the law schools to the bar examiners.

The Medieval Cartel as a Model of the Modern Legal Profession

The legal profession in its traditional form is a cartel of providers of services related to society's laws.[9] The theory of cartels explores the circumstances under which firms are, and are not, able to increase their prices above competitive levels and make the higher prices stick, at least for a time.[10] Cartels come in a great variety of forms, today ranging from furtive short-lived bid-rigging conspiracies in the highway-construction industry to the OPEC oil cartel, and including regulatory cartels such as that of the dairy farmers. Few cartels have a mystique or an ideology, as restricted professions in general and the legal profession in particular have; for that we must go to the medieval craft guilds, early cartels that in periods both of flourishing and of decline resemble the corresponding phases of the legal profession. As my interest in the medieval guild is limited to the light it sheds on one of its remote descendants, it will be convenient to bring out the salient features of the guild system through a composite portrait of a fictitious guild.[11]

9. The cartel explanation for professional restrictions is of course not new. See Brown, note 8 above, at 63–64; Milton Friedman, *Capitalism and Freedom*, ch. 9 (1962); D. S. Lees, *Economic Consequences of the Professions* (1966); *Regulating the Professions: A Public-Policy Symposium* (Roger D. Blair and Stephen Rubin eds. 1980); S. David Young, *The Rule of Experts: Occupational Licensing in America* (1987). For criticism, see Mark J. Osiel, "Lawyers as Monopolists, Aristocrats, and Entrepreneurs," 103 *Harvard Law Review* 2009 (1990).

10. *Economic Analysis of Law* 265–271.

11. For sources of this composite portrait, see Steven A. Epstein, *Wage Labor and Guilds in Medieval Europe* (1991); John H. Mundy, *Europe in the High Middle Ages: 1150–1309* 131–138 (2d ed. 1991); Antony Black, *Guilds and Civil Society in European Political Thought from the Twelfth Century to the Present* (1984); Sylvia L. Thrupp, "The Gilds," in *Economic Organization and Policies in the Middle Ages* (vol. 3 of the *Cambridge Economic History of Europe*), ch. 5 (M. M. Postan, E. E. Rich, and Edward Miller eds. 1965); Edgcumbe Staley, *The Guilds of Florence* (1906); Lujo Brentano, *On the History and Development of Gilds, and the Origin of Trade-Unions* (1870); Toulmin Smith, *English Gilds: The Original Ordinances of More Than One Hundred Early English Gilds* (1870). For a particularly good discussion, see Henri Pirenne, *Economic and Social History of Medieval Europe* 178–191 (1933). The literature is summarized and criticized in Charles R. Hickson and Earl A. Thompson, "A New Theory of Guilds and European Economic Development," 28 *Explorations in Economic History* 127 (1991). Lawyers' guilds were rare, although there was a powerful lawyers' guild in Florence from the fourteenth to the sixteenth centuries. Lauro Martines, *Lawyers and Statecraft in Renaissance Florence*, ch. 2 (1968). Its structure and practices were similar to those of other guilds.

The linen weavers' guild of the Duchy of Guermantes in twelfth-century France operates under a charter from the Duke of Guermantes. The charter authorizes the guild to manufacture and sell linen fabrics and forbids the manufacture or the importation into the duchy of linen fabrics other than those made by guild members and imprinted with the guild's exclusive mark. The guild obtained this monopoly charter by agreeing to give the duke an annual present of its best fabrics. In exchange the guild is enabled by the prohibition against competitive entry to fix prices that assure handsome remuneration to its members even after subtraction of the cost of the gift to the duke. But guild and duke alike are reluctant to justify the monopoly charter in the stark terms of mutual economic self-interest. Even in a nondemocratic polity, public opinion counts for something, and usually a lot. Privilege is resented, and may also have ominous political implications. The monopolist in the famous "Case of Monopolies," in which the English judges sided with Parliament in its opposition to the Crown's practice of raising revenue without parliamentary consent by selling monopolies, defended his monopoly of playing cards by arguing that monopoly kept the quality up and also that permitting cheap foreign imports would take jobs away from Englishmen.[12]

So it is no surprise that the charter of the weavers' guild recites that monopoly is necessary to protect the public from deceptively cheap—because shoddy, but difficult to recognize as such—merchandise sold by foreigners and other undependable people. A precocious guild theoretician has pointed out that if consumers lack good information about the quality of a product they will perforce assume that every brand of the product, regardless of its price, is of average quality. They will therefore buy the cheapest brand—which being of lowest quality will probably cost the least to make. Producers of the higher-quality, costlier brands, unable to recoup their additional costs by charging a higher price, will be driven from the market unless they reduce the quality and hence the cost of their brand. Quality will spiral downward, and consumers will end up receiving a lower quality of product than they want and would be willing to pay for.[13]

12. Darcy v. Allein, 11 Co. Rep. 84b, 77 Eng. Rep. 1260 (K.B. 1602).
13. Hayne E. Leland, "Quacks, Lemons, and Licensing: A Theory of Minimum Quality Standards," 87 *Journal of Political Economy* 1328 (1979); for criticism, see Keith B. Leffler, "Commentary," in *Occupational Licensure and Regulation* 287 (Simon Rottenberg ed. 1980). In the case of a producer of personal services, such as a lawyer, the analysis in the text implies

Although prohibiting entry is necessary if the guild is to have supracompetitive profits, it is not sufficient. If the members of a guild are numerous (and perhaps even if they are few), each will have an incentive to expand his output until the cost of the last unit that he produces is equal to the market price, because until that point is reached a greater output will increase his profits. But eventually all this additional output will drive the market price down to the competitive level. One might suppose that this result could easily be averted by the guild's fixing a minimum price for its members' output at the level that maximizes their profits as a whole, and by punishing cheaters, that is, price cutters. The weavers' guild has done this. But even though outright cheating by members—the slight shading of the fixed minimum price to enable the sale of a much larger output at a profit per unit only slightly lower than selling at the price fixed by the cartel would yield—has been prevented, the temptation to engross a larger share of the guild's profits led some members of the guild in its early days to work longer hours, or hire more workers, in order to sell more at the fixed price. And it led others to increase the quality of their output in order to wrest business from their competitors by offering the consumer more for the same, guild-fixed price.

The guild has acted more vigorously against the first practice (increasing quantity) than against the second (increasing quality). This is partly for reasons of practicality and partly for reasons of public relations, or mystique. It is relatively easy for the guild to fix and even to enforce limits on hours of work and on number of workers; and in fact the guild has forbidden its members to work at night or on holidays or to hire workers beyond the minimum number of apprentices necessary to assure the guild's continuation after its present members retire or die. Although the guild's profits have, nevertheless, eroded some because its members persist in competing in quality, this is not entirely

---

that the client may get a less able practitioner than he wants and would be willing to pay for. Carl Shapiro, "Investment, Moral Hazard, and Occupational Licensing," 53 *Review of Economic Studies* 843 (1986). The economic case for regarding guilds as a response to a problem of consumer uncertainty about quality is argued in Bo Gustafsson, "The Rise and Economic Behavior of Medieval Craft Guilds: An Economic-Theoretical Interpretation," 35 *Scandinavian Economic History Review and Economy and History* 1 (1987). I shall not try to evaluate the overall economic efficiency or social value of the guild system or of the counterpart restrictions in the legal profession, but shall glance at the issue in Chapter 4. For an interesting discussion, see Ronald J. Gilson, "The Devolution of the Legal Profession: A Demand Side Perspective," 49 *Maryland Law Review* 869 (1990).

a bad thing from the guild's standpoint. Quality competition reinforces the quality-protection argument that is the cornerstone of the guild's claim of legitimacy. The guild really *is* producing a superior product. In fact, it is producing a better product than consumers want; they would be happier with a product of slightly lower quality at a lower price. But they don't know the optimal price-quality combination because they are offered no alternative. What they do know and what the guild does not let them forget is that they are getting a product of superior quality along such dimensions as tightness of weave, strength, softness, appearance, and durability.

The restrictions on employment, although primarily intended to limit output, reinforce the quality argument for the guild's monopoly. Because a member of the guild cannot hire a flock of workers—cannot operate on the factory system—he is, perforce, a craftsman, a handicrafter. The weavers' guild has vigorously propagated a norm of craftsmanship, of hand-madeness, as an index of quality. It is a plausible norm in an era before department stores and enforceable warranties. Each swatch of linen fabric bears the mark not only of the guild but also of the member who produced it. The consumer knows infallibly who the producer is. There is no divided responsibility, no possibility of mutual finger-pointing, when any of the guild's output proves defective.

The real danger to the guild is not that the members will compete away all available profits by increasing the quality of their product, but that they will try to increase their profits by reducing that quality and, with it, their costs. Such competition would destroy the quality rationale for the guild's monopoly, engender consumer dissatisfaction in the long run (in the short run, consumers may not notice the deterioration in quality), and threaten the survival of the guild and therefore of its higher-cost members by creating irresistible pressure to abandon the minimum price fixed by the guild. The guild has responded to this menace by fixing minimum standards of quality of workmanship and materials. Members are required to adhere to these standards under threat of expulsion from the guild. The guild has gone so far as to specify the tools that its members must use. These standards, these requirements, have provided, in turn, additional support for the quality rationale for guild restrictions—the guild is policing the quality of its members' work directly rather than merely excluding putatively lower-quality competitors.

The guild cannot expect the threat of sanctions to prevent all violations of guild restrictions. It has sought therefore to encourage social cohesiveness among its members in order to bring altruism and informal sanctions to bear in support of compliance with the guild's restrictions. It has excluded from membership Jews and other aliens believed not to share a common core of basic tastes and values with the members. It has become a social as well as a business alliance, with frequent intermarriage among the families of members and with generational competition muted by drawing apprentices exclusively from the ranks of the sons and nephews of the guild's present members. The guild talks up pride in one's calling, the leading of a blameless life, loyalty to the guild, and equality among its members—seeks in other words to imbue its members with moral precepts and values, communal rather than individualistic, calculated to reduce the likelihood that members will cheat on the restrictions that the guild imposes on them. Tradition, not innovation; uniformity, not variety; emphasis on input rather than emphasis on output, hence emphasis on quality rather than on quantity and on doing one's own work rather than contracting it out or delegating it to employees—in short on making, on crafting, rather than on supervising the work of others—all are attitudes and values that the guild has been sedulous to cultivate.

We must take a closer look at apprenticeship. Its significance lies not only in its training function,[14] but also in the fact that a guild must make provision for its continuation into the indefinite future. Even if the members have no concern about its flourishing after they are dead, the guild cannot hope to retain its privileged status under the laws of Guermantes if it does not hold out reasonable assurances of being able to supply the duchy's linen needs for the indefinite future. But how can it assure that there will be a next generation of guild members without sharing its monopoly rents with a class of new entrants? Apprenticeship is the answer. Entry into the potentially lucrative occupation of being a member of the weavers' guild is rationed to persons willing to put in long years of work at low wages. In effect they buy a share of the master's share of the guild's profits, much as the modern purchaser of stock in a corporation that has a patent or other monopoly buys a right to receive a proportionate share of the firm's expected

---

14. Emphasized in Bernard Elbaum, "Why Apprenticeship Persisted in Britain But Not in the United States," 49 *Journal of Economic History* 337 (1989).

monopoly profits. The right yields him only a competitive expected return on his investment, not a monopoly return, because the expected monopoly profits have been discounted in the purchase price of the stock.

The length of the apprenticeship limits the rate at which the guild expands. Varying that length enables the supply of labor to be adjusted continually to meet changes in the demand for the guild's output and hence in its derived demand for labor and other inputs, while the meager level of the wages paid apprentices prevents the dissipation of guild rents to newcomers. The length of the apprenticeship also reinforces the quality argument. Apprenticeship is in part a period of training, so the longer the apprenticeship, the more plausibly the guild can represent to the public that the manufacture of a high-quality product is a task requiring unusual skill which can be acquired only by lengthy training. Apprenticeship also facilitates the screening and indoctrination of new members. Uniformity of outlook, and with it a greater likelihood of conformity to the established norms of pricing, workmanship, and output, are fostered by a system in which new producers have spent many years as students, wards, and understudies of the old. The weavers' guild could auction off new memberships, as was later to be done with seats on the New York Stock Exchange, another cartel. But that would bring into the guild producers unlikely to internalize the guild's values—values designed to limit competition among the members. The apprenticeship system of acquiring new members minimizes this risk.

From Guild to Factory

Even if, as I believe, the best explanation for the guilds is that they were devices for maximizing the net earnings of their members, the efforts that the guilds bent to this end fostered both a particular personal morality and a particular institutional mystique. The personal morality emphasized such values as loyalty, equality, conformity, personal responsibility, and patient craftsmanship, implying scrupulous attention to detail and to quality. The institutional mystique involved celebration of the production of high-quality goods or services as unique handicrafts by highly trained specialists, and the abhorrence of cheapness and shoddiness. This mutually reinforcing combination of morality and mystique is the ideology of guild production. An industry ideology, however, does not survive the transition to mass production. The conditions of such production may, as Marx argued, foster the creation of a workers' ideology, over and against which we observe a diffuse business ideology shared by many business executives. But there is no ideology of the producing unit; as we are about to see, there *is* no single producing unit any more. A guild of weavers has an ideology; a cartel, and especially a competitive market, of textile manufacturers does not.

Mass production involves a change from the handcrafting of small quantities of individualized, high-quality goods by highly trained specialists to machine production of large quantities of goods of average quality, often by unskilled workers performing simple, repetitive operations, under the direction of supervisors and ultimately executives.[15] The division of labor within the producing unit, by breaking up into its constituent operations the process of manufacture that was the guild's craft, enables a greater output to be produced by a work force that may lack anyone with the range of skills and the depth of training of a master craftsman in a guild system.[16] The importance of instilling traditional craft values in the work force is therefore diminished, along with the value of protracted training as under a system of apprenticeship. The workers are more like the different parts of a machine, or the different cells of an organism, than they are like handcraftsmen, for none of them produces an entire product. The values required of supervisors and executives are especially remote from those of the guild—they are leadership values and related "people skills," specific talents for maneuvering in large organizations, and financial and marketing acumen. Those talents are of little use to a person who works

15. An intermediate stage between guild and mass production is the "craft" union, in which guild-like organization of the "skilled" work force is combined with modern methods of organizing production. The apprenticeship rules and exclusionary practices of the craft unions are reminiscent of guild practices. An analogy is to the "in-house" lawyer, who, being a corporate employee, is simultaneously a subordinate figure in an industrial work force and an independent professional—which means that his independence is compromised. Cf. Diana Chapman Walsh, *Corporate Physicians: Between Medicine and Management* (1987).

16. Harry Braverman, *Labor and Monopoly Capital: The Degradation of Work in the Twentieth Century* 79–80 (1974). It would be a mistake however to suppose that modern methods of production imply a wholesale "deskilling" of the labor force. Paul Attewell, "The Deskilling Controversy," 14 *Work and Occupations* 323 (1987).

slowly and painstakingly, by himself or with at most the aid of one or two apprentices.

The diversity of tasks in the modern business firm dooms the moral uniformity secured by the guild system. And with quality de-emphasized and handcrafting a thing of the past, the quality-centered mystique of the guild disappears as well. Not only the work force but the management force is mobile, possessed of general-purpose production and managerial skills rather than anchored to a particular industry by a patient accretion of unique handicraft skills. Once, a weaver might have been thought a kind of artist; no one would describe the modern textile manufacturing firm as an *atelier*.

We must be wary of overstatement. There is craft, and not just craftiness, in the organizational skills of the modern business executive and in the technical skills of the modern factory worker, who with the growth of the "total quality management" concept and Japanese-style team production is less and less likely to be a Charlie Chaplinesque assembly-line automaton. I need a better word than "craft" to distinguish the work of medieval guild craftsmen from that of modern manufacturing personnel. That word is "artisanality."[17] It is at once broader and narrower than craft—broader because not limited to a member of a medieval (or any) guild; narrower because the terms *craft, craftsman,* and *craftsmanship* can be applied to nonartisanal activities, persons, and skills. The guild craftsman, however, was an artisan.

The industrial counterpart of the painter or sculptor, the artisan makes things with his hands, with at most limited aid from machinery. He has the satisfaction of observing a direct connection between his input and his output—the satisfaction of having something tangible to show for his efforts. The spirit of artisanality is captured in the nineteenth-century "arts and crafts" movement, which "emphasized the human touch—the care, craftsmanship and attention to detail that go into a piece of furniture or a decorative object that is crafted by hand. The art of creating something, it was thought, should be a joyful, exhilarating experience, not just a way of earning money."[18] In addition, the artisanal mode of production promotes a stable cartel organization of industry by limiting output.

17. See, for example, Paul S. Seaver, *Wallington's World: A Puritan Artisan in Seventeenth-Century London,* ch. 5 (1985).

18. Beth Sherman, "A Celebration of Beauty," *Newsday,* March 31, 1988, p. 3. For a similar sentiment expressed by a modern judge, see Chapter 4.

The Rise of the Legal Profession's Cartel

Something like the evolution of the textile industry from guild production to mass production, and the concomitant decline of artisanality, is occurring today in the market for legal services.

By the end of the thirteenth century a distinct legal profession had emerged in England that had definite affinities to a craft guild on the one hand and to the modern English legal profession on the other, and by the time of our Revolution the English legal profession had assumed something remarkably like its present form.[19] It was divided between courtroom lawyers (the barristers) and office lawyers (the solicitors). To become a barrister an aspirant had to be "called to the bar" after a period of residing and studying in an inn of court. Because such residence was costly and because a barrister could not work for another barrister but instead had to depend on cases referred to him by solicitors, who were naturally reluctant to refer cases to a beginner, the career of a barrister was largely limited to persons of independent means. As a result, the supply of barristers was restricted, and while many barristers had, therefore, very high incomes, those who lost out in the barrister lottery by failing to obtain cases from solicitors eked out a meager living, often supplemented by moonlighting, for example as a journalist. The large dispersion of lawyers' income remains a characteristic of both the English and the American legal profession.

The successful barristers and the royal judges (who were former barristers) formed a small, cosy, homogeneous community. The common law is the expression of the values of this community.[20] The lack of a felt need to systematize the common law by reducing it to a code is a reflection of the community's homogeneity. Its members had no

19. The historical sketch that follows is based on *Lawyers in Early Modern Europe and America* (Wilfrid Prest ed. 1981); Gerald W. Gawalt, *The Promise of Power: The Emergence of the Legal Profession in Massachusetts 1760–1840* (1979); Robert Stevens, *Law School: Legal Education in America from the 1850s to the 1980s* (1983); Richard L. Abel, *American Lawyers* (1989); Paul Brand, *The Origins of the English Legal Profession* (1992). The support that the "craft" analogy gives to traditional jurisprudential thinking receives suggestive treatment in Pierre Schlag, "The Problem of the Subject," 69 *Texas Law Review* 1627, 1662–1663 (1991). A wealth of comparative and historical information about the legal profession can be found in *Lawyers in Society* (Richard L. Abel and Philip S. C. Lewis eds., 3 vols., 1988–1989).

20. A. W. Brian Simpson, "The Common Law and Legal Theory," in *Legal Theory and Common Law* 8 (William Twining ed. 1986), reprinted in Simpson, *Legal Theory and Legal History: Essays on the Common Law* 359 (1987).

more need for a code than the native speakers in a language community need a grammar book to know how to speak.

To become a solicitor in eighteenth-century England one had to serve a period of years as an articled clerk, that is, as a solicitor's apprentice. So entry into the solicitors' branch of the profession was controlled too. Solicitors were allowed only one articled clerk at a time, which limited the growth of the profession.

The situation in the colonies and, later, in the new nation was more fluid. Although lawyers had played a prominent role in the founding, and constituted in Tocqueville's view the nearest thing that the United States had to an aristocracy, the public was hostile to guild-like restrictions and privileges. The division between barristers and solicitors never took hold. Many judges were elected rather than appointed; most of them didn't wear the robe—the symbol of the judge's, as of the clergyman's, specialness; and their powers over juries were severely limited. In short, the idea of a legal caste was resisted. Before the Civil War, two states abolished all restrictions on entry into the legal profession other than that the entrant be an adult of good moral character.[21] Other states were more restrictive, generally requiring an apprenticeship (clerking in a lawyer's office, the equivalent of the English articled clerkship) as a condition to becoming a member of the bar. But there were no educational requirements and no bar exam, and probably the principal limitation on the size of the profession was simply the generally low standard of education in nineteenth-century America. Law was then as it is today an intellectually demanding profession. (Whether it has to be is a separate question.) A brilliant man like Abraham Lincoln could become a successful lawyer with little formal education. But the pool from which such lawyers could emerge must have been small, just like the pool of persons from which opera singers and professional athletes emerge—two occupations in which a few "stars" earn very high salaries even though there are no legal restrictions on entry.

Educational standards rose, endangering the lawyers' scarcity rents (see note 26), and whether for that or other reasons the latter part of the nineteenth century witnessed a movement, rich in parallels to developments occurring at the same time in the medical profession, toward making the American legal profession a restricted occupation. We may date the beginning of this movement to 1870 when Christo-

21. Stevens, note 19 above, at 17.

pher Columbus Langdell became dean of the Harvard Law School. His program of educational reform[22] was explicitly based on the premise that law was a science.[23] That premise made it natural to suppose that lawyers should undergo a lengthy period of preparation at a university—where else would one develop scientists? From there it is but a step, though a big step (and one not taken by real sciences), to *making* them undergo that preparation as a condition of being permitted to engage in professional activity. The step was not complete until apprenticeship as an alternative route to qualifying to take the bar exam was abolished and until bar cram schools were disaccredited, although they survive to this day as the bar-review courses of a few weeks in length that newly graduated law students take before sitting for the bar exam. As late as 1951, 20 percent of American lawyers had not graduated from law school and 50 percent had not graduated from college.[24] But by 1960 four years of college (more precisely, a college degree, which rarely is earned in fewer years), plus three years at an accredited law school, plus receipt of a passing grade on the bar exam administered by the state in which the candidate wanted to practice, plus satisfying a bar committee that the candidate was of sound moral character, formed a series of hoops through which almost everyone who wanted to become a licensed practitioner of law in this country had to jump.

The barrier to new entry created by these requirements would have been porous, however, had it not been for the prohibition against the unauthorized practice of law. Not only were persons who had not been admitted to the bar of a state forbidden to call themselves lawyers; they could not perform the services that the state defined as the practice of law—mainly the representation of litigants before courts and most administrative agencies, and the sale of legal advice. Nonlawyers were kept from circumventing this prohibition by being forbidden to enter into partnership with lawyers or otherwise obtain an ownership interest in enterprises selling legal services.

States also limited competition *within* the profession, by forbidding most methods of soliciting business (including "ambulance chasing"

22. For which, however, Harvard President Charles W. Eliot may deserve much of the credit. Anthony Chase, "The Birth of the Modern Law School," 23 *American Journal of Legal History* 329, 332 (1979).

23. Albeit of a curious sort, as we shall note in Chapter 5.

24. Dietrich Rueschemeyer, *Lawyers and Their Society: A Comparative Study of the Legal Profession in Germany and in the United States* 105 (1973).

and advertising), by encouraging lawyers to price their services according to fees set by the state bar association, and by limiting interstate mobility of lawyers. A lawyer was permitted to practice only in the courts of a state of which he was both a resident and, by virtue of having passed the state's bar exam and satisfied the state's other requirements for licensing, a member of the state's bar. Some states admitted to the bar applicants who had not taken the state's bar exam if the applicant had practiced law in a state that provided reciprocal privileges, but only if he moved to the state in which he was seeking admission. The prohibitions against "lay intermediaries" (the employment of a lawyer by a nonlawyer, for example by a corporation seeking to market legal services to clients), and against unauthorized practice, limited competition within as well as with the legal profession by making it more difficult for law firms to expand.

The restrictions on competition within the profession were also restrictions on new entry into professional submarkets. Advertising and access to efficient capital markets are more important for new entrants than for existing firms, because the latter already have established their reputations and accumulated their capital. Even if an enterprising lawyer, perceiving unusual profit opportunities in a state in which the supply of legal services was especially restricted, went to the bother of obtaining a license in that state—and the bother might be considerable, might be the reason the supply of lawyers in the state *was* so restricted—he would not be able to use the common methods by which a new firm in a market seeks to wrest customers from the existing firms.

When one is speaking of markets of thousands of sellers, concern over limitations on entry into the profession's markets may seem academic. Were there not bound to be enough licensed sellers of legal services in every significant locality to guarantee vigorous competition—and thus thwart any efforts at cartelization—even if new entry were blocked completely? To answer this question requires distinguishing between a cartel of producers of goods and a cartel of providers of personal services. The latter is likely to have a larger membership, which will increase the costs of coordination and of preventing cheating. But it is much more difficult for an individual to increase his output of a personal service than it is for a firm to increase its output of a product. A firm can hire additional workers, build a larger factory, buy more machinery and supplies, add more executives; only gradually will it encounter diseconomies of scale that limit its growth. Personal services are different. There are only so many hours in the year, and therefore only so many operations a highly skilled surgeon can perform, only so many trials that even the best trial lawyer can conduct, only so many clients that the best legal counselor can advise. Even the world's best and cheapest lawyer, assisted by the most skilled and serviceable assistants, can supply only a tiny fraction of the market's demand for trial counsel. Some Renaissance artists expanded their output significantly by having assistants, apprentices, or students paint the lesser figures or landscape backgrounds in their paintings. Even so, the amount of personal attention required of the master was generally too great for him to be able to engage in mass production.[25]

So even if it is infeasible to fix the price of legal services—a further difficulty being the heterogeneous character of those services—or to limit the output of individual lawyers or law firms, as long as the *number* of lawyers is limited some lawyers will enjoy monopoly returns.[26] Limiting entry therefore becomes the focus of the professional cartel. This in turn makes government assistance more important to professional cartels than to ordinary producer cartels. The latter can by fixing prices or limiting output make monopoly profits for a time, although new entry will squeeze out those profits eventually. But control of entry is essential to a professional cartel, because the large number of its members is bound to make the coordination of prices and output and the detection of cheaters very difficult. And despite a vast theoretical literature on the use of predatory tactics to discourage entry, instances of successful use of such tactics are rare and almost all involve single-firm monopolies rather than cartels, since the coordinated employment of predatory tactics is particularly difficult to pull off. Government on the other hand, through a requirement that

25. Rubens was an exception. "He developed a painting factory: assistants specialized in certain skills—landscapes, animals, and so on—and the master devised a mode of invention employing a clever combination of oil sketches and drawings. These permitted his inventions to be executed by others, sometimes with final touches to hands or faces by the master himself . . . Rubens, unlike Rembrandt, did not sign the works that were sold from his studio. Only five of the thousands of works produced were signed." Svetlana Alpers, *Rembrandt's Enterprise: The Studio and the Market* 101 (1988).

26. Even with no restrictions, some lawyers would earn economic rents (returns greater than they could earn in any other activity), just as some opera singers, who compete in an unregulated industry, earn economic rents. But a rent to a factor of production that is in irremediably short supply relative to demand must be distinguished from a rent to a factor of production the supply of which is limited by agreement or regulation. It is the latter rent, the true monopoly rent, that concerns us here.

providers of a specified service have a license, can limit entry rather easily. So we should expect to find that durable, effective professional cartels are government-supported.

Another difference between professional and producer cartels is that it is generally easier to distinguish among products than among professional services. Steel, aluminum, automobiles, oil, plumbing fixtures, and coffee are both visible and visibly distinct from one another in a way in which many legal services and medical services are not. If a lawyer hires a professional actor to read the script, written by the lawyer, of the lawyer's closing argument to the jury, is the actor practicing law? (An interpreter wouldn't be; nor the lawyer's tailor—yet clothes are a form of statement, as we shall see in Chapter 24.) Is drafting a will the practice of law? Creating a trust? Giving legal advice? Doing legal research for a lawyer? Indexing the record in a trial? Ghostwriting a judge's opinions? Teaching law to law students? To business students? Proofreading a bond indenture? Representing litigants in a tax court or before a social security or veterans' disability tribunal? Bringing business into a law firm? Collecting overdue bills? Insuring real estate titles? Conveying real estate? Conveying an automobile? Interviewing potential witnesses? Serving as an arbitrator? Is public sanitation the practice of medicine? Is setting simple fractures? Performing first-trimester abortions? Treating neuroses? Administering enemas? Giving flu injections? Faith healing? Prescribing exercises for a sore back? Correcting vision? Pulling teeth? Prescribing a diet for losing weight? To limit entry into a profession, it is not enough to place obstacles in the path of those who want to *call* themselves lawyers or doctors or whatever. The profession must be defined in a way that prevents sellers of substitute services from taking away the profession's business in the way that psychologists have taken away much of the medical and religious professions' business of ministering to people's mental health and that banks and trust companies have taken away much of the legal profession's probate and conveyancing business.

I have called the demarcation of professional services entry-limiting, but it could equally well be called demand-increasing. The demand for a profession's services will be greater the greater the scope of those services. Defining an increase in demand as economists do, as the willingness of consumers to buy more of a product at any given price, we can see that an increase in the demand for a cartel's product or service could increase the cartel's output without causing price to fall, so that the cartel's profits would increase. Another way in which a cartel can increase demand is by inducing the government to subsidize that demand, for example by paying for a poor person's lawyer. But demand-increasing measures are double-edged swords from a cartel's standpoint, a fact that helps explain the long opposition of the medical and legal professions to government subsidization of their services. When demand is rising, a cartel has more difficulty detecting the cheaters in its ranks because the "honest" members may not be losing sales but may merely be growing more slowly than the cheaters—and they may not even know they are growing more slowly. If, moreover, a professional cartel, in the interest of preserving its cohesiveness, does not expand output in response to growing demand, public and competitive pressure to allow new entry may become overpowering as prices soar to ration the existing and now insufficient supply to the newly expanded demand. Because it is so difficult for an individual to expand his output of personal services, the only way to expand the supply of professional services to meet an increased demand may be to admit new members. But increasing the size of the professional cartel can magnify the disintegrative pressures that afflict all cartels, not only by making it more difficult to identify cheaters but also by forcing the profession to admit new members who do not share the values of the old, perhaps because they are drawn from ethnic groups formerly barred from the profession. Thus it might be in the interest of the existing members of the profession that demand remain at a lower level.

My description of the guild system emphasized the intimate relation between cartelization and quality. Cartelization can improve a profession's average quality even if the selection or credentialing mechanism operates randomly with respect to quality (it could be a lottery system, for example). All that is necessary is that it limit the number of persons in the profession. For then their average income will be higher, which will raise the average quality of candidates for the profession by making it more attractive to people who have good prospects in other fields, unless the profession's existing members are able to use apprenticeship requirements to prevent newcomers from sharing in the monopoly rents that cartelization generates.

Another source of upward pressure on quality in the legal profession is the adversary character of legal services. The better the lawyer on one side of a case (or a negotiation) is, the greater will be the value to the opposing party of having a good lawyer on his side. Since better quality of lawyers may conduce to better quality of decisions, quality competition among lawyers is not a zero-sum game. If cartelization results in higher-quality lawyers who produce higher-quality briefs, judges' decisions will tend to be of higher quality and this will confer benefits on the community as a whole—maybe. "Quality" is an elusive concept when one is speaking of legal services. Highly intelligent lawyers may create intricate doctrinal structures that, while ingenious, even in a sense rigorous, have no social utility. For example, brilliant lawyers create, discover, and enlarge tax loopholes. This activity is purely redistributive; there is no social gain. In fact there is a net social loss, not only because lawyers' time has an opportunity cost but also because their beaver-like activities require more carefully drafted and complex tax codes. Social welfare might increase if the IQs of all tax lawyers could be reduced by 10 percent.

This point illustrates a difference between craft guilds and professions. More dimensions of quality are hidden in the case of the latter. Professional services require interpretation, not inspection, to determine private and social value, and this magnifies the role of ideology and rhetoric in securing a high economic and social position for a profession.[27] As medicine becomes more scientific and law more competitive—both developments that facilitate the monitoring of professional services—we can expect the ideological and rhetorical components of these professional services to diminish.

A complete economic analysis of professional cartelization would require an explanation of how a group composed of hundreds of thousands of individuals can overcome free-rider obstacles to collective action to the extent of being able to obtain governmental support for a cartel. (But we know they can: think of farmers.) Because the profession is so large, because a perceptible if small fraction of its members have a palpable self-interest in maintaining the professional cartel, and because the social costs of such a cartel are both diffuse and only dimly perceived, the problem of free riding need not be insoluble. Provided that existing practitioners are grandfathered whenever some new entry barrier is created (such as graduation from an accredited law school), the entire cost of the barrier will fall on prospective entrants to the profession—many of whom have not begun to think about entering

27. As emphasized in Brown, note 8 above, ch. 1.

the profession and some of whom have not even been born—and on consumers of legal services.

Some states have an "integrated" bar, meaning that every lawyer must belong to the state bar association. In effect he is taxed to support the cartel-enhancing activities of the association, and so the free-rider problem is overcome. But we must ask how a state comes to have an integrated bar; whose self-interest was served by taking a leading role in advocating such an institution? A possible answer is that a part-time investment in bar association activities pays dividends in legal fees by making a lawyer better known to other lawyers, increasing the likelihood of their referring cases to him that they don't have the time or skills to handle themselves or are barred from handling by conflict of interest rules.

Ever since the adoption of Langdell's system of case law instruction, which is feasible (some think optimal) with a very low ratio of faculty to students and therefore is cheap, universities that have law schools have had a pecuniary interest in promoting a requirement that lawyers have to be graduates of a three-year law school.[28] Existing universities also have a pecuniary interest in accreditation standards that limit competition from new schools, such as the dreaded "proprietary" (profit-making) professional schools. Law professors have an interest in raising the quality of the legal profession, too, because better students are more rewarding to teach, and (subject to the qualification in note 28) in preserving the system of regulation that requires people who want to practice law to attend law schools for a lengthy fixed period. One rarely finds law professors, whether they are radicals or libertarians, inveighing against the legal profession's cartelistic restrictions.

The role of judges in encouraging and maintaining those restrictions should not be overlooked. Brand argues (see note 19) that the legal profession emerged in England in response to the growing professionalization of the judiciary. As knowledge of and experience in law became recognized qualifications for judicial office, litigants found it more difficult to present their cases without the assistance of similarly knowledgeable and experienced persons. (So one is not surprised at the absence of a legal profession in ancient Athens, where, as we shall see

28. A qualification is necessary. Reducing the length of law school to, say, two years could, by making a legal education much cheaper, so increase the number of entering students as to offset the loss of students in the third year.

in Chapter 14, there were no professional judges.) The other side of this coin is that professional lawyers make the task of the professional judge much easier. The judges' self-interest in the quality of the bar makes them sympathetic to pleas for regulations that raise that quality; cartelization does that, as we have seen. And the judges are not merely passive sympathizers with professional efforts at cartelization. They have played an active role in the formulation and administration of standards of professional conduct, including standards governing licensure and thus controlling entry into the profession. We judges who vigorously enforce sanctions against unprofessional behavior by the lawyers practicing before us are protecting the consumer of legal services in one sense but are also raising the price of those services and, by tending to exclude the less able practitioners, restricting entry into the profession.

Guild and Profession Compared

We can begin to sense ideological parallels, and to understand their common material basis, between the medieval craft guild and the modern legal profession as it stood on the eve of the transformation of the market for legal services that began in about 1960. In both forms of market organization, cartelization is facilitated by the creation of an ideological community that genteelly resists the "commodification" of its output—resists, that is, the commercial values of competition, innovation, consumer sovereignty, and the deliberate pursuit of profit. Professions advance "claims to esoteric knowledge and unselfish service."[29]

"Plumbing is still prosecuted too largely for the plumber's profit. It is therefore a handicraft, not a profession."[30] We can hear the echo of the quality argument for restricting competition. For an ethic of individuality and rivalry is substituted one of cooperation and solidarity. "A profession is a brotherhood—almost, if the word could be purified of its invidious implications, a caste. Professional activities are so definite, so absorbing in interest, so rich in duties and responsibilities that they completely engage their votaries. The social and personal lives of professional men and their families thus tend to organize around a profes-

29. Marie Haug, "The Sociological Approach to Self-Regulation," in *Regulating the Professions,* note 9 above, at 61, 63.

30. Abraham Flexner, "Is Social Work a Profession?" 1 *School and Society* 901, 905 (1915). See also Louis D. Brandeis, *Business—A Profession* 2 (1914).

sional nucleus. A strong class consciousness soon develops."[31] Central to this consciousness, despite Flexner's dismissive attitude toward mere "handicrafts," is a mystique akin to artisanality. Brandeis liked to boast that judges—unlike other high government officials, who preside over bureaucracies similar to those of large business firms—do their own work; and Henry Hart wrote, with what in retrospect seems astonishing naiveté, that "writing opinions is the most time-consuming of all judicial work, and the least susceptible of effective assistance from a law clerk."[32] He either did not know or would not say that by 1959 a majority of the Supreme Court's opinions were being written by law clerks; today, a judge-written opinion, at any level of the American judiciary, is rare. The fact that legal services are personal services rather than products, and hence resistant to automation, made plausible the idea that artisanship, epitomized in the "handcrafting" of a judicial opinion, supplies the criterion of professional excellence. Some personal services, it is true, have become highly standardized. But the arts remain a bastion (albeit an embattled one) of artisanship, and to its votaries law is an art. So acknowledgment that neophytes can, after only three years of professional instruction and no professional experience, do much of the principal work of judges more or less satisfactorily, or at least not shockingly badly, still has the capacity to undermine professional self-esteem. It is a little as if brain surgeons delegated the entire performance of delicate operations to nurses, orderlies, and first-year medical students—and patients were none the worse for it. Of course only judges who allow their law clerks to dictate the judges' votes are delegating the *entire* performance of the "operation." Nor is the judicial function exhausted in voting and opinion writing; there are also conferring, editing, questioning counsel, and other tasks. Still, so central has judicial opinion-writing seemed to the conception of legal "craft" that revelations about how heavily appellate judges, notably including U.S. Supreme Court Justices, rely on ghostwriters[33] continue to roil the smooth surface of professional self-esteem.

Law is an art, but also a mystery. Emphasis on formal education attracts intellectually agile aspirants whose forensic and analytic efforts

31. Flexner, note 30 above, at 904.

32. Hart, note 2 above, at 91.

33. See, for example, Jeffrey Rosen, "The Next Justice," *New Republic,* April 12, 1993, p. 21; Paul M. Barrett, "If There Is Blood in an Opinion, We Know Who Wrote It," *Wall Street Journal,* Oct. 4, 1993, p. A1.

intellectualize professional activity, making that activity increasingly impenetrable by the lay understanding. One is put in mind of the relation between clerisy and laity in the medieval Church. Like many clerics, professionals practice "unworthy arts to raise their importance among the ignorant," including "an affectation of mystery in all their writings and conversations relating to their profession; an affectation of knowledge inscrutable to all, except the adepts in the science; an air of perfect confidence in their own skill and abilities; and a demeanor solemn, contemptuous and highly expressive of self-sufficiency."[34]

The homogeneity of professional training produces a degree of consensus on professional issues that tricks the practitioners into believing they have a pipeline to the truth. The complexity of law's doctrines, the obscurity of its jargon, and the objectifying of "the law" are in part endogenous to the organization of the legal profession, rather than being exogenous factors to which the profession has adapted by setting high and uniform standards for qualification. People who have the same training and experiences tend to look at things the same way, but are less likely to believe that they agree because they are alike than to believe that they agree because they have the training and skills necessary to penetrate appearances to a uniform reality that exists outside themselves and guides their inquiries. When religious zealots succeed through the persecution of dissenters in enforcing uniformity of belief, they do not infer that consensus is the result of persecution. They infer that theirs is the true faith. The more heterogeneous in training and background the legal profession is, the less likely it is to reach consensus on important legal issues and therefore to delude itself that legal opinion is, as it were, coerced by external reality; so, with the profession in fact becoming more heterogeneous in recent decades, belief in "the law" has diminished.

All this is not to say that either members of a homogeneous profession or religious fanatics are "irrational" by virtue of succumbing to a degree, perhaps a very high degree, of self-delusion. People are more likely to believe what they believe because it is useful for them to believe those things than because the things they believe are true. It can be dangerous to base action on false beliefs; but what is the good of a bad conscience, from the standpoint not of morality but of rational utility maximization, unless it leads one to alter one's actions in a direction

34. Jeffrey Lionel Berlant, *Profession and Monopoly: A Study of Medicine in the United States and Great Britain* 89 (1975), quoting an eighteenth-century Scottish professor of medicine, John Gregory.

that will increase one's utility? Why should a prosperous and respected member of a restricted profession torment himself with doubts about the social utility of his actions or about the soundness of the foundations of his beliefs? The natural human tendency to think well of oneself should be distinguished from ostrichism, sometimes called the avoidance of cognitive dissonance, whereby a person in a bad situation, rather than taking steps (which he could do) to ameliorate it, convinces himself that it actually is a good situation. This is different from the harmless delusion—harmless to the deluded, that is—that the behavior and beliefs that promote one's own happiness are consistent with truth and social welfare.

The organization of the legal profession is not the only determinant of legal thought. Plato believed in the objectivity of law before there was a formal legal profession. And long before the organized profession began to come apart at the seams there were doubters of law's objectivity, such as Holmes and the realists, though the profession has shown a remarkable capacity for domesticating, co-opting, and where necessary ignoring its critics. Felix Frankfurter, the authorized keeper of the Holmes flame, made his hero stand for things important to professional autonomy and self-esteem but not important in Holmes's actual thinking, such as rigorous compliance with jurisdictional and procedural niceties and the efficacy of legal procedure in bringing about substantively just outcomes. Other features of the legal process school of which Frankfurter was the pioneer are, however, authentically Holmesian. They include a decent respect for precedent and an emphasis on comparative institutional competence as a guide to principled limitations on judicial assertiveness.

The radical wing of the legal profession is contemptuous of the traditional lawyer's belief in the objectivity of his inquiry. Yet the deregulation of the legal-services industry is not a prominent plank in its platform. Duncan Kennedy, who has urged the random assignment of faculty and students to law schools and a Chinese Cultural Revolution style rotation of law jobs among lawyers and janitors, accepts "the forced exclusion of many aspirants to legal careers."[35] For him the

---

35. Kennedy, *Legal Education and the Reproduction of Hierarchy: A Polemic against the System* 53 (1983). Another "crit," Richard Abel, is, it is true, extremely critical of restrictions on competition and entry in the legal services industry. Abel, note 19 above. Yet Mark Kelman's book, *A Guide to Critical Legal Studies* (1987)—the closest thing we have to a treatise on critical legal studies—contains no index reference to "legal profession" or "profession," or for that matter to Richard Abel.

injustice is not that people can buy legal services only from licensed sellers but that the licenses are not assigned to the right people. Self-interest is not the only cause of this blind spot in the radical critique of the legal profession. There is also nostalgia for the communitarian ideology of a craft guild or a professional cartel, an ideology that elevates solidarity and cooperation over individualism and competition.

The Jurisprudence of the Cartelized Profession

With the benefit of hindsight, 1960 can be identified as the highwater mark of the American legal profession's cartel, and hence of jurisprudence as a guild ideology. It was the year Karl Llewellyn, quondam legal realist, can be said to have thrown in the sponge by publishing a book in which he celebrated in extravagant terms the ineffable "craft" (a word used obsessively throughout the book) of appellate judging.[36] All the restrictions that the organized bar had striven for were in place and the number of lawyers who had hurdled the fence before it had been raised—that is, who had become lawyers before protracted formal education had become a prerequisite to admission to the profession—was in irreversible decline. Potentially rival systems of regulation and dispute resolution, such as the administrative process and arbitration, which the judiciary and the legal profession had once fought, had been successfully lawyerized and were no longer a threat. Among symptoms of noncompetitive pricing and other monopolistic behavior in the heyday of the cartel were the prevalence of "value of service" pricing (billing by the hour became common and eventually dominant only after 1960),[37] the cult of meticulous craftsmanship and of long hours (representing the transformation of price into nonprice competition), the queuing for places in law school classes and for admission to the bar in desirable locations such as California and Florida, and discrimi-

36. *The Common Law Tradition: Deciding Appeals* (1960). See Anthony T. Kronman, *The Lost Lawyer: Failing Ideals of the Legal Profession* 211–225 (1993), for a sympathetic summary of Llewellyn's book.

37. William G. Ross, "The Ethics of Hourly Billing by Attorneys," 44 *Rutgers Law Review* 1, 11 (1991). On price-fixing by lawyers, see Richard J. Arnould, "Pricing Professional Services: A Case Study of the Legal Service Industry," 38 *Southern Economic Journal* 495 (1972). Hourly billing is currently under challenge, as increased competition pushes lawyers to offer more competitive and incentive-compatible billing, including fixed and capped fees, discounts, contingent fees, and budget ceilings. Margot Slade, "Billable Hours, a Centerpiece of American Law, Is Fading," *New York Times*, Oct. 22, 1993, p. A1.

nation by elite firms against Jews,[38] women, and other "nongentle-manly" sorts who might, lacking the values and outlook of gentlemen, be less prone to cooperate in preventing and avoiding competition, and whose presence might in addition reduce the nonpecuniary income of the members of these firms by requiring undesired personal associations.[39] The "ethical" obligation of lawyers to devote a certain amount of their time to "pro bono" (nonfee) work—an obligation that has no counterpart in competitive markets and that is now in decline as the legal profession has become more competitive—limits the supply of legal services to the market while jacking up the demand. For the more legal assistance indigents have, the more paid legal assistance their adversaries (mainly prosecutors, landlords, finance companies, and installment sellers) need.

The condition of the profession in 1960 helps explain not only the fulsome celebration of traditional legal craftsmanship by Henry Hart but also, though less obviously, the puzzling discomfiture of the professional elite with the decision in *Brown v. Board of Education*.[40] The problem with *Brown* from the perspective of professional ideology was fourfold:

1. The minor premise of the decision—that segregation was harmful to blacks, whether by stamping them with a badge of inferiority, depriving them of a quality education, denying them valuable associations with white persons, or all three, and that this stigmatization and these deprivations were the original and continuing objectives of segregation—was obvious and had been so from the inception of the practice. This was embarrassing in two ways. First, if so palpable a form of deliberate and invidious racial discrimination had existed for as long as it had, why had the Supreme Court taken so long to invalidate it?

---

38. Though already on the wane by 1960, it was an old concern. Stevens, note 19 above, at 181 n. 14, records concerns voiced in 1929 about the entry of "Russian Jew boys" into the profession. Wigmore urged "a requirement of two years of college" as "a beneficent measure for reducing hereafter the spawning mass of promiscuous semi-intelligence which now enters the bar." John H. Wigmore, "Should the Standard of Admission to the Bar Be Based on Two Years or More of College-Grade Education? It Should," 4 *American Law School Review* 30, 31 (1915).

39. For analogies in medicine, see Reuben A. Kessel, *Essays in Applied Price Theory*, chs. 1–3, 9 (R. H. Coase and Merton H. Miller eds. 1980).

40. See, for example, Herbert Wechsler, "Toward Neutral Principles of Constitutional Law," 73 *Harvard Law Review* 1, 31–35 (1959). Wechsler's article was published in book form as *Principles, Politics, and Fundamental Law* (1961), but my page references will be to the article.

Why in particular had it upheld segregation in 1897, in the *Plessy* opinion which *Brown* in effect overruled?[41] Neither the *Brown* opinion itself nor the uncomfortable professional commentary remarked this point. Second, a judicial decision that is based on a ground obvious to the lay public is professionally uninteresting, even a little threatening. Nothing in Chief Justice Warren's opinion marked it as the product of a first-rate legal mind. It lacked subtlety, elegance, and eloquence. In fact the opinion, probably written by Warren himself rather than by a law clerk, was not the product of a first-rate legal mind. Much intelligent lawyerly maneuvering had occurred behind the scenes, and the "all deliberate speed" remedial formula announced in the second *Brown* opinion was a neat bit of legal legerdemain.[42] But the Supreme Court's main opinion in the most important judicial decision of the century was—banal.

2. More obvious than the effect of compulsory public school segregation on blacks (for it was only one of the forms of discrimination to which blacks were subject, and disentangling the effects of the other forms was difficult to do) was the intention behind it, which was to maintain blacks in a subordinate position. It would have been awkward for a court, especially a federal court dominated by northerners, to say to the southern legislators, "We see through the reasons you give for segregation to your real motivations, which are evil."

3. While the minor premise of the decision was too obvious to be congenial, the major premise was too difficult. It was unclear, to say the least, that the framers or ratifiers of the Fourteenth Amendment had intended the equal protection clause to prevent racially segregated public education. To decide whether their intentions should count— even how their intentions should be characterized (because they could have had general intentions, such as to promote racial equality, that were inconsistent with their specific intentions, such as to preserve the subordinate social position of blacks)—would have required a theory of interpretation that the legal profession lacked in 1954 and lacks today, so that the debate over the soundness of *Brown v. Board of*

41. Plessy v. Ferguson, 163 U.S. 537 (1896).
42. Brown v. Board of Education, 349 U.S. 294 (1955). See Richard Kluger, *Simple Justice: The History of Brown v. Board of Education and Black America's Struggle for Social Justice* (1976); Philip Elman and Norman Silber, "The Solicitor General's Office, Justice Frankfurter, and Civil Rights Litigation, 1946–1960: An Oral History," 100 *Harvard Law Review* 817 (1987); Mark Tushnet, "What Really Happened in *Brown v. Board of Education*," 91 *Columbia Law Review* 1867 (1991).

Education as constitutional interpretation continues.[43] The suspicion persists that the Court outlawed public school segregation because it thought it an evil practice rather than because it suddenly woke up to the fact that the practice had been declared unlawful in a constitutional amendment ratified almost a century earlier.

4. Whatever its motive or juridical content, *Brown* was politically highly consequential—it thrust the Supreme Court into the midst of a power struggle between the southern and the nonsouthern states and in that respect could be thought a reprise of the Dred Scott decision. The Court's reluctance to come to grips with what might have seemed the central issue—the intentions of southern legislators in imposing segregation—and its delay in ordering compliance with its ruling are other political aspects of the decision. (The determination to avoid seeming political may itself be politically motivated.) The artisanal perspective is resolutely antipolitical. It wants law for law's sake (like art for art's sake), not for politics' sake. Alternatively, the further the courts steer clear of political controversy, the more likely judicial inquiry is to resemble scientific truth-seeking. The professional is happy to be thought a kind of artist or scientist, even a kind of social scientist or a "social engineer," but not a politician. He is even content to be thought an artisan, surrendering any claim to originality, vision, or audacity in exchange for society's acknowledging his possession of unchallengeable expertise within a limited domain of social governance.

One might suppose that these points against *Brown* would be thought merely costs to be traded off against the social benefits from invalidating an unjust institution. But it is no part of professional ideology to run risks for the sake of social gains. The risks are to the profession, the gains to the larger society. Lawyers, like other people, tend to set their own welfare and that of their profession above the interests they have in common with the population at large.

The Crisis of the Profession

Thus stood the American legal profession in 1960, on the eve of revolution. Today all is changed, changed utterly.[44] Although the pro-

43. See, for example, Lino A. Graglia, "'Interpreting' the Constitution: Posner on Bork," 44 *Stanford Law Review* 1019, 1037–1043 (1992); Bernard H. Siegan, *The Supreme Court's Constitution: An Inquiry into Judicial Review and Its Impact on Society* 93–107 (1987).

44. For documentation, see, most recently, Kronman, note 36 above, at 274–314, and

fession has not been thrown open to free entry, an accelerating accumulation of legal and especially economic changes over the past three decades has transformed the profession in the direction of competitive enterprise. It is not so profound a transformation as the change from medieval weavers' guilds to the modern mass-production textile industry—it does not signify the deprofessionalization, let alone the proletarianization, of the legal profession.[45] But there are sufficient parallels to make the analogy an illuminating one.

Although part of a larger movement aptly described as the industrialization of service,[46] the transformation of the profession is the proximate consequence of a surge in demand for legal services. The causes of this surge are not well understood, though some causal factors, such as the creation of new rights, much higher crime rates, greatly relaxed rules of standing, more generous legal remedies (including relaxed standards for class actions) as part of a general tilt in favor of civil plaintiffs and against civil defendants, and the increased subsidization of lawyers for indigent criminal defendants and indigent civil plaintiffs, can be identified. The most conspicuous manifestations of the surge in demand for legal services are the litigation explosion and the concomi-

---

Sharyn L. Roach Anleu, "The Legal Profession in the United States and Australia: Deprofessionalization or Reorganization?" 19 *Work and Occupations* 184 (1992); also Abel, note 19 above; Marc Galanter and Thomas Palay, *Tournament of Lawyers: The Transformation of the Big Law Firm* (1991); Robert A. Rothman, "Deprofessionalization: The Case of Law in America," 11 *Work and Occupations* 183 (1984); Richard H. Sander and E. Douglass Williams, "Why Are There So Many Lawyers? Perspectives on a Turbulent Market," 14 *Journal of Law and Social Inquiry* 431 (1989); Robert L. Nelson, *Partners with Power: The Social Transformation of the Large Law Firm* (1988). Of course lawyers have been crying "crisis" for a long time. Rayman L. Solomon, "Five Crises or One: The Concept of Legal Professionalism, 1925–1960," in *Lawyers' Ideals/Lawyers' Practices: Transformations in the American Legal Profession* 144 (Robert L. Nelson, David M. Trubek, and Rayman L. Solomon eds. 1992). But the wolf is finally at the door.

45. Anleu, note 44 above, points out sensibly that specialization, large firms, advertising, and other trends in the legal profession need not result in "deprofessionalization" in the sense of loss of autonomy and status, though it is likely to alter the distribution of rewards within the profession.

46. Theodore Levitt, "The Industrialization of Service," *Harvard Business Review*, Sept./Oct. 1976, p. 63. Levitt points out that the service sector was built on the model of the traditional relation between a servant and his master. The idea of the lawyer as a high-class servant of the rich is traditional; it is illustrated by Dickens's depiction of the lawyer Tulkinghorn in *Bleak House*. The idea that American law is undergoing a process of "industrialization," with consequences for legal thought as well as practice, is noted in J. M. Balkin, "What Is Postmodern Constitutionalism?" 90 *Michigan Law Review* 1966, 1983–1986 (1992).

tant rapid growth in the number of lawyers.[47] While it is popularly believed that lawyers create their own demand, the vast expansion in legal rights and regulations in recent decades cannot be the consequence of an increase in the number of junior lawyers. When the legal profession expands, it does so much less by lateral entry of mature, influential persons than by an expansion in the number of law students, which gradually works its way through the profession.

The accommodation of the increased demand for legal services has taken a variety of forms, all of which involve expanding the supply of those services. This was not an inevitable response. The greater demand could have been accommodated if not exactly satisfied by price rationing that would have shunted people into other systems of dispute resolution—political, arbitral, informal, even internal (a merger between firms standing in a supplier-customer relation to each other will transform disputes between supplier and customer from legal disputes into intrafirm disputes resolved by the fiat of supervisors). Instead the supply of legal services was expanded through increases in the number of suppliers, increased competition among suppliers, and technical and organizational innovations that enhanced the productivity of legal services. The first response is illustrated by the creation of new law schools, the expansion of existing ones, and the reduction in the rate of flunking out students—developments that together enabled an enormous increase in the size of the legal profession, which grew from 213,000 lawyers and judges (mostly of course the former) in 1960 to 772,000 in 1991.[48] The motor for this expansion in supply was competition among law firms to add lawyers in order to cope with the higher demand for legal services. The competition increased the incomes of lawyers, attracting more students to law school. The surge in demand for places in law school enabled law schools to expand (and new law schools to be created) and to screen applicants more carefully, since the pool was larger and abler, increasing the percentage of students that actually graduated and became lawyers.

The second response to the rising demand for legal services—in-

47. For documentation, see Sherwin Rosen, "The Market for Lawyers," 35 *Journal of Law and Economics* 215 (1992).

48. Richard A. Posner, *The Federal Courts: Crisis and Reform* 80 (1985); U.S. Bureau of the Census, *Historical Statistics of the United States: Colonial Times to 1970*, pt. 1, p. 140 (Bicentennial ed. 1975) (ser. D233–682); U.S. Bureau of the Census, *Statistical Abstract of the United States* 392 (112th ed. 1992) (tab. 629).

creased competition within the profession—is the result in part of a
series of decisions by the Supreme Court that invalidated on one
ground or another a number of traditional restrictions on competition
among lawyers.[49] The judge-made exemption of the learned professions
from antitrust law has gone, and with it price-fixing by bar associations.
Most limitations on lawyers' advertising, not only media advertising
but also the personal solicitation of legal business from persons having
potential legal claims, have been invalidated, as have many barriers to
lawyers' relocating to states other than the ones in which they were
originally licensed.

Technical and organizational innovations have increased the vigor of
competition in the legal-services market, but they have also an independent significance for the transformation of the profession. The rise
of the paralegal has demonstrated that much of the traditional work of
lawyers can be done by nonlawyers. It has also made the production
of legal services a less homogeneous activity. The use of computers for
document preparation, indexing, and legal research, and of facsimile
machines and other communications equipment, has increased the
traditionally low capital requirements of law firms, raising the minimum
efficient size of firms and hence contributing to the astonishing growth
in the average size of firms, some of which now have more than a
thousand lawyers.[50] Another factor in that growth has been the increasing importance of litigation in law firms' mix of business, a change due
in part to corporate clients' taking more of their nonlitigation legal
business in house. The incidence and demands of litigation are inherently unpredictable, so an increase in the size of a firm enables a
smoothing of the firm's load.

Old believers in antitrust law might suppose that a growth in average
firm size would conduce to monopoly or oligopoly. That has not been
the experience of the legal-services industry. The growing size of firms
has facilitated their expansion into different geographic and service

49. Bates v. State Bar, 433 U.S. 350 (1977); Supreme Court of New Hampshire v. Piper,
470 U.S. 274 (1985); Zauderer v. Office of Disciplinary Counsel, 471 U.S. 626 (1985);
Shapero v. Kentucky Bar Association, 486 U.S. 466 (1988); Supreme Court of Virginia v.
Friedman, 487 U.S. 59 (1988); Peel v. Attorney Registration and Disciplinary Commission,
496 U.S. 91 (1990); but see Ohralik v. Ohio State Bar Association, 436 U.S. 447 (1978).

50. The increasing sophistication of personal computers, and the falling price of electronic
products generally, may limit the increase in minimum efficient firm size. If there were steep
diseconomies of scale, an increase in the demand for legal services would tend to cause an
increase in the number rather than in the size of law firms.

markets, increasing competition. (The analogy is to banking: an unregulated banking industry that had 10 banks in it would probably be more competitive than our regulated industry of 14,000 banks.) As the legal problems of business firms grow, more firms find it profitable to create large in-house legal staffs. These staffs not only provide greater competition for law firms but also enable corporate clients to engage in shrewder negotiations with them—to play off one against the other, to solicit competitive bids, and so forth—thus further stimulating competition among law firms. We should not be surprised that the price of legal services fell (in real, that is, inflation-adjusted, terms), rather than, as popular and professional opinion alike supposes, rose, between 1970 and 1985.[51] The growing ratio of associate to partner income is consistent with the hypothesis of growing competition: reduction in monopsony power has increased law firms' labor costs.

As law firms grow, opportunities for professional specialization—for a more complete division of labor—grow apace. I mentioned the paralegal. Large law firms also hire professional managers, English professors, accountants, economists, computer experts, and other nonlawyer specialists to perform services formerly performed by lawyers. Lawyers become proficient in narrow fields of law or in particular techniques, learn to work in large teams, and engage in activities characteristic of competition—such as marketing—or of large enterprises—such as supervision. Competition makes them work harder, too, and reduces their security of tenure. There are more cases of firms dissolving, restructuring, regrouping; of firms firing associates and even partners; and of wide fluctations in earnings within firms.

These changes have psychological consequences. Harder work, even when well remunerated, greater uncertainty of tenure, and the inevitably bureaucratic "feel" of practicing law in a huge organization all reduce job satisfaction. Many lawyers claim with evident sincerity not to enjoy the practice of law as much as they once did. Many say they wouldn't have gone to law school had they known what the practice of law would become. The increasingly competitive character of the legal-services market makes lawyers feel like hucksters rather than the proud professionals they once were, and brings forward to positions of leadership in the profession persons whose talents, for example for marketing ("rainmaking"), are those of competitive business rather than of pro-

51. Sander and Williams, note 44 above, at 451.

fessionalism. Gone are the joys of artisanality and the security of the guild.

We can find traces of the changes in lawyers' work in two characteristic products of the legal profession—the appellate brief and the appellate opinion. Both types of document used to be the product of a legal professional, whether mature lawyer or judge, working essentially by himself, though with advice from others. The author of the brief or opinion was not only—it went without saying—an experienced professional; he was an experienced legal writer; the craft of writing legal-rhetorical documents, such as briefs and opinions, was central to his professional self-image. No longer. Brief writing in large law firms, government agencies, and other influential legal enterprises is now generally delegated to the least experienced lawyers. They work, it is true, under supervision; theirs is first-draft, not final-draft, responsibility. But the writer of the first draft usually controls to a great extent the final product. The craft of the senior lawyer in relation to brief writing is now that of a supervisor skilled at eliciting and improving the best work of his juniors.

As part of the research for my book *Cardozo: A Study in Reputation* (1990), I read the briefs that had been submitted to Cardozo's court (the New York Court of Appeals) in the twenty cases, decided mainly in the 1920s, that I planned to discuss in the book. Although Cardozo's opinions owed little to the briefs, I was impressed by the briefs' individuality, their thoroughness, their meticulous grammatical and typographical accuracy. The authors were not legal geniuses (with the possible exception of Robert Jackson, who wrote one of the briefs), but they were legal artisans. I was struck by the contrast with the mass-produced uniformity, the characterlessness, the impersonality, and the evident hastiness of the vast majority of the "good" briefs submitted in Seventh Circuit cases in the 1980s.

A parallel though not identical evolution has occurred in opinion writing. The appellate judge's main role, that of deciding the case, is largely unimpaired; but for the secondary role of writer the judge has substituted that of supervisor. This division of labor, with its echo of the transformation from guild to factory production, enables the judiciary to dispose of a vastly larger number of cases with no marked (perhaps no) diminution in average quality. It is an efficient adaptation to the greater demand for the subset of legal services that consists of judicial decision-making. But we should not expect from judge-editors the literary or rhetorical gems of Holmes, Hand, Cardozo, and Jackson, or the powerful essays in political or social theory of John Marshall or Brandeis. There is craft in supervision; and perhaps in the fullness of time the profession will recognize a new sort of master judge, one who elicits an outstanding product from a staff as distinct from producing his own carefully wrought opinions. But it is different from the artisanal craft of the judges of yore.

Although the average quality of judicial opinions may not have diminished as a result of the delegation of the opinion-writing function to law clerks, the *variance* in quality has. Law clerks, who mostly are recent law school graduates with outstanding academic records but no legal or other vocational experience, are more homogeneous than judges. The tendency to uniformity of output, which is also characteristic of legal briefs from large law firms, has its counterpart in the evolution toward mass production of industrial products. Despite the emphasis laid by the medieval craft guilds on the importance of uniformity, handicrafts are less likely to be of uniform quality than machine-made products because machine production facilitates standardization and testing. Law clerks are not machines, but the division of labor in the judiciary as elsewhere facilitates a comparable type of standardization. It buffers the differences between individual judges. The Bachrach studio is not Van Gogh or even Brady (and Brennan is not Brandeis), but modern photography provides a more uniform quality of portraiture than the artisanal methods that preceded it.

Do not suppose, however, that the growing uniformity of legal output spells a growing uniformity of lawyers' earnings. A competitive legal profession offers an opportunity for entrepreneurial returns that a cartelized one does not, just as the advent of mass production offered profit opportunities that dwarfed the monopoly returns of guild producers. Indeed, one thing that makes cartels, including professional cartels, fragile is that some producers can make more money as members of a competitive industry. When legal restrictions made it impossible to create a nationwide law firm, lawyers whose talents ran to the organization of large enterprises and the penetration of new markets were unable to cash in on their talents. Thus, the fact that some lawyers continue to command extremely high incomes in the more competitive environment of the present-day profession does not show, as Derek Bok believes, that competition is not working.[52] Bok also overlooks the

52. Bok, *The Cost of Talent: How Executives and Professionals Are Paid and How It Affects America*, ch. 7 (1993).

relation between risk and remuneration. He claims that partners in law firms can maintain their high incomes when business sags by laying off the less productive partners.[53] If so, this makes those continued high earnings in part illusory, since the earner may find himself one of those less productive partners who is laid off.

The Twilight of Jurisprudence

In discussing *Brown v. Board of Education* I offered a glimpse of the world of legal thought as it stood on the eve of law's industrial revolution, described above. It is the world of thought epitomized by Wechsler's article on neutral principles. The analytical shortcomings of the article, one of the most heavily cited in legal history,[54] have been documented by others[55] and need not detain us here. It is its representative character that interests me. What it is representative of is the juristic counterpart of artisanality.

The form is that of a personal statement. "Let me begin by stating that I have not the slightest doubt respecting the legitimacy of judicial review [of the constitutionality of federal or state legislative or executive actions]."[56] This would be a curious beginning for a scientific or social scientific article, because it assumes that the author's inner mental state, his doubts or confidences, have a significance independent of the reasoning or evidence that he offers in support of his views. When craft is a mystery, the identity of the craftsman conveys valuable information. The article identifies Wechsler as the holder of a named professorship in constitutional law at a major law school, Columbia's, and explains that the article is the text of the Oliver Wendell Holmes Lecture, given annually at the Harvard Law School, then the world's preeminent law school. The lecture series was named after the Anglo-American world's

53. Id. at 146. For other criticisms, see the review by Andrew Hacker, "Unjust Desserts?" *New York Review of Books,* March 3, 1994, p. 20.

54. The article was published in 1959. Between 1960 and the end of 1992, it had been cited a remarkable 1,102 times in law reviews. This figure is computed from the *Social Sciences Citation Index* for 1960 through 1986 and from the LEXIS law review database for the remaining years, *SSCI* being years behind in its tabulation of data. According to a study based on a slightly different database, as of March 1985 Wechsler's was the second most frequently cited law review article in history. Fred R. Shapiro, "The Most-Cited Law Review Articles," 73 *California Law Review* 1540, 1549 (1985) (tab. 1).

55. See, for example, Gary Peller, "Neutral Principles in the 1950's," 21 *Journal of Law Reform* 561 (1988).

56. Wechsler, note 40 above, at 2.

most illustrious jurist, himself the most famous graduate of, briefly a professor at, and long identified with that law school. Wechsler mentions in his first paragraph that the previous year's Holmes lecturer had been Learned Hand, the greatest judge in the history of the federal courts of appeals. Wechsler's is the lead article of Volume 73 of the *Harvard Law Review*, at the time the nation's foremost legal journal. The article is thus more (or less) than an effort at scholarly analysis; it is the self-conscious performance of a master craftsman of the guild of lawyers.

We should not be surprised that Wechsler's tone is patronizing. The conception of the Supreme Court "as an ever-open forum for the ventilation of all grievances that draw upon the Constitution for support," a plausible conception one might have thought as an original matter, is derided as the view of "the uninstructed." They ignore the need for "rigorous insistence on the satisfaction of procedural and jurisdictional requirements"—an insistence "fundamental in the thought and work of Mr. Justice Brandeis"—so nothing more need be said in justification of it.[57] The cynic might have wondered whether Brandeis's insistence on these technicalities may not have been intended to inhibit the Court from reaching substantive questions that a majority of the Justices were likely to answer in a way unpleasing to Brandeis, a man of emphatic substantive views. But the idea that Brandeis might not have been a perfectly disinterested professional, might in fact have been influenced by political and strategic considerations, is not allowed to intrude; it would be like imputing the profit motive to a respected member of a medieval craft guild.

It soon becomes clear that one of the most important duties of judges is to resist the pull of common sense and laymen's justice. Even a lay person should be able to understand that judges have not been given a blank check on which to write their personal and political preferences and call them the Constitution. But Wechsler wants to identify cases in which lay intuition fails because they involve palpable, or at least plausible, violations of the Constitution yet the judges refuse to do, or at least they *should* refuse to do, anything about them: infringements of the guarantee of a republican form of government; gerrymanders, and legislative malapportionment generally; laws forbidding marriage between persons of different races; laws prohibiting

57. Id. at 6.

blacks from voting in the Democratic or Republican primaries; and laws prohibiting blacks from attending the same public schools as whites (and vice versa). Wechsler's objection to judicial rectification of any of these apparent denials of the equal protection of the laws is that he cannot find an adequately general principle to cover them. A principle is adequately general, he believes, only if it treats consistently not only the case at hand but any hypothetical or actual case within the principle's semantic scope. We can see in this proposal the technique of the law school classroom—where students' attempts to formulate legal principles are challenged by the teacher's putting hypothetical cases that test the scope of the principle—being elevated to a methodological requirement of constitutional adjudication. "I found myself developing the neutral principles idea as a pedagogical instrument for pushing students into subjecting their own immediate reactions of approval or disapproval of the results of a particular decision to a more searching type of criterion of evaluation."[58]

The use of hypothetical cases to test and limit a theory or principle is more than a pedagogical technique. But it does not have the normative power that Wechsler believes, for all but the first of the constitutional violations that he thought could *not* be corrected by the Supreme Court without a betrayal of neutrality have been corrected by the Court, yet without the sky falling.[59]

One might have supposed that the central question in *Brown v. Board of Education* was not the scope of some abstract principle of freedom of association but whether racial segregation of public facilities in the South was intended or likely to keep the blacks in their traditionally subordinate position. This was a factual question, the answer to which was obvious, although it might as I have said have been impolitic for the Supreme Court to utter it. That may be why the Court focused not on the motives or political consequences of public-school segregation but instead on the consequences for the educational attainments and psychological well-being of blacks. Wechsler is not interested in the motives for or the effects of segregation, except that in typical lawyer's

58. Quoted in Norman Silber and Geoffrey Miller, "Toward 'Neutral Principles' in the Law: Selections from the Oral History of Herbert Wechsler," 93 *Columbia Law Review* 854, 925 (1993).

59. The Court still refuses to enforce the guarantee of a republican form of government, but there is a serious question what the guarantee means and whether any state has ever actually infringed it. See Chapter 9.

fashion he speculates on the possibly deleterious effects of integration—that is, the only consequences he is interested in are speculative bad consequences of the position that he questions. He emphatically endorses the principle that the motives of legislators are irrelevant to the validity of the legislative product. He wants to restate the constitutional question as whether there is a principle of freedom of association that would permit blacks to complain about being kept out of white schools but forbid whites to complain about having to go to school with blacks.

That is *a* way of looking at the case. But the only reason I can imagine why Wechsler thought it *the* way is that it is more congenial than factual inquiry to the type of rhetoric characteristic of lawyers, with their fondness for abstract concepts ("freedom of association"), arguments from logic, and hypothetical cases.[60] Professionals do not want to risk undermining their claim to professional autonomy by getting into areas where they do not command all the tools of inquiry. They want to do well what they do well, even if they could make a greater social contribution by performing a more important task, such as rendering social justice, less well. Implicitly they place the welfare of the profession above the welfare of the community; the rationalization is that they are hoarding their prestige for the day when it is needed to save the country. (We have been waiting more than two centuries for the day to arrive.) The analogy is to the medieval physicians who emphasized prognosis so that they could decline patients likely to die and concentrate on those who were likely to recover with or without medical attention.

I call what lawyers do in their argumentative or justificatory capacity *rhetoric* rather than *reasoning* because so much legal writing, even of the most celebrated sort, has only the form and not the substance of intellectual rigor.[61] Wechsler's article does not explain, or adequately

---

60. The case method "puts a premium on verbal manipulation and encourages a tendency to look inward at the consistency of the system rather than outward at the relation of the system to the real world, and at its impact on people and events." Erwin N. Griswold, "Intellect and Spirit," 81 *Harvard Law Review* 292, 299 (1967).

61. To set rhetoric in opposition to logic and science in this way may seem decidedly unpragmatic; for justification and qualification, see Chapter 24.

Concerning a later specimen of scholarship of the legal process school, Gerald Gunther's article "In Search of Judicial Quality on a Changing Court: The Case of Justice Powell," 24 *Stanford Law Review* 1001 (1972), Mark Tushnet remarks: "His sentences parse well enough and seem to be saying something, and yet they turn out to have almost no content. Their tone and manner of presentation *do* say something, though not perhaps what Gunther consciously intended. The article is very much written for insiders, who are assumed to share

define, or indicate the provenance of, or defend, his central concept of "neutral principles." All he means, apparently, is that decisions should be "principled," and all that that seems to mean to him is that judges should avoid grounds of decision that would require them to engage with the messy world of empirical reality—to inquire for example into the motives and consequences of public school segregation. So a comparable decision by a legislature might be principled. That is, the term may be relative to the capabilities and traditions of the institution making the decision in question, although Wechsler forbids courts to inquire into the actual competence of the legislature—he assigns spheres of competence in an empirical void. He may have thought that the decision in *Brown* was redistributive in character—shifting wealth from whites to blacks—and that redistributive judgments, however just, are for legislatures to make rather than courts.

Wechsler never gets around to sorting out these matters because his preferred method of argument is the posing of rhetorical questions, of which I count 60 in his 35-page article. The rhetorical question is the literary counterpart to the coerced confession: it forces the reader's agreement. The cascades of rhetorical questions force upon the reader a predetermined choice: agree with Wechsler, or join the idiots who "perceive in law only the element of fiat," or, even worse (in an image that has come to seem almost obscene), who believe "that the courts are free to function as a naked power organ."[62]

The rhetorical question is not the only rhetorical technique used heavily by Wechsler. The article does not fail to mention the famous cases that he had argued in the Supreme Court, and it harps on the deep liberal sympathies that make it painful for him to expose the inadequacies of the Supreme Court's racial jurisprudence[63]—but his sense of craft permits no less. Assisted by its occasion and its setting, the article richly illustrates the "ethical appeal" of classical rhetoric, in

a way of looking at the world and the laws that ought to regulate it. Gunther implicitly says that we can finesse the difficulties of choosing a level of generality in describing a situation or characterizing interests, and of selecting what amount of unification a principle must provide, because all of us know what good judges ought to do. And in this he may well be correct, if 'all of us' is defined in a certain way." Tushnet, *Red, White, and Blue: A Critical Analysis of Constitutional Law* 184 (1988).

62. Wechsler, note 40 above, at 11, 12.

63. As Wechsler has said, "Indeed, one of the elements of rhetorical effectiveness in the piece was precisely that I persuaded people that I liked the results [of the race cases] and still felt it important to question the grounds." Silber and Miller, note 58 above, at 926.

which the speaker enhances the persuasive power of his argument by persuading the audience that he is the kind of person who ought to be believed whatever he says. And there is a teasing coyness, the lawyer's traditional evasion of straight talking. For Wechsler never does say that the decision in *Brown* was actually wrong but only that no one had yet been able to come up with a persuasive rationale—not even he.

Like an artist or an artisan, the traditional legal advocate, professor, or judge produced neither a replicable or otherwise verifiable argument or proof nor a standardized product that could be readily evaluated in the marketplace for legal services or academic scholarship. He produced an essentially literary product in which he displayed mastery of the rhetorical skills that are the distinctive fruit of the lawyer's talent, training, and experience. Holmes was never further off the mark than when he called law the calling of thinkers, not poets.[64] Much of Holmes's own celebrity, like that of the other great figures in the history of the Anglo-American legal profession, including Herbert Wechsler, is due to the power of his rhetoric.[65]

I have been picking on Wechsler not out of malice or envy but because, like Henry Hart, he is a leading figure of the "legal process" school,[66] Harvard's answer to legal realism—a synthesis of Langdell and Holmes. Wechsler is not at all a strict constructionist and I daresay would not like to be called a formalist. Yet rather little of substance separates the Harts and the Wechslers from the Langdells and the Beales. The vocabulary is different, more modern; the touchstones are reasonableness and institutional competence rather than authoritative legal texts and fundamental jural concepts. But at bottom there is the same unspoken conviction that the relations among legal concepts are rightly the focus of legal analysis, the same unacknowledged depend-

---

64. Oliver Wendell Holmes, Jr., "The Profession of Law" (1886), in *The Essential Holmes: Selections from the Letters, Speeches, Judicial Opinions, and Other Writings of Oliver Wendell Holmes, Jr.* 218 (Richard A. Posner ed. 1992).

65. I argue this point in *Cardozo: A Study in Reputation* 133–134 (1990), and in *Law and Literature* 281–289. The role of bluff and posturing in the success of the professions is not limited to law—how else to explain the prestige and profitability of medicine in the many centuries before scientific advances finally made the net expected benefits of medical treatment positive? See Brown, note 8 above; Freidson, note 8 above, at 16. I do not claim that even modern science is completely free from rhetoric. See Chapter 24.

66. For descriptions of this school, see Neil Duxbury, "Faith in Reason: The Process Tradition in American Jurisprudence," 15 *Cardozo Law Review* 601 (1993); William N. Eskridge, Jr., and Philip P. Frickey, "An Historical and Critical Introduction to 'The Legal Process'" (unpublished, Georgetown and Minnesota law schools, Jan. 26, 1994).

ence on homogeneity of outlook and of values as the real motor of consensus, the same comfortable illusion of analytical rigor, the same intimation that the judge or Supreme Court Justice is a kind of failed law professor, the same indifference to the empirical world, and the same antipathy to legal novelty because a genuinely new case is not continuous with precedent or the other conventionally authoritative materials for legal judgment. For the reflexive but unreflective hostility of an earlier generation of establishment jurists to legislation and the administrative process, the legal process generation substituted an unreflective, indeed naive, faith in the probity and wisdom of legislators and administrators. Legal fiction flourished as before, but bromides about federalism and institutional competence replaced the ones about freedom of contract.[67]

Am I wrong to sense, in the following passage from the work of another distinguished practitioner of "process jurisprudence," a certain warmed-over Langdellism?

> In a society so complex, so pragmatic as ours, unity is never realized, nor is it necessary that it should be. Indeed, there is no possibility of agreement on criteria for absolute unity; what is contradiction to one man is higher synthesis to another. But within a determined context there may be a sense of contradiction sufficient to create social distress; and it is one of the grand roles of our constitutional courts to detect such contradictions and to affirm the capacity of our society to integrate its purposes . . . An [administrative] agency is not an island entire to itself. It is one of the many rooms in the magnificent mansion of the law. The very subordination of the agency to judicial jurisdiction is intended to proclaim the premise that each agency is to be brought into harmony with the totality of the law.[68]

There is acknowledgment that ours is a pragmatic society, foreclosing the possibility of a totally unified conception of law that is the dream of antediluvian formalists. But the dream dies hard. Our courts have the "grand" role of "affirm[ing] the capacity of our society to integrate its purposes." The law itself is a "magnificent mansion," a "totality" among whose parts the courts can bring about "harmony." This is the music of the spheres; it is not the discourse of pragmatism.

67. For parallel criticism of the legal process school, noting the "inbreeding" of the leading legal process scholars and their resulting blindnesses, see Akhil Reed Amar, "Law Story," 102 *Harvard Law Review* 688, 702–710, 719 (1989).

68. Louis L. Jaffe, *Judicial Control of Administrative Action* 589–590 (1965).

A charming irony of the legal process school is that Henry Hart's belief in the rationality and efficacy of law appears to have grown out of his experience as a lawyer for the agency that enforced our World War II price controls.[69] We now know that evasion of the controls was rampant and that although inflation was controlled the cost may have been a dramatic and, because inflation could equally well have been prevented by a tight monetary policy, unnecessary reduction in employment and output. "Price controls hindered the war effort and made many households worse off."[70]

It is not easy to imagine an article with the self-conscious *authority* of Wechsler's being written today. The complacent faith in the trenchancy of legal reasoning has lost its grip and the Harvard Law School, wracked by internal political struggles unthinkable in the 1950s, its unchallenged preeminence. The *Harvard Law Review*, with its epicycles of affirmative action, is on the way to becoming a laughing stock. The Holmes Lectures have lost much of their luster. And there is no longer anyone in the legal profession who has the kind of stature that a Wechsler achieved, with his service at Nuremberg, his Supreme Court advocacy, his coauthorship of the most famous casebook in legal history (the Hart and Wechsler federal courts book), his authorship of the Model Penal Code, and his directorship of the American Law Institute when that institution had an eminence that it has lost. Of course giants are not always visible to contemporaries; the necessary perspective is lacking. But as the legal profession becomes larger, more specialized, more diverse, more commercial, one has difficulty imagining a career, a confidence, a consciousness of authority, of self-sufficiency, like Wechsler's, that would enable a member of the profession to mount the rhetorical high horse from which Wechsler declaimed the neutral-principles paper.

The mission of jurisprudence was to show that law was more than politics and rhetoric. Writing at a time when most intelligent lawyers no longer believed (or found it expedient to believe or claim) that the text of the Constitution provided an algorithm for deciding all cases, Wechsler proposed "neutral principles" as an alternative to strict con-

69. Eskridge and Frickey, note 66 above, at 57 n. 120.

70. Paul Evans, "The Effects of General Price Controls in the United States during World War II," 90 *Journal of Political Economy* 944, 965 (1982). See also Geoffrey Mills and Hugh Rockoff, "Compliance with Price Controls in the United States and the United Kingdom during World War II," 47 *Journal of Economic History* 197 (1987).

struction as a guarantor of law's freedom from politics and public opinion. The homogeneity of the elite professional community that Wechsler addressed assured an audience predisposed to agree with one of its leaders. Not only the messenger, but the message, was welcome. So the article was not at first scrutinized critically, even though its analytical faults are both very great and very near the surface of the piece, and, as I have argued, it subordinates analysis to rhetoric: what oft was thought (the conventional, guild-edged wisdom of the professional elite) but ne'er so well expressed.

There was some scholarly dissent from Wechsler's thesis. It came primarily,[71] as one would expect, from professors at the Yale Law School, the heirs of legal realism. The title of former dean Charles E. Clark's dissent suggests, however, that Wechsler had succeeded in seizing the rhetorical high ground. The title is "A Plea for the Unprincipled Decision,"[72] and few legal professionals would be tempted by such a title to read beyond it. Louis Pollak rose to Wechsler's bait and wrote an alternative opinion in support of the result in *Brown*.[73] To avoid having to examine the consequences of public school segregation, Pollak resorted to the unedifying lawyer's tactic of shifting the burden of proof—requiring the school districts to prove that segregation was *not* stigmatizing and then finding that they had not carried the burden. Of course not; they didn't know they *had* such a burden. The most eloquent scholarly defense of *Brown* was that of Charles Black, who saw the challenge to the opinion writer as that "of developing ways to make it permissible for the Court to use what it knows." Yet he did not indicate what those ways are, and in the end resorted to such formalisms as that the Fourteenth Amendment made blacks "citizens" of their states and "it is hard for me to imagine in what operative sense a man could be a 'citizen' without his fellow citizens' once in a while having to associate with him."[74]

The criticisms of Wechsler's article made possible by the new per-

71. Though not exclusively. Several members of the "legal process" school wrote in favor of *Brown*, see Eskridge and Frickey, not 66 above, at 103–107, although much of this writing preceded Wechsler's article, and Hart and Sacks's *Legal Process* text, the movement's bible, did not mention *Brown*. Eskridge and Frickey, note 66 above, at 102.

72. 49 *Virginia Law Review* 660 (1963).

73. Louis H. Pollak, "Racial Discrimination and Judicial Integrity: A Reply to Professor Wechsler," 108 *University of Pennsylvania Law Review* 1, 24–30 (1959).

74. Charles L. Black, Jr., "The Lawfulness of the Segregation Decisions," 69 *Yale Law Journal* 421, 428–429 (1960).

spective created by the dissolution of the traditional legal ideology may seem to miss his basic point—which (*pace* Judge Clark) no right-thinking person can disagree with—that judicial decisions should be principled. Yet this insistence itself bespeaks guild thinking. As the hearings on the nomination of Robert Bork to the Supreme Court showed, the American people want two things from judges: they want particular results (such as capital punishment and the decriminalization of abortion), and they want judges who find rather than make law. These things are incompatible. Judges nevertheless find it easy enough to satisfy the public's demands by giving them the results they want, clothed in the rhetoric of passive obeisance to "the law" (including law the judges may have made up last week). This lends a hypocritical tone and illogical content to many judicial opinions, offending guild norms, or, what is closely related, professional norms, of lofty personal morality and scrupulous craftsmanship. It is steadfast adherence to those norms, not, as Wechsler thought, the failure to adhere to them steadfastly, that endangers popular support for judicial independence.

I predict that as the legal profession opens up to diverse viewpoints and backgrounds, as paralegals become authorized (as I hope and believe they someday will) to form their own law firms and compete with "real" lawyers,[75] as bankers, accountants, statisticians, economists, computer engineers, and management consultants play an increasing role in the formulation and application of law, as law firms grow, diversify, and become increasingly international, as legal education becomes more optional, hence more practical, and its frills are discarded, as judiciaries become larger and more specialized, and as law, like the rest of social life, becomes more and more quantitative and computerized, the traditional preoccupations that go by the name of jurisprudence will seem and be increasingly irrelevant. The sort of people who believe that the important thing is to police the boundaries of law— who think it rewarding to ask whether the "law" applied at the Nuremberg trials of the Nazi war criminals was "really" law—who think it illuminating to list the "ten major criteria [that] may be relevant to evaluating the appropriateness of a given type of substantive reason for use in the law"—to wit, "(1) intrinsic justificatory force, (2) conventional justificatory force, (3) commensurability with other reasons, (4)

75. This is beginning. See Jana Eisinger, "Nonlawyers Claim a Growing Swath of Legal Turf," *New York Times,* July 16, 1993, p. B10. There is a parallel movement to permit nurses to compete with doctors in the provision of certain types of medical treatment.

intelligibility and persuasiveness, (5) transmutability into stable rules, (6) 'guidesomeness,' (7) efficient constructability, (8) possible arbitrariness of 'boundary conditions,' (9) general 'range' of the reason, and (10) suitability for court use"[76]—will come to seem as irrelevant to the theory and practice of law as the lesser medieval canonists, whom they resemble. Their hermetic discourse befits a profession that seeks to justify its privileges by pointing to the high obscurity of its thought. I think too that academic lawyers will abandon the hope expressed by Rakowski that jurisprudence can produce roadmaps for judges.[77] Like most philosophy, all that jurisprudence can do is to arm one against philosophical arguments. It is therapeutic, but not curative. I am speaking of the kind of jurisprudence that takes its cues from analytic philosophy. When jurisprudence is defined more broadly, as legal theory,[78] the limitations of conventional jurisprudence are even plainer.

76. Robert S. Summers, "Judge Richard Posner's Jurisprudence," 89 *Michigan Law Review* 1302, 1333 n. 73 (1991).

77. Eric Rakowski, "Posner's Pragmatism," 104 *Harvard Law Review* 1681 (1991).

78. As in, for example, Gary Minda, "The Jurisprudential Movements of the 1980s," 50 *Ohio State Law Journal* 599 (1989), a useful survey.

chapter 2

The Triumphs and Travails
of Legal Scholarship

AT THE center of the web of restrictions that maintains the (fast-weak-ening) professional cartel is the law school. It is also the principal site for the production of legal theory and knowledge. Virtually all law schools today are university law schools; and the American university, despite its well-known faults, is without peer in the world. But we should not allow complacency about the American university system to blind us to weaknesses in legal education. Many fields of university scholarship, particularly but not only in the humanities, are declining, stagnant, or adrift. Theology (if we take a long view—comparing its position today with that which it occupied in the thirteenth century) is not an improving field. Nor education. Nor (and here I turn con-troversial) anthropology, geography, English literature, or architecture.

The situation in law is complex. The law schools are more or less holding their own as far as quality of teaching is concerned, though that most distinctive and, I think, most valuable technique of legal teaching, the Socratic method, is endangered, in part because of affir-mative action. By "affirmative action" I do not mean merely trading off adherence to conventional standards of evaluation against perceived gains in diversity of outlook and experience. I mean treating the possession of a particular racial, or ethnic, or gender identity, or sexual orientation, or some other nonmeritocratic factor, as per se a favorable factor in the decision on whether to admit a student or hire a faculty member. Affirmative action so defined entails the admission of minority students less qualified on average than the law school's nonminority students and therefore more likely to be embarrassed by the "cold call" method of Socratic teaching. The taking and grading of written exams are more private activities; the danger of public humiliation is slighter.

Academic Law on the Eve of the Revolution

The changes in legal teaching are slight compared to what has happened since about 1960 in legal scholarship.[1] It used to be that law professors were *in* the university but *of* the legal profession. Usually they had spent the first few years after graduating from law school in some branch of the practice of law. Whether they had or not, they thought of themselves primarily as lawyers training the next generation of lawyers and through scholarship—through law review articles, treatises, model laws, and restatements of the law—guiding judges and practicing lawyers in the path of sound legal reasoning. The superior intellects of these academic lawyers, in combination with their greater leisure for research, reflection, and the formulation of a personal professional agenda, enabled them to attain that synoptic view of an individual field which must forever elude the practitioner and judge immersed in a sea of particular cases. These intellects, this depth and breadth of knowledge, were, however, strictly at the service of the practical profession—the judges and practicing lawyers.

The demeanor and attire of the law professor were professional, worldly (as was his income), in comparison to the mild bohemianism by which the true don proclaims his independence from the quotidian. Law professors moved easily between the practical and academic worlds, an example being the references to his practice before the Supreme Court that dot Herbert Wechsler's article on neutral principles.

1. I discussed some of these changes, which were already well in train more than a decade ago, in my article "The Present Situation in Legal Scholarship," 90 *Yale Law Journal* 1113 (1981). See also "The Decline of Law as an Autonomous Discipline, 1962–1987," 100 *Harvard Law Review* 761 (1987), which appears in revised and amplified form as chapter 14 of *The Problems of Jurisprudence*.

The self-identification of the professoriat with the practical profession was a source of strength for the former. It provided anchor, balance, and goal. The job of the professor was to produce knowledge useful to the practitioner. To be useful it had to have a credible source and to be packaged in a form the practitioner could use. The source was the law professor viewed as a superior lawyer. The form was the law review article or treatise or model law or restatement or casebook, which respected the practitioner's preoccupation with decided cases, his methodological conservatism, his deep-seated (as well as self-serving) belief in the autonomy of law as a subject of thought and practice, the high valuation he placed on tradition, convention, and stability, and hence his aversion to any but incremental change. It implied too—this *useful* academic law that I am considering—a broad political congruence between the academy, on the one hand, and the judiciary, the bar, and the society as a whole, on the other. The ultimate premises of legal doctrines are political. Without a minimum of political agreement between the professoriat and the profession, therefore, neither party to their symbiotic relationship will respect the objectivity, the professionalism, of the other.

There was always some tension between the professoriat and the judiciary. The relation between the law professors who analyze judicial decisions and the judges who make these decisions, like the relation between literary critic and literary author which it resembles, has an inescapably adversary element. The judge, like the literary author, wants to conceal his technique—wants to pretend that the decision flowed as if without human mediation from a previous decision or from the words of a statute or the Constitution. The professor's business is to unmask the technique, to reveal (often disapprovingly) the falsification of fact or precedent, the omission of facts and arguments, the polemical or rhetorical thrusts over emptiness, that are the standard methods of judicial creativity.

The traditional law professor is above all a student of legal doctrine. What he does, mainly, in a legal system such as that of the United States which is oriented toward case law is to read judicial opinions and try to find the pattern in the cases or, failing that, to impose one of his own. Doctrinalists are law's Talmudists. They proceed from the welter of particular cases. The theory that guides their inquiry is muted, tacit, traditional. When they make arguments for reform they make them from within the tradition, using fragments of ethical or policy analysis found in the cases. The enterprise of doctrinal scholarship is heavily interpretive and rhetorical, often polemical, sometimes historical, never empirical or scientific. Now casuistry, as Socrates in Plato's *Gorgias* famously observed, is a knack, and it is one that bright law students pick up quickly. When edited by bright students, therefore, law reviews are competent institutions for screening, correcting, improving, and even creating (in student-written notes) doctrinal scholarship. As legal scholarship has moved away from the doctrinal, merit as measured by law school grades has become a less important criterion for the selection of law review editors (though the causality works in both directions, and other factors are at work as well, including affirmative action) and the number of faculty-edited law journals has increased.

No one doubts that the *practice* of law is a distinct profession. It is not economics, or psychology, or philosophy. It is an autonomous professional activity. The closer the law professor hews to the professional model, the more academic legal scholarship is an autonomous department of academic scholarship, set apart from the other departments of the university: a secure monopolist of legal studies.

The Deprofessionalization of Legal Scholarship

Doctrinal scholarship has been in relative decline for many years,[2] having been abandoned by many law professors, especially young ones and especially at elite law schools. The breaking up of the traditional professional norms and structures, discussed in Chapter 1, is one cause; here I want to emphasize two others that are, however, closely related to it. The first is the rise of disciplines that, by challenging the methods and results of doctrinal scholarship, have chipped away at the autonomy of academic law from other academic fields. The second is the decline of political consensus within the profession.

Among the disciplines that have challenged the legal doctrinalists'

---

2. A decline increasingly criticized. See, for example, Harry T. Edwards, "The Growing Disjunction between Legal Education and the Legal Profession," 91 *Michigan Law Review* 34 (1992); Edward L. Rubin, "On Beyond Truth: A Theory for Evaluating Legal Scholarship," 80 *California Law Review* 889 (1992); Paul D. Carrington, "Butterfly Effects: The Possibilities of Law Teaching in a Democracy," 41 *Duke Law Journal* 741, 800–805 (1992); Mary Ann Glendon, "What's Wrong with the Elite Law Schools," *Wall Street Journal*, June 8, 1993, p. A14. (I discuss Judge Edwards's article later in this chapter.) For statistical evidence of the decline, see William M. Landes and Richard A. Posner, "The Influence of Economics on Law: A Quantitative Study," 36 *Journal of Law and Economics* 385 (1993).

monopoly of legal studies, pride of place belongs to economics, which has made great progress in the last thirty years and, applied to law, has revolutionized the profession's understanding of fields of law as disparate as antitrust, torts (mainly accidents), contracts, corporations, and bankruptcy. At the academic level it has made inroads into most other legal fields as well, ranging from adoption to zoning. Fields closely related to economics, notably finance theory, public-choice theory, and game theory, are also making inroads into law. Finance theory has transformed academic thinking about corporations, securities, bankruptcy, secured lending, and trust investment; public choice is influencing the legal understanding of legislation and constitutional law; game theory is influencing the understanding of contracts, procedure, bankruptcy, and antitrust.

Another discipline that is being widely applied to law is political and moral philosophy. Especially when broadly defined to include at one end hermeneutics (the study of interpretation—more precisely, the study of the *pervasiveness* of interpretation as a mode of understanding, implying the social and in some versions the political construction of reality) and at the other end political theory, moral and political philosophy has undergone a renascence. Stages in this renascence include the growing receptivity in American intellectual circles to the Continental philosophical tradition; the continuation of that tradition by Foucault, Derrida, Gadamer, and others; the recognition of affinities between that tradition and our own native pragmatist tradition; and the revival, led by John Rawls, of interest in both Kantian and contractarian political theory. Rawls's work forms a bridge to the theoretical side of political science, where scholars such as Jon Elster, Stephen Holmes, and Jeremy Waldron do work on or abutting law.

The Continental savants have given critical legal studies some of its leading ideas, but their influence on law has not stopped there. The recent interest in legal interpretation has been spurred in part by the legal professoriat's discovery of hermeneutics. And feminism, which did not exist as an organized academic field thirty years ago but which today, in part under the influence of Continental social constructionists, flourishes across the humanities, has under the banner of feminist jurisprudence obtained an expanding lodgment in the legal academy. Feminism has influenced academic legal thinking not only about women's legal rights but also about the nature of legal reasoning, and bids fair to push critical legal studies out of the academic limelight.

Through the efforts of Catharine MacKinnon and other feminists (not all of them lawyers—Andrea Dworkin, Carol Gilligan, and Martha Nussbaum are among the nonlawyer feminists who have influenced legal thinking), feminist jurisprudence has had an impact on the world outside the university. For example, it has persuaded judges to recognize sexual harassment as a legal wrong (a form of sex discrimination) and legislatures to recognize marital rape as a crime and to make proof of rape easier.

Another new academic discipline shaped by the perspective of a group believed to have been slighted by the conventional disciplines is black and ethnic studies. It too has its academic legal branch, called critical race theory, at which I shall glance later in this chapter and in Chapter 18 as well. Gay and lesbian legal studies are beginning to emerge, and I shall take note of them too (Chapters 16 and 26).

The Continental tradition has had a further impact on academic legal thought through its effect in making over literature departments into departments of interpretive theory from which English professors like Stanley Fish and Walter Benn Michaels sally forth to joust with Ronald Dworkin and other legal philosophers over issues of objectivity in interpretation. Feminist interest in literature, as well as the interest of old-fashioned New Critics turned law professors like James Boyd White, has joined with the new literary theory to make the interplay and overlap of law and literature still another interdisciplinary field of legal studies (see Chapter 23). Legal anthropology has received new impetus from the work of David Cohen, John Comaroff, and William Ian Miller, among others; legal sociology from the work of Richard Abel, Robert Ellickson, Kim Scheppele, and others. And work in probability theory, statistics, and psychology is transforming legal academic thinking about the rules of evidence and the role of juries.

The legal doctrinalists are being crowded by economic analysts of law, by other social scientists of law, by Bayesians, by philosophers of law, by political theorists, by critical legal scholars, by feminist and gay legal scholars, by the law and literature people, and by critical race theorists, all deploying the tools of nonlegal disciplines. (There is some double or even triple counting here; for example, critical legal studies and feminist jurisprudence overlap both each other and conventional legal philosophy.) In addition, a political gulf has opened between the doctrinalists, on the one hand, and the profession, the judiciary, and the larger society, on the other hand. The faculties of the leading

American law schools are now substantially to the left of the judiciary, especially the federal judiciary, and of the public at large; and they are moderately to the left of the practicing legal profession.[3]

Presidents Reagan and Bush appointed appellate judges disproportionately from the right-hand tail of the political distribution within the legal profession. The effect was to siphon conservative lawyers from the academy to the judiciary and thus at one and the same time to tug the academy leftward and the judiciary rightward. This effect has been reinforced by the self-selection of leftward-leaning lawyers into academic law. The financial rewards of a commercial practice for top-flight lawyers are very great, and naturally the law students most drawn to such a practice are those with conventional career goals, which emphasize financial success. Opportunities to practice law in an interesting and remunerative fashion in fields like constitutional, poverty, and environmental law are slight unless you're working for the bad guys, and federal legal service in the era of Reagan and Bush was not a congenial alternative for persons of liberal or left inclination. This will now change. But for many years left-leaning lawyers often felt they had no alternative to teaching and so gravitated there and found themselves in an antagonistic relation to the courts, especially the federal courts. The law reviews reek of the smell of cordite from the salvos with which today's law professors bombard today's Supreme Court Justices.

Constitutional law remains the most prestigious field in the legal academy. It draws many of the ablest doctrinalists. But they have lost their principal audience, the judges. They now write for each other. Doctrinalists who do not share the basic political premises of the judges whose work they analyze do not produce a scholarship that those judges, or the lawyers who are trying to move those judges by their advocacy, find useful, either in a critical or in a constructive sense. Nondoctrinalists, with some exceptions, especially among economic analysts of law and legal feminists, do not produce scholarship of even potential interest to practitioners or judges. But that is not a critical problem for nondoctrinalists. They identify with the university anyway

3. This is without regard to the leftward pull exerted by critical legal scholars, feminists, and critical race theorists. But none of these groups is as yet a large fraction of the legal professoriat, and their pull to the left is partly offset by the slight rightward tug exerted by the economic analysts of law, who are on average more conservative than other members of law faculties, and in part by the tiny band of social conservatives among law professors.

rather than with the legal profession. It is the doctrinalists who have a sense of exile.

The political gulf has a further significance for the morale of doctrinal scholarship. It exposes the epistemic shallowness of the enterprise. The main premises from which the legal reasoner proceeds are ethical, political, or ideological, and in a pluralistic society this spells trouble for anyone who insists on objectivity in law. The roots of legal doctrines are in such norms as freedom of contract, personal liberty and responsibility, and racial and sexual equality, which today are contested. The egalitarian, the libertarian, and the social conservative can use respectable methods of legal analysis to reach opposite conclusions across the whole range of legal controversy, because such values as freedom, responsibility, and equality crop up in every area of law, not just in constitutional law. It is true that people sometimes reason to the same conclusion from different, even opposite, premises, as where both the radical feminist and the religious fundamentalist agree that pornography should be outlawed, or the civil libertarian and the Seventh Day Adventist that the free exercise clause of the First Amendment should be construed broadly. But these are not examples of the power of legal reasoning to bring persons of disparate views to an agreement; they are fortuitous convergences or political compromises.

There is still more to discomfit today's legal doctrinalist. He is a student of texts, and the hermeneuticist has exposed the naiveté of legal interpretation (so there is no longer a consensus even on the methodology of legal reasoning), while the economist has derided the doctrinalist's grasp of policy and the feminist and the critical legal scholar have exposed the unconscious biases that permeate legal scholarship. The new learning is not only competitive with the old but antagonistic to it. It has put the doctrinalist on the defensive. And the very texts that are the material of his study and the source of his knowledge are deteriorating. With the vast majority of judicial opinions now being written by law clerks, almost all of whom are very recent law school graduates, increasingly the law professor's exegesis of the latest Supreme Court decision belongs to the same genre as his comments on his students' papers.

Increasingly, too, traditional legal scholars are unable to answer the most pressing questions about law. In an era of rapid social change, systemic questions sometimes become more interesting, more urgent, than doctrinal ones. The period since 1960 has seen an enormous upsurge in the amount of legal activity in the United States. Why has this happened, and what has been the effect? Are lawyers in the number in which we have them today a drag on economic growth? Are they overpaid? Have lawyer-initiated reforms in bankruptcy and employment law, in criminal sentencing and in the rights of civil rights plaintiffs, criminal defendants, juveniles, and the insane increased or reduced social welfare? Have they, perhaps, had few consequences of any kind?[4] To these vital questions the close study of judicial opinions yields no answers.

Take the question whether there are "too many" lawyers. Two studies by economists find that the more lawyers a nation has, other things being equal, the lower its rate of economic growth.[5] The United States has the most, even on a per capita basis (obviously population is one of those other things that must be held constant in the comparison of nations). The studies are superficial, however, because they ignore the contributions that lawyers make to nonmarket output.[6] Such output is ignored in the usual measures of economic activity not because it is not "economic" but because it is difficult to attach a dollar value to. For example, the regulation of pollution is a lawyer-intensive activity the principal outputs of which—clean air and clear water—are not included in conventional measures of economic output, such as GNP. Deterring police brutality is another example of a nonmarket good that lawyers play a significant role in producing. Moreover, a lawyer-driven increase in access to legal remedies is the equivalent of giving the population potentially valuable options to invoke those remedies should the need arise. The options are separate from their exercise; people who never in their lives bring a lawsuit may nevertheless derive value from knowing that should their legal rights ever be invaded they will be able to find a lawyer and get into court without waiting for many years, just as people derive utility from having fire insurance who never have a fire.

4. Gerald N. Rosenberg, *The Hollow Hope: Can Courts Bring about Social Change?* (1991).

5. Kevin M. Murphy, Andrei Shleifer, and Robert W. Vishny, "The Allocation of Talent: Implications for Growth," 106 *Quarterly Journal of Economics* 503 (1991); Samar K. Datta and Jeffrey B. Nugent, "Adversary Activities and Per Capita Income Growth," 14 *World Development* 1457 (1986).

6. For other criticisms, see George L. Priest, "Lawyers, Liability, and Law Reform: Effects on American Economic Growth and Trade Competitiveness," 71 *Denver University Law Review* 115 (1993). The popular "too many lawyers" literature is effectively criticized in Marc Galanter, "News from Nowhere: The Debased Debate on Civil Justice," 71 *Denver University Law Review* 77 (1993).

Of course, the threat of legal liability, a kind of negative option, or tax, is also greater, the easier it is to bring a lawsuit; and who knows how the two option values net out? For that matter, who knows whether, if the nation's economic output were measured correctly, the growth in lawyers would be found to have increased or reduced that output? My point is only that there are many important questions about law that traditional lawyers, even when they are professors at the best law schools, do not and cannot answer, instead deferring to experts in other disciplines who may not know enough about law to answer them either.

The interdisciplinarians have highlighted the *narrowness* of professional knowledge. Legal training and experience equip lawyers with a set of essentially casuistic tools and a feel for legal doctrines, but not with the tools they need in order to understand the social consequences of law. Maybe casuistry has gotten too bad a press.[7] But legal casuistry, at least, seems to give out just when one needs it. The enormous amount of academic legal ink spilled on the issues of abortion and gay rights has been largely wasted. The legal understanding of issues of sexuality and reproduction has improved only because of the recent emergence of new *interdisciplinary* fields of legal scholarship—feminism, the economics of the family, gay and lesbian studies, and the study of human sexuality in relation to issues of law and public policy generally.

It is instructive to compare traditional academic law with typical humanities fields such as literature and philosophy, on the one hand, and typical science fields such as physics and biology, on the other. The professor of literature or of philosophy is a student of texts created by some of the greatest minds in history,[8] and some of the greatness rubs off on the student. The professor of biology or physics deploys upon his rather less articulate subject matter mathematical and experimental methods of great power. The professor of law is immersed in texts—primarily judicial opinions, statutes, and miscellaneous rules and regulations—written by judges, law clerks, politicians, lobbyists, and civil

7. As forcefully argued in Albert R. Jonsen and Stephen Toulmin, *The Abuse of Casuistry: A History of Moral Reasoning* (1988), esp. pp. 16–19. I examine their argument in Chapter 24.

8. Of course in both fields many practitioners confine their study to a radically truncated subset of the canon; some branches of modern philosophy, such as formal logic and philosophy of mind, are not heavily text-dependent at all; and literary theorists and critics are increasingly interested not in the classics but instead in popular culture, with which we shall have a brush in Chapter 23.

servants. To these essentially, and perhaps increasingly, mediocre texts he applies analytical tools of no great power—unless they are tools borrowed from another field. The force and reach of doctrinal legal scholarship are inherently limited.

Is the Gap between the Academy and the Profession Widening Dangerously?

Judge Harry Edwards of the U.S. Court of Appeals for the District of Columbia Circuit believes that law schools should train ethical practitioners and produce scholarship that is useful to lawyers and judges, while law firms should practice law ethically, and that neither type of institution is doing either of these things any more.[9] Especially but not only at the elite law schools, faculty, especially young faculty, have, he argues, become disdainful about the practice of law and the judging of cases and about the forms of legal scholarship that assist in practice and judging. Uninterested in producing ethical or for that matter any practitioners or any professionally relevant scholarship, these faculty spend their time using theories drawn from other fields such as economics and philosophy to make fun of law. "We see 'law professors' hired from graduate schools, wholly lacking in legal experience or training, who use the law school as a bully pulpit from which to pour scorn upon the legal profession."[10] Law firms are becoming ever more interested in making money rather than in maintaining high ethical standards, being abetted in this by the law schools' growing indifference to instilling those standards in their students. As for the scholarship that the new-fashioned law school faculty members are producing, it has, in Edwards's opinion, little value. Law professors are unlikely to be able to do economics or philosophy or literary theory as well as people who are trained in and work full time in those disciplines.

There is an amusing paradox here. Judge Edwards's article is not about legal doctrine, although as a judge and former law professor that is presumably the only type of article that he would consider himself competent to write, or that he believes a law review competent to publish, under the austere standards that he has set down for the profession. It is an article in the sociology of legal education and

9. Edwards, note 2 above. Edwards's article has received extensive commentary. See *Symposium: Legal Education*, 91 *Michigan Law Review* 1921 (1993).

10. Edwards, note 2 above, at 37.

practice. The author relies heavily on a traditional sociological technique, the survey, but admits that his survey did not produce "statistically reliable data."[11] That is an understatement. The survey was confined to Judge Edwards's former law clerks. He does not tell us what percentage responded or what precise questions they were asked to respond to; evidently the responses were not anonymous, although the names of the respondents are not revealed in the article.

So even doctrinalists cannot resist writing the occasional nondoctrinal article and in so doing tumbling into the pitfall of amateurism that Edwards rightly decries; but that is a trivial observation and I shall move on to more serious matters. Edwards is closer to the mark with respect to academic law than with respect to the practice of law. About the latter he remarks revealingly, "The tremendous pressure to create revenues, which so many of my former clerks describe, is a wholly novel phenomenon. When I practiced law at a large firm, some twenty years ago, I felt no such pressure, nor did my colleagues. We enjoyed our work."[12] That "tremendous pressure to create revenues" could equally well be described as competitive pressure to work hard. The practice of law has become more competitive since Edwards's days in practice. Naturally it is less fun. Competitive markets are no fun at all for most sellers; the effect of competition is to transform most producer surplus into consumer surplus and in more or less time to drive the less efficient producers out of business.

The implications for legal ethics are complex. It is necessary to distinguish between two types of ethical obligation. One is to the client and is illustrated by rules against overbilling and conflicts of interest and above all by the rule that the lawyer is the fiduciary of his client, whom he must therefore treat as he would himself rather than as he would treat the other party to a normal arm's-length contract. The other type of ethical obligation is to the court or the community and is illustrated by rules against suborning perjury and abusing pretrial discovery. Competition will not greatly erode the first kind of ethical obligation; competitive markets are not notable for disserving their customers. It is true that by reducing the profitability of lawyering, competition will reduce the penalty for being caught out in unethical conduct and expelled from the profession. The major penalty is simply

11. Id. at 42.
12. Id. at 72.

the loss of future professional income when one is expelled, and that loss will be greater, on average, the more profitable the profession.[13] But this is an esoteric point, and on balance competition should make the consumers of legal services better off. It may, however, erode the second type of ethical obligation significantly. The lawyer's performance of his ethical obligations to people and institutions that are not his clients disserves his clients, his customers; and competition implies the subordination of other interests to those of the consumer. But Edwards does not allude to the trade-off between the gains to clients from greater competition and the losses to others—he does not have the consumer's perspective—and as a result he conveys an unduly negative impression of the current practice of law.

Professor Kronman offers a different perspective on this issue. He argues that the recent changes in the profession, by increasing lawyers' preoccupation with making money, have undermined their ability to render imaginative advice to their clients. "By contrast, a culture that downplays the importance of money, in the way that most large firms did thirty years ago, deploys its normative resources not on behalf of but in opposition to self-interest, and thereby empowers the capacity for sympathy, instead of blocking it as the regnant culture of large firms now tends to do."[14] Kronman appears to associate what he believes to be the increasingly mercenary and indeed rapacious character of the practice of law with the opening up of jobs in large law firms to Jews, women, and persons from a working-class background.[15] As we saw in Chapter 1, a positive correlation between social homogeneity and avoidance of price competition is plausible. But to want to increase that homogeneity in order to reduce price competition is a symptom of the guild mentality, and Kronman does not show that such a mentality is likely to serve clients or the society better than a competitive ethos would do. He does argue that the greater turnover of clients that we

13. See Gary S. Becker and George J. Stigler, "Law Enforcement, Malfeasance, and Compensation of Enforcers," 3 *Journal of Legal Studies* 1, 6–13 (1974). Becker and Stigler suggest that persons entering such occupations be charged an entrance fee designed so that their lifetime earnings would not exceed a competitive return. This is done automatically by the private market when costly education, low-paid apprenticeship, or queuing is used to depress initial earnings by way of compensation for expected monopoly returns later in one's career.

14. Anthony T. Kronman, *The Lost Lawyer: Failing Ideals of the Legal Profession* 299 (1993).

15. See id. at 291–300.

can expect under competition will make it harder for lawyers to get to know them well enough to render "statesmanlike" advice, advice that helps a client clarify his goals. But if such advice really is valuable and valued, this will check the tendency to excessive turnover of clients. Not all contracts in competitive markets are spot contracts. Competitive firms often establish durable relations with suppliers or customers. They do so when the benefits of such relations exceed the costs. Why should law be different?

Judge Edwards is on stronger ground in his criticisms of the law schools than in his criticisms of the practicing profession. He is right to criticize those brash youths who radiate disdain for conventional, which is to say doctrinal, legal scholarship. He is also right to note a shift away from doctrinal legal scholarship at the leading law schools, but he exaggerates both the shift and its significance. Such scholarship continues to be written at those schools—even in the form of treatises (Areeda's multivolume antitrust treatise, Farnsworth's three-volume contract treatise, and Currie's treatise on the Clean Air Act come immediately to mind). Some younger scholars at those schools have signed on as coauthors (notably Kaplow, on the Areeda treatise), and many write doctrinal articles (such as Meltzer and Sullivan at Harvard and Brilmayer at N.Y.U.). Many distinguished nondoctrinalists such as Sunstein write doctrinal articles, and some doctrinal articles, such as McConnell's on freedom of religion, are so permeated with extralegal insight as to dissolve the distinction between the two genres. The decline in doctrinal scholarship is relative, not absolute, and perhaps not even relative; all that may be occurring is a shift in the production of doctrinal scholarship toward scholars at law schools of the second and third tier. Is that a bad thing? Edwards thinks so because it is the only type of legal scholarship that he regards as useful or as likely to be done well by law professors, and because he thinks that the law professors who have turned their backs on it are unlikely to have much interest in instilling high standards of ethical practice of law in their students. Implicitly he believes that the leaders of the bar are likely in the future as in the past to be drawn disproportionately from the ranks of graduates of the top-tier law schools. So the fact that old-fashioned legal scholarship and old-fashioned indoctrination in the folkways of the traditional profession continue and even flourish in many lower-tier schools is not much consolation for him.

Edwards's threnody overlooks a lot, such as that there are more and larger law schools since his day, that as a result law school faculties have expanded greatly, and that the quality of these faculties has improved as law, becoming a more lucrative profession, has attracted abler young people to it, some fraction of whom become law professors. It is true that during this period American law has become more ramified and complex. But no area of practice or doctrine is beyond the intellectual competence of the increasingly able faculties of the lesser law schools. The shift in legal doctrinal scholarship toward those faculties can hardly be considered a disaster for the profession.

The percentage of doctrinal articles that are useful to the profession probably has fallen. Part of the reason may be that nondoctrinalists place more emphasis on writing than on teaching. This is an aspect of their taking their cues from the university community rather than the professional community; the former emphasizes the growth of knowledge, the latter the training of lawyers. So for nondoctrinalists it is publish or perish, and they have tried with some success to impose this norm on their doctrinalist colleagues. The latter, who used to publish only when they had something useful to say to the profession, now are under pressure to publish to gain tenure and academic recognition. So they publish more, and the addition flunks the test of professional utility. The political divergence between the law professoriat and the judiciary, which is new, has further reduced the utility of academic legal writing in the practice of law, although doctrinalists tend to be less political than nondoctrinalists.

As for failing to instill legal ethics in law students at elite, or for that matter at any, law schools, few things are more futile than trying to make people good by preaching at them. "We learn how to behave as lawyers, soldiers, merchants, or what not by being them. Life, not the parson, teaches conduct."[16] Since not all ethical principles are intuitive, instruction in legal ethics performs an informational function. But Edwards is concerned about the lack of inspirational precepts and examples in the teaching of legal ethics at the elite schools rather than about a failure to impart prudential warnings.

Again there is irony. An exciting course in legal ethics, aimed at students at the best law schools, could not be limited to a careful exegesis of the American Bar Association's code of professional ethics.

16. Letter from Oliver Wendell Holmes to Frederick Pollock (April 2, 1926), in *Holmes-Pollock Letters: The Correspondence of Mr. Justice Holmes and Sir Frederick Pollock 1874–1932*, vol. 2, p. 178 (Mark DeWolfe Howe ed. 1941).

It would have to bring to bear on law the Western philosophical tradition of ethical reflection. It would have to confront the student with ethical questions about agency and advocacy raised by Plato in the *Gorgias* and answered by Aristotle in the *Rhetoric;* with discussions of the role of lawyer as statesman and as friend by scholars of jurisprudence such as Charles Fried and Anthony Kronman; with the philosophical literature on loyalty, commitment, detachment, and candor; with the profound depiction of the lawyer's role and character in literary works by Dickens and Tolstoy; with the criticisms of the traditional conceptions of the lawyer's role by legal realists, critical legal scholars, and feminist legal scholars; and with the behavior of the legal profession in crisis, for example in Nazi Germany (see Chapter 4). Could a doctrinal scholar teach such a course well?

The most interesting question raised by Edwards's article is whether the shift in the emphasis in legal scholarship at the leading law schools from the practical to the theoretical has caused a net decline in the social value of legal scholarship. He is convinced that it has. His evidence is that he, and many of his former law clerks who responded to his survey, regard interdisciplinary scholarship as useless to the legal profession, even to its judicial branch of which Judge Edwards is a distinguished representative.[17] Offered as it is without particulars, this verdict is extraordinary. Consider some of the developments in interdisciplinary legal scholarship over the past two or three decades. The application of economics to law is generally believed to have transformed antitrust law. One can argue that all it has really done has been to provide conservative judges with a vocabulary and conceptual apparatus that has enabled them to reach the results they were drawn to on political grounds. Even if this were all, it would be far from negligible; to enable is to do much. Law and economics has also contributed significantly to the deregulation movement, which has transformed the legal landscape in a number of fields of law, such as transportation law, communications law, and the regulation of the legal profession itself. It is a factor in the courts' increasing hospitality to claims of constitutional protection for commercial speech. It has influenced environmental regulation, and the proof of commercial damages. It has underwritten the movement toward awarding "hedonic" damages in

---

17. To similar effect, see Carrington, note 2 above, at 802 ("theorizing about law is perhaps the activity of law professors least likely to bear on the course of events").

personal injury cases, that is, damages for loss of the pleasure of living. It has armed divorcing women to argue that a husband's professional degree is a (human) capital asset to which the wife contributed and in which she should be recognized as having an interest. It has greatly influenced the proof of injury and damages in securities cases. It has changed the way in which lost earnings are computed in tort cases. It has suggested new lines of proof in employment-discrimination cases (again through the human-capital model of earnings), while at the same time casting doubt on theories of comparable worth. It has influenced the design of the federal sentencing guidelines (an economist was a member of the Sentencing Commission which promulgated the guidelines), which has transformed the sentencing practices of the federal courts. It is powering a gathering movement to reform the Bankruptcy Code. It is even influencing the way in which courts deal with indigent litigants. Judge Edwards discusses none of these examples.[18]

He does not discuss the criticisms that Bayesian probability theorists and cognitive psychologists have made of the rules of evidence, jury instructions, and burdens of proof:[19] criticisms of immediate practical import, made by scholars who have as much to say about these matters as judges and practicing lawyers. He does not discuss the impact of feminist jurisprudence on rape law, sexual harassment, and the debate over the legal protection of pornography. (He does not mention feminist legal writing at all.) He ignores the important role that political scientists play as expert witnesses in reapportionment litigation. And he is silent on the growing literature, which is informed by philosophy and literary theory and also by political theory, economics, and the theory of public choice, on the interpretation of constitutions and statutes, even though interpretation is the major function of the court on which Judge Edwards sits.

The philistinism of the highly educated is captured in the slogan, "What I do not know is not knowledge." That is, in truth, how most of us think. We lawyers—especially ones of Judge Edwards's and my generation, who were trained at a time when the legal process school

18. For confirmation, by a distinguished legal scholar who is emphatically not an economic analyst of law, of the influence of economics on law's practical side, see Robert W. Gordon, "Lawyers, Scholars and the 'Middle Ground,'" 91 *Michigan Law Review* 2075, 2084–2085 (1993).

19. For a useful review of this scholarship, see Roger C. Park, "Evidence Scholarship, Old and New," 75 *Minnesota Law Review* 849 (1991).

of jurisprudence was in the ascendancy—find it comfortable and indeed natural, the path of least resistance, to believe that law is an autonomous discipline and that what there is to know about law is therefore a monopoly of legal professionals that must not be allowed to be broken by interlopers from other fields or, even worse, by legal professionals treasonably seduced by other fields. But professional knowledge is narrow; this is the characteristic deformation of professionalization. Most physicians are narrowly focused on using orthodox treatment methods to treat a stereotyped list of crisis situations. Preventive methods of an unorthodox character such as diet and exercise, or unorthodox treatments such as acupuncture and meditation, are slighted or disparaged, while whole fields of medicine broadly understood, such as securing a safe water supply or improving dental health, are placed outside the boundaries of medicine and derided as lesser pursuits.[20] As a result, many of the advances in human health, as well as most critiques of the medical profession, have come from outside the profession. It is the same with law. Conventional legal education puts blinders on the students, enabling them to tread doggedly a well-trodden path of professional success, and generates forms of scholarship that accept the borders of the path as the boundaries of the legal universe. It places too narrow a construal on "law," which when construed as it ought to be supports the proposition "that most legal academics . . . are among the few people left in their profession who take law seriously."[21]

I am not starry-eyed about the new interdisciplinary legal scholarship. Much of it is bad, in part because a form of scholarship that is so difficult for most law students to understand places a severe strain on the system for publishing legal scholarship, a system dominated by student-edited law reviews, and by doing so impedes the gatekeeper function that scholarly journals are supposed to perform. But when Samuel Johnson said that a writer is judged by his worst work when he is alive and by his best work when he is dead, he was not intending to pay a compliment to contemporaries' evaluations of achievement. We should consider whether legal scholarship would be enriched or impoverished if (to speak only of living nonyoung lawyers whose principal academic appointment is in a law school) such scholars as Bruce Ackerman, William Baxter, Robert Bork, Guido Calabresi, Ronald

---

20. Diana Chapman Walsh, *Corporate Physicians: Between Medicine and Management* 117–119 (1987).

21. Gordon, note 18 above, at 2104.

Dworkin, Frank Easterbrook, Robert Ellickson, Richard Epstein, William Eskridge, Marc Galanter, Mary Ann Glendon, Robert Gordon, Thomas Grey, Henry Hansmann, Morton Horwitz, Thomas Jackson, Duncan Kennedy, Anthony Kronman, Sanford Levinson, Saul Levmore, Catharine MacKinnon, Henry Manne, Frank Michelman, William Ian Miller, Martha Minow, John Noonan, George Priest, Matthew Spitzer, Cass Sunstein, Roberto Unger, Robin West, G. Edward White, James Boyd White, and others almost too numerous to mention had either been deflected to other fields altogether or been apprenticed to Corbin, Wigmore, Williston, Prosser, or Scott. With many of those whom I have listed I have sharp disagreements. But I do not believe that the legal profession would be better without them, or that they could be made to plow the narrow groove prescribed for legal scholars by Judge Edwards and his law clerks.

Granted, much of what these first-rate interdisciplinary scholars do makes no contribution to the work of a judge or a practitioner. William Ian Miller writes about medieval Icelandic society (see Chapter 14). Kronman has written extensively about Aristotle and Max Weber, Noonan about Catholic doctrine, James Boyd White about Jane Austen, Grey about the poetry of Wallace Stevens (Chapter 23). But where is it written that all legal scholarship shall be in the service of the legal profession? Perhaps the ultimate criterion of all scholarship is utility, but it need not be utility to a particular audience, or even to a contemporary audience. It is common in many fields of scholarship for professors to follow research paths that do not interest many of their students. Judge Edwards lacks a conception of *basic* research, research that precisely because it lacks immediate application—a market for its fruits—is unlikely to be conducted elsewhere than in a university setting. A new approach to law, such as the economic approach, may take a generation or more to alter professional thinking (in fact it has taken much less time than that); that does not make it useless.

I suggested that the new legal scholarship should be judged by its best rather than by its worst examples. Judge Edwards might reply that the important thing is the ratio of the one to the other; that if most of the stuff is garbage, the price of the occasional pearl is too high. But there are few more elusive or problematic concepts than that of "waste."[22] Out of 6,000 eggs laid by a female salmon and fertilized by

22. We shall encounter in the next chapter the ambiguity of "wasting time."

the male, on average only two salmon are born who live to adulthood.[23] Does this mean that 5,998 eggs are "wasted"? Only if there is a more efficient method of perpetuating the species. Scholarship, like salmon breeding in the wild, is a high-risk, low-return activity. American universities are the finest in the world, but the vast majority of their scholarly output is trivial, ephemeral, uncited, forgettable and soon forgotten. Even in physics, almost 40 percent of all journal articles are not cited within the first four years after publication—which probably means, since physics is a rapidly changing field, that they are never cited. This figure rises to 72 percent in engineering, 75 percent in the social sciences, and an astonishing 98 percent in arts and humanities.[24] We should not be surprised or unhappy that so much of the new legal scholarship is of little value to anyone. That is the price of a body of creative scholarship that has more practical relevance than Judge Edwards will admit and a value as theory that his criteria for worthwhile scholarship, criteria understandably but nevertheless excessively narrow, prevent him from acknowledging.

When I said I was not starry-eyed, I did not intend merely a polite bow to the widespread professional skepticism, crystallized in Edwards's article, about the new legal scholarship. Academic law is artificially sustained, indeed bloated, by the requirement in most states that persons who want to become lawyers spend three years at an accredited law school. This requirement creates in turn a demand for law professors who will teach advanced courses to keep the students occupied for the full three years. Law is a prosperous profession, and stiff accreditation standards limit the entry of new law schools, while proprietary (that is, profit-making) law schools rarely can obtain accreditation at all. Relative to most other departments in a university, law schools are awash in tuition income and in gifts from wealthy alums. Every law school sports its own law review, and many have

23. Robert Trivers, *Social Evolution* 12 (1985).
24. These figures are from David P. Hamilton, "Research Papers: Who's Uncited Now?" 251 *Science* 25 (1991). The citing database consists of the thousands of journals tabulated by the Institute for Scientific Information, which publishes citation indexes for the natural sciences, the social sciences, and the arts and humanities. Among subdisciplines, the lowest noncitation rate is 9.2 percent for atomic, molecular, and chemical physics. The highest is theater—99.9 percent. American literature is close behind, with 99.8 percent. History and philosophy have surprisingly high noncitation rates as well—95.5 and 92.1 percent, respectively. David Pendlebury of the Institute has kindly computed for me the noncitation rate in law; it is 57 percent for articles published in 1987.

several. Law professors can find publication outlets for their scholarship too easily, especially since the editors of the law reviews are students few of whom are competent to evaluate nondoctrinal scholarship. Some crazy stuff is being published in law reviews nowadays.

The problem was less serious when most legal scholarship was doctrinal. The criteria for such scholarship were clear and evaluation therefore straightforward. The new legal scholarship borrows its ideas and methods from other fields but does not subject itself to evaluation by the trained specialists in those fields, the real pros. This is what makes it so difficult to judge, and to separate the experts in it from the tyros and the charlatans. Law review editors cannot judge. Neither can the doctrinal scholars, who, despite their relative decline and the crisis of confidence that afflicts some of them, continue to dominate most law school faculties.

Most American law professors, even nondoctrinalists, have the identical legal training as practitioners. Only the continuity between the practice of law and *traditional* legal scholarship made this a defensible method of preparing law professors. Nondoctrinalists also lack cadres of graduate students to extend their work by writing dissertations in areas of the professor's interest. Though technically graduate students because they have graduated from college, law students are legal undergraduates and do not write dissertations.

I am not a degree-monger. The essence of most graduate education is not the courses and the exams, but the preparation for a career in scholarship that is afforded by the experience of writing a dissertation. Few law professors, even when they are practitioners of the new legal scholarship, have that experience.

The problem of evaluating the new legal scholarship is made more acute by the fact that the methods and objectives in the different fields of nondoctrinal legal scholarship are different. How to compare practitioners in different fields? How to judge whether a critical race theorist's narratives of discrimination are superior or inferior, as scholarship, to an economist's rational model of discrimination? Only when the practitioners of an academic discipline agree on criteria of excellence will a discipline—here I am treating the entire spectrum of nondoctrinal legal scholarship as a single field—be able to claim objectivity for its output.

Yet we should not mourn the decline in the objectivity of academic law any more than we should mourn the increased heterodoxy of religious opinion that followed the abolition of the Inquisition. The objectivity of academic law in the 1950s was the result of a homogeneity of background, training, experience, and outlook among academic lawyers and the poverty of competition from other fields. Of course every community of reasoners must be homogeneous to a degree; you must know the rules of chess to recognize illegal moves. But too much homogeneity, or homogeneity of the wrong kind, can produce a fragile, sterile objectivity. Some truths (as we now believe them to be) are not credible, and hence are not believed. Some beliefs that are credible to the entire community of interested inquirers turn out to be false. The credence accorded false beliefs must reflect features in the social organization of knowledge. The academic legal profession used to be organized in such a way that a body of beliefs concerning the autonomy of the law, the criteria for evaluating legal decisions, the scope and meaning of the Constitution, and so forth commanded such widespread agreement as to be thought unquestionably true. The expansion of the legal profession, the greater diversity of its membership, political turmoil, and the rise of competing disciplines have shattered the consensus on which law's objectivity rested. A certain professionalism, a certain dependability, a certain craftsmanship has been lost, but intellectual sophistication has been gained along with a broadening of legal scholarship that has for the first time enabled it to touch, and potentially to enrich, neighboring fields. Competent lawyers lured by the siren song of Theory have wrecked their academic careers. But a few have had careers that could not have been envisaged when academic legal scholarship was at once a solid professional service and a complacent academic backwater.

Affirmative Action in Law School Faculty Hiring

An "objective" discipline, parading however misleadingly under the banner of truth, will be perceived (not least by its own practitioners) as "strong." And the stronger a field is perceived to be, the weaker will be the felt grounds for suspicion that able members of a minority group are being excluded for invidious reasons, or for believing that ethnic or racial or sexual diversity is likely to improve the field—a strong field isn't apt to seem in need of improving—or that hiring the apparently less well-qualified applicant won't really dilute quality. Academic law is no longer a strong field in the sense of having objective standards, though it may be a better and more interesting field. So one should not be surprised that it is riven by affirmative action.

These observations provide background to Duncan Kennedy's suggestion that law schools should give preferential treatment in hiring to minorities in the interest of increasing the quality of legal scholarship.[25] Affirmative action in faculty hiring is often defended as providing role models for minority students, rectifying historic injustices, preserving social peace, and exposing students to diverse viewpoints and backgrounds. Rarely is it defended on Kennedy's ground, that it will raise the quality of scholarship.

Before this claim can be evaluated, several preliminary questions must be addressed. One is whether to distinguish between public and private law schools. Wholly apart from the different constitutional status of state action and private action, we should be more wary—on pragmatic grounds duly regardful of history—about allowing or encouraging public institutions to engage in racial discrimination, however well intentioned. I shall therefore confine my discussion to affirmative action by private law schools.

Which racial, ethnic, or other groups shall be entitled to preferential treatment? Asians are underrepresented on the faculties of American law schools, yet their average income exceeds that of white Americans by a wide margin[26]—should they nevertheless be entitled to a leg up in law school hiring? If so, what about the Jews? They are as much a race as Hispanics are, and they have a longer history of being discriminated against—we recall that they were expelled from Spain, Hispania itself, in 1492. Of course it would be extremely odd for law schools to decide to discriminate in favor of Jews. If any group is "overrepresented" from a population standpoint on law school faculties, it is Jews—indeed, they comprise so large a fraction of the faculties of elite

25. Kennedy, "A Cultural Pluralist Case for Affirmative Action in Legal Academia," 1990 *Duke Law Journal* 705, reprinted as chapter 2 of Kennedy's book *Sexy Dressing Etc.* (1993). My page references are to the article version.

26. Thomas Sowell, "*Weber* and *Bakke* and the Presuppositions of 'Affirmative Action,'" in *Discrimination, Affirmative Action, and Equal Opportunity* 46 (W. E. Block and M. A. Walker eds. 1982); U.S. Bureau of the Census, *Statistical Abstract of the United States* 39 (111th ed. 1991) (tab. 44); U.S. Bureau of the Census, *Current Population Reports,* ser. P-60, no. 174, p. 3 (1991) (tab. A). Of course there is great diversity within the Asian community; not all Asian groups have had the success in America of the Japanese, Chinese, Vietnamese, and Indians. Another diverse minority is the Hispanic. It includes a number of persons of undiluted Spanish or Portuguese ancestry, who encounter little or no discrimination yet are included in some programs of affirmative action.

law schools that if the "major minorities" to which Kennedy alludes are to be hired in substantial numbers, the Jewish representation in law school faculties will drop precipitously. Unconsciously substantiating his stated concern with the insensitivity of "white ruling class males" such as himself, Kennedy makes a comment bound to grate on Jewish sensibilities: "We usually think of assimilation as very different from being 'born into' a culture. There are always doubts about 'authenticity,' or the possibility that the assimilated person is 'neither fish nor fowl'" (p. 741).[27]

It is necessary to distinguish between requiring and permitting law schools to engage in affirmative action. Although Kennedy denies that he is talking about the former, it is plain that he would very much like to see *all* law schools practice the high degree of affirmative action that he thinks desirable. But to believe, however earnestly, that an educational reform would be a very good idea does not entail recommending that every school in the country adopt it. If they all do, we shall lose the benefit of controlled experimentation. That is an important fruit of diversity, and Kennedy applauds diversity.

Another distinction is among affirmative action in law school admissions, in initial and lateral faculty hiring, and in promotion to tenure. These have to be examined separately because they raise different issues, but then put back together because they are interrelated. Concerning admissions, it is necessary to distinguish between two degrees of affirmative action. One involves making small departures from the usual criteria based on grade point averages and law school aptitude test scores in recognition of the fact that these measures are not perfect predictors of performance in law school or the legal profession. Even the small departures are questionable from a purely academic standpoint, because college grades and LSAT scores rarely underpredict law school grades of minority students. Altogether more questionable are the large departures from the normal admission standards that would be necessary to admit blacks to law schools at a rate equal to their percentage of the overall American population, the college-age population, or even the college population.[28] That sort of affirmative action causes significant tension in elite law schools, where blacks admitted

27. He deleted this passage about assimilation when he reprinted his article in *Sexy Dressing Etc.*, note 25 above. See id. at 66.

28. In 1989, blacks were 9.8 percent of the college student population in the United States. U.S. Bureau of the Census, *Statistical Abstract of the United States*, note 26 above, at 158 (tab. 263).

with seriously subpar records cluster at the bottom of the class. But if a law school decides not to set a high quota for black students, it will find it awkward to set a high quota for black teachers. As a practical, political matter the two sorts of quota go hand in glove, and so the objection to high racial quotas in student admissions is also one to high racial quotas in faculty hiring.

The reason for distinguishing between, on the one hand, new and lateral faculty hiring and, on the other hand, promotion to tenure from within is that if a school bends its standards at the entry level, things become dicey when the entrants come up for promotion. That is not a serious problem with admissions. It is enough for most law students if they graduate, and most students who are admitted to law school as beneficiaries of affirmative action can graduate, even if not at the top of their class. Tenure is different. Not every competent untenured faculty member can expect to achieve tenure; and tenure is a commitment to lifetime employment (literally, with the abolition of mandatory retirement ages for professors). What are to be the tenure standards for those hired through affirmative action? If they are to be the same as for white males, a disproportionate number of blacks will be turned down, and this will be more than awkward. Are there to be two tracks, therefore? If so, will voting on tenure in the affirmative action track be limited to blacks?

Let me put these questions to one side and concentrate on entry-level hiring of blacks, and ask whether Kennedy is right that the bending of standards necessary to hire a substantial number will raise rather than lower the quality of legal scholarship. It is not a ridiculous suggestion. I do think his invocation of "the general democratic principle that people should be represented in institutions that have power over their lives" (p. 705) is ridiculous. It implies that all law schools should be public institutions so that the public at large, whose lives are affected by law and lawyers and hence by legal education, can be represented in law school governance. But Kennedy is right that academic law has great room for improvement, and this opens up the possibility that existing standards for faculty appointment, which emphasize law school grades and verbal quickness, should not be thought immutable and that a diversity of approaches, a multiplication of perspectives, a dislocation of the settled ways of thinking could improve the field. Law and economics has had this effect, and feminist legal scholarship as well. Maybe minority scholarship will too.

Maybe. But there are problems. One arises from the fact that race itself, unlike economics or feminism, is not an approach, any more than gender is an approach. There is a positive correlation between being black and having distinctive life experiences, and it may create a distinctive perspective. It is these experiences, this perspective, that Kennedy is after. But not all blacks are culturally black. Some are completely assimilated to the dominant white Eurocentric culture. Especially if they are uninterested in teaching or writing about racial questions, they do not add the diversity that Kennedy seeks. But there will be pressure from faculty members who do not share Kennedy's desire for cultural diversity at the price of conventional credentials to focus racial hiring precisely on assimilated blacks. To work, therefore, his scheme would require a cultural definition of blackness (Hispanic-ness, American Indian-ness, Asian-ness) and thus discriminate against those blacks, Hispanics, American Indians, and Asians who have adopted the dominant culture. One might expect similar pressure to apply a cultural definition to femaleness, and thus hire only radical feminists, but such pressure has not materialized, because there are plenty of qualified female candidates for law teaching across the entire spectrum of attitudes toward feminism. There are not many qualified black candidates, and a law school willing to bend its normal standards only so far as necessary to hire one or two blacks may find itself under great pressure to hire the one or two who are more "authentically" black. The effect is to confine most black law professors to the academic ghetto of critical race theory.

Discrimination against assimilated blacks is a disagreeable corollary to Kennedy's proposal, but I do not think he would shrink from it. He deems them victims of false consciousness. "We coerce minorities who want the rewards we have to offer into 'being like us'" (p. 720). I do not doubt that there are people who have been habituated by tradition or an oppressively homogeneous social environment to believe things that are contrary to their best interests. But Kennedy is not talking about peasant women in Bangladesh. He is talking about highly educated Americans. They have a clearer idea of what is best for them to believe than he does.

Kennedy overlooks the potential of his proposal to sap the self-esteem of black academics. The larger the quotas, the farther down in the pool of eligibles the law schools will have to dip to fill them, so the average quality of black academics will fall. What is less often remarked is that every increase in a minority faculty quota raises the average quality of the nonminority faculty; there are now fewer places for them to fill and, if merit criteria of selection are used, average quality will rise. A falling average quality of minority faculty will cross a rising average quality of nonminority faculty, widening the gap between the two groups and fostering perceptions of minority inadequacy.

Is this a price worth paying—to improve legal scholarship? Kennedy does not mention a single idea that critical race theory—the legal scholarship of the self-consciously nonassimilationist minority legal scholars—has produced. Gary Peller's long article on critical race theory in the same issue of the *Duke Law Journal* in which Kennedy's article appears is similarly evasive.[29] In fact critical race theory has produced ideas. In particular, critical race theorists have been in the forefront of the movement for universities to adopt sweeping rules against "hate speech."[30] But maybe this field of legal scholarship is not *mainly* in the business of producing ideas. Its favorite expository technique is the "narrative," a literary rather than an analytical genre well represented by Patricia Williams's book, *The Alchemy of Race and Rights,* which I shall examine in Chapter 18. It is a respectable genre, but one unlikely to transform legal scholarship. Kennedy's faith that if only more blacks were law professors they would produce a scholarship that would "knock our socks off" (p. 715) (but would it all be about race?) is a false and sentimental faith, reflecting a lack of realism that is a constant feature of Kennedy's work and is further represented in his article by such fantasies as that there are "millions of people who might be able to do the job of law professor better than those who end up getting it," that modern civil rights law is the creation of black lawyers (rather than of black lawyers plus white lawyers plus white judges plus white legislators), that "facially neutral categories can accomplish almost anything a confirmed racist would want," and that law school teaching positions are a "small but significant part of the wealth of the United States" (pp. 712, 717, 737).

But I do not want to argue with Duncan Kennedy over which of us is better connected to reality. I want experimentation. I think it's a good thing that Santa Monica, Cambridge, and New York have rent

---

29. "Race Consciousness," 1990 *Duke Law Journal* 758.

30. See, for example, Mari J. Matsuda et al., *Words That Wound: Critical Race Theory, Assaultive Speech, and the First Amendment* (1993). For other references, summary, and critique, see Charles W. Collier, "Cultural Critique and Legal Change," 43 *Florida Law Review* 463 (1991); Henry Louis Gates Jr., "Let Them Talk: Why Civil Liberties Pose No Threat to Civil Rights," *New Republic*, Sept. 20 and 27, 1993, p. 37.

control—a good thing not for the people of those cities but for the rest of us, who can judge from these natural experiments whether rent control has the effects that economists predict or those the Left predicts.[31] It is a good thing for those of us who have an academic bent that socialism was tried in the Soviet Union and Eastern Europe, Sweden, Great Britain, Israel, Cuba, and elsewhere, because now we know that incentives do matter, private property does matter, prosperity matters, price matters. Let one of the leading law schools establish the kind of racial quotas for its faculty that Kennedy advocates, and we shall learn whether the diversity and perspectivism that Kennedy believes such quotas would engender will raise the quality of legal scholarship enough to atone for their ugliness.

31. The former. See Chapter 18.

chapter 3

What Do Judges Maximize?

The Ordinary Judge

FROM Hobbes to Blackstone to Dworkin to the economic analyst of law, the actual and the appropriate role of the judge—his incentives and constraints, the balance he should seek to maintain between discretion and obeisance, between creativity and conformity, the conditions of judicial greatness, the sources of judicial wisdom, the twin shoals of usurpation and passivity—has occupied center stage in the drama of Anglo-American jurisprudence. Whether a fighter for liberty or a master of self-restraint, an oracle of the law or a prescient economic analyst, the hero of this drama is—heroic; the spotlight, consistent with the profession's inflated self-image, is on the judicial titan. I take a different tack in this chapter by proposing a theory of judicial behavior focused on the "ordinary" appellate judge with secure tenure, for example a federal court of appeals judge or a Supreme Court Justice. The shift of focus from the extraordinary to the ordinary judge exemplifies the pragmatist's interest in the world of fact, for most judges are, in fact, ordinary.[1] They are not, for the most part, either power seekers, like

---

1. We are beginning, at last, to get a glimpse from judges of some of the unvarnished realities of a judicial career. Besides *The Problems of Jurisprudence*, passim, see Frank H. Easterbrook, "What's So Special about Judges?" 61 *University of Colorado Law Review* 773

some politicians—only a small minority of judges have a visionary or crusading bent[2]—or truth seekers, like most scientists. The methods of selection and reward, and other institutional constraints that make truth-seeking a plausible though not completely realistic goal to ascribe to scientists, do not characterize the judicial environment.[3]

Because there are so many ordinary judges, and because anti-intellectualism, democratic egalitarianism, and suspicion of officials run deep in the American soul, there is even a cult of ordinariness in judging. Exceptionally able judges arouse suspicion of having an "agenda," that is, of wanting to be something more than just corks bobbing on the waves of litigation or umpires calling balls and strikes. Some judges have had political agendas, but there is no correlation between being exceptionally able and having such an agenda.

We know that the framers of the Constitution tried to design a government that could be operated by moral and intellectual mediocrities. The inclusion in the design of life tenure for federal judges suggests that the framers believed that judges could not be counted on to behave with consistent courage, although some of course have, such as the judges who supervised public school desegregation in the South after *Brown v. Board of Education*. Politics, personal friendships, ideology, and pure serendipity play too large a role in the appointment of federal judges to warrant treating the judiciary as a collection of sainted genius-heroes miraculously immune to the tug of self-interest. By treating judges as ordinary people, my approach makes them fit subjects for economic analysis; for economists have no good theories of genius. Fortunately for economic analysis, most law is made not by the handful of great judges but by the mass of ordinary ones, although I shall extend my analysis briefly to extraordinary judges.

I concentrate on federal appellate judges, not only because I am one and know this group of judges best[4] but also because efforts to strip

(1990); Patricia M. Wald, "Some Real-Life Observations about Judging," 26 *Indiana Law Review* 173 (1992).

2. Hence the common criticism of the Supreme Court in the Burger years as lacking any "vision" or sense of mission. This is true of most courts most of the time, but is not necessarily a good criticism.

3. "Most judges, even Supreme Court Justices, have been plucked from well deserved intellectual obscurity." Charles W. Collier, "The Use and Abuse of Humanistic Theory in Law: Reexamining the Assumptions of Interdisciplinary Legal Scholarship," 41 *Duke Law Journal* 191, 221 (1991). From political obscurity as well, one might add.

4. In so saying I do not mean to suggest that judges have privileged access to the judicial

away incentives have progressed furthest with them. Article III of the Constitution erects such a high hurdle to removing a federal judge from office that pretty much the only thing that will get him removed is criminal activity. A federal judge can be lazy, lack judicial temperament, mistreat his staff, berate without reason the lawyers who appear before him, be reprimanded for ethical lapses, verge on or even slide into senility, be continually reversed for elementary legal mistakes, hold under advisement for years cases that could be decided perfectly well in days or weeks, leak confidential information to the press, pursue a nakedly political agenda, and misbehave in other ways that might get even a tenured civil servant or university professor fired; he will retain his office. His pay cannot be lowered, either—and neither can the pay of a good judge be raised. All judges of the same rank are paid exactly the same, and so the carrot is withdrawn along with the stick. Another reason there is no carrot is that a judge is forbidden to accept bribes from litigants, to pocket filing fees or other fees levied on litigants, or to collect royalties from people who cite his opinions. He gets a fixed salary, period.

Well, there is a small carrot. Supreme Court Justices are often appointed from the ranks of federal court of appeals judges; indeed, at present all but two of the Justices—Rehnquist and O'Connor—are former federal court of appeals judges. Although the probability of such an appointment is low for any particular judge even if he or she is one of the relatively few who are talked about for such a promotion, it figures in the thinking of some judges. The impact of a single judicial decision on the prospects for such a promotion is normally very slight, however. Some decisions have no impact at all on those prospects, and in the case of almost all the remaining ones the impact is unpredictable—the decision may offend as many influential people as it delights.

Efforts by federal judges to enhance their prospects for promotion to jobs outside the judiciary are discouraged by the structure of judicial compensation, which is heavily backloaded.[5] The pension is extraordinarily generous (one's final salary, for life, including annual cost-of-liv-

---

utility function. A utility function is not a psychological or phenomenological concept but a device for generating hypotheses. I doubt that *any* judge subjectively experiences his job in the way modeled in this chapter. I don't.

5. On the effect of backloading compensation on the turnover of federal civil servants, see Richard A. Ippolito, "Why Federal Workers Don't Quit," 22 *Journal of Human Resources* 281 (1987).

ing increases), but there is no vesting till age 65, so anyone who quits sooner gives up a large expected benefit. The attractive pension arrangements are important for inducing judges of advanced age to retire. Article III presumably outlaws mandatory retirement for Article III judges, and makes it very difficult to force judges to retire even for cause. A carrot must do all the work.

The compensation and tenure structure for federal district judges is the same as that for appellate judges except that the salary is slightly lower and they have greater prospects for promotion,[6] although for the most part only to the court of appeals. More important in keeping them in line is the fact that a district judge presides more or less continuously at trials and other proceedings in open court in which he is required to make rulings and talk to lawyers and jurors. If he isn't on the ball this soon becomes known, and he gets a bad reputation in the legal community. Appellate judges, in contrast, are largely although not entirely shielded from direct evaluations of their work. They never have to make rulings in open court, or indeed open their mouth in court. As long as they can pick competent law clerks they will be able to churn out, regardless of their own efforts or ability, professionally adequate opinions—and opinions are virtually their only public product and hence virtually the only basis upon which the legal profession, or the rest of the world, can evaluate them. It is the unique insulation of federal appellate judges from accountability that makes their behavior such a challenge to the economic analysis of law, and more broadly to the universalist claims of the economic theory of human behavior.[7]

The Nonprofit Analogy

The natural starting point for discussing the behavior of federal judges might seem to be the behavior of other government bureaucrats, an

6. Mark A. Cohen, in his article "The Motives of Judges: Empirical Evidence from Antitrust Sentencing," 12 *International Review of Law and Economics* 13 (1992), presents some empirical evidence that desire for promotion affects the behavior of district judges. Another article by Cohen provides additional empirical evidence for a district-judge utility function that contains such arguments as desire to exercise discretion, aversion to heavy workloads, and desire for promotion to the court of appeals. Cohen, "Explaining Judicial Behavior or What's 'Unconstitutional' about the Sentencing Commission?" 7 *Journal of Law, Economics, and Organization* 183 (1991).

7. For previous efforts to analyze judicial behavior in utility-maximizing terms, see, besides Cohen's two papers cited in note 6, Robert D. Cooter, "The Objectives of Private and Public Judges," 41 *Public Choice* 107 (1983); Jeffrey N. Gordon, "Corporations, Markets, and

area in which there is a growing literature in political science and in economics. But I do not think that the conventional bureaucrat provides the most fertile analogy to the (nonelected) judge. The latter has more secure tenure and is largely free from control by superiors and from legislative oversight. A more promising analogy is to the nonprofit form of enterprise, commonly used when buyers cannot observe an enterprise's output.[8] If to help the starving people of Somalia you make a contract with a food distributor to provide X amount of soybeans to those people, you will find it very difficult to determine whether the distributor has done this. He is a little more likely to do it if he is forbidden to pocket the residual income (after paying all expenses—a big loophole, as we are about to see) from the distribution, the profit in other words. For then the benefit to him of cheating on the contract is reduced.

The nonprofit form does not solve, it merely alleviates, the problem of the disloyal agent. The nonprofit provider has less incentive to be efficient than a profit-maximizing provider would have, because cost savings do not accrue to him as profit. We therefore expect more slack in a nonprofit enterprise and also more transforming of profits into salary and other employee perquisites, a normal consequence of constraining monetary profits.[9] Why don't *all* the profits get transformed into salary or perks? First, although extravagant perks are more difficult

Courts," 91 *Columbia Law Review* 1931, 1967–1971 (1991); Richard S. Higgins and Paul H. Rubin, "Judicial Discretion," 9 *Journal of Legal Studies* 129 (1980); Bruce H. Kobayashi and John R. Lott, Jr., "Judicial Reputation and the Efficiency of the Common Law" (unpublished, George Mason University School of Law, 1993); Thomas J. Miceli and Metin M. Coşgel, "Reputation and Judicial Decision-Making," 23 *Journal of Economic Behavior and Organization* 31 (1994); Erin O'Hara, "Implicit Collusion or Social Constraint: Toward a Game Theoretic Analysis of Stare Decisis" (unpublished, Clemson University Departments of Legal Studies and of Economics, n.d.); and Eric Rasmusen, "Judicial Legitimacy as a Repeated Game" (Indiana University Working Paper 93–017, July 1992). Kobayashi and Lott point out that a judge who wanted to maximize citations to his decisions would have an incentive to upset existing precedents—and to replace them not only with his own decisions but with his own *inefficient* decisions, because, other things being equal, inefficient decisions are likely to generate more litigation, hence more occasions for citing the judge's decisions. Such a judge, however, belongs more to the Promethean than to the ordinary category, and it is the latter on which I focus. I leave aside the question whether a true Promethean would be likely to be a simple citation maximizer.

8. Henry B. Hansmann, "The Role of Nonprofit Enterprise," 89 *Yale Law Journal* 835 (1980); see also Hansmann, "Ownership of the Firm," 4 *Journal of Law, Economics, and Organization* 267 (1988).

9. This has long been a staple observation in the literature on the regulation of public utilities. See, for example, Armen A. Alchian and Reuben A. Kessel, "Competition, Monopoly, and the Pursuit of Money," in *Aspects of Labor Economics* 157 (National Bureau of Economic

to expose than extravagant salaries, beyond a point perhaps soon reached the utility conferred by a perk (a large office, for example) may be only a small fraction of its cost. Second, people will not donate to a nonprofit organization whose employees are known to have astronomical salaries or to overindulge in perks. Third, a form of enterprise that constrains profitmaking may attract as employees people less preoccupied with moneymaking than the comparable employees of profitmaking enterprises. They may be more risk-averse and hence more willing to trade money income for job security, or their utility functions may be dominated by nonpecuniary sources of utility. In either event, given their preferences (or "character") they are not as likely to try to squeeze the last penny of pecuniary advantage from their situation. I do not put much weight on this point, in view of the empirical evidence against it.[10]

The parallel between the nonprofit enterprise and the federal courts should be apparent. The public would find it difficult, should it attempt to hire judicial services from a profitmaking organization, to determine the extent to which its contractor was producing "justice." There is, it is true, a good deal of private judging. But an arbitrator or other private judge is hired by the parties to a dispute to resolve that dispute, not to produce the full range of judicial services. The full range includes rulemaking through the issuance of opinions that interpret statutes, common law principles, rules and regulations, and constitutional provisions; the provision of a stand-by dispute-resolution service for people who can't agree on a neutral arbiter; the interposition of a neutral body between the state and the citizen—and the enforcement of arbitration awards, making the public judge a backstop to the private one. The arbitrator's or other private judge's output is more readily observable than the more complex, largely invisible or at least unmeasurable output of a "full service" public judicial system.[11] The incentive effect of conditioning the private judge's compensation on satisfying a market

Research 1962); *Economic Analysis of Law* 350, 653. "Slack" is better viewed as leisure, a perquisite, than as something separate from perquisites; and that is the approach I shall take.

10. Summarized in Edwin G. West, "Nonprofit Organizations: Revised Theory and New Evidence," 63 *Public Choice* 165, 168–169 (1989).

11. Well, not entirely. The absence of an opinion (commercial arbitrators, as the theory predicts, generally do not issue opinions, though labor arbitrators generally do) makes it more difficult to evaluate the quality of a judge's work. A related point is that arbitrators are understood to exercise broad discretion, and, as I shall note shortly, discretionary judgments are more difficult to evaluate than "ruled" ones.

demand may therefore enable the slack associated with the counterpart nonprofit service to be avoided at reasonable cost, so that in some areas of dispute resolution private judging can compete effectively with public judging even though the latter is subsidized.[12] The coexistence of profit and nonprofit firms is common in other industries as well, despite the tax advantages that nonprofits enjoy.[13]

Since the output of a full-service judiciary cannot readily be evaluated, a rational public is reluctant to buy that output from a profit-making enterprise, which would be tempted to grab for big profits by skimping on the costs of the service. Nor can the public easily delegate the evaluative function to the legislative or executive branches; they are not trustworthy or easily monitored agents either. The Justice Department *could* evaluate judicial performance by neutral criteria, but it would have an incentive to use political criteria as well, and if it fired or demoted judges allegedly for professional incompetence the public would find it difficult to evaluate the evaluation.

Hiring *competitive* judicial firms is not the answer either, quite apart from the difficulty of maintaining consistency of legal decisions. Competition doesn't work well when customers cannot determine even roughly the quality of the output offered by the competing firms and when warranties or equivalent guarantees are infeasible. Unable to rely on the market or on incentive compensation, the public forbids judges to take monetary profits from judging not only by accepting bribes or being paid out of court fees, fines, or other revenues generated by the judicial process but also by sitting on a case in which a relative, or a company in which the judge owns stock, is a party. Thus, as the discretionary power of the judiciary increases, the rules on conflict of interest become more stringent, because the more discretion judges exercise the more difficult it is to determine the quality of judicial output.

Because the judiciary has been placed on a nonprofit basis, we should expect judges on average not to work as hard as lawyers of comparable age and ability. I believe that this is true, at least of appellate judges.[14]

---

12. On the economics of arbitration, and of private judging generally, see William M. Landes and Richard A. Posner, "Adjudication as a Private Good," 8 *Journal of Legal Studies* 235 (1979); Cooter, note 7 above.

13. Burton A. Weisbrod, *The Nonprofit Economy*, ch. 8 (1988).

14. Compare the finding that members of Congress who have announced that they are retiring vote less in their last term of office—the penalty for shirking is less. John R. Lott, Jr., "Political Cheating," 52 *Public Choice* 169, 179–182 (1987).

The enormous caseload increases of recent decades have been accommodated mainly by expansions in staff, though judges today do work harder than judges thirty or forty years ago did. Judicial "moonlighting" is rightly limited so that judges cannot easily transform judicial leisure into cash income, which by increasing the value of that "leisure" would induce some judges to do less judicial work.

Judicial slack can also be limited by careful screening of judicial candidates. Especially if behavior has a habitual component, a person known to be a hard worker in his present job may be a good bet to continue working hard even when incentives to work hard are removed. In fact the screening of candidates for federal judicial appointment is elaborate (just as—and for a similar reason—premarital search is more protracted the more difficult it is to get a divorce), and most judges are appointed at an age at which their work habits have had many years to become fixed. This may be one reason why persons under 40 are rarely appointed to federal judgeships. Although academic tenure is usually awarded at a younger age, academic salaries are not fixed or outside earnings effectively constrained and there is more than one academic employer, so academics retain monetary incentives to work hard.

Nonprofit organizations are not constrained to pay all employees of the same rank the same compensation. Nor for that matter is the federal judiciary. Secretaries and other support personnel can receive quality raises and bonuses, and there is even an annual cash prize (the $15,000 Edward J. Devitt Distinguished Service to Justice Award) for federal judges, though only one is awarded. But aside from the prize, federal judges of the same rank (and apart from the Supreme Court Justices all Article III judges are in one of just two ranks—district judge or circuit judge) are all paid the same regardless of their productivity and stature and even regardless of their years of service.[15] The difference in treatment between judicial and support personnel reflects the fact that the former have much more discretionary power, which ultimately is what makes judicial output so difficult to value. To recognize differences in the quality or value of that output would resurrect the problem that gave rise to the nonprofit organization of the judiciary in the first place. Suppose a judge who increased his case output by 1 percent

15. Except that the older a judge is, the greater the expected value of his pension. This is a big exception to the uniformity of judicial salaries, but it is not something over which the individual judge has any control.

received an extra $5,000 a year. His monetary incentive would be to reduce the time he spent on each case by 1 percent, so that he could decide 1 percent more cases in the same amount of time. For then, assuming that he was not working more intensively (and why should he be?), the $5,000 bonus would represent a pure profit enabled by the difficulty encountered by the "buyers" of his decisions in evaluating their quality. I assume that the judge has nonmonetary incentives to do judicial work; otherwise, why did he wait for the bonus to reduce the amount of that work? But these incentives (explored next) are compatible with his reducing the amount of work he does per case without reducing his judicial work overall.

The Judicial Utility Function

I said that I do not think that federal appellate judges work as hard as comparable lawyers in private practice. Most of them, however, work quite hard—often at an age when their counterparts in private practice have retired and are living in Scottsdale or La Jolla. They must be deriving utility from the work of being a judge, and not just from the status of being a judge, which they could retain while doing very little and sometimes—when they have reached retirement age—nothing. Their utility function must in short contain something besides leisure and the judicial salary. Let us consider some possibilities.

Popularity. Robert Cooter suggests that judges "seek prestige" among "the lawyers and litigants who bring cases before the judges."[16] They do this, he believes, "by ignoring [the] effects [of their decisions] upon parties other than the disputants." What he calls prestige sounds more like popularity. No matter; he is correct that many federal appellate judges, although in no way dependent upon the goodwill of practicing lawyers (unlike their counterparts in elected state judiciaries), are sensitive to their popularity with them, especially if, as is common, many of their friends are lawyers. People like to be liked. Few judges, however, care whether they are popular with the litigants themselves. How could they be? Virtually every decision produces a happy winner and an unhappy loser. (Lawyers are more philosophical about losing.) Judges' desire to be popular with lawyers may express itself in reluctance to impose sanctions upon or even to criticize lawyers who per-

16. Cooter, note 7 above, at 129.

form below reasonable professional standards, but I believe not otherwise.

Prestige. In a sense distinct from popularity on the one hand and deference (outward shows of respect, discussed later) on the other, prestige is unquestionably an element of the judicial utility function. The thirst for prestige is manifested primarily in opposition to any large increase in the number of judges, at least high-level judges, and to extending the title "judge" to lower-level judicial personnel, such as magistrates and bankruptcy referees (now called "magistrate judges" and "bankruptcy judges," to the dismay of many Article III judges). Judges normally reluctant to ascribe base motives to their group have been vocal in insisting that a substantial increase in the number of judges would, by diluting judicial prestige, increase the difficulties of recruitment.[17] But judges are quite willing to delegate the performance of judicial duties to nonjudges, such as law clerks—a form of delegation which does not dilute judicial prestige. Apart from opposing an increase in the number of judges or a dilution of the title "judge," however, there is little an individual judge can do to enhance his judicial prestige. That prestige inheres in the whole judiciary. Free-rider problems make it unlikely that any one judge will exert himself strenuously to raise the prestige of all.

Public interest. To include in the judicial utility function desire to promote the public interest would be inconsistent with treating judges as "ordinary" people. Although views concerning the public interest undoubtedly affect judicial preferences, just as they affect voter preferences (more on this shortly), they do so, I assume, only insofar as decisions expressing those views enhance the judge's utility.

Avoiding reversal. Judges don't like to be reversed (I speak from experience), but aversion to reversal does not bulk large in the judicial utility function. It is nonexistent in the case of Supreme Court Justices, and fairly unimportant in the case of court of appeals judges because reversals of appellate decisions by the Supreme Court have become rare[18] and most reflect differences in judicial philosophy or legal policy

---

17. Gordon Bermant et al., *Imposing a Moratorium on the Number of Federal Judges: Analysis of Arguments and Implications* (Federal Judicial Center 1993).

18. Not because the Court is affirming a higher percentage of decisions, but because the interaction of a growing lower-court caseload with a relatively fixed Supreme Court decisional capacity has resulted in the Court's accepting for review a declining fraction of lower-court decisions. Of more than a thousand majority opinions that I have written for the Seventh

rather than mistake or incompetence by the appellate judges.[19] Reversal rates apparently do not affect district judges' chances of promotion.[20]

Reputation. As my reference to criticism implies, a potentially significant element in the judicial utility function is reputation, both with other judges, especially ones on the same court—one's colleagues (and here reputation merges with popularity)—and with the legal profession at large. Reputation is a function of effort, but, for the judge of ordinary abilities, only of a minimum level of effort. Effort beyond that level will not make an ordinary judge great, any more than hard work will turn a journeyman mathematician into a math whiz, and it may make the judge unpopular with his colleagues and thereby reduce his utility. Employers like a Stakhanovite; fellow employees do not—he makes them look bad. And a workaholic judge is apt to increase rather than reduce his colleagues' workloads by making nitpicking comments on their opinions and by writing frequent concurring and dissenting opinions.

So concern with reputation does not explain why judges don't always retire at the earliest opportunity, which would be financially the wisest course. Some do, but many do not. I am speaking, however, of the ordinary judge. For the extraordinary judge, as we shall see later, reputation may be a dominating objective and may be highly correlated with effort.

Voting. The elements of the judicial utility function that I have discussed so far are, I believe, less important for the average federal appellate judge than the one I want to highlight here, which is best understood by analogy to voting in political elections.[21] Although vot-

---

Circuit, the Supreme Court has granted certiorari in only about ten (and has affirmed some of them). I believe that this is a representative percentage.

Some Supreme Court decisions are overruled legislatively, William N. Eskridge, Jr., "Overriding Supreme Court Statutory Interpretation Decisions," 101 *Yale Law Journal* 331 (1991), but the Justices are apt to perceive such overruling as the product of political or policy disagreement, rather than as responsible criticism of their work.

19. The remarkable fact that the Supreme Court had not reversed a single one of the 400 majority decisions that Judge Robert Bork had written or joined at the time of his nomination to the Supreme Court was deemed irrelevant in a report commissioned and relied on by Senator Biden, the Chairman of the Senate Judiciary Committee. "Response Prepared to White House Analysis of Judge Bork's Record: Statement of Committee Consultants," reprinted in 9 *Cardozo Law Review* 219, 238–242 (1987).

20. Higgins and Rubin, note 7 above.

21. The analogy is used for a different purpose—to explain with the aid of Kenneth Arrow's impossibility theorem the difficulty of a court's achieving consistency across deci-

ing is not compulsory in this country, vast numbers of people vote in elections in which the likelihood that their vote will affect the result of the election is vanishingly close to zero. This suggests that voting is for many people a valued consumption activity. Well, judges are constantly voting. A federal appellate judge votes several hundred times a year. Although his votes frequently are "wasted" because the case would have been decided the same way without him (he was not the swing vote), they have more impact than the votes of ordinary electors. A judge's vote sometimes decides the outcome of a case, and the outcome of a case is usually important to at least a few people and, in some court of appeals cases and many Supreme Court cases, to many—even millions of—people. So if voting in elections is a source of utility, we should not be surprised that voting in cases is a source of utility.

An alternative explanation for electoral voting is that people do it out of a sense of duty, and activity so motivated is different from ordinary consumption.[22] No doubt many do vote out of duty. But the pure consumption element is important, perhaps especially for judges. A federal judgeship remains a coveted job, and most judges enjoy their work. They are not reluctant conscripts of conscience.

Another source of judicial utility turns out to be derivative from voting. It is the deference that judges receive from lawyers and from the public generally.[23] Like that accorded wealthy people, this deference is of the shallowest kind: as soon as the judge loses office, as soon as the wealthy person loses money, the deference ceases.[24] Sensitive people realize this, but it does not eliminate the pleasure of being treated in

---

sions—in Frank H. Easterbrook, "Ways of Criticizing the Court," 95 *Harvard Law Review* 802 (1982).

22. Amartya Sen, "Rational Fools: A Critique of the Behavioural Foundations of Economic Theory," in Sen, *Choice, Welfare and Measurement* 84, 97 (1982). Elsewhere, however, Sen has described voting, much in the spirit of the present analysis, as being guided by a desire to record one's true preference. Sen, *Collective Choice and Social Welfare* 195–196 (1970). The duty and consumption explanations for voting are merged in William H. Riker and Peter C. Ordeschook, "A Theory of the Calculus of Voting," 62 *American Political Science Review* 25, 28 (1968).

23. Lawyers, like other sellers of services, are, in contrast to judges, deference givers rather than deference receivers. I suspect, therefore, that a higher percentage of practicing lawyers than of judges are former salesmen.

24. Well, not entirely. Retired judges (even judges who have resigned to pursue a career in practice) usually retain the title "judge," and the title commands some deference even when separated from the office.

a respectful manner. The republican simplicity of manners—the "I'm no better than the next guy" deportment—that most American judges affect is intended to be admired rather than to be taken seriously. Judges receive deference because they have power, and the power resides in their votes. They don't have much power (Supreme Court Justices are an important exception, and the petty tyranny of the trial judge is well known) and they are not much deferred to (with the same exceptions). But such deference as they do receive comes from their being, like wealthy people, more powerful than most people, not from being—like athletes, popular entertainers, war heroes, saints, and scientists—admired. Most judges are quickly forgotten after they leave office.

Previous economic analyses of judicial behavior have also been concerned with judges' power,[25] but not as a source of deference or as the garnish on voting, as I am using it here; rather as a source of satisfaction, or even of exhilaration, akin to that experienced by creative people. Artists make works of art that change sensibility; judges make decisions that change social or business practices. Artists impose their aesthetic vision on society; judges impose their political vision on society. They do this mainly through the precedential force of their decisions, since a single decision rarely has a great impact.

There is a trade-off between the loss of power that results from judges' following their predecessors' decisions rather than innovating and the loss of power that results if, by refusing to follow their predecessors' decisions and thus weakening the practice of decision according to precedent, they reduce the likelihood that their successors will follow their decisions.[26] There is, it is true, a serious free-rider problem. One judge's flouting precedent will be unlikely to damage the practice seriously. The problem can be held in check by the highest court in the

---

25. For a notable example, see Rafael Gely and Pablo T. Spiller, "A Rational Choice Theory of Supreme Court Statutory Decisions with Applications to the *State Farm* and *Grove City* Cases," 6 *Journal of Law, Economics, and Organization* 263 (1990); also Eugenia Froedge Toma, "Congressional Influence and the Supreme Court: The Budget as a Signaling Device," 20 *Journal of Legal Studies* 131 (1991).

26. Lewis A. Kornhauser, "Modeling Collegial Courts I: Path Dependence," 12 *International Review of Law and Economics* 169 (1992); Kornhauser, "Modeling Collegial Courts II: Legal Doctrine," 8 *Journal of Law, Economics, and Organization* 441 (1992); Rasmusen, note 7 above; Edward P. Schwartz, "Policy, Precedent, and Power: A Positive Theory of Supreme Court Decision-Making," 8 *Journal of Law, Economics, and Organization* 219 (1992); *Economic Analysis of Law* 534–536, 541–542.

jurisdiction. That court can reverse lower-court decisions that display an insufficient respect for precedent. The members of that court will be few enough to be concerned about the impact of their own behavior toward precedent on the survival of the practice of decision according to precedent in their jurisdiction.[27] If they flout precedent they will be criticized, which for any judge who cares about his reputation is a cost, though one that may well be outweighed by the gain to him from changing policy in the direction he desires. Their successors, however, will not be criticized, or will be criticized less, for flouting precedent, both because their flouting will be defensible as a method of correcting or punishing the misbehavior of their predecessors and because they will have a "precedent" for not following precedent! Since criticism imposes a cost on the person criticized, the reduction in criticism of precedent-defying successors that is brought about by the predecessor judges' flouting of precedent will increase the likelihood that the precedents created by those judges will themselves be flouted. The predecessors thus incur a future loss from their flouting of precedent, and knowing this they have a greater incentive than they would otherwise have to refrain from that behavior.

This is a side issue, however, when the focus is on the ordinary judge. He is not interested in shaping the future, and so needn't worry about finding the point at which adhering to precedent yields a gain in power over the future brought about by the greater likelihood that judges will adhere to his precedents that is just equal to the loss in power from allowing past precedents to override his own preferences.

For the handful of judges who today still write their own opinions, and for some who do not, there is additional utility, akin to that which a literary or scholarly author obtains, from being a published author. There is also the intrinsic pleasure of writing, for those who like to write. But these things are not important to most judges today; they are happy to cede opinion-writing to eager law clerks, believing (consistent with my analysis) that the core judicial function is deciding, that is, voting, rather than articulating the grounds of decision. This readiness to delegate judicial duties to nonjudges, such as law clerks, has enabled the federal judiciary to increase its output enormously with

---

27. *Economic Analysis of Law* 542; Rasmusen, note 7 above. If this is correct, we might expect a comparison of the different state supreme courts (which differ in size) to show that the smaller the court, the less frequently it overrules its previous decisions.

only a modest increase in judicial effort; it thus may illustrate the operation of leisure preference in the judicial utility function.

Judicial Behavior Explained

People who vote in elections the outcomes of which they cannot influence nevertheless do not vote randomly. The utility is not in the act of voting but in voting for someone or something. It is related to the utility that people derive from speaking their mind about some subject even though nothing will be changed by what they say. But judges, unlike ordinary voters, derive power as well as the pure consumption value of voting from judicial activity, and power is no less when it is exercised randomly—indeed, arbitrary power is especially feared, and perhaps therefore especially powerful. So we might expect judges to vote *less* responsibly than the ordinary voter. Of course if most judges voted randomly the whole caboodle of judges would be got rid of eventually. But random voting by a single judge would not endanger that judge's tenure. Yet it is rare. Why? As I have been emphasizing, for judges as for ordinary citizens voting has a consumption value that is independent of its instrumental, power-exercising value (which as I have said is negligible for the ordinary citizen—yet he votes); this consumption value depends on making a deliberate choice of whom to vote for.

Moreover, the cost of nonrandom voting to judges sitting in panels, as appellate judges do, is low. Even in a three-judge panel, provided that at least one judge has a strong opinion on the proper outcome of the case, or even that a law clerk of one judge has a strong opinion on the matter, the other judges, if not terribly interested in the case, may simply cast their vote with the "opinionated" judge. This will not be random behavior and will incidentally be leisure-serving since if both indifferent judges vote against the opinionated one he may write a fierce dissent that will either make them look bad or require them to spend time revising the majority opinion to blunt the points made by him. Notice that if one indifferent judge decides to go along with the opinionated one, the other indifferent one is likely to go along as well. Otherwise he will be forcing himself to write a dissenting opinion, given the taboo (relatively new and, I admit, somewhat mysterious) against dissenting without giving any reasons.

The larger the panel, the cheaper it is to dissent because the likelier it is that there will be more than one dissenter; only one need write an opinion and the others can join it. We should therefore expect that, if differences in the difficulty of cases are corrected for, dissent will be found to be more frequent in courts that sit in panels of five, seven, or nine judges than in those that sit in panels of three.

"Going-along" voting is only one example of the influence of leisure-seeking on judicial behavior. Another—once leisure is defined for these purposes, as it should be, as an aversion to any sort of "hassle," as well as to sheer hard work—is the insistence by judges that their decisions are coerced by "the law" and hence that the judge shouldn't be blamed by the losing party or anyone else distressed by the outcome. Call this the theory of power without responsibility.

A third example of the operation of leisure preference is the norm of equality in appellate-court assignments. Judges of the same court hear the same number of cases and generally are assigned the same number of decisions to write, though in the latter regard the Supreme Court is more flexible than the courts of appeals. An effort by one judge to hear more than his proportional share of cases or snag more than his proportional share of writing assignments is resented and rebuffed.

A fourth example is the distinction between "holding" and "dictum"—the latter being anything in a judicial opinion which is not essential to the outcome. Dicta, unlike holdings, are not considered binding in subsequent decisions. This principle can be rationalized in various ways; leisure-seeking is a neglected one. Because dictum is nonbinding, a judge can, without thereby mortgaging his future votes, join an opinion by one of his colleagues that contains much with which he disagrees. In exchange, other judges will join his opinions even though they disagree with much in them. This "live and let live" attitude made possible by the difference in authority between holding and dictum reduces the amount of effort that judges need invest either in their own opinions (to meet objections by other judges to dicta) or in the opinions of their colleagues (to purge those opinions of objectionable dicta).

Consider now the multitude of devices, most invented by judges, for ducking issues presented by the parties to appeals: the issue is moot or unripe, or calls for an "advisory opinion," or presents a nonjusticiable political question, or the party pressing it lacks standing, or the appeal was filed a day late, or the appellant had failed to exhaust some administrative or judicial remedy. These devices enable judges to reduce their workload as well as to avoid the hassle involved in wrestling with difficult, politically sensitive issues. The workload benefits are probably the less important. Screening all appeals to identify the handful that can be denied without reaching the merits is itself a time-consuming task. (But of course without such screening the number of cases might soar. Imagine if every potential litigant were entitled to obtain an advisory opinion from a court!) And the more expeditious dispatch of judicial business that is enabled by limiting the number of cases reviewable on the merits may, by reducing court queues (which are a cost of using the courts), increase the demand for judicial services, just as building a new highway may by reducing highway congestion induce an increase in traffic.

My approach may help explain why judges adhere to stare decisis but not rigidly. If they adhered rigidly, realistically they would not be voting as often, because voting implies discretion; if there is no felt choice, there is no pleasure in choosing. That may be why so many district judges held the federal sentencing guidelines unconstitutional.[28] They believed that the guidelines would turn criminal sentencing, formerly an area of almost unlimited district-judge discretion, into a process of mechanical, but laborious, computation.

Yet if judges considered every case afresh they would, if conscientious, have to work harder; deciding a case conscientiously without reading the previous decisions would be like writing a serious, thoughtful article without doing any research to discover what had already been written on the subject. The judges would also lose the protection from criticism and attack that comes from being able to blame an unpopular decision on someone else (that is, on earlier judges). And there might be more litigated cases because of the greater uncertainty of legal rights and duties in a system not stabilized by stare decisis. The last two points—more hassle and more uncertainty—may be more important than the first—more work on each case—because following precedent requires research.

"Going-along" voting and "live and let live" opinion-joining are practices related to vote trading ("logrolling") but distinct from it because they are leisure-serving rather than power-maximizing. That

---

28. Cohen, "Explaining Judicial Behavior or What's 'Unconstitutional' about the Sentencing Commission?" note 6 above.

may be why vote trading by judges is condemned (as depriving the litigants and the community of the judge's independent judgment on the case), and is in fact rare, while the other practices, which are common, are condoned or ignored. Legislators have a different utility function from judges, in part because they face reelection. Power and influence are more important to them than to judges, and therefore they engage in logrolling.[29] Here is an economic reason to suppose, contrary to the extreme claims of some legal realists and critical legal scholars, that judges are not just legislators in robes. This analysis also predicts, however, that vote trading may be common among elected judges.

Both "going-along" voting and "live and let live" opinion-joining can be explained alternatively as devices for increasing judicial productivity, for by saving time they enable judges to decide more cases in the same amount of time as well as to reallocate time from work to leisure. Such policies as flexible deference to precedent and forbearance to decide premature cases also have public-interest justifications.[30] A task for future research is to disentangle self-interest from other sources of judicial practices.

The Judge as Spectator—and as Player

We have yet to consider how a judge decides to vote for one side rather than another, or to vote for one interpretation of a statute or legal doctrine rather than another, or to adopt one judicial philosophy (such as "conservative," "liberal," "activist," or "restrained") rather than another. The traditional objection to the secret ballot—that it fosters irresponsible voting—has carried the day with respect to voting by judges. Judicial votes are public,[31] although sometimes a judge will tell his friends that he joined an opinion with which he disagreed because he didn't think the issue significant enough to warrant the preparation of a dissenting opinion. The public character of judicial voting facilitates

29. Barry R. Weingast, "The Political Institutions of Representative Government: Legislatures," 145 *Journal of Institutional and Theoretical Economics* 693 (1989).

30. See, for example, William M. Landes and Richard A. Posner, "The Economics of Anticipatory Adjudication," 23 *Journal of Legal Studies* 683 (1994).

31. Not a universal feature of judging: most courts in most civil law systems (such as those of Japan and Continental Europe) do not publish dissents or make the votes of the judges public.

criticism, which can be expected to have a greater effect on behavior when ordinarily more powerful incentives, such as money, are not in play. Yet most judges are pretty insensitive to criticism other than by other judges, believing conveniently that most of it is motivated by political disagreement, envy, self-promotion, or ignorance (willful or otherwise) of the conditions under which judges work. And public comment on judicial decisions other than by the Supreme Court is rare. Only a tiny fraction of the thousands of other appellate opinions published each year receive any sort of critical attention that might get back to the judge and alter his future behavior.

Choices of the kind that face a judge who must vote in a case—choices that cannot be made on the basis of wanting to increase one's pecuniary income, leisure, fame, or other forms of utility—are common in other areas of living. They are for example the choices we make when watching dramatic or cinematic performances. Athletic contests are different, mainly because of the built-in bias in favor, normally, of the "home" team, a bias that makes the judicial analogy strained. Such bias is relevant to state court adjudication, however, and can help explain not only the federal diversity jurisdiction but also the exclusive federal jurisdiction over many types of case that pit a state resident against federal taxpayers.

The audience for a play or movie is detached, having no tangible stake in the outcome of whatever struggle is being depicted on stage or screen. Yet it is induced to "choose" one side or the other. Usually the choice is manipulated by the author—he "tells" us as it were to side with the hero against the villain. But in dramatic works of deep ambiguity, which often are highly popular among intellectuals on that account, such as *Hamlet,* or *Measure for Measure,* or *Pygmalion,* the choice offered to the spectator is a real one. The author either has not resolved in his own mind the central tension in the situation dramatized or has not been able (or has not wanted) to communicate the resolution clearly. The interest that such irresolutions arouse explains the popularity of revisionist interpretations of literature, such as William Blake's proposal that the real hero of *Paradise Lost* is Satan. The spectator or, in the last example, the reader (but a "live" performance provides a closer analogy to the judicial process, though today many cases are submitted for decision without any oral argument or other hearing—much as when a play is read rather than performed) has to weigh the evidence and come to a decision. The position of the judge is similar.[32] If spectators get consumption value out of such choices, it is not surprising that judges do.

Spectators make choices about the meaning of a play or movie by bringing to bear their personal experiences and any specialized cultural competence that they have obtained from study of or immersion in the type of drama that they are watching, and often by discussing their reactions with friends who may have a similar competence. The judge brings to bear on his spectatorial function not only a range of personal and political preferences but also a specialized cultural competence—his knowledge of and experience in "the law." And if he is an appellate judge he will consult with his professional colleagues before making up his mind.

Of course few legal cases have the rich ambiguities of *Hamlet*. Many cases involve puzzles soluble with the technical tools of legal analysis— here the judge is like the reader of a detective story. The jury as factfinder performs a similar function. It is a different kind of spectatorship from the one I am stressing here, that of the appellate judge asked to decide not where truth lies but which party has the better case. But in either case the choice, like that of the theater audience, is a disinterested one; the judge's or jury's income is not affected by it. A further point is that the less informed the tribunal is, the more "dramatic" the trial must be to hold the "audience's" attention. It is not surprising that Anglo-American trials, historically dominated by juries, are more dramatic than Continental trials, historically dominated by professional judges.

The voting and spectatorship analogies to judicial decision-making are similar (though, as we shall see, not identical). In a large audience the clapping of a single spectator contributes little more to the decibel level than a single vote in an election contributes to the outcome. And the voter is the spectator in a contest between candidates,[33] much as

32. The analogy between the judge and the literary reader or spectator is developed, though for a different purpose, in Martha C. Nussbaum, "Equity and Mercy," 22 *Philosophy and Public Affairs* 83 (1993). On the dramaturgical character of trials, see Milner S. Ball, "The Play's the Thing: An Unscientific Reflection on Courts under the Rubric of Theater," 28 *Stanford Law Review* 81 (1975), and on the forensic character of drama, see Kathy Eden, *Poetic and Legal Fiction in the Aristotelian Tradition* 176–183 (1986).

33. Geoffrey Brennan and Loren Lomasky, "The Impartial Spectator Goes to Washington: Toward a Smithian Theory of Electoral Behavior," 1 *Economics and Philosophy* 189 (1985).

the reader or viewer of *Antigone* is the spectator of a contest between Antigone and Creon. It is no surprise that voter turnout is higher, the more publicized and the closer an election is (even though not so close that one vote is likely to affect the outcome),[34] just as the audience for a heavily advertised, highly dramatic play is likely to be larger than the audience for a meagerly advertised, undramatic play.

Why has the spectatorship analogy to judging been overlooked?[35] One reason is the piety in which most public discussion of judges is wrapped. The analogy seems to give judging a frivolous air. But serious engagement with the arts as reader or viewer is not a frivolous activity. Nor is "play" (contrasted with work) incompatible with adherence to rules. A chess player would reduce rather than enhance the pleasure he received from the game if he violated its rules, and so would the theatergoer who refused to enter into the lives of the stage characters because they are not real people; and likewise the judge who violates the rules of the judicial game. Sports fans, theater fans, movie fans, and opera fans often develop a degree of connoisseurship which enhances their pleasure. In other words, they learn the rules (broadly understood) of the game they are watching and respond in accordance with those rules. Judges do the same thing, with the important difference that more of the rules of the judicial game are likely to be uncertain or contested.

A second reason why the spectatorship analogy to judging has been overlooked is that most analysis of judicial behavior is done by legal academics. The academic is a spectator too, but he is a spectator not of the little drama that the judge witnesses—the trial or other contest that the judge resolves—but of the judge's opinion. The academic usually does not attend oral argument or even read the briefs in the cases that he writes about or teaches. Naturally, therefore, he tends to ascribe more importance to the opinion, to its reasoning, its rhetoric, and so forth, than to the decision itself. Yet these are secondary factors

34. John H. Aldrich, "Rational Choice and Turnout," 37 *American Journal of Political Science* 246, 266–268 (1993); Gary W. Cox and Michael C. Munger, "Closeness, Expenditures, and Turnout in the 1982 U.S. House Elections," 83 *American Political Science Review* 217 (1989).

35. Not *completely* overlooked. See Yosal Rogat, "The Judge as Spectator," 31 *University of Chicago Law Review* 213 (1964). Rogat's article is a criticism of Justice Holmes for having been *too* detached, too much an observer of rather than a participant in life (like his friends Henry Adams and Henry James)—in short an insufficiently empathetic spectator.

for most judges. For the judge, as for Hamlet, the play's the thing.[36] When judges got busy, the first thing they delegated was opinion-writing; yet even today it would be considered a scandal if judges delegated the hearing of testimony or argument, though actually there is growing delegation of these functions to magistrates and special masters.

The analogy to spectatorship can help us see how judicial outcomes reflect both the judges' preferences going in *and* the quality of the briefing and argument in particular cases. It can also help us understand the function of confirmation hearings in enabling legislators to ascertain a judicial candidate's policy preferences, since those preferences can be expected to guide or at least influence a judge's decisions. We might also expect that "ideologues" would be appointed to judgeships at an earlier age on average than other candidates. Not only may it be difficult to determine the trajectory of the nonideologue's views except by inference from behavior over a long career, but to the extent that an ideologue is inherently more predictable there is less worry about the fact that if appointed young he will have a long time in which to change his views.[37]

Most political campaigners appeal primarily, though not exclusively, to the voter's self-interest.[38] The judge, in contrast, like the theatrical spectator, is asked to cast a disinterested vote. It is easy to see why the spectator's vote is likely to be disinterested; what has he—being powerless—to gain by refusing to play the spectator's game? But a judge has some power. Supposing that the conflict of interest rules are effective in insulating his decision from any consequences for his personal or family wealth, one can still imagine a host of inappropriate considerations that might enter into his utility function: personal dislike of a lawyer or litigant, gratitude to the appointing authorities, desire for advancement, irritation with or even a desire to undermine a judicial colleague or subordinate, willingness to trade votes, desire to be on good terms with colleagues, not wanting to disagree with people one likes or respects, fear for personal safety, fear of ridicule, reluctance to

36. Cf. Joseph Bensman and Robert Lilienfeld, *Craft and Consciousness: Occupational Technique and the Development of World Images* 19–22 (1973).

37. Cf. John R. Lott, Jr., and W. Robert Reed, "Shirking and Sorting in a Political Market with Finite-Lived Politicians," 61 *Public Choice* 75, 87–88, 91 n. 26 (1989).

38. Brennan and Lomasky, note 33 above, emphasize the element of disinterest in political voting. (Compare the discussion of deliberative democracy in the Introduction.) They follow Adam Smith's *Theory of Moral Sentiments* in arguing that disinterested actions are likely where the cost of such actions to the actor is low.

offend one's spouse or close friends, and racial or class solidarity. These are common factors in the decisions of everyday life—why not in the decisions of judges, unless we ascribe to them a utility function different from that of the ordinary person?

Such factors do influence judicial decisions, but less often than the suspicious layman thinks. The reason is not that judges have different utility functions from those of other people; it is that the utility they derive from judging would be reduced by more than they would gain from giving way to the temptations that I have listed. It is the same reason why many people do not cheat at games even when they are sure they could get away with cheating. The pleasure of judging is bound up with compliance with certain self-limiting rules that define the "game" of judging. It is a source of satisfaction to a judge to vote *for* the irritating litigant, *for* the lawyer who fails to exhibit proper deference to the court, *for* the side that represents a different social class from that of the judges. It is by doing such things that you know you are playing the judge role, not some other role; and judges for the most part are people who want to be—judges. This is consistent with most judges' not wanting to work too hard, for working as hard as a lawyer in private practice is not one of the rules of the judicial game, not only because most judges are older than most lawyers but also because judges tend to think of themselves as performing primarily a stand-by rather than a piecework function, a little like firemen, and needing to keep their heads clear for the exercise of good judgment. Playing by the rules is also consistent with judges' often voting their policy preferences and personal convictions. For in our system the line between law and policy, the judging game and the legislating game, is blurred. Many cases cannot be decided by reasoning from conventional legal materials. Such cases require the judge to exercise a legislative judgment, although a more confined one than "real" legislators are authorized to exercise.[39]

The general approach of this chapter may seem to undermine the theory that the common law and other areas of judge-made law are on the whole efficiency-enhancing,[40] by disparaging the ability and the will of judges to conceive and impose so singular and ambitious a vision,

---

39. The legislative function of the judge is one of the reasons (I argue in Chapter 23) why a judge is not permitted to use random methods, such as coin flipping, for deciding even cases that are truly indeterminate from a conventionally "legal" standpoint.

40. See, for example, *Economic Analysis of Law*, pt. 2.

as well as one so remote, it might seem, from normal conceptions of the rules of the judicial game.[41] But awareness of the legislative function of the judiciary may enable this tension to be dissolved. When a really new case arises, the rules of the judicial game require the judge to act the part of a legislator and therefore vote his values, although the rules do not require and may even him forbid him to acknowledge that this is what he is doing. Efficiency—not necessarily by that name—is an important social value and hence one internalized by most judges, and it may be the only social value that judges can promote effectively, given their limited remedial powers and the value pluralism of our society. So it should be influential in judicial decision-making when judges are called upon to exercise a legislative function. The decision of a really new case establishes a precedent to guide future cases, and the rules of the judicial game require the judges to follow precedent (though not slavishly) rather than to decide each future case from the ground up. The subsequent cases may bear no visible imprint of economic thinking, yet they will be efficient decisions if the precedents that influence them, reflecting the judges' legislative activity, were based implicitly or explicitly on a desire to enhance efficiency. Law can thus be efficient even if only a small minority of cases concern themselves with efficiency.

I want to say more about the analogy between judging cases and playing games. Rules are not always irksome restraints. They may be constitutive. It is difficult to write a sonnet, because the sonnet is a genre with rigid rules; but without the rules there would be no sonnets, and this would be a loss not only for the reader but for the sonneteer. And similarly with a game,[42] for example chess. If you decided that your bishops should be allowed to make the same moves as your queen, or

41. But see Kobayashi and Lott, note 7 above.

42. For pertinent discussions, see Bernard Suits, "What Is a Game?" 34 *Philosophy of Science* 148 (1967); Arthur Allen Leff, "Law and," 87 *Yale Law Journal* 989, 998–1003 (1978); J. Huizinga, *Homo Ludens: A Study of the Play-Element in Culture,* chs. 1, 4 (1950); Thomas Morawetz, "The Concept of a Practice," 24 *Philosophical Studies* 209 (1973); Morawetz, "The Epistemology of Judging: Wittgenstein and Deliberative Practices," in *Wittgenstein and Legal Theory* 3 (Dennis M. Patterson ed. 1992). The notion of "game" that I am using here is unrelated to that used in game theory, which is concerned with strategic behavior. For my purposes, solitaire is a good example of a game, but it is not a game in game-theory terms because it does not involve an interaction between persons. My discussion of judging as a game is related to H. L. A. Hart's emphasis, in his book *The Concept of Law* (1961), on the internal perspective. The game player, viewing the rules from within, considers himself bound by them. The nonplayer does not. Morawetz thinks "practice" describes judging better than "game" does, but such a refinement is unnecessary for my purposes.

that some of your pieces should be allowed to make moves off the chessboard, you would no longer be playing the game of chess. It is true that people sometimes cheat at games when they think they can get away with it. But that is because the pleasure of the game is not the only argument in their utility function. A person might cheat at tennis because he saw an advantage from winning, but if at all reflective he would realize that his pleasure from playing the game itself was diminished, that he was trading off that pleasure against another source of utility. The judicial game has rules that lawyers learn in law school and then in practice or teaching. Both self-selection and the careful screening of federal judicial candidates help to assure that most lawyers who become federal judges will be lawyers who enjoy this particular game. They are therefore likely to adhere, more or less, to the rules limiting the considerations that enter into their decisions. This is just Wittgenstein's point that rules bind because they are accepted, rather than being accepted because they bind. Nothing *in* a rule imposes an obligation to follow it. The decision to obey comes from outside, from force or socialization or the fact that the rule is constitutive of a pleasurable activity.[43]

The rules of judging of which I am speaking are not the rules of substantive law, to which the community is subject but to which judges in their judicial capacity relate differently, as law givers and law appliers. They are the institutional rules of judging, to which only judges are subject. These rules, as I have said, are not altogether clear or uniform. Some judges play by "activist" rules, others (a larger number) by rules of "restraint" because those rules are more congenial to the legal profession's self-image; and judges, like other game players, sometimes bend or break the rules for the sake of other values, such violations being in fact rather common because detection and sanctioning are difficult. Nevertheless most judicial decisions do have a "ruled" quality. The analogy to games helps show how this is consistent with utility maximization and how it therefore does not presuppose heroic self-abnegation on the part of the judges.

A further point is that in creating games, as in creating art, people create a temporary refuge from, by imaginative transformation of, the sinister realities of ordinary life, the realities of hatred, disease, crime, betrayal, war, poverty, bereavement, despair. The judicial game has

---

43. Cf. Sabina Lovibond, *Realism and Imagination in Ethics* 55–57 (1983).

aspects of this refuge and transformation. Its raw materials are the ugly realities of life, but the judicial game transmutes them into intellectual disputes over rights and duties, claims and proofs, presumptions and rebuttals, jurisdiction and competences. And that is a comfort; among other things it spares the judge who inflicts or upholds the death penalty of thinking of himself as a killer. But to get this comfort, the judge must play by the rules of the judicial game, because the rules constitute the game.

It is because judges play by the rules of the judicial game that legislatures can control judicial behavior, though not perfectly, by substituting rules (now I am speaking of rules of law, not rules of the judicial game) for standards. Standards authorize a judge to bring his intuitions of policy to bear on the decision of a case. Rules tell him not to. Because obedience to the rules laid down by the legislature is itself a rule of the judicial game, a legislature can expect a fair degree of compliance by the judges with its rules even though there is no sanction for noncompliance.

Elected judges play the judge game too, and legislators play a related game called statesmanship or public service. But unlike life-tenured federal judges, these players face higher costs (and obtain no greater benefits) from abiding by the rules of their games and therefore break those rules more often. Not always, which is why many and indeed most decisions by nonelected judges have a ruled quality and why much legislation has a genuine public-spirited character—not necessarily because the voters are public-spirited but because legislators derive satisfactions from acting in the public interest that may outweigh the costs when those costs are small.

An important question is the extent to which judges' willingness to play what I am calling the judicial game is a function of the professional ideology discussed in Chapter 1. Traditional legal education and practice do tend to filter out of the profession, or at least the part of the profession from which most judges are appointed, persons radically uncomfortable with traditional legal roles, including that of the judge. As the restrictions that define the legal profession erode, as law becomes more like a policy science, will a point be reached at which neither screening nor self-selection assures that most judges play the judicial game? I suggest a partial answer later.

Here is another application of the concept of games. At various places in this book I criticize the rhetoric of legal scholars; elsewhere I employ that rhetoric. There is no inconsistency. The argument game is different from the critique-of-argument game, just as the judicial game is different from the critique-of-judging game. More broadly, the theory game is different from the practice game. This is not to suggest that there are watertight bulkheads between them. My criticism of scholarly rhetoric has made me more self-conscious about the use of that rhetoric in my own scholarly writing. Stanley Fish believes that my judicial practice could not possibly be influenced by my pragmatic jurisprudence. Pragmatism is purely a method of description, so I am guilty of "the mistake of thinking that a description of a practice has cash value in a game other than the game of description."[44] But he gives no indication that he has tested this assertion by reading my judicial opinions.

A Very Simple Formal Model of the Judicial Utility Function

The implications of the analysis in this chapter for concrete problems in judicial administration can be elucidated by means of a simple formal model. The model is also helpful in distinguishing between the question whether judicial behavior is consistent with rationality, which I hope I have succeeded in showing, and the more difficult question whether judicial behavior *is* rational. That judges with secure tenure nevertheless do *some* work can hardly be considered a robust demonstration of the applicability of rational-choice theory to judges.

Consider the following judicial utility function, in which effort is proxied by time:[45]

$$U = U(t_j, t_l, I, R, O). \tag{1}$$

t_j is the number of hours per day that the judge devotes to judging, t_l is the time he devotes to leisure[46] (here defined as all activities other than judging, so that $t_j + t_l = 24$), I is pecuniary income, initially limited

---

44. "Almost Pragmatism: Richard Posner's Jurisprudence," 57 *University of Chicago Law Review* 1447, 1469 (1990). He has made this argument in many different contexts. See, for example, Fish, *There's No Such Thing as Free Speech* (1994); Fish, "Comments from outside Economics," in *The Consequences of Economic Rhetoric* 21 (Arjo Klamer, Donald N. McCloskey, and Robert M. Solow eds. 1988).

45. A richer model would consider energy or intensity as an additional choice variable, as in Gary S. Becker, *A Treatise on the Family* 64–79 (enlarged ed. 1991). I shall come back to this point.

46. Leisure need not be consumed off the premises, as it were. Loafing on the job is a form of leisure in my model.

to judicial salary, R is reputation, and O represents the other sources of judicial utility besides that of judicial voting itself—popularity, prestige, and avoiding reversal. R, O, and especially I can be assumed to be invariant to t_j above a low threshold (presumably a judge who refused to do any work at all would be impeached and removed, making $I = 0$ in such a case); and let us assume that the average judge is safely above it. On these assumptions, the judge will allocate his time between leisure and judging so that the last hour devoted to judging yields him the same utility as the last hour devoted to leisure, since otherwise he could increase his total utility by reallocating time from the less to the more valuable activity.

In this first cut at a model of judicial utility, pecuniary income is assumed to have no effect on the utility of judging and of leisure. Economists ordinarily expect an increase in annual income to lead to an increase in the utility of leisure relative to work, because of the diminishing marginal utility of money.[47] This expectation depends, however, on the assumption that work generates no utility apart from that of the income it produces. If work produces nonpecuniary utility, just like leisure, it is not obvious that an increase in income will cause a reallocation of time from work to leisure. Indeed, pleasurable work like judging might be considered a form of leisure.[48] A more discriminating analysis of the effect of income on leisure is necessary.

A higher income will affect leisure in two potentially offsetting ways. The first is by reducing the time devoted to household production. Remember that leisure, in the model, includes all nonjudging activities. An increase in income will enable the purchase of additional labor-saving appliances and the hiring of additional household help. This will free up time for other activities, not only pleasurable leisure activities

47. The qualification implicit in "annual" is important. An increase in hourly income would increase the cost of leisure by increasing the amount of money lost by substituting leisure for work, and the resulting incentive to work harder might offset or even exceed the disincentive to work harder resulting from the diminishing marginal utility of income. This qualification will become important when we consider judges' moonlighting income, which unlike their judicial income varies with the time they devote to producing it.

48. Another example of "productive consumption" would be the business lunch. Gary S. Becker, "A Theory of the Allocation of Time," 75 *Economic Journal* 493, 504 (1965). Economic analysis of the nonpecuniary amenities or disamenities of work goes back to Adam Smith's discussion of the compensating wage differential for dangerous or dirty work. The modern literature is illustrated by B. K. Atrostic, "The Demand for Leisure and Nonpecuniary Job Characteristics," 72 *American Economic Review* 428 (1982), and by F. Thomas Juster and Frank P. Stafford, "The Allocation of Time: Empirical Findings, Behavioral Models, and Problems of Measurement," 29 *Journal of Economic Literature* 471, 495–496 (1991).

but also judging, itself a source of utility in my model. Second, a higher income increases the utility generated by pleasurable leisure activities, such as travel, by enabling a higher quality of those activities to be bought. A trip to the South Seas is more fun than sitting in a rocking chair on the back porch. Of course, increased *quality* of leisure need not translate into increased *time* devoted to leisure; an alternative would be the substitution of an expensive for an inexpensive vacation of the same length.[49] But probably people who have more money to spend on leisure activities will increase the time devoted to, as well as the quality of, those activities.

The effect of a higher income in increasing the demand for leisure time can be expected to predominate in the case of a person whose income was already high enough to enable him to eliminate most of his household chores. I therefore predict that a higher judicial salary is likely to reduce the amount of work done by existing judges. The qualification "existing judges" is important. By increasing the field of selection and specifically by attracting persons who set a higher value on income, and hence on work, relative to leisure, an increase in judicial salary may enable a harder-working class of judges to be recruited. And by reducing turnover, especially of the judges with the best private-sector opportunities (who are probably on average the best judges), the higher salary may conduce to a more experienced, higher-quality judiciary. But the possible cost in reduced effort should not be ignored—though here we must bear in mind that time and effort are not synonyms. If energy is limited and leisure requires less of it than judging, a reallocation of time from judging to leisure activities may actually increase the energy that the judge devotes to judging and hence the quality of his judicial output. This is the economic interpretation of Brandeis's dictum, in explaining why he took a month's vacation every summer: "I can do twelve months' work in eleven months but not in twelve."

Let us now allow the judge to obtain some income from moonlighting. The opportunities for such income have been greatly curtailed.[50] Judges no longer can accept payment for speeches or articles, and their

49. Cf. John D. Owen, *The Price of Leisure: An Economic Analysis of the Demand for Leisure Time* 22 (1969).

50. Title VI of the Ethics Reform Act of 1989, 5 U.S.C. app. 7 §§ 501–505, effective January 1, 1991. See also Regulations of the Judicial Conference of the United States under Title VI of the Ethics Reform Act of 1989 concerning Outside Earned Income, Honoraria, and Outside Employment.

income from teaching has been capped at a modest percentage (approximately 15 percent) of their judicial salaries. Book royalties are not limited, however—so one predicts that judges will give fewer speeches and write more books.

The effect of curtailing nonjudicial income can be modeled by partitioning judges' income into a fixed and a variable component, the second representing moonlighting income. With this refinement, and ignoring the arguments in the judicial function (other than judicial income) that are not likely to be significantly responsive to changes in the amount of time invested in judging, we can rewrite the judicial utility function as

$$U = U(I_f, I_v(t_v), t_j, t_l). \tag{2}$$

I has now a fixed and a variable component. The former is the judge's judicial salary. The latter is his moonlighting income, and depends on the time he allots to moonlighting (t_v). So $I = I_f + I_v(t_v)$, where $t_j + t_l + t_v = 24$. In deciding how much time to allocate to judging, the rational judge will consider not only the negative impact on his leisure but also the negative impact on his nonjudicial income. That impact will be less, the fewer lawful opportunities the judge has to obtain such income. Hence we can expect that the curtailment of judicial moonlighting has increased both the judicial effort of the existing judges (except for the book writers!) and their leisure, since the opportunity to moonlight makes leisure more costly. The prediction with respect to leisure is solider. Moonlighting income at time $t + 1$ may be a positive function of judicial effort at time t, so curtailing opportunities for moonlighting income may reduce the return to judicial effort and, as a result, the amount of that effort. Furthermore, moonlighting judges may work harder at judging than they otherwise would in order to avoid becoming unpopular with their nonmoonlighting colleagues. If so, the more their moonlighting is curtailed by limitations on moonlighting income, the less judicial work they will do, though this effect may be offset by the greater time they have for judging as well as for leisure.

Although my analysis predicts that the curtailment of moonlighting income, coupled with the increase in judicial salaries,[51] has increased

---

51. The curtailment of judicial moonlighting was coupled with a substantial judicial pay raise (nominally 25 percent, effectively almost 40 percent), also as of January 1, 1991.

judges' consumption of leisure, this prediction is difficult to test empirically unless the increased leisure has come at the expense of judicial work as well as of moonlighting. If it has, we can expect a lengthening of court queues unexplained by any other factor.

As before, the effects on judicial selection and retention must be considered in a total evaluation, as must any reduction in government tax revenues from curtailing judges' opportunities to earn outside income. If in order to limit the effects on selection and retention the curtailment of moonlighting is coupled with an increase in judicial salaries, there may be no net reduction in tax revenues. But there will be a net increase in government spending, to fund the salary increase.

Another point to note is that the judicial pay raise would probably have reduced the amount of judicial moonlighting even if no limitations on moonlighting income had been imposed. For, if diminishing marginal utility of income is assumed, the raise reduced the increment of utility contributed by money-making activities.

Let us consider more carefully the selection of judges. A person will accept a judgeship if his net expected utility from it is positive, which is to say if that utility exceeds the utility that he obtains in his present employment (in the practice of law, let us assume) plus the cost (other than the forgone income from practice) of becoming a judge, for example the inconvenience, exasperation, and loss of privacy entailed in filling out elaborate forms and undergoing a searching investigation by the FBI and possibly a severe grilling by the Senate Judiciary Committee, with always some risk of embarrassment or even rejection. Formally, then, the condition for accepting the offer of a judgeship is that

$$U_J(t_j,\ t_l,\ I_J,\ R_J,\ P_J) - U_L(t_L,\ I_L) - C > 0, \tag{3}$$

where U_J is the utility from being a judge, I_J is the judicial salary, P_J is the prestige of being a judge, U_L is the utility of practicing law, t_L is the time a lawyer devotes to his work, C is the cost of becoming a judge, and the other terms are either as before or self-explanatory. Lawyers are assumed to have no leisure—more realistically, l_J should be viewed as the judge's added leisure. The other arguments in the judicial utility function (that is, the components of O other than prestige) have been dropped as not particularly helpful to the analysis of judicial selection. The utility terms should be translated into present values to be comparable to C, but I omit this detail.

Certain points are obvious. The more costly it is to become a judge and the lower judicial income is relative to income in practice, the less likely a lawyer is to accept a judgeship. Hence the fact that federal judges of the same rank are paid the same no matter where they live, even though the cost of living and the salaries of lawyers vary widely across the country, enlarges the field of selection in low-cost versus high-cost areas. So we should expect judges in low-cost areas to be abler relative to the practicing lawyers in their areas than is the case in high-cost areas. And the more a lawyer values leisure, prestige, and judging versus lawyering, the more likely he will be to accept a judgeship.

A subtler point is that if in order to enlarge the field of selection steps are taken to increase judicial prestige by limiting the growth in the number of judges, the amount of leisure that a judge can enjoy without imperiling his reputation will fall and as a result the field of selection may not, on balance, be enlarged. That field will be larger, the greater the expected utility of being a judge. So far as relevant here, that expected utility is a positive function of judicial prestige and of the amount of leisure time a judge has. Both factors are affected by the number of judges, but in opposite directions. An increase in the number of judges increases judges' leisure by reducing the average judicial workload, but reduces the prestige of judges. If these effects are perfectly offsetting, the field of selection will not be enlarged. But its composition will be altered in favor of judges who attach less weight to prestige and more to leisure. The net effect will be a reduction in the propensity of judges to work. This analysis has relevance to policy in view of recent calls to limit the number of federal judges, and is empirically testable because it predicts that, other things being equal, judicial output increases less than proportionately to an increase in the number of judges.

Although my focus is on the ordinary judge, there have been of course some extraordinary judges; is this consistent with the model? One does not expect large quality differences between employees paid the same wage in the same job by the same employer. Such a wage would either overpay the lower-quality employees or underpay the higher-quality ones (it could of course do both), and in the latter event the higher-quality employees would leave, unless their skills were not transferable to another employer. One possibility is that the judicial wage has been set at a level that is compensatory for the extraordinary judge but overpays the ordinary one; then we would expect queuing for the job by the ordinary candidates—and there is queuing for federal judgeships.[52] Another possibility, however, is that although the wage is the same for the ordinary and the extraordinary judge, the full income (U) is as high or even higher for the latter, because R_J in his judicial utility function is higher than R_J in the judicial utility function of the ordinary judge. (The more talented judge is more likely to obtain a greater reputation.) The higher R_J in the left-most term of inequality (3) might offset the higher I_L in the next term, in which event U_J would exceed U_L by the same amount as in the case of the ordinary judge.

Along similar lines it has been argued that an increase in judicial salaries could actually reduce the quality of the judiciary, by diluting the effect of low judicial salaries in screening out candidates who do not anticipate large nonpecuniary gains as a result of being able to develop a reputation for being a superior judge.[53] Moreover, an increase in judicial salaries could, by making a judgeship a richer patronage plum, increase the role of political as distinct from merit considerations in the selection of judges. These are only partial effects, however. An increase in judicial salaries will also make it easier to attract candidates who have good incomes in the private practice of law, or in law teaching or other law-related activities, and these lawyers are probably on average the abler candidates.

If judges do not pay sufficient attention to precedent, this may seem a compelling argument for low judicial salaries. Such salaries will be attractive to leisure-lovers, and adherence to precedent is, as we saw earlier, an effort-minimizing method of judicial decision-making. At the same time, the effect of low salaries in causing self-selection of candidates who anticipate nonpecuniary income (which need not be limited to leisure) from judging may bring into the judiciary more people who want to make new law rather than merely apply existing law. If, as seems plausible, low salaries would attract both types of judge—leisure-lovers and bomb-throwers, sheeps and wolves—the consequence might be to accelerate legal change, as discussed below.

Should we expect systematic behavioral differences between ordinary

---

52. The very low rate of turnover among federal judges might seem additional evidence that they are overpaid, but it may simply reflect the heavily backloaded character of federal judicial compensation.

53. Paul E. Greenberg and James A. Haley, "The Role of the Compensation Structure in Enhancing Judicial Quality," 15 *Journal of Legal Studies* 417 (1986).

and extraordinary judges? I conjecture that the function relating judicial work to judicial ability is U-shaped. Very weak judges must work hard to reach the threshold above which judicial prestige does not vary greatly with output; very strong judges have an incentive to work hard because hard work can be expected to have a multiplicative rather than merely an additive effect on ability.

It might seem that strong judges would be less likely than weak ones to adhere to precedent because they would not want to feel themselves bound by the decisions of previous judges who were on average weaker than they. But this is not clear, and not only because these strong judges want the precedents *they* create to be followed. If abandonment or erosion of stare decisis increased judicial workloads, which we recall is plausible although not certain, more judges would be appointed, and the influence of each judge would be diluted.[54] Moreover, we should recall the earlier point that judges, strong as well as weak, enjoy playing the judicial "game." That game has certain rules, of which one (in the Anglo-American legal system) is that judges should give great although not controlling weight to precedents as authorities. Two of the strongest judges in our history, Oliver Wendell Holmes and Learned Hand, were deferential toward precedent.

But notice that the more, and the more strongly, ordinary judges are committed (for whatever reason) to following precedent, the weaker may be the extraordinary judge's incentive to do so. His departures from precedent will be both more likely to be followed, thus magnifying his influence, and less likely to undermine the practice of decision according to precedent and therefore less likely to impair the precedential effect of his decisions. I say his incentive to follow precedent "may be" weaker the more precedent-observing the ordinary judge is, rather than "will be," because the ordinary judge will be less likely to join an opinion that departs from the existing precedents the more he is committed to abiding by precedent. Nevertheless, this discussion may provide a partial answer to the question I raised earlier of whether the decline of the legal profession's traditional ideology may lead to more violations of the rules of the judicial game. A situation in which most but not all judges conform to those rules may increase the incentives of some judges to violate them. The adventurous judges of the Earl Warren era departed from precedent unusually frequently, but with

54. O'Hara, note 7 above, at 14.

some confidence that their tradition-minded colleagues and successors would follow the radical new precedents rather than try to turn the clock back.[55]

Inequality (3) can be used to predict behavioral differences between court of appeals judges and Supreme Court Justices. Since I_J, $U_J(t_j)$, and especially P_J are substantially higher for the latter than for the former, we expect, and observe, that there is more vigorous "campaigning" for Supreme Court appointments and that refusal to accept appointment to the Court is rare. Moreover, Supreme Court Justices are less likely to resign to pursue other careers than lower-court judges are (even after correction is made for differences in age) or to retire at the earliest possible date. Although they have better opportunities in private practice than lower-court judges (that is, a higher I_L), their loss in voting power and in prestige would be greater. And because $U_J(t_j)$ (the utility of time devoted to judging) is greater for Supreme Court Justices than for court of appeals judges (the average vote in the Supreme Court has more impact than the average vote in any of the courts of appeals, and the Justices decide which cases to hear rather than having to hear all appeals within their jurisdiction, as court of appeals judges do), while $U_J(t_l)$ (the utility of time devoted to leisure) presumably is the same, we can expect Supreme Court Justices to devote more time to their work than court of appeals judges do to theirs. (This is only on average, however, and is subject to other important qualifications, discussed below.) The analogy is to the greater propensity to vote in closely contested elections for high offices such as the Presidency than in one-sided elections for unimportant offices.

It might seem that since there are more Supreme Court Justices than the number of judges on most lower-court panels—in the federal courts of appeals, for example, the vast majority of cases are heard and decided by panels of only three judges—a Supreme Court Justice is less likely to be the swing vote and so less likely to make a difference in the outcome of the case. But because of the greater controversiality of Supreme Court cases a much higher fraction of decisions are decided by a single vote than in the courts of appeals, where dissents are relatively infrequent.

The prediction that Supreme Court Justices work harder than other

---

55. On this "precedent ratchet," see my book *The Federal Courts: Crisis and Reform* 217 (1985).

judges is plausible only if allowance is made for differences in age and workload between them and other judges. Supreme Court Justices are older on average than court of appeals judges (implying that they have a lower energy level and hence a diminished capacity for hard work) and they have (possibly as a concomitant) a lighter workload, in major part because their jurisdiction is discretionary, which enables them to limit their workload. If greater age and lighter workload are assumed to cancel out—the average Justice works fewer hours but his hours are divided among fewer cases—we are left with a simple prediction that the average Supreme Court Justice does work harder per case than the average court of appeals judge does. If, however, as seems plausible, judicial effort has a diminishing effect on the satisfactions from judicial voting, a reduction in workload will reduce total judicial effort rather than merely redistribute it among fewer cases, and then we might expect the Justices to work less hard than court of appeals judges do, even on a per-case basis. If as I believe the average Justice works harder, this implies that the diminishing marginal utility of judicial effort is offset by the higher average utility resulting from the greater power and case selectivity of the Supreme Court compared to the courts of appeals.

A further difference in workload should be noted. Cases decided by the Supreme Court tend to be more sensitive and controversial than cases (even the same cases) decided by lower courts. So we can expect the Justices, in order to reduce the element of hassle in their work, to be adept at using decision-avoidance doctrines, such as mootness, ripeness, political question, and absence of a real case or controversy, as well as the power of choice that they enjoy by virtue of having a discretionary jurisdiction, to avoid many difficult and controversial cases. Making life easier for themselves is of course not the only motivation of Supreme Court Justices or other judges. But it is one, and I have tried in this chapter to show how economics—aided by fields of learning with which most economists are unfamiliar, such as literature and philosophy—can help us to a disciplined understanding of this and other intensely human factors in adjudication.

chapter 4

The Profession in Crisis:
Germany and Britain

STUDENTS of jurisprudence have long been fascinated by the pressures that a national crisis exerts on the ideals and behavior of the legal profession. Two books, one on judges and lawyers in the Third Reich, the other on executive detention in wartime Britain, cast light on the subject and in doing so provoke disturbing reflections on the morality of a pragmatic jurisprudence.

Nazi Judges

No legal profession has faced the challenge that faced the German legal profession in the period of Hitler's rule. Here is the conventional account of how the profession responded: Before, after, and even to some extent during this period, German justice maintained its traditional Prussian rectitude and efficiency. Hitler, to be sure, subverted the norms of legality; but he did so by bypassing the regular courts and establishing Nazi institutions, such as the SS, the Gestapo, and the People's Court that tried the July 20, 1944, conspirators, to exterminate his political enemies and implement his racist and eugenic policies. Within their diminished sphere, largely though of course not completely untouched by Nazi ideology and personnel, the ordinary judges and the ordinary lawyers conducted the ordinary business of the law in the ordinary way, sometimes indeed offering at least passive resistance to the regime. If these judges did not resist more—if, indeed, they often enforced Nazi laws in an unquestioning manner—it was not only because they were afraid for their lives but also because they had been schooled in the ingrained positivism of German legal thought: The content of the law is exhausted in the enactments of the duly constituted authorities. The judge cannot bend, let alone nullify, such enactments by appealing to principles of natural law.[1]

This is the story that the German legal establishment has told throughout the postwar period; and although it has never gone unquestioned and has for some time been the subject of a critical literature in Germany,[2] it is still widely accepted in this country. It is forcefully challenged in a book by a German lawyer that tells an ugly story of moral corruption and professional degradation.[3] Müller's story begins—surprisingly—shortly after the creation of the German Empire in 1871 and continues—even more surprisingly—until a quarter-century after the death of Hitler, and has very little to do with legal positivism. It begins with Bismarck's packing the German judiciary with ultraconservative statists whose motto was, "What the army is at our borders, our decisions must be within it!" (p. 9). These statists still dominated the judiciary when the Weimar Republic decided to retain all the imperial judges in their jobs and to guarantee them against dismissal. They proved a subversive force, bending and twisting the law so that it descended with savage force on the heads of leftwingers, but letting off far more dangerous rightwingers. For Hitler's treasonous participation in the Munich "Beer Hall Putsch" of 1923 the minimum sentence prescribed by statute was five years in prison, and because Hitler was

---

1. On the distinction between positive and natural law, see *The Problems of Jurisprudence*, ch. 7. The argument that positivism paved the way for Nazism is, in American academic legal circles, most prominently associated with Lon Fuller. See his article "Positivism and Fidelity to Law—A Reply to Professor Hart," 71 *Harvard Law Review* 630, 657–661 (1958).

2. For extensive references, see Markus Dirk Dubber, "Judicial Positivism and Hitler's Injustice," 93 *Columbia Law Review* 1807, 1811 n. 17 (1993). Illustrative are the essays in *Rechtsgeschichte im Nationalsozialismus: Beiträge zur Geschichte einer Disziplin* (Michael Stolleis and Dieter Simon eds. 1989) ("National Socialist Legal History: Contributions to the History of a Discipline").

3. Ingo Müller, *Hitler's Justice: The Courts of the Third Reich* (Deborah Lucas Schneider trans. 1990), first published (in German) in 1987.

already on probation for another offense the sentence could not be suspended even in part. The statute further required that a foreign offender be deported, and Hitler was still a citizen of Austria rather than of Germany. Nevertheless the court suspended all but six months of his sentence, with the brief period of imprisonment to be served in comfort in a lavishly appointed castle. And it refused to order him deported, because "in the case of a man whose thoughts and feelings are as German as Hitler's, the court is of the opinion that the intent and purpose of the law have no application" (p. 16).

Although German law made it an offense to vilify publicly the constitutionally established form of government (that is, the Weimar Republic), the German Supreme Court permitted the use of the term "Jew republic" on the ground that "it can denote the new legal and social order in Germany which was brought about in significant measure by German and foreign Jews" and "the disproportionate influence which, in the opinion of many citizens, a small number of Jews, relative to the total population actually wields" (p. 18). Yet a worker who carried a sign reading "Workers, burst your chains!" was sent to prison for inciting class hatred. Müller gives other examples of the blatant partiality of the German judiciary during the Weimar period, in light of which one is not surprised that Hitler saw no need to make wholesale changes in the judiciary when he took power.

The Jews and the handful of social democrats in the judiciary were of course expelled then and Jews were gradually extruded from the practicing legal profession as well, along with such questionable characters as the non-Jewish attorney who continued to consult a physician to whose treatment she owed her life, even though she had "acquired knowledge that Dr. M. was a member of the Jewish race" (p. 66). In 1938 the remaining Jewish lawyers were reclassified as "Jewish legal advisers" and confined to acting on behalf of Jews. "The German guardian of the law for the German! The Jewish adviser for the Jew! Once again German lawyers can take pride in the title of attorney!" (p. 62). A third of the nation's law professors—the Jewish third—were dismissed, replaced by young men who, still teaching and writing in the 1960s, constituted a powerful cadre of apologists for the behavior of the profession during the Hitler era. Yet it was not one of these youngsters, but a law professor who had held his chair since 1919, who in 1933 exhorted his colleagues "to extol the Führer as a figure of light and a hero who is leading the German soul out of the depths into the light, showing it the safe path to Valhalla, to God the Father in the true German homeland, setting an example of this Gothic life to his own brothers, offering them help to help themselves, so that all Germans may become brothers before God the Father" (p. 70).

Purged of its Jews and its democrats, the judiciary put its shoulder to the Nazi wheel with enthusiasm. The Reichstag arson trial, conducted before the German Supreme Court in the fall of 1933, was a portent. Although four of the five defendants were acquitted, the prosecutor had requested the acquittal of three of them, apparently out of concern for foreign reactions to Nazi justice. The court condemned the fifth defendant to death under a law that had been passed after the fire. The court dismissed the suspicion that the Nazis themselves were the arsonists: "The [National Socialist] party's ethical principles of restraint preclude the very possibility of such crimes and actions as are ascribed to them by unprincipled agitators" (p. 33).

Flexible interpretation was used to nazify laws inherited from the previous regime and to amplify the effect of the Nazi laws themselves. As one judge put it, "Eliminating the last traces of the enemy within is undoubtedly a part of the restoration of German honor. German judges can participate in this task through generous interpretation of the penal code" (p. 52). In upholding the convictions of members of the banned Social Democratic Party, a decision handed down in 1934 took judicial notice that "the activities of the Social Democrats who have fled abroad are intended to prepare the violent overthrow of the constitution, which has been guaranteed by the new government with the support of the entire population" (p. 54). The constitution to which the court was referring was the Weimar constitution, although the "new government"—Hitler's—far from guaranteeing the Weimar constitution was busy subverting it.

It was for the most part establishment conservatives rather than Nazi hotheads who fashioned the new jurisprudence (in fact, as we shall see, its roots were pre-Hitler), in which, as leaders of the profession explained, judges were to "make value judgments which correspond to the National Socialist legal order and the will of the political leadership," in which people could be punished for an act that while not expressly punishable by any law "deserves punishment according to the fundamental principle of a criminal statute and healthy popular opinion," in which the maxim "no crime without punishment" trumped the older maxim "no punishment without law," and in which the criminal law's "ultimate function is to exterminate" (pp. 73–76). The initiative for the Nuremberg race laws was Hitler's, but the judiciary enforced them with relish in opinions full of angry references to "Jewish effrontery, Jewish contempt for German laws, Jewish lasciviousness, and Jewish unscrupulousness" (p. 104).

> It is a monstrous instance of shamelessness that in November 1937 a Jew, in full knowledge of the unbending determination of the German people to secure its future for all time by maintaining the purity of its blood, and in full knowledge of the severe sentences widely known . . . to be given to defilers of the race, spoke in the street to a girl clearly and immediately recognizable as being of German blood and made her his mistress (id.).

Despite the reference to "clearly and immediately recognizable as being of German blood," a Jew could be guilty no matter what the lengths to which he had gone to determine whether his sexual partner was Jewish. Nor was it necessary that German "bloodlines" actually be in peril. One Jewish man was sent to prison for "the offense of looking across the street at the 15-year-old ('German-blooded') Ilse S., 'if not importunately, then at least so as to attract notice'" (p. 111). Another Jewish man, who may have become sexually excited when being massaged by a German woman though she noticed no signs of such excitement, was sentenced to two years in prison, in an opinion, signed by a judge who was still sitting in 1975, that described the Jew as "an inferior human being. The offense in this case was committed approximately three years after the Nuremberg laws took effect. It represents an extraordinary piece of effrontery on the part of the accused to have dared, at this date, to abuse the witness as the object of his sexual lust" (p. 103).

New courts, such as the Special Courts and the Hereditary Health Courts as well as the People's Court, were created by the National Socialist regime to share the dirty work with the regular courts, eventually taking over much of their criminal jurisdiction. But this devolution of authority does not mitigate the legal profession's complicity with the regime. For the new courts were staffed by regular judges. Roland Freisler, the notorious president of the People's Court, was no professional pariah, but "an expert whom law professors were fond of citing" (p. 152).

Things were bad enough before World War II, but after the war broke out and even before it began to go badly for Germany they got much worse. The treatment of Jews and Poles by the German courts in occupied Poland was particularly vile. Proceedings were conducted in German whether or not the defendant understood the language. Jews and Poles were not permitted to testify under oath, their testimony being considered inherently unworthy of belief. One young Polish woman was sentenced to death for having received as a present a fur jacket that had been stolen from the winter collection of clothing for the eastern front, even though she neither knew nor had reason to know that it was stolen. Another Polish woman was sentenced to death for having struck, probably accidentally, a German woman in a scuffle started by the German. The German woman was not injured. The court found the Pole's "claim that she did not realize she was dealing with a German 'unconvincing,' since she ought to have recognized that Mrs. Baschek's self-confident demeanor was 'clearly and beyond doubt the manner of a German'" (p. 162).[4]

But the courts treated Germans badly enough. A German who in the course of courageously saving the contents of a burning building helped himself to a bottle of perfume and a knockwurst was sentenced to death along with a companion who had taken two bars of soap. Several German soldiers were executed for desertion after Germany's unconditional surrender to the Allies had taken effect—a curious echo of Kant's dictum that a society would be morally obligated to carry out a death sentence even if, the society being on the point of dissolution, no deterrent interest would be served. Müller estimates that by the end of the Nazi era German courts had sentenced 80,000 persons to death and that 80 percent of the sentences had been carried out.

Müller's research revealed only one judge who had refused to serve the regime from the bench. His name was Dr. Lothar Kreyssig, a county court judge. A series of acts of insubordination by this upstanding man (a devout Lutheran) culminated in his issuing an injunction against several hospitals that were shipping patients to concentration camps for extermination under the Nazi euthanasia program and in his attempting to get a Nazi Party leader prosecuted criminally for the leader's part in the program. When the Reich Minister of Justice ordered Kreyssig to withdraw the injunction, Kreyssig refused and requested early retirement. Not only was the request granted, but Kreyssig was given his full

---

4. It is odd that the judges should have been so eager to embrace the stereotype of the arrogant German.

pension—and this was in 1942. He was allowed to live out the war in peace.

With the war over and Germany occupied, the Allies made some efforts to cleanse the judiciary and in doing so to make room for Jewish and other judges and law professors who had been driven into exile by the Nazis. The German legal establishment fought this campaign tooth and nail, and ultimately won. The exiles who had received judicial or university appointments right after the war were fired a few years later when the newly formed German Federal Republic passed a law guaranteeing reemployment to all members of the civil (including judicial) service of the Third Reich other than a handful who had occupied "political" posts. (Shades of Weimar's decision to retain the members of the imperial judiciary.) That handful, including some who had been convicted at the Nuremberg "judges' trial,"[5] received generous pensions. Franz Schlegelberger, for example, undersecretary of the Ministry of Justice and for a time acting minister during the Nazi era, a man deeply implicated in the various exterminations conducted by the Nazis and sentenced to life imprisonment at Nuremberg (but released in 1951), was awarded a monthly pension of 2,894 Deutsche marks (seven times the average monthly wage of a skilled laborer), plus 160,000 DM in back pension, even though Hitler had given him 100,000 Reischmarks upon his retirement in 1942.[6]

A decided lack of tact was evident in some of the postwar appointments. One judge of the Hitler era "was named presiding judge of a board in Hamburg to hear the cases of war victims claiming damages; here he decided claims filed by the survivors of his own earlier trials, and by the relatives of those he had sentenced to death" (p. 215). The judge I mentioned earlier who was still sitting in 1975 rendered a decision that year barring a member of the Communist Party from teaching, on the ground that she knew "that the federal government considers the goals of this political party opposed to the constitution" (p. 218), just as the Jew had known about the racial policy of Hitler's government, as embodied in the Nuremberg laws. The judge was joined in this decision by a colleague who had been a high-ranking ss police officer in the occupied territories during World War II. None of

5. On which see Telford Taylor, "The Nuremberg War Crimes Trials," *International Conciliation*, April 1949, pp. 241, 286–292.

6. For more on Schlegelberger, see Ted Harrison, "Political Police and Lawyers in Hitler's Germany," 10 *German History* 226, 226–228 (1992).

the judges whose egregious decisions during the Nazi period Müller quotes lost his job after the war.

As part of its population policy the Nazi regime had expanded the definition of illegal homosexual relations and made the punishment more severe. A postwar statute forbade judges to enforce Nazi laws that had increased the punishment of preexisting crimes but permitted the enforcement of laws newly enacted in the Nazi era provided they had not been based on National Socialist principles. To get around these limitations the postwar German judges first classified the Nazi amendment of the homosexual statute as a new law rather than as a law punishing a preexisting crime more harshly and then declared that the new law had been "justified on objective grounds and can thus not be regarded as part of National Socialist doctrine" (p. 228), even though repression of homosexuality had been a particular project of Himmler's as well as a cornerstone of Nazi population policy.

Yet when the defendants were Nazis rather than homosexuals or leftwingers, the full armamentarium of legal casuistry was, in a reprise of the Weimar experience, placed at the disposal of the defendants. So a man who had been a Gestapo chief in Danzig during the war and had personally killed four English prisoners was acquitted of the charge of being an accomplice to murder because "with reference to the killing of these four officers in Danzig, the perpetrator was the former Führer and chancellor of the Reich, Adolf Hitler." Applying the doctrine of lenity to Hitler (!), the court proceeded to hold that "it cannot be proven with sufficient certainty that Hitler had an even limited premeditation or malicious intent" (p. 251). So the Gestapo chief was merely an accomplice to manslaughter and was sentenced to two years.

People who tried to reopen cases from the Nazi era were uniformly rebuffed, since "every government, even a totalitarian one, has a right to defend its own interests. No reproach may be made of the fact that in times of crisis, it resorts to extraordinary measures" (p. 288). (This is like saying that a bank robber has a right to defend himself against the police.) Müller tells us that "a West German court has never summoned the courage to declare a single Nazi decision 'null and void,'" not even the decision by the People's Court condemning the July 20 conspirators, although "Hitler had publicly announced their forthcoming executions even before the verdict was reached" (pp. 285–287). But a West German court did declare a postwar trial of Nazis void because of procedural irregularities.

West Germany's reparations law, applicable to persons who had suffered "because of their opposition to National Socialism or because of their race, creed, or ideology," was narrowly interpreted, making gypsies ineligible because "in spite of the occurrence of racial considerations, the measures taken were based not on race as such but rather on the Gypsies' asocial characteristics." Yet the Nazi position had been that, "as a rule, in Europe only Jews and Gypsies [are] of alien blood," and Himmler had instructed the SS and the police that it was time "to deal with the Gypsy question in connection with the nature of the race" (pp. 263–264).

How does Müller explain what he believes to be a century of betrayal of the norms of legality and justice by the German judiciary? Having emphasized the judges' refusal to be cabined by a narrow literalism, he naturally does not endorse the hackneyed proposition that German legal education and culture were too positivistic. His book refutes the proposition, once popular in jurisprudential circles in this country (particularly Catholic jurisprudential circles), that legal positivism, through its rejection of natural-law constraints on the making and application of law, was a factor in the rise of totalitarianism.[7] He does point out that the "fixation on government [that was] characteristic of such a large part of the judiciary" made it easy for them to adapt to conditions in the Third Reich (p. 297). His main explanation, however, is simply that the judges whom Hitler inherited from Weimar were a highly nationalistic, ultraconservative group deeply offended by conditions under Weimar and broadly sympathetic to the goals and methods of the Nazi regime. Along with the judges and law professors appointed in the Hitler era, they carried Nazi habits of thought forward into the postwar era. Moreover, they wanted to whitewash the judicial performance during the Nazi era.

So far I have allowed *Hitler's Justice* to speak for itself. But there are two large questions that must be asked about the book. The first is whether it gives an accurate and balanced picture of the German legal and judicial scene before, during, and after the Nazi era. The second is whether, if so, it gives a convincing explanation for that scene.

I have no reason to doubt the book's accuracy, although Markus Dubber, who knows more about German law and jurisprudence than

---

7. Edward A. Purcell, Jr., *The Crisis of Democratic Theory: Scientific Naturalism and the Problem of Value* 164–171 (1973).

I, believes that Müller has exaggerated the continuity of that jurisprudence throughout the period covered by the book.[8] The more general issue is balance.[9] *Hitler's Justice* is anecdotal, not systematic. It quotes scores of decisions, but out of thousands, prompting the reader to wonder how representative the decisions are that Müller discusses. He notes that during the Nazi era most criminal appeals were by prosecutors, complaining of erroneous acquittals or too lenient sentences, rather than by defendants. Shouldn't the authors of those lower-court decisions (invariably reversed) be commended?

Even I know of a humane decision by a German court during the Nazi period.[10] The decision, which was affirmed on appeal and is not discussed by Müller, held that a half-Jewish woman who attended Jewish New Year's services in order to preserve family peace did not have a sufficient tie to the Jewish community to be classified as a Jew under the Nuremberg laws.[11] Was this the only such decision in twelve years? Müller also fails to consider the possibility that judges may have occasionally meted out long prison sentences to protect the defendants, who could expect to be carted off to concentration camps by the Gestapo upon the completion of their prison sentences.[12] Müller's discussions of the Weimar and modern eras are skimpy, and the ugly decisions of those eras that he cites and quotes from may be isolated— though he is not the first to have pointed out that judges undermined the Weimar regime.[13] Then too, despite the benign treatment of Judge Kreyssig, we soft, sheltered Americans can have no conception of the physical and moral courage that a German had to have in order to resist Hitler's regime, especially after the war began.[14] But the author has

8. Dubber, note 2 above, at 1816–1822.

9. Id. at 1814–1815. See also Walter Otto Weyrauch, "Limits of Perception: Reader Response to *Hitler's Justice*," 40 *American Journal of Comparative Law* 237, 243–248 (1992), and Marc Linder, *The Supreme Labor Court in Nazi Germany: A Jurisprudential Analysis* (1987). Linder argues that this court, at least, adhered to traditional norms of legality even when that meant bucking Nazi labor policy. See, for example, id. at 61–63, 184–185.

10. Harrison, note 6 above, at 227, mentions another.

11. See *Law and Literature* 172–173. Half-Jews were not classified as Jews if they were nonobservant.

12. Weyrauch, note 9 above, at 244, provides support for this conjecture.

13. See Judith Shklar, *Legalism: Laws, Morals, and Political Trials* 72 (1964).

14. This point is emphasized by Weyrauch, note 9 above, at 247–248, recounting an incident of passive resistance by a German law professor. We should not blame judges for not being brave, but neither should we forget the barb: the highest law for the German judges was self-preservation. Nor should we forget the examples of judicial courage by Colombian judges threatened by the drug cartels and Italian judges threatened by the Mafia, and even

made a prima facie case that the German judiciary was rotten for a century or more, and it is now up to its defenders to reply. I hear no replies.

Müller's explanation for the rot is more convincing than the conventional view, which ascribes it to the positivistic character of German legal education and tradition. German judges in the period studied by Müller, as doubtless in any period—as is true of our judges today—did engage in hair-splitting casuistry, strict construction, disavowal of personal responsibility, and the other tricks of the legal positivist. But they did so opportunistically, to give their decisions the appearance of legality and to still any stirrings of conscience. They were not acting under the compulsion of a reflex induced by miseducation. They were not victims of brainwashing by law professors. In fact they repeatedly rejected positivism, and did so with a brutal forthrightness that should make our judicial activists, realists, utilitarians, and pragmatists squirm. (I am one of those pragmatists, and I'm squirming.) "Abstract" thinking was denounced in favor of the "teleological" method, "which encouraged judges to identify a particular ideological meaning and intent underlying a given law and then to use this intent to determine" the law's meaning (pp. 80–81); or the holistic method, in which, as leaders of the profession explained, cases are decided "not on the basis of an analytical investigation of their elements, but only as wholes, concretely, after grasping their essence" (p. 73). "The courts to which the Third Reich has assigned responsibility for administering justice can carry out this task . . . only if they do not remain glued to the letter of the law, but rather penetrate its inner core in their interpretations and do their part to see that the aims of the lawmaker are realized" (p. 220). With judges so helpful as this, the Nazis were saved the trouble of rewriting the statute books from cover to cover.

One law professor wrote that "behavior is unlawful when its general tendency in the judgment of jurisprudence does more harm than good to the state and its members." Another dismissed the possibility of misdiagnosing conditions warranting involuntary sterilization (a procedure that carried with it a five percent risk of death) by remarking that "for family members the loss is naturally very severe, but the human race loses so many members to errors that one more or less hardly

---

by the U.S. judges in the South who enforced desegregation decrees in the wake of *Brown v. Board of Education*. There is such a thing as judicial courage, but it has not been conspicuous in Germany.

matters" (pp. 76, 121). The balancing approach taken by these jurists reminds one of such decisions as *Lochner* and *Buck v. Bell* ("Three generations of imbeciles are enough").[15]

The roots were, as usual, pre-Hitler. Particularly noteworthy was a decision by Germany's supreme criminal court in 1927, the heyday of American legal realism, expanding the defense of necessity in, of all things, an abortion case.[16] A doctor, convinced that his patient, a pregnant woman, might because she suffered from depression kill herself if forced to carry her fetus to term, performed an abortion on her and was prosecuted. The relevant statute recognized a defense of necessity, but it probably required a greater showing of actual danger than the facts presented and it definitely did not allow the defense to be asserted by a person, such as the doctor, who was not himself endangered. Nevertheless it was an appealing case, and the court created an extrastatutory defense of necessity and let the doctor off. The opinion, and even more the scholarly commentary on it, offered justifications couched in the statist-oriented interest-balancing terms that would characterize opinions by the judges of the Third Reich. One commentator, for example, said that the important question was whether—in light of such (unconventional) sources of legal obligation as "the trends of the times"—"this general type of behaviour serve[s] the interests of the State more than it harms such interests."[17]

It is tempting to turn the conventional story on its head and attribute some of the misconduct of the judiciary during the Hitler period to legal realism and pragmatism. For these are approaches that seem, because of their skepticism and relativism,[18] to lack an unwavering moral compass and an ironclad commitment to the rule of law, and, because of their instrumentalist character, to lend themselves to treating people as pawns on a social chessboard. But a "pawn" is a symbol, and should not the pragmatist's concern with consequences lead him to consider the human consequences of treating people as pawns? Is not empathetic awareness of other human beings therefore as pragmatic as moral skepticism? Doesn't utilitarianism insist that *everyone's* welfare

15. 274 U.S. 200, 207 (1927).
16. See the discussion of the case and its aftermath in David Cohen, "The Development of the Modern Doctrine of Necessity: A Comparative Critique," 4 *Rechtshistorisches Journal* 215, 225–228 (1985).
17. Quoted in id. at 227 from a 1929 article by Eberhard Schmidt.
18. Even when these attributes are suitably qualified. See my Introduction.

must be counted in the social calculus, even the welfare of criminals and animals? Anyway it seems unlikely that "isms" had much to do with the German judges' behavior. The judges were swept up in powerful emotional and political currents that probably owed little to legal theories.

It is natural to wonder whether traces of the vicious behavior depicted in Müller's book can be found in our own legal system. Our retention, indeed our expanding use, of capital punishment, our other exceptionally severe criminal punishments (many for intrinsically minor, esoteric, archaic, or victimless offenses), our adoption of pretrial detention, as a result of which some criminal defendants languish in jail for years awaiting trial, and our enormous prison and jail population, which has now passed the one-million mark, mark us as the most penal of civilized nations. This is a disturbing state of affairs—justifiable perhaps, remote from Nazi justice, but problematic all the same.

"Remote from Nazi justice . . ." Of course. But we should not suppose that our judges have a margin of moral superiority over our political leaders greater than the margin that the German judges of the Third Reich had over their Leader. The United States has never had a Hitler, so it has never had a judiciary complicit with a Hitler. But we have had slavery, and segregation, and criminal laws against miscegenation ("dishonoring the race"), and Red Scares, and the internment in World War II of tens of thousands of harmless Japanese-Americans; and most of our judges went along with these things without protest.[19] The German judges were not worse, certainly, than Germany's political leaders; they were ordinary Germans of the educated middle class. Our judges for the most part are ordinary Americans of the educated middle class.

Two of the lasting impressions that *Hitler's Justice* conveys are the extraordinary plasticity of legal rhetoric, which enables a clever judge to find a plausible form of words to clothe virtually any decision, however barbarous; and the German judges' overidentification with the Nazi regime. These are dangers for us. We have the same rhetorical resources the German judges had. We also have some judges, fortunately not many, who impose savage penalties on minor drug dealers with obvious relish, and who in thereby enlisting in the "war against

19. See, for example, Mark Tushnet, "The American Law of Slavery, 1810–1860: A Study in the Persistence of Legal Autonomy," 10 *Law and Society Review* 119 (1975).

drugs" may remind readers of *Hitler's Justice* of the German judges' self-description as fighters on the internal battlefront.

Perhaps in the fullness of time the growing of marijuana plants, the "manipulation" of financial markets, the sale of pornographic magazines, the bribery of foreign government officials, the facilitation of suicide by the terminally ill, and the violation of arcane regulations governing the financing of political campaigns will come to seem objects of criminal punishment not much more appropriate than "dishonoring the race." Müller's book can help us see that judges on the one hand should not be eager enlisters in popular movements, but on the other hand should not allow themselves to become so immersed in a professional culture that they are oblivious to the human consequences of their decisions, and in addition should be wary of embracing totalizing visions that like Gradgrind's Benthamism in *Hard Times* reduce individual human beings to numbers or objects—and not with the innocent purpose of facilitating academic analysis. Müller's book contains no suggestions for avoiding these dangers but can help us understand why most of our judges treat criminal defendants, even after conviction, with a rather elaborate show of courtesy and why the criminal justice system tries to make capital punishment, even of the worst monsters, a dignified and even humane procedure. German judges had an "us versus them" mentality. Violators of laws were not errant members of the community; they were "the enemy within"—the equivalent of a fifth column or an infestation. To exclude a person from the community (as in the slavery and genocide games), whether the national community or the human community, is to make him an outlaw to whom no consideration is due. And therefore to enable a person or other creature (an animal, for example, or a human fetus) to be mistreated with a good conscience, the person or creature is first excluded from the relevant community. So a society that wants to permit infanticide may decide that a child does not become a human being until it is some number of months or years old.[20]

Yet in Raul Hilberg's analysis of the psychology of the Germans who participated in the implementation of the Final Solution, the casting of the Jews as a subhuman species plays a relatively modest role, as only one of a number of beliefs by which these Germans rationalized their participation. Other beliefs or feelings were that they were doing their

20. See *Sex and Reason* 289.

duty (so here positivism rears its head, after all), that they were not obtaining any personal benefit, that they had no personal animus against Jews, that their refusing to participate would make no difference, that they regretted what they were doing, that it was fate, that they had drawn a line across which they would not step (for example, they would transport Jews, but not participate in the actual killing; or they would kill foreign Jews but not German Jews, or unbaptized Jews but not baptized Jews).[21] Not only is the capacity to rationalize unlimited, but there is no reliable technique for expanding the community, for enlarging human sympathies; nor would it make any sense to try to expand the bounds of community indefinitely. Imagination is not a panacea for xenophobia, since imagination can magnify fears as much as sympathies; and expanding the community of concern may hurt the members of the narrower community, as when animal-rights advocates prevent animal experiments that may help human beings. Still, one of the extraordinary features of the Nazi regime was the narrowing of the national and human communities by extruding groups previously considered to be part of both, and against *that* at least we should be warned. The opponents of abortion contend that we have not heeded the warning, and they might point out that the German Constitutional Court, more mindful of the dangers involved in expelling members of the community, has refused to recognize a general right of abortion— to which the defenders of abortion rights might reply that the attitudes of the German court are the product of a particular national experience and that there is more to be said for protecting Jews than for protecting fetuses. As debate moves to particular issues the disquieting implications of *Hitler's Justice* recede, but they remain visible in the distance, an ominous reminder of the precariousness of civilization and the fragility of a legal culture.

Executive Detention in Wartime Britain

I have suggested that the difference in character between our judges and those of the Third Reich is the difference between the United States and the Third Reich, not the difference between Anglo-American and German judges. For support, and also to enable a further exami-

---

21. Raul Hilberg, *The Destruction of the European Jews*, vol. 3, pp. 993–1029 (rev. ed. 1985).

nation of the criticisms of legal pragmatism suggested by Müller's book, I turn to the study by the English legal historian Brian Simpson of Britain's program of executive detention during World War II.[22]

The legal vehicle for the program was a regulation (Regulation 18B) promulgated by the Cabinet pursuant to an emergency defense bill passed by Parliament a week before Germany invaded Poland. A similar regulation had been in force in World War I, when the Home Secretary had argued successfully against drawing a strict line between German aliens and naturalized British citizens born in Germany, between naturalized British citizens born in Germany and native-born British citizens of German descent, and, finally, between British citizens of German origin and British citizens of whatever origin who had "hostile associations" (p. 13): they were all dangerous, and should be subject to detention without trial. About this eminently pragmatic approach Simpson comments: "Nobody seriously committed to the rule of law could possibly accept [this] argument. Law is just in the business of drawing firm lines of demarcation—between mine and thine, between guilt and innocence, between citizens and non-citizens" (pp. 13–14).

Regulation 18B authorized the Home Secretary to detain any person if there was "reasonable cause to believe" him "of hostile origin or associations or to have been recently concerned in acts prejudicial to the public safety or the defence of the realm or in the preparation or instigation of such acts."[23] The person detained was entitled to lodge objections with an advisory committee appointed by the Home Office. The chairman of the committee was "to inform the objector of the grounds on which the order [of detention, or some lesser restriction, such as house arrest or confinement to a particular locality] has been made and to furnish him with such particulars as are in the opinion of the chairman sufficient to enable him to present his case." After hearing the objector's case, the advisory committee would advise the Home Secretary whether to continue or lift the detention order. No right of judicial review was specified.

Of the total of 1,847 detention orders executed, 1,145 were against "straightforwardly British citizens" (p. 223) as distinct from aliens, persons who had been born in nations with which Britain was at war, and persons of uncertain nationality. The vast majority of orders were

22. A. W. Brian Simpson, *In the Highest Degree Odious: Detention without Trial in Wartime Britain* (1992).
23. The regulation is reprinted in id. at 424–425.

issued in May, June, and July of 1940, the nadir of Britain's fortunes in the war; the peak month was June, when 826 orders were issued, although not all were executed. The names of persons to be detained were supplied to the Home Office by the Security Service, more commonly known (to this day) as "MI5" because it had once been a branch of military intelligence. The Security Service's recommendation was reviewed, though often perfunctorily, by the Home Secretary, and if it was approved the person to be detained was immediately arrested, without any warning, and imprisoned. If a detainee filed an objection he would be given a hearing, though often not for several months, before one of the advisory committees. The objector could seek the advice of a lawyer, but the lawyer was not permitted at the hearing. The advisory committees were composed of distinguished private citizens; the chairmen were lawyers. The hearing would often lead the Home Secretary to recommend the release of the detainee; the recommendations, though often opposed by the Security Service, were generally followed. Most detainees were released after some months; very few were held to the end of the war. Some challenged their detention in court, mainly by habeas corpus proceedings, but they were uniformly unsuccessful.

The largest group of citizen detainees were members or ex-members of the British Union of Fascists, headed by Sir Oswald Mosley (he and his wife were among the detainees), or of other pro-Nazi or fascistic associations. Among the persons detained were a Member of Parliament, a retired admiral, and a peer. The Security Service believed that the people it wanted detained represented a potential Fifth Column which would erode the British will to fight and, in the event of a German invasion, assist the German army. In retrospect it is plain that the Security Service greatly exaggerated the danger of Fifth Column activities in Britain. The potential Fifth Columnists were few and the vast majority of them were harmless cranks, like the veterinarian who after his release wrote an autobiography that he entitled *Out of Step: Events in the Two Lives of an Anti-Jewish Camel Doctor.* Even the leaders and hard core members of the BU were, with only a few exceptions, loyal to their country, though prone to admire Germany and to criticize Britain for having entered the war on the side of France and Poland. The Security Service's mistake was soon evident even to it, and the failure to rescind Regulation 18B after the summer of 1940 was largely a sop to the Labour Party, which was fiercely hostile to the BU.

Churchill was an early skeptic about the existence of a Fifth Column in Britain. It was he who later in the war described executive detention as "in the highest degree odious" and "the foundation of all totalitarian government whether Nazi or Communist" (p. 391).

The number of detentions, in a nation of 47 million people engaged in a desperate struggle for survival, was small, the detentions mostly brief, and the exaggeration of the Fifth Column danger understandable—for it was an article of faith at the time that the collapse of most of Germany's enemies like ninepins had been due to the "enemy within." Indeed the Germans themselves, who as we saw in the first part of this chapter were preoccupied with their own "enemy within," attributed their sudden collapse in the fall of 1918 to such machinations, and the term "Fifth Column" had originated in the recently concluded Spanish Civil War, in which Franco had credited it as a factor in his victory. In far more perilous circumstances than faced the United States after Pearl Harbor, the British responded to the danger of the "enemy within" with greater restraint than our government did when it decided to intern U.S. citizens of Japanese origin living on the West Coast.[24]

Simpson was a child during World War II, but an old enough one to retain in adulthood vivid memories. So it is a tribute to his detachment that he is so critical of Britain's program of wartime detention. And critical he is. He concentrates on three institutions involved in the program: the Security Service, the Home Office, and the courts. The key to his assessment of the Security Service is his statement that "intelligence organizations attract peculiar and unreliable people" (p. 92),[25] at least in time of peace. The Security Service had been a backwater between the world wars and thus was not adequately staffed at the outset of the second war to perform the duties heaped on it, including enforcement of Regulation 18B. It was "engaged in the pursuit of phantoms" (p. 92). But then "those who believe in the enemy in our midst," as the Security Service was naturally disposed to do, "have minds insulated against evidence; its absence proves the

24. This and other wartime suspensions of civil liberties in the United States are discussed in J. Gregory Sidak, "War, Liberty, and Enemy Aliens," 67 *New York University Law Review* 1402 (1992).

25. Such as Harold Kurtz, later "employed to record the dying words of the Nazi war criminals incompetently hanged by the American executioner, an assignment which did not improve his drink habit" (p. 368).

extreme skill of the enemy" (p. 108). "The mechanisms which insulate [security services] from public accountability contribute to their unreliability" (pp. 410–411).

The Home Office comes off better in Simpson's account. (The Security Service was not part of the Home Office; apparently it reported directly to the Cabinet.) "In general Home Office officials seem to have genuinely respected legality, though there was a willingness to stretch things and break the rules when it seemed in the public interest to do so" (p. 415). Simpson's major criticism is that the civil servants of the Home Office were implacably hostile to open government and judicial review. But he is also critical of the sudden arrests, which were made by officers of the Special Branch of Scotland Yard, a part of the Home Office, and of the conditions in the prisons (also run by the Home Office) in which the detainees were held. "An arrest was rather like a heart attack, or indeed a visit from the Gestapo, in its immediate social consequences" (p. 87). No provision had been made for informing relatives that a person had been detained or where he was being taken. Although detained persons, not having been charged with or convicted of any crime, were supposed to be treated with consideration, in fact they were treated much like ordinary prison inmates, at least in the period of mass detentions. Mothers were sometimes separated from young children. The medical needs of detainees were not always properly attended to. Simpson attributes "the apparent inhumanity" of the detentions to the callousness of Home Office officials: "A great deal of what the Home Office did, or still does, is intrinsically very unpleasant . . . A certain detachment is needed to preside over such things . . . Civil Servants deal with files, not people" (p. 415).

The legal profession fares very badly in Simpson's account. "The courts did virtually nothing for the detainees, either to secure their liberty, to preserve what rights they did possess under the regulation, to scrutinize the legality of Home Office action, or to provide compensation when matters went wrong. The legal profession too, as a profession, did nothing; I am told that it was not easy to persuade lawyers to act for detainees at all" (pp. 418–419). The basic judicial position was that so long as the Home Office had acted on the basis of reasonable suspicion that the detainee fell under one of the criteria of the regulation, his detention was legal. Since, however, the courts did not require the Home Office to submit the evidence on which its suspicion was based, the judges could not determine whether the suspicion was reasonable and were therefore helpless to give detention orders meaningful review. The evidence consisted mainly of files of the Security Service. The files were secret, but the judges could have examined them *in camera*. They did not. They intoned "the traditional judicial humbug on the liberty of the subject" (p. 364) but were content to accept "the Home Office affidavit [that reasonable grounds for the order existed] as conclusive so long as no formal irregularities appeared" (p. 328). One judge did dissent from the denial of a habeas corpus, saying that "judges should not be 'mice squeaking under a chair in the Home Office'" (p. 328), but he deleted this memorable phrase from his published opinion. Anyway "his concern was not so much with civil liberty as with judicial status" (p. 329). "The only circumstance capable of galvanizing the judges into action was blatant lack of respect for their status . . . The judges were prepared to behave like mice, so long as they were treated like lions" (p. 331).

I have no basis for quarreling with Simpson's specific criticisms. But I think his overall verdict on the wartime detention program is too severe—and unpragmatic. The severity is evident from the passages I have quoted, but it comes out even more clearly in the summary assessments sprinkled throughout the book. According to Simpson, the role appointed to law in the scheme that became Regulation 18B was to be "the instrument with which the rule of law was to be abolished, to be replaced by executive discretion, exercised by gentlemen, in secret, in pursuance of the public interest" (p. 44). "The legal regime under which Britain fought the war was that of a totalitarian state" (p. 46). "Britain had, within a very few weeks, become, in the name of liberty, a totalitarian state" (p. 190). "During the war Britain was not, in any real sense, a democratic state" (p. 282).

There are several reasons for the severity of Simpson's assessment. One is an uncritical use of the terms "democracy" and "totalitarian." Implicitly for him these are the only possible forms of government, so that anything that is not one is the other and in particular anything that does not conform to a particular conception of democratic government is totalitarian. This binary classification obscures important distinctions. That for a short period during the war Britain in effect suspended habeas corpus does not equate to the wholesale extinction of liberty, legality, and democracy by Nazi Germany and the Soviet Union in war and peace alike. We should not forget that the British electorate threw out Churchill and the Conservative Party before the

war ended—an unthinkable dénouement in a totalitarian state. The
United States did not cease to be a democracy in 1942, even though
it interned thousands of its citizens on flimsy grounds.

To say that democracy is suspended when executive detention is
permitted is to miss the tension that I noted in the Introduction
between legality and democracy. As Simpson acknowledges, there was
no popular pressure to abrogate Rule 18B even when the emergency
had passed. Fascists and fascist sympathizers were, unsurprisingly, intensely unpopular; the British people were *happy* to see them detained;
the popular will was fulfilled rather than thwarted by this "undemocratic" regulation. It is true that even popular measures for the repression of the politically unpopular can undermine democracy; plebiscitary
democracy, even Athenian democracy (which was notably lacking in
legal protection of rights), is not the best form of democracy. But it is
a little much to pronounce a regime *totalitarian* merely because it does
not adequately *limit* democratic preference. Liberal democracy is a
means, not an end, and one of the ends to which it is a means is
national survival in the face of a totalitarian nation bent on conquest.[26]
It is no more "totalitarian" for a liberal democracy to suspend some
civil liberties in wartime than it is for army officers in a liberal democracy to be appointed rather than elected.

Another source of Simpson's negative assessment of Britain's wartime detentions is an unwillingness to accept people and institutions
for what they are. It is a fact and a readily understandable one that an
intelligence service would attract peculiar and unreliable people in
peacetime and thus be inadequately prepared for the strains of war. It
is a fact and again a readily understandable one that civil servants resent
political and judicial interference with their work, and that police and
prison work attracts people less delicate than professors and that the
work itself makes them more callous; as Hamlet put it, "the hand of
little employment hath the daintier sense." It is also a fact that judges
care about their status and are reluctant to check the executive in
matters of national security. Our vaunted independent judiciary upheld
the Japanese relocation, upheld the constitutionality of the Smith Act
until the wind had gone out of the Act's sails, and has devised ingenious
doctrines for minimizing judicial intervention in military and foreign

---

26. Compare Justice Jackson's warning, in his dissent in Terminiello v. City of Chicago,
337 U.S. 1, 37 (1949), against turning the Bill of Rights into a suicide pact.

policy. People being what they are, with their human failings and professional deformations, it is not to be expected that the administration of a program of executive detention in wartime will be a model of efficiency and rectitude. The question is whether the program, given the inevitable abuses, is on balance worthwhile. If it is, the abuses are still worth pointing out but they do not condemn the program.

The absence of a comparative dimension is a closely related source of Simpson's disparagement of his country's response to national emergency. Peacetime civil liberties are a luxury that nations engaged in wars of survival believe, not unreasonably, that they cannot afford. Even if the German judges' extravagant conception of *raison d'état* is rejected, as it should be, the realistic question for the civil libertarian to ask is not whether Britain curtailed civil liberties more than either seemed at the time or was in retrospect necessary but whether it reacted more or less temperately than other nations in comparable circumstances would do or had done. So far as I can judge, the answer is more temperately[27]—than the United States, for example, which was far less endangered. Of course there are risks in using a purely relative standard; it is unpragmatic to assume that we can never improve on existing practices. The administration of Regulation 18B caused many hardships and in hindsight at least seems not to have contributed materially to Britain's survival or to have shortened the war. If there are lessons in this experience that might enable Britain or the United States to deal more effectively with the problem of internal security in wartime the next time the problem arises, we should try to draw them. The only lesson Simpson draws, however, is that Britain should not have destroyed "about 99 per cent of public records dealing with detention, which is in line with general practice" (p. 422), and should not be refusing access, half a century later, to most of the rest. I am sure that this is right, but it makes an anticlimactic ending to the book. Can it be that the British government's greatest sin with respect to the wartime detention program was to make it difficult for academics to write the program's history?

I am not sure how many of these points Simpson would reject, because his book displays considerable ambivalence about Regulation 18B. He notes official fears before World War II "that the horror of the trenches had produced a state of affairs, symbolized by the cele-

27. Simpson does remark this (p. 413), but he quickly drops the point.

brated King and Country motion in the Oxford Union in 1933, in which it might be extremely difficult for the government to conduct war at all" (p. 46). He acknowledges "the widespread"—although, again, erroneous—"belief that Norway's collapse was brought about by 'Quislings'" (pp. 98–99). He acknowledges that the British Union of Fascists "was pro-German and undermined morale, and might get up to mischief" (p. 167), and that in fact "a British Fifth column, that is a number of individuals who were, with some element of organization, clandestinely assisting the enemy, actually existed" (p. 171). While regarding "the acceptance by the [House of] Commons of the detention of one of its own members in conditions of complete secrecy" as "quite bizarre in a liberal democracy," Simpson acknowledges that "the times were desperate" (p. 282). And "common sense would also suggest that detentions under 18B may have in some instances prevented individuals with pro-German sympathies from attempted acts of espionage or sabotage, and been useful in contributing to the control of the IRA or in preventing leakage of information about the Normandy landings" (p. 412). Regulation 18B may even "have saved some individuals from violence, from long prison terms, or even from death sentences," since it provided a relatively mild way of dealing with people who were hated and thought dangerous (p. 422).[28] And the judges "may have been right in conceiving the conflict [between them and the Home Office] in terms of status: not so much their personal status, but that of the institution to which they belonged."

Most important, the Cabinet had been advised in May 1940 that Britain could fight even if France fell "so long as British morale held . . . A consequential recommendation was ruthless action against the Fifth Column" (p. 185). This "special sort of political necessity—to exhibit a ruthless determination to continue the war against Germany at whatever cost" (p. 412) furnishes the strongest justification of Regulation 18B. As for those who "view executive detention as simply wrong in principle . . . it is perhaps worth remembering that any absolute objection to detention without trial runs into problems unless it also excludes the pre-trial detention of persons accused of crimes, and the detention of the mentally ill, or at least explains why these practices may nevertheless be justifiable" (p. 413). Despite Simpson's claim that

28. A little like the German prison sentences that saved some people, for a time anyway, from the Gestapo.

no one committed to the rule of law could accept the kind of redrawing of the traditional legal bright lines that was brought about by Regulation 18B, ultimately he rests his doubts about the need for the regulation on "pragmatic scepticism" (id.).

Simpson's ambivalence enables readers to form their own judgment. If, as he implies, the right test is a pragmatic one, my judgment is that the British government was right (ex ante, not ex post—ex post we can be fairly sure that the program was a mistake) to promulgate and enforce Regulation 18B, and that the mistakes and injustices and suffering that resulted were no more than were inevitable given the nature of the program and the human and institutional resources available for its administration. No doubt at some level of generality the pragmatic justifications for Regulation 18B and the pragmatic justifications for Nazi jurisprudence merge, as Simpson's broad use of "totalitarian" invites us to consider. But at too high a level. Pragmatism demands closer engagement with the facts. The facts justify the British program; they condemn the German one.

PART TWO

Constitutional Theory

chapter 5

Legal Reasoning from the Top Down and from the Bottom Up

THE five chapters in this part of the book examine a stellar array of contemporary constitutional theorists. The common preoccupation of these theorists, as of most constitutional theorists today, is with the soundness or legitimacy of a relative handful of famous Supreme Court decisions concerning individual rights. That constitutional theory should have so confined, and so relentlessly normative, a focus is not inevitable even if we ignore the fact that the Constitution does much more than confer rights; it also defines the respective powers of the different branches of government. It would be good if students of the Constitution paid more attention to the positive aspects of their subject—in particular the causes and consequences of constitutional rights, duties, powers, and structure.[1] But that is not to the point here. I mean to take the theorists on their own terms and show that their constitutional theories are no more satisfactory than that of Herbert Wechsler, examined in Chapter 1. The reasons include the inadequacy of conven-

---

1. Richard A. Posner, "The Constitution as an Economic Document," 56 *George Washington Law Review* 4 (1987). For a good example of the positive literature on constitutionalism, see Donald J. Boudreaux and A. C. Pritchard, "Rewriting the Constitution: An Economic Analysis of the Constitutional Amendment Process," 62 *Fordham Law Review* 111 (1993), discussed in Chapter 7.

tional legal reasoning, which pervades constitutional theorizing however unconventional the theorist's pose, and of the methods of analytic philosophy, which conventional legal reasoning resembles; the under-specialization of constitutional theorists; and, related to both points, the weak sense of fact that is so marked a characteristic of legal scholarship in general. However politically advanced these theorists, the dead hand of the professional cartel retains a strong grip on their thinking.

Two Styles of Legal Reasoning

The dominant style of modern constitutional theorizing is what I call reasoning from the "top down." I shall illustrate it mainly with Ronald Dworkin's arguments for abortion rights,[2] contrast it with "bottom-up" reasoning, and reject both types in favor of the pragmatic approach.

In reasoning from the top down, the judge or other legal analyst invents or adopts a theory about an area of law—perhaps about all law—and uses it to organize, criticize, accept or reject, explain or explain away, distinguish or amplify the decided cases to make them conform to the theory and generate an outcome in each new case as it arises that will be consistent with the theory and with the cases accepted as authoritative within the theory. The theory need not be, perhaps never can be, drawn "from" law; it surely need not be articulated in lawyers' jargon.

In bottom-up reasoning, which includes such familiar lawyers' techniques as "reasoning by analogy" and interpretation according to "plain meaning," one starts with the words of a statute or other enactment, or with a case or a mass of cases, and moves from there—but one doesn't move far. The top-downer and the bottom-upper do not meet.

I am associated with several top-down theories. One, which is primarily positive (descriptive), is that the common law is best understood on the "as if" assumption that judges try to maximize the wealth of

2. Dworkin, "Unenumerated Rights: Whether and How *Roe* Should Be Overruled," 59 *University of Chicago Law Review* 381 (1992); Dworkin, *Life's Dominion: An Argument about Abortion, Euthanasia, and Individual Freedom,* chs. 1–6 (1993). We now know (especially with the replacement on the Supreme Court of Justice White, one of the *Roe* dissenters, by Judge Ginsburg) that *Roe v. Wade,* insofar as it holds that the Constitution forbids government to prohibit adult women from having abortions early in pregnancy, will not be overruled in the foreseeable future. Planned Parenthood v. Casey, 112 S. Ct. 2791 (1992). But that does not affect the theoretical issues raised by Dworkin's analysis.

society. Another, primarily normative, is that judges should interpret the antitrust statutes to make them conform to the dictates of wealth maximization. In the development of the latter theory, Robert Bork—Ronald Dworkin's *bête noire*[3]—was a pioneer. Bork called his theory "maximization of consumer welfare,"[4] but that is just a reassuring term for wealth maximization. He divided the Supreme Court's antitrust cases into a main tradition informed by the principles of wealth maximization and a deviant branch of that tradition, and he argued for lopping off the branch.[5]

Dworkin himself is prominently associated with a theory of constitutional law that makes such law the expression of liberal, which for him entails egalitarian, principles. Richard Epstein has a broadly similar view of constitutional law, but he weights his liberalism not with egalitarianism but with economic freedom. John Hart Ely has a different but equally ambitious theory of constitutional law, one that yokes the various clauses together to draw the plow called promoting the values of a representative democracy. Bruce Ackerman has still another, and Bork himself another, though it might better be described as an anti-theory. (Bork's, Ackerman's, and Ely's constitutional theories are the subject of subsequent chapters.) A famous common-law top-downer from an earlier generation was Christopher Columbus Langdell, for whom leading cases were portals through which the pure concepts of law could be discerned by the discerning.[6] And before him Hobbes.

Yet legal reasoning from the bottom up is the more familiar, even the more hallowed, type.[7] The endlessly repeated refrain of modern judicial opinions that in interpreting a statute the judge must start with its words is in this tradition. And we lawyers all remember our first day in law school, when we were asked to read for each course not an overview or theoretical treatment of the field but a case—a case, more-

---

3. See the following articles by Dworkin: "Reagan's Justice," *New York Review of Books,* Nov. 8, 1984, p. 27; "The Bork Nomination," *New York Review of Books,* Aug. 13, 1987, p. 3, reprinted in 9 *Cardozo Law Review* 101 (1987); "From Bork to Kennedy," *New York Review of Books,* Dec. 17, 1987, p. 36; "Bork's Jurisprudence," 57 *University of Chicago Law Review* 657 (1990).

4. Robert H. Bork, *The Antitrust Paradox: A Policy at War with Itself* 7 (1978).

5. Bork, "The Rule of Reason and the Per Se Concept: Price Fixing and Market Division (Part I)," 74 *Yale Law Journal* 775 (1965); Bork, "The Rule of Reason and the Per Se Concept: Price Fixing and Market Division (Part II)," 75 *Yale Law Journal* 373 (1966).

6. Cf. Thomas C. Grey, "Langdell's Orthodoxy," 45 *University of Pittsburgh Law Review* 1, 16–20 (1983).

7. The classic statement is Edward H. Levi, *An Introduction to Legal Reasoning* (1949).

over, lying in the middle rather than at the historical or logical beginning of the field. Those of us who are appellate judges also remember
our first day in that job, when we were handed a sheaf of briefs in cases
from fields we may have known nothing about and told that in a few
days we would be hearing oral argument and would then take our
tentative vote.

There is a question whether legal reasoning from the bottom up
amounts to much. Dworkin thinks not. His extensive writings evince
little interest in the words of the Constitution, or in its structure (that
is, in how its various parts—the articles, sections, clauses, and amendments—work together), in the texture and details of the complex
statutes that his works discuss, such as Title VII of the Civil Rights Act
of 1964, or in any extended body of case law. His implicit legal universe
consists of a handful of general principles embodied in a handful of
exemplary, often rather bodiless, cases. He contrasts a constitution of
"principle" with one of "detail" and leaves no doubt that he prefers
the former. He goes so far as to say that he wants and we have
"government not by men and women, or even under law, but government under principle"—principle fashioned by the Supreme Court in
the name of the Constitution.[8]

I do not myself see the law in quite that way, but I agree there isn't
much to bottom-up reasoning. We don't ever "start" from a mass of
cases or from a statute or from a clause of the Constitution. To read a
case, to read a statute, a rule, or a constitutional clause presupposes a
vast linguistic, cultural, and conceptual apparatus. And more: One
doesn't see judicial opinions that say, for example, "On page 532 of
Title 29 of the U.S. Code appears the following sentence . . ." The
opinion invariably gives the name of the statute ("The Sherman Act
provides . . ." or "ERISA provides . . .") and immediately the reader
is primed to react to the words in a particular way. And if, as is so
common, the case or statute or other enactment is unclear, and maybe
even when it seems quite clear, the reader, to extract or more precisely
to impute its meaning, must *interpret* it; and interpretation is as much
creation as discovery.[9]

Nor is it clear what it means to reason "from" one case to another,
the heart of bottom-up reasoning in law. It sounds like induction,

8. *Life's Dominion*, note 2 above, at 124.
9. See *The Problems of Jurisprudence*, chs. 9–10; and Chapter 19 of the present book.

which from Hume to Popper has taken hard knocks from philosophers. Most so-called reasoning by analogy in law is actually an oblique form of logical reasoning. Cases are used as sources of interesting facts and ideas, and hence as materials for the creation of a theory that can be applied deductively to a new case. But not (one hopes) as the *exclusive* materials for the creation of the theory. That would unjustifiably exclude whole worlds of other learning and insight.

Reasoning by analogy also has an empirical function. If case A is canonical within your theory, and along comes B, and the theory implies that the outcome of B should be different from A, you had better be sure that the two outcomes are logically consistent; otherwise you have a problem with the theory. So cases accepted within a theory provide testing instances for its further application. But there must be a theory. One cannot just go from case to case, not responsibly anyway. One cannot say: I have no theory of privacy or due process or anything else, but, given *Griswold, Roe* follows. One has to be able to say what in *Griswold* dictates *Roe*. *Griswold* does not tell one how broadly or narrowly to read *Griswold*.[10]

Unenumerated Constitutional Rights, with Special Reference to Abortion

No right to an abortion, or right of privacy, is stated in the Constitution. These are unenumerated constitutional rights. Their scope and legitimacy are at the forefront of modern constitutional controversy— and look different when they are approached from the bottom up rather than from the top down.

If we are top-downers, we would proceed as have Dworkin, Epstein, Ely, and many others. We would create from a variety of sources—the text, history, and background of the Constitution (with the text given no particular primacy, because people who are sophisticated about interpretation know that text does not come first in any illuminating sense), the decisions interpreting the Constitution, and sundry political, moral, and institutional values and insights—a comprehensive theory of the rights that the Constitution should be deemed to recognize. Armed with such a theory, we would select a main tradition of cases and discard or downplay the outliers, and we would decide new cases

10. For a fuller discussion of reasoning by analogy, see Chapter 24.

in a way that would be consistent both with the theory and with the (duly pruned) precedents.

Were I to attempt such a project I might come out closer to Dworkin than many would expect who are not familiar with the full range of my judicial and academic writings. Although I weight economic freedom more and equality less than Dworkin and would be more inclined than he to give the states and the nonjudicial branches of government generous room for experimentation, the practical differences between us might be small, especially in regard to personal rights, such as freedom of speech, religious freedom, and sexual and reproductive liberty. And then indeed, as Dworkin contends, the right to use contraceptives and the right to burn the American flag (provided you own the flag you burn), a right affirmed by many scholars and judges, such as Justice Scalia, who believe that *Roe v. Wade* was decided incorrectly, would be seen to stand on the same plane as far as the distinction between enumerated and unenumerated rights is concerned.[11] For the distinction has no significance to a comprehensive constitutional theory. Such a theory may use the text as one of its jumping-off points, but it goes beyond and eventually submerges textual distinctions because specific constitutional rights such as the right to burn the flag or to use contraceptives come out of the theory rather than (directly) out of the text.

The situation is different if one follows a bottom-up approach. For then one will start by paging through the Constitution and one will find nothing that seems related to contraception, sex, reproduction, or the family. One will find no mention of the flag either but one will find a reference to freedom of speech, and it is easy to move analogically from literal speech to flag-burning, as in the following interior Socratic dialogue:

"I see nothing here about flags or about the use of fire. Speech is verbal. Flag-burning is not a verbal act."

"Well, to begin with, must speech be oral? Sign language is speech— doesn't this show that speech is more than words, that it includes gestures? And what about communication with semaphores? Semaphores *are* flags, as a matter of fact."

---

11. The Supreme Court has held that statutes which forbid flag-burning violate the First Amendment. Texas v. Johnson, 491 U.S. 397 (1989); United States v. Eichman, 496 U.S. 310 (1990).

"Sign language and semaphores are alternative methods to spoken language for encoding words—as is Morse code, or writing itself. Fire is not."

"But what about the chain of fires that in Aeschylus's *Agamemnon* is used to signal the fall of Troy to Clytemnestra hundreds of miles away?"

"That's not *quite* speech, because the fires do not encode a particular form of words, although they do communicate a simple message."

"But is not the essence of constitutionally protected speech the communication of a message?"

"Yes."

"So wouldn't the signal fires be protected speech (provided there were no safety concerns, etc.)?"

"I suppose so."

"Doesn't flag-burning, when employed as an element of a protest or a demonstration rather than as a method of discarding a piece of worn-out cloth or starting a (literal) conflagration, communicate a message?"

"Perhaps so, but it involves the destruction of property, and that's different."

"People are allowed to destroy their own property, aren't they? And flag-burning for demonstrative purposes is not even wanton destruction. In fact, it's consumption—it's like the destruction of a forest to produce the *Sunday New York Times*."

This method of "proof," though irresistible to most lawyers because it enables them to reach conclusions without reading much beyond what is in law books, is spurious. It shows that there is a sense of "speech" that embraces flag-burning—just as there is a sense of the word that embraces a right of association and a right not to be forced to express support for a cause one disfavors.[12] But it supplies no reason for preferring that sense to a narrower one. One must range wider and consider the differences, not just the similarities, between burning a flag and engaging in the other forms of communication that the courts have held or would surely hold to be constitutionally protected. One must, in fact, develop or adopt a theory of free speech and then apply

12. See NAACP v. Alabama, 357 U.S. 449, 460 (1958); West Virginia State Board of Education v. Barnette, 319 U.S. 624, 633 (1943).

it to the case at hand. The development of such a theory was Bork's project in an article that he later retracted in part.[13]

Yet even if bottom-up reasoning is not reasoning but is at best preparatory to reasoning, and even if legal reasoning worthy of the name inescapably involves the creation of theories to guide decision, we have still to consider the appropriate scope of such theories. Must they embrace entire fields of law, such as federal constitutional law or the common law? Must they, perhaps, embrace all of law? Or can they be limited to narrower slices of legal experience, such as particular clauses of the Constitution, or particular statutes, or clusters of related statutes? Can they be so confined even if the result is a set of theories that are not consistent with one another, so that different clauses of a statute or the Constitution will sometimes pull in different directions?

Dworkin answers "no" to the last two questions. An interpretation of individual clauses that fails to achieve consistency of principle across clauses is illegitimate. A theory of constitutional law must take in the whole Constitution, or at least the whole of the Bill of Rights plus the Fourteenth Amendment—must to that extent be coherent, holistic. "The Supreme Court has a duty to find some conception of protected liberties, some statement defining which freedoms must be preserved, that is defensible both as a political principle and as consistent with the general form of government established by the Constitution."[14] Dworkin's basic criticism of Bork is that Bork has no constitutional philosophy.[15] But as Dworkin well knows, Bork has a notable theory of free speech, and a notable theory of antitrust as well.[16] And these are

13. Robert H. Bork, "Neutral Principles and Some First Amendment Problems," 47 *Indiana Law Journal* 1 (1971). See "Nomination of Robert H. Bork to Be Associate Justice of the Supreme Court of the United States: Hearings before the Senate Committee on the Judiciary," 100th Cong., 1st sess., pt. 1, 268–271 (1989).

14. Dworkin, "Reagan's Justice," note 3 above, at 30. Alternatively, "the system of [constitutional] rights must be interpreted, so far as possible, as expressing a coherent vision of justice." Dworkin, *Law's Empire* 368 (1986). The qualification "so far as possible" enables Dworkin to make room for some pragmatic compromises. See, for example, id. at 380–381.

15. "I am interested . . . in a different issue: not whether Bork has a persuasive or plausible constitutional philosophy, but whether he has any constitutional philosophy at all." Dworkin, "The Bork Nomination," note 3 above, at 3. Bork's "constitutional philosophy is empty: not just impoverished and unattractive but no philosophy at all . . . He believes he has no responsibility to treat the Constitution as an integrated structure of moral and political principles . . . He has no theory at all, no conservative jurisprudence, but only right-wing dogma to guide his decisions." Id. at 10.

16. Bork's article on free speech began: "A persistently disturbing aspect of constitutional law is its lack of theory." Bork, note 13 above, at 1.

very much top-down theories. Bork does not go case to case. He derives an overarching principle which he then applies to the cases, discarding many. But his theories are tied to specific provisions; they lack the political and moral generality and ambition that Dworkin prizes. Bork's only *general* theory of constitutional law is, as we shall see in Chapter 9, that there are no general theories of constitutional law.

The question of the proper scope of a constitutional theory connects with another much discussed issue, what level of generality of the framers' intentions should guide judges in interpreting the Constitution. If you ask what the intention behind the equal protection clause was, you will find that it was both to benefit blacks in some ways but not others and to promote an ideal of equality that may be inconsistent with aspects of the framers' more specific intention, which was to entitle blacks to civil but not social equality with whites. The choice of which intention to honor determines for example whether the Supreme Court was correct to outlaw racial segregation in public schools. But it is a question about the level of generality of intention behind a single clause. To pass beyond that to intentions concerning the Constitution as a whole, a sheaf of documents written at different times and covering a variety of discrete topics—to suppose it possible to extract a single unifying intention or theme from the sheaf—is to enter cloud-cuckoo-land. This is not to disparage the holistic approach but to distinguish it from one that depends on the framers' intentions, whether broadly or narrowly construed. Yet it is a considerable demerit of the holistic approach, in the eyes of many legal professionals, that it cuts free from those intentions.

The issue of holistic versus clause-by-clause constitutional reasoning is not merely aesthetic or methodological. Despite the efforts that Dworkin makes to ground *Roe v. Wade* in a particular clause of the Constitution, he cannot have great confidence that the rights he especially cherishes can be generated by theories limited to individual clauses, such as the due process clause, *Roe*'s original home. The substantive construal of that clause stinks in the nostrils of modern liberals and modern conservatives alike, because of its association with Dred Scott's case[17] and with *Lochner* and the other freedom of contract cases, because of its formlessness, because of its being rather buried in

17. Scott v. Sandford, 60 U.S. (19 How.) 393 (1857).

the Fifth Amendment (making one wonder whether it can be all that important—though, granted, it is featured more prominently in the Fourteenth Amendment), and because it makes a poor match with the right to notice and hearing that is the procedural content of the clause. If we must go clause by clause in constructing our constitutional theory (actually theor*ies*, on this approach), we are conceding, Dworkin must believe, too much rhetorical ammunition to the enemies of sexual liberty.

Could the Ninth Amendment dissolve the tension between the clause-by-clause and holistic approaches? It is a chunk of the text, after all. It says, "The enumeration in the Constitution, of certain rights, shall not be construed to deny or disparage others retained by the people." Could this be a warrant for judges to recognize new rights, both against the federal government and against the states? The extensive literature on this question[18] has had little impact because, with rare exceptions, neither the clause-by-clausers nor the holists are happy with basing decisions on the Ninth Amendment. The amendment does not identify any of the retained rights, or specify a methodology for identifying them. If it gives the courts anything, it gives them a blank check.[19] Neither judges nor their academic critics and defenders want judicial review to operate *avowedly* free of any external criteria. Even "due process" and "equal protection" seem directive compared to the Ninth Amendment—or for that matter to "privileges and immunities," another constitutional orphan. So, not only is there not enough textual support for unenumerated constitutional rights; there is too much.

Roe v. Wade has been the Wandering Jew of constitutional law. It started life in the due process clause, but that made it a substantive due process case and invited a rain of arrows. Laurence Tribe first moved it to the establishment clause of the First Amendment, then recanted.[20] Dworkin now picks up the torch, but relies upon the free exercise and establishment clauses in combination.[21] Feminists, as we are about to

---

18. See, for example, *The Rights Retained by the People: The History and Meaning of the Ninth Amendment* (2 vols., Randy E. Barnett ed. 1989).

19. Alternatively, it just negates any inference that the failure of the framers of the Bill of Rights to specify additional rights signified their understanding that all other rights had been placed in the control of the federal government. Raoul Berger, "The Ninth Amendment," 66 *Cornell Law Review* 1 (1980).

20. Laurence H. Tribe, *American Constitutional Law* 1349–1350 and nn. 87–88 (2d ed. 1988).

21. *Life's Dominion*, note 2 above, at 165. The free exercise clause forbids government

see, have tried to squeeze *Roe v. Wade* into the equal protection clause. Others have tried to move it inside the Ninth Amendment (of course—but if I am right it has no inside); still others (including Tribe) inside the Thirteenth Amendment, which forbids involuntary servitude.[22] I await the day when someone shovels it into the takings clause, or the republican form of government clause (out of which an adventurous judge could excogitate the entire Bill of Rights and the Fourteenth Amendment), or the privileges and immunities clause of the Fourteenth Amendment. It is not, as Dworkin suggests, a matter of the more the merrier; it is a desperate search for an adequate textual home, and it has failed.

Consider the equal protection argument for abortion rights.[23] It begins by noting that a law forbidding abortions weighs more heavily on women than on men. Granted. But a difference in treatment does not violate the equal protection clause if it is justifiable, and this particular difference in treatment seems, at first glance anyway, justified by the fact that men and women are differently situated in relation to fetal life by virtue of their biology. To show that the difference is not substantially related to an important governmental interest, and is therefore unconstitutional under the prevailing standard for reviewing sex discrimination challenged under the Fourteenth Amendment, re-quires consideration of the social value or moral weight of fetal life. But that is an intractable inquiry, or at least one that the defenders of *Roe v. Wade* are reluctant to undertake.

They try to shut the door on the inquiry either by placing an unrealistic burden of justification on the state—an arbitrary tactic—or by arguing that, whatever justifications *might* be offered for laws for-bidding abortion, the support for those laws *in fact* comes from people

---

to interfere with religious freedom; the establishment clause forbids it to create an established church, but has been broadly interpreted to forbid most lesser forms of government assistance to religion as well.

22. Tribe, "The Abortion Funding Conundrum: Inalienable Rights, Affirmative Duties, and the Dilemma of Dependence," 99 *Harvard Law Review* 330, 337 (1985); Andrew Koppelman, "Forced Labor: A Thirteenth Amendment Defense of Abortion," 84 *Northwestern University Law Review* 480 (1990). Notice the pun in Koppelman's title. For more on the Thirteenth Amendment, see the next chapter.

23. See, for example, Catharine A. MacKinnon, "Reflections on Sex Equality under Law," 100 *Yale Law Journal* 1281, 1309–1328 (1991); Sylvia A. Law, "Rethinking Sex and the Constitution," 132 *University of Pennsylvania Law Review* 955 (1984); Cass R. Sunstein, "Neutrality in Constitutional Law (with Special Reference to Pornography, Abortion, and Surrogacy)," 92 *Columbia Law Review* 1, 29–44 (1992).

who want to keep women down; and an invidious purpose can condemn a law. Realistically, an invidious purpose can condemn only a marginal law, such as a law imposing a poll tax or requiring a literacy test for prospective voters. Judges are not going to deprive the community of essential legal protection just because some supporters of such laws (laws criminalizing rape, for example) had bad motives. The principal support for anti-abortion laws, moreover, comes not from misogynists or "macho" men (Don Juan would favor abortion on demand because it would reduce the cost of sex), but from men and, particularly, women who, whether or not Roman Catholic (many of them of course *are* Roman Catholic), believe that abortion is sacrilegious.[24] That is not a sexist or otherwise discriminatory or invidious belief, even though it is positively correlated with a belief in the traditional role of women, a role that feminists, with much support in history, consider subordinate. It is true that for many, perhaps most or even all, opponents of abortion, opposition to abortion is commingled with opposition to a broader set of practices and values—call it feminism.[25] But for many supporters, abortion on demand is the very symbol of feminism. Should the courts take sides in this clash of symbols?

Behind symbols, ideology, even religious belief may lurk concrete interests. The debate over abortion, and over the sexual and reproductive freedom of women more broadly, is in part a debate between women who lose and women who gain from that freedom.[26] The more reproductive autonomy and sexual freedom women have, the less interest men have in marriage, because secure paternity is one of the principal benefits of marriage for a man; men generally don't want to support or care for other men's children. Women who would prefer to specialize in household rather than market production are therefore harmed by sexual freedom, while women who prefer specializing in market production are helped by anything that gives them fuller control over their reproduction, though they too pay a price in reduced marital opportunities. The conflict between these two classes of women is a clash of interests, the sort of thing usually left to legislatures, as the registers of political muscle, to resolve. This conflict within the protected group helps to distinguish the issue of sex equality from that of

24. Kristin Luker, *Abortion and the Politics of Motherhood* 186 (1984).
25. See id. at 158–175, 214–215.
26. Cf. id. at 217.

racial equality, since few if any blacks are helped by denying blacks full equality, although I noted in Chapter 2 that affirmative action in law school faculty hiring might hurt culturally assimilated blacks.

Dworkin takes a different tack from the feminists. He considers a person's view of the sanctity of life a religious view even if the person is an atheist, and he says that the government cannot, without violating the free exercise clause, make a person act on one religious view rather than another. Dworkin realizes that some (I would have said most) women who have abortions do so not because they believe they have a sacred right to pursue their life plans without the impediment of an unwanted child, or a sacred duty to prevent an unwanted child from coming into the world, but because they value their own interests above those of their unborn child. Egoism is fine, but hardly sacral.[27] Nevertheless he argues that to deny the right of abortion to women who choose abortion for reasons that "cannot be traced to even submerged views about the sanctity of life" would put the government in the position of "commanding one essentially religious position over others," contrary to the establishment clause.[28]

The idea that a person's opinion about—including an opinion denying—the "sacredness" or "sanctity" of life is inherently religious confuses figurative with literal uses of religious terms. A person who says "Holy cow!" is not necessarily a votary of Hinduism. Anyone prepared to conceive of religion as broadly as Dworkin does should allow for a religion of free markets (economic freedom *is* a religion in Dworkin's sense to the likes of Murray Rothbard, Milton and David Friedman, Friedrich Hayek, and Ayn Rand), a religion of animal rights, of environmentalism, of art, and so on. Dworkin could then place every aborting mother under the free exercise clause by citing Nietzsche and Emerson for the proposition that self-assertion is a moral duty so profound as to deserve the status of a religious duty. An ordinance that forbade an aesthete to alter the exterior of his landmark house would be an infringement of religious freedom. The progressive income tax would be a sacrilege. The protection of endangered species would be an establishment of religion.

Dworkin tries to distinguish these cases by making the test for whether a belief is religious its "content." The test is applied to a

27. "The pro-choice world view is not centered around a Divine Being." Id. at 188.
28. *Life's Dominion,* note 2 above, at 165.

particular belief "by asking whether it is sufficiently similar in content to plainly religious beliefs."[29] The practical meaning of "religion," however, is belief in a supernatural being or beings, and once that is dropped as the touchstone the content of religious belief becomes infinitely various. Not only personal conduct but also art, animals, the nation, the race, and the environment are frequently endowed with religious significance in this extended sense. For the only things that distinguish religious from nonreligious beliefs once the theistic element is removed are the grounds on which and the intensity with which they are held. A woman's belief that she should be free to place her interests above those of her unborn child has less of a religious character than a belief—if deeply, unshakably held—that art constitutes an eternal order of beauty and meaning that has greater value than an individual human life, or an unshakable belief in utilitarianism, secular humanism, Marxism, or Social Darwinism. In all these examples belief takes the form of an unswerving commitment to some force or concept of metaphysical heft and urgency and cannot be dislodged by arguments or proofs. Some decisions to have an abortion have this character. A woman might consider it a sacrilege to have a child who would be born seriously deformed or whom she could not take care of adequately. But Dworkin does not propose to confine the right of abortion to such cases, and they are a minority. The most common reason that women who have had an abortion give for why they had it is concern "about how having a baby could change her [the mother's] life."[30]

The law defines religion much more narrowly than Dworkin does. The Internal Revenue Service will not grant a new religion the tax exemption for religious organizations unless the religion is—organized; that is, unless it has at least traces of conventional sectarian structure.[31] And the Supreme Court will not allow a nontheist conscientious objector to claim the exemption from military service for those whose religion forbids them to serve unless his system of ethical beliefs plays the same role in his life as conventional religious beliefs play in the lives of the conventionally religious.[32] There is no organized religion of

29. Id. at 155; see also id. at 163–165.

30. Aida Torres and Jacqueline Darroch Forrest, "Why Do Women Have Abortions?" 20 *Family Planning Perspectives* 169, 170 (1988) (tab. 1).

31. See 26 U.S.C. § 501(c)(3); Terry L. Slye, "Rendering unto Caesar: Defining 'Religion' for Purposes of Administering Religion-Based Tax Exemptions," 6 *Harvard Journal of Law and Public Policy* 219, 259–261 (1983).

32. United States v. Seeger, 380 U.S. 163 (1965).

abortion rights, and few women base their decision to have an abortion on a comprehensive ethical system.

Almost no one in our society thinks that religious beliefs, however fervidly held, justify or excuse violating the ordinary criminal laws. Dworkin is able to make abortion a matter of the varying opinions that Americans hold about the sanctity of life, rather than an issue of homicide, only because he will not allow states to define the fetus as a person and therefore abortion as murder. (If he did allow this, he would not be able to distinguish abortion from infanticide.) Yet the states are allowed to decide what is property and (in the case of prisoners for example) what is liberty, for purposes of the due process clause; why not what is a person? May not a state decide that death means brain death rather than a stopped heart? And if it may decide when life ends, why may it not decide when life begins? An Illinois statute makes abortion murder, and on the civil side wrongful death.[33] The supremacy clause of the Constitution prevents the application of the statute to abortions privileged by *Roe v. Wade,* but with that qualification (which in any event cannot be used to defend *Roe v. Wade*) the constitutionality of the statute cannot be doubted. It shows that the states are already in the business of defining human life. They can, thus, classify a fetus as a human being, and the question is then the strength of the state's interest in protecting that newly recognized human being against various menaces to it. Dworkin concedes that the states can forbid abortion after the fetus becomes viable.[34] He does not explain why states should be forbidden to move the point at which the fetus becomes a full-fledged rights-bearing human a little closer to conception.

Apart from specific objections to Dworkin's attempt to ground a right of abortion in the religion clauses of the First Amendment, it blurs his holistic approach. There is no actual inconsistency, because his interpretation of those clauses draws on values derived from his reflections on other provisions in the Constitution, consistent with his insistence on the integrity of the document as a whole. But his position would be clearer, and I think more persuasive, were he content to derive a right of abortion from his general theory of constitutional law, in which the clauses merge and lose their distinctness and the issue of the right of abortion becomes the place of such a right in the liberal

33. Homicide of an Unborn Child, 720 ILCS 5/9–1.2; Fetal Death—Cause of Action, 740 ILCS 180/2.2.

34. *Life's Dominion,* note 2 above, at 114–115. "Viability" refers to the point in the pregnancy at which the fetus theoretically could live outside the womb.

theory of the state. *Griswold,* the first of the sexual liberty cases, actually started down this road. Justice Douglas, albeit in his usual slipshod way, tried to extract a general (or at least generalizable) principle of sexual liberty from a collection of seemingly unrelated constitutional clauses. But no judge has picked up this particular spear and tried to throw it farther.

The arguments against the holistic approach are familiar. The basic one is that it gives judges too much power. When you think of all those constitutional theories jostling against one another—Epstein's that would repeal the New Deal, Ackerman's and Sunstein's that would constitutionalize it, Michelman's that would constitutionalize the welfare state, Mark Tushnet's that would make the Constitution a charter of socialism, Ely's that would resurrect Earl Warren, and some that would mold constitutional law to the Thomists' version of natural law—you see the range of choice that the approach legitimizes, the instability of constitutional doctrine that it portends. It is no good saying that Epstein is wrong, or Michelman is wrong, or St. Thomas is wrong. The arguments made against their theories cannot slay any of them or even wound them seriously in the eyes of those drawn to them because of temperament, emotion, or personal experience. If the only constraints on constitutional decision-making are good arguments, the embarrassment is the plenitude of good arguments on all sides of the hot issues.

Heat is important. A person who is indifferent to the outcome of a dispute will weigh up the arguments on both sides and give the nod to the side that has the stronger arguments, even if the weaker side has good arguments too. But someone who had a strong emotional commitment to one side or the other would be acting not only unnaturally, but imprudently, in abandoning that commitment on the basis of a slight, or even a not so slight, preponderance of counterarguments. Our deepest commitments are not so weakly held. Hence there can be practical indeterminacy about an issue even if a disinterested observer would not think the competing arguments evenly balanced.[35]

A comprehensive theory of constitutional law will infringe a multitude of deeply held commitments without being supportable by decisive arguments. That is why the situation with respect to constitutional theory is one of practical indeterminacy, driving the cautious jurist back

35. See *The Problems of Jurisprudence* 124–125.

to the clause-by-clause approach. It is much easier to impute a purpose to a particular clause and then use that purpose both to generate and circumscribe the meaning of the clause—which is all I meant in speaking of Bork's "theories" of free speech and of antitrust—than to impute a purpose to the Constitution as a whole and make a convincing case for the imputation. The problem with the modest approach is that it opens up large gaps in constitutional protection. As the eighteenth century recedes, and the original text becomes a palimpsest overlaid with the amendments of two centuries, not only the vision but the very identity of the framers blurs, and by going clause by clause one could end up with a document that gave answers only to questions that no one was asking any longer. Americans like to think that the Constitution protects them even against political enormities that do not fit comfortably into one clause or another. This is the practical appeal of an approach that makes of the Constitution a tire that seals up automatically when it is punctured or gashed. In 1791 such an approach might well have been otiose; the modest top-down, the ambitious top-down, the bottom-up approaches might all have coincided. No more. They diverge further with every passing year, and the ambitious top-down approach becomes more attractive with every passing year. It is not just academic fashion that has made constitutional theorizing a bigger activity today than a century ago.

The most remarkable aspect of Dworkin's analysis of the issue of abortion rights has yet to be noted: his confidence that it is an *analytical* issue. He claims that "the right of procreative autonomy follows from any competent interpretation of the due process clause and of the Supreme Court's past decisions applying it."[36] One of those decisions of course is *Roe v. Wade* itself. But he does not mean that the right of procreative autonomy follows from *Roe v. Wade,* and from the *Casey* decision, which reaffirmed *Roe v. Wade*'s central holding. He means that *Roe* and *Casey* follow from any competent interpretation of the due process clause and the Supreme Court's earlier due process decisions. This amounts to saying that the thousands of lawyers, many of them highly expert and distinguished and several of them Justices of the U.S. Supreme Court, who believe that the abortion cases do *not* follow from a competent interpretation of the due process clause and of due process jurisprudence are—incompetent, maybe even deluded.

36. *Life's Dominion,* note 2 above, at 160.

Dworkin thinks the uncompromising positions taken by the "pro-choice" and "right to life" movements are a product of "intellectual confusion,"[37] a confusion between the personhood of the fetus and the sacredness of human life that his book will clear up. The abortion controversy is founded on a *mistake.*

The idea that even the most passionate political and ideological disagreements rest on mere analytic errors is the faith of a certain kind of analytic philosopher well illustrated by Dworkin. It helps to explain what at first glance seems incongruous—that many of these analysts, despite their great faith in reason, find their opponents exasperating, and sometimes turn downright abusive. A person who equates disagreement with error will tend to find opponents unreasonable and therefore exasperating, just as he would be exasperated by someone who insisted that 2 + 2 = 5.

If the anti-abortion people have merely been confused all these years, it is curious that no one was able to set them to rights until Dworkin wrote his book. I agree with Dworkin that some of the arguments against abortion, including some of the theological arguments, are contradictory or otherwise flawed.[38] And this is worth pointing out. But none of the weapons in the armory of the analytic philosopher or expert legal reasoner will or should deflect a person who believes that the fetus is a human being and the abortionist a murderer. Those beliefs, like other fundamental beliefs, live below reason and are not the less worthy for doing so. The best study of public attitudes toward abortion that I have found identifies a variety of factors as influencing those attitudes, including charismatic leadership, media advertising, and personal experiences. Intellectual debate and discussion are not among them.[39]

Some Other Analytic Defenses of the Right to Abortion

John Rawls, like Dworkin, disagrees that the abortion controversy transcends analysis. He believes that a woman's constitutional right to

37. Id. at 10–11.

38. *Sex and Reason* 272–290. *Life's Dominion,* note 2 above at 35–50, contains an excellent discussion of the tensions and ambivalence in the religious condemnation of abortion.

39. Hyman Rodman, Betty Sarvis, and Joy Walker Bonar, *The Abortion Question,* ch. 8 (1987); cf. Luker, note 24 above, at 225–226.

have an abortion during the first three months of pregnancy is entailed by the most abstract version of liberalism, which he calls political liberalism and believes should command the assent of every reasonable person in our society. Political liberalism abstracts from every comprehensive doctrine of how we should live—utilitarianism, Catholicism, evangelical Protestantism, Marxism, Islam, even Millian liberalism. It consists of the limited set of political principles upon which adherents to all reasonable comprehensive doctrines ("reasonable" in, for example, conceding the incorrigible pluralism of comprehensive doctrines in our society today) can be brought to agree. These principles, Rawls believes, lead ineluctably to a constitutional right to abortion. He suggests that we consider the constitutional issue "in terms of these three important political values: the due respect for human life, the ordered reproduction of political society over time, including the family in some form, and finally the equality of women as equal citizens." Without further argument or analysis he declares that "any reasonable balance of these three values will give a woman a duly qualified right" to an abortion in the first trimester of pregnancy because "at this early stage of pregnancy the political value of the equality of women is overriding, and this right is required to give it substance and force."[40] Rawls considers respect for human life a legitimate political value but one lacking in weight when the fetus is too small to have much weight itself. He does not explain why. The proposition that sex equality would lack substance and force without a right of abortion is also assumed rather than defended. Unless women are irrational or an unwanted pregnancy and birth are much less costly to women than the advocates of abortion rights maintain, the principal effect of forbidding abortion, supposing unrealistically that such a prohibition could be enforced, would be to make women more careful about sex—less willing to have sex when not wanting to have a child, more discriminating in the choice of sexual partners and of occasions for sexual intercourse, and more diligent in learning about and properly using effective techniques of contraception—rather than to keep them out of the labor force, reduce their educational opportunities, depress their earnings, discourage them from voting, or otherwise deprive the equality of the sexes of substance

40. Rawls, *Political Liberalism* 243 n. 32 (1993). He does not claim that the three political values he discusses are the only political values that bear on the issue of abortion. But "other political values, if tallied in, would not, I think, affect this conclusion [that women have a constitutional right to early-pregnancy abortions]." Id.

and force. If this is incorrect, Rawls should provide some evidence. I do not mean that he should have written a chapter on abortion for *Political Liberalism*. But he should not have suggested that the question of the unconstitutionality of laws forbidding abortion could be established by lightning-fast reasoning from a handful of unexceptionable basic principles.

We all have the weaknesses of our strengths. It is hardly a surprise that people who have powerful intellects tend to have an exaggerated faith in the power of intellect to solve social problems. It is the same perspectival deformity that leads intellectuals to model democracy as a form of intellectual discussion or to set freedom of thought and debate far above economic freedom. It is well illustrated by another defense of abortion rights, this one by David Strauss. To the argument that abortion is murder he replies that the moral status of the fetus is so uncertain that it cannot be used to justify the subordination of women, which he believes is the effect of forbidding abortion. The fetus's moral status is radically or fundamentally uncertain in part because "abstract moral theories have difficulty dealing with the status of fetal life . . . The reason moral theories have trouble with this question is that no one really knows how to think about it systematically," and as a result "we have few reasons we can offer to try to persuade each other."[41] The implication is that a social or legal norm cannot be considered well grounded unless we can give good reasons for having it, and gender equality is therefore a trump because Strauss thinks he can give reasons for it but not for competing values such as fetal life. So opponents of abortion are checkmated. But ungroundedness is characteristic of many of our most firmly held norms. The issue of the moral status of fetal life is one of a host of boundary issues to which reason does not speak with a clear voice—issues about who is to be considered a member of the community and therefore a person whose welfare must be considered. The question arises with respect to foreigners, animals, the profoundly deformed and retarded, murderers, trees, infants, Jews in a Christian society, Christians in a Jewish society, slaves, and eight-month-old fetuses, as well as first-trimester ones. The notion that a society should hesitate to make judgments about such issues because people differ about them and neither side can offer reasons to persuade

41. David A. Strauss, "Abortion, Toleration, and Moral Uncertainty," 1992 *Supreme Court Review* 1, 10.

the other exaggerates the role that reasoning does or should play in social ordering. We reason from our bedrock beliefs, not to them. Infanticide and slavery are not forbidden in our society because the arguments against these practices are stronger than the arguments in favor of them, but because the practices revolt us. We would not listen to anyone who cared to make arguments in favor of them. Strauss's argument implies that at the time when a substantial minority of the nation favored Negro slavery it would have been wrong to deprive slaveowners of their property rights, since "abstract moral theories have difficulty with the status of" persons whose membership in the community is not conceded.

Frances Kamm bites the bullet and argues that even if the fetus is a person, abortion is justified, and not only in extreme cases, such as rape or incest, or where the fetus is profoundly deformed or the mother's life at risk. She is reluctant, however, to acknowledge that the fetus is not only a "person" but an "infant," because that might make us "more resistant to killing it from merely biological or sentimental motives."[42] No doubt it would. Our primary motives for not killing children are indeed biological and sentimental—and provide a solider basis for a civilized morality than philosophical reflection, which notoriously has difficulty drawing moral distinctions among computers, talking apes, and retarded human beings.

I have been knocking the arguments for abortion rights, but I would not like to leave the impression that I think the arguments against are any stronger. It is just that most of the academic brainpower is on the pro-abortion side. Not because that side is inherently stronger, but because the material interests of highly educated women are served by abortion rights, and academics are either highly educated women or the spouses, friends, and professional colleagues of such women.

The Pragmatic Approach

Although I am inclined to reject as imprudent, overambitious, excessively contentious, and in the end too inconclusive the task of fashioning a comprehensive theory of constitutional law, an "immodest" top-down theory intended to guide judges through every clause of the

42. F. M. Kamm, *Creation and Abortion: A Study in Moral and Legal Philosophy* 6 (1992). The motives to which she is referring are, of course, the motives of those who oppose abortion.

Constitution and its amendments, I do not object to judges' stretching clauses—even such questionable candidates as the due process clause—when there is a compelling practical case or imperative felt need for intervention. This was Holmes's approach, and later that of Cardozo, Frankfurter, and the second Harlan. Holmes said (though only privately) that a law was constitutional unless it made him want to "puke."[43] If we follow this approach we must be careful not to appoint judges whose stomachs are too weak. Of course Holmes was not speaking literally; nor am I. The point is only that our deepest values—Holmes's "can't helps"[44]—live below thought and provide warrants for action even when we cannot give those values a compelling or perhaps any rational justification. This holds even for judicial action. It is a comfort to a judge to know that he does not have to ratify a law or other official act or practice that he deeply feels to be terribly unjust, even if the conventional legal materials are not quite up to the job of constitutional condemnation. He preserves that role for conscience that we would have liked the German judges to play during the Third Reich.

It is easy for legal professionals, and intellectuals of every stripe, to ridicule so pragmatic an approach—which, by the way, transcends both top-down and bottom-up reasoning by locating a ground for judicial action in instinct rather than in analysis. They can ridicule it for its shapelessness, its subjectivity, its noncognitivism, its relativism, its foundationlessness, and its undemocratic character unredeemed by pedigree or principle. But the alternatives are unpalatable (to continue the digestive metaphor); and maybe what was good enough for Holmes should be good enough for us. The approach need not be quite so formless, so visceral as I have implied. Certainly it need not be inarticulate (in this respect the digestive metaphor is inapt); Holmes was the most eloquent judge in our history. The responsible judge will not be content with a naked statement of values. He will not ignore objections, or fail to test the consistency of his values by exploring hypothetical cases within the semantic domain of his statement. And

43. Letter to Harold Laski (Oct. 23, 1926), in *Holmes-Laski Letters: The Correspondence of Mr. Justice Holmes and Harold J. Laski 1916–1935,* vol. 2, p. 888 (Mark DeWolfe Howe ed. 1953). The "puke test" gives new meaning to the joke that to a legal realist the most important predictor of a judicial ruling is what the judge had for breakfast.

44. In another letter to Harold Laski (Jan. 11, 1929), Holmes had written, "When I say that a thing is true I only mean that I can't help believing it—but I have no grounds for assuming that my can't helps are cosmic can't helps." *Holmes-Laski Letters,* note 43 above, vol. 2, p. 1124.

he will seek to inform himself through empirical inquiry more searching than is normal in judicial opinions. Prudence dictates that before you react strongly to something you try to obtain as clear an idea as possible of what that something is.

The *Griswold* case, for example, in part because of the excellent brief of the lawyers for the birth control clinic (one of whom was Thomas Emerson of the Yale Law School faculty), provided an opportunity— which the Court didn't take—to deploy data in support of a professionally more respectable precedent than what emerged from Douglas's majority opinion and the concurrences. The brief highlights some striking facts which subsequent research[45] has confirmed. One is that statutes forbidding contraceptives had been passed in a wave in the late nineteenth century but had been repealed in all but two states, Connecticut and Massachusetts. In both states, repeal, though repeatedly attempted, had been blocked by the vigorous lobbying of the Catholic Church working on the large Catholic population. The only efforts to enforce the Connecticut statute, however—and they were entirely successful—were directed against birth control clinics, whose clientele was dominated by the poor and the uneducated; middle-class women preferred to go to their private gynecologist for contraceptive advice and devices. So the clinics were closed down and of course abortion was illegal at the time, making the sexual and reproductive dilemmas of poor women acute, whereas middle-class women had unrestricted access to contraceptives, and probably to safe illegal abortions as well if contraception failed—but it was less likely to fail for them.

As the law made no distinction between married and unmarried persons, it placed a burden on marriage—specifically marriage by the poor and the working class—and did so arbitrarily. The law had been founded on Protestant (indeed, such are the ironies of history, on anti-Catholic) concern with fornication, adultery, and prostitution, and with the supposed immorality of immigrants and of the lower class generally. Yet the law may actually have discouraged marriage—and fostered immorality—among the poor. The law's survival owed everything to a belief, by 1965 limited essentially to Catholics and by no means shared by all of them, that it is sinful to impede the procreative outcome of sexual intercourse, coupled with legislative inertia which makes it difficult to repeal legislation supported by a vigorous minority

45. Summarized in chapters 7 and 12 of *Sex and Reason*.

even if that minority would not be strong enough to get the statute reenacted.

Sectarian in motive and rationale, capriciously enforced, out of step with dominant public opinion in the country, genuinely oppressive, a vestige maintained by legislative inertia, the Connecticut contraceptive law was a national embarrassment—as would be a law forbidding re-marriage, or limiting the number of children a married couple may have, or requiring the sterilization of persons having genetic defects, or denying the mothers of illegitimate children parental rights, or forbid-ding homosexuals to practice medicine, or forbidding abortion even when necessary to spare a woman from a crippling or debilitating illness, or requiring the tattooing of people who carry the AIDS virus, or—coming closest to *Griswold* itself—requiring married couples to have a minimum number of children unless they prove that they are infertile. It is not the worst thing in the world to have judges who are willing to strike down such laws in the name of the Constitution. The sequelae to *Griswold* show that the risks in this approach are enormous too, but smaller I think than those that would be entailed by the totalizing approach that Dworkin defends with such elegant tenacity.

Dworkin believes that only his approach can prevent constitutional doctrine from changing with every change in the composition of the Court. This belief, another example of the intellectualist fallacy, exag-gerates both the possibility of cogent theorizing at the high level of abstraction implied by the holistic approach, and the fidelity of judges, especially Supreme Court Justices, whose decisions are unreviewable, to the doctrines (as distinct from narrow holdings) of their predeces-sors. Nothing but *force majeure* can prevent judges from giving vent to their political and personal values, if that is what they want to do. They may not want to, if they are thoroughly imbued with the old-fashioned formalist virtues of stare decisis and strict construction. But of course Dworkin does not want that. He approves of *Brown,* and *Griswold,* and *Roe.* He wants to package novelty as orthodoxy.

I remind the reader, in support of my suggested approach, that judicial decision precedes articulate theory—because the duty to resolve the dispute at hand is primary—that few judges are equipped to create or even evaluate comprehensive political theories, that our judges are generally not appointed on the basis of their intellectual merit, and that instinct can be a surer guide to action than analysis. I may seem to be indulging in paradox in proposing an approach that accepts the role of personal values in adjudication and asks only that they be yoked to empirical data. But personal values, while influenced by temperament and upbringing, are not independent of adult personal experience. Research—into facts, not just into what judges have said in the past— can substitute for experience, enlarge and correct the factual materials on which temperament and outlook react, and thus bring home to a judge the realities of a law against contraception or against abortion or against sodomy. Most judges can handle facts better than they can handle theories. Of course that is what bottom-up reasoners say in defense of their approach. But bottom-up reasoning only *pretends* to be reasoning.

Unless we abandon such pretenses we may have to expel Holmes from the juristic pantheon, even though he not only is the greatest judge and scholar in the history of our law but also possessed the finest *philosophical* mind in the history of judging. His most famous judicial opinion is the dissent in *Lochner,* which judged by conventional standards of legal reasoning is a flop—an example of Holmes's inveterate tendency "to substitute epigrams for analysis: instead of taking *Lochner* as the opportunity to show what the due process clause was all about, Holmes contented himself with the smug assertion that the clause did not 'enact Mr. Herbert Spencer's "Social Statics.""""[46] As I have remarked elsewhere, I agree that Holmes's dissent in *Lochner* is not "a good judicial opinion. It is merely the greatest judicial opinion of the last hundred years."[47] There is something radically incomplete about the conventional standards: They miss the vital essence of legal growth and insight. We need to move beyond Holmes not in becoming more legalistic and less eloquent, but in becoming more empirical.

If Holmes had the finest philosophical mind in the history of judging, one might think him the prime candidate to have worked out the sort of comprehensive top-down theory that Dworkin wants to bring to bear on questions of constitutional interpretation. But Holmes's philosophical bent did not express itself in attempting to fashion a comprehensive theory of constitutional law—a constitution of "principle," as distinct from one of "detail," in Dworkin's terminology. It was

---

46. David P. Currie, *The Constitution in the Supreme Court: The Second Century: 1888– 1986* 82 (1990). See also id. at 81–82, 130. This type of criticism is akin to criticizing Shakespeare for failing to observe the classical unities of time and place. And what *is* due process "all about," anyway? Is that even a meaningful question?

47. *Law and Literature* 285.

manifested in Holmes's bringing to bear on discrete constitutional issues the curious mélange of pragmatism, Social Darwinism, logical positivism, existentialism, vitalism, and other "isms" that is his rich but far from univocal philosophical legacy.[48] A sense of the Darwinian character of the struggle of interest groups for legislative supremacy, coupled with hostility to natural law, made Holmes reluctant to invalidate legislation as contrary to freedom of contract regarded as an absolute of natural law—even though the "nature" from which the concept of freedom of contract was drawn was itself the (Social) Darwinian law of the (economic) jungle, *real* nature. Holmes's positivism made him doubt that there was such as thing as "the common law" existing apart from the decisions of particular state courts. His pragmatist fondness for experimentation led him to look with favor on federalism, the philosophy of limited national government, while his pragmatist distrust of final truths made him reluctant to countenance government's superseding the market—his metaphor—of ideas and opinions. In his most notable opinions Holmes did not reason from authoritative texts, with or without the aid of a comprehensive legal theory. Those texts, along with values shaped by extensive nonlegal reading and life experience, were resources for a decision-making style more intuitive than analytic.

In drawing, inexplicitly for the most part but nevertheless unmistakably, on philosophical doctrines for the substance of many of his constitutional views, did Holmes violate Rawls's injunction against basing political, including judicial, judgments on comprehensive doctrines as distinct from that spare outline, what Rawls calls political liberalism, that inhabits the intersection of all reasonable comprehensive doctrines held in the society? Rawls believes that the Supreme Court should limit the fund of ideas on which it draws to what he calls "public reasons," reasons drawn from within political liberalism.[49]

> The justices [of the Supreme Court] cannot, of course, invoke their own personal morality, nor the ideals and virtues of morality generally. Those they must view as irrelevant. Equally, they cannot invoke their or other people's religious or philosophical views. Nor can they cite political values without restriction. Rather, they must appeal to the political values they

48. See Introduction, in *The Essential Holmes: Selections from the Letters, Speeches, Judicial Opinions, and Other Writings of Oliver Wendell Holmes, Jr.* ix, xvii–xx (Richard A. Posner ed. 1992).

49. Rawls, note 40 above, at 231–240.

think belong to the most reasonable understanding of the public conception and its political values of justice and public reason. These are values that they believe in good faith, as the duty of civility requires, that all citizens as reasonable and rational might reasonably be expected to endorse.[50]

Since not "all citizens" could "reasonably be expected" to subscribe to the various elements of Holmes's philosophy, the passage I have quoted implies that Holmes overstepped the proper bounds in basing his judicial views on them; not only Holmes but every great judge in our history. That can't be right. No doubt a judge ought not to use the freedom of his office to try to impose wholesale the natural-law views of Aquinas, or for that matter of Herbert Spencer, or the utilitarian philosophy of Bentham, or even that of Mill, on the nation in the name of the Constitution. Tolerance and restraint are important virtues in judging. But a judge's philosophical or religious or economic or political views are bound to shape his response to specific cases in the open area where judicial decision-making is discretionary. How else are such cases to be decided? The values that all reasonable and rational people in our society endorse make too thin a gruel to resolve the difficult cases. The danger of judicial tyranny should not be exaggerated: The heterogeneity of our society, which is reflected in the composition of the judiciary, prevents judges from legislating comprehensive doctrine. Appellate judges sit in panels, so a majority opinion in a difficult case will generally reflect a compromise among comprehensive doctrines.

Rawls's effort to place limits on political (including judicial) discourse is unpragmatic. If a judge can reason only from the meager set of premises that *all* reasonable people in the United States can be expected to share, the creative judge is an oxymoron. Holmes's influential conception of free speech as an open marketplace of ideas owes more to Mill and Darwin than to the values that all reasonable Americans could or can be brought to agree on. The great judges have enriched political thought and practice precisely by bringing controversial values, whether of an egalitarian, populist, or libertarian cast, into the formation of public policy. Marshall, Holmes, Brandeis, and Black, to name only a few of the most important American judges, are major figures in the history of American political liberalism because they used their judicial office to stamp the law with a personal vision.

50. Id. at 236.

chapter 6

Have We Constitutional Theory?

Democracy and Distrust

WHEN John Ely's book was first published[1] it seemed another in a spate of books and articles about constitutional law written by liberals nostalgic for the days when Chief Justice Warren (to whom the book is dedicated) led a like-minded group of Justices in remaking that law; and I confess that, not being a liberal in the relevant sense, I read the book less carefully than I should have done.[2] Reread more than a decade later the book stands forth as a work of outstanding merit—but also, especially when read in conjunction with other works of constitutional theory, as an exemplar of deep problems with such theory.

Ely's book is best known for proposing a unifying principle for understanding and extending the program of the Warren Court; it is another example of top-down constitutional theorizing. But that is the project of the last three chapters of the book. The first three constitute a critical monograph of independent significance. Their aim is to affirm the necessity for tethering constitutional law—in the sense of the body

1. John Hart Ely, *Democracy and Distrust: A Theory of Judicial Review* (1980).
2. And as a result failed to make proper attribution to Ely of some of the criticisms of judicial activism and restraint that I made in chapter 7 of *The Federal Courts: Crisis and Reform* (1985), and chapter 7 of *The Problems of Jurisprudence*.

of principles actually applied by judges—to the Constitution's text and history against those who would make constitutional law a vehicle for enforcing "fundamental values" discovered by judges as an exercise in moral philosophy,[3] but at the same time to knock down the interpretive approach variously called "strict construction," "textualism," and "originalism," but which Ely calls "clause-bound interpretivism." The "fundamental values" approach gives judges too much discretion, and "clause-bound interpretivism" too little; the middle way is a moderate interpretivism.

Ely's book has helped me see, though in the teeth of his own intentions, that there is no middle way. Rather, there are these two ways that he stresses (of course there are countless others as well) in which judges can go wrong. The "fundamental values" approach goes wrong by being too willing to make political judgments. "Clause-bound interpretivism" goes wrong by not being willing enough to make political judgments, with the result that substantive injustices are ratified, even reveled in, in the name of the rule of law. The first mistake invites charges that the judges are being lawless, the second that they are being heartless. The first invites charges that the judges are elitist, antidemocratic, arrogant in setting their judgment against that of the people's representatives, the second that they are too quick to yield to populist pressures, too insensitive to the danger of tyranny by the majority, too pious and credulous about the ideology of democracy, too callous, too servile—even cowardly. The objection to naming the avoidance of these extremes "interpretivism" is that it implies the existence of an objective technique, such as cryptography, or translation (see Chapter 23), or reading a chest X-ray for signs of pulmonary disease, that, if only judges would adhere to it, would prevent them from going to either of the bad extremes. If there is such a technique—something to lift free constitutional "interpretation" above the reading of palms and the interpretation of dreams—no one has discovered it.

Not Ely, in any event. The second half of the book is his proposal for a moderate interpretive approach to constitutional law. What he

---

3. The "fundamental values" school is the target of Ely's best sallies. "The Constitution may follow the flag, but is it really supposed to keep up with the *New York Review of Books?*" (p. 58). "We may grant until we're blue in the face that legislatures aren't wholly democratic, but that isn't going to make courts more democratic than legislatures" (p. 67). "The notion that the genuine values of the people can most reliably be discerned by a nondemocratic elite is sometimes referred to in the literature as 'the Führer principle'" (p. 68).

does, or at least purports to do, is to search for values that can fairly be said to be "in" the Constitution and that judges are equipped by experience and by the nature of their office to promote. What he finds, reading the text of the Constitution in light of what its framers said about it in the *Federalist Papers* and elsewhere, is that the document's basic purpose—also that of the principal amendments from the Bill of Rights to the present—is to create a system of government in which elected representatives will do a sincere and competent job of representing the interests of all the people. Representative government presupposes two values, both procedural in a broad sense—participation by all competent adults in the election of government officials, and fair representation of all by those officials. Judicial decisions that promote these values are lawful because consistent with the spirit of the document being interpreted, and they cannot be criticized as antidemocratic, because the values they promote are democratic.

So Ely has done more than find in the Constitution the very values whose vigorous deployment by the Supreme Court in the heyday of Earl Warren's chief justiceship called down upon the Court charges of elitism; any defender of the Warren era could do that, working imaginatively upon the plastic material for interpretation that an ancient document provides. Ely's trick is to argue that the Court, far from acting in elitist fashion with or without the permission as it were of the framers, was making America more democratic by promoting the foundational democratic principles of participation and representation. Participation was promoted, for example, by judicial decisions that required apportionment on the basis of "one man, one vote," that outlawed poll taxes, that limited the power of states to discriminate against nonresidents (who have no political voice in the state), and that protected freedom of political advocacy and association. Representation was promoted by identifying minority groups whose interests were unlikely to be weighed sympathetically by representatives drawn primarily from the majority and by forbidding government to place unequal burdens on such groups without a compelling and noninvidious reason for doing so. Discrimination against aliens illustrates both forms of democratic failure against which Ely's program is directed. Aliens have no voting power; and legislators—citizens all—lack the sort of firsthand experience with aliens (except as maids and nannies) that would enable them to empathize with their problems and needs.

Ely does a superb job of relating the clauses of the Constitution (including the amendments) to the values of participation and representation. He points out, for example, that the constitutional right of travel which the Supreme Court found implicit in the privileges and immunities clause of Article IV and in the equal protection clause of the Fourteenth Amendment—a right, for example, to move to another state without having to reside there for a minimum period of time in order to qualify for welfare benefits—serves to add "exit" to "voice" as a mode of participation in the political process. He points out that the commerce clause, in its "negative" or "dormant" aspect, limits a state's power to shift the costs of government to residents of other states by means of a tax on a scarce commodity produced within the state but consumed mainly elsewhere. Similarly, the free exercise clause has been used for the most part to protect marginal, unpopular sects, such as Jehovah's Witnesses. And the protections that the Bill of Rights extends to criminal defendants ensure a form of representation for the denizens of the despised and poorly understood social margin from which most criminals come. At times, it is true, Ely's analysis is circular. The negative commerce clause, for example, is a free (some believe an unsound) judicial interpretation of the textual commerce clause, so one cannot use *that* text to argue that Ely's approach is immanent in the Constitution. On the other hand, a number of constitutional provisions, such as the equal protection clause, the privileges and immunities clause of Article IV,[4] the voting rights amendments, and the republican form of government clause, fit his model without strain. Of course, he is treating as an integrated whole a set of documents written in three different centuries, and of course it is an embarrassment to his project that nowhere in this layer cake can be found a right to vote *tout court*. But these are not decisive objections. They merely underscore the radical uncertainty of constitutional interpretation.

The body of constitutional law that Ely's approach generates bears, as one would expect from the book's dedication, a general resemblance to the constitutional jurisprudence of the Warren era. But there are interesting differences, not all of which are merely extrapolations from that jurisprudence to the problems of the 1970s:

1. Women, being an electoral majority, are entitled to no special constitutional solicitude. By the same token, however, laws discriminat-

---

4. There is another privileges and immunities clause, which no one can make sense of, in the Fourteenth Amendment. See Chapter 9.

ing against women that were enacted before they got the vote are unconstitutional—but if those laws are reenacted after being found unconstitutional, they are okay.

2. Affirmative action is unproblematic since it is a matter of whites discriminating against themselves. Obviously whites are adequately empathetic toward the problems of fellow whites adversely affected by policies that favor blacks.

3. There is no constitutional right to privacy. The "privacy" decisions (really decisions about the sexual and reproductive freedom of women), culminating in *Roe v. Wade*, have no relation to a "participation-oriented, representation-reinforcing approach to judicial review" (p. 87). There is no other "interpretivist" basis for them either; they are the product of "fundamental rights" jurisprudence, nothing more.

4. In apparent tension with point 3, discrimination against homosexuals is suspect because legislators are unlikely to empathize with their problems and concerns. But if satisfied that the laws criminalizing homosexual behavior are founded on "a sincerely held moral objection to the act (or anything else that transcends a simple desire to injure the parties involved)" (p. 256 n. 92), judges should uphold the laws unembarrassed by any claim that homosexuals have a right to sexual freedom because Ely believes that no one has a constitutional right to sexual freedom. Aliens are even more clearly entitled to judicial solicitude than homosexuals since they are not entitled to vote.

5. It is strongly arguable that capital punishment is unconstitutional because murderers drawn from the affluent, educated class that supplies our representatives, judges, and other public officials are never executed.

The foregoing list does not, of course, exhaust the content of constitutional law according to Ely. He recognizes that some provisions of the Constitution confer substantive rights wholly unrelated to participation or representation, and naturally he endorses the participation-oriented and representation-reinforcing decisions and doctrines of the Warren and Burger eras, such as the reapportionment, poll tax, and political speech decisions. The propositions in my list are, however, the *distinctive* product of his theory.

How persuasive is this, even taken on its own terms and thus with its "interpretive" character conceded? It is true that the framers, both of the original Constitution and of most of the amendments, were concerned about problems of representative government. It is also true that two of the problems that dog this form of government are lack of participation and lack of effective representation. But, to begin with, these really are one problem, not two. If some people are not effectively represented because they are not allowed to vote or because their candidates are jailed for espousing their interests, or if they are not represented on equal terms because their vote is weighted less heavily in the election than other people's, or if they are not represented adequately because their nominal representatives do not understand or care about their problems and their needs because they are importantly different sorts of people from the representatives (they are aliens or blacks or homosexuals, for example), then, in all of these cases, there is a defect in representation.

But the defect is found in a number of other cases as well, cases that Ely does not discuss. Interest-group politics often enable a compact group to use the political process to transfer wealth to itself from a larger, more diffuse group—consumers or taxpayers, for example—whose members are, as a practical matter, helpless to protect themselves against this mulcting. A large and amorphous majority may be at the mercy of the very sort of interest group that Ely conceives it to be the fundamental purpose of the Constitution to protect. So the fact that women are an electoral majority does not guarantee that the political process will reflect their preferences, or the fact that blacks are a minority that the political process will not reflect their preferences. A related point is the electorate's pervasive ignorance of the effects of public policies. Furthermore, representatives are not perfect agents of the electors. They have their own interests, selfish and otherwise, and it would be sheer luck if self-interest and interest-group pressures generally offset each other, leaving the public interest to determine the representative's vote. And except in states that permit referenda or initiatives, we vote for candidates rather than for policies—which means that, at best, we are voting for a package of policies—and it is easy to show that as a result particular policies may end up being adopted that are not the preference of a majority of the voters.

Most of the problems of representation are beyond the capacity of the courts to solve. But if they are left unsolved, it is by no means clear that the judicial initiatives that Ely commends will improve the functioning of representative government, or even that those he opposes will *not* improve it. As an illustration of the first point, consider affirmative action. Forget that there are cities in which blacks are an electoral majority. Grant that notwithstanding "white guilt," white legislators do not ignore the costs of affirmative action to whites. It does not follow that affirmative action passes Ely's representation test. Affirmative-action programs are intended to give a leg up to traditionally disfavored minorities. The leg up might take the form of an award of super-seniority or of extra points on a civil service exam, or a lowering of the test score required for admission to a prestigious school. Who is hurt by such thumb-on-the-scale tactics? It is the *marginal* white—the white who is uncertain about being rehired in the event of layoff, or who is the last to be hired, or who is the last to be admitted to the school. Is it realistic to assume that *his* plight is uppermost in the thinking of the upper-middle-class legislators and educators who support affirmative action? And can we exclude the possibility of coalitions between blacks and whites to advance some blacks at the expense of some whites for selfish political reasons, unrelated to social justice?

And *Griswold v. Connecticut*—had it, as Ely believes, nothing to do with representation? Was it not a case about the power of an interest group, consisting of the Catholic Church and devout Catholics, to block legislative reform that would have benefited lower-class and lower-middle-class women primarily—a diffuse group, not all of voting age, with a weak political voice—whose access to family planning services was barred by the Connecticut statute? In discussing legislation discriminating against women that was passed before they got the vote and has not yet been repealed, Ely displays sensitivity to the inertial character of the political process; but it was inertia that prevented Connecticut from repealing its archaic ban on contraception.

Consider the issue of reapportionment. At first glance there might appear to be no more palpable affront to the principles of representative government than to make the votes of people from one part of a state count for more than the votes of people from another part by failing to adjust the boundaries of voting districts so that each district has roughly the same voting population. But on reflection it is apparent that people rarely have the same voting power even when state legislative districts have equal voting populations. There are more senators per capita in Delaware than in New York; so each Delaware voter has more voting power in United States Senate elections than each New York voter. That is constitutionally privileged malapportionment, but I live in a congressional district in which Republicans have no voting power in the election of a representative simply because there are too few Republicans in the district to induce the Republican Party to put up a plausible candidate. And voting power is only one element of political power; others include money, education, age, membership in or good access to a constitutionally privileged class, such as the press, and membership in a politically effective interest group. So various is the allocation of political power wholly apart from whether state legislatures are malapportioned that it is difficult to predict whether reapportionment will have any systematic impact on policy outcomes. It is no surprise that political scientists disagree over whether it *has* had any such impact.[5] Ely ignores the empirical issue.

The flaws these examples expose are at once internal to his argument (the "malapportioned" character of the United States Senate suggests that the Constitution embodies a different democratic theory from the one Ely would impose on the states in the name of the Constitution) and illustrative of a weak sense of fact (for example in his discussion of *Griswold*). They are also weaknesses at the level of theory. Almost the only political scientist whom Ely cites is Robert Dahl, who did his major work in the 1950s. He cites none of the political science literature on the effects of reapportionment or other constitutional decisions, none of the political science or economic literature on interest groups, and none of the literature of public choice, though all these literatures existed when he wrote his book.[6] He does cite Gordon Allport and other psychologists on the nature of prejudice to bolster his contention that we may have trouble empathizing with persons of a different race or religion or social class or sexual orientation, but neither the psychologists nor Ely presents evidence that failures of empathy are com-

---

5. The studies through 1980 are reviewed in David C. Safell, "Reapportionment and Public Policy: State Legislators' Perspectives," in *Representation and Redistricting Issues* 203, 204–210 (Bernard Grofman et al. eds. 1982). Safell, while noting the disagreement in his profession, sides with the "counterskeptics." Since he wrote, however, the skeptical literature has been augmented by Larry M. Schwab, *The Impact of Congressional Reapportionment and Redistricting* 196–200 (1988), and William H. Riker, "Democracy and Representation: A Reconciliation of *Ball v. James* and *Reynolds v. Sims*," 1 *Supreme Court Economic Review* 39, 41–55 (1982).

6. See, for example, besides the studies cited in Safell, note 5 above, David B. Truman, *The Governmental Process: Political Interests and Public Opinion* (2d ed. 1971); James M. Buchanan and Gordon Tullock, *The Calculus of Consent: Logical Foundations of Constitutional Democracy* (1962); Mancur Olson, Jr., *The Logic of Collective Action: Public Goods and the Theory of Groups* (1965); George J. Stigler, *The Citizen and the State: Essays on Regulation* (1975).

mon in the political arena. Whatever their manifold other failings, politicians are specialists in discerning the interests of their constituents.

So the book is not a masterpiece of social science; but so what? Ely is engaged in interpretation, isn't he? Do you need social science to *interpret* the Constitution? Ely calls his approach interpretive, but it is that only in the sense of being connected, by however long a chain, to a document. The Constitution created a representative form of government. Ely believes that by correcting some defects of representation judges could make government even more representative than it is. The almost embarrassing plenitude of vague constitutional provisions gives judges ample power to carry out this program. They can do, in fact, *anything*—abolish capital punishment, force the states to allow homosexual marriage, force them to extend the franchise to nonresidents and maybe even to aliens—all in the name of the Constitution's participation-oriented, representation-reinforcing theme. They could, I have suggested, though Ely demurs, bring the sexual privacy cases, some of them anyway (and not just ones filed by homosexuals), under that umbrella.

If this is interpretation, then what exactly is "noninterpretivism" or "fundamental rights" jurisprudence? You need a handle in the constitutional text to be able to say that you are interpreting—but liberty, surely, could do as well in that role as representation—and then you're off and running. It is true that if you run from the liberty side of the field you run into the argument that the courts are elitist. There is more open ground on the representation side. But to run well there you need more social science than Ely deploys in *Democracy and Distrust*. Ely may seem to have finessed this point, for despite the citations to Dahl and Allport one reason he prefers the theme of representation to that of liberty is that he thinks lawyers and judges better equipped to deal with questions of process than with questions of substance. This would be correct if Ely were speaking at the level of trials. But he is speaking of the design of political institutions. About this level of political governance lawyers and judges know as much or as little as they know about our society's fundamental values. The effects of apportionment, the political dynamics of affirmative action, the conditions for effective minority politics, the significance of conflicting interests within a group, the force of inertia in the political process—these and other matters central to the construction and evaluation of a participation-oriented representation-reinforcing jurisprudence are issues in social science.

They are not issues of "process" rather than "substance" in any sense relevant to lawyers' capacities.

When "interpretation" is used in the sense of decoding, all you need is the text and the code. When it is used in the sense of creating new meanings, you need more—more than what is in a lawyer's kitbag.

Why Constitutional Theory Is So Weak

In the end one is not convinced by Ely, though impressed by his ambition and panache. The reasons for his (magnificent) failure have ultimately to do, as I have hinted, with the nature of constitutional law and of the academic study of law rather than with any failure of intelligence on Ely's part. The Constitution is an old document that was drafted by men who, despite much civic piety to the contrary, were not clairvoyant. Two centuries of amendments have muddied the waters still more. A document that as a result is inscrutable with respect to most modern problems has been overlaid by hundreds of thousands of pages of judicial interpretation, much of it internally inconsistent. The sum of all this verbiage is not a directive but a resource; further interpretive ventures, therefore, whether by Ely or by his opponents to the left and right, are bound to illustrate interpretation as creation, not as constraint. One cannot choose among these interpretations on semantic or conceptual grounds. Choice must be based on which interpretation seems best in a sense that includes but also transcends considerations of fidelity to a text and a tradition. The interpretive question is ultimately a political, economic, or social one to which social science may have more to contribute than law.

At least this is the case when law is treated in so provincial a fashion as is the accepted mode even at the best of our law schools. How absurd that constitutional law should be considered a single specialty, so that a John Ely is presumed to be able to speak knowledgeably about the social treatment of aliens and of illegitimate children, of homosexuals and of women, of political agitators, religious dissenters, and murderers on death row. Academic law is clause-bound in its own way. Because government programs dealing with aliens, children born out of wedlock, members of racial minorities, indigent criminal defendants, veterans, and women are all challenged and litigated under one tiny clause of the Constitution—the equal protection clause of the Fourteenth Amendment—it is natural to think that one person should be able to evaluate all those programs, together with laws and policies affecting fetuses, homosexuals, and others whose rights or claims to have rights are litigated under the adjacent due process clause; natural, but wrong. The programs are heterogeneous and their social consequences complex.

Constitutional lawyers know little about their proper subject matter—a complex of political, social, and economic phenomena. They know only cases. An exclusive diet of Supreme Court opinions is a recipe for intellectual malnutrition.

Consider David Strauss's article on the Supreme Court's decision in the *DeShaney* case.[7] A social worker employed by a public agency had failed to remove a child named Joshua DeShaney from the custody of his abusive father, despite unmistakable signs of abuse. The father later beat Joshua into a vegetative state. The mother brought a civil rights suit against the agency, seeking damages. The Supreme Court held that the state's failure to protect Joshua from his father did not violate the due process clause of the Fourteenth Amendment. The state had done nothing to Joshua DeShaney; it had failed to protect him from private violence. The liberty that the Fourteenth Amendment protects, the Court held, is negative liberty—the right to be let alone by the state— rather than positive liberty, the right to state services. Strauss is critical of the Court's decision but relegates to a footnote a discussion of one of the Court's principal grounds, the practical one as it happens—that making the state's inaction actionable would place social workers on a razor's edge. They would be suable not only for depriving parents of their parental rights (a component of Fourteenth Amendment liberty) if the child was removed from parental custody unnecessarily (as settled by previous decisions), but also for failing to deprive parents of their liberty if the child should have been removed from parental custody. "Why," says Strauss in the footnote, "is it bad for society that government employees are confronted with this dilemma?" And if, contrary to his priors, it is bad, "the proper way to deal with the dilemma is to design substantive and immunity doctrines that produce the correct

---

7. DeShaney v. Winnebago County Department of Social Services, 489 U.S. 189 (1989). The article is "Due Process, Government Inaction, and Private Wrongs," 1989 *Supreme Court Review* 53. I have a judicial as well as academic interest in the *DeShaney* case, having written the court of appeals decision, which the Supreme Court affirmed. See 812 F.2d 298 (7th Cir. 1989).

incentives."[8] No clue to the content of these doctrines is offered. Why the solution of the dilemma cannot be left to the states is also ignored; as Strauss does not mention, the states provide damages remedies for persons injured as a result of the negligence of child welfare workers.[9] Nor does he consider the possibility that the costs of increased litigation against welfare agencies might, in a period such as the present when government budgets are tight, cause a curtailment of benefits.

Now as it happens the University of Chicago Law School, where Strauss teaches, is one block east of the university's School of Social Service Administration, the nation's premier school of social work. A two-minute walk would have brought Strauss into the presence of experts with whom to explore the practical consequences of a decision the other way in *DeShaney*.[10] One block east of the law school is the university's School of Public Policy Studies, where Strauss could have consulted experts in public administration and finance to determine the consequences of using the federal courts to enforce, in the name of civil rights, standards of right conduct for public employees engaged in rescue services, broadly defined. For if social workers have a constitutional duty to protect children against their parents, presumably they have a constitutional duty to rescue people who fall off bridges or drive into trees or have heart attacks; if so, the federal courts will become enmeshed in the administration of police and fire departments as well as social welfare agencies. Would that be a good thing? To a pragmatist, the answer to this question is not irrelevant to evaluating the soundness of the *DeShaney* decision, for it is not as if the correct decision is obvious from the text of the Fourteenth Amendment. The answer is within Strauss's intellectual capacity to give, but he would have to immerse himself in what is after all a mere corner of modern constitutional law. His wings would be clipped. He would be demoted in the

8. Strauss, note 7 above, at 80 n. 63.

9. See *Liability in Child Welfare and Protection Work: Risk Management Strategies* (Marcia Sprague and Robert M. Horowitz eds. 1991), esp. chs. 1, 2, and 6.

10. An illustrative discussion of the liability of child welfare workers from the social service perspective, expressing concern about the razor's-edge problem, is Rudolph Alexander, Jr., "The Legal Liability of Social Workers after *DeShaney*," 38 *Social Work* 64, 68 (1993). See also James Strickland, "Risk Reduction Techniques for Child Welfare and Protective Service Programs: 'Putting in Stop Bells and Whistles,'" in *Liability in Child Welfare and Protection Work*, note 9 above, at 105, 106; cf. Jim Strickland and Stuart Reynolds, "The New Untouchables: Risk Management of Child Abuse in Child Care," *Exchange*, April 1989, pp. 51, 52.

legal-academic pecking order from an expert on the Constitution to an expert on welfare.

Strauss might riposte that the judges (I, for example) should have done the necessary factual research before denying Joshua DeShaney's claim; that when we judges talk about the consequences of placing social workers on a razor's edge we too are merely speculating with the aid of metaphor. That is true. But judges are not allowed to have private consultations with academics about pending cases; nor do judges have the time or the resources required for competent empirical research, though Brandeis tried in some of his dissenting opinions.[11] Judges rely for their knowledge of the facts of or bearing on a case on the briefs and record and on published materials. In any sensible division of responsibilities among branches of the legal profession, the task of conducting detailed empirical inquiries into the presuppositions of legal doctrines would be assigned to the law schools. Too many constitutional scholars conceive their role as that of shadow judges, writing, in the guise of articles, alternative judicial opinions in Supreme Court cases.

Given Joshua DeShaney's vegetative state, a victory in the lawsuit would have done very little for him. Given the existence of state tort remedies against negligent child care workers and the agencies that employ them, the incremental deterrent effect of a federal tort remedy might be slight, and the social benefit produced by that effect might well be offset by the razor's-edge problem or by a curtailment of welfare benefits in reaction to an expansion in liability. And since Joshua's mother probably cannot afford the cost of maintaining Joshua in an institution, the state might have ended up paying for the catastrophe whether it won or lost the suit. Perhaps only attorney's fees were actually at stake (a prevailing plaintiff in a civil rights suit is usually entitled to obtain reimbursement of his attorney's fees from the defendant). But Strauss may not care about the practical significance of *DeShaney*. He may be reacting against the conception of limited government—a government legally obligated only to protect negative, not positive, liberties—that informed the Court's interpretation of the due process clause in *DeShaney*. Valuing active government, Strauss would like symbolic confirmation of the duty of government to be active even

11. Without conspicuous success, if one may judge from his ambitious dissent in the Oklahoma ice-monopoly case, New State Ice Co. v. Liebmann, 285 U.S. 262, 280 (1932). See *Economic Analysis of Law* 626–628.

in affairs of the family. But the defense of a symbolic justification for the plaintiff's position, like an empirical one, would require different tools from those of the conventional constitutional scholar, however accomplished a one.

At first glance, Amar and Widawsky's article on *DeShaney* escapes these criticisms.[12] Where Strauss, in the abstractly analytical manner of Dworkin, Rawls, and Ely, had tried to show that the judges' attempted distinction between positive and negative liberties collapses on inspection, Amar and Widawsky make what appears to be a close-grained textual and well-documented historical argument that Wisconsin's failure to protect Joshua DeShaney from his father violated the Thirteenth Amendment,[13] which provides that "neither slavery nor involuntary servitude, except as a punishment for crime whereof the party shall have been duly convicted, shall exist within the United States, or any place subject to their jurisdiction." From the amendment's "sweeping words and underlying vision" Amar and Widawsky extract the following definition of "slavery": "a power relation of domination, degradation, and subservience, in which human beings are treated as chattel, not persons."[14] Ordinary parental custody, while it could be said to involve a power relation of domination, is not slavery because it does not involve degradation or subservience, and the child, while not free, is treated as a person rather than a thing. But when the parental custodian physically abuses the child, he supplies the missing elements of the definition of slavery. The authors do not argue that Joshua DeShaney was the state's slave; he was his father's slave. But unlike the due process clause of the Fourteenth Amendment, the Thirteenth Amendment does not prohibit action only by the state; the slaveowners at whom the amendment was centrally aimed were private individuals rather than state agents.

Objections to Amar and Widawsky's startling thesis crowd the mind. To begin with, the authors have confused an entity and its attributes.

12. Akhil Reed Amar and Daniel Widawsky, "Child Abuse as Slavery: A Thirteenth Amendment Response to *Deshaney*," 105 *Harvard Law Review* 1359 (1992).

13. Although DeShaney's lawyers had not argued the Thirteenth Amendment, perhaps for fear that the courts would have thought it a legally frivolous, hence sanctionable, argument, as well they might have. The Amar-Widawsky article is presumably the sort of scholarship that Judge Edwards would dismiss as useless (Chapter 2). And not only Judge Edwards. See, for example, J. M. Balkin, "What Is a Postmodern Constitutionalism?" 90 *Michigan Law Review* 1966 (1992).

14. Amar and Widawsky, note 12 above, at 1365.

No doubt they are correct that the brutal, degrading, and dehumanizing character of Negro slavery was one of the reasons the Thirteenth Amendment was adopted.[15] But it does not follow that every relation that is brutal, degrading, and dehumanizing is a form of slavery, any more than it follows from the fact that all judges are wise that all wise men are judges. Negro slavery in the United States is only one form of slavery, and the Thirteenth Amendment outlawed the others as well. But when we talk about "wage slaves," or say that some husband has made a "slave" of his wife, or call an executive a "slave" of his job, or describe prostitution as "white slavery" (the official title of the Mann Act was originally the "White Slave Traffic Act"), we are conscious of using "slavery" metaphorically rather than literally. We mean in fact that these relations or practices are not slavery[16] but have something in common with it. To treat constitutional terms metaphorically is, like using a pun on "labor" to bring the right to an abortion under the Thirteenth Amendment (see Chapter 5), to remove any textual check to constitutional interpretation. This is a paradoxical result of what purports to be a close reading of the Thirteenth Amendment, and shows that even clause-by-clause theorizing can quickly get out of hand.

It is true that by changing the focus of DeShaney's claim from the Fourteenth to the Thirteenth Amendment, Amar and Widawsky avoid the farthest-reaching implication of Strauss's analysis: that we all have a federally enforceable right to some level of competently performed state social services—to decent police and fire protection, ambulance service, the prevention of child abuse, and so forth. There is no way in which a right to be rescued from the car that you drove into a lake could be extracted from the Thirteenth Amendment. But this is small comfort to the constitutional conservative, who will be appalled to discover that Amar and Widawsky read "slavery" so broadly that the Thirteenth Amendment "may provide a cause of action for battered wives who are unprotected by the state."[17]

And even if Joshua DeShaney was his father's slave within the meaning of the amendment, it does not follow that by failing to protect him from his father the state violated the amendment. It is not as if the

15. Another was that, as Lincoln had seen before the Civil War, as a practical matter the nation could not hold together if some states permitted slavery while others forbade it.

16. See the discussion of metaphor in Chapter 24.

17. Amar and Widawsky, note 12 above, at 1385 n. 112.

state condoned the father's conduct; indeed, it prosecuted him for it. To reply that "despite its knowledge of Joshua's victimization, the state turned a blind eye to de facto slavery within its jurisdiction and violated the Amendment just as much as if its judges had simply ignored habeas [corpus] writs filed on Joshua's behalf"[18] is to speak the language of legal fiction. "The state" did not know anything. A social worker employed by the state stupidly though not maliciously failed to remove DeShaney from his father's custody. Is Wisconsin therefore a slave state?

A reader more sympathetic to Amar and Widawsky's article than I might be persuaded that the authors had shown that Joshua DeShaney's plight was similar to enslavement and even that the language and history of the Thirteenth Amendment permit a broad reading that would treat his situation as one of actual slavery and that might *even* entitle his mother to obtain in federal court monetary redress from the state. But there would still be a missing link. To say that the amendment could be read as broadly as Amar and Widawsky propose is not to say that it must or should be read that way. The missing link is a reason for preferring the slavery analogy to the alternatives. DeShaney's case could just as readily be analogized to one in which a mugger beats up his victim in the presence of a police officer who, having been inadequately trained, is unable to prevent the crime. That would be a pure case of negligent failure by the state to prevent private violence. No one would try to connect it to the Thirteenth Amendment. Is DeShaney's plight more like that of the mugging victim or more like that of a slave on a cotton plantation in Mississippi in 1850? To choose between the analogies requires consideration of a number of factors ignored by Amar and Widawsky, notably the empirical questions that I raised in connection with David Strauss's article.

Amar has been commended for providing a more lawyerly alternative—one that pays due regard to constitutional "text, history, and structure"—to Dworkin's treatment of constitutional provisions as "abstract moral principles."[19] So Amar is a liberal's Bork; a left-wing originalist.[20] But isn't all this business of constitutional method just a lot of shadow-boxing? Shouldn't Dworkin be commended for the

18. Id. at 1381.

19. Jeffrey Rosen, "Jeffrey Rosen Replies," in "'Life's Dominion': An Exchange," *New Republic*, Sept. 6, 1993, pp. 44, 45; see also Rosen, "A Womb with a View," *New Republic*, June 14, 1993, p. 35.

20. Not an adequate characterization of Amar's work as a whole, I admit.

candor of his position—for not always pretending that he's just a better reader, a better mole, whose personal values and political philosophy have nothing to do with his interpretations?

Strauss and Amar-Widawsky are subject to a further criticism: failure to consider the total effect of their proposals. Liberal constitutional theorists want the Supreme Court to recognize a number of new constitutional rights, such as the right to be protected from private violence. Amar and Widawsky's interpretive method would make the Constitution a cornucopia of new rights. A responsible defense of a program for increasing the number of constitutional rights would require the proponent to consider what the aggregate impact, whether on judicial workloads or on the political legitimacy of the Supreme Court or on the distribution of power among the different branches of government, would be if *all* the rights he wants to see recognized were recognized. Suppose that if the aggregate impact of an approach that would dictate a different result in *DeShaney* and a host of other "conservative" constitutional decisions were estimated, it would be plain that the approach was mistaken, that the courts would be biting off much more than they could chew. Liberal constitutional theorists ignore this possibility. Implicitly they assume that the incremental social cost of indefinitely expanding federal judicial capacity is zero. They have no sense of priorities. They are piecemeal analysts, like the judges themselves.

Notice, finally, the *belatedness* of the type of constitutional theorizing illustrated by Strauss and Amar-Widawsky, and in the case of abortion by Dworkin as well. Constitutional issues percolate in the lower courts for years before they reach the Supreme Court. Yet scholarly interest in the issues rarely perks up until the issue has not only reached the Supreme Court but been decided by it. So mesmerized are constitutional scholars by the Supreme Court—which is to say by power, because few constitutional scholars have an inflated opinion of the quality of Supreme Court Justices—that often they delay too long in writing to have a chance of having an impact on constitutional law. By the time they reach the battlefield, the battle is over.

The multitude, for the moment, is foolish, when they act without delib-eration.[1]

chapter 7

Legal Positivism without Positive Law

YEARS ago Bruce Ackerman advanced the startling—to legal profes-sionals, the incredible—thesis that the constitutional turmoil of the 1930s—the Supreme Court's invalidation of key New Deal programs, Roosevelt's "Court-packing" plan, and the "switch in time that saved nine," which presaged the retirement of the older Supreme Court Justices and their replacement by New Dealers—constituted a legal amendment of the Constitution. In the first volume of a projected trilogy, Ackerman extends and defends this thesis and embeds it in a larger view of constitutional legitimacy that I want to examine.[2]

Ackerman first outlines the rival approaches that he seeks to supplant. One, which he calls "monism," sees the task of constitutional theoriz-ing as one of reconciling the authority of unelected, life-tenured judges to invalidate legislation with America's commitment, seen as primary, to democracy. The usual monistic solution is a presumption of legisla-tive validity. One leading monist, however, John Ely, attempts to dis-solve the tension inherent in judicial review of legislation by arguing,

---

1. Edmund Burke, "Speech on the Reform of Representation of the Commons in Parlia-ment," in *The Philosophy of Edmund Burke: A Selection from His Speeches and Writings* 211 (Louis I. Bredvold and Ralph G. Ross eds. 1960).
2. *We the People*, vol. 1: *Foundations* (1991).

as we have seen, that constitutional rights are designed to make democracy work better, as by removing obstacles to the franchise and to free debate. A second approach, which Ackerman calls "rights foundationalism," sees the task of constitutional theorizing as that of identifying principles worthy of preempting democratic choice. One prominent rights foundationalist, Ronald Dworkin, tries monist-like to dissolve the tension with democracy by arguing that "the American conception of democracy is whatever form of government the Constitution, according to the best interpretation of that document, establishes."[3] Since the Constitution implicitly authorizes judicial review of the validity of legislation, such review cannot be antidemocratic—nothing allowed by the Constitution can be. This is a conversation stopper all right. It disables us from saying not only that Athens was more (or less) democratic than modern America, but also that America would be more democratic if judges were less willing than they are to invalidate legislation.

Ackerman's solution, which he calls "dualism," posits two sorts of democratic political activity, a higher and a lower. Monists believe that democracy is primary, and so does he. The difference is that they think democracy is one thing and he thinks it two things. The higher lawmaking occurs in periods of revolutionary self-consciousness, as he believes the founding period, the period of the Civil War and Reconstruction, and the New Deal all to have been. It is the expression of a deep, broad, genuine, and unimpeachably legitimate popular will, when people are thinking and acting as private *citizens*. The lower form of political activity occurs in normal times, when people are thinking and acting as *private* citizens; it is the quotidian horse-trading and intrigue of ordinary politics.[4] When judges use principles adopted in periods of revolutionary self-consciousness to invalidate the legislative products of ordinary politics, they are not being undemocratic; they are being faithful to a deeper conception of democracy than mundane representative democracy, heeding a popular will tested and refined in the crucible of public debate and earnest deliberation.

Ackerman argues from the *Federalist Papers* that the founders be-

3. Ronald Dworkin, "Unenumerated Rights: Whether and How *Roe* Should Be Overruled," 59 *University of Chicago Law Review* 381, 385 (1992).

4. The analogy to Thomas Kuhn's distinction between "revolutionary" and "normal" science is noted in Frank Michelman, "Law's Republic," 97 *Yale Law Journal* 1493, 1522–1523 (1988).

lieved both that there was a difference between revolutionary and normal politics and that they were practicing the first sort. He defends the possibility of genuinely public-spirited politics—the sort he finds, and for his thesis to persuade must find, in the nation's revolutionary periods—against public-choice theorists who argue that free-rider problems and difficulties in aggregating preferences by means of voting prevent democratic politics from expressing a genuine, informed popular will. He thinks it a detail whether the authentic popular will that emerges in periods of revolutionary consciousness is embodied in a document that complies with the prescribed formalities for a legally binding enactment. Some perfectly regular amendments, such as the amendments creating and repealing Prohibition, are to him mere "superstatutes" that have no radiations beyond their language,[5] while some invalid and even invisible amendments have transformative force because they are manifestations of the higher lawmaking.

Both the original Constitution and the Reconstruction amendments were adopted irregularly, even illegally—the constitutional convention of 1787 exceeded its terms of reference from the Continental Congress, and the southern states were required to ratify the Reconstruction amendments as a condition of having their congressional representation restored—making those amendments, in Ackerman's words, merely "amendment-simulacra" (p. 51). So it does not matter that the third great constitutional revolution, that of the 1930s, produced no piece of paper to tack on to the Constitution as an amendment except the repeal of Prohibition. The only thing that matters is that by invalidating New Deal statutes the Supreme Court forced the American people to think hard about what kind of constitutional structure they wanted, with the result that the reelection of Roosevelt by a huge plurality in 1936 was a genuine expression of the popular will—the will to big government. Ackerman insists on the parity of these constitutional revolutions. "The Republican Reconstruction of the Union was an act of constitutional creation no less profound than the Founding itself,"

---

5. Cf. Donald J. Boudreaux and A. C. Pritchard, "Rewriting the Constitution: An Economic Analysis of the Constitutional Amendment Process," 62 *Fordham Law Review* 111 (1993). Boudreaux and Pritchard argue that constitutional amendments are best understood as a species of interest-group legislation most likely to be sought when an interest group, anticipating *future* opposition to its preferred policy, wishes to embody it in an enactment that will be difficult to repeal. If there is present opposition, the amendment route is unlikely to be feasible. See also W. Mark Crain and Robert D. Tollison, "Constitutional Change in an Interest-Group Perspective," 8 *Journal of Legal Studies* 165 (1979).

while in the New Deal the Supreme Court "began to build new constitutional foundations for activist national government" (pp. 46, 49).

The wicked Reagan tried to precipitate a fourth constitutional revolution by nominating Robert Bork—who "could supply the intellectual firepower necessary to write judicial texts that would shape the law as fundamentally as had the great New Deal opinions" (p. 52)—to the Supreme Court. The effort failed, as have many similar efforts, such as William Jennings Bryan's populism and Joseph McCarthy's lumpen anticommunism. Bork, an "originalist," would have tried to restore the founders' constitution—a restoration that would be revolutionary, because it would overturn the second and third constitutions.[6]

Ackerman believes that between periods of revolutionary excitement the Supreme Court plays and should play only a preservationist role—preserving the structure created in the preceding such period. The role requires great interpretive skill, because what is to be interpreted is not a text but a revolution that need leave no documentary traces, at least in the form of constitutional amendments. The modern judge, moreover—the judge of the New Deal era, which is our era because there has been no successful constitutional revolution since the New Deal—must interpret three revolutions rather than just one, because numbers two and three did not sweep number one away entirely. This interpretive challenge is "the problem of multigenerational synthesis" (p. 88).

Ackerman's analysis of the judicial function enables him to rescue *Lochner v. New York* from the traditional charge of usurpation. Although the decision went far beyond the founding fathers' understanding of national power, it reflected the Supreme Court's awareness that the Civil War and Reconstruction had created a new constitution, one in which states no longer had a free hand to curtail liberty. No longer could they countenance slavery; that much was clear. But in addition (so Ackerman interprets *Lochner* as deciding) no longer could they permit those lesser but still significant interferences with freedom of property and contract brought about by paternalistic laws, such as laws fixing wages or hours of work.

Two decisions exemplify for Ackerman interpretation of the New Deal constitution. *Brown v. Board of Education* he thinks pivots on the

---

6. Ackerman overlooks the fact that Justice Scalia has the same basic beliefs as Bork and adequate intellectual firepower to embody them in transformative judicial opinions.

expanded importance that the New Deal gave to public school education, while *Griswold v. Connecticut* transformed the contract and property rights that had been important in the first and second constitutions into a right of privacy responsive to the altered balance between governmental power and personal liberty that had been brought about by the third, the New Deal, constitution.

Both the normative and the positive adequacy of Ackerman's ingenious analysis can be questioned. To begin with, he does not explain *why* we should bestow legitimacy on revolutionary excitement. Suppose that in some future period of economic crisis, akin to that which spawned the New Deal, a Hitler-style demagogue is elected President and persuades Congress to enact plainly unconstitutional statutes sweeping away basic civil liberties. The courts duly invalidate these statutes, but the demagogue is reelected on the crest of a wave of public indignation at judicial obstructionism and within a few years is able to pack the courts with judges who share his views and uphold his laws. This sequence would for Ackerman create a constitutional revolution that the next generation of judges would be *legally* obligated to preserve—even though it entailed their disregarding the written Constitution, which had never been amended—until another constitutional revolution erupted. Why would one want to encourage judges to behave in this way by telling them that otherwise they would be acting lawlessly? Ackerman does not answer this question but is sufficiently alert to the concern behind it to propose that the Constitution be amended to forbid amending it to repeal the Bill of Rights. He wants, in short, to "entrench" the Bill of Rights against a future Hitler. In so proposing he both flinches from the implications of his approach and contradicts it, for he forgets his basic point that an amendment does not have to conform to the constitutionally prescribed procedure for amending the Constitution in order to bind the judges. All that entrenchment can do is prevent formal amendments, but on Ackerman's own account the most important amendments are informal, and it is profoundly unclear what form of words could rule them out. Entrenchment presupposes—what he denies—the legal paramountcy of formal amendments.

Legal positivism is controversial enough, as we glimpsed in Chapter 4. Ackerman is proposing that we bestow the mantle of legitimacy on something far more questionable: legal positivism without positive law. "During both Reconstruction and the New Deal, the Court recognized

that the People had spoken even though their political leaders refused
to follow the technical legalities regulating constitutional amendment"
(p. 195). Ackerman thinks it a good thing, rather than merely a pru-
dent thing, that the Court did this; but he does not defend his position.
He should at least have asked *why* the nation's political leaders did not
employ the amendment process. Because it would have taken too long?
Because a proposed amendment would have failed of enactment? Are
these not reasons for doubting whether "the People" had actually
spoken?

The original Constitution is a detailed document, and the *Federalist
Papers* explained the meaning of the various provisions and the political
theory behind them in detail. The antifederalists set forth their objections in detail too. The people who elected delegates to the state
ratifying conventions therefore had the benefit of a full debate. No one
could have doubted the importance of the issues debated. So if the
restricted nature of the eighteenth-century franchise is ignored
(women, slaves, and the unpropertied could not vote), the original
Constitution can fairly be thought a considered expression of informed
public opinion. Not so Ackerman's two subsequent "constitutional
moments." The Reconstruction amendments do not on their face
appear to revolutionize the relation between the national government
and the states; their principal thrust is to abolish the racial caste system
of the southern states. The amendments were vague enough that aggressive judges, without being laughed out of court, could transform
them from a protection of the freedom of black people against oppression by the southern states to a protection of economic freedom from
state regulation anywhere.[7] But Ackerman has not shown that this
diversion actualized the popular will expressed in the amendments.

Although there was strong popular support for the New Deal programs, there was strong public antipathy, expressed in the successful
opposition to Roosevelt's Court-packing plan, to coercing the Supreme
Court to uphold those programs. The popular support for the New
Deal, moreover, was not well informed; and this should matter to
Ackerman. Much of it was motivated by the belief that the New Deal
would bring the country out of the Depression. The belief was mis-

7. We saw an extreme example of the Reconstruction amendments' potential fluidity in
Chapter 6 when discussing Amar and Widawsky's proposal to turn the Thirteenth Amendment against child abuse.

taken.[8] Many New Deal programs were aimed at raising prices and wages, and by thus reducing economic growth and employment programs delayed the recovery from the Depression, as did (in all likelihood) the spirit of restless experimentation and of hostility to business that was characteristic of Roosevelt's pre–World War II Presidency. And many New Deal programs, whatever their motives and their macroeconomic significance or insignificance, were microeconomically unsound; they prevented an efficient allocation of resources. Examples are the separation of commercial and investment banking, the breaking up of public utility holding companies, the attack on chain stores, the creation of farm price supports and acreage restrictions, the regulation of truck and airline routes and fares, the increased regulation of telecommunications, the encouragement of unionization,[9] and perhaps even federal deposit insurance.

Maybe the nation could have done no better in the circumstances. But beginning with the Administrative Procedure Act and the Taft-Hartley Act, and continuing to this day, much federal legislative activity has had to be devoted to pruning the excesses of the New Deal. Ackerman regards the New Deal as a coherent effort to create a modern welfare state by throwing off the shackles of laissez-faire. Actually it was a collection of partisan, ad hoc, opportunistic responses to a frightening and poorly understood economic crisis and to relentless interest-group pressures. A consistent commitment to social justice is not easy to discern in this welter. New Deal tax policies reduced the after-tax income of the very wealthiest *and* of the poorest, leaving the income distribution largely unchanged.[10]

8. See, for example, Robert Aaron Gordon, *Economic Instability and Growth: The American Record* 72 (1974); Herbert Stein, *Presidential Economics: The Making of Economic Policy from Roosevelt to Reagan* 62–63 (1984); Ellis W. Hawley, *The New Deal and the Problem of Monopoly: A Study in Economic Ambivalence* (1966), esp. chs. 7, 14, and 20; Stanley Lebergott, *The Americans: An Economic Record*, ch. 35 (1984); Bradford A. Lee, "The New Deal Reconsidered," *Wilson Quarterly*, Spring 1982, p. 62. For a more favorable view of the impact of early New Deal macroeconomic policies, see Peter Temin, *Lessons from the Great Depression: The Lionel Robbins Lectures for 1989* 96–100 (1989); yet even Temin blames the deep recession of 1937 on government policy. Id. at 121–122.

9. Even those who think very well of unionization in principle are critical of the actual design and consequences of the Wagner Act. See, for example, Mark Barenberg, "The Political Economy of the Wagner Act: Power, Symbol, and Workplace Cooperation," 106 *Harvard Law Review* 1379, 1489–1496 (1993).

10. Mark H. Leff, *The Limits of Symbolic Reform: The New Deal and Taxation, 1933–1939*

All that this shows, though, is that the popular will can be mistaken; and the fact that it *is* the popular will might be enough to confer legitimacy upon it. But you need an *argument* that democracy is normative, and Ackerman makes none and would have trouble making one since he wants courts to feel free to override current democratic preferences on the basis of a wave of popular emotion that crested more than half a century ago. No doubt, the more earnest and extensive the deliberations leading up to a democratic enactment are, the more likely the enactment is to be an authentic expression of popular opinion (and what else could democratic preference mean?). But it does not follow that judges should genuflect to strong currents of public opinion *before* those currents express themselves in positive law, and use their reading of those currents to limit the power of democratically elected officials.

Ackerman's own faith in "deliberative democracy" is distinctly limited. It is his fear that due deliberation is no guaranty against error or even viciousness that motivates his suggestion for placing certain fundamental rights beyond the possibility of removal from the Constitution. So the grounding of his populism cannot be epistemological— cannot be the idea that, given ideal conditions for the formation of an educated and reflective public opinion, that opinion is the closest we can get to truth. And though Ackerman is an expert on liberal theory,[11] he does not seek to derive his populism from it. He grounds his populism in—populism (in "dualist America" it is "the People who are the source of rights" [p. 15]), and in the views of the framers of the original Constitution. That is an odd line for him to take. It is antidualist: it allows the framers of the original Constitution to control the future.

Ackerman's theory asks too little of judges in one sense (they are not to exercise conscience), too much in another. They are to determine the "meaning" of amorphous historical "moments." Maybe that formidable bit of jargon, "multigenerational synthesis," is apt after all—as connoting the remoteness of what Ackerman wants judges to do from what they are able to do. It is difficult enough to interpret texts in light of historical events without having to interpret the whole of American political history before you can decide a case.

3–7 (1984). None of this does Ackerman discuss; he keeps as aloof from facts as Strauss or Amar.

11. See his book *Social Justice in the Liberal State* (1980).

Another objection to dualism is that some niceties are nicer than others. Such illegalities as attended the adoption of the original Constitution and the Reconstruction amendments took place in the turbulent wakes of major internal wars. And what was adopted, in both cases, was a text. The New Deal was not a product of war and did not produce a constitutional text. It produced collectivist federal legislation and a liberal judiciary that proceeded to remake constitutional law.

Ackerman might respond that he is describing, not applauding, our constitutional regime; that his analysis is positive rather than normative. To the extent that he wants to entrench certain rights against even supermajorities, he obviously does want to go beyond dualism. But he describes the project of transcending dualism as "Utopian." Dualism is not Utopia, and maybe it best describes the structure of the Constitution and the practice under it, in which judges are interpreters of revolutionary moments.

I doubt it. The same forces that shape the thinking of statesmen (as we call politicians whose efforts produce large and durable changes in public policy) shape the thinking of judges. The nationalist impulse that swept the Union to triumph in the Civil War produced Supreme Court Justices who thought that a strong national economy unimpeded by parochial local regulations, such as the maximum hour law struck down in *Lochner*, was more important than justice to blacks and who interpreted the plastic language of the Fourteenth Amendment accordingly. The medley of "liberal" ideas that produced the New Deal produced Justices who, naturally enough, changed the focus of constitutional law to the promotion of those ideas. The judges at these various stages were not interpreting a revolution. They *were* the (or rather some of the) revolutionaries. Their place in history is determined not by their fidelity to their revolution but by the success of that revolution—which is why Holmes (who opposed the second revolution and anticipated the third), Jackson, Stone, and Warren are heroes; Taney, Brown, and Peckham villains.

Decided just five years after the adoption of the Fourteenth Amendment, the *Slaughter-House Cases*[12] rejected the argument that the amendment protected businessmen from state regulation that interfered with freedom of contract. The Court held that the Reconstruction amendments had altered the balance of federal and state relations

---

12. 83 U.S. 36 (1873).

only in the area of race. Ackerman explains the decision as "initiat[ing] one of the two fundamental approaches to [multigenerational] synthesis that defined middle [that is, second] republican jurisprudence. This involves *particularizing* the constitutional principles announced at Time Two in a way that restricted their impact upon the older principles of Time One" (p. 95; emphasis in original). The Justices of the Reconstruction era had learned about the (first) Constitution through law books, and the books had built a conceptual structure, a structure of broad principles. But they had "gain[ed] access to the meaning of the Reconstruction texts in a very different way—through lived experience of the greatest political events of their time." Naturally, therefore, "to them, Reconstruction was the culmination of something concrete and particular—the struggle against slavery" (pp. 96–97). It was only in the next generation, with "the fading of lived experience and the rise of legal dialectic" (p. 97), that judges raised the Reconstruction amendments to the level of general principle that could engender *Lochner* and like cases.

Some might think "lived experience" a better interpretive guide than "legal dialectic." But a stronger bit of evidence that the judges of the *Lochner* period were not engaged in something usefully described as interpretation is their abandonment of blacks. Fastening on the infamous remark in the majority opinion in *Plessy v. Ferguson* that segregation would stigmatize blacks only if they chose to regard it as stigmatizing,[13] Ackerman argues that the decision reveals the grip of laissez-faire thinking as surely as *Lochner.* But the law upheld in *Plessy* forbade blacks to make contracts with railroads on mutually agreeable terms. Ackerman does not explain how the Reconstruction amendments could have been thought, by an *honest* judge, simultaneously to forbid states to interfere with the freedom of contract of whites and to permit states to interfere with the freedom of contract of blacks. The judges of the *Plessy-Lochner* period were not interpreting the Reconstruction amendments; they were inverting them.

Neither were *Brown* and *Griswold* syntheses of the New Deal "constitution" with the previous constitutions. It is true that in distinguishing *Plessy* the Court in *Brown* emphasized the greater importance of public education in 1954 than in 1868, when the Fourteenth Amendment was adopted, or in 1896, when *Plessy* was decided. But the

13. 163 U.S. 537, 551 (1896).

reasons for this emphasis had nothing to do with the New Deal. They were rhetorical: to explain why the Court need not be bound by the legislative history of the Fourteenth Amendment, a history which indicated that the amendment had not been understood by its framers or supporters to require blacks to attend school with whites,[14] and to justify overruling a decision on which the South had erected its public institutions. Proof of the rhetorical function of invoking the growth of public education is that in the years following *Brown*, in a series of per curiam (unsigned) decisions that offer no explanation for their result, as if it were obviously dictated by *Brown*, the Supreme Court invalidated a host of segregation laws that had nothing to do with public education; that involved the segregation of beaches, golf courses, parks, buses, and other noneducational facilities.[15]

The Court's mention of public education could have had nothing to do with the New Deal. Although public education was more widespread in the 1950s than it had been at the end of the nineteenth century, it had been important enough back then for the Court in *Plessy* to use the legality of public school racial segregation—conceded by Plessy's lawyer—to justify the segregation of transportation facilities.[16] And the New Deal had given public education no push at all. Both total school enrollment and public school attendance fell between 1932 and 1940.[17] When "Roosevelt and his associates put together the congeries of programs that came to be known as the New Deal, it was not primarily to the schools that they turned in developing educational

14. In an unpublished monograph, Michael W. McConnell has challenged this reading of the legislative history. McConnell, "Originalism and the Desegregation Decisions" (unpublished, University of Chicago Law School, 1993). But it was the conventional wisdom at the time of *Brown*.

15. See, for example, Mayor and City Council of Baltimore City v. Dawson, 350 U.S. 877 (1955); Holmes v. City of Atlanta, 350 U.S. 879 (1955); Gayle v. Browder, 352 U.S. 903 (1956); New Orleans Parks Improvement Association v. Detiege, 358 U.S. 54 (1958); State Athletic Commission v. Dorsey, 359 U.S. 533 (1959).

16. 163 U.S. at 544–545, 551.

17. U.S. Bureau of the Census, *Historical Statistics of the United States: Colonial Times to 1957* 207 (1960) (ser. H 223–233); Joel Spring, *The American School 1642–1990: Varieties of Historical Interpretation of the Foundations and Development of American Education* 277–280 (2d ed. 1990); David Tyack, Robert Lowe, and Elisabeth Hansot, *Public Schools in Hard Times: The Great Depression and Recent Years,* ch. 3 (1984) ("A New Deal in Education?"). Such New Deal programs as the Civilian Conservation Corps and the National Youth Administration emphasized learning by doing. There were also special programs in adult literacy. But public school education was not emphasized, and there was tension between the Roosevelt Administration and the educational establishment.

programs. They saw the 'youth problem' as one of the critical issues facing the nation, but they conceived of it in terms of youth unemployment; and, suspicious of the people they associated with the 'educational establishment,' they were inclined to bypass the formal apparatus of schooling."[18] Ackerman's timing is off when he says that "with the New Deal, the public schools could take on a new symbolic meaning. They were no longer anomalous, but paradigmatic of the new promise of activist government" (p. 148). It had been a long time since public schools had been considered anomalous, and Roosevelt did not consider public schools paradigmatic of anything.

Granted, the New Deal was more than its legislative product. It was also the empowerment at the national level of certain "outs"—Catholics, Jews, workers, intellectuals, Southerners. It had an egalitarian component, one manifestation of which was the appointment to the Supreme Court of men like Douglas and Frankfurter who had liberal views on race. The views of these Justices, and the heightened consciousness of racism generated by Hitler and World War II, set the stage for *Brown*. But the decision is not usefully viewed as an interpretation of the New Deal, or of the Reconstruction amendments in the light of the New Deal. Ackerman is very much a Yale Law School product: he has New Deal nostalgia, as well as legal realist disdain for legal formalities such as the constitutionally prescribed process for amending the Constitution.

It requires as big a stretch to tie *Griswold* to the New Deal. Laws forbidding contraceptives had been enacted in the latter part of the nineteenth century, as part of the purity movement—an expression of Victorianism—and by 1965, when *Griswold* was decided, had been repealed in all but two states. The wave of repeals reflected the decline of Victorian sexual morality and the rise of the birth-control movement; both trends antedated the New Deal. Since the Connecticut law was enforced only against birth-control clinics, whose primary clientele consisted of poor and working-class women, the law was inequitable. But the Court did not mention this aspect of it. Nor does Ackerman. He tries to relate the decision to the New Deal differently, arguing that the bigger government is, the more urgent is the need for courts to protect individuals, through the recognition of new rights, from being

---

18. Lawrence A. Cremin, *American Education: The Metropolitan Experience 1876–1980* 311 (1988).

ground down by it. Under the "second Constitution," people had had robust contract and property rights, which automatically protected their privacy from invasion by the states. The New Deal took these away, and by doing so made the right of privacy more important than it had been.

But if bigger government empowers groups that formerly were politically impotent, the need of those groups for judicial protection may be less rather than more. It was in the era of lynching and Jim Crow that blacks needed judicial protection the most, and they didn't get it then—their abandonment by the courts having been announced with characteristic forthrightness by Holmes in an opinion which held, two years before *Lochner,* that the federal courts would not provide a remedy for the disenfranchisement of blacks in the southern states.[19] In any event the point is wide of *Griswold.* The law struck down in that case was not a manifestation of big government but a hangover from the era of small government. It is true that if the "second Constitution" had *really* protected freedom of contract, a married couple would have had no need to invoke a constitutional right of privacy in order to be able to buy contraceptives; their constitutional right of contract would have sufficed to enable them to buy anything that sellers were offering. But no one in the "middle Republic" had thought that laws forbidding the sale of contraceptives denied constitutionally protected freedom of contract. Such laws, which spread like wildfire in the heyday of constitutional doctrines influenced by laissez-faire principles, were considered comfortably within the states' regulatory power.

I do not want to exaggerate my disagreement with Ackerman. I agree that we should interpret the Constitution in light of our whole experience, including the dramatic upheavals of the Civil War, Reconstruction, the New Deal, and World War II. I agree that an amendment can alter a provision whose words it does not change (and thus the Supreme Court may have been justified in *Bolling v. Sharpe*[20] in holding that the equal protection clause of the Fourteenth Amendment had enlarged the concept of due process in the Fifth Amendment so that it now forbade federal segregation of public schools in the District of Columbia). The point has been made by thinkers as otherwise diverse as T. S. Eliot, who said that "what happens when a new work of art is created

19. Giles v. Harris, 189 U.S. 475 (1903).
20. 347 U.S. 497 (1954); see *The Problems of Jurisprudence* 144–146.

is something that happens simultaneously to all the works of art which preceded it,"[21] and Ronald Dworkin, who describes law by the metaphor of a chain novel, in which authors of successive chapters are both constrained by and alter the meaning of the earlier chapters.[22] I agree that judges are properly (as well as inevitably) influenced by deep and broad currents of public opinion. These are familiar points, but they are dramatized by Ackerman's thesis.

But the thesis itself is wrong and even dangerous. Wrong because the history of constitutional law since 1868 cannot be explained as the effort of judges to interpret and preserve moments of revolutionary consciousness. Dangerous because it invites judges to treat the popular will as a form of higher law entitling them to disregard ordinary concepts of legality. That is what Hitler's judges did, as we saw in Chapter 4. They correctly sensed a sea change in public attitudes (Hitler was immensely popular in Germany until the outbreak of war, and indeed retained much of his popularity until the collapse), and enforced the new outlook with minimum regard for legal niceties. It is worth recalling that what Ackerman deems the informal but legitimate amendment of the Constitution by the New Deal occurred at the same time.

21. "Tradition and the Individual Talent," in Eliot, *Selected Essays* 3, 5 (new ed. 1950).
22. Dworkin, *Law's Empire* 228–250 (1986).

chapter 8

What Am I? A Potted Plant?

I HAVE been lashing liberals for several chapters. But not in order to clear the way for conservative constitutional theory. This chapter and the next apply the lash to the most influential conservative approach to the Constitution. The core of that approach is a belief, by no means confined to people of conservative bent, that modern American judges are too aggressive, too "activist," too prone to substitute their own policy preferences for those of the elected branches of government. Maybe so, but many who complain about judicial activism espouse a view of law that is too narrow. And a good cause will not hallow a bad argument.

The legal theory that takes off from a rejection of judicial activism is sometimes called "strict constructionism"; applied to constitutional law, "originalism" or "textualism"; in its broadest signification, "formalism." Its best-known modern proponents are Robert Bork and Antonin Scalia. I shall discuss Bork's views in the next chapter. My text for this one is a forceful polemic by the political scientist Walter Berns.[1]

---

1. "Government by Lawyers & Judges," *Commentary,* June 1987, p. 17.

A less elaborate and sophisticated version of Bork's position, it exhibits the weaknesses of that position with stark clarity.[2]

"Questions about the public good," Berns argues, can "be decided legitimately only with the consent of the governed." Judges have no legitimate say about these issues. Their business is to address issues of private rights, that is, "to decide whether the right exists—in the Constitution or in a statute—and, if so, what it is; but at that point inquiry ceases." The judge may not use "discretion and the weighing of consequences" to arrive at his decisions, and he may not create new rights (p. 17). The Constitution is a source of legally enforceable rights only to the extent that it sets forth "fundamental and clearly articulated principles of government" (p. 19). There must be no judicial creativity or "policy-making" (p. 20). In short, there is a political sphere, where the people rule, and a domain of fixed rights, administered but not created or altered by judges. The first is the sphere of discretion, the second of application. Legislators make the law; judges find and apply it.

There has never been a time when the courts of the United States, state or federal, behaved consistently in accordance with this ideal. Nor could they, for reasons rooted in the nature of law and legal institutions, in the limitations of human knowledge, and in the character of a political system.

"Questions about the public good" and "questions about private rights" are separable when one is dealing with established rights that are well defined. But society, especially in periods of change, keeps throwing up to the courts questions about the scope of the established rights, and those questions cannot be answered without consideration of the public good. Can a rescuer claim a reward under the law of contract if he didn't know about it? The effect on the number of rescues is not irrelevant to answering this qustion. Should an heir who murders his benefactor have a right to inherit from his victim? The

2. The article on which this chapter is based was published in the *New Republic* on the day when the confirmation hearing on Bork's nomination to the Supreme Court began, and was taken in some quarters as an oblique expression of opposition to the nomination. Nothing could have been more remote from my intentions. The article was written and mailed to the *New Republic* before Justice Powell announced his resignation, creating the vacancy that Bork was nominated to fill; it is sheer happenstance that the article was published when it was. Although I have my differences with Bork, I thought when he was nominated and I think today that he should have been confirmed and would have been an outstanding Justice.

public good that results from discouraging murders is a relevant consideration. Almost the whole of so-called private law, such as property, contract, and tort law, is instrumental to the public end of obtaining the social advantages of free markets. And since most private law is common law—that is, law made by judges rather than by legislators or by constitution-framers—judges have been entrusted from the start with making policy. Can nonpossessory rights be acquired in water, oil, gas, and other "fugitive" resources? A sensible answer will not be insensitive to the consequences for efficient resource allocation, a policy consideration. If a locomotive spews sparks that set a farmer's crops afire, has the railroad invaded the farmer's property right or does the railroad's ownership of its right-of-way implicitly include the right to emit sparks? If the railroad has such a right, shall it be conditional on the railroad's taking reasonable precautions to minimize the danger of fire? If, instead, the farmer has a right to be free from sparks, shall it be conditional on his taking reasonable precautions? These questions, too, cannot be answered sensibly without considering the social consequences of alternative answers, and yet it is courts that, typically, have been delegated to answer them. Private law is inseparable from notions of the public good, especially for us classical liberals, for whom society is the aggregate of its members rather than something standing apart from them and having its own interests.

When a constitutional convention, a legislature, or a court promulgates a rule of law, it necessarily does so without full knowledge of the circumstances in which the rule might be invoked in the future. When the unforeseen circumstance arises—it might be the advent of the motor vehicle or of electronic surveillance, or a change in attitudes toward religion, race, or sexual propriety—a court asked to apply the rule must decide, in light of information not available to the promulgators of the rule, what the rule should mean in its new setting. Realistically, it is being asked to make a new rule, in short to legislate. This entails a creative decision, involving discretion, the weighing of consequences, though, properly, a more circumscribed decision than one made by a real legislature. A court that decides that copyright protection extends to the coloring of old black-and-white movies is making a creative decision, because the copyright laws do not mention colorization. It is not being lawless or usurpative merely because it is weighing consequences and exercising discretion. A court that decides (as the Supreme Court has done in one of its less controversial modern rulings)[3] that the Fourth Amendment's prohibition against unreasonable searches and seizures shall apply to wiretapping, even though no trespass is committed by wiretapping and hence no property right is invaded, is creating a new right and making policy. In a situation not foreseen or expressly provided for by the framers of the Constitution, a simple reading out of a policy judgment made by them is impossible.

The Constitution does not say that the federal government has sovereign immunity—the traditional right of governments not to be sued without their consent. Nevertheless the Supreme Court has held that the federal government has sovereign immunity.[4] Is this interpolation usurpative? The Federal Tort Claims Act, a law waiving sovereign immunity so that citizens can sue the federal government, makes no exception for suits by members of the armed services who are injured through the negligence of their superiors. Nevertheless the Supreme Court has held that the act was not intended to provide soldiers with a remedy.[5] The decision may be right or wrong, but it is not wrong just because it is creative. The Eleventh Amendment to the Constitution forbids a citizen of one state to sue "another" state in federal court without the consent of the defendant state. Does this mean that you can sue your own state in federal court without the state's consent? That is what the words imply, but the Supreme Court, concluding that the amendment was intended to preserve the sovereign immunity of the states more broadly, answered the question "no."[6] The Court thought this result entailed by the federal system that the Constitution created. Again, the Court may have been right or wrong, but it was not wrong just because it was creative.

Opposite the unrealistic picture of judges who apply law but never make it, Walter Berns hangs an unrealistic picture of a populist legislature that acts only "with the consent of the governed" (p. 17). (That Right and Left invoke "democracy" with equal facility may suggest a certain emptiness in the word.) Speaking for myself, I find that many of the political candidates whom I have voted for have failed to be elected and that those who have been elected have then proceeded to vote for a great deal of legislation that I did not want to see enacted.

3. Katz v. United States, 389 U.S. 347 (1967).
4. United States v. Lee, 106 U.S. 196 (1882).
5. Feres v. United States, 340 U.S. 135 (1950).
6. Hans v. Louisiana, 134 U.S. 1 (1890).

Given the effectiveness of interest groups in the political process, much of this legislation probably didn't have the consent of a majority of citizens. Politically, I feel more governed than self-governing, and this is one reason why I think more warmly of limited government than of popular government. In considering whether to shrink what are now understood to be constitutional safeguards to the slight dimensions implied by a literal interpretation of the Constitution, we should be careful to have a realistic, not an idealized, picture of the legislative and executive branches of government, which would be even more powerful than they are today if those safeguards were reduced.

The framers of a constitution who want to make it a charter of liberties and not just a set of constitutive rules face a difficult choice. They can write specific provisions and thereby doom their work to rapid obsolescence, or they can write general provisions, thereby allowing substantial discretion to the authoritative interpreters, who in our system are the judges. The U.S. Constitution is a mixture of specific and general provisions. Many of the specific provisions have stood the test of time well or have been amended without much fuss. This is especially true of the rules establishing the structure and procedures of Congress. Most of the specific provisions creating rights, however, have fared poorly. Some have proved irksomely anachronistic—for example, the right conferred by the Seventh Amendment to a jury trial in federal court in all cases at law if the stakes exceed $20. Others have become dangerously anachronistic, such as the right to bear arms. Some have even turned topsy-turvy, such as the provision for indictment by grand jury. The grand jury has become an instrument of prosecutorial investigation, rather than being the protection for the criminal suspect that the framers of the Bill of Rights expected it to be. If the Bill of Rights had consisted entirely of specific provisions, it would no longer be a significant constraint on the behavior of government officials.

Many provisions of the Constitution, however, are drafted in general terms. This creates flexibility in the face of unforeseen changes, but it also creates the possibility of alternative interpretations, and this possibility is an embarrassment for a theory of judicial legitimacy that denies that judges have any right to exercise discretion. A choice among semantically plausible interpretations of a text, in circumstances remote from those contemplated by its drafters, requires the exercise of discretion and the weighing of consequences. Reading is not a form of deduction; understanding requires a consideration of consequences. If

I say, "I'll eat my hat," one reason why my listeners will "decode" the meaning of this statement in nonliteral fashion is that I couldn't eat a hat if I tried. The broader principle, which applies to the Constitution as much as to a spoken utterance, is that if one possible interpretation of an ambiguous statement would entail absurd or terrible results, that is a good reason to reject it.

Even the decision to read the Constitution narrowly, and thereby to "restrain" judicial interpretation, is not a decision that can be read directly from the text. The Constitution does not say, "Read me broadly," or, "Read me narrowly." The decision to do one or the other must be made as a matter of political theory and will depend on such things as one's view of the springs of judicial legitimacy and the relative competence of courts and legislatures in dealing with particular types of issue.

The Sixth Amendment provides that "in all criminal prosecutions, the accused shall enjoy the right . . . to have the Assistance of Counsel for his defense." Read narrowly, this just means that the defendant can't be forbidden to retain counsel. If he cannot afford counsel, or competent counsel, he is out of luck. Read broadly, it guarantees even the indigent the effective assistance of counsel. It becomes not just a negative right to be allowed to hire a lawyer but a positive right to demand the help of the government in financing one's defense if one cannot do it oneself. Either reading is compatible with the semantics of the provision, but the first better captures the specific intent of the framers. When the Sixth Amendment was written, English law forbade a criminal defendant to have the assistance of counsel unless his case presented abstruse questions of law. The framers wanted to do away with this prohibition. But, more broadly, they wanted to give criminal defendants protection against being railroaded. When they wrote, government could not afford, or at least did not think it could afford, to hire lawyers for indigent criminal defendants. Moreover, criminal trials were short and simple, so it was not completely ridiculous to expect a lay person to be able to defend himself competently from a criminal charge without a lawyer if he couldn't afford to hire one. Today the situation is different. Not only can the society afford to supply lawyers to poor people charged with crimes, but modern criminal law and procedure are so complicated that an unrepresented defendant is usually at a great disadvantage.

I do not know whether Berns thinks the Supreme Court was usurping legislative power when it held that a poor person has a right to the assistance of counsel at the state's expense.[7] But he clearly thinks it a mistake that the Supreme Court invalidated racial segregation in public schools. Reading the words of the Fourteenth Amendment in the narrowest possible manner in order to minimize judicial discretion, and noting the absence of evidence that the framers wanted to eliminate segregation, Berns argues that "equal protection of the laws" just means nondiscriminatory enforcement of whatever laws are enacted, even if the laws themselves are discriminatory. As for the proposition that "separate educational facilities are inherently unequal," that is "a logical absurdity" (p. 20).

On Berns's reading, then, the promulgation of the equal protection clause was a trivial gesture at giving the recently freed slaves (and other blacks in the South, whose status at the time was similar to that of serfs) political equality with whites, since the clause in his view forbids the denial of that equality only by executive officers. The state may not withdraw police protection from blacks (unless by legislation?), but it may forbid them to sit next to whites on buses. This is a possible reading of the Fourteenth Amendment but not an inevitable one, unless judges must always interpret the Constitution as denying them the power to exercise judgment.

No competent person believes this. Everyone professionally involved with law knows that, as Holmes put it, judges legislate "interstitially," which is to say they make law, only more cautiously, more slowly, and in more principled, less partisan, fashion than legislators. Attempts to deny this truism entangle strict constructionists in contradictions. Berns says both that judges can enforce only "clearly articulated principles" (p. 19) and that they may invalidate unconstitutional laws. But the power to invalidate laws is not "articulated" in the Constitution; it is merely implicit in it. Berns believes that the courts have been wrong to interpret the First Amendment as protecting the publication of foul language in school newspapers, yet the words "freedom of speech, or of the press" do not appear to exclude foul language in school newspapers. Berns says he deduces his conclusion from the principle that expression, to be within the scope of the First Amendment, must be related to representative government. Where did he get that principle from? He did not read it in the Constitution.

7. Gideon v. Wainwright, 372 U.S. 335 (1963).

The First Amendment also forbids Congress to make laws "respecting an establishment of religion." Berns says that this does not mean that Congress "must be neutral between religion and irreligion" (p. 22). But the words will bear that meaning, so on what basis does he decide they should be given a different meaning? On the basis of Tocqueville's opinion of the importance of religion in a democratic society. In short, the correct basis for decision in his view is the consequence of the decision for democracy. Yet consequences are not—in the strict constructionist view that it is the particular objective of his article to defend—a fit thing for courts to consider. Berns expresses regret that the modern Supreme Court is oblivious to Tocqueville's opinion "of the importance of the woman . . . whose chastity as a young girl is protected not only by religion but by an education that limits her 'imagination'" (p. 21). A court that took such opinions into account would be engaged in aggressively consequentialist thinking.

The liberal judicial activists may be imprudent and misguided in their efforts to enact the liberal political agenda into constitutional law. But it is no use pretending that what they are doing is not interpretation but "deconstruction," not law but politics, just because it involves the exercise of discretion and a concern with consequences and because it reaches results not foreseen two hundred years ago. It may be bad law because it lacks firm moorings in constitutional text, or structure, or history, or consensus, or other legitimate sources of constitutional law, or because it is reckless of consequences, or because it oversimplifies difficult moral and political questions. But it is not bad law, or no law, just because it violates the tenets of strict construction.

chapter 9

Bork and Beethoven

$COMMENTARY$ magazine, as we glimpsed in the preceding chapter, is distinguished by the lucidity and forthrightness of its articles and by its single-minded advocacy of a "neoconservative" philosophy built around the related themes of conservative social and cultural values, aggressive anticommunism, and determined opposition to the egalitarian programs espoused by liberal Democrats and university radicals. It does not knowingly publish articles that deviate from this party line. Yet the February 1990 issue contained two articles that took opposite positions on originalism in the sense of interpretive fidelity to a text as the text was understood by its authors. The tension between the articles is masked by the fact that one was about Robert Bork and the other about musical performance and that both embrace the neoconservative creed. Nevertheless there is a deep and illuminating fissure between them.

"Bork Revisited" by Terry Eastland,[1] the Justice Department's director of public relations during the Reagan era, discusses three books about the Bork debacle, including Bork's own.[2] Eastland's main pur-

1. *Commentary,* Feb. 1990, p. 39.
2. Robert H. Bork, *The Tempting of America: The Political Seduction of the Law* (1990).

poses are to show that there really was an unprecedented as well as unsavory left-wing campaign against Bork's confirmation and that the Justice Department should not be blamed for Bork's defeat since the handling of the confirmation process had been assigned to the White House staff. The latter point, while important to Eastland's *amour propre,* is of no general interest, not least because Bork would have been defeated (it is clear in hindsight) even if his campaign had been handled more adroitly, which the Department of Justice might or might not have done. It is a fact that Bork was the target of a scurrilous scare campaign orchestrated by left-wingers, but Eastland is wrong to suppose that this is something new. Vicious political battles over Supreme Court nominees took place at the very outset of our constitutional history.[3] This should matter to an originalist, and therefore to Eastland, who praises Bork's book to the skies—a book whose project is the defense of originalism, in Eastland's paraphrase the "recovery of the once dominant view of constitutional law, which is that courts should apply the Constitution according to the principles intended by those who ratified the document."[4]

One might expect reinforcement of the originalist approach from "Cutting Beethoven Down to Size," by *Commentary*'s music critic, Samuel Lipman.[5] For it is an article about the authentic-performance movement, which is to musical interpretation what originalism is to legal interpretation. The movement involves "the required employment of original instruments—instruments resembling as closely as possible those on which the music was to be played at the time of its composition"; "reliance on what remains of the composer's original text, freed of all inadvertent error in transmission and publication, and of all subsequent editorial emendation"; and "the use of original performance styles—the complete observance of the composer's explicit indications, and an untiring attempt to recover all that can be known of the unwritten, customary, and taken-for-granted methods of deciphering and implementing his written notation" (p. 53). Thus, "in authentic performances the sought-after styles, including details of rhythmic execution, instrumental techniques, and concert pitch, are those contemporaneous with the composer—the exact way a composer might

3. James E. Gauch, "The Intended Role of the Senate in Supreme Court Appointments," 56 *University of Chicago Law Review* 337, 365 (1989).

4. Eastland, note 1 above, at 43.

5. *Commentary,* Feb. 1990, p. 53.

have heard his works when they were first rendered, at the time of their composition or shortly thereafter, by the best and most representative executants of the day" (p. 54).

This sounds much like Bork's originalism. Yet Lipman *hates* the authentic-performance movement. "Whereas the new approach is based on the use of scholarship to recapture a lost material reality of physically existing instruments, written texts, and definable styles, the best that has gone on over the past century and more in concert halls and opera houses has stressed spiritual insight—the empathic projection of the minds and talents of performers into the creative souls of great composers" (p. 54).[6] Lipman's *bête noire* is the English conductor Roger Norrington, whose performances of Beethoven's symphonies

> are short-winded, the music does not breathe. Because the music does not breathe, this quintessentially passionate music conveys no passion . . . These performances are, in short, consistently bad—and what is bad about them is precisely the result of the fleshing-out of all the absurd musico-intellectual pretensions of the authentic-performance movement . . . It is no defense . . . to adduce Beethoven's metronome markings as justification for these musical crimes. Any musician with experience in playing music by living composers knows that of all their performance directions, metronome markings are the least viable, consistent, and trustworthy. (pp. 56–57)

The reasons for the unreliability of composers' metronome markings "include distance in time from the work's actual composition, inexperience with the requirements of performance, a frequent disdain for the very fact of performance, and above all the composer's preexisting and complete knowledge of the content and structure of the music, a knowledge which no audience—and few performers either—can be expected to possess" (p. 57).[7]

A striking feature of Lipman's essay—redeeming it for *Commentary* orthodoxy—is his attributing the authentic-performance movement

6. Lipman is not alone in this view. "A young student, inclined at first always 'to respect the printed note' and to be wary of seemingly unmotivated or unjustified flights of fancy or free abandon of the formal rails, soon discovers that good teachers, and a majority of composers too—especially composers of an earlier period than ours—expect from him above all a living and breathing response to the printed ideas." Desmond Shawe-Taylor, "Keeping to the Score," *Times Literary Supplement*, Nov. 5, 1993, p. 6.

7. Lipman's strictures on strict metronomic regularity in the performance of Beethoven's music are supported by George Barth, *The Pianist as Orator: Beethoven and the Transformation of Keyboard Style* 1–2, 161–162 (1992).

not, as one might expect, to cultural conservatism but instead to cultural radicalism, aesthetic relativism, and the egalitarian obsessions of intellectuals. Norrington's "all-out attack on the foundations of Beethoven's greatness" is part of "the postmodern effort to humble once-mighty artists, thinkers, and values" (p. 56).

I do not want to be understood as endorsing Lipman's criticisms of the authentic-performance movement; evaluation of the movement raises many difficult questions.[8] Nor do I believe that if one is an originalist in one domain of interpretation, one must be an originalist in all.[9] Moreover, if the originalist and the nonoriginalist approach to musical interpretation both have some merit, they can coexist happily, and there is no need to choose between them, whereas when judges cannot agree on how to interpret statutes and the Constitution, law may become unpredictable. What I do contend is that originalism is neither the inevitable nor even the natural method of interpreting a given body of texts, or even the method of interpretation that is natural or inevitable for conservatives to follow.

The Tempting of America defends the position that "all that counts" to a judge interpreting the Constitution "is how the words used in the Constitution would have been understood at the time [of enactment]" (p. 144). But rather than produce convincing reasons why society should want its judges to adopt originalism as their interpretive methodology in constitutional cases, Bork seems almost to want to place the issue outside the boundaries of rational debate. How else to explain the pervasive religious imagery? It begins with the title of the book. Any doubt that the reference is to *the* temptation is dispelled by the title of the first chapter—"Creation and Fall"—which begins, "The Constitution was barely in place when one Justice of the Supreme Court cast covetous glances at the apple that would eventually cause the fall" (p. 19). (This must have been the original constitutional sin.) Bork embraces the idea that the Constitution is "our civil religion,"

---

8. For an excellent discussion, see Peter Kivy, *The Fine Art of Repetition: Essays in the Philosophy of Music,* ch. 6 (1993). Michael Krausz, in a fascinating essay on musical interpretation in which the lawyer will recognize innumerable parallels to the literature on constitutional and statutory interpretation, notes the tension between "the principle of faithfulness to the score" and "the principle of aesthetic consistency" as guides to interpretation and remarks judiciously that "there is no meta-standard in virtue of which literalism or aesthetic consistency can be conclusively ranked." Krausz, "Rightness and Reasons in Musical Interpretation," in *The Interpretation of Music: Philosophical Essays* 75, 79–80 (Michael Krausz ed. 1993).

9. See *Law and Literature* 209–268.

and, he never tires of repeating, originalism is its "orthodoxy" (pp. 6, 153). Naturally, then, Bork's opponents are guilty of "heresy," a term he elucidates with quotations from the Catholic apologist Hilaire Belloc (pp. 4, 11). Since it is heresy, "it is crucial . . . to root it out," and therefore "no person should be nominated or confirmed [for the Supreme Court] who does not display both a grasp of and devotion to the philosophy of original understanding" (pp. 9, 11). Bork adjures the Supreme Court to "'go and sin no more,'" calls Cardinal Newman and St. Thomas More to his aid along with Belloc, and in a surprising twist compares *himself* to the heretic: "If the philosophy of political judging is a heresy in the American system of government, it is the orthodoxy of the law schools and of the left-liberal culture. I would have done well to remember that in the old days nobody burned infidels, but they did burn heretics" (pp. 159, 343, 352, 354).[10]

A summons to holy war is not an *argument* for originalism. Bork's militance and dogmatism will buck up his followers and sweep along some doubters, but it will not persuade neutrals. One especially wants a better ground than piety for genuflecting to originalism because Bork rightly if incongruously reminds us of the danger of "absolutisms" and "abstract principles," criticizes reliance in constitutional law on "history and tradition," and implies in his interesting discussion of originalism's historical roots that the nonoriginalist heresy may be part of the original understanding of the Constitution (pp. 19–27, 119, 353). Apparently there was no Eden. Terry Eastland must have been wrong to describe originalism as the "once dominant" view of constitutional interpretation.

Bork thinks originalism necessary in order to curb judicial discretion, and curbs on that discretion necessary in order to keep the handful of unelected federal judges from seizing the reins of power from the people's representatives. But if democracy is the end, originalism is a clumsy means. Bork notes that in the wake of the New Deal the Supreme Court read out of the Constitution the limitations that the commerce clause of Article I appears to place on the regulatory powers of the federal government. By the test of originalism, the Court erred. But by erring it transferred power to the people's representatives.

And democracy is not the end, at least not the unalloyed end. The

10. Not quite nobody: During the Crusades, the Inquisition, and other periods of Christian zealotry, many Jews, Turks, Arabs, and other infidels were killed on religious grounds, often by being burned at the stake.

democratic (really Bork means the populist) principle is diluted in our system of government. Policies are made by agents of the people rather than by the people themselves—precisely so that raw popular desire will be buffered, civilized, guided, mediated by professionals and experts, informed through deliberation. Even the representatives do not have a blank check. They are hemmed in by the Constitution—itself representing, to be sure, popular preferences, but those of a sliver of a tiny population two centuries ago. As Dworkin would say, the question posed by an originalist versus an activist or a pragmatist judiciary is not one of democracy or no democracy, but of the *kind* of democracy we want.

On the evidence of the book, Bork himself is not an admirer of popular government. And why should he be? His appointment to the Supreme Court was rejected by the Senate of the United States, which with all its manifest faults, well documented in Bork's book, is a legislative body of above-average quality, albeit not so representative as many other such bodies (no "one person, one vote" there). And he was rejected because of a grass-roots political campaign that he devotes a quarter of the book to denouncing. The first page of the book warns against "the temptations of politics" and laments that "politics invariably tries to dominate" the professions and academic disciplines "that once possessed a life and structure of their own." Later Bork denounces populism, although his implicit definition of democracy is populism—the conforming of public policy to the popular preferences that he is so distressed to find the courts now and then thwarting in the name of the Constitution. He does not explain how increasing the power of legislatures by diminishing that of judges who are trying to limit legislative power could be the antidote to the rampant politicization of American life that he deplores, or how politics and democracy can be separated.

In further tension with his celebration of democracy Bork claims that originalism is necessary to the very existence of the Supreme Court, that undemocratic institution. He expresses concern that those who succeed in ousting originalism "will have destroyed a great and essential institution"—the Court (p. 2; see also p. 349). But on Bork's account the Court has wrought mainly mischief in its two centuries of existence, and he points out that other Western nations, which do not have courts comparable to our Supreme Court, have roughly the same set of liberties that we have. The implication is that we could do quite nicely without a constitutional court.

Anyway there is no evidence that the Court's authority depends on adherence to originalism. Bork knows this, for he says (in great tension with his remark about the destructibility of the institution) that "the Court is virtually invulnerable"; it "can do what it wishes, and there is almost no way to stop it, provided its result has a significant political constituency" (p. 77). That is a sensible observation. The Court's survival and flourishing depend on the political acceptability of its results rather than on its adherence to an esoteric philosophy of interpretation. The Court has never been consistently originalist, yet has survived. Maybe the Justices know more about survival than their critics do; we economist types believe that people generally know more about how to protect their own interests than a kibitzer does.

Bork argues that if the only criterion for evaluating the Supreme Court's decisions is their political soundness, anyone who thinks the Court is politically wrong "is morally justified in evading its rulings whenever he can and overthrowing it if possible in order to replace it with a body that will produce results he likes" (p. 265). He adds ominously: "The man who prefers results to processes has no reason to say that the Court is more legitimate than any other institution capable of wielding power. If the Court will not agree with him, why not argue his case to some other group, say the Joint Chiefs of Staff, a body with rather better means for enforcing its decisions? No answer exists" (p. 265).

Actually there are plenty of answers, and one is that Bork is posing a false dichotomy: a court committed to originalism versus a court that is a "naked power organ" (p. 146);[11] blind obedience versus rebellion. These dichotomies imply, implausibly, that the *only* method of justification available to a court, the only method of channeling judicial discretion and thus of distinguishing judges from legislators, is the originalist. No other method—one that emphasizes natural justice, sound justice, social welfare, or neutral (but not necessarily originalist) principles—so much as exists. "The judge who looks outside the historic Constitution always looks inside himself and nowhere else" (p. 242).

And it may be doubted whether the forbearance of the Joint Chiefs

11. Recall Wechsler's use of the phrase in his article on neutral principles (Chapter 1).

of Staff to attempt a takeover of the government of the United States is dependent to the slightest degree on the Supreme Court's adherence to originalism. If one may judge by the evidence that Bork arrays, the Court has since the beginning strayed repeatedly from the originalist path, yet the Joint Chiefs (or their predecessors) have never tried to take over the government. Nor are they likely to try. It is not true that the Joint Chiefs have better means of enforcing their decisions than the Supreme Court has of enforcing its decisions. If they ordered the army to take over the government, their order would not be obeyed. Bork believes that the Court has issued a parallel order, "taking over" the government from the elected branches, and that its order *has* been obeyed. This implies correctly that, other than in times of general war, the Supreme Court is more powerful than the Joint Chiefs.

Bork's invocation of the Joint Chiefs shows only that he is almost as fond of military as of religious imagery. He especially likes the Leninist metaphor of seizing the "commanding heights" or "high ground" (pp. 3, 338). Military and religious terms are a common part of our speech ("war," "coup d'état," "anathema," and so forth); it is the *density* of these systems of imagery in Bork's book that gives the book its militant and dogmatic tone and much of its polemical power.

Although Bork derides scholars who try to found constitutional doctrine on moral philosophy, it should be apparent by now that he is himself under the sway of a moral philosopher, by name of Hobbes, who also thought that the only source of political legitimacy was a contract among people who died long ago. A progressive idea in an era when kings claimed to rule by divine right, it is an incomplete theory of the legitimacy of the modern Supreme Court. There are other reasons for obeying a judicial decision besides the Court's ability to display, like the owner of a champion Airedale, an impeccable pedigree tracing the decision to its remote eighteenth-century ancestor.

The idea of the Constitution as a binding contract is an incomplete theory of political legitimacy, not an erroneous one. A contract induces reliance that can make a strong claim for protection; it also frees people from having continually to reexamine and revise the terms of their relationship. These values are independent of whether the original contracting parties are still alive. But a long-term contract is bound eventually to require, if not formal modification (which in the case of the Constitution can be accomplished only through the amendment process), then flexible interpretation, to cope effectively with altered circumstances. Modification and interpretation are reciprocal; the more difficult it is to modify the instrument formally, the more exigent is flexible interpretation. Bork is aware of the practical impediments to amending the Constitution but is unwilling to draw the inference that flexible interpretation is therefore necessary to prevent constitutional obsolescence.

He places great weight on the argument from hypocrisy, conceived as the tribute that vice pays to virtue. The dominant rhetoric of judges, even activist judges, is originalist, for originalism is the legal profession's orthodox mode of justification. The judge is the oracle through which Law speaks. This stance may reflect a queasiness about the legitimacy—less grandly, the public acceptability—of nonoriginalist decisions; or it may simply be that judges, like most other people, want to foist responsibility for difficult and unpopular decisions on others. The long-dead framers are a convenient group to whom to pass the buck. But although judges are not immune from the all too human tendency to deny responsibility for actions that cause pain, the significance of this fact is another matter. It is a considerable paradox to suggest that the false reasons which uncandid judges give for their actions are the only legitimate grounds for judicial action.

If the result-oriented or activist judge is queasy about the title deeds of his rulings, the originalist is (on the evidence of *The Tempting of America*, at any rate) queasy about the consequences of originalist rulings. And rightly so. A theory of constitutional interpretation that ignores consequences is no more satisfactory than one that ignores the political importance of building a bridge between the contemporary judge's pronouncement and some authoritative document from the past. It is difficult to argue to Americans that in evaluating a political theory they should ignore its practical consequences. Bork is not prepared to make such an argument. He continually reassures the reader that originalism does not yield ghastly results, while at the same time denouncing judges who are "result-oriented." The argument from hypocrisy can be turned against originalism: Bork is not a practicing originalist.

The doctrine of incorporation holds that the Fourteenth Amendment makes some or all of the provisions of the Bill of Rights constraints on state governments. About the validity of the doctrine Bork says only, "There is no occasion here to attempt to resolve the controversy concerning the application of the Bill of Rights to the states"

(p. 93). Why not? The issue is central to determining the contemporary reach of the Constitution, and Bork is not elsewhere bashful about discussing controversial issues. His diffidence is all the more surprising because a rejection of incorporation is clearly entailed by his discussion of the only clauses of the Fourteenth Amendment that might be thought to incorporate the Bill of Rights. The Supreme Court has used as the vehicle of incorporation the Fourteenth Amendment's due process clause. But Bork is emphatic that all that this clause requires is that states use fair procedures in applying their substantive law. The Court could not, therefore, properly use it to require the states to respect free speech or the free exercise of religion or any of the other substantive liberties in the Bill of Rights. As for procedural liberties, since the due process clause of the Fifth Amendment is, if it is purely a procedural clause, only one of the procedural clauses of the Bill of Rights, it is hardly likely, on an originalist construal, that transposed to the Fourteenth Amendment it stands for all the other procedural liberties in the Bill of Rights.

The other clause of the Fourteenth Amendment that might provide a vehicle for the incorporation of the Bill of Rights against the states is the privileges and immunities clause, which guarantees to the citizens of the states the privileges and immunities of U.S. citizenship. But Bork regards this clause as a "dead letter," a "cadaver," a "corpse," because its meaning is, he believes, unascertainable (pp. 166, 180). Even to an originalist, bound to respect the dead hand of the past, a corpse is not a seemly vehicle for imposing the Bill of Rights on the states; nor does Bork suggest that it could properly be used for this purpose.[12] One objection to deriving the doctrine of incorporation from the privileges and immunities clause is that it would make the due process clause of the Fourteenth Amendment superfluous, for the privileges and immunities clause would have incorporated along with everything else in the Bill of Rights the due process clause of the Fifth Amendment, which is identical to the due process clause of the Fourteenth except in not referring to the states.

Bork is unwilling to follow the logic of his analysis to its inevitable conclusion, which is that the doctrine of incorporation is thoroughly illegitimate. On the contrary, throughout most of the book he takes

---

12. In this he is correct. David P. Currie, *The Constitution in the Supreme Court: The First Hundred Years, 1789–1888* 344–351 (1985); see also pp. 181–182 of Bork's book.

the doctrine for granted, as something he has no wish to disturb. He knows that his originalist position would be rejected out of hand were it understood to make the Bill of Rights totally inapplicable to the states. He is being pragmatic, not originalist.

No constitutional theory which implies that *Brown v. Board of Education* was decided incorrectly will receive a fair hearing nowadays, though on a consistent application of originalism it *was* decided incorrectly.[13] Yet on its face the equal protection clause guarantees not legal equality but merely equal protection of whatever laws there may happen to be, and its background was the refusal of law enforcement authorities in southern states to protect the freedmen against the private violence of the Ku Klux Klan. Language and background combine to suggest that, as Walter Berns believes, all that the clause forbids is the selective withdrawal of legal protection on racial grounds: a state cannot make black people outlaws by refusing to enforce the state's criminal and tort law when the victims of a crime or tort are black. To the consistent originalist that should be the extent of the clause's reach. Bork adds that the framers and ratifiers of the Fourteenth Amendment did not intend to bring about social equality between the races and would not have cared if the failure to achieve such equality inflicted psychological wounds on blacks. And he objects to extracting from a constitutional provision "a concept whose content would so dramatically change over time that it would come to outlaw things that the ratifiers had no idea of outlawing" (p. 214).

Yet having built an unanswerable case (on his own terms) against *Brown*, he flinches (p. 82):

> By 1954, when *Brown* came up for decision, it had been apparent for some time that segregation rarely if ever produced equality. Quite apart from any question of psychology [an irrelevant question, on Bork's reading of the Fourteenth Amendment], the physical facilities provided for blacks were not as good as those provided for whites. That had been demonstrated in a long series of cases. The Supreme Court was faced with a situation in which the courts would have to go on forever entertaining litigation about primary schools, secondary schools, colleges, washrooms,

13. As acknowledged by Bork's admirer and fellow originalist, Lino A. Graglia, in his article "'Interpreting' the Constitution: Posner on Bork," 44 *Stanford Law Review* 1019, 1037–1043 (1992), as well as by Walter Berns, as we saw in Chapter 8, and by Bernard H. Siegan, *The Supreme Court's Constitution: An Inquiry into Judicial Review and Its Impact on Society* 93–107 (1987). Graglia and Siegan were prevented from becoming federal judges by their views on *Brown*.

golf courses, swimming pools, drinking fountains, and the endless variety of facilities that were segregated, or else the separate-but-equal doctrine would have to be abandoned. Endless litigation, aside from the burden on the courts, also would never produce the equality the Constitution promised. The Court's realistic choice, therefore, was either to abandon the quest for equality by allowing segregation or to forbid segregation in order to achieve equality.

So the Court chose equality, and Bork approves. The talk of "equality" places Bork on the side of the angels, but the quoted passage shows that the only reason Bork favors desegregation is that he believes it the only way of sparing the courts the bother, likely to be futile, of monitoring segregated schools (and other facilities) to make sure they are physically equal. This is an unconvincing reason. Measurement of physical equality, even when understood broadly as including all inputs, other than racial integration itself, into the provision of a public service is easier than many things courts do. It would have been easier than preventing the southern states from circumventing the *Brown* decree by the variety of imaginative devices that they employed to this end. Physical equality of schools could be measured by per-pupil expenditures, teacher salaries, teacher-student ratios, size of school divided by number of students, and other dimensions of investment or effort. Concern with the feasibility of monitoring a regime of separate but equal schools is also a petty, makeweight sort of reason for *Brown*. Imagine the tinny sound that would have been emitted by an opinion that made the decision turn on the difficulty of measuring physical equality, coupled with indifference to the psychological impact of segregation. Bork's ground for defending *Brown* is also inconsistent with his criticism of the decision that imposed the "Miranda" rule on the states[14]—a decision explicitly premised on the administrative costs of assuring compliance with the Constitution's implied prohibition of coerced confessions. Bork does not explain why those costs should be decisive in race law but illegitimate in criminal law.

The grudging quality of Bork's defense of *Brown* is further shown by his assimilation of the decision to "liberal" and "egalitarian" policy measures (pp. 92–93), for Bork considers himself neither a liberal nor an egalitarian. To him, a liberal is a modern welfare state liberal, and an egalitarian is someone who believes in equality of result, not of

14. Miranda v. Arizona, 384 U.S. 436 (1966).

opportunity. He overlooks the older tradition of liberalism, that of the classical liberals who believed in a limited state and would have disapproved of the efforts of our southern states to use law to back a caste system. This tradition provides a footing for *Brown* that does not require the embrace of the egalitarian principles which Bork deplores. But it is not a footing available to Bork. For while the libertarian, or classical liberal, is not an egalitarian, neither is he a social conservative. The defining elements of social conservatism—religious ideas and attitudes, nostalgia, suspicion of intellect, and fear of change—are not elements of classical liberalism. *Commentary*'s neoconservatism is one form of social conservatism; James Fitzjames Stephen's attack on Mill, the subject of the next chapter, is another. The spirit of social conservatism broods over Bork's book and is crystallized in such remarks as "no activity that society thinks immoral is victimless. Knowledge that an activity is taking place is a harm to those who find it profoundly immoral" (p. 123). This is the philosophy of *On Liberty* with a negative sign placed before it.

Brown is not the only sacred cow that Bork refuses to kick. He says he would use the obscure, and usually assumed to be nonjusticiable, "guarantee" clause of the Constitution (guaranteeing each state the right to a republican form of government) to correct extreme forms of legislative malapportionment. This suggestion confuses republican with democratic and contradicts Bork's own statement that the clause left the states free to experiment with different forms of government, provided only that state governments did not become "'aristocratic or monarchical'" (p. 87, quoting Madison). He suggests that the clause might also be used to require states "to avoid obvious and egregious deviations from their own laws" (p. 86 n.). If adopted, this suggestion, by making federal judges the final arbiters of state law, would license a degree of judicial activism to make the ghost of Earl Warren blush.

Bork notes with apparent approval the suggestion that "if anyone tried to enforce a law that had moldered in disuse for many years, the statute should be declared void by reason of desuetude" (p. 96). He is referring to the statute banning contraceptives that was struck down in *Griswold v. Connecticut*, but the logic of "desuetude" applies equally to the long-unenforced sodomy statute upheld in *Bowers v. Hardwick*—a decision of which Bork thoroughly approves. He does not tell us where in the Constitution we should look for the desuetude clause.

He hints that there is a residual power, lurking in some unspecified provision of the Constitution, to invalidate "horrible" laws (p. 97),[15] and he believes that courts have the power to create "buffer zone[s]" around constitutional rights "by prohibiting a government from doing something not in itself forbidden but likely to lead to an invasion of a right specified in the Constitution" (p. 97). In other words, explicit constitutional rights create penumbras of further constitutional protection. Yet he is derisive about Justice Douglas's use of the penumbra concept in *Griswold* and also says that a judge "may never create new constitutional rights" (p. 147), even by extrapolation from old ones.

Bork even appears to believe—this is his most startling backsliding from originalism—that "any challenged legislative distinction [must] have a rational basis" and hence that "all legislative distinctions between persons [must] be reasonable" or stand condemned under the equal protection clause (p. 330). This is the approach of Justice Stevens, and it differs from what has become (pardon the expression) the orthodox approach because it jettisons reference to fundamental rights. Bork hates the approach of judges' deciding which rights are fundamental (for example, the right not to be discriminated against on grounds of sex or by reason of illegitimate birth or of alienage, and the right to access to the courts) and which are not (for example, the right to an education) and giving the former more protection than the latter. But he likes Stevens's approach. "Justice Stevens' formulation might not in fact cause any major change in the application of the equal protection clause but it would focus judges' attention on the reasonableness of distinctions rather than on a process of simply including or excluding groups on criteria that can only be subjective and arbitrary" (p. 330). In other words, for all his fulminations against fundamental rights jurisprudence, Bork appears to accept the bulk of modern equal protection law, the epitome of fundamental rights jurisprudence.[16] He just objects to the subjectivity of fundamental rights talk compared to the

---

15. Although he can find no constitutional basis for the decision in Skinner v. Oklahoma, 316 U.S. 535 (1942), which invalidated a statute that authorized the sterilizing of larcenists, but not of embezzlers, on the basis of an unexamined notion of the heritability of selected criminal tendencies.

16. Though elsewhere in the book he flirts with the idea that the equal protection clause forbids only discrimination based on race or ethnicity. For "the Constitution does not prohibit laws based on prejudice *per se*," and "how is the Court to know whether a particular minority lost in the legislature because of 'prejudice,' as opposed to morality, prudence, or any other legitimate reason?" (p. 60). If this is what Bork believes, he cannot accept Justice Stevens's view of equal protection.

(imagined) objectivity of a standard of reasonableness. He does not discuss the originalist foundations, if any, of Justice Stevens's approach.

Originalism's bark (at least this originalist's bark), it appears, is worse than its bite. Originalism may indeed be completely plastic; for besides the examples I have given, apparently it is acceptable originalist argumentation to defend a statute that forbids defacing the American flag by pointing out that "nobody pledges allegiance to the Presidential seal or salutes when it goes by" (p. 128). Originalism is not an analytic method; it is a rhetoric that can be used to support any result a judge wants to reach. The conservative libertarians whom Bork criticizes (Richard Epstein and Bernard Siegan) are originalists; his disagreement with them is not over method, but over result. The Dred Scott decision—to Bork, the very fount of modern judicial activism—is permeated by originalist rhetoric.[17]

We should, of course, distinguish between good originalism and bad originalism. As Bork reminds us, the key holding of the Dred Scott decision—that the Missouri Compromise was unconstitutional—was an unabashed application of the concept of substantive due process.[18] And while Bork is not prepared to reject the possibility that the due process clause of the Fourteenth Amendment incorporates the Bill of Rights, he never wavers in his rejection of the possibility that the clause, in either the Fifth or Fourteenth Amendments, might license the creation of new rights in the name of substantive due process. Yet there is a lesson, in the bad originalism of *Scott v. Sandford,* that the good originalist may wish to ponder. Some of the most activist judges, whether of the right or of the left, whether named Taney or Black, have been among the judges most drawn to the rhetoric of originalism. For it is a magnificent disguise. The judge can do the wildest things, all the while presenting himself as the passive agent of the sainted Founders—don't argue with me, argue with Them.

I have hinted with deliberate paradox that the problem with Bork's originalism may be that it is not originalist enough.[19] As a public man,

17. For example: "No one, we presume, supposes that any change in public opinion or feeling, in relation to this unfortunate race, in the civilized nations of Europe or in this country, should induce the court to give to the words of the Constitution a more liberal construction in their favor than they were intended to bear when the instrument was framed and adopted." Scott v. Sandford, 60 U.S. (19 How.) 393, 426 (1856).

18. See 60 U.S. (19 How.) at 450; Currie, note 12 above, at 263–273.

19. One of his orginalist allies has also pointed this out: "Bork can be faulted for not always following his own prescription and for defining originalism in a way that leaves judges with overly broad discretion." Graglia, note 13 above, at 1044.

and one who tried to conciliate critics and reassure doubters at his confirmation hearing, Bork may have disabled himself from pressing originalism to its logical extreme; and perhaps the exigencies of writing a popular book preclude complete intellectual rigor. For a pure originalism, a consistent originalism, a rigorous originalism, we may have to look elsewhere. But the impurities of Bork's originalism are a strength rather than a weakness of his book, for in his concessions to practicality and public opinion, and in other remarks scattered throughout the book, one can find materials for constructing an alternative to strict originalism. Call it pragmatism, not in its caricatural sense of deciding today's case with no heed for tomorrow, but in my sense of advocating the primacy of consequences in interpretation as in other departments of practical reason, the continuity of legal and moral discourse, and a critical rather than pietistic attitude toward history and tradition.

Introducing Bork the—uncertain—pragmatist:

1. "Results that are particularly awkward, in the absence of evidence to the contrary, were probably not intended [by the framers]" (p. 165). Fortunately, such results can be avoided by flexible interpretation: "The Constitution states its principles in majestic generalities that we know cannot be taken as sweepingly as the words alone might suggest" (p. 147).

2. "Law will not be recognized as legitimate if it is not organically related to the 'larger universe of moral discourse that helps shape human behavior'" (p. 354). Here an interpretive problem arises because Bork doubts "that there are any moral 'facts'" (p. 121) yet on the next page denounces "moral relativism" and later denies emphatically that he is a "radical moral skeptic" (p. 259). And he believes that "moral outrage is a sufficient ground for prohibitory legislation" (p. 124). It is as if he considered the raw preferences of the people to have great moral weight but the moral views of judges to be mere raw preferences having no moral weight (see pp. 125, 257, 259). Probably all he means is that there is insufficient moral consensus in our society for judges to have solid grounds for using moral principles to invalidate in the name of the Constitution legislation that reflects whatever moral theory has temporarily gained the upper hand in the political branches of government. Inevitably the judges would be imposing their own, possibly idiosyncratic, moral preferences on the society.

3. Obedience to the past has pitfalls: "Not all traditions are admira-

ble" (p. 235). "History is not binding, and tradition is useful to remind us of the wisdom and folly of the past, not to chain us to either . . . Our history and tradition, like those of any nation, display not only adherence to great moral principles but also instances of profound immorality" (p. 119). Yet on the same page Bork remarks approvingly that "because homosexual sodomy has been proscribed for centuries, Justice White said [in *Bowers v. Hardwick*] the claim that such conduct was 'deeply rooted in this Nation's history and tradition' was 'at best, facetious.'" The entire discussion is facetious, in an unintended sense. Homosexual sodomy has been widely practiced since the earliest societies that have left records, and probably since we came down from the trees—and before—and in that sense, which of course was not White's sense, is deeply rooted in every nation's history and tradition. Although it has generally been disapproved, efforts to suppress it have been sporadic. The verdict of history and tradition thus is ambiguous, and in any event should not be controlling, for precisely the reasons that Bork eloquently states. Yet Bork himself, like Justice White, appears to regard the suggestion that efforts to suppress homosexuality might raise constitutional questions as the *reductio ad absurdum* of judicial activism, for he suggests that the moral claims of homosexuals to be left in peace are no stronger than those of kleptomaniacs (p. 204).

The originalist faces backwards but steals frequent sideways glances at consequences. The pragmatist places the consequences of his decisions in the foreground. The pragmatist judge does not deny that his role in interpreting the Constitution is interpretive. He is not a lawless judge. He does not, in order to do short-sighted justice between the parties, violate the Constitution and his oath, for he is mindful of the systemic consequences of judicial lawlessness. Like Samuel Lipman's ideal conductor, however, the pragmatist judge believes that constitutional interpretation involves the empathic projection of the judge's mind and talent into the creative souls of the framers rather than slavish obeisance to the framers' every metronome marking. In the capacious, forward-looking account of interpretation that I am calling pragmatic, the social consequences of alternative interpretations often are decisive; to the consistent originalist, if there were such a person, they would always be irrelevant.

Speaking of the consequences of judicial decisions, I think Bork misreads the lesson of his defeat in the Senate. He attributes it to the machinations of the "new class"—the "knowledge class" or "intellectual class" of left-liberal academics and journalists (pp. 337, 339). That there is such a group of people, that its members collectively have great influence in American universities and in the mass media, and that it played a role in Bork's defeat are all true. But I do not think its role in that debacle was decisive. The decisive factor, besides Reagan's being a lame duck crippled by the Iran-Contra affair and the Senate's being controlled by the Democrats, was that a large number of Americans (I do not say a majority—but passionate and articulate minorities can be very powerful in a system of representative government, and a number of otherwise conservative Democratic Senators from the South owed their seats to black voters) do not want the Constitution to be construed as narrowly as Bork would construe it. They do not think that states should be allowed to forbid abortion (Bork says that *Roe v. Wade* is "the greatest example and symbol of the judicial usurpation of democratic prerogatives in this century [and] should be overturned" [p. 116]) or to enforce racial restrictive covenants (invalidated in *Shelley v. Kraemer,*[20] which Bork argues was decided incorrectly). They do not think that the federal government should be free to engage in racial discrimination. (Bork thinks that *Bolling v. Sharpe* [see Chapter 6] was erroneously decided too.) They do not think that states should be free to enact "savage" laws, or that a judge should practice "moral abstention," as Bork urges (p. 259). They doubt whether minorities whose rights are not expressly protected by the Constitution should be at the mercy of the majority. They do not lose sleep over the fact that "no Justice renounces the power to override democratic majorities when the Constitution is silent" (p. 240). (Bork argues that no current member of the Supreme Court is a genuine originalist, and, so far as one can gather from the book, he does not believe that there has *ever* been a consistent originalist on the Court.) They do not believe that under Chief Justice Rehnquist as under his predecessors "the political seduction of the law continues apace" (p. 240). They do not believe that the books should be closed on judicial innovation, preventing the creation of new rights, which is what Bork means when he tells the Supreme Court to sin "no more." They consider results more important than theory, and they don't like the results that Bork would be

20. 334 U.S. 1 (1948). He adds that to apply the principle of *Shelley* in a neutral fashion "would be both revolutionary and preposterous" (p. 153).

likely, on the evidence of his book as well as of his earlier writings, to reach.

Our fellow citizens may be morally or politically immature to think such things and they may also have—I think they do have—an incomplete picture of the consequences of some of the decisions that Bork criticizes. The conception of law held by lay people may even be incoherent, because they believe both that judges' decisions should be dictated by positive law rather than by moral principles and that the decisions should yield results which conform to such principles, so that at one level they agree both with Bork and with his fiercest foe, Ronald Dworkin, and at another level they reject both. Finally, it is not certain that a majority of Americans agree with the particular views of policy that I have described.

But these are details. In a representative democracy, the fact that many (it need not be most) people do not like the probable consequences of a judge's judicial philosophy provides permissible, and in any event inevitable, grounds for the people's representatives to refuse to consent to his appointment, even if popular antipathy to the judge is not grounded in a well-thought-out theory of adjudication. The people are entitled to ask what the benefits to them of originalism would be, and they will find no answers in *The Tempting of America*. If, to echo Samuel Lipman again, originalism makes bad music despite or perhaps because of its scrupulous historicity, why *should* the people listen to it?

PART THREE

Variety and Ideology
in Legal Theory

chapter 10

The First Neoconservative

T H E variousness, and ideological stamp, of legal theory are my themes in this part of the book. I devote most of my attention to leftist legal theories, but I am going to begin at the other end of the political spectrum, with an unjustly neglected figure who can fairly be judged the original of Walter Berns and Robert Bork. Sir James Fitzjames Stephen, who was born in 1829 and died in 1894, was simultaneously or successively a barrister, prolific essayist, moralist, political thinker, writer of influential treatises on criminal law, colonial official, and High Court judge—as well as the brother of Leslie Stephen and, therefore, the uncle of Virginia Woolf. He is the subject of a superb biography, written by his brother and published the year after his death, which accomplishes the impossible in being both pious and critical, intimate and detached.[1] Fitzjames Stephen's best-known work is his book *Liberty, Equality, Fraternity* (1873), an attack on the normative political theory of John Stuart Mill as developed in *On Liberty* (1859) and other works and a sketch of an alternative theory. It will be the focus of my discussion in this chapter.[2]

1. Leslie Stephen, *The Life of Sir James Fitzjames Stephen* (1895). There is a fine recent biography: K. J. M. Smith, *James Fitzjames Stephen: Portrait of a Victorian Rationalist* (1988).
2. A second edition of *Liberty, Equality, Fraternity* was published in 1874. The book was

Liberty, Equality, Fraternity is a magnificent period piece: as vivid and revealing a document of British imperialism in its heyday as John Buchan's novel *Prester John* and Kipling's verse would be a generation later. Written immediately after Stephen had completed his service as a member of the Indian Council—the governing body of the jewel of the British Empire—the book radiates a self-consciously imperial confidence fairly describable as Roman. The tip-off is Stephen's defense of Pontius Pilate, from which I quote a brief passage: "If . . . it is said that Pilate ought to have respected the principle of religious liberty as propounded by Mr. Mill, the answer is that if he had done so he would have run the risk of setting the whole province in a blaze . . . If this should appear harsh, I would appeal again to Indian experience" (p. 115). Anyone who thinks that man is the imperialistic animal, or that modern America is imperialistic, or that economists are imperialistic because they, or some of them, seek to extend their sway over other fields such as law or history or sociology, will learn what the real thing is from Stephen's book: it is utter willingness to rule other peoples, rooted in supreme confidence in the superiority of one's own civilization. "It is impossible to lay down any principles of legislation at all unless you are prepared to say, I am right, and you are wrong, and your view shall give way to mine, quietly, gradually, and peaceably; but one of us two must rule and the other must obey, and I mean to rule" (p. 90). Britain's astonishing success—which Stephen had witnessed at first hand and to which indeed he had contributed—in ruling India with a handful of soldiers and civil servants may explain much of the authoritarian cast, as well as confident tone, of *Liberty, Equality, Fraternity.*

Forceful, pithy, aphoristic, Stephen was a magnificent prose stylist in the English tradition of brook-no-disagreement plain speaking. "To be able to punish, a moral majority must be overwhelming" (p. 159). "Struggles there must and always will be, unless men stick like limpets or spin like weathercocks" (p. 111). "Parliamentary government is simply a mild and disguised form of compulsion. We agree to try strength by counting heads instead of breaking heads, but the principle

---

not republished until 1967, after having long been out of print. The 1967 edition (edited, with an introduction and notes, by R. J. White, and published by Cambridge University Press) was allowed to go out of print as well but was reprinted in 1992 by the University of Chicago Press; and in 1993 the Liberty Fund published an edition edited by Stuart D. Warner. My page references are to the Chicago edition.

is exactly the same . . . The minority gives way not because it is convinced that it is wrong, but because it is convinced that it is a minority" (p. 70). "The difference between a rough and a civilised society is not that force is (or ought to be) guided with greater care in the second case than in the first. President Lincoln attained his objects by the use of a degree of force which would have crushed Charlemagne and his paladins and peers like so many eggshells" (p. 71). "The result of [intellectual] warfare is that the weaker opinion—the less robust and deeply seated feeling—is rooted out to the last fibre, the place where it grew being seared as with a hot iron; whereas the prison, the stake, and the sword only strike it down, and leave it to grow again in better circumstances" (p. 121).

Rhetoric prigs believe that only truthful and edifying rhetoric is worthy of praise; but we true descendants of Protagoras (see Chapter 24) can delight in and acclaim Stephen's wit, verve, and confidence even when he is at his most snobbish and shortsighted: "It is also a question, which I cannot do more than glance at in two words in this place, whether the enormous development of equality in America, the rapid production of an immense multitude of commonplace, self-satisfied, and essentially slight people is an exploit which the whole world need fall down and worship" (p. 220).

If American lawyers, including law professors and judges, were more intellectual than they are, they would be eager to acknowledge this vivid intellectual figure as an ancestor. And in fact Stephen is, to an unsuspected degree, a significant figure in the history of American legal thought, through his influence on Holmes. I refer not to the impact of his theory of criminal law on Holmes,[3] though it may have been considerable, but to qualities of style and thought that *Liberty, Equality, Fraternity* exhibits with particular clarity. One is Stephen's direct, muscular, witty, vivacious, economical style of writing, so different from American writing of any era yet so similar to Holmes's style. The Bostonians of Holmes's time and class took their cultural cues from England, which Holmes visited frequently until he was an old man and in which he met and became acquainted with Stephen.[4] I imagine that

3. On which see Mark DeWolfe Howe, *Justice Oliver Wendell Holmes: The Proving Years, 1870–1882* 213, 227, 267–268 (1963). Smith, note 1 above, at 63–65, emphasizes the differences between their approaches to criminal law.

4. "No friendship ever developed" between the two, however (Smith, note 1 above, at 63), as it did between Holmes and Leslie Stephen.

Holmes modeled his style on that of the best contemporary English prose writers.[5] Stephen was not only a notable member of that class but a fellow lawyer and a personal acquaintance. He was also of a suitable age to be Holmes's mentor. Twelve years older than Holmes, he was 44 when *Liberty, Equality, Fraternity* was published, and Holmes had only recently begun doing scholarly writing. Holmes may also have acquired from Stephen—though it is more likely that he merely found in Stephen a prestigious confirmer of his own tendencies—such dispositions characteristic of both writers as moral hardness. Stephen's God

> is an infinitely wise and powerful Legislator whose own nature is confessedly inscrutable to man, but who has made the world as it is for a prudent, steady, hardy, enduring race of people who are neither fools nor cowards, who have no particular love for those who are, who distinctly know what they want, and are determined to use all lawful means to get it. Some such religion as this is the unspoken deeply rooted conviction of the solid, established part of the English nation. They form an anvil which has worn out a good many hammers, and will wear out a good many more, enthusiasts and humanitarians notwithstanding. (p. 252)

Closely related to this hardness is the belief that the world is ruled by force, which notwithstanding Stephen's preoccupation with religion is the dominant motif of his book as it is of Holmes's jurisprudence.

Stephen's book (here providing a lead that Holmes was not to follow) is a powerful defense of the idea that it is a proper office of the law, although, given law's practical limitations, one to be employed very circumspectly—Stephen calls criminal law "the roughest engine which society can use for any purpose" (p. 151)—to improve people's morals and not just to prevent tangible harms to third parties. The debate over the proper scope of criminal law has continued, as in the famous exchange between H. L. A. Hart and Patrick Devlin, with Devlin taking Stephen's position[6]—but so much less eloquently. Not only does Devlin echo Stephen but Hart echoes Holmes, thus placing Holmes and Stephen on opposite sides in the debate despite their other similarities. Notably in "The Path of the Law," Holmes exhorted the law to work

5. The Harvard Law School library has a recording of a brief radio address that Holmes delivered as part of the celebration of his ninetieth birthday. Listening to it, I was struck by the fact that Holmes spoke with what to the modern ear, at least, is an English accent.

6. Hart, *Law, Liberty and Morality* (1963); Devlin, *The Enforcement of Morals* (1965).

itself free from morality, and he was as committed an atheist as Stephen was a Christian, though Stephen, as we are about to see, was a Christian of rather a peculiar sort. Both thought force the ultimate arbiter, but only Stephen believed that a moral code rooted in Christian belief was an indispensable part of a system of public values designed to keep people in line and society together.

But the greatest significance of *Liberty, Equality, Fraternity* is the audacious challenge to Mill, which has made the book a (neglected) classic of conservative thought.[7] To understand and evaluate Stephen's challenge we must fix Mill's place in the history of classical liberalism. One foundation of classical liberalism is the utilitarian principle of Jeremy Bentham, from which with some auxiliary principles can be derived the kind of laissez-faire approach associated with economic libertarians such as Milton Friedman. But Bentham's principle is multifaceted, and Mill emphasized the aspect of respect for diversity of human preferences—Bentham's slogan of everybody to count for one and nobody to count for more than one. This is the most important egalitarian element in utilitarianism (another, stressed by some modern utilitarians, is diminishing marginal utility of income), and it leads directly to belief in popular government. But while greatly indebted to Bentham, Mill did not make the cornerstone of the classical-liberal edifice democracy. He made it liberty. Liberty is the principle—which trumps democracy by setting tight limits on the scope of government— that people should be free to do what they want, think what they want, say what they please, worship whom they want to worship, or not worship at all, and fashion and follow the life plan that they want, provided only (granted, it's a big and vague proviso) that they refrain from doing things that interfere unreasonably with the liberty of other people to do the same things. The libertarian principle[8] is at the heart of Mill's political philosophy but is not the whole of it even if his intermittent socialist sympathies are ignored. He believed that there are higher (intellectual, artistic, altruistic) and lower pleasures and that through education, the protection of property rights and economic

7. Not completely neglected. Russell Kirk, in his introduction to a 1955 edition of *On Liberty*, proclaims *Liberty, Equality, Fraternity* a decisive refutation of Mill.

8. But we must be careful to distinguish this Millian libertarianism from the dogmatic and extreme libertarianism, founded on metaphysical notions of human freedom, that is associated with the followers of Ayn Rand, with some of the followers of Hayek and von Mises, and with "anarcho-capitalists" such as Murray Rothbard.

liberty as pathways to prosperity, and the encouragement of civic responsibility in such forms as suffrage and jury service, society can change people's preferences from lower to higher and ought to do so. As the social bottom rises through the substitution of higher for lower pleasures among an increasing fraction of the population, people will become more equal to one another in a good sense. Among the higher pleasures (reinforcing the egalitarian tendency) is benevolent regard for the well-being of other people. So: liberty, equality, fraternity—though it was naughty of Stephen to apply the slogan of the French Revolution to Mill and the Millians.

We modern Millians are apt to be classified as conservatives rather than as liberals because we are not strongly egalitarian—not as strongly as Mill himself was, allowing for the changed political climate—and oppose various features of the welfare state, whose supporters, though they ought to be called socialists or collectivists, have managed to appropriate the term "liberal" and to retain it even when they advocate restricting liberty of expression in the name of racial or sexual equality. The real conservatives are not the Millians; they are social and religious conservatives and neoconservatives, such as Irving Kristol, Allan Bloom, William Bennett, William Buckley, Walter Berns, Russell Kirk, and Robert Bork. They believe with Plato and with Leo Strauss that the state should not be content with protecting property and personal rights and access to education and civic participation all to the end of fostering material prosperity and a climate of free inquiry and debate, of diversity and experimentation (including experiments in living), and a mild benevolence. The state should inculcate virtue, promote piety, punish immorality, discourage hedonism. It is among believers that the state has a moral mission—that the state must know right from wrong and impose its view of the right—that we find the Stephen of *Liberty, Equality, Fraternity.*

I have called his book an audacious challenge to classical liberalism. It might better be called pugnacious. Having separated the liberty, equality, and fraternity (altruism, benevolence, fellow feeling) strands in classical liberalism, Stephen replaces each with its opposite. For liberty (which he calls a "negation") he substitutes power and restraint, noting that "power precedes liberty," which, "from the very nature of things, is dependent upon power . . . It is only under the protection of a powerful, well-organized, and intelligent government that any liberty can exist at all" (p. 166). For equality Stephen substitutes the natural inequality, physical and intellectual, of human beings (for example, what he believes to be the natural inequality between men and women). For fraternity he substitutes enmity: "If in the course of my life I come across any man or body of men who treats me or mine or the people I care about as an enemy, I shall treat him as an enemy with the most absolute indifference to the question whether we can or cannot trace out a relationship either through Adam or through some primeval ape" (p. 240). And for humanism, as the overarching guide of a just government, Stephen substitutes the tyrannies of force, public opinion, and hellfire.

Does this make Stephen the English version of Dostoevsky's Grand Inquisitor? Both the Grand Inquisitor chapter of *The Brothers Karamazov* and *Liberty, Equality, Fraternity* bring us into the presence—with startling immediacy, because without the usual veils—of the authentic authoritarian tradition. But Stephen's is for us the more interesting critique because he was an Englishman steeped in the liberal thought of Bentham and Mill, both of whom he greatly admired. His is criticism from within. Unwittingly it shows how fine the line is that separates the liberal from the antiliberal.

The disagreement between Mill and Stephen is at bottom over human nature. Of all his predecessors in English political thought, Stephen most admired Hobbes. Mill thought people would be improved by discussion. Stephen thought not. "Estimate the proportion of men and women who are selfish, sensual, frivolous, idle, absolutely commonplace and wrapped up in the smallest of petty routines, and consider how far the freest of free discussion is likely to improve them. The only way by which it is practically possible to act upon them at all is by compulsion or restraint" (p. 72). (No fan of "deliberative democracy" he.) Like the Grand Inquisitor (and also like Nietzsche, another great nineteenth-century antiliberal), Stephen believed both that most people were like children or domestic animals, and hence were natural slaves, and that the significance of religion was not that it was true but that it was an effective goad. "All experience shows that almost all men require at times both the spur of hope and the bridle of fear, and that religious hope and fear are an effective spur and bridle, though some people are too hard-mouthed and thick-skinned to care much for either" (p. 98). The situation of children—"a state of submission, dependence, and obedience to orders the objects of which are usually most imperfectly understood by the persons who receive them"—is for

Stephen an apt model of that "union of love, reverence, and submission" that provides "a far better conception of the essential conditions of permanent national existence and prosperity" than "the motto Liberty, Equality, and Fraternity" (p. 193).

Religion as goad implies a particular form of religious doctrine. The Grand Inquisitor rejected Christ; so did Stephen. "No sane nation ever did or ever will pretend to believe the Sermon on the Mount in any sense which is inconsistent with the maintenance to the very utmost by force of arms of the national independence, honour, and interest. If the Sermon on the Mount really means to forbid this, it ought to be disregarded" (p. 261). Even to believing Christians, the Sermon on the Mount is "a pathetic overstatement of duties" (p. 259). But the question of religious belief doesn't really arise for Stephen. His view of religion is instrumental. Religion is an adjunct of the police. God, in Stephen's conception, inspires awe rather than love. He is like a human judge, only more powerful and more accurate.

I quoted the wonderful passage in which Stephen describes intellectual warfare as more destructive than persecution. It is an aspect of his general tendency to see force everywhere. "Disguise it how you will, it is force in one shape or another which determines the relations between human beings" (p. 209). Law, of course, "is nothing but regulated force" (p. 200). And "persuasion, indeed, is a kind of force," as "it consists in showing a person the consequences of his actions" (p. 129). (In emphasizing the continuity between power and persuasion, Stephen foreshadowed the theory of free speech that Holmes would articulate many years later.)[9] For Stephen, progress does not diminish the role of force in society; it merely changes its form. "The first impression on comparing [medieval with modern Scotland] is that the fourteenth century was entirely subject to the law of force, and that Scotland in the nineteenth century has ceased to be the theatre of force at all" (p. 203). But the contrary is true: the force of government is greater in modern Scotland—so much so that "deliberate individual resistance to the law of the land for mere private advantage is in these days an

---

9. Abrams v. United States, 250 U.S. 616, 630 (1919) (dissenting opinion); Gitlow v. New York, 268 U.S. 652, 673 (1925) (dissenting opinion). Especially apt is Holmes's language in *Gitlow:* "If, in the long run, the beliefs expressed in proletarian dictatorship are destined to be accepted by the dominant forces of the community, the only meaning of free speech is that they should be given their chance and have their way." Never mind what exactly this means or whether it is a becoming fatalism.

impossibility which no one ever thinks of attempting" (p. 204). "To say that the law of force is abandoned because force is regular, unopposed, and beneficially exercised, is to say that day and night are now such well-established institutions that the sun and moon are mere superfluities" (p. 206).

Stephen's emphasis on force rather than on consent, tradition, inertia, or mutual advantage as the cement of society implied to him a natural and radical inequality among persons. There has to be an elite to wield the lash, and hence a division between masters and slaves. He is emphatic about the inevitability of this division, but what is particularly interesting is his claim (oddly Marxist in its flavor, and later much emphasized by Max Weber) that Mill-style bourgeois liberty amplifies rather than mitigates the consequences of inequality (pp. 207–208):

> If in old times a slave was inattentive, his master might no doubt have him maimed or put to death or flogged; but he had to consider that in doing so he was damaging his own property . . . If a modern servant misconducts himself, he can be turned out of the house on the spot, and another can be hired as easily as you would call a cab. To refuse the dismissed person a character [reference] may very likely be equivalent to sentencing him to months of suffering and to a permanent fall in the social scale. Such punishments are inflicted without appeal, without reflection, without the smallest disturbance of the smooth surface of ordinary life.

"It is quite true that we have succeeded in cutting political power into very little bits, which with our usual hymns of triumph we are continually mincing" (p. 207), but the result "is simply that the man who can sweep the greatest number of them into one heap will govern the rest" (p. 211). "In a pure democracy the ruling men will be the wirepullers and their friends; but they will no more be on an equality with the voters than soldiers or Ministers of State are on an equality with the subjects of a monarchy" (p. 211).

Stephen agreed with his friend Henry Maine that there had been a movement from status to contract as the regulator of human relations. But it had merely exacerbated inequality (p. 209):

> Let us suppose, to take one illustration, that men and women are made as equal as law can make them, and that public opinion followed the law. Let us suppose that marriage became a mere partnership dissoluble like another; that women were expected to earn their living just like men; that the notion of anything like protection due from the one sex to the other

was thoroughly rooted out; that men's manners to women became identical with their manners to men; that the cheerful concessions to acknowledged weakness, the obligation to do for women a thousand things which it would be insulting to offer to do for a man, which we inherit from a different order of ideas, were totally exploded; and what would be the result? The result would be that women would become men's slaves and drudges, that they would be made to feel their weakness and to accept its consequences to the very utmost. Submission and protection are correlative. Withdraw the one and the other is lost, and force will assert itself a hundred times more harshly through the law of contract than ever it did through the law of status.

The awful thing that Stephen feared—the legal and to a great extent the practical equality of men and women—has come to pass, yet without making women "men's slaves and drudges." In this respect, as in his denigration of the United States, history has falsified Stephen's political vision. And in another: At the heart of that vision was the belief that law must have a moral basis, that morals must have a religious basis, that for government to side with no religion was tacitly to accept the skeptical, the irreligious view, and hence that government must choose between religions, selecting the one that contains the moral code that the government wants to inculcate, supporting that religion, ignoring the others. Yet, since Stephen's time and particularly since World War II, the people of Europe, despite their retention of established churches, have for the most part lost religion yet without ceasing to be moral, while the American people, despite the rigid separation of church and state, have remained intensely religious without surpassing the moral standards of Europeans.[10]

Mill's is the more realistic, as well as—a conjunction as happy as it is rare—the more edifying, vision of a political community, despite Mill's "wetness," as it seemed to Stephen. Yet if it misses its main target, *Liberty, Equality, Fraternity* contains important insights that make it more than a period piece and rhetorical tour de force. Like Adam Smith, Stephen was right to be skeptical about fraternity and thus to doubt that he or anyone else could be made "to care about masses of men with whom I have nothing to do" (p. 240). He was right to note

10. On the relative religiosity of Europeans and Americans, see *Gallup Report* No. 236, May 1985, p. 50; Richard A. Posner, "The Law and Economics Movement," 77 *American Economic Review* 1, 9–12 (Papers and Proceedings issue, May 1987); *Sex and Reason* 161.

the devil-take-the-hindmost character of a free-market system (and in this he sounded a note that should resonate with modern communitarians). And if equality has not made women slaves and drudges, it has had its downside: the feminization of poverty in the United States is a function in part of easy divorce.[11]

Stephen, here breaking with Bentham as well as with Mill, was also right to point out that considerations of deterrence do not exhaust the policy of the criminal law; for that law is among other things "an emphatic assertion of the principle that the feeling of hatred and the desire of vengeance . . . are important elements of human nature which ought in such cases to be satisfied in a regular public and legal manner" (p. 152). That is why "a considerable number of acts which need not be specified are treated as crimes merely because they are regarded as grossly immoral" (p. 154).[12]

He was right to emphasize the practical limits of the criminal law as a regulatory device. "Before an act can be treated as a crime, it ought to be capable of distinct definition and of specific proof, and it ought also to be of such nature that it is worth while to prevent it at the risk of inflicting great damage, direct and indirect, upon those who commit it" (p. 151). Though skeptical about liberty, he believed that

> there is a sphere, none the less real because impossible to define its limits, within which law and public opinion are intruders likely to do more harm than good. To try to regulate the internal affairs of a family, the relations of love or friendship, or many other things of the same sort, by law or by the coercion of public opinion, is like trying to pull an eyelash out of a man's eye with a pair of tongs. They may put out the eye, but they will never get hold of the eyelash. (p. 162)

"A law which enters into a direct contest with a fierce impetuous passion, which the person who feels it does not admit to be bad, and which is not directly injurious to others, will generally do more harm

11. Lenore J. Weitzman, *The Divorce Revolution: The Unexpected Social and Economic Consequences for Women and Children in America* xiv (1985); H. Elizabeth Peters, "Marriage and Divorce: Informational Constraints and Private Contracting," 76 *American Economic Review* 437, 449 (1986) (tab. 6).

12. R. J. White says Stephen had in mind sodomy and other "unnatural acts" (p. 154 n. 13). We need not agree with Stephen that these acts should be criminal in order to recognize the justness of Stephen's observation as a description of the sentiments that shape the criminal law.

than good; and this is perhaps the principal reason why it is impossible to legislate directly against unchastity, unless it takes forms which every one regards as monstrous and horrible" (p. 152).

These passages may make one wonder what side Stephen really was on in the debate over whether law should try to regulate morals or just try to prevent palpable harms. Could it be that intelligent authoritarians and intelligent libertarians are at one on most practical questions? The answer may be "yes" when the common starting point is Bentham. For we must not forget Bentham's hard side[13]—the defense of torture, the admiration for the Court of Star Chamber, the proposal to imprison beggars, the belief in surveillance and indoctrination, the depreciation of rights, all revealing a considerable streak of authoritarianism, a proclivity for top-down reform, and an enthusiasm for force and fraud as methods of social control and betterment. Authoritarianism is not the complete story of Benthamism, but we can see—for example in Stephen's emphatically instrumental conception of religion—the logical working out of this strand in Bentham's thought. So *Liberty, Equality, Fraternity* is a document of utilitarianism as well as of conservatism, and we recall that for all his hardness Bentham believed that the pain inflicted on criminals by punishment was an evil that could be justified only if it prevented greater pain to others. A utilitarian like Stephen who knew the criminal law at first hand would not be likely to overlook its practical limitations as a utility-maximizing instrument of social control, and, as we have seen, he did not. We should not overlook his pragmatic strain, the danger of pigeonholing creative thinkers, and the many respects in which he and Mill were at one.[14]

13. See "Blackstone and Bentham," in my book *The Economics of Justice* 13, 33–47 (1981).

14. See also Smith, note 1 above, at 170–172.

chapter 11

The Left-Wing History of American Legal Thought

MORTON HORWITZ, a legal historian and a founder of the critical legal studies movement, made his scholarly reputation with a history of American legal thought before the Civil War.[1] He focused on the evolution of the American common law—the body of originally English judge-made doctrines dealing mainly with accidents, property, contracts, and commercial instruments. Horwitz argued that after Independence, bold, innovative American judges had recast doctrines designed for a static post-feudal agrarian economy in a mold that facilitated—indeed, that subsidized—industrialization and economic growth. The process of transformation was complete by 1850. After that the judges sought to obfuscate, mystify, and legitimate the inegalitarian redistribution of income and wealth which had accompanied the nation's transition from an agrarian to an industrial economy,[2] and which the judges themselves had fostered, by abandoning their free-wheeling goal-oriented decision-making methods in favor of legal for-

1. Morton J. Horwitz, *The Transformation of American Law, 1780–1860* (1977, reprinted 1992).
2. By the eve of the Civil War, "the law had come simply to ratify those forms of inequality that the market system produced." Id. at 210.

malism—"a scientific, objective, professional, and apolitical conception of law."[3]

Plausible, arresting, Marxian (if not quite Marxist), and clearly argued, Horwitz's thesis nevertheless was vulnerable to several criticisms. His use of evidence had been careless, selective, even tendentious.[4] He had romanticized eighteenth-century law and by doing so had exaggerated the exploitative character of nineteenth-century law.[5] He had overlooked efficiency justifications for legal doctrines and misunderstood the concept of subsidization,[6] which to be meaningful requires a baseline that he had failed to specify—for it is hardly useful to describe every legal change as the conferral of a "subsidy" on those who benefit from it. And if the judges had been bent on putting one over on the public, why had the great "redistributive" decisions been so forthright in grounding legal doctrine on economic policy rather than just on the usual obfuscatory talk about rights, justice, and precedent?[7] Why had these judges not tumbled to the rhetorical advantages of legal formalism long before 1850? The invention of formalism had not waited upon the development of a differentiated, organized, intellectualized legal profession, as Horwitz supposed. It could be traced back to Cicero, and more proximately to the *Federalist Papers* and the opinions of John Marshall.

3. Id. at 266. "The paramount social condition that is necessary for legal formalism to flourish in a society is for the powerful groups in that society to have a great interest in disguising and suppressing the inevitably political and redistributive functions of law." Id.

4. A. W. B. Simpson, "The Horwitz Thesis and the History of Contracts," 46 *University of Chicago Law Review* 533 (1979); R. Randall Bridwell, "Theme v. Reality in American Legal History: A Commentary on Horwitz, *The Transformation of American Law, 1780–1960,* and on the Common Law in America," 53 *Indiana Law Journal* 449 (1977).

5. See, for example, Simpson, note 4 above, at 600–601.

6. Stephen F. Williams, "Transforming American Law: Doubtful Economics Makes Doubtful History," 25 *UCLA Law Review* 1187 (1978); Herbert Hovenkamp, "The Economics of Legal History," 67 *Minnesota Law Review* 643, 670–689 (1983); Gary T. Schwartz, "Tort Law and the Economy in Nineteenth-Century America: A Reinterpretation," 90 *Yale Law Journal* 1717 (1981), esp. pp. 1772–1774; *Economic Analysis of Law* 256–260.

7. Consider the following quotation from Massachusetts Chief Justice Lemuel Shaw's famous opinion in Farwell v. Boston & Worcester R.R., 45 Mass. (4 Met.) 49, 58 (1842): "In considering the rights and obligations arising out of particular relations, it is competent for courts of justice to regard considerations of policy and general convenience, and to draw from them such rules as will, in their practical application, best promote the safety and security of all parties concerned." Horwitz, note 1 above, at 209, calls *Farwell* a "landmark" in the free-market revolution in American law. On the policy-saturated, nonformalist character of Shaw's judicial opinions, see Leonard W. Levy, *The Law of the Commonwealth and Chief Justice Shaw* (1957), esp. ch. 2.

These criticisms did not demolish Horwitz's book; it stood as a formidable synthesis of historical materials and a powerful if partial vision of the development of American legal thought. They were nonetheless substantial criticisms to which Horwitz might have been expected to react by reexamining his thesis. Instead, after many years he wrote a book that picks up the story in 1870, a decade after the point at which he had left it at the end of the earlier book, and carries it through to 1960 as if only chronology distinguished the two books.[8] Much more does.[9]

Although the second book contains no direct reference to the criticisms of the first, they may not have left the author's thinking unaffected. The preface to the second book confesses the author's deep misgivings about the possibility of objective, determinate causal explanations of historical phenomena. The first book had been an essay in economic determinism. Horwitz had argued that class bias rooted in economic interest and increasingly disguised by formalist rhetoric had made nineteenth-century legal doctrine what it was—a well-honed tool for redistributing wealth from agriculture to business, passive to active, weak to strong, Labor to Capital. In the second book class bias and exploitation are intermittent causes of legal change, but equal emphasis is placed on politically neutral changes in the economic environment, such as the growth of new forms of property (intellectual property, for example), on emotional or psychological factors, including—remarkably—love and its vicissitudes, and on changes in the *Weltanschauung*, mysteriously including the development of quantum theory, as causal factors in legal change. Equal emphasis does not mean great emphasis. Horwitz's diminished faith in Marxian explanations is not completely offset by his newly acquired interest in Freudian and other psychological modes of explanation. He has grown shy about all causal explanations of history.

The first book examined the major doctrinal developments in a reasonably discrete period in American legal history—from Independence to the Civil War. This was the period, as Horwitz conceived it, of the reception of English common law by American judges, the transformation of that law in favor of the commercial interests, and the capping of that transformation by the judiciary's adoption of the for-

8. *The Transformation of American Law, 1870–1960: The Crisis of Legal Orthodoxy* (1992).
9. As also noted in G. Edward White's review of the later book, 91 *Michigan Law Review* 1315 (1993).

malist style. The book's coverage was comprehensive (although not complete) because, while it was limited to the common law, most American law of the period *was* common law; and the period is recognizably "historical" because it ended more than a century ago. The second book begins *in medias res*—decades into the long reign of formalism—and, ending as it does in 1960, neither brings the story up to the present nor cuts it off at a natural break in historical continuity.

In some respects, it is true, 1960 could be thought a watershed year in American legal history; I treated it as such in Chapters 1 and 2. It is the approximate beginning of the brief but memorable heyday of the "Warren Court," of the vast expansion in federal litigation that ensued and that continues to this day, and of profound changes in the profession. But these are not watershed events in American law as Horwitz understands it. The book has little to say about such far-reaching doctrinal and institutional developments of the tumultuous near-century of American law that is the book's ostensible subject as the vast expansion of tort liability, the procedural revolution wrought by the Federal Rules of Civil Procedure, the rise of new fields of law such as antitrust, labor, public utility regulation, income taxation, securities law, and workmen's compensation, the growing concern with civil liberties and the extraordinary growth of civil-rights law and litigation, increased specialization within the legal profession, the shifting interface between federal and state judicial power, the advent of huge national and even international law firms, the shift from apprenticeship to classroom education as the dominant method of entry into the profession, the rise of the judicial law clerk, and the codification of commercial law. American law for Horwitz consists of a handful of confused or tendentious conceptual entities, such as "property," "causation," "corporation," and "police power." Perfected by reactionaries and their apologists, mainly in the last quarter of the nineteenth century, the precarious formalist edifice that Horwitz calls "Classical Legal Thought" was first undermined by social and economic change, then unmasked by legal realists and other Progressive legal thinkers psychologically disposed to rebel. Oliver Wendell Holmes, having contributed both to the creation of the classical edifice and to the attack on it, is the key transitional figure—transformed by a love affair. Eventually the Realists became the victims of their own conceptualizations, such as "judicial self-restraint"; by the 1950s, the Progressives had become the reactionaries. I am burlesquing the book a bit, but only a bit.

While the first book had focused on the most important legal doctrines of the era it discussed, the second, pitched at a higher level of abstraction, focuses on a debate in jurisprudence—the debate between formalists and realists. That debate petered out in the 1940s, so that the temporal as well as the thematic scope of the second book is more truncated than the title would lead one to expect. Much of the book is devoted to legal realism, which even when conceived as broadly as Horwitz conceives it is a thread in the intricate tapestry of American legal history that only law professors, and precious few of them, would consider central. But then the book is primarily about what law professors (or judges writing extrajudicially, professorially) said, secondarily about judicial doctrines, and virtually not at all about the operating level of law. While one might have supposed that "law" meant a type of social control different from ethics on one side and politics on the other, or the people and organizations that comprise the legal system, or merely the body of legal rules—the last being the implicit conception of law in Horwitz's first book—Horwitz has come to think of law in a fourth sense: as the discourse of law professors and other jurists. The real subject of the book is "American legal thought as a coherent scholarly field separate from constitutional history" (p. 273).

I do not want to exaggerate the discontinuity between Horwitz's two books. In the first, naughty realists like Lemuel Shaw turn into formalist butterflies after 1850. In the second, naughty boys like Jerome Frank and Karl Llewellyn chase the formalist butterflies until they turn into formalist butterflies themselves. Still, they are very different books; and I want first to consider whether the principal criticisms of the first apply to the second. I must leave it to specialists to determine whether Horwitz still is careless with historical evidence, but I have a concern on this score arising from his discussion of Holmes's view of contract. Horwitz points to "three sentences" in Holmes's most famous essay "which were as influential as any [Holmes] wrote" (p. 38). They are, "You always can imply a condition in a contract. But why do you imply it? It is because of some belief as to the practice of the community or of a class, or because of some opinion as to policy, or in short, because of some attitude of yours upon a matter not capable of exact quantitative measurement, and therefore not capable of founding exact logical conclusions."[10] The suggestion that this passage is as

10. "The Path of the Law," 10 *Harvard Law Review* at 466.

influential as *any* sentences of Holmes—the author of "The life of the law has not been logic: it has been experience" and "The Fourteenth Amendment does not enact Mr. Herbert Spencer's Social Statics"—is reckless, especially in the mouth of a professed skeptic about ascriptions of causality. But my concern with accuracy lies elsewhere. Horwitz says that these three sentences mark "the revolutionary moment" at which a "paradigm shift" occurred from a theory of contract as founded on the will of the parties to a theory of contract as the imposition of "some policy on the parties regardless of any supposed intention" (p. 38). Yet the sentence that precedes the three which Horwitz quotes reveals that Holmes was not making a point about the role of intent in contract law. The sentence is: "You can give any conclusion a logical form." The following sentences illustrate this proposition with the example of "implying" a condition in a contract, that is, of using deduction to derive the condition, when in fact, Holmes believes, the decision to interpolate conditions in contracts reflects a judgment of social policy. The policy could, however, be one of enforcing contracts in accordance with the parties' intentions, so far as they can be discerned, and, in cases in which those intentions cannot be discerned, in accordance with a surmise about what the parties would have agreed upon had they negotiated with reference to the point in dispute. This is clear enough with respect to the most important contract condition—that the duty of one party to perform is conditional on the other party's substantially performing *his* side of the bargain.

It is true that elsewhere in the essay Holmes emphasizes that the law does not proceed on the assumption that a contract is a literal meeting of minds—judges have no way of crawling into people's minds; they act on the basis of external signs. This is not, however, a denial that the social function of contracts and contract law is to facilitate agreement (sometimes by filling a gap in the parties' express contract as the court believes the parties would have filled it had they thought about the question when they made the contract) rather than to tell people how to conduct their lives. It is not even a change in Holmes's thinking. Many years earlier he had written that the decision about what step in the performance of a contract shall be regarded as a precondition to the other party's having to perform can be made "only by reference to the habits of the community and to convenience . . . An answer cannot be obtained from any general theory . . . The grounds of decision are purely practical, and can never be elicited from grammar or from logic.

A reference to practical considerations will be found to run all through the subject [of conditions]."[11]

Granted there is a difference between seeking to determine at all costs the intent of *these* parties to *this* contract and seeking to develop rules of contract law that over the general run of cases will minimize costs of making and enforcing contracts. The first approach has a Kantian or natural law flavor, the second a utilitarian or economic one. A court taking the second approach might refuse to enforce an unwritten contract, utterly disregarding evidence of the parties' intentions, because it believed that requiring a writing would reduce the likelihood of erroneous determinations of contractual intent in the generality of cases. The triumph of the second approach, an approach indeed more congenial to Holmes though not the point of the quoted passage, might count as an important change in legal doctrine. But it was not a change in Holmes's own thought. The next step in this evolution might be an approach that sought to achieve substantively desirable results rather than to facilitate the process of voluntary transacting— that sought in short to transcend freedom of contract. That was a step Holmes never took, despite Horwitz's contrary suggestion.

As evidence of the "overwhelming" influence of the three sentences, Horwitz offers two articles by the forgotten Clarence Ashley. Horwitz tells us that these articles attack freedom of contract, and among the telling quotations that he offers in support of this characterization we read: "There does not seem to be any difference . . . between the obligation of Tort and Contract" (p. 39).[12] Beware a Horwitz bearing ellipses.[13] The missing words between "difference" and "between" are "in this respect." Ashley's point was merely that, once parties express their mutual assent to be bound by a contract, the law decides the legal consequences. "In Tort the law annexes to certain actions an obligation, namely, to pay damages. In Contract the law annexes to certain other actions an obligation, namely, contract." This is authentically Holmesian, but it is not revolutionary.

The second major criticism of the first book—that Horwitz's ignorance of economics had led him to ascribe redistributive motives to

---

11. *The Common Law* 337–338. The practical considerations to which Holmes is referring in this passage concern the facilitative role of contracts and contract law in market transactions.

12. Quoting Clarence D. Ashley, "Mutual Assent in Contract," 3 *Columbia Law Review* 71, 78 (1903).

13. For a similar example from the first book, see Simpson, note 4 above, at 591.

concepts that are as likely to have reflected efficiency considerations—is less applicable to the second book because he has become less interested in economic explanations for intellectual change. It crops up occasionally, though, especially in reference to corporations. Horwitz subscribes uncritically to the proposition that "oligarchic" directors and officers (he uses the word repeatedly) exploit shareholders and consumers and that states compete to offer corporate-law principles that will facilitate this exploitation—this competition being the "infamous 'race to the bottom'" (p. 84) of which Horwitz writes in apparent ignorance of an extensive scholarly literature on the question.[14] His most serious economic error is to suppose that the use of a reproduction-cost, rather than an original-cost, standard for public-utility ratemaking creates monopoly windfalls. Competitive pricing is based on current, not sunk, costs, so that if a utility is planning to replace its plant the cost of replacement is the proper cost to reflect in the utility's rates, assuming the ratemaking process is trying to simulate competitive pricing. This is not an important error in itself. But it illustrates something that is important—that people who don't understand economics exaggerate the monopolistic and exploitative character of unregulated markets. A feeling that capitalism is a gigantic con game, that private enterprise exists mainly to rip off workers, consumers, and other vulnerable people, permeates the book—it informs, for example, Horwitz's uncritical approbation of all Progressive assaults on business—although it rarely crystallizes into a falsifiable proposition about the economic consequences of a legal doctrine.

The book's main theme is that in every generation since at least 1850, conventionally minded, methodologically conservative, establishment jurists have created a logical, tidy, self-contained, satisfyingly professional or "scientific" system of legal concepts from which specific outcomes could be derived deductively, thus sparing the jurist a messy encounter with reality. Although these concepts actually are shallow rationalizations, rife with internal contradiction because generated by political or psychological yearnings that have no intellectual coherence,

14. See, for example, Ralph K. Winter, Jr., "State Law, Shareholder Protection, and the Theory of the Corporation," 6 *Journal of Legal Studies* 251 (1977); Roberta Romano, "Law as a Product: Some Pieces of the Incorporation Puzzle," 1 *Journal of Law, Economics, and Organization* 225 (1985); Romano, "The State Competition Debate in Corporate Law," 8 *Cardozo Law Review* 709 (1987); Lucian Arye Bebchuk, "Federalism and the Corporation: The Desirable Limits on State Competition in Corporate Law," 105 *Harvard Law Review* 1435 (1992).

the contradictions are at first overlooked. But eventually the tides of social change erode the flimsy conceptual structure, clearing the way for a few daring thinkers to appear and unmask the fundamental contradictions, thus precipitating "a crisis of legitimacy" that is temporarily resolved when the old conceptualists make peace with the insurrectionists and a new set of conceptualisms is spawned. After a while, however, the fundamental contradictions resurface and a new crisis of legitimacy erupts. "Each generation continues frantically to hide behind unhistorical and abstract universalisms in order to deny, even to itself, its own political and moral choices" (p. 272). In opposition to that unhistorical and abstract universalism "liberty of contract," which conservative turn-of-the-century judges used to invalidate restrictions on free enterprise (as in *Lochner*), Progressives embraced "judicial self-restraint," which later inhibited them from supporting *Brown*. So the great Progressive jurist Learned Hand is found in his old age denouncing *Brown* as an affront to self-restraint (and likewise, as we saw in Chapter 1, Herbert Wechsler, another Progressive). Progressives who had trumpeted administrative discretion when wielded by the National Labor Relations Board during the New Deal were embarrassed to find it wielded with equal vigor by McCarthyite loyalty boards after World War II, while Progressives who had plumped for balancing tests as the antidote to formalist classification games were dismayed to discover that the balancing metaphor was well suited to justifying restrictions on free speech. The only way to break the circle of sterile and reified abstraction, Horwitz believes, is to acknowledge that law is an instrument of politics rather than a self-perfecting, autonomous conceptual structure. *Lochner* was wrong because maximum hours of work are a good thing; *Brown* was right because public school segregation is a bad thing.

But if each generation, Left or Right, succumbs to the siren song of abstraction, it becomes difficult to affix a definite political sign to this vice; it is more a cognitive or psychological deficiency. So it is in the realm of the cognitive and the psychological, rather than of the political or the social scientific, that we should look for clues to "critical" thought, the thought of Holmes and the Progressives, of legal realists, and today of the practitioners of critical legal studies, who are mentioned in passing in the conclusion as the heirs of the realists. Horwitz equivocates, however, between the old-fashioned intellectual historian's view that ideas collapse of their own weight—Holmes abandoned freedom of contract (as Horwitz erroneously supposes him to have done) because the scales fell from his eyes—and the view that people give their assent to particular ideas because of some quirk of personal psychology. In the long footnote that ends the chapter on Holmes (pp. 142–143 n.), Horwitz tells us that after completing the text of that chapter, which ascribes Holmes's supposed change of mind to pragmatism's "fundamental break with theological and doctrinal modes of thought" (p. 142), he discovered Holmes's letters to Lady Castletown, with whom Holmes had—or didn't have—an affair in the 1890s.[15] There was *something* between them—no doubt about that. Holmes wrote a number of passionate love letters to her, several while he was composing "The Path of the Law." On the basis of these letters Horwitz says in his footnote, "Now one must ask whether and to what extent it was the discovery of some deep—and previously unfulfilled—love that produced in Holmes what Freud called an 'oceanic' feeling, inducing him to transcend the prior categories of his thought."

Horwitz declares Jerome Frank and Karl Llewellyn the founders of legal realism. Frank's book *Law and the Modern Mind,* written we are told "in the midst of [Frank's] own psychoanalysis," diagnosed formalism as the product of arrested development—of a "childish longing" for "Father-as-Infallible Judge" (quoted on p. 177). Frank pronounced Holmes "the Completely Adult Jurist" for having outgrown that longing and thus got "rid of the need of a strict father" (p. 178). As for Llewellyn—self-proclaimed rebel, freak, and nonconformist—Horwitz points to his three marriages and his alcoholism for confirmation of "this picture of a soul in conflict" (p. 186). He adds that Llewellyn and Frank "appear to have been drawn to each other's emotional volatility, exhibitionism, and rebelliousness" (p. 187).

Horwitz is correct in perceiving an abiding tension between conceiving law as a set of objective, autonomous, politically disinterested concepts from which specific case outcomes can be derived by the methods of logic and conceiving law as a practical instrument of government to be evaluated by its consequences. But he is incorrect to think that the first conception is the property of a party or a school. When, some years after writing *Law and the Modern Mind,* Jerome Frank became a federal court of appeals judge, his rebelliousness drained away. His judicial opinions differed from those of his colleagues

---

15. See G. Edward White, *Justice Oliver Wendell Holmes: Law and the Inner Self* 230–252 (1993), for a detailed though speculative discussion of their relationship.

mainly in being even longer and more heavily larded with case citations. Llewellyn went on to write the Uniform Commercial Code and to praise state appellate judges. Among other famous legal realists, Thurman Arnold, after deriding the antitrust laws, became an energetic trust-buster and later a founder of a Washington law firm, while William Douglas, until he became bored with being a Supreme Court Justice, wrote conventional enough opinions. Frank, Llewellyn, and Arnold became establishment figures along with Learned Hand, Felix Frankfurter, Henry Hart, Herbert Wechsler, and others who had chafed under the formalisms of an earlier era; only Douglas retained his bad-boy rebelliousness.

The first generation of crits, the self-proclaimed heirs of the legal realists, is likewise becoming co-opted by the legal establishment. Many of the older crits are comfortably ensconced in the tenured ranks of leading law schools, and one is a dean of such a school (Paul Brest of Stanford). And even in the flush of youth, realists and especially the crits had really just exchanged one set of reified abstractions—Property and Contract—for another and equally unexamined set—Equality, Liberation, Socialism, and Democracy. A reified abstraction that Horwitz recites with evident relish is that all private action is a delegation of public power to private individuals,[16] making the latter in effect public officials, so that levying a general income tax is merely cutting government salaries (pp. 163–164). When I eat a potato chip I am really eating the government's potato chip with its permission, since it is the government that created, recognizes, and protects my property right in the chip. This is a valid thrust against anyone who asserts a metaphysical concept of privateness. But the idea that everything is *really* public is as metaphysical and unpragmatic as the idea that there *really* is a realm of purely private action. It is not even true that the state precedes property and contract.[17]

Horwitz does not understand that the tension between formalism and realism is creative. This oversight is connected with his hostility to science. He will have no truck with the branch of legal realism that

16. The invention of Robert Hale, the "crits'" favorite legal realist. See Robert L. Hale, "Coercion and Distribution in a Supposedly Non-Coercive State," 38 *Political Science Quarterly* 470 (1923); also Neil Duxbury, "Robert Hale and the Economy of Legal Force," 53 *Modern Law Review* 421, 439–444 (1990).

17. See my book *The Economics of Justice*, pt. 2 (1981), discussing the legal doctrines and institutions of prepolitical societies.

sought (abortively, to be sure) to apply the methods of social science to law. For him the significance of realism is its "cognitive relativism," that is, its skepticism about established structures of thought. He commends Jerome Frank for "bad manners" and "bad taste," viewed as a contribution to "cultural politics" (p. 177). He loves images of destruction; "disintegration" is one of his favorite words. The drive to abstraction, generalization, and systematization of legal doctrine in the last half of the nineteenth century "ultimately sowed the seeds of its own destruction" because it "simply exposed contradictions that earlier compartmentalized structures had been able successfully to suppress" (p. 15). The word "simply" suggests that Horwitz does not understand the function of abstraction, generalization, and systematization in bringing anomalies to the surface and setting the stage for new revolutions in thought. To him, science is Platonic, and thus allied to religion. Not for him the fallibilist picture of science painted by Karl Popper, which has affinities with pragmatism that might have been expected to commend it to Horwitz. Not for him, either, pragmatic recognition that rules in the normative rather than descriptive sense are useful features for even a just legal system to have—that they are not *only* instruments of mystification and oppression. Horwitz the self-declared pragmatist (p. 271) is interested in nothing so practical as an actual legal system. He is interested in what legal intellectuals say about the legal system.

He sheds no light on the role that deep personal maladjustments, or sudden psychological jolts, have played in revolts against formalism. His speculation about the effect of Holmes's possible affair with Lady Castletown on the dramatic change of position announced in "The Path of the Law" founders on the absence of a dramatic change of position. There are differences in emphasis between *The Common Law* and "The Path of the Law," but they have mainly to do with the different scope and occasion of the two works and with the difference in perspective between a scholar and a judge. Horwitz claims that not until 1894 did Holmes come to realize that "Law is the product of social struggle. Nothing stands between the state and the individual" (p. 130). Yet two *decades* earlier Holmes had written that

> the struggle for life . . . does not stop in the ascending scale with the monkeys, but is equally the law of human existence . . . And this is as true in legislation as in any other form of corporate action. All that can

be expected from modern improvements is that legislation should easily and quickly, yet not too quickly, modify itself in accordance with the will of the *de facto* supreme power in the community . . . The more powerful interests must be more or less reflected in legislation; which, like every other device of man or beast, must tend in the long run to aid the survival of the fittest.[18]

The continuity of Holmes's thought is more remarkable than its eddies.

But if I am wrong about that continuity I still do not accept Horwitz's psychologizing. It is irresponsibly amateur. If there is a body of psychological scholarship, or of imaginative literature, or of biography, psycho- or otherwise, that predicts that a middle-aged love affair will cause a person to throw over his whole system of thought, Horwitz ought to cite it to us. The proposition is hardly intuitive, and Horwitz does not furnish his reader with enough details to make it plausible as an interpretation of a specific relationship between the specific people involved. As for Frank and Llewellyn, I grant that a psychiatrist would have a field day with them. But their psychiatric problems seem unrelated to anything involved in Holmes's relationship with Lady Castletown, so what is the psychological lowest common denominator that explains the convergence (as Horwitz would have it) of the thought of these three men? And if one picked a larger sample of the progressive-realist movement I doubt that one would find a higher proportion of oddballs in it than in any random cross-section of human beings. Horwitz's broader psychological generalizations, such as "the ideal of neutrality represents a form of denial: As the level of social conflict produced ever more anxiety, the yearning to believe in an idealized oasis of neutrality became correspondingly greater" (p. 20), are merely asserted. Not only the jargon but the theme of *Law and the Modern Mind* is Freudian, and for all one knows Frank got both from his psychoanalyst; but you don't have to have a psychological problem to hold a psychological theory.

Horwitz would have been better advised to search for an explanation of the patterns of legal thought that he describes in the structure of the legal profession, which is something different from either the social class of its clients or the psyches of its members. A profession's claim to monopolize a service, such as the treatment of illness or the administration of the laws, is strengthened by persuading the public that the

18. Holmes, "The Gas-Stokers' Strike," 7 *American Law Review* 582, 583 (1873).

profession commands a body of difficult, demanding, and distinctive techniques, which in the case of law consist of logical and classificatory operations performed upon a family of concepts represented to be capable of generating exact and objective results. It is difficult for a member of a profession to thumb his nose at the norms and practices that are the source of the profession's self-esteem and social importance. Hence the backsliding into formalism of realists such as Frank and Llewellyn; hence the marginalization of that unregenerate realist Fred Rodell. Hence, too, as we saw in Chapter 1, the professional elite's discomfiture with the decision in *Brown*.

Even a Horwitz cannot escape the lure of formalism. The inseparability of public and private is, as we saw, as much a dogma for him as their separability is a dogma of classical liberals. He seems unable, moreover, to visualize an alternative to legal formalism,[19] and this failure of imagination leads him into a formalist trap. All law for Horwitz is divided into formalism and politics, with the latter viewed as an arena of power, of inarticulate struggle. The spirit of "people's justice" broods over the book: get rid of the judges and the lawyers, let the populace rule, judge, and punish. But isn't this a kind of formalism? We recall that the realists, in reaction to *Lochner*, made a shibboleth of democratic choice expressed through legislative enactments, and of expertise enshrined in the administrative process. Uncritical belief in the wisdom either of experts or of "the people" is of a piece with uncritical belief in the wisdom of legal professionals. It evades responsibility for making up one's mind on difficult questions of policy, which is just what formalism does. A reason for doubting that hostility to Lochnerism necessarily is hostility to formalism is that the majority opinion in *Lochner* is not formalistic. It balances the interest of workers and employers in being able to make contracts with each other on mutually agreeable terms with the interest of the state in protecting the public health, and finds the former interest weightier in the particular circumstances, noting in passing the numerous cases in which the Court had found the balance to incline the other way. By treating American legal thought as synonymous with academic legal thought, Horwitz exaggerates the formalistic character of judicial decisions. Until the Supreme Court began turning conservative in the

---

19. Cass R. Sunstein, "Where Politics Ends," *New Republic,* Aug. 3, 1992, p. 38.

1970s, judges had rarely made as big a fetish of logic as law professors had done; they had not had the same incentive to do so.

Populism is only one interpretation of Horwitz's preferred alternative to legal formalism. Another is leftism. Perhaps the relevant political and moral choices are those not of the people but of the judges, and what is at fault are the criteria for selecting judges and the formalism-induced timidity that prevents "good" judges from expressing their political and moral values forthrightly in their decisions. A third possibility—that judges would do better if they brought to their endeavors the open-mindedness, curiosity, intellectual breadth, imagination, willingness to reconsider their views in the light of new experience, and theoretical and empirical rigor and freshness characteristic of the better social and natural scientists—has not occurred to Horwitz.

Subordinate to the major—actually, the excruciatingly minor—theme of the book is a theme better documented, less conjectural, and more closely connected to the earlier book. This is the story of the struggle to adapt legal categories to changed social or economic conditions. When a new institution emerges, such as the corporation, it must be fitted into preexisting categories of legal analysis by a process of analogy, extension, or redefinition; and the process of adjustment may, by altering the categories, alter thinking about other institutions. At first it seemed natural to analogize the corporation to a partnership, with the shareholders as the partners. But to give the shareholders the rights of partners, when really all they are or want to be (in large corporations, anyway) is passive investors, would defeat the purposes of the corporate form. A corporation is not an experiment in democracy or solidarity; it is a device for raising capital. Gradually judges realized this. They began to treat the corporation as a "natural entity," much like an individual. This was more appropriate than the partnership analogy to the economic function of the modern corporation. But the corporation is not a natural entity. It is an artifactual entity recognized and protected by the state. The state endows it with many of the same rights that individuals have, but does so for instrumental ends.

As people began to understand that the corporation, far from being a "natural" rights-bearing entity, had been given rights for instrumental ends, it began to occur to them that maybe even *individuals* had been endowed by the state with rights, specifically property rights, for functional, instrumental ends, rather than having been born with rights. In this way the effort to give the corporation a secure legal status could undermine the belief, widespread in the nineteenth century, that the right of property was a "natural," that is, a prepolitical, right, with which the state could not tamper without compelling justification. Why anyone should care whether rights are "natural" is a bit of a puzzle. They could be prepolitical—even natural in some literal sense—but still alterable. Holmes liked to illustrate the meaning of rights by pointing out that a dog will fight for its bone; he was not paying a compliment to rights by finding their root in nature. Equally, rights could be thoroughly artifactual yet too precious, or simply too engrained in the culture, to tamper with. But "nature" has normative force, at least rhetorically, with many people. Reactionary judges, aware that a realistic conception of the corporation was the crest of the slippery slope at the bottom of which lies my potato-chip example, resisted "modern" ideas of the corporation—and proto-legal-realists embraced those ideas for the same reason. This is the kind of story that Horwitz tells well.

There is nothing either good or bad, but thinking makes it so.[1]

chapter **12**

Pragmatic or Utopian?

T H E animating principle, recognizably pragmatic, of Martha Minow's book[2] about law in relation to traditionally disadvantaged persons, primarily the physically and mentally handicapped but also women and racial minorities, is distrust of categorization. Especially categorization that makes a sharp distinction between "us," the "normal," the benchmark—in fact, often just the average, the majority, or the politically, socially, or economically dominant—and some class of others, the subnormal or abnormal or marginal, as they appear to us to be. White and nonwhite, man and woman, able-bodied and disabled, normal and retarded, whole and crippled, healthy and sick, sane and insane, majority and minority, normal and deviant, even adult and child: such dichotomies, however useful they may be in ordering the chaos of our perceptions, by framing perceptions limit them and by limiting them rationalize insensitive, even oppressive, treatment of people who are different from the average member of society and who do not have much, and sometimes have no, political or economic power.

Such dichotomies have this effect in part because they appear to be

1. Hamlet to Rosencrantz in *Hamlet,* Act II, sc. ii, ll. 251–252.
2. *Making All the Difference: Inclusion, Exclusion, and American Law* (1990).

natural, intrinsic, inevitable, rather than, as in fact they are, socially constructed, for the sake of expedience or policy or even exploitation. Of course, there are real—"natural" (in fact biological)—as well as merely social differences between whites and blacks, men and women, adults and children, the healthy and the sick, the bright and the retarded. But the social significance of these biological differences is given by society rather than by nature. To be crippled has a different meaning in a society that has staircases than in one that does not. Likewise, the ascription of legal rights and duties on the basis of biological differences is a social act rather than a command of nature and is therefore contestable, revisable. Not easily, though. In part this is because what is familiar seems natural and what is natural seems immutable, so we must keep up our guard against complacency. We can do this only by becoming self-critical, by multiplying our skepticisms, our perspectives, our empathies.

All this is true, and important, and still resisted so strenuously as to be worth reiteration. It is a lesson particularly worth emphasizing to lawyers because legal reasoning is a bastion of dichotomous classifications that oversimplify social reality and confuse local, transient, sometimes uninformed public opinion with durable, even metaphysical, reality. But it is a lesson that is cautionary rather than constructive. This is so whether it is set out in the garb of the American pragmatist philosophers or that of feminists who do not think it enough for the law to treat women as if they were men and therefore to refuse, as the Supreme Court once did, to consider pregnancy a disability for which an employer who has a medical benefits plan for his employees should have to pay.[3] Both garbs are on display in Minow's book.

In popular understanding a pragmatist is a doer, a problem solver. But a pragmatist *philosopher* is a debunker of metaphysical and other occult entities, of philosophical foundations such as the real and the ideal, and of essentialist concepts such as the natural. Feminist theoreticians, taking their cue in part from these philosophers, are debunkers of traditional ideas, often felt as natural and immutable by those who hold them, about the proper role of women. The great challenge is to put something in place of the jejune dichotomies that Minow, wielding the weapons of pragmatist and feminist thought, effectively undermines. To this challenge her book does not rise. It is an "on the one

3. General Electric Co. v. Gilbert, 429 U.S. 125 (1976).

hand, on the other hand" kind of book. On the one hand, forcing an immigrant child to speak English from his first day in public school exemplifies an uncritical norm of English-language competence. On the other hand, bilingual education may handicap the immigrant child in developing what is after all the essential language competence in an English-speaking nation. On the one hand, segregating deaf children in special classes classifies them and, by classifying, stigmatizes them as abnormal. On the other hand, ignoring their "differentness" by putting them in the same classes with children of normal hearing makes it harder, maybe impossible, for the deaf children to learn. On the one hand, affirmative action for minorities stigmatizes them as handicapped. On the other hand, a "colorblind" public policy may keep them behind the societal eight ball. The differences in the way society treats the foreign-born and the native-born, the deaf and the nondeaf, the non-white and the white are not inscribed in the book of nature. But efforts to eliminate them may make the disadvantaged group worse off rather than better off or may impose other unacceptable costs.

What is to be done? Minow is reluctant to say. For the most part she confines herself to stating dilemmas, posing questions, and exhorting her readers to set aside their prejudices, to transcend sterile dichotomies, to reason together. Her hesitation about taking sides on tough social questions is understandable, and if it gives the book an indecisive air, this is better than choosing recklessly on inadequate facts. Minow's lawyerly caution (I am tempted to say "innate" lawyerly caution) is reinforced by her awareness of the checkered history of social reform. The juvenile-court movement was intended to spare children the cruelty and stigma of adult punishment and place their fates in the hands of experts; in fact it merely denied them their procedural rights. The fixing of minimum wages and maximum hours for women, and their exclusion from dangerous occupations, may have been intended to protect women's health and welfare, and no doubt did so to some extent. But it also reduced their job opportunities and promoted the view that a woman's proper place is either in the home or in traditional women's jobs such as teaching or nursing.

Minow makes some concrete proposals, but the results of these forays into the practical are not reassuring. With regard to the deaf child, for example, she suggests in all seriousness that the child be placed in a class with nondeaf children and the class conducted in sign language. The proposal fits her conceptual framework nicely because it reverses our "natural" tendency to take the nondeaf as the norm; the deaf becomes the norm. But at least in the unelaborated form in which the book presents it, the proposal is unpersuasive, a gimmick. Before the class could be conducted in sign language the children would have to be taught both to understand and to "speak" sign language. A protracted course of instruction would be required, which would take time away from subjects of greater utility to the children and arouse the resentment of parents at what many of them would consider irresponsible experimentation with their children's education. Minow does not tell the reader whether, once the children had mastered sign language, all classes in which the deaf child was enrolled would be conducted in sign language, or some, or only one, and for how long the program would continue. And is there to be similar instruction in Braille, in the operation of a wheelchair, and in the dialect of inner-city blacks?

A pragmatist is interested in the consequences of reform proposals, and one consequence is cost. Minow does not examine the costs of a school's treating the exceptional as the normal or of treating pregnancy and active parenting as the normal condition of a worker to which the organization of the workplace should adapt with generous maternity and paternity leaves, flexible hours, and "free" day care. These adaptations are expensive, and it is particularly important for a pragmatist who like Minow is also an egalitarian to consider, as she does not, who will pay for them. Primarily it is workers. Their wages will fall because the cost of labor will rise if employers have to pay for maternity leave and paternity leave and day care and flex time. Consumers—to whom the employers will pass on a portion of their higher costs in the form of higher prices—will suffer too, and the poor more than the rich. An increase in price is like an increase in sales tax, which unless confined to luxury goods is regressive. A reduction in wages is similar in its distributive consequences, and will be felt most keenly by the nonworking wives of male workers and by childless women, married and unmarried; for these groups will not benefit from the pregnancy and maternity benefits that employers are forced to provide.[4] The perspectives of the childless, of the housewife, of the taxpayer, of the consumer are barely reflected in the book; Minow's empathy is truncated.

She is articulate about the dilemma presented by the baby who is

---

4. The effect on workers of government regulation of the employment relation is discussed further in the next chapter.

born with a profound physical or mental defect. The "right to life" enthusiasts want to save the baby at all costs, regardless of the quality of the life that the child, if it survives, can be expected to lead. The "quality of life" enthusiasts want to let the baby die if it is unlikely to be able to lead a normal human life. Minow sides with the right-to-lifers, relegating to a footnote the resulting tension with the right of abortion, which she also supports. But her real hope is that the dilemma posed by the defective baby can be transcended and everyone made happy. In this vein she offers the (real) case of a child born with Down (or Down's) syndrome, a child who in the old days would have been called, cruelly and inaccurately, a "Mongoloid Idiot." A frequent component of Down syndrome is a serious heart defect nowadays reparable by surgery. In the case that Minow discusses, the child's parents withheld their consent to the surgery. They thought their child would be better off dead. A couple who did volunteer work at the institution in which the child was living while its fate was being decided became deeply attached to the child and fought the parents, successfully, to be appointed his guardians, in effect his parents, the natural parents being limited to rights of infrequent visitation. The surgery was performed, and the child, now a teenager, is doing well. The Cinderella ending[5] persuades Minow that society can resolve the dilemma of difference without having to embrace either horn. But the case was an easy one: the parents in effect abandoned the child, and the state quite rightly reassigned the parental rights to a couple who were optimistic about the child's prospects. Minow makes an easy case seem hard in order to make the hard cases seem soluble.

Those who believe that "reality" is constructed rather than found are prone to forget that not every social construction is arbitrary. This tendency is conspicuous in Minow's book, sometimes amusingly, as when she expresses wonderment at the couple who conducted elabo-

---

5. Which however Minow exaggerates. The outlook for children with Down syndrome is not good. Of those with congenital heart anomalies, such as the child Minow writes about, only 50 percent survive to age 30. Patricia A. Baird and Adele D. Sadovnick, "Life Expectancy in Down Syndrome," 110 *Journal of Pediatrics* 849 (1987); Richard K. Eyman, Thomas L. Call, and James F. White, "Life Expectancy of Persons with Down Syndrome," 95 *American Journal of Mental Retardation* 603, 610 (1991). Those who do make it past early adulthood are highly likely to become afflicted with Alzheimer's disease in their thirties or forties. Marlis Tolksdorf and H.-R. Wiedemann, "Clinical Aspects of Down's Syndrome from Infancy to Adult Life," in *Trisomy 21: An International Symposium* 3, 23–28 (G. R. Burgio et al. eds. 1981). Minow does not refer to the medical literature on Down syndrome.

rate funeral obsequies for their son's pet mouse while at the same time setting traps for the pet's wild cousins. She might as well be baffled that the nation mourned Lincoln's death but not that of his assassin. Minow quotes with approval a sociologist's statement that "social groups create deviance by making the rules whose infraction constitutes deviance" (p. 174), as if the murderer were an artifact of the criminal law, which in a sense he is, but not a useful sense. And she mentions "elderly people suffering from what has been called senility" (p. 127), as if senility were merely an epithet. She describes the mentally retarded as persons who are merely "delayed in their progress along the path of development followed by every human being" (p. 134), as if with time and patience we can all be Einstein; yet elsewhere she affirms the existence of real differences in mental capacity.[6]

It might seem all the clearer that there are real differences in physical capacity. Yet to Minow the able-bodied are merely the "temporarily able" (which in a sense they are, since they'll die eventually and probably become disabled well before then), and she takes at face value—rather credulously, it seems to me—the answer given by a severely crippled person to the question of what he would do first if he could leave his wheelchair: "Get right back in" (p. 155).[7] Minow likes fables but has forgotten the one about the fox without a tail, a fable whose moral is nowadays called cognitive dissonance. She seeks both to minimize the differences between normal and handicapped persons so that the normal won't look down on the handicapped and to maximize the sympathy of the normal for the handicapped—which requires, however, that the former retain a lively perception of real differences that are highly disadvantageous to the latter.

The implication of rejecting "the view of the disabled as lacking—and wanting—something that those with abilities have" (p. 155 n. 25) is that we should stop spending money on cures for cleft palates, harelips, club feet, spinal injuries, dwarfism, and other sources of disfigurement or immobility, since people who have these conditions are not afflicted, they are merely different. It is unlikely that Minow actually believes

6. Sufferers from Down syndrome do not catch up with normal people; they get worse with age, as noted in the preceding footnote.

7. Cf. Felicity Barringer, "Pride in a Soundless World: Deaf Oppose a Hearing Aid," *New York Times*, May 16, 1993, p. 1, attributing to "leading advocates for the deaf" the view that it is "brutal" to insert an inner-ear implant in a deaf child "just to rob that child of a birthright of silence."

this, but that means that she is insufficiently critical about her premises. There is also something deeply unpragmatic about encouraging people to be content with their lot.

She would be on stronger ground if she distinguished between two situations: a disability with which a person is born, and which does not become curable until many years later, when the person is fully mature; and a disability that is curable shortly after its onset, whatever the stage of life at which the onset occurred. (The intermediate cases do not present an analytically distinct issue.) In the first situation—for example that of a person who has been blind from birth and recovers his sight in middle age—the person may have become so completely adapted to the disability that it is part of his identity, so that the cure would be a kind of death. But it is only in that unusual situation that it makes any sense to speak of the disabled as merely different.

Minow says that "children *no less than adults* can participate in the legal conversation that uses rights to gain the community's attention" (p. 308; my emphasis). She does not mean this, for she has just acknowledged that courts might have to appoint not just one legal guardian, but "multiple representatives," for a child caught in a legal proceeding, in order "to offer contrasting views of children's interests and rights" (p. 306).[8] Children are inarticulate; adults must speak for them. True enough; but to talk then of children's "rights" is as misleading as to talk of children participating in the legal conversation. The issue is how far the law should protect children, and by what means. The language of rights may actually be inimical to children's interests. Minow is concerned about the prevalence of sexual abuse of children, yet her repeated affirmations of children's rights, children's competence, and children's parity with adults could be thought to imply that the age of consent should be drastically lowered, which would have the effect of decriminalizing most child abuse. She may answer that you can be competent yet powerless, which is true. But the distinction is more pertinent to the rape of children than to the seduction of children, the more prevalent abuse.

Commenting on Carol Gilligan's finding that girls and boys react differently to ethical problems,[9] Minow simultaneously affirms and

8. The lawyer's propensity for casually proposing ways of making legal proceedings ever more complex, protracted, and expensive, well illustrated by Minow's proposal for multiple guardians, is the sort of thing that makes the lay person shudder.

9. Gilligan, *In a Different Voice: Psychological Theory and Women's Development* (1982).

denies that women are different from men: "Gilligan's study thus does not assert inherent or even descriptive differences between males and females so much as it posits an alternative perspective that is enabled when the researcher includes women in studies and builds frameworks of analysis from their statements rather than judging them in relation to frameworks constructed with men in mind" (p. 196 n. 84). If women's statements reflect a conceptual or moral framework different from men's, men and women are different. A further example of Minow's backsliding into essentialism is that while derisive about basing public policy on biology, she criticizes the term "surrogate mother" because it "obscures the fact that it applies to the person who is actually the biological mother"—the "real" mother (p. 4 n. 5).[10]

Minow is intelligent, conscientious, hard-working. The flaws in her book—neglect of issues of cost and incidence (that is, who pays?), indecision, wishful thinking, contradictions born of a desire to have things both ways at once, lapses into essentialist thinking, a certain thinness wearing the guise of judiciousness—are the failings of a system more than of an individual. That system is academic law, which, as we saw in discussing the work of Ely, Strauss, and Amar in Chapter 6, does not contain the answers, or the resources for generating the answers, to social questions of the kind that engage Minow's interest.

Minow is not a narrow lawyer. She has read widely in philosophy, history, sociology, and other fields, and she is steeped in feminist scholarship; what she is not is an expert on mental retardation, labor markets, physical handicaps, or public finance. Minow's engagement with the actual subject matter of her book is mediated by a vast secondary literature written by historians, philosophers, law professors, and others who are themselves not experts in mental retardation, labor markets, physical handicaps, or public finance. She writes less about the problems of the disadvantaged than about the writers about those problems, and, as is sadly characteristic of American lawyers, she displays no interest in the experience of foreign countries with the same problems. The only exception is a brief, laudatory reference to the "respectful attitudes toward bilingualism and, indeed, multilingualism in other countries" (p. 27 n. 22). Ask a Belgian, a Malaysian, a Cana-

---

10. Equivocation about the "natural" is common in feminist thought. No feminist would accept the argument that since women in wealthy modern nations like the United States live longer than men on average, medical resources should be reallocated from women to men in order to eliminate this "natural" inequality.

dian, or a resident of what used to be Yugoslavia about the joys of a multilingual society. The essential facts and figures concerning the subject matter of Minow's book—such as how many persons with serious physical or mental handicaps there are, of what sort, mitigable at what cost paid by whom—are missing. The gap is not closed by the voluminous citations to feminists, postmodernists, law professors, and judges. The book is not policy analysis but discourse about policy analysis. It is properly critical of abstraction, of generality, but is itself abstract, general.

Minow's book underscores a weakness not only of academic law but of pragmatic social thought more generally. I said in the Introduction that pragmatists tend to have an equivocal attitude toward common sense. They do not despise it merely because it often lacks articulable foundations, and their practical orientation requires them to take it seriously. But precisely because they are aware of its lack of foundations and of its unpredictable mutability, neither do they venerate it, and indeed they are inclined to question it. When the skeptical view of common sense is emphasized to the exclusion of the common-sense vein in pragmatism, pragmatism veers into social constructionism and even Utopianism. Common sense tells us that the disabled are—disabled. Minow rejects this, and her audacious rejection is a source of insight but also as we have seen of occasional naïveté and ostrichism.

Self-conscious Utopianism is a growing though still tiny voice in the cacophonous chorus of modern legal scholarship. Consider an article by Leonard Jaffee deceptively entitled "The Troubles with Law & Economics."[11] The title is deceptive because while the article does contain criticisms of the economic approach to law, these criticisms are merely the prolegomenon to the real "work" of the article, which is to promote anarcho-vegetarianism. To Jaffee, capitalism, epitomized by economic analysis of law, is the philosophy of greed; vegetarianism is the antidote to greed; if greed were cured, we wouldn't need government.

It probably is true that if the human race turned vegetarian, then after the inevitable transitional dislocations the cost of feeding the race would be lower than it is today; perhaps medical costs would be lower

---

11. Leonard R. Jaffee, "The Troubles with Law & Economics," 20 *Hofstra Law Review* 777 (1992). For another specimen of self-consciously Utopian legal scholarship, see Robin West, "Law, Literature, and the Celebration of Authority," 83 *Northwestern University Law Review* 977 (1989).

too. It does not follow—this is a standard mistake of Utopians—that there would be less greed. The cost of many things is lower than it once was—the cost of transportation for example, or of communications, or of illumination, or of listening to music—without the greed index having declined as a consequence. If the cost of one type of good or service goes down, this frees up resources for the purchase of other goods and services. For that matter the fraction of the family budget that goes for food is less than half what it was at the beginning of the twentieth century[12] even though we are, most of us, still omnivores—and still greedy. There is a moral argument for vegetarianism, based on the capacity of animals to suffer,[13] but Jaffee does not press it.

The Utopian is forever casting longing eyes toward simpler societies. Jaffee praises the American Indians and the poor of China. He thinks finance did bad things to the character of German Jews. He is very down on television, fast food, food preservatives, unfertilized eggs, vitamin supplements, white bread, and bottle-feeding. He is in fact down on the West, viewed as the symbol of progress, modernity, and their handmaiden, technology. He wants us to adapt to our environment, rather than changing the environment to make it suit our wants better and at the same time multiplying our wants. He is even critical of the wheel, and would no doubt reject Christopher Marlowe's dictum (in *The First Part of Tamburlaine the Great*), great Renaissance commonplace that it is, that "Nature . . . doth teach us all to have aspiring minds." Jaffee says, "Look not to Europe's heritage, but to Hunzas, traditional Georgians, Peru's Andean Indians, and China's simple folk. They do not want because they don't demand."[14]

We all know who the Georgians, the Peruvians, and the Chinese are, though one would have liked Jaffee to comment on the civil wars in Georgia and Peru and on the rapid *embourgeoisement* of the Chinese. But who are the Hunzas? Jaffee might have told his readers, few of whom I daresay have heard of the Hunzas. The Hunzas or Hunzukuts are inhabitants of a mountainous region in what is now northern Pakistan.[15] When first discovered by the British, at the end of the

12. Eva Jacobs and Stephanie Shipp, "How Family Spending Has Changed in the U.S.," *Monthly Labor Review*, March 1990, pp. 20, 22 (tab. 2).

13. James Rachels, *Created from Animals: The Moral Implications of Darwinism* 211–212 (1990).

14. Jaffee, note 11 above, at 912.

15. Hermann Kreutzmann, "Challenge and Response in the Karakoram: Socioeconomic Transformation in Hunza, Northern Areas, Pakistan," 13 *Mountain Research and Develop-*

nineteenth century, the Hunzas were living in extreme poverty, subsisting on a diet mainly of apricots. But according to the British ethnographers who studied—and were charmed by—them, they were serene, extraordinarily healthy, and free from crime and other social problems; and the treatment of men and women was remarkably egalitarian.[16] The beauty of the country and the idyllic way of life of its people (as it seemed to ethnographers and other Westerners) made it the model of the fictional Shangri-La. The idyll was not perfect, though. The Hunzas had a caste system and before the British came had been renowned as warriors, brigands, and slave traders. After Pakistan became independent, and especially after a highway linking the Hunza region to the rest of Pakistan was completed in the late 1970s, the region began to modernize. Tourist and other commercial facilities sprang up and, with easier access to the outside world, many Hunzas found more lucrative employment outside the region. I don't think Jaffee means us to emulate *those* Hunzas.

The usual complaint about the politics of nostalgia is that it overlooks the bad features of the good old days—polio, the Inquisition, the Pale of Settlement, the slave trade, the Black Death, the exclusion of blacks and women from many occupations: the list is endless. Jaffee seeks to finesse this complaint by pushing his Golden Age *way* back: not to the 1950s, not to the nineteenth century, not to Cathay or Byzantium or the Roman Republic, but, as his reference to the Hunzas intimates, to the Stone Age.[17] Yet even Heidegger didn't want to go back much before Socrates. And the Hunzas were quick to embrace modernity when the opportunity came to them with the highway. They had been vegetarian only because they couldn't afford meat, pacific only because the British had pacified them, egalitarian only because they were poor.

Jaffee's basic idea, that of dealing with scarcity by limiting our wants rather than by upping our production, has a distinguished pedigree that goes back to Epicurus. So Jaffee is in some good company. Unfortu-

---

ment 19 (1993); Sabrina Michaud and Roland Michaud, "Trek to Lofty Hunza—and Beyond," 148 *National Geographic* 644 (1975); Timothy J. O'Leary, "Burusho Cultural Summary" (Human Relations Area Files, unpublished, 1965); E. O. Lorimer, "The Burusho of Hunza," 12 *Antiquity* 5 (1938). The Hunzukut population is about 30,000.

16. There are affinities to William Miller's description of medieval Iceland, discussed in Chapter 14.

17. This doesn't quite work, because the Hunzas were slave traders and because Stone Age people were not vegetarians.

nately he has no suggestions for how to get from where we are back to the Stone Age. His imagination has wings, but it has no feet. There are more than five billion people in the world. Their happiness—their very survival—depends on modern technology, the division of labor, the existence of governments, and even the science of economics.

Jaffee looks to a change in the human spirit rather than to a change in institutions for solutions to social problems.[18] He is a preacher, a prophet. He wants the American people, turned off law and economics and, more broadly, capitalism by the first part of his paper, to be inspired by the second part to change their lives—to stop eating meat, being vaccinated, consuming fast foods, and watching television. Not the least unrealistic feature of Jaffee's article is his supposition that it is an effective clarion.

Minow is not Jaffee, but like him she does not have a tight grip on the world of fact. Jaffee has reached the end of the road on which Minow has taken the first tentative steps. The lesson from reading their very different but related works is the same. We cannot wish away physical and mental abnormalities merely by inverting accepted categories, or build intelligent social policies merely by ripping up foundations.

18. Cf. George Orwell, "Charles Dickens," in *Collected Essays, Journalism and Letters of George Orwell*, vol. 1, p. 413 (Sonia Orwell and Ian Angus eds. 1968).

chapter 13

Hegel and Employment at Will

A TOWERING figure not only in general philosophy but also in jurisprudence, Hegel, like James Fitzjames Stephen whom he otherwise
does not resemble in the least, is too little known to Anglo-American
legal scholars. Drucilla Cornell is one of the handful of such scholars
who are trying to domesticate him for American legal thought.[1] Particularly noteworthy, because it has a concreteness seldom encountered
in Hegelian jurisprudence, is Cornell's effort to apply Hegel's thought
to the important common law doctrine of employment at will.[2] That
effort is the focus of this chapter. As in other chapters, I try to clear
away thick theoretical underbrush to create a space for empirical in-

---

1. See, for example, her article "Institutionalization of Meaning, Recollective Imagination
and the Potential for Transformative Legal Interpretation," 136 *University of Pennsylvania
Law Review* 1135, 1178–1193 (1988); also Michel Rosenfeld, "Hegel and the Dialectics of
Contract," 10 *Cardozo Law Review* 1199 (1989). Both Rosenfeld's article and the article by
Cornell that I discuss in this chapter (see note 2) appear in the ambitious, book-length *Hegel
and Legal Theory Symposium,* 10 *Cardozo Law Review* 847 (1989).

2. Cornell, "Dialogic Reciprocity and the Critique of Employment at Will," 10 *Cardozo
Law Review* 1575 (1989). The best introduction to the controversy over employment at will
is Paul C. Weiler, *Governing the Workplace: The Future of Labor and Employment Law,* ch. 2
(1990), and the most thorough and rigorous economic analysis of the institution is Edward
P. Lazear, "Employment-at-Will, Job Security, and Work Incentives," in *Employment, Unemployment and Labor Utilization* 39 (Robert A. Hart ed. 1988).

quiry. The question we ought to be asking about employment at will is not whether it is un-Hegelian, but what would be the likely consequences of abolishing it.

Employment at will means employment terminable by either party, employer or employee, at any time and without grounds. Cornell uses several strands in Hegel's thought to argue, primarily against Richard Epstein,[3] that employment at will should be outlawed. Every employee would be entitled after successful completion of a brief probationary period to retain his or her job for life unless economic adversity required layoffs or an arbitrator or some other neutral adjudicator determined that the employer had good cause to discharge the employee. This is the type of job security enjoyed at present by tenured college and university teachers, civil servants (including public school teachers), and workers covered by collective bargaining agreements. Cornell's particular proposal is that statutes be enacted that would specify forbidden grounds for discharging an employee, so that all discharges would be for "rational cause." The list of forbidden grounds, on which Cornell is surprisingly casual, must be specified precisely before one can be sure whether her proposal would curtail the freedom of action of employers substantially. But probably it would; and assuming it would, I am against it; it is inefficient and regressive. And I doubt whether Hegel can be squeezed hard enough to yield persuasive reasons for it.

I grant the force of Hegel's argument, which Cornell emphasizes, that individualism, upon which Epstein founded the ethical part of his argument for employment at will,[4] is socially constructed rather than presocial. Individuals do not have "natural" rights to make contracts. The natural state of human beings is one not of equality but of de-

---

3. Richard A. Epstein, "In Defense of the Contract at Will," 51 *University of Chicago Law Review* 947 (1984). Epstein defends employment at will on both economic and ethical grounds. Other economic defenses of the institution are Lazear, note 2 above; Mayer G. Freed and Daniel D. Polsby, "Just Cause for Termination Rules and Economic Efficiency," 38 *Emory Law Journal* 1097 (1989); and Gail L. Heriot, "The New Feudalism: The Unintended Destination of Contemporary Trends in Employment Law," 28 *Georgia Law Review* 167 (1993).

4. Epstein, note 3 above, at 951–955. I use the past tense because he has since abandoned the effort to ground his jurisprudential views on natural-rights philosophy in favor of a utilitarian-economic approach. See, for example, his articles "A Last Word on Eminent Domain," 41 *University of Miami Law Review* 253, 256–258 (1986); "The Utilitarian Foundations of Natural Law," 12 *Harvard Journal of Law and Public Policy* 713 (1989); and "Holdouts, Externalities, and the Single Owner: One More Salute to Ronald Coase," 36 *Journal of Law and Economics* 553 (1993).

pendence on more powerful human beings. Economic freedom, including freedom of contract, in the classical liberal sense is one of the luxuries enabled by social organization. The long life, wide liberties, and extensive property of the average modern American are the creation not of that American alone but of society, that is, of a vast aggregation of individuals, living and dead; and of luck—in geography, climate, natural resources. To this extent, Robert Hale and Morton Horwitz are right to question the distinction between the public and the private spheres. If there are two equally able and hard-working people, one living in a wealthy society and the other in a poor one, the former will have a higher standard of living; and the difference will be due to the efforts of other members, living and dead, of the wealthier society and to other factors external to the character, capacity, and efforts of the two individuals. The individual's "right" to property in such a society is not "natural," because, even if we ignore the role of luck, his possessions are a product of social interactions rather than of his skills and efforts alone, and those skills may be, in part or whole, a social product too. I thus stand with Hegel and Cornell, and against Hobbes and (1984 vintage) Epstein, in believing that freedom of contract—the principle that undergirds the institution of employment at will—cannot be defended persuasively by reference to natural liberty.

But this concession will not carry the day for opponents of employment at will. To knock down one of the doctrine's philosophical struts is not to show that the doctrine should be abandoned. It would be odd to conclude—although this is the character of Rawls's famous "difference principle"—that because individual well-being is, in an important sense, a social product, the state ought to be empowered to take away the difference between my income and that of the average resident of Bangladesh. That would be the same *reductio ad absurdum* as supposing that recognition of the artificiality of the distinction between private and public action makes all private property, such as the computer keyboard on which I am typing this sentence, public property. Employment at will is a corollary of freedom of contract, and freedom of contract is a social policy with a host of economic and social justifications, even though nature is not one of them. Employment at will happens to be the logical terminus on the road that begins with slavery and makes intermediate stops at serfdom, indentured servitude, involuntary servitude, and guild restrictions. That should be a point in its favor. Hegel himself, as Cornell notes, would have thought employment at will a fine idea. Just the pragmatic success of free markets in "delivering the goods"[5] warrants a presumption in their favor, preventing Cornell from resting her case with Hegel's demonstration that rights are social rather than natural.

She knows she cannot stop there, and she is therefore led to place great emphasis on Hegel's belief that the possession of property is an element of a person's sense of himself as a person.[6] Taken literally (but Cornell does not take it literally), this is an odd and implausible idea. But what is true or at least plausible is that we are scarcely persons unless we are able to intervene in the external world. An individual who cannot have any effect on his environment may not be aware of himself as a person, that is, aware of himself as being distinct from his environment. These interventions constitute personality in the further sense that our sense of ourselves as persons is a function in part of our recollections of past experience, and, as Proust taught us, those recollections are kept fresh by the objects and activities associated with them. That is why it can be a terrible wrench (over and above the inconvenience) to lose one's house and personal possessions in a fire even if they are fully insured.

It may therefore be the case empirically that a person who has no property has a fainter awareness of himself as a separate person than one who does have property—is it not a purpose of monastic life to make its adherents feel themselves a part of a larger organism? To Margaret Jane Radin, Hegel's analysis of property implies that heirlooms should receive greater legal protection than cash or other fungible property.[7] This may seem a curious suggestion, but insolvency law does place some of the bankrupt's personal property—including, in some states, his heirlooms—beyond the reach of his creditors. Radin also suggests that Hegel's theory of property provides support for

5. On which, see, for example, Samuel Brittan, "How British is the British Sickness?" in Brittan, *The Role and Limits of Government: Essays in Political Economy* 219 (1983); Alan Ryan, "Why Are There So Few Socialists?" in Ryan, *Property and Political Theory* 118 (1984); and discussion in Chapter 22 of the present book.

6. Hegel's theory of property is well described in Alan Ryan's essay "Hegel and Mastering the World," in Ryan, note 5 above, at 194.

7. "Property and Personhood," 34 *Stanford Law Review* 957 (1982); see also Radin, "Time, Possession and Alienation," 64 *Washington University Law Quarterly* 739, 741 (1986) ("the claim to an owned object grows stronger as, over time, the holder becomes bound up with the object"). This was also Holmes's theory of property. See "The Path of the Law," 10 *Harvard Law Review* at 477.

entitling tenants to renew their leases indefinitely, provided they behave themselves.[8] This suggestion is far more problematic. Carried to its logical extreme, it would destroy the institution of tenancy by giving the tenant a right almost as extensive as outright ownership. It is difficult to see how the interests of people who cannot afford to own their homes would be helped by the destruction of tenancy. Existing tenants would benefit, but what of persons who will be seeking rental housing in the future?

Cornell's version of Hegel's theory of property rights is less literal than Radin's version, although neither has much bearing on employment at will. The employee at will can quit whenever he wants and go work for someone else. He can also, it is true, be fired at will. But the consequences of being fired, in our society at any rate, do not include becoming someone's slave. Given unemployment insurance and welfare, they do not even include becoming a poor person, in the sense of someone utterly destitute and without property—the sort of fell consequence that we recall Fitzjames Stephen associating with the loss of a job (see Chapter 10). Poor people in the United States have enough goods to retain a lively sense of themselves as persons. It is patronizing to suggest otherwise.

But by pushing a little harder the idea that our sense of personality is embodied in our accustomed possessions and activities, we can begin to see a loosely Hegelian argument for job tenure, as for tenant rights. The person who has had the same job for a long time, like the tenant who has lived in the same place for a long time, albeit under a succession of one-year leases, may develop such an attachment that termination is wrenching. But we are now a long way from the idea that people who lack any property (the monk, the conscript soldier, the pauper) may in consequence have a precarious sense of self. We are now saying merely that everyone dislikes losing what he had grown accustomed to having. We have turned Hegel into a superficial utilitarian, who does not consider the long-range consequences of his happiness-maximizing proposals.

The right of property, moreover, implies the right of alienation. If I own my labor I should be entitled to rent it on whatever terms I see fit. We shall see that the employee at will is likely to have a higher wage

8. "Property and Personhood," note 7 above, at 991–996; see also Radin, "Residential Rent Control," 15 *Philosophy and Public Affairs* 350, 362–368 (1986).

than he would if he had a term employment contract or any other form
of job tenure, including Cornell's proposed "rational cause" protection.
With the higher wage he can acquire additional property. To force him
to forgo his preferred wage-tenure package and accept a lower wage in
exchange for greater job security is, one might think, a denial of his
personhood. This analysis would fail if employees did not *realize* they
were employees at will. But especially nowadays, with so many well-
publicized mass discharges by large employers, few employees at will
think they have job tenure; being dismissed from a job is not, or at
least is no longer, such a low-probability event that people have trouble
thinking rationally about it. Maybe we need heavier sanctions on employers who mislead their employees into thinking they have job protection when they don't. But this would be far different from abolishing employment at will.

To suggest that one's right in one's labor should be freely alienable
may seem inconsistent with the fact that people are not allowed to sell
themselves into slavery. The ban against self-enslavement is connected
with notions of essential personhood, but an additional, pragmatic
consideration is that most of us cannot think of any reason why a sane
person in our affluent society would make a contract to become a slave.
However generous the price were for surrendering his freedom, as a
slave the person would derive no benefit unless he were intensely
altruistic toward his family or others *and* they were either truly desperate or did not reciprocate his concern—for if they did they would suffer
from seeing him a slave, and his altruistic gesture would fail. And if
they are so indifferent to his own welfare as to be untroubled by seeing
him a slave, he is unlikely to be so altruistic toward them as to be willing
to make that sacrifice for them. The surprising implication is that
sacrifice is likely to be more rational, the less grateful the person for
whom the sacrifice is made is to the person making the sacrifice.

I would not put too much weight on utilitarian arguments pro and
con allowing self-enslavement. Our reaction to slavery is both culture-
bound and semantically influenced. We are unlikely to say that a captive
in ancient times who chose slavery over death surrendered his personhood. And today when a person does outwardly rather similar things
to self-enslavement, but for what is considered a good reason—joins
the army, becomes a Catholic priest, or even, having robbed a bank,
becomes a "slave" of the state, maybe for life—we do not say that he
has surrendered his essential personhood. Slavery has become the name

of the forms of involuntary servitude that we abhor, and what those are owes almost everything to the history of Negro slavery in the United States. The word does not signify the abhorrence of all forms of involuntary servitude. And none of this has anything to do with employment at will, which lies at the other end of the spectrum of labor contracts from slavery.

Cornell emphasizes the importance of reciprocal symmetry in personal relations: "The image is of two people looking one another in the eye, knowing the other is looking back. No one is on top."[9] This is not a bad description—of the regime of freedom of contract. The employer and employee meet as free individuals and can strike any deal they want; presumably it will be mutually advantageous. It may or may not involve job tenure, as the parties prefer. If, perhaps by virtue of a statute, the employee could dictate the terms, he would be on top, and this would violate reciprocal symmetry.

Cornell understands reciprocal symmetry differently, as entitling each of us to demand that someone who proposes to harm us, as by firing us, must have and give us a compelling reason for doing so. Carried to its logical extreme, this is an unworkable principle. Each of us is harmed every day by the actions of unknown others and harms unknown others by our own actions, if only through the operation of competition in economic and other marketplaces. It would be absurd to require that all the harmed—the jilted boyfriend, the writer whose book is reviewed unfavorably, the consumer faced with an increase in the price of anchovies, the loser in a tennis match—be given notice and a hearing. Granted, losing one's job is apt to be a greater blow. But it is a known risk, and anyone who desires—and is willing to pay for—protection against it can negotiate for an employment contract; or, more realistically (because asking one's employer for a contract may signal to the employer that one is apt to be an unsatisfactory worker), can enter the sector of the work force where such protection comes with the job.

Let us pause for a moment to consider conditions in that sector. For the truth is that millions of American workers have job tenure. Does their experience suggest that universalizing the practice would improve human relations? Does the union worker have a greater sense of personality than the nonunion worker? Does the civil servant have a

9. Cornell, note 2 above, at 1587.

greater sense of personality than his counterpart who works without tenure in a private-sector job? Do public school teachers have a greater sense of personality than private school teachers? Even if there is something to the Hegelian notion that property is a part of personality, or to the notion that people should interact on terms of reciprocal symmetry, it is far from clear that Cornell's proposal would if adopted cause these notions to be more fully actualized than they already are. What it clearly would do is curtail freedom of contract, an important part of Hegel's notion of freedom.

Another objection to entitling a person to demand a reason for being fired is that it logically entails giving the employer the right to demand of the employee a reason for quitting—and if this seems to be pushing logic too hard, consider that in the Netherlands neither party to an employment relationship can terminate the relationship without cause, and workers can be sent to jail for trying to do so.[10] The resemblance of the just-cause principle to slavery is nowhere clearer than in this example: the employee who could not show just cause for leaving his employment might be forced to spend his whole life in a job he hated. This is unlikely, of course; the costs of monitoring the effort of an unhappy worker would be too high. That is one reason why slavery has gone out of fashion. Nevertheless, what is sauce for the goose should be sauce for the gander. Cornell does not deny that an employee can sometimes hurt his employer, and hurt him badly, by quitting without notice or just cause. She thinks a discharge will on average hurt the employee more than a quit will hurt the employer, but this is not clear, as we are about to see. Even if she is right, this would not provide a compelling justification for denying the employer a remedy in those cases where he *was* hurt by the resignation of a key employee.

She makes one good argument against employment at will (or at least against an argument made in favor of employment at will), and it would be petty to object that the argument owes nothing to Hegel. The economic defense of employment at will builds on the fact that an employment relationship is often one of bilateral monopoly.[11] (This was implicit in my reference to quits by key employees.) The employee develops skills that are specialized to the particular job he is doing for his particular employer. As a result, he would be less productive work-

10. Donald L. Martin, "The Economics of Employment Termination Rights," 20 *Journal of Law and Economics* 187, 188–189 (1977).

11. Epstein, note 3 above, at 973–976.

ing for another employer; and knowing this, his current employer may be able to threaten him, explicitly or implicitly, with discharge if he demands a wage equal to his marginal product for this employer. But precisely because this employee is more productive than his replacement would be, he can threaten the employer with quitting if the employer does not pay him his full marginal product. It is a game of chicken, likely to end in a stand-off, in which case both parties are protected, to some extent anyway, against overreaching by the other.

There is an alternative path to this conclusion. Suppose a worker would be more valuable if he developed skills specialized to this employer. If the employer incurs the full costs of developing these skills, the worker can hardly complain if the employer refuses to pay him the higher marginal product made possible by the employer's own investment in the worker's skills; and to the extent that the worker (by threatening to quit) can extract any part of that higher marginal product in the form of a higher wage, the employer has been "had." Conversely, if the worker pays for the acquisition of these skills himself (maybe by accepting a lower wage initially), he will be at the mercy of the employer, who can expropriate the worker's investment by refusing to pay him his full marginal product. If the worker quits he will have lost his entire investment, since by definition the skills are worth nothing in another employment. Consideration of these alternatives leads to a prediction that the costs of developing specific human capital (as skills specialized to a particular employer are called) will be shared between worker and employer.[12] Then neither party has as much to gain or lose from a termination of the employment relationship, so there is less incentive to engage in bluffing and other gaming, and less turnover, even if neither party has contracted protection against termination by the other.

But the assumption is that the worker develops specialized skills; and, as Cornell rightly points out, not every employee is so fortunate. This is a good point, but incomplete. If the employee lacks specialized skills, he loses a club over his employer's head, it is true, but by the same token the employer loses a club over the employee's head. The employee's wage will be as high in another job as it is in this one, since his skills, such as they are, are by hypothesis mobile. Were there a vast

---

12. Gary S. Becker, *Human Capital: A Theoretical and Empirical Analysis, with Special Reference to Education* 40–49 (3d ed. 1993).

labor surplus the wages of unskilled labor would be very low, but this situation would not be alleviated by job tenure.

There are other reasons for doubting whether employment at will is exploitative. The employer who encourages employees to develop a specialized skill and then takes advantage of their resulting immobility by refusing to compensate them adequately will find that he has to pay higher wages to induce people to work for him in the future. (A similar concern with reputation may restrain key employees from taking advantage of their employer's vulnerability by walking off the job without notice, or by demanding a raise not to do so.) The employer will also find that his employees are highly susceptible to the enticements of labor unions. One of the curious by-products of the universal "rational cause" rule that Cornell proposes is that it would weaken labor unions by giving every worker the kind of protection that could be got through a union only at the cost of having to pay union dues. I had thought that Cornell, a former union organizer, was a supporter of unions for reasons that went beyond the tenure provisions in collective bargaining contracts. But I said she is a *former* union organizer. She may have come to regard unionization as a lost cause.

Although not every employer in the United States is an effective profit-maximizer (and hence cost-minimizer), a free-market institution as persistent and widespread as employment at will is presumptively more efficient than an alternative imposed by government would be. The reason it might be more efficient is not hard to find. Litigation, even when conducted before arbitrators rather than before judges and juries, is costly. To these direct costs of legally enforceable tenure rights must be added the indirect costs from the weakening of discipline in the workplace when workers can be fired only after a costly and uncertain proceeding. The sum of these costs should not be underestimated. If they did not outweigh the benefits to workers, why would employers not offer just-cause protection voluntarily, the way they offer other fringe benefits? Are the employers that do offer such protection—government agencies, unionized firms, and universities—the most efficient producers in the marketplace? Do law professors know more about the efficient management of labor than business people? One is amused to be told by another advocate of abolishing employment at will that we need not be afraid that it would be inefficient, because "under the British system, for example, industrial tribunals determine whether an employee has been improperly discharged."[13] The "British system" of employment regulation is no more promising a model for our economy than the employment practices of our nonprofit and governmental sectors are. And while it is plausible that cooperative relations between labor and management are more conducive to increases in productivity than antagonistic relations,[14] it is implausible that granting workers tenure is an efficient method of fostering that cooperation. If it were, why would not companies adopt it without prodding by government?

We must not neglect the *incidence* of the costs of a just-cause or rational-cause principle. Consumers would be hurt to the extent that the employer passed on any part of these costs to its customers in the form of higher product prices. Workers would be hurt the most. In figuring what he can afford to pay, an employer considers not only the direct costs of labor but indirect costs as well (such as the employer's social security tax, unemployment insurance premiums, and workers' compensation insurance premiums), of which the costs of tenure would be one. The higher the indirect costs of employment, the lower the wage the employer will be willing to pay.[15] Since just-cause protection is itself a fringe benefit (like severance pay or unemployment compensation), the worker does not lose out completely. But if he had preferred such protection to a higher wage, the employer would have offered it to him. Just-cause protection may force employers to provide what from the average employee's standpoint is an inferior compensation package.

If, because of union contracts, minimum-wage laws, custom, inertia, or other factors, employers were prevented from charging back the full cost of job protection to workers in the form of lower wages or fewer (other) benefits, unemployment would rise because the cost of labor would now be higher.[16] Employers would have an incentive to hire less,

13. Arthur S. Leonard, "A New Common Law of Employment Termination," 66 *North Carolina Law Review* 631, 677 (1988).

14. For evidence, see Robert Buchele and Jens Christiansen, "Industrial Relations and Productivity Growth: A Comparative Perspective," 2 *International Contributions to Labour Studies* 77 (1992).

15. This is an application of the Coase Theorem, discussed in Chapter 20.

16. For empirical evidence that job-protection laws do increase the number of unemployed (including all able-bodied workers who do not have a job, not just jobless workers who are still searching for jobs, the narrow definition used in computing unemployment statistics), see

automate more, and relocate plants to foreign countries that do not have such protection. Since, as we saw in Chapter 3, job tenure causes people to work less hard, the employer might actually need more workers under a just-cause regime to get the work done; but this prospect would accelerate his flight to automated and foreign plants.

Some workers would keep their jobs who would have lost them under a regime of employment at will, but presumably not many. A rational employer will not fire an employee without cause. Although most dismissals are made by lower-level supervisors, who may not be perfect agents of the enterprise, irrational firing of workers does not appear to be widespread,[17] especially in profit-making enterprises, which are penalized by the market for making mistakes. (This may be the reason why employment at will is so much less common in the non-profit and governmental sectors.) At all events it is not one of the grounds on which Cornell defends her proposal.

In a regime of universal tenure, a rational employer would search longer before hiring a worker[18] because the cost of firing the worker if he did not pan out would be higher. This effect would be mitigated but not eliminated by postponing just-cause protection until the worker had completed a probationary period of employment.

The brunt of any disemployment effect of just-cause laws would be

---

Martin, note 10 above, at 199–201; Richard Layard and Stephen Nickell, "Unemployment in Britain," 53 *Economica* (n.s.) S121, S165 (1986); and Layard, Nickell, and Richard Jackman, *Unemployment: Macroeconomic Performance and the Labour Market* 508 (1991). The evidence, however, is weak. Id. at 508; Organisation for Economic Co-Operation and Development, *Flexibility in the Labour Market: The Current Debate: A Technical Report* 123 (1986). (No surprise, in view of the Coase Theorem.) Daniel S. Hamermesh concludes in a judicious review of the empirical literature on European job-protection laws that they "offer an industrialized economy a choice between greater employment stability (with fewer total hours worked on average) and greater employment fluctuations (with more total hours worked on average). Moreover, to the extent they cover only part of the labor market, they help create a two-tier labor market consisting of secure jobs in a declining sector and insecure jobs in an expanding sector." Hamermesh, "The Demand for Workers and Hours and the Effects of Job Security Policies: Theory and Evidence," in *Employment, Unemployment and Labor Utilization*, note 2 above, at 9, 29–30.

17. James E. DeFranco, "Modification of the Employee at Will Doctrine—Balancing Judicial Development of the Common Law with the Legislative Prerogative to Declare Public Policy," 30 *St. Louis University Law Journal* 65, 70–72 (1985).

18. For evidence, see W. W. Daniel and Elizabeth Stilgoe, *The Impact of Employment Protection Laws* 78 (Policy Studies Institute, June 1978).

borne by newcomers to the work force and other marginal workers.[19] In the United States, most of these newcomers would be women, nonwhites, or handicapped—the very people whom Cornell would most like to protect in the interest of reciprocal symmetry. Employers would be less willing to take chances on problem workers or on workers who lacked an impressive job history, because it would be harder for an employer to correct mistakes in hiring than it is under the system of employment at will. They might therefore prefer encouraging overtime work by their existing workers to hiring additional ones, and this too would reduce employment.[20] And if, as has been the pattern with European job-protection laws, temporary and part-time workers were exempted, employers would tend to substitute them for full-time workers, creating a tier of second-class workers.[21]

The short of it is that the adoption of Cornell's proposal might move the United States farther down the road of "Eurosclerosis"—high long-term unemployment due to excessive regulation of labor markets.[22] Or might not. I shall not pretend that all economists would accept the analysis that I have presented, or even that, if all did, this would show it was correct. My objection to her proposal is not that it is demonstrably wrong, but that it is irresponsible, because if adopted it might very well impose immense social costs—and costs born mainly by workers themselves, the intended beneficiaries of the proposal—that she has not considered. She has tried to substitute political theory, in the person of Hegel, for the study of consequences. She illustrates the flight from fact so characteristic of even the ablest academic lawyers.

19. For evidence from Europe, see, for example, Franco Bernabè, "The Labour Market and Unemployment," in *The European Economy: Growth and Crisis* 159, 179, 185 (Andrea Boltho ed. 1982).

20. For evidence, see Wolfgang Franz and Heinz König, "The Nature and Causes of Unemployment in the Federal Republic of Germany since the 1970s: An Empirical Investigation," 53 *Economica* (n.s.) S219, S243 (1986).

21. For evidence, once again from Europe, see Samuel Bentolila and Guiseppe Bertola, "Firing Costs and Labour Demand: How Bad is Eurosclerosis?" 57 *Review of Economic Studies* 381, 395 (1990); Bernabè, note 19 above, at 185; and recall Hamermesh's observation on the issue, in note 16.

22. See generally David Henderson, "The Europeanization of the U.S. Labor Market," *Public Interest*, Fall 1993, p. 66.

chapter 14

Postmodern Medieval Iceland

I F J U D G E Harry Edwards[1] knew (perhaps he does know) that a law professor at the school (Michigan) at which he taught before becoming a judge was devoting his career to the study of medieval Iceland, he would think his direst fears about the trend in legal education confirmed. He would not be reassured to discover that before going to law school William Miller, rather than being a historian or a student of Germanic languages, was an English professor; or that Miller's latest book on Iceland[2] flirts with postmodernism and displays a nostalgia for simple societies that might remind unkind readers of Leonard Jaffee (see Chapter 12).

Bloodtaking and Peacemaking is about the social and political institutions of medieval Iceland, with specific reference to its methods of dispute resolution. Miller has written for two audiences. One consists of the tiny handful of specialists in medieval Icelandic studies, the other of social historians, academic lawyers, political scientists, and other social scientists interested in dispute resolution and in social control more generally, including the foundations of the state. For the second

1. See Chapter 2.
2. William Ian Miller, *Bloodtaking and Peacemaking: Feud, Law, and Society in Saga Iceland* (1990).

group, the relative simplicity—political, social, and religious—of medieval Icelandic society lends fascination to the social institutions found in it because they are observed under laboratory conditions. As a member of Miller's second audience, I am not in the best position to evaluate the accuracy of his scholarship. But a comparison of the book with what I understand to be leading modern works of Icelandic scholarship on the subjects that he discusses[3] suggests that his book is in no wise deficient on the score of scholarship.

Miller is writing about the period of Iceland's independence, A.D. 930–1262, the period depicted in the sagas, our main source of knowledge about medieval Iceland. A simple pastoral society, it lacked the gorgeousness, and the hypertrophy of social forms, characteristic of the Middle Ages. It had no king or nobles, no chivalry or courtly love, no jousts, wars, or armies, no cities or even villages, and none but the simplest art, architecture, and decor. The Catholic Church was so weak that it was forced to adopt a policy of peaceful coexistence with paganism. But of course it is the very simplicity of medieval Iceland, in particular its political simplicity, that is its fascination. Although not quite a stateless society, it was weaker than the weakest nightwatchman state. The formal institutions of government were limited to courts and an assembly that, like their ancient Athenian counterparts, were staffed by ordinary citizens rather than by professionals. In effect there were jurors but no judges; there were no appeals, either. The speaker of the assembly was the only salaried official in Iceland. There were virtually no taxes, the speaker being paid out of a fee for marriage. There was, crucially, no executive branch of government, so there were no sheriffs, police, soldiers, or prosecutors. All lawsuits, including criminal suits, were prosecuted by private individuals, and, what was the greater innovation in the art of minimizing government—for a number of societies that we would not call stateless, including those of ancient Greece and Rome and Anglo-Saxon England, left prosecution of criminal cases to private individuals[4]—all judicial decrees were enforced, if at all, privately.

3. Jesse L. Byock, *Feud in the Icelandic Saga* (1982); Byock, *Medieval Iceland: Society, Sagas, and Power* (1988). See also Henry Ordover, "Exploring the Literary Function of Law and Litigation in *Njal's Saga*," 3 *Cardozo Studies in Law and Literature* 41 (1991). Further evidence of the thoroughly professional character of Miller's Icelandic scholarship is his coauthored work, Theodore M. Andersson and William Ian Miller, *Law and Literature in Medieval Iceland: "Ljósvetninga saga" and "Valla-Ljóts saga"* (1989).

4. See, for example, Douglas M. MacDowell, *The Law in Classical Athens* 237–240

Adjudication was not the only lawful method of resolving disputes. The feud was lawful too, and so (less surprisingly) was private arbitration, in which a dispute was submitted for binding resolution to one or more men selected by the disputants. And because people looked to both near and remote relatives for help in enforcing decrees and conducting feuds, concepts of kinship were far more elaborate than in modern society. The help of relatives might not be enough, so less powerful men rendered services to the more powerful, the chieftains, in exchange for support and protection. Here was the germ of a feudal system. But the elaboration of feudal duties, ranks, ceremonies, and obligations that we find in medieval Europe was missing. And chieftainships could be sold—an intrusion of the market that would have been unthinkable in a feudal system.

Icelanders were great amateur lawyers, and their law codes were as complex and ingenious as most of the rest of their culture was simple and monotonous. Njal, the hero of the best-known saga, was one of those amateur lawyers. The procedures for finding facts were more rational than those used in most medieval legal systems, little reliance being placed on supernatural methods. Yet the system was surprisingly inflexible on the remedial side. The only sanctions that the Icelandic courts meted out, other than for the most trivial infractions (which were punished by a fixed fine), were outlawry and lesser outlawry. Outlawry made a man an outlaw in the literal sense: anyone could kill him with impunity. Lesser outlawry meant banishment from Iceland for three years. The inflexible character of the legal remedies made arbitration an attractive alternative to ordinary litigation, because arbitrators could impose fines or fashion what we would call equitable decrees, tailored to the particular circumstances of the case. Refusal to obey an arbitral decree was punishable like other serious wrongdoing.

This strikingly decentralized system of governance survived for more than three centuries. No one knows just how much violence there was, but the society was not anarchic, although the institutional structure sketched above might seem a recipe for anarchy. Nor did saga Iceland lapse into tyranny, despite the seeming fragility of its institutions. Even feuds were governed by norms (for example, that the killing of an

---

(1978). On the history of private criminal prosecution in Anglo-American jurisprudence, see Harold J. Krent, "Executive Control over Criminal Law Enforcement: Some Lessons from History," 38 *American University Law Review* 275, 290–295 (1989).

outlaw should not be revenged—should not, that is, occasion a feud)
that despite the absence of formal sanctions were obeyed with some,
though far from complete, regularity.

All this Miller sets forth with great clarity. It is at the level of theory
that he runs into problems. The book is at once too theoretical and
not theoretical enough. It is too theoretical in gesturing toward two
bodies of theory, or more accurately literatures, that are useless for an
understanding of medieval Iceland; the result is some bad patches of
jargon, some laboring of the obvious, and some superfluous bows to
the norm of political correctness for which Miller's university is notorious.[5] One is the historical and particularly the anthropological literature on dispute resolution, which, while a mine of interesting information about societies that resemble medieval Iceland in the weakness of
their state institutions, is for the most part a- or pre-theoretical, occasionally venturing interesting generalizations but usually emphasizing
the uniqueness of the particular society under consideration. (Anthropologists, like historians, have a vested interest in the particularity of
the individual culture that they have taken such pains to understand.)
General knowledge is not the only knowledge, even if you don't agree
with William Blake's dictum that to generalize is to to be an idiot. But
knowledge without an organizing theory is difficult to deploy, and
Miller seems stumped by what to do with the anthropological and
historical parallels that he has found.

The other body of theory that Miller invokes is postmodernism; and
we should pause for a moment to consider what this term means. Most
fundamentally it signifies disillusionment with modernity, conceived of
as the triumph of Enlightenment values, but a disillusionment that
resists nostalgia for premodern values such as religion and caste. Basic
to the Enlightenment, in the postmodernist critique, is the dichotomy
between knower (or subject) and known (or object): the latter the inert
domain of physical and even social reality (society as an aggregation of
"rational" men and women robotically responsive to incentives), the
former the domain of the active, autonomous self, deploying intellect
and language for understanding, communication, and control, and thus
for intellectual and material progress. Physics, medicine, economics,
engineering, and law are examples of fields built on the presuppositions

5. See Doe v. University of Michigan, 721 F. Supp. 852 (E.D. Mich. 1989), invalidating
the university's hate-speech code.

of Enlightenment thought, while liberalism, with its emphasis on individual autonomy, is the political theory built on those presuppositions. Postmodernism challenges this picture by rejecting the dichotomy between subject and object. The rejection takes place on two levels, which I shall call, loosely, historical and philosophical. The first is based on observation of contemporary American culture. Whatever may have been true fifty or a hundred or two hundred years ago, *this* culture, says Balkin in an article that I have already cited twice in this book, is postmodern because of material developments that have destroyed the preconditions of Enlightened society.[6] Examples he gives are that modern advertising (including political advertising) manipulates preferences and beliefs, thus undermining the autonomous self, and that the "industrialization" of legal services has brought about a fracturing of legal tasks, including the assignment of opinion-writing to law clerks as a result of which a judicial opinion no longer establishes a direct path of communication between judge and reader.

Philosophical postmodernism, which has its roots in Nietzsche and Wittgenstein and of which its best-known exemplars are Foucault and Derrida in France and in this country Rorty and Fish, is the use of logic, rhetoric, historical and sociological investigation, and other methods of argument or analysis to debunk the philosophical tenets and assumptions of the Enlightenment—objectivity, observer independence, and the rest. Philosophical postmodernism denies both the givenness of the object and the freedom of the subject, and depending on which denial is emphasized can thus be either Utopian or quietistic. When the contingent, constructed character of social and in some versions even physical reality is emphasized, the radical transformation of the world and society is seen as possible and desirable. Much radical feminism is of this character; likewise the social-constructionist view of sexuality. But when the ethnocentric, embedded, socially constructed character of the self is emphasized, social criticism becomes an oxymoron; it presupposes an external standpoint that postmodernism denies. So we have both politically radical postmodernism, and political radicals' criticism of postmodernism as a roadblock to social critique.[7]

Postmodernism in what I am calling its historical aspect has affinities

6. J. M. Balkin, "What Is Postmodern Constitutionalism?" 90 *Michigan Law Review* 1966 (1992).

7. Sabina Lovibond, "Feminism and Postmodernism," 178 *New Left Review* 5 (1989). Both Rorty and Fish, the latter more emphatically, are in the quietist camp.

with the economics of nonmarket behavior, because both disciplines study the effects of material developments on thought and are skeptical of idealizing pictures of social practices, such as language and reputation.[8] And postmodernism in its philosophical aspect has obvious affinities with pragmatism, of which Rorty and Fish are distinguished exponents (see Chapter 19). Yet I would not describe myself as a postmodernist thinker. Postmodernism is the excess of pragmatism. Postmodernists are not merely antimetaphysical, which is fine, but also antitheoretical.[9] Almost all of them are infected by the virus of political correctness, as well. And, though with notable exceptions, they write in an ugly, impenetrable jargon,[10] sometimes with the excuse that to write clearly is to buy into the Enlightenment mythology of unmediated communication between author and reader.

Postmodernism in law has so far meant little more than threatening conventionally minded law professors with "deconstruction,"[11] though Balkin's article and the recent writings of Pierre Schlag and Steven Winter hold promise of something better. All that William Miller seems to have gotten from postmodernism is an unpleasant though happily very intermittent jargon, a desire to mystify common sense, a conviction that the world is a very complicated and mysterious place resistant to comparative study aimed at uncovering regularities analogous to those found by science in nature, and a fear of being thought judgmental. Such expressions in *Bloodtaking and Peacemaking* as "the negotiability of significations" (p. 3), "the philology of residence" (p. 115), "fostering was the social construct within which the circulation of children was comprehended" (p. 123), kinship as "an organizing metaphor" (p. 154), "the balanced-exchange model, to give it a name, served as a kind of constitutive metaphor" (p. 184), "power is a difficult concept, at least since Foucault made it one" (p. 245), "power did indeed have a strong discursive component" (p. 246), and "can the 'private' as an analytic category exist unless it is paired with and distinguished from 'public'?" (p. 305) illustrate how postmodernist

---

8. See, for example, Pierre Bourdieu, *Language and Symbolic Power,* pt. 1 (1991); Gary Taylor, *Reinventing Shakespeare: A Cultural History, from the Restoration to the Present* (1989).

9. Recall the discussion of Fish in Chapter 3.

10. Amusingly discussed in Bert O. States, "Notes on the Poststructural Code," *American Scholar,* Winter 1994, p. 111.

11. *Law and Literature* 210 n. 3.

tendencies can lead an author away from clear-headed analysis of social institutions and into a terminological miasma.

In the last quotation Miller is trying to save his Icelanders from the clutches of the libertarians, who advocate the privatization of law enforcement and find it exemplified in the society depicted in the sagas.[12] But the idea that "private" is not a meaningful term in a society that lacks a "public" sector is, unless amplified, nonsense parading as paradox. The libertarian point is after all a simple though potentially misleading one: the history of Iceland shows that a society can maintain some minimum of law and order without a public monopoly of force. That point is not touched by Miller's rhetorical question. But maybe what he means is that if there is no coercive government other coercive institutions will take its place, and these—a numbing traditionalism, perhaps, or the petty tyranny of family heads, or intimidation by grandees—may, as John Stuart Mill believed, curtail liberty just as much as the modern welfare state does. Were old people less dependent before social security?

An earlier quotation illustrates, once its context is restored, Miller's tendency to wrap a simple and sound, sometimes even obvious, point in postmodernist cotton: "Because power was so intimately linked with reputation and specifically with the reputation for having power (that is, power did indeed have a strong discursive component), its loss was often gradual, requiring both a slow cumulation of discomfitures and a consequent community reassessment of one's standing relative to others" (p. 246). This is an obscure and plethoric way of saying that political power, being latent force, will often persist after the actual willingness or ability to apply force has ceased, because it will take time for knowledge of that cessation to filter out. The United States could continue to exert power over other countries for quite a time after its officials secretly agreed never again to employ force in aid of foreign policy.

Some of Miller's points may not be worth making at all, as distinct from being made clearly. For example, he says that "law never eschews violence either in early Iceland or in modern industrial societies" (p. 232). That's true, because it is always possible that force may have to be used to compel obedience to a legal judgment, and physical force

---

12. Actually, one libertarian: David Friedman, "Private Creation and Enforcement of Law: A Historical Case," 8 *Journal of Legal Studies* 399 (1979).

exerted against a resisting organism is violence. It does not follow, as Miller appears to believe, that in a comparison of early Iceland to modern us there is nothing to choose between on the score of law and order. In his conclusion, worrying the question whether Iceland was a more or a less violent society than ours is, Miller asks: Does it merely seem violent in comparison to ours because of

> the fear and anxiety we imagine we would feel at the prospect of having no state to enforce our rights for us or to protect us from those bent on enforcing their own? In other words, does their culture seem more violent because the responsibility for actually doing acts of violence was more evenly distributed than it is now, there being no state agents to delegate the dirty work to or to claim a monopoly on the dirty work? (p. 304; see also p. 256)

These questions suggest that a bloodfeud society merely makes transparent the conditions of our own society. In the same vein Miller remarks that "the sagas do not show people continually living with the anticipation of violence, rape, or expropriation that many American urban dwellers must live with daily" (p. 304) and that "early state formation, I would guess, surely tended to involve redistributions, not from rich to poor, however, but from poor to rich, from weak to strong" (p. 306). Miller's own account of medieval Iceland belies this attack upon the idea of progress. A lot of bystanders get killed in the feuds that he describes. Despite the poverty of the society there is plenty of inequality—there are chiefs, and at the other end of the social scale there are slaves. And while the institutions of medieval Iceland were remarkably adaptive to the requirements of human survival in a peculiar ecological niche, they are not anything that we, who live in a different environment, should want to imitate, any more than we should want to adopt the Hunzas' diet of apricots. If Miller means merely to underscore the Icelanders' adaptation to their environment, I have no quarrel. But particularly in his concluding chapter he seems to be doing something else—burnishing his postmodernist credentials, establishing his political inoffensiveness, by denying that anything in his book should be thought to give aid and comfort to libertarians, or to whiggish liberals, and even trying to redeem medieval Iceland for feminism by pointing out, Jaffee-like, that the status of women was higher than elsewhere in medieval Europe.

Where Miller's book is insufficiently theoretical is in failing to explore more deeply the character of a revenge society, a society in which people keep greed and violence within bounds, yet without a state security apparatus. The essential restraining device is the threat of retaliation by potential victims of aggression. But to be a fully credible deterrent, such a threat requires that the victim have allies; otherwise there would be no deterring murder. This point shows the importance not only of kinship but also, as Miller emphasizes, of rhetoric. Even kin may be reluctant to risk their necks on your behalf, so you have to be able to put the offender in the wrong in the eyes of your kin and demonstrate the importance of retaliation to the future security of your kin group.

Kinship has a double (actually a triple, as we shall see) significance in a revenge society. It expands not only the ranks of the potential violators but also the range of potential targets for the revenger. If X kills Y, Y's family may decide to go after X's brother rather than after X himself—maybe the brother is not as well protected as X. In other words, responsibility is collective, which gives people an incentive to police their kin lest a kinsman's misbehavior lead to retaliation against them rather than against him.

Like other writers about the feud, Miller emphasizes the importance of a sense of honor. Shame, the reaction to being dishonored, helps overcome fear, making it more likely that a victim will retaliate if attacked or abused—and if he doesn't retaliate he will be easy game and the system of revenge will fail to keep the peace. Hence the importance of keeping score and the connection of the sense of honor with notions of exchange, balance, and reciprocity.

The difficulty with an economy of threats is that it is likely to be unstable, although there are counterexamples, such as the nuclear balance of terror. Deterrence rarely works perfectly, so there will be some wrongdoing and therefore some retaliation, each act of which may be perceived by the original aggressor or by his kin as an act of aggression requiring retaliation against the aggressor-retaliator. The resulting feud can spiral out of control, creating a demand for a protective group powerful enough to deter retaliation. Competition to form such groups, with fictive kinship sometimes used to expand the ranks of relatives, may result in a monopoly of force after all and hence in the formation of a state. This happened eventually in Iceland. But the fact that it took three centuries to happen suggests that the Icelanders must have had norms or institutions that played the same role in the bloodfeud system as graphite rods play in the core of a nuclear reactor: to slow down the chain reaction.

One such institution was law. Legal judgments were not self-executing, and if the convicted defendant thumbed his nose at a judgment the plaintiff would have to rally his kin to enforce the judgment by force, much as if he had decided to retaliate directly against the defendant for whatever wrong had precipitated the suit. But as Miller explains, a legal judgment might have enough suasive force to enable the plaintiff to rally his allies and also to make it easier for the defendant's potential allies to beg off, thus isolating the defendant and so vindicating the plaintiff's decision to go to law rather than fight. And the bilateral character of Icelandic kinship—Icelanders reckoned kinship through both the father and the mother, whereas many societies reckon it only through the father and some only through the mother—made it more likely that a disputant would have kin on both sides of the dispute. Caught in the middle, these kin were naturals to try to make peace between the disputants.

All this is not so exotic as it seems. Holmes thought law the next stage in social ordering after revenge.[13] Ancient Athens had a legal system not unlike the one Miller describes. Prosecutions even for such serious offenses as murder and treason were instituted and conducted by private persons ("denouncers") and tried before panels of citizens chosen at random, with no professional judges and no appeals. There were no lawyers as such, though litigants hired rhetoricians to write speeches for them. Enforcement of criminal judgments was by public officers, unlike the procedure in Iceland; and the juries were larger. There were other differences. But the parallels are striking, and even include the use of banishment as a sanction and a propensity to protracted and repetitive litigation by "feuding" factions. It would have profited Miller to consult the extensive scholarly literature on the Athenian system, including the role of forensic oratory in it.[14]

The ancient Greek society that most resembles saga Iceland, however, is not Athens; it is the society depicted in the Homeric epics. (And there is the same problem of disentangling fact from fiction in works

13. *The Common Law*, lect. 1.

14. See, for example, Robert J. Bonner and Gertrude Smith, *The Administration of Justice from Homer to Aristotle*, vol. 2 (1938); other references cited in *Law and Literature* 110 n. 57; and Thomas C. Brickhouse and Nicholas D. Smith, *Socrates on Trial* (1989).

of imaginative literature.) That society reveals only rudimentary government institutions and exhibits the same emphasis found in the sagas on revenge as the basic principle of social order. Some years ago I tried to extract the system of social order from the Homeric epics much as Miller does with the sagas.[15] But my approach differed from Miller's in using economic theory to apprehend the basic character of a revenge system.[16] Others have applied economic theory to medieval Iceland itself,[17] as well as to other stateless regimes, such as the mining communities that sprang up during the California Gold Rush to maintain order at a time and in a place where governmental authority was essentially nonexistent.[18]

Economists are interested in incentives and hence in deterrence, and Miller recognizes the centrality of these factors to the social system of saga Iceland. He puzzles over the relation between honor and the feud but quickly recognizes that the key is deterrence: "honor is the ability to make others believe that you will indeed be tough the next time" (p. 303). He intuits the essential economic logic of a revenge system but could have written a shorter and clearer book, rich with comparisons of medieval Iceland to other societies with rudimentary or weak state institutions, had he equipped himself with some economic theory and (what is closely related) game theory—the systematic study of strategic interactions, prominently including threats and counterthreats. He glances at game theory in a single note, citing Axelrod's book, which found on the basis of computer games that the optimal strategy for achieving cooperation in a decentralized system is "tit for tat": if you act noncooperatively toward me I'll retaliate in kind, but I won't escalate the retaliation.[19] Miller gives Axelrod the brush-off: "Axelrod's analysis of computerized strategies for the Prisoner's Dilemma game is remarkably suggestive, but does not seem to be readily applicable to the Icelandic feud without considerable qualification"

15. "The Homeric Version of the Minimal State," 90 *Ethics* 27 (1979), reprinted in my book *The Economics of Justice* 119 (1981).

16. See also "Retribution and Related Concepts of Punishment," reprinted in *The Economics of Justice*, note 15 above; and chapter 1 of *Law and Literature* ("Revenge as Legal Prototype and Literary Genre").

17. Friedman, note 12 above; Thráinn Eggertsson, *Economic Behavior and Institutions* 305–310 (1990).

18. See, for example, Robert C. Ellickson, *Order without Law: How Neighbors Settle Disputes* (1991); Gary D. Libecap, *Contracting for Property Rights* (1989).

19. Robert Axelrod, *The Evolution of Cooperation* (1984).

(p. 374). He does not say why not, but adds, "I am not a student of game theory, so the points I am making here may well have easy answers I do not know about." That won't do. Game theory is the science of conflict and conflict resolution. If you want to write about conflict resolution it behooves you to look into this science to see whether it might have something in it that you can use. (I shall glance at game theory in Chapter 25, in discussing blackmail.)

Economics may be able to solve the puzzle of why the stateless equilibrium persisted for as long as it did in Iceland but not longer. Iceland had no foreign enemies—there were no threats of invasion until Norway began throwing its considerable weight around toward the end of the period of Icelandic independence. Until then, the benefits of a large protective association were smaller than they usually are. And the country was very poor, which made it difficult for anyone to support an entourage of retainers, feudal-style, who in exchange for food and shelter would place an armed force at the disposal of their liege; lacking that armed force he had little to offer in the way of protection to other people in the society. Little, but not nothing; there were chieftains. But the pitifully small forces at their disposal—a handful of relatives, dependents, and clients taking the afternoon off from tending their flocks—limited their power to the execution of piecemeal revenge. None was able to offer a king's peace.

A community needs an economic surplus to support specialists in coercion. Once the surplus comes into being, however, the stateless state's days are numbered. Eggertsson suggests that toward the end of the period of Icelandic independence the Church was able at last to collect a heavy tax yet unable to keep the bulk of the revenues out of the coffers of a handful of major chieftains. Six of them grew to the point where they could engage in civil war on a respectable scale, and they did, at which point the population was happy to turn to the King of Norway for protection, and Icelandic independence ended.[20]

Bloodtaking and Peacemaking is interesting not only in its own right but also as an illustration of the change in legal scholarship that I described in Chapter 2. Within a year after it was published appeared Ellickson's book on extralegal dispute settlement, Grey's book on the poetry of Wallace Stevens, Rosenberg's study of the effects of landmark

20. Eggertsson, note 17 above, at 309–310. Eggertsson's analysis is extended in Birgir T. R. Solvason, "The Evolution of the Institutional Structure of the Icelandic Commonwealth" (unpublished, Dept. of Economics, University of Iceland, June 25, 1992).

legal cases, and Cohen's study of the legal and moral regulation of sexuality in ancient Athens.[21] Ellickson and Grey are law professors, Rosenberg a political scientist, Cohen the chairman of a department of rhetoric. These are all books published by distinguished university presses and on the whole warmly reviewed despite what might appear to the pedantic to be in each case a mismatch between the author's professional credentials and his subject matter.[22] Yet this is the age of specialization. Did not Max Weber warn almost a century ago that "limitation to specialized work, with a renunciation of any Faustian universality of man which it involves, is a condition of any valuable work in the modern world"?[23] So what is going on? Five things, I believe:

1. The academic market for legal books, other than textbooks, is small, in part because law professors, being habituated to excellent library facilities, are not natural book buyers, despite their affluence. As a result, university presses, which generally do not publish textbooks, are reluctant to publish law books that do not spill over into other fields. So spillover books are overrepresented in these presses' law lists.

2. The job of a law professor, being by current American academic standards extremely well paid, undemanding, and noncompetitive, attracts a number of bright people whose true love is for a different subject, as is plainly the case for Miller. A fraction of these people turn out to be highly motivated scholars despite their having an easy berth.

3. Being subject rather than method, law is amenable to study by people in other disciplines, such as economics, political science, and even literary criticism, or by lawyers employing the tools of these disciplines.

4. Specialization begets a demand for generalists and interdisciplinarians. The proliferation of arcane subspecialties creates a space for bridge builders and translators who will meld approaches or use an approach developed in one specialty to study problems in another.

21. Ellickson, note 18 above; Thomas C. Grey, *The Wallace Stevens Case: Law and the Practice of Poetry* (1991); Gerald N. Rosenberg, *The Hollow Hope: Can Courts Bring about Social Change?* (1991); David Cohen, *Law, Sexuality and Society: The Enforcement of Morals in Classical Athens* (1991). I discuss Grey's book in Chapter 23.

22. Least so in the case of Cohen, who has both a doctorate in classics and a law degree.

23. *The Protestant Ethic and the Spirit of Capitalism* 180 (Talcott Parsons trans. 1958). He had a point, as I noted in Chapter 6, discussing the underspecialization of constitutional theorists.

5. The rapid progress of the social sciences, and the increasing emphasis on theory in fields such as literature and history that had for so long resisted it, have multiplied the opportunities for bringing other fields to bear on law. The result is a growing and improving interdisciplinary legal scholarship. That it is also improvable is not the least of its virtues.

PART FOUR

Of Gender and Race

chapter 15

Ms. Aristotle

THE enemy of my enemy is my friend. Liberalism is my enemy. Therefore Aristotle, insofar as he is antiliberal, is my friend. And my friend's ethical insights will help me show that women should serve in the armed services on terms of equality with men, while his ethical blindness and biological ignorance will help me show that surrogate motherhood is an evil. That is Linda Hirshman's argument in a nutshell,[1] and it provides an apt introduction to radical feminist jurisprudence.

Hirshman's argument invites a number of questions. The first is why liberalism should be thought antagonistic to feminism. Common to most forms of liberalism is a belief in personal liberty and to all forms of feminism a belief that the position of women should be improved. It is difficult to see why there should be any conflict. Women have fared much better in liberal societies than in traditional or otherwise antiliberal ones. Liberalism fosters economic and scientific progress, which has powered the emancipation of women in modern societies. For that emancipation is mainly due to the reduction in infant mortality (no longer must a woman be continually pregnant to have a reasonable

1. Linda R. Hirshman, "The Book of 'A,'" 70 *Texas Law Review* 971 (1992).

prospect of producing children who will survive to adulthood), to the advent of household labor-saving devices, to improved methods of contraception, to the growth of light work (the "service economy"), and to an improved understanding of the biology of sex and reproduction. Technological progress is not always emancipatory; the invention of the cotton gin, far from emancipating the slave, increased the demand for slavery. But technological progress *has* removed the principal causes of female subordination (see the next chapter as well on this point).

Liberalism, even in its narrowest "classical" form, is antagonistic to immutable status, restricted entry into occupations, and the infusion of religious dogma into political decision-making. This antagonism, and the corresponding favor with which liberals look upon competition (including competition for public offices), free entry into markets and occupations, and social mobility, create a friendlier climate for the emancipation of women from traditional bonds and prescribed roles than the ideologies of antiliberal societies. John Stuart Mill was an ardent feminist,[2] while Aristotle, with whose aid Hirshman hopes to "break the liberal frame,"[3] held views concerning the status of women that were conservative even for his time. He was notably less progressive than Euripides, Aristophanes, the author of the *Odyssey,* and Plato—on the evidence of the *Republic* and the *Laws,*[4] the first radical feminist.[5]

What Hirshman dislikes about liberalism is abstraction, which she

2. John Stuart Mill, "The Subjection of Women," in *On Liberty and Other Writings* 117 (Stefan Collini ed. 1989).

3. Hirshman, note 1 above, at 1003.

4. David Cohen, "The Legal Status and Political Role of Women in Plato's Laws," 34 *Revue internationale des droits de l'antiquité* (3d ser., pt. 2) 27 (1987).

5. "The temperance [*sophrosynē*] of a man and of a woman, or the courage and justice of a man and of a woman, are not, *as Socrates maintained,* the same; the courage of a man is shown in commanding, of a woman in obeying. And this holds of all other [virtues]." Aristotle, *Politics* (B. Jowett trans.), in *The Complete Works of Aristotle,* vol. 2, p. 1999 (Jonathan Barnes ed. 1984) (p. 1260, col. a, ll. 20–23 in Bekker's Greek edition) (emphasis added). The reason, Aristotle explained, is that the deliberative part of the woman's soul, unlike the man's, lacks full command over the person. Id. (ll. 11–14). On Aristotle's view of women contrasted with Plato's, see also Nicholas D. Smith, "Plato and Aristotle on the Nature of Women," 21 *Journal of Historical Philology* 467 (1983); Maryanne Cline Horowitz, "Aristotle and Woman," 9 *Journal of the History of Biology* 183 (1976); Stephen R. L. Clark, "Aristotle's Woman," 3 *History of Political Thought* 177, 179–180, 182 (1982); Martha C. Nussbaum, "Comments," 66 *Chicago-Kent Law Review* 213, 221, 227, 230 (1990); Nancy Sherman, *The Fabric of Character: Aristotle's Theory of Virtue* 153–154 (1989).

considers the essence of scientific realism on the one hand and of individualism on the other. Hirshman sees Aristotelian practical reason (in the sense, no longer orthodox, of a combination of the methods of reasoning and persuasion that Aristotle classified under dialectic and rhetoric)[6] combating abstraction on its epistemological side, while Aristotelian ethics, with its emphasis on virtue and community, does battle with the political side of abstraction. Yet the strongest link between science and liberalism (an ethical and political ideology, not an epistemology) is not a love of abstraction; it is a belief, which is fundamental both to scientific progress and to political liberty, in the virtues of free inquiry. The philosophical tradition that emphasizes not the correspondence of scientific theories to objective reality but the importance of such scientific virtues as open-mindedness, respect for evidence, rejection of dogma, diversity of opinion, intellectual independence, and wide-open debate is, of course, pragmatism, which feminists, including Hirshman, have generally found congenial. Science encourages and rewards the pragmatic virtues.[7] And so does the political side of liberalism, with its ideal of tolerance for different points of view and different styles of life, its secularism, its accommodating attitude toward social and political change, and its rejection of totalizing theories of the Good and other fanaticisms. It is not in Islamic nations such as Iran, or in India, or in tribal Africa that the liberated woman finds social, political, and economic space to pursue her heterodox personal and ideological projects. It is in the wealthy liberal states of the West.

Aristotle's thought is complex. Many of its strands nourish the liberal ideology. Hirshman, however, is consistent in using the illiberal strands to support her view of specific policies. She says that a better argument for equal treatment of women with regard to military service is not equality at all but the role of military service as "one of the rites by which the moral force of the law is brought to command the shaping of a virtuous self" or as "the quintessence of participation in the community."[8] This assumes that it is a proper task of government to seek through coercion (universal military service) to imbue the citizenry with specific virtues, such as courage, discipline, obedience, and self-sacrifice, so that anyone who is not subjected to this program of

6. See *The Problems of Jurisprudence* 71–72.
7. Richard Rorty, "Is Natural Science a Natural Kind?" in Rorty, *Philosophical Papers: Objectivity, Relativism, and Truth* 46, 61–62 (1991).
8. Hirshman, note 1 above, at 994–995.

indoctrination cannot hope to be regarded as a full-fledged citizen. This is not an absurd idea. The creation of a pervasive garrison-state mentality may make perfectly good sense for a nation that is in serious danger of being attacked. But the role of women in such a state will depend not on abstract conceptions of citizenship but on concrete considerations of where women can contribute most to the national defense—and it might be as draft labor in factories rather than in the front line. To nations such as ours, which happily do not face acute military threats at present and in which for this and other reasons universal military training would be an enormous waste of resources, the relevance of Athenian militarism is not easy to see. We face other threats of course, but a state-sponsored ideology—even if it were feasible in so politically and morally heterogeneous a society as ours, which it is not—would do little to repel them.

All this is not to deny that there are good reasons for admitting women to our (volunteer) armed forces on terms of equality with men. The remaining doubts on this score were dispelled by the performance of our female soldiers in the Persian Gulf War. But the key is, precisely, performance, not anything to be found in Aristotle. Again it should be noted that Plato, not Aristotle, favored (in the *Laws*) military service for women.

Hirshman believes that Aristotelian biology, though discredited—in fact, *because* discredited—can be brought usefully to bear on the controversy over surrogate motherhood. Aristotle believed that the father provides the seed and the mother the soil, so that from a genetic standpoint (as we would say) the child really is the father's—the father's clone.[9] This belief has long been understood to be erroneous, but Hirshman thinks that the same fallacy contaminates efforts to defend surrogate motherhood. Her idea of surrogate motherhood is that the father pays the surrogate mother to produce "his" child, that is, a child over whom the surrogate mother will have no parental rights. Hirshman thinks that this is like the ancient Greek view—a view indeed supported by Aristotle's biology—that the father had sole rights over his children, so that if, for example, he divorced the mother he would have full custodial rights and she would have no rights at all.

---

9. This is something of a caricature of Aristotle's view. See Johannes Morsink, "Was Aristotle's Biology Sexist?" 12 *Journal of the History of Biology* 83 (1979). But it is sufficiently accurate for my purposes.

Critical differences are overlooked.[10] The surrogate mother rents her reproductive capacity, it is true, but she is compensated for doing so. She rents it not for life (or until the man tires of her and casts her off) but for one pregnancy. And she rents it not to the prospective father alone, but to his wife as well, who becomes the adoptive mother.[11] Assuming as Hirshman appears to do that the three adults involved in the transaction are well-informed, mentally competent, and not acting under physical or economic coercion, both the surrogate mother and the father's wife—the two women in the picture—are made better off by the surrogacy arrangement, as is the father, and presumably the child as well, who wouldn't be born otherwise. Hirshman alludes to reasons that other feminists have given why on balance such arrangements might nevertheless make women worse off, but her own reason—that there is an analogy between surrogate motherhood and Aristotle's exploded theory of reproduction—is not a good reason, if it is a reason at all. She also has some dark words about "commodification" and the desirability of rebuilding social relations on the model of civic friendship, conceived as a halfway house between market relations and social hierarchy. She does not explain what this might mean in practice.

Hirshman overlooks the tension between attacking surrogate motherhood by emphasizing the connectedness of the biological mother and her child and defending abortion by treating the mother and child as strangers, as in the influential article by Judith Jarvis Thomson, who compares a mother to a complete stranger required to spend nine months in bed connected by tubes to a famous violinist who has a potentially fatal kidney disease.[12] I do not see how a feminist can simultaneously emphasize and slight the biological role of the mother in this fashion. But in any event I do not think Hirshman must, to save Aristotle for feminism, show that even his misogyny[13] can be used to

10. For a fuller discussion, see *Sex and Reason,* ch. 15.

11. We shall see that the same mistake—ignoring the wife—is made by Patricia Williams in discussing surrogate motherhood in her book *The Alchemy of Race and Rights,* discussed in Chapter 18.

12. Judith Jarvis Thomson, "A Defense of Abortion," 1 *Philosophy and Public Affairs* 47, 48–49 (1971). See also Laurence H. Tribe, *Constitutional Choices* 243 (1985), describing pregnant women as "incubators"—a view close to Aristotle's.

13. If that is what it should be called. Morsink thinks that Aristotle's view of the biology of men and women was the most scientific one possible given the state of science in his time. See Morsink, note 9 above, at 110–112.

advance the feminist agenda. Several years ago a distinguished professor emeritus of the University of Chicago Law School gave an after-dinner speech in which he expressed astonishment that feminists should use Hegel's thought in the making of their theories when Hegel was such a misogynist. He should not have been astonished; there was no inconsistency. The thought of Hegel, of Aristotle, of Nietzsche—for that matter of Ezra Pound and Salvador Dali—is not a seamless web, so that if you pull out one thread the whole thing unravels. You can throw away huge chunks of their belief systems without undermining the remainder. You can jettison Aristotelian biology and Aristotle's aristocratic values without jeopardizing what he has to say about reasoning in the face of uncertainty or about corrective justice or about the interpretation of laws. But what is left after the necessary pruning does not undermine liberalism or advance the dubious cause of antiliberal feminism.

chapter 16

Biology, Economics, and the Radical Feminist Critique of *Sex and Reason*

FEMINISM, as a branch of learning, is the study of women in society from an angle that emphasizes the effects on them of social practices and public policies, that pays careful attention to what they themselves, often ignored, have said or say, that is sincerely concerned for their welfare, and that is duly skeptical of theories of a theocratic or otherwise dogmatic cast that teach that women are predestined to be subordinate to men. On this construal of feminism, John Stuart Mill is a feminist as well as Catharine MacKinnon, Mary Wollstonecraft as well as Andrea Dworkin, Martha Minow and Martha Nussbaum as well as Martha Fineman and Linda Hirshman. On this construal, rejection of biological and economic science, rejection of liberalism, rejection of the evidence of one's senses, a left-wing vocabulary thick with words like "patriarchal," "hegemonic," "colonizing," and "classism," and dislike of men or at least suspicion of heterosexuality, are adventitious rather than organic characteristics of feminism; they reflect the temporary dominance of radical feminism in the academy. On this construal, MacKinnon's equation of radical feminism to feminism is wrong.[1]

---

1. Catharine A. MacKinnon, *Feminism Unmodified: Discourses on Life and Law* 137 (1987); see also Katharine T. Bartlett, "Feminist Legal Methods," 103 *Harvard Law Review*

My book *Sex and Reason* has been a lightning rod for radical feminist criticism.[2] I had tried to show that a simple economic model could explain the broad patterns of sexual behavior and norms across different cultures and epochs and could also generate new, counterintuitive, testable hypotheses concerning the incidence of different types of sexual behavior. My model (further described in the last chapter of this book) treated sexual behavior as the consequence of rational choices made in light of the relevant costs (mostly nonpecuniary), including search, expected punishment, fertility, and disease costs, and of benefits influenced by innate or otherwise unshakable sexual preferences, for example for same-sex relations or for variety in sexual partners. I did not insist dogmatically that economics is *the* key to the secrets of human sexuality. I recognized the dependence of an economic theory of sexuality on the descriptive and analytical work of psychologists, historians, and sociologists, including specialists in women's and gay studies. I was interested in what biology could contribute to an understanding not only of the physiological properties of human sexuality but also of the social dimensions, including differences between male and female sexual behavior and the preference of some men and women for homosexual over heterosexual relations. I wanted to compare scientific and social scientific approaches generally with the moral theories of sexuality that have seemed to shape sexual mores and public policy. And I wanted to evaluate judicial performance in dealing with such issues of public policy as what (if anything) to do about homosexual sodomy, surrogate motherhood, abortion, marital rape, and pornography.

829, 833 and n. 8 (1990). MacKinnon's attack on pornography is the subject of the next chapter.

2. See Katharine T. Bartlett, "Rumpelstiltskin," 25 *Connecticut Law Review* 477 (1993); Margaret Chon, "Sex Stories—A Review of *Sex and Reason*," 62 *George Washington Law Review* 162 (1993); Martha Ertman, "Denying the Secret of Joy: A Critique of Posner's Theory of Sexuality," 45 *Stanford Law Review* 1485 (1993); Martha Albertson Fineman, "The Hermeneutics of Reason: A Commentary on *Sex and Reason*," 25 *Connecticut Law Review* 507 (1993); Gillian K. Hadfield, "Flirting with Science: Richard Posner on the Bioeconomics of Sexual Man," 106 *Harvard Law Review* 479 (1992); Hadfield, "Not the 'Radical' Feminist Critique of *Sex and Reason*," 25 *Connecticut Law Review* 533 (1993); Jane E. Larson, "The New Home Economics," 10 *Constitutional Commentary* 443 (1993); Ruthann Robson, "Posner's Lesbians: Neither Sexy Nor Reasonable," 25 *Connecticut Law Review* 491 (1993); Carol Sager, "He's Gotta Have It," 66 *Southern California Law Review* 1221 (1993); Robin West, "Sex, Reason, and a Taste for the Absurd," 81 *Georgetown Law Journal* 2413 (1993). Hadfield cannot be considered a radical feminist *tout court,* but her position on the issues discussed in my book is similar to that of acknowledged radical feminists.

The result is a long book, and an eclectic one, although economics occupies center stage. The emphasis is descriptive and explanatory— hence positive rather than normative. But not exclusively. The book also offers opinions on a number of normative issues, arguing, in the spirit of John Stuart Mill, that adults, generously defined to include much of the teenage population, should be free to engage in consensual sexual relations and related conduct, such as the consumption of pornography and the formation and enforcement of surrogate-mother-hood arrangements, unless there are palpably adverse consequences for nonconsenting third parties.

A book of such broad scope,[3] dealing with so controversial and emotional a subject, and one on which firm data are so difficult to come by, is sure to contain errors and omissions,[4] misplaced emphases, manifestations of bias and insensitivity, incomplete logic, and warps reflecting the limitations of the author's personal experience and the quirks of his psychology. Moreover, the book is aligned with none of the vocal schools of sexual theorizing—not the Foucaldian constructionist, or the radical feminist, or the Thomist, or the neoconservative, or the paleoconservative, or the Marcusan, or the gay and lesbian liberationist. It takes its inspiration from a branch of economics, the economics of nonmarket behavior, that is controversial even within the economics profession and is detested as "imperialistic" by most other social scientists. And it draws on the most controversial branch of evolutionary biology—sociobiology, the application of Darwinian principles to social behavior. Such a book could not fail to attract criticism from many quarters; and the criticism by the radical feminists tells us much about that movement.

Ships Passing in the Night

Martha Fineman questions three specific claims made in *Sex and Reason*. One is that lesbian couples have intercourse less frequently on average than heterosexual couples, who in turn have intercourse less

3. One review of the book is 101 pages long. C. G. Schoenfeld, Book Review, 20 *Journal of Psychiatry and Law* 515 (1992).

4. My review of the previous economic literature (*Sex and Reason* 33–36) missed Ray C. Fair, "A Theory of Extramarital Affairs," 86 *Journal of Political Economy* 45 (1978), an empirical study based on a rational-choice model of adultery, and Thomas J. Meeks, "The Economic Efficiency and Equity of Abortion," 6 *Economics and Philosophy* 95 (1990), a normative economic study of abortion.

frequently on average than male homosexual couples. Fineman does not argue that the statement—which is supported by feminist scholars of lesbian sexuality[5]—is false, but only that it contains buried assumptions about the definition of sexual intercourse and its relation to other forms of sexual expression. That is a fair point. For what, after all, *is* "lesbian intercourse"? Could not the very term be thought an attempt to force a homosexual activity into a heterosexual mold? The question is not answered by substituting for intercourse as the unit of sexual activity the number of sexual acts in which at least one of the partners has an orgasm. For while the relation that I posit between frequency of sexual activity and the presence of a male would still hold,[6] it could be objected that the definition remained arbitrary. If, however, it were thought arbitrary on the ground that the orgasm is less central to the female than to the male expression of erotic feeling,[7] I would consider this a confirmation of the basic biological point, that the male sex drive is on average stronger than the female. I had never suggested that women love less intensely than men; yet if orgasmic activity (or genital stimulation more broadly) is a less characteristic, urgent, desired, and frequent activity for women than for men, this is an important, and plausibly a biologically programmed, difference. Fineman's underlying point survives, however: the inescapable arbitrariness of picking a particular erotic experience or class of such experiences as the unit of sexual activity for comparing male and female sex drives.

The second claim that Fineman questions is that capacity for breast-feeding is positively correlated with size of breasts. She is right to question it;[8] I withdraw it. Last, she takes issue with my reference to

5. Lillian Faderman, *Odd Girls and Twilight Lovers: A History of Lesbian Life in Twentieth-Century America* 248 (1991) ("lesbians tend to have less sex than heterosexuals or gay men"); Marilyn Frye, "Lesbian 'Sex,'" in *Lesbian Philosophies and Cultures* 305, 313 (Jeffner Allen ed. 1990) (lesbian relationships are "relationships in which there is a lowish frequency of clearly delineated desires and direct initiations of satisfactions"). See also Federman, above, at 246–248, 254.

6. Unless, perhaps, the measure of sexual activity is sheer *number* of orgasms, since women, unlike men, are physically capable of multiple orgasms in close, almost immediate, succession. Robson says that lesbian intercourse frequently is multi-orgasmic. Robson, note 2 above, at 498–499.

7. Sarah Lucia Hoagland, *Lesbian Ethics: Toward New Values* 167–168 (1988), depicts lesbian sexuality as subordinating the orgasm to a more diffuse eroticism.

8. This claim, also questioned by Hadfield, "Flirting with Science," note 2 above, at 492 n. 33, was based on a single article and probably is incorrect. See Joan M. Bedinghaus and Joy Melnikow, "Promoting Successful Breast-Feeding Skills," 45 *American Family Physician*

the "common observation" that homosexual men and heterosexual women are on average better dressed than heterosexual men or homosexual women. Her objection is not that my assertion is false but that it is not adequately documented. She is correct about the lack of documentation. I shall now rectify it. The *Encylopedia of Homosexuality* informs us that "gay men have often used clothing to indicate that they were potential sexual partners for other males." The various types of "signal" clothing used by gay men are then described. Lesbians receive only a brief paragraph, referring to their former preference for "male formal dress" and to a more recent preference for "somewhat shapeless garments and no makeup," although it is pointed out that "other gay women prefer more elegant dress, of which there are several versions."[9] A treatise on fashion contains an index entry for "Gay males, dress of," but nothing concerning lesbians.[10] It would be odd to describe men's formal dress or women's shapeless garments as "sexy," yet that is a recognized category of heterosexual women's clothing, as well as of gay men's clothing.[11] I anticipate the objection that lesbians don't dress as well as heterosexual women or homosexual men[12] because they have lower incomes than either heterosexual women or homosexual men. Men generally have higher incomes than women, and many heterosexual women are supported, in part anyway, by a man.[13] But the stereo-

---

1309, 1310 (1992); Barbara K. Popper and Constance K. Culley, "Breast Feeding Makes a Comeback—For Good Reason," *Brown University Child Behavior and Development Letter*, Feb. 1989, p. 1.

9. "Clothing," 1 *Encylopedia of Homosexuality* 246, 247 (Wayne R. Dynes ed. 1990). See also Lisa M. Walker, "How to Recognize a Lesbian: The Cultural Politics of Looking Like What You Are," 18 *Signs: Journal of Women in Culture and Society* 866, 867 (1993).

10. Susan B. Kaiser, *The Social Psychology of Clothing and Personal Adornment* 491 (1985). The treatise supports another of my challenged sartorial points—that high heels have a symbolic function similar to that of Chinese foot-binding: impeding female mobility. For Kaiser remarks that women's shoes are considered attractive only if they appear to be uncomfortable. Id. at 243. Although a later edition omits the reference to homosexuals' clothing choices, it retains the reference to uncomfortable shoes. Kaiser, *The Social Psychology of Clothing: Symbolic Appearances in Context* 88 (1990).

11. Mary K. Ericksen and M. Joseph Sirgy, "Employed Females' Clothing Preference, Self-Image Congruence, and Career Anchorage," 22 *Journal of Applied Social Psychology* 408, 411 (1992). Cf. Fred Davis, *Fashion, Culture, and Identity* 35 (1992).

12. If "better dressed" is thought hopelessly vague for social scientific research, one can substitute fraction of income spent on clothing, cosmetics, and grooming, perhaps "normalized" by reference to the spending of heterosexual members of the same sex.

13. *Sex and Reason* touches on the effect of income on sex-related behavior (at pp. 133–136), but the touch may be too light, as argued in Martha C. Nussbaum, "'Only Grey

type of poor lesbians is outmoded, now that most women work outside the home. Today the average lesbian has more education than the average heterosexual woman and probably a higher income.[14]

Fineman's greatest concern is with what she deems a pattern of "misogynistic conceptualization and thought patterns."[15] She illustrates this by my statement that in very poor societies female infanticide may, by reducing the number of adult women, increase the welfare of the surviving females.[16] Katharine Bartlett points out that these survivors' welfare, broadly construed as it should be to include psychic as well as material well-being, may be reduced by knowledge of the practice. Another valid feminist point is that girls may be too costly to raise and thus candidates for infanticide only because the society refuses to allow women to do productive work. But Fineman does not question the accuracy or completeness of my discussion of female infanticide on these or other grounds. The misogyny of which she accuses me consists in my remarking an unpleasant fact: to utter uncomfortable truths is, apparently, to be misogynist. Yet my discussion of infanticide is in the spirit of a distinguished feminist anthropologist who has emphasized the *mother's* initiative in infanticide because the mother bears the heavier burden of care for an infant who, if allowed to survive, may impair the mother's ability to take care of her present or future offspring.[17]

Fineman criticizes me for saying that most rape (more, even, were it

---

Matter'? Richard Posner's Cost-Benefit Analysis of Sex," 59 *University of Chicago Law Review* 1689, 1726–1728 (1992).

14. Ertman, note 2 above, at 1500, 1510 n. 168.

15. Fineman, note 2 above, at 512.

16. A related though less ominous phenomenon is that a fall in the ratio of young women to men will reduce the amount of dowry demanded by prospective husbands—that is, will reduce the price of a husband, thus making it easier for women to marry. For empirical evidence of the inverse ratio between the number of young women (relative to men) and dowry levels, see Vijayenda Rao, "The Rising Price of Husbands: A Hedonic Analysis of Dowry Increases in Rural India," 101 *Journal of Political Economy* 666 (1993).

17. Sarah Blaffer Hrdy, "Fitness Tradeoffs in the History and Evolution of Delegated Mothering with Special Reference to Wet-Nursing, Abandonment, and Infanticide," 13 *Ethology and Sociobiology* 409 (1992). On the feminist character of Hrdy's work, see her essay "Empathy, Polyandry, and the Myth of the Coy Female," in *Feminist Approaches to Science* 119 (Ruth Bleier ed. 1986). Larson, note 2 above, at 456–457, argues that recent primate studies by Hrdy and others undermine the sociobiological analysis of human sexuality by showing that nonhuman primates exhibit a variety of sexual behaviors many of which do not conform to the aggressive, promiscuous male/coy female pattern that (to oversimplify) sociobiologists find to be the innate tendency in human sexuality. The real significance of these studies, however, is in showing how the biological differences among primate species

not a criminal offense) is sex theft—meaning that the man obtains sexual gratification without having to negotiate for it in the "market" for voluntary sexual relationships—rather than a device for expressing the male will to dominate women. She does not say that this view is incorrect but only that it has been employed to the end of advocating the decriminalization of rape; so here I have veered from uttering uncomfortable truths to uttering dangerous ones. Yet since no one proposes to decriminalize theft I am puzzled by the suggestion that characterizing rape as sex theft arms the advocates of decriminalizing rape. Who are those advocates? The tide is running strongly in the opposite direction. Rape-shield laws and the criminalization of marital rape are recent developments. The term "sex theft" might be thought to deflect attention from the violent character of rape, since most theft is not violent, though some of course is. But my use of the term was not intended to deny the violent, sometimes sadistic, character of rape—indeed I emphasized those aspects of the crime. Some forms of theft are crimes of violence, and rape is one of them. I denied only that rapists are, as it were, agents of the rest of the adult male population, appointed to keep women in a state of terrified dependency.[18] Of course women fear being raped, and this fear causes psychological distress and limits their freedom of action. But men also fear being victims of violent crime.

Ruthann Robson disclaims any attempt to refute my factual assertions (although she implies that she could easily do so) because the very attempt would endanger the survival of lesbianism, and she describes her scholarly ambition in frankly political terms as "contribut[ing] toward the survival of lesbians, both as individuals and as identity."[19] She adds a twist to Fineman's criticism of my suggestion that the average lesbian is less well dressed than the average heterosexual woman or homosexual man by treating the suggestion as a personal affront. One might have expected feminists to decry the social pressure

---

dictate differences in sexual strategy and behavior. *Sex and Reason* 20 n. 7, 97, and esp. 260. Larson writes as if all primates constituted a single species, so that any set of primate behaviors could be "natural" for humans.

18. A variant of this view is that all men benefit from rape because fear of rape "makes the practice of consensual heterosexuality and the institution of marriage desirable measures of safety" for women. Robin L. West, "Legitimating the Illegitimate: A Comment on 'Beyond Rape,'" 93 *Columbia Law Review* 1442, 1454–1455 (1993).

19. Robson, note 2 above, at 504–505.

on women to dress attractively, and applaud lesbians' defiance of that norm, rather than to accept the norm and deny that lesbians defy it.

There are baffling assertions in Robson's paper, such as "the 'fact' of lesbians as [being] 'not very sexual' may be perceived as a mandate, or at least a reason, to regulate lesbian sexuality."[20] I thought on first reading this passage that she might be making the not ridiculous point that if lesbians (or simply all women) were believed "naturally" unsexual, then lesbian sex would seem all the more "unnatural." But the passage will not bear that interpretation, leaving me to wonder why anyone would think that the *less* sexually active a group was the *more* the state should try to restrict the group's sexual activity. I have no idea where Robson got the impression that I believe that lesbians "are not very reasonable."[21] (Later she says, equally without basis, that I believe that lesbians are more rational than male homosexuals.) Rational behavior is behavior guided by costs and benefits, broadly conceived. If a person has an intense sexual preference, the benefit from trying to satisfy it may exceed the costs even if those costs are high because of social stigma, discrimination, or disease risk.[22] Even if the preference is much less intense—even if a person is merely opportunistically homosexual (see Chapter 26)—a homosexual act may, if opportunity beckons, be substituted for a heterosexual one even if society disapproves of homosexuality. Incidentally, Robson's suggestion that 10 percent of women are lesbians is plainly exaggerated, perhaps by a factor of ten. The 10 percent figure that homosexual-rights advocates have tried to convince the public is the true percentage of homosexuals both male and female is based on a questionable interpretation of Kinsey's figure for *male* homosexuals, and is probably three times too high even for males.[23] It is a political statistic.

Martha Ertman ascribes to me the view that lesbianism is a matter of choice rather than of biology.[24] All I said was that opportunistic

---

20. Id. at 500.

21. Id. at 501.

22. So the AIDS epidemic has reduced the cost of lesbian sex relative to heterosexual sex.

23. *Sex and Reason* 294–295; see also Chapter 26 of this book. Admittedly the problem discussed earlier of the arbitrariness of definitions of sexual activity complicates any effort to estimate the number of homosexuals. The basic issue is whether to define a homosexual by activity or by preference, and if the former what activities to count. There are exquisitely difficult borderline cases. For example, if a divorced woman who never enjoyed sex with her husband dislikes men and associates only with women some of whom she hugs or kisses but with none of whom she has any genital contact, is she a lesbian?

24. See also Larson, note 2 above, at 459, 461

lesbianism is a larger fraction of all lesbianism than opportunistic male homosexuality is of all male homosexuality; I did not say, and I do not believe, that it is anywhere near 100 percent.[25] She reasons from this erroneous characterization of my position that economic analysis implies that all women should be lesbians, since, given how badly men treat women, the benefits of lesbian sex greatly exceed those of heterosexual sex, provided there is no strong preference for the latter over the former. She cannot make up her mind, however, whether it is politically more advantageous to claim that lesbianism is innate or chosen, and actually seems to prefer that it be neither.[26] This is a standard feminist equivocation, as we shall see.

Like Robson, Ertman is a promoter of lesbianism, so she is distressed by the suggestion in *Sex and Reason* that homosexuality is likely to be a less happy condition than heterosexuality even after discrimination against homosexual men and women is extirpated, if it ever is.[27] She denies that even today homosexuals are less happy than heterosexuals, but contradicts herself by pointing to the high rate of suicide among homosexuals and to evidence that "as much as 25% of the adolescent street population is lesbian or gay," a situation she attributes to "rejec-

---

25. For recent evidence of the biological basis of lesbianism, see J. Michael Bailey et al., "Heritable Factors Influence Sexual Orientation in Women," 50 *Archives of General Psychiatry* 217 (1993). The fact that some, perhaps much, lesbianism is not biological but is instead a reaction to bad experiences with men (*Sex and Reason* 179) is damaging to Adrienne Rich's conjecture that the *normal* orientation of women is lesbian—that if it weren't for brainwashing and intimidation by men, all or most women would be lesbians. "Compulsory Heterosexuality and Lesbian Existence," in *Powers of Desire: The Politics of Sexuality* 177 (Ann Snitow, Christine Stansell, and Sharon Thompson eds. 1983).

Ertman mischaracterizes my views in a number of other respects as well. I do not claim that lesbians have never been persecuted or otherwise discriminated against—only that they have less frequently been subjected to criminal punishment. For example, lesbian relations were not criminal at all in England at a time when homosexual sodomy was a capital offense. I did not say that women are "uninterested in heterosexual sex" (Ertman, note 2 above, at 1516), but only that they have on average a less intense sex drive than men. Ertman says that because I described the traditional Catholic view that homosexual intercourse is "unnatural" as "not absurd," *Sex and Reason* 226, quoted in Ertman, note 2 above, at 1519, I believe the view to be sound; in fact *Sex and Reason* rejects the Catholic view of sex. She has me saying there were no male homosexuals in ancient Greece except opportunistic ones. On the contrary, I believe that "real" as distinct from opportunistic homosexuals are found in every society. (A "real" or "preference" homosexual, in my terminology, is one who prefers same-sex relations even if opposite-sex relations are available at the same "cost," broadly interpreted to include nonpecuniary as well as pecuniary costs.) And I do not urge parents "to indoctrinate their children into heterosexuality." Ertman, note 2 above, at 1513.

26. See id. at 1505.

27. I said this was especially true of *male* homosexuality (*Sex and Reason* 307); Ertman ignores this qualification.

tion by their families."[28] She wants me to "advocat[e] an end to this estrangement."[29] But if I am right—and she presents no evidence that I am not—this estrangement is rooted in the genes and will not be easily rooted out by advocacy.

Nature and Culture

Robson makes in passing a point emphasized by Bartlett and Hadfield, that despite all my disclaimers my ostensibly economic analysis depends on the truth of sociobiology. What is true is that some of what I say about homosexuality depends upon my belief that homosexual preference is largely or entirely innate, rather than acquired as a result of personal choice, cultural influences, seduction, advocacy, or rape. But nothing depends on whether it is innate because a gene or complex of genes for homosexuality might somehow enhance inclusive fitness or because some more or less regular percentage of infants are born with or acquire in early infancy a neurological or psychological condition that will cause them when they reach sexual maturity to be attracted sexually to persons of the same sex. Much of my economic analysis of homosexuality, such as the analysis of homosexual search costs mentioned by Bartlett, Hadfield, and Robson and the analysis of opportunistic or situational homosexuality, is completely independent of theories about the causes of homosexual preference. The same is largely true of my discussion of women's sexuality. For example, it is a fact, whether or not it has a genetic or a purely cultural explanation, that women have generally pursued a more conservative sexual strategy than men. And for the most part that is all that my analysis of the differences between male and female sexual behavior requires.

Of course, if the reason for the more conservative strategy is cultural rather than biological, it may be an economic reason, and an economic analysis that failed to explain it would be incomplete. But most economic analysis is partial, and therefore incomplete, seeking to explain a part of the social world rather than the whole of it. *Sex and Reason* does try to explain the difference in male and female sexual strategies in economic as well as in biological terms, emphasizing the tendency of the strategies to converge when women's occupational profile con-

28. Ertman, note 2 above, at 1500 and n. 99; see also id. at 1505–1506.
29. Id. at 1500–1501.

verges with men's, as in modern Sweden. Bartlett is therefore wrong to say that it is crucial to my theory to regard men and women as subject not to social factors but only to evolutionary forces. The opposite is true: it is crucial to my theory that human sexual behavior and mores have been shaped by economic forces and not merely by biological ones.

My book is open to attack from the opposite direction—from evolutionary biologists who believe that the differences in sexual behavior and customs that I attribute to economic factors are the product of evolution. Pointing to the variance in sexual behavior and especially customs across human societies is only a superficial response, because animals display different behaviors in different ecological niches. A house cat behaves very differently from an alley cat—for example, eats fewer mice, and, more pertinently, usually has fewer offspring—and while it may be possible to explain the differences in economic terms (the house cat has a cheaper source of food but higher sexual search costs), a biological explanation would probably be adequate. The strongest evidence against a biological explanation for the patterns of human sexual activity is what is called the demographic transition, meaning the tendency for birth rates to fall very sharply when a society crosses some threshold of wealth. If human beings, like other animals, are reproduction machines, as the evolutionary biologist considers them to be, their tendency to reproduce less when they can afford to reproduce more is deeply puzzling. There may be a biological explanation, though it is one that opens a space for economic analysis. Human beings reached their present state of biological development before they understood the mechanics of reproduction. Selection was therefore in favor not of reproductive activity per se but of sexual activity and some affection and caring for offspring. When sex and reproduction are decoupled by contraception, abortion, artificial insemination, and other practices presumably unknown in the evolutionary period of human development (abortion may be an exception), the "reproduction machine" model of human behavior is bound to lose much of its explanatory value, opening the way for economic explanations of human sexual phenomena.

Bartlett makes a good point about the possible psychological effects on women and children of allowing a market in parental rights. She is also right to observe that some men derive pleasure from thinking that they belong to the dominant sex, and to point out that when I claim to be presenting a "nonmoral" or "morally indifferent" conception of sex I am in fact presenting a conception based on a specific morality, that of Mill.[30] Yet a morality of morally indifferent sex is not really an oxymoron. To regard sex as morally indifferent is to regard it in the same light in which we regard driving cars. Driving is a potentially dangerous activity, to self and to others, but ethical and policy analysis of it is not encumbered by taboos, stigmas, or appeals to nature or to the deity. Driving is recognized as useful, pleasurable, rational, and thus as, in the main, private in the sense of properly being subject to only limited constraints of law and social pressure. Purging, so far as it is possible to do, the moral charge from sex clears the way for the Millian approach to it, which comes naturally when we discuss morally indifferent subjects like driving, eating (for those of us who are neither vegetarians nor adherents to religions that impose dietary restrictions), and playing bridge.

It is not incorrect, but it is misleading, to represent me as saying "that it is appropriate for society to withhold its endorsement of homosexual marriage and disfavor child custody by homosexuals."[31] I discuss the pros and cons of homosexual marriage without reaching a conclusion, and I argue that homosexuals should *not* be categorically forbidden to have custody of children. The best interests of the child may sometimes be served by such custody; the matter should be considered on a case-by-case basis rather than straitjacketed by rules. I do not dismiss the moral objections to abortion or suggest that they can be refuted by rational arguments. I point out inconsistencies in the moral objections but acknowledge, indeed emphasize, that beyond a point they are not profitably discussable. I also acknowledge that abortion cannot be rationally justified to "an individual who puts a high (if not the highest) value on fetal life,"[32] but I suggest (as Bartlett momentarily forgets) that the opponents of abortion in fact do *not* place the highest value on fetal life. If they did, they would have to oppose abortion even when the mother's life was endangered. They do not.

I should not have thought it necessary to give reasons for doubting

30. This point is also made in Nussbaum, note 13 above, at 1701–1709, and in Hadfield, "Flirting with Science," note 2 above, at 489.

31. Bartlett, note 2 above, at 481.

32. Id. at 486. See also Chapter 5 of this book, discussing Dworkin's and Rawls's arguments for abortion rights.

that a woman who says that "daughters of lesbians, like freedom fighters everywhere, need to be enlisted in infancy, and protected against heterofemininity by words and actions,"[33] is *automatically* to be assumed a fit parent if her fitness is questioned in a custody contest. The more difficult question is whether the answer should be the same if "heterosexuals" is substituted for "lesbians" and "lesbianism" for "heterofeminity." No categorical answer is possible. It would be bizarre, given public opinion in this society, to pronounce automatically unfit any mother who wanted to do what she could to prevent her daughter from becoming a lesbian, futile as her efforts are likely to be. But one can imagine situations in which the mother's efforts to steer her daughter away from lesbianism would take so destructive a form as to make the mother an unfit parent.

I do not define companionate marriage as marriage in which "the wife must be made desirable (or here, 'companionable') enough to keep him [her husband]."[34] The passage on which Bartlett bases this interpretation is an attempt not at describing companionate marriage but at assessing the impact on it of access to effective contraception. Companionate marriage is described in other chapters. I do not discount what Bartlett calls "irrational altruism" (altruism not based on an expectation of reciprocal favors) as a factor in sexual and family behavior or deride it as "naive."[35]

I do not consider it "soft and sentimental" to talk about "the welfare of others" but neither do I get much out of the assertion that "the social conditions that perpetuate women's subservience to men are unfair and should be changed."[36] Not many people nowadays acknowledge defending conditions "that perpetuate women's subservience to men." The problem is in defining "subservience" and identifying the conditions that promote it and designing appropriate means of eliminating it. We won't get far with "a commitment to women's control over their reproductive decisions . . . or to improving the quality of life for children who are born"[37] if, as the quoted passage suggests, the

33. *Sex and Reason* 429.
34. Bartlett, note 2 above, at 487.
35. Id. at 488, 494. Nor for that matter do I consider nonreciprocal altruism (interdependence of utility functions, so that an increase in A's utility may increase B's utility) irrational.
36. Id. at 493.
37. Id.

commitment involves simultaneously urging the woman's right to kill her child until the moment of birth[38] and the child's right to a high-quality life from the moment of birth forward. I do not say that even so abrupt a discontinuity could not be defended; but Bartlett disables herself from defending it by remarking a few sentences later that "society benefits most when individuals fight rather than give in to whatever tendencies they might have to think of themselves first."[39] One might have supposed that many abortions resulted from women's "tendencies . . . to think of themselves first." Before Bartlett embraces selflessness as the beacon for social policy she may wish to ponder the implications. Many feminists believe that one of the problems of women is that they have been *too* selfless.

Feminist Criticism Purportedly from within Economics

Gillian Hadfield does not question the pertinence of economics to the understanding of sexuality. But she finds everywhere in my book "the pitfalls of a male-centered vision of what sex is all about."[40] Hadfield offers few clues to what a proper economic analysis of sexuality would look like, but I infer, despite some backpedaling in her second paper,[41] that it would treat the oppression of women as the most important causal factor in sexual attitudes and behavior. In other words, "what sex is all about" is male domination.

Hadfield makes several good points. One is that I neglect some potentially significant endogeneities in an economic analysis of sexuality.[42] The sexual practices of women not only are influenced by women's occupational choices, as I emphasized, but also influence those choices. If women are sequestered, in order to assure their virginity (before marriage) or their chastity (after), they will be deprived of opportunities to work in the market. This is an overlooked point in my analysis, but

---

38. That may not be Bartlett's position. For all I know, she would restrict abortion when the pregnancy is far advanced. But she does not indicate any such qualification of women's right to "control over their reproductive decisions."

39. Bartlett, note 2 above, at 494.

40. "Flirting with Science," note 2 above, at 502.

41. "Not the 'Radical' Feminist Critique of *Sex and Reason*," note 2 above.

42. An endogenous factor in an economic model, as distinct from an exogenous one, is one that is affected by the variables in the model rather than just affecting them. So price is an endogenous factor in a model of the wheat market, but weather is an exogenous factor in that market.

probably a minor one. Women do not go to work because men stop sequestering them; men stop sequestering them because the opportunity cost of sequestration becomes prohibitive.

Hadfield argues that contraception is a function not only of the cost and efficacy of contraceptive methods but also of a desire to limit family size and a taste for particular sexual practices, not all of which are procreative. The first half of this proposition—that desire to limit family size can induce contraception even if the cost is high, as it was before the invention of modern contraceptives—obviously is true, is indeed a commonplace in the literature on fertility, and is discussed in the book. I said that contraception must be understood broadly to include non-technological methods such as coitus interruptus, occasional abstinence, and the various forms of nonvaginal intercourse, such as oral and anal intercourse. It is true that when I wrote about how the fall in the full price of contraception has facilitated women's liberation from the household I disregarded the possibility that this liberation would have occurred earlier if people had had different preferences concerning contraceptive sexual practices such as oral intercourse. The possibility is real, but of limited significance because most men and women will run a substantial pregnancy risk if necessary in order to engage in vaginal intercourse. Other elements of endogeneity in the market for contraceptives are more important. The advent of the contraceptive pill lowered the cost of premarital sex and therefore increased the demand for it, but higher demand for premarital sex was also a factor in increasing the demand for the pill. I grant that much more can be done with the economics of contraception than I attempted to do in *Sex and Reason*.[43]

Less justly, Hadfield criticizes me for ignoring the social organization of child care; in fact it is central to the discussion in chapter 6 of *Sex and Reason* of the evolution of sexual morality. And in attributing to me the belief that all women in ancient Greece were regarded merely as breeders, she ignores the fact that I was discussing upper-class women, who were not permitted to work. Elsewhere the book emphasizes the productivity of women in traditional agricultural societies and discusses the impact of that productivity on sexual mores.[44] Yet I should

43. See Tomas J. Philipson and Richard A. Posner, *Private Choices and Public Health: The AIDS Epidemic in an Economic Perspective*, ch. 9 (1993).

44. *Sex and Reason* 129, 170. I should however have mentioned that wives of the poorer Greek citizens apparently did often work outside the home.

have said even more about the social organization of child care, and in particular about the role of slavery in shaping sexual mores. Where, as in ancient Athens or Rome or the antebellum American South, slaves are available to be used, and are used, for child care, the productivity of (free) women who are not permitted to engage in agricultural or other laboring activities is reduced. Their essential role is limited to breeding. Companionate marriage—the marriage of equals joined by a deep emotional bond—is rare in a system in which the wife's only function is to be a breeder, and this functional limitation is more likely the more that slaves are available to do work that free women otherwise would do. So slavery fosters noncompanionate marriage. Noncompanionate marriage in turn fosters the familiar double standard of sexual freedom, because where there is little intimacy or affection in marriage the husband has an incentive to sequester the wife in order to secure his paternity of her children, and to seek elsewhere the erotic satisfaction not available to him in marriage. He can do that all the more readily because the availability of slaves for child care excuses him from potentially burdensome household duties,[45] and because female slaves are a ready source of extramarital sexual gratification. With the decline of slavery, a decline that was a marked feature of the transition from classical antiquity to the Christian Middle Ages, the wife's household duties increased, and the husband's too.[46] Christianity placed new emphasis on the role of parents—both parents—in the education of children.[47] It became natural to think of marriage as a full-time, working

45. For evidence, see Richard Saller, "Slavery and the Roman Family," in *Classical Slavery* 65 (M. I. Finley ed. 1987); Keith R. Bradley, *Discovering the Roman Family: Studies in Roman Social History* 55–56, 127 (1991). It should be noted, however, in some tension with the argument I am making here, that upper-class Roman wives, though relatively uninvolved in child-rearing, especially of their young children (Suzanne Dixon, *The Roman Mother* 109–111 [1988]), had a high social status and considerable freedom. Id. at 233–236; *Sex and Reason* 176. For a stab at an economic explanation consistent with the argument here, see id. at 177.

46. Some speculative evidence is the decline in average household size, which has been attributed to the difference between a slave and a free society. Andrew Wallace-Hadrill, "Houses and Households: Sampling Pompeii and Herculaneum," in *Marriage, Divorce, and Children in Ancient Rome* 191, 204 (Beryl Rawson ed. 1991).

47. H. I. Marrou, *A History of Education in Antiquity* 314–315 (1956). In ancient Greece, in contrast, "The family could not be the educational centre. The wife was kept in the background; she was considered fit enough to look after the baby; but no more: when the child was seven, it was taken out of her hands. As for the father, he was absorbed in public affairs, for we must not forget that we are speaking of what was orginally an aristocracy; he was a citizen and a man of politics before he was head of the family." Id. at 31. Compare Charles de La Roncière, "Tuscan Notables on the Eve of the Renaissance," in *A History of*

partnership of equals, a partnership incompatible with sequestration of women but also with extramarital activity, heterosexual or homosexual, of men.

Hadfield makes some odd claims about *Sex and Reason*—for example that it slights women by having an index entry for women but not for men, by devoting more space to male homosexuality than to lesbianism, and by giving "disproportionate" attention to male homosexuality[48] relative to female sexuality, the disproportion apparently consisting in the fact that there are so many more women than there are male homosexuals. Hadfield ignores most of my discussion of women, and while pouncing on me for acknowledging that I do not attempt a *systematic* economic analysis of prostitution ignores the dozens of index entries under "Prostitution." What is correct is that because men (apparently in all societies) are more promiscuous than women, women do not incur search costs for sex (streetwalkers are an exception), unless expenditures on enhancing attractiveness, broadly understood, are counted. That important qualification, not remarked by Hadfield, to one side, an analysis that focuses on search costs because they are one of the less intractable issues in the nascent economic analysis of sex is bound to seem preoccupied with male behavior. She ignores the further point that we can learn things about heterosexuality by studying relationships in which the "hetero" element is missing. Male homosexual relationships can teach us a lot about what women bring to a relationship, lesbian relationships about what men bring to a relationship.

Like Fineman and Bartlett, Hadfield believes that biology is the linchpin of my analysis. This is a puzzling mistake for her to make, given her complaint that I devote too much space to male homosexuality; my theoretical analysis of homosexuality (as distinct from my policy recommendations) has nothing to do with whether it has a genetic basis. Her mistake prejudices her against me, because she confesses to an unexplained general skepticism about biological explanations of human behavior.[49] She seems irritated at the suggestion that

---

Private Life, vol. 2: *Revelations of the Medieval World* 157, 279–281 (Philippe Ariès and Georges Duby eds. 1988), describing the personal role of both parents, even in wealthy families, in the education of children in fourteenth- and fifteenth-century Italy.

48. "Flirting with Sex," note 2 above, at 485 n. 16, 490–491. "Posner seems to believe that the central phenomenon for which a theory of sexuality must account is the choice of a man's anus from the range of available options." Id. at 490.

49. Compare Larson, note 2 above, at 463, expressing concern with the "moral effect of sociobiological arguments." I am concerned by her concern. Scholarship is compromised

women have on average a less overmastering lust, a less intense sexual itch, than men. *Why* that should be irritating is mysterious. As a prop of the ideology of women's natural subordination to men, the erroneous belief that women are greater slaves to their sexual desire than men are has alternated with the erroneous belief that normal women lack any sexual desire at all.[50]

Lest the pendulum swing too far to the other side, it should be noted that the phenomenon of prostitution may result in the underestimation of the sexual interest of the *average* woman. One would expect prostitutes to be drawn disproportionately from women who derive more than average pleasure from frequent sex, because the costs of being a prostitute are, other things being equal, lower for such women. There is more to a decision to become a prostitute than a taste for frequent sex or for multiple sex partners; but if the other factors are assumed to be randomly distributed with respect to such tastes, the generalization that the average prostitute has more sexual interest than the average woman should hold. It would follow that the average wife would have less sexual interest than the average woman, since most prostitutes are unmarried. And since there is virtually no female (though some male) demand for male prostitutes, the average sexual interest among married men will not be diminished by the siphoning off into prostitution of men who derive the greatest pleasure from frequent sex or multiple sex partners. Such men may be somewhat less likely to marry, but the same is true of men at the other end of the distribution of sexual desire; the distribution of married men will therefore be truncated at both ends,

---

when scholars are deflected by political or moral concerns from pursuing otherwise promising paths of research and analysis. I acknowledge the relevance of moral concerns when the question is whether to conduct experiments on human beings or to build weapons, but not when the question is whether to engage in pure armchair research.

Science skepticism is a leitmotif of radical feminism. Janet Halley's criticisms of the scientific evidence for a biological basis of homosexuality, in her article "Sexual Orientation and the Politics of Biology: A Critique of the Argument from Motibility," 46 *Stanford Law Review* 503 (1994), remind one of the cigarette companies' arguments that smoking has not been "proved" to cause lung cancer. Science skepticism has played a disastrous role in the recent history of homosexuality. When AIDS was first discovered, a number of advocates for homosexual rights denounced the discovery as a plot against homosexuality, and campaigned against safe sex and the closing of homosexual bath houses. Randy Shilts, *And the Band Played On: Politics, People, and the AIDS Epidemic* (1987), passim.

50. See, for example, Thomas Laqueur, *Making Sex: Body and Gender from the Greeks to Freud* (1990).

that of women mainly at only one end. So generalizations drawn from observation of "respectable" women will tend to underestimate female sexual interest; and yet the phenomenon responsible for this distorted impression—prostitution—is itself persuasive evidence that female sexual desire is on average less than male. With trivial exceptions, only the male population, though usually no larger than the female, has unsatisfied sexual needs great enough to support a prostitution industry.

Comparison of male and female sexual demand requires qualification in other respects, some insufficiently emphasized in my book: the definitional respects that I mentioned in connection with lesbianism; the fact that polygyny creates an artificial shortage of women; differences over the life cycle, because male sexual desire diminishes with age more precipitously than female. A further point, which bears on my suggestion that the absence of a female demand for prostitution reflects an asymmetry in the intensity of male and female sexual desire, is that men's sexual interest is more strongly focused on young women than women's on young men, creating a "shortage" of women that prostitution helps alleviate. The difference in preference with respect to the age of one's sexual partner is further evidence, however, for a biological theory of human sexual activity, since it suggests that sexual interest is correlated with fertility, as men are fertile until a greater age than women.

Radical feminists like to emphasize, as part of their project of equating ostensibly consensual heterosexual intercourse to rape,[51] that women frequently consent to sex without really desiring it.[52] This is exactly what one would expect if men have on average a stronger sex drive than women. Yet no inference of coercion need be drawn. When people have different tastes, they maximize their satisfactions by trading. Willing though undesired sex is a currency of payment for services rendered women by men,[53] and would be even if there were complete economic, political, and social equality between the sexes. We can see this most clearly by imagining a lesbian couple in which one of the women has a more intense sexual drive than the other. She will want to have sex more often, and to get it she will have to offer compensation on some other front, perhaps by assuming a larger share of the

51. See the next chapter, discussing MacKinnon on pornography.
52. This is the theme of West, note 18 above. See esp. id. at 1455–1457.
53. Douglas W. Allen and Margaret Brinig, "Sex, Property Rights, and Divorce" (unpublished, Simon Fraser and George Mason universities, Nov. 1993).

housework or deferring to the other's preferences in housing or entertainment. From this perspective, Robin West's question about heterosexual marriage, "Why is it okay for her to have sex even though she does not want to, but not okay for him not have sex even though he wants to?"[54] suggests that she does not understand barter.

Another point that Hadfield taxes me with omitting—that the larger the optimal paternal investment in child rearing, the more costly a promiscuous sexual strategy is for a man—is actually one that I emphasize.[55] Not only in discussing the biology of sex; it is fundamental to my discussions of polygamy and (as I suggested earlier) of companionate marriage. Both a promiscuous and nonpromiscuous (call it "uxorious") male sexual strategy could be optimal for different men, the difference corresponding to the economic distinction between cultivating the extensive and the intensive margin. The promiscuous male has many children, but does not stick around to protect them, so their chances of survival are diminished (I am speaking of course of the evolutionary era, not of today), reducing his inclusive fitness (that is, inclusive of descendants beyond those of the first generation). The uxorious man has fewer children, but protects them, increasing their chances of survival and therefore his own inclusive fitness. Both types of men, not to mention men pursuing a mixed strategy, could end up with the same number of grandchildren. Women, however, are constrained to cultivate the intensive margin, because of their inherently limited reproductive capacity. A promiscuous sexual strategy does not make reproductive sense for them, so the genes of women who followed such a strategy during the evolutionary era would have tended to be weeded out of the population eventually.

Sex and Reason argues that biology, including male sex drive and paternity anxiety, along with the high level of child mortality in a society without knowledge of modern medicine and hygiene, goes far to explain the high degree of subordination of women that is found in many ancient and primitive societies, while technological and economic development, including improvements in medicine and hygiene that greatly reduced infant mortality, in household labor-saving devices, in contraception, and in job opportunities for women, has enabled women in modern Western societies to progress toward full social, political,

54. West, note 18 above, at 1456.
55. See, for example, *Sex and Reason* 95.

economic, and sexual equality with men. Hadfield, here echoing the radical feminist line, regards male power and exploitativeness as more important factors than biology and technology in the history of women and in the character of female sexuality. (Does the possibility that women's liberation from their traditional subordination to men may be due primarily to technological advancements made by men rankle so?) Consistent with that view, she thinks that rape illustrates the continuing desire and capacity of men to use sex to intimidate women.

I find it plausible to imagine fully informed women in a society in which technological conditions deny them any career other than motherhood freely agreeing to exchange reproductive control for male economic support. The result would be a subordinate role for women but one preferable from their own point of view to the only alternatives feasible in their society even if no man ever used or threatened violence against a woman. I do not find it plausible to suppose that women were excluded from the combat branches of our armed forces until recently because of phallocracy. Recent changes in the technology of warfare have reduced the role of brawn, stamina, and aggressiveness. The armed forces' demand for people able to march through mud carrying hundred-pound packs on their back and to kill at short range with fists or knives or rifle butts or submachine guns has not vanished, but it has shrunk. We live in an age of push-button warfare. Women can push buttons as well as men.

A theory of human sexuality that stresses male power and violence is a rival hypothesis to the economic one. If Hadfield had said I should have given it more attention I could only have pleaded limitations of space, the difficulty of fitting the hypothesis to the standard economic model of human behavior, its implausibility in the absence of any explanation of why the male grip has suddenly loosened, its logical puzzles (for example, if men control society and all men benefit from rape, why is rape illegal?), and the counterevidence that I marshaled and that she ignores.[56] Radical feminists believe that women's subordi-

---

56. For example, evidence that the subordination of women to men is greater in societies with little pornography or rape or both than in the United States. See *Sex and Reason*, chs. 13–14, and the next chapter of this book. For empirical evidence that women's status is relative to their economic contributions even in primitive societies, see Gary S. Becker and Richard A. Posner, "Cross-Cultural Differences in Family and Sexual Life: An Economic Analysis," 5 *Rationality and Society* 421 (1993). See also Ester Boserup, "Economic and Demographic Interrelationships in Sub-Saharan Africa," 11 *Population and Development Review* 383, 388–389 (1985).

nate position is due to male violence. But if so how have women been able to get free from this coercive domination? One answer is that they haven't; that the seemingly dramatic progress of women in recent years is illusory, that the rape-shield laws, the criminalization of marital rape, and so forth, are all phony. Nothing in Hadfield's article suggests that she believes this. But if women have made dramatic or at least definite progress, this implies, if the domination hypothesis is correct, that they have done so because male domination somehow slackened. How did that happen? We know, more or less, the reasons why the slaves were freed, Louis XVI deposed, the czar overthrown, the shah forced to abdicate; what enabled women suddenly to throw off, if not all their chains, many of them? The economist can point to the expansion of jobs in the service sector, improved household labor-saving devices, improvements in contraception, and other economic or technological factors as causes of women's increasing emancipation from dependence on men. To what can the dominance theorist point? Her own writings?—a clarion that has awakened women from thousands of years of dumb passivity?

chapter 17

Obsessed with Pornography

THE title of Catharine MacKinnon's book[1] is intended as an ironic commentary on the belief that pornography is "only words" and therefore, unlike sticks and stones, can never hurt anyone. It is ironic in a further sense that is unintended. *Only Words* is a rhetorical rather than an analytical production; it is only words. It is eloquent and passionate, yet, like much radical feminist jurisprudence, it lacks the careful distinctions, scrupulous weighing of evidence, and fair consideration of opposing views that one is entitled to expect in a work off scholarship.[2] It is a verbal torrent that, much like pornography itself as MacKinnon conceives of it, appeals to elemental passions (fear, disgust, anger, hatred) rather than engaging the rational intellect. There is no nuance, no qualification, no sense of proportion. "You grow up with your father holding you down and covering your mouth so another man can make horrible searing pain between your legs. When you are older, your husband ties you to the bed and drips hot wax on your nipples and brings in other men to watch and makes you smile through it" (p. 1). "The message of [pornography] . . . is 'get her' . . . This message is

---

1. Catharine A. MacKinnon, *Only Words* (1993).
2. We saw other examples in the preceding chapter, and shall see still another example in the next.

addressed directly to the penis, delivered through an erection, and taken out on women in the real world" (p. 21). "Society is made of language" (p. 106), and "speech . . . belongs to those who own it, mainly big corporations" (p. 78), which are complicit in the production of pornography because they are managed by men and have a financial stake in being free to publish anything that is profitable. We live in "a world made by pornography" (p. 67). "'Pornography'"—MacKinnon is quoting with approval her frequent collaborator Andrea Dworkin— "'is the law for women'" (p. 40).

Beneath the indignation, the hyperbole, the sarcasm, and the innuendoes—"some [consumers of pornography] undoubtedly write judicial opinions" (p. 19), and the Supreme Court might not have held child pornography illegal if the children in the case[3] had been girls rather than boys (p. 91)—an argument can be discerned. Pornography both destroys the lives of the women who appear in it and causes its male consumers to commit rapes and sexual murders, abuse female children sexually, and disvalue and intimidate women. "Sooner or later, in one way or another, the consumers want to live out the pornography further in three dimensions," want "to keep the world a pornographic place so they can continue to get hard from everyday life" (p. 19).

Since pornography "impels behaviors in ways that are unique in their extent and devastating in their consequences" (p. 37), why do the courts throw the cloak of the First Amendment over it? Partly because most judges are men, partly because in laudable reaction to Joe McCarthy they made a dogma of the First Amendment's free speech and free press clauses. This dogma has blinded male judges to the fact that "women are far more likely to be harmed through pornography than the U.S. government is to be overthrown by communists" (p. 39). Judges do not realize, moreover, that there is no tenable distinction between words and deeds: "*Saying* kill to a trained attack dog is only words" (p. 12). The courts have never been able to explain "why, if pornography is protected speech based on its mental elements, rape and sexual murder, which have mental elements, are not [protected speech] as well" (p. 94).

The incoherence of the judicial approach is further shown, MacKinnon argues, by the fact that laws against sexual harassment in the workplace have been upheld even though much of that harassment is

3. New York v. Ferber, 458 U.S. 747 (1982).

verbal; for why should women be protected *only* in the workplace? Above all, the courts have failed to recognize the tension between equality, which is protected by the Fourteenth Amendment, and freedom of expression, which is protected by the First. When free expression is used to demean or intimidate a vulnerable group—as in the case of racial epithets and other "hate speech," including teaching that the Holocaust never happened—prohibiting that expression may be necessary to the achievement of full equality and should therefore be authorized. We should not regret that if this argument is accepted, members of minority groups will have more freedom of speech than white males. "The more the speech of the dominant is protected, the more dominant they become" (p. 72). We should not succumb to "the studied inability to tell the difference between oppressor and oppressed that passes for principled neutrality" (p. 86). The possibility of oppressed turning oppressor through reckless and unsubstantiated charges of rape, child abuse, and workplace harassment, through speech codes and norms of political correctness, through quotas and affirmative action, through bloc voting and interest-group politics and demonstrations and censorship—the possibility, in short, of p.c. witch hunting—has not occurred to MacKinnon.

In ordinary language the word "pornography" denotes a sexually graphic representation, verbal or pictorial, heterosexual or homosexual, designed to titillate or arouse the reader or viewer. What MacKinnon means by the word is not entirely clear. In this book, although not in the antipornography ordinance that she drafted with Andrea Dworkin (pp. 121–122 n. 32) and that was adopted by Indianapolis and invalidated by the courts as a violation of the First Amendment, she seems to mean all live erotic performances (such as striptease dancing) and all photographs of women either nude or engaged in a sexual act, real or simulated. She says that "all pornography is made under conditions of inequality based on sex" (p. 20), and this seems to exclude a purely verbal or cartoon presentation. Although to count as pornography the representation must depict women as "subordinated" to men in some fashion, this requirement would probably be satisfied by almost any nude photograph of a woman, since MacKinnon considers *Playboy* pornographic (pp. 22–23).[4] She is most concerned about violent pornography, especially when it involves actual rather than simulated vio-

---

4. See also MacKinnon, *Feminism Unmodified: Discourses on Life and Law*, ch. 12 (1987).

lence perpetrated upon the pornographic models or actresses, but her implicit definition sweeps far more broadly.

It is odd that she should leave the definition of pornography implicit. Odder still that she should let her book create the impression that *all* pornography, as she defines it, except that in which child models are used, is legal in the United States. This is not true. The sale of "hard core" pornography—primarily the explicit photographic depiction of actual or realistically simulated sex acts or of an erect penis, with no pretense of aesthetic or scientific purpose[5]—is illegal even when the persons photographed are adults.[6] MacKinnon does not complain as she might that the enforcement of the laws is so listless that the hard-core pornographic film industry operates pretty much in the open, believing that a thin veneer of aesthetic pretension will ward off prosecution.[7] Since MacKinnon believes that men control the legal system and have an immense stake in pornography, she cannot conceive that there might actually be laws against the stuff. Still, her conception of pornography reaches far beyond current law and would forbid much that is indeed protected by the First Amendment. *Playboy*'s stock in trade consists of retouched nude photographs of smiling, voluptuous young women in suggestive poses. If these photographs are pornographic and should be suppressed, much of the production of the U.S. film and theater industry, a fair amount of cable-television programming, a huge number of videocassettes, some greeting cards, some advertising, a fair amount of high art (possibly not excepting such works as Titian's *Rape of Europa*), even an occasional opera (for example *Salome* when the Dance of the Seven Veils is done as a striptease), are pornographic and should be suppressed.

That is a lot to remove from the market. It would require, as

5. The qualification is important. See, for example, Piarowski v. Illinois Community College, 759 F.2d 625, 627 (7th Cir. 1985), discussing Aubrey Beardsley's sexually explicit drawings.

6. See, for example, Miller v. California, 413 U.S. 15 (1973); Walter v. United States, 447 U.S. 649 (1980); Alexander v. United States, 113 S. Ct. 2766, 2770 (1993); Kucharek v. Hanaway, 902 F.2d 513 (7th Cir. 1990); United States v. Bagnell, 679 F.2d 826, 833, 837 (11th Cir. 1982); Dunlap v. State, 728 S.W.2d 155 (Ark. 1987); State v. Simmer, 772 S.W.2d 372 (Mo. 1989); City of Urbana ex rel. Newlin v. Downing, 539 N.E.2d 140 (Ohio 1989); Minnesota v. Davidson, 481 N.W.2d 51 (Minn. 1992); Butler v. Tucker, 416 S.E.2d 262 (W. Va. 1992); Catherine Itzin, "A Legal Definition of Pornography," in *Pornography: Women, Violence and Civil Liberties* 435, 446–447 (Catherine Itzin ed. 1992).

7. See Gary Indiana [a pseudonym?], "A Day in the Life of Hollywood's Sex Factory," *Village Voice*, Aug. 24, 1993, pp. 27, 35.

MacKinnon fails to mention, not a smattering of Indianapolis-style local ordinances but a law enforcement effort on the scale of Prohibition or the "war on drugs," and with the same dubious prospects of success. Would it be worth it? In MacKinnon's distinctive idiom, "How many women's bodies have to stack up here even to register against male profit and pleasure presented as First Amendment principle?" (p. 22). In more neutral language, what is the harm of "soft core" pornography à la *Playboy,* or for that matter hard-core pornography, that would justify an Iran-style crusade against the photographic display of the female body? On this critical question, the book is largely a blank. A footnote (pp. 119–120 n. 27) cites several studies that have found that pornography can incite aggressive behavior by men. To this evidence MacKinnon adds anecdotes, for example that of a sexual murder committed in a manner that had been depicted in a magazine published eight months earlier, though there is no evidence that the murderer had seen the magazine.[8] MacKinnon tries to get some mileage from the decision invalidating the Indianapolis ordinance by noting that it accepted the ordinance's premise that pornography harms women. But as the court explained, "In saying that we accept the finding that pornography as the ordinance defines it leads to unhappy consequences, we mean only that there is evidence to this effect, that this evidence is consistent with much human experience, and that *as judges we must accept the legislative resolution of such disputed empirical questions.*"[9]

The United States is a nation of more than a quarter-billion people closely watched by a horde of journalists. Every bad thing that can happen does happen and much of it is reported in the media, so that a piling on of anecdotes can make any bad thing, however rare, seem common. MacKinnon does not acknowledge the limitations of anecdotal evidence. Or the limited scope of the nonanecdotal evidence, almost all of which concerns violent pornography, although she wants to forbid the nonviolent as well. Or the counterevidence.[10] Denmark,

8. For a more extensive, but not less one-sided, canvas of the evidence of pornography's harm, see *Pornography: Women, Violence and Civil Liberties,* note 6 above, pt. 3. Criticisms similar to mine of MacKinnon's use of evidence are made by Ronald Dworkin, "Women and Pornography," *New York Review of Books,* Oct. 21, 1993, pp. 36, 38.

9. American Booksellers Association, Inc. v. Hudnut, 771 F.2d 323, 329 n. 2 (7th Cir. 1985), affirmed without opinion, 475 U.S. 1001 (1986) (emphasis added).

10. Summarized in *Sex and Reason* 366–374, and in Nadine Strossen, "A Feminist Critique of 'the' Feminist Critique of Pornography," 79 *Virginia Law Review* 1099, 1176–

which has no law against even hard-core pornography (other than child pornography), and Japan, in which pornography is sold freely and is dominated by rape and bondage scenes, have rape rates far lower than that in the United States. The rape rate in the United States has probably been falling or steady,[11] and it certainly has not been increasing as fast as the rate of violent crimes generally, even though the consumption of hard-core pornography has been increasing because of the videocassette. Women's status is generally much lower in societies such as those of the Islamic nations that repress pornography than in societies, such as those of the Scandinavian nations, that do not.[12] Some of MacKinnon's conservative allies in the fight against pornography believe that pornography deflects men from intercourse to masturbation rather than spurring them to rape: in economic terms that pornography is a substitute for intercourse (including rape) rather than a complement to it. And on the left we find Duncan Kennedy quoting with approval the assertion that pornography provides a "victimless outlet" for the "basic sexual rage" that many men feel toward women, a rage that would otherwise be "vented" in rape.[13] MacKinnon herself says that "pornography is masturbation material" (p. 17).

It would be a mistake to conclude that pornography has been shown to be harmless. The evidence is inconclusive. Our present knowledge does not warrant a confident conclusion that eliminating pornography would reduce, increase, or leave unchanged the incidence of sex crimes and other mistreatment of women. It is especially reckless to conclude that pornography in the United States today is a *major* cause of harm

---

1185 (1993). Even one of MacKinnon's strongest academic supporters, after a sympathetic review of the evidence on which she relies, finds no more than "a plausible connection between exposure to sexually violent material and sexually violent acts." Cass Sunstein, *Democracy and the Problem of Free Speech* 218 (1993). "Plausible" is not "proven," and MacKinnon's conception of pornography is not limited to violent material. If "plausible" harms justify censorship, we have no freedom of speech.

11. Official statistics show a sharp increase in the per capita incidence of rape during the 1970s, and a small increase since then. U.S. Bureau of the Census, *Statistical Abstract of the United States* 195 (113th ed. 1993) (tab. 306). But a study by the Justice Department found a big decrease in the incidence of rape and attempted rape between 1978 and 1987. *Sex and Reason* 33 n. 39. The increase shown by the official statistics may be due entirely to better reporting of the crime.

12. Even without the international evidence, her dictum "No pornography, no male sexuality" (MacKinnon, *Toward a Feminist Theory of the State* 139 [1989]), would be fantastic.

13. Duncan Kennedy, *Sexy Dressing Etc.* 247 n. 93 (1993), quoting David Steinberg, "The Roots of Pornography," in *Men Confront Pornography* 54, 57 (Michael S. Kimmel ed. 1990).

to women. The issue of magnitude is critical; it would not pay to devote major social resources to extirpating a minor source of harm.

It is not on behalf of the multitudinous consumers of pornography (not all heterosexual males),[14] who will be deprived of a source of possibly harmless pleasure if MacKinnon's proposal is accepted, that I raise this question. My concern is that she is plumping for an enormously ambitious and possibly quixotic program of law enforcement in order to bring about what for all anyone knows might be only a small, or no, or even a negative, improvement in the life of American women. Apart from the direct costs, always considerable, of trying to eliminate a consensual activity (such as the drug trade, gambling, or prostitution), a crusade against pornography defined as it is defined in *Only Words* would impose heavy indirect costs in the form of infringement of civil liberties. High art would occasionally be caught in the dragnet,[15] and any campaign against "victimless" crimes endangers civil liberties because of the necessarily heavy reliance on searches, on wiretapping and other means of surreptitious surveillance, on broad interpretations of conspiracy, and on undercover agents, paid informers, and sting operations. An ineffective campaign would be cheaper, but what would be the point?

MacKinnon's blindness to the fact that hard-core pornography is already illegal in this country vitiates her emphasis on the brutal treatment of pornographic models and actresses. For that is exactly what one expects in an illegal market. We know from Prohibition, prostitution, the campaign against drugs, and the employment of illegal immigrants that when an economic activity is placed outside the protection of the law, the participants will resort to threats and violence in lieu of the contractual and other legal remedies denied them. The pimp is an artifact of the illegality of prostitution, and the exploitation of pornographic actresses and models by their employers is parallel to the exploitation of illegal immigrant labor by its employers. These women would be better off if all pornography were legal. Oddly, MacKinnon

14. *Only Words* does not discuss homosexual pornography, but the MacKinnon-Dworkin ordinance forbids pornography whenever a man as well as a woman is "subordinated," and regardless of the sex of the subordinator (p. 122 n. 32). This is extremely odd, since the main premise of MacKinnon's attack on pornography is that it is a method by which men harm women.

15. "If a woman is subjected, why should it matter that the work has other value?" MacKinnon, note 12 above, at 202. And see discussion of Canada's new obscenity law, below.

does not express any concern with the potential of pornographic performances to spread AIDS. She should.[16]

She misses another critical distinction when she complains about the asymmetrical treatment of pornography on the one hand and verbal sexual harassment of women in the workplace on the other. If words are deemed actionable harm in the latter context, why, she asks, not in the former as well? An obvious answer is overlooked. In the case of harassment, at least when properly circumscribed,[17] the words are aimed at a woman; she is the target of a verbal assault. In the case of pornography, the words (pictures are MacKinnon's actual concern) are aimed at a man, the reader or viewer of the pornography, and the aim is to please, not to insult or intimidate. Since a woman is not the intended and rarely the actual viewer or reader, she can be harmed only if a voluntary male consumer of the pornography is incited by it to mistreat her. The effect is indirect; whether it is substantial is the essential issue that MacKinnon fails to confront. It is facile to equate child pornography to adult pornography on the ground that the objection to child pornography is the inequality between children and adults and that adult pornography is based similarly on inequality, that between women and men (p. 36). And it is nonsense to argue that because murder and pornography both involve mental elements, it would be anomalous to punish one and not the other.

MacKinnon wants to associate women with other traditional victim groups, so she compares pornography to the shouting of racial epithets and to Nazi marches and Holocaust revisionism, all of which are expressive sources of pain. But these comparisons, especially the last, cause her to equivocate over the difference between the form and the content of expression. Most of the time she treats pornography as something that bypasses the rational intellect (the "message is addressed directly to the penis"). Misogynistic messages not conveyed by sexually explicit representations fall outside the scope of her pornography ordinance; "pornography [is] more than mere words, while the words of communism *are* only words" (p. 39). Mere words are privi-

16. See Indiana, note 7 above, at 34, 36.

17. The reason for this qualification is that some cases have found harassment in situations where no woman was an actual target; for example, pin-ups in the workplace have been held to create a hostile environment, for which the employer is legally responsible, for female employees. See Kingsley R. Browne, "Title VII as Censorship: Hostile-Environment Harassment and the First Amendment," 52 *Ohio State Law Journal* 481 (1991).

leged. But then she applauds Canada for punishing the propagation of the thesis that the Holocaust did not occur, even though these teachings like "the words of communism *are* only words." In the same vein she says that "the current legal distinction between screaming 'go kill that nigger' and advocating the view that African-Americans should be eliminated from parts of the United States needs to be seriously reconsidered" (p. 108). But if the line between incitement and advocacy, and between obscenity and misogyny, is erased, censorship will become a pervasive feature of American public life. The communist case will then be an easy one—communism has done more harm to more people than pornography has—so that I cannot understand why MacKinnon regards the protection of the free speech of communists as one of the shining moments of American constitutionalism.

She endorses *New York Times Co. v. Sullivan*,[18] which limited the right of public figures to sue for defamation, only because the public figures involved were white racists; had they been black they should, she believes, have been granted a broader right to sue (pp. 79–80). She is derisive about the courts' refusal to distinguish between oppressor and oppressed and to grant more rights to the latter. Yet it is not always clear which is which. Some people believe that criminals, who in this country disproportionately are black, and who are of course the perpetrators of rape and other sex crimes, are an oppressed group. German judges in the Weimar and Hitler eras thought that Germans were an oppressed group and that Jews were their oppressors. Stalin exterminated so-called oppressors by the million. Religious fundamentalists in the United States have as much claim to being oppressed by the derision with which their beliefs are met in influential quarters as do Jews angered by the lunatic Holocaust deniers. Do we want judges to be picking their favorite groups, pronouncing them oppressed, and giving them extra rights?

Canada's supreme court has upheld the constitutionality of an obscenity law modeled on the MacKinnon-Dworkin ordinance.[19] MacKinnon is enthusiastic about this decision (pp. 101–106), but has not examined the operation of the law. A novella by the distinguished French author Marguerite Duras was seized by Canadian customs officials because it contains scenes in which a woman is beaten.[20] And

18. 376 U.S. 254 (1964).
19. Butler v. Regina, [1992] 2 W.W.R. 577.
20. Sarah Lyall, "At Canada Border: Literature at Risk?" *New-York Times,* Dec. 13, 1993,

"it is books for gay and lesbian readers that are most often seized by the authorities."[21] A book by a distinguished woman; books, some of undoubted literary merit, for gay and lesbian readers: Canada's law is being enforced in a manner that MacKinnon if she troubled to study it would surely consider perverse.

But would that stop her? Naturally she is prepared to accept large social costs to save women from oppression. But are *American* women an oppressed class? Still? Can MacKinnon be oblivious to the changes in the status of women that have occurred in recent years? Is she in a time warp? If American women are still an oppressed class, is *pornography* responsible? Can it be, as she suggests, pornography that is responsible for "feminity" (p. 7)? If censorship is the answer to women's problems, shouldn't we censor the forms of feminity-encouraging expression that women actually watch, like television commercials in which housewives wax kitchen floors happily, or Doris Day films?

The increase in the number of working women in recent years has focused public attention on employment conditions, such as sexual harassment and lack of generous provisions for child care and maternity leave, that are disadvantageous to many female employees. That increase, both cause and effect of women's increasing emancipation from household duties, has in turn increased women's demands for sexual freedom and reproductive autonomy, and hence for secure protection against rape and for the right of abortion. Less dependent on men, better educated, better paid, more conscious of alternatives to marriage, women have become politically more assertive, more powerful. Politicians cater to them; some of them *are* influential politicians. The result has been an avalanche of laws designed to help women who want sexual freedom, reproductive autonomy, and careers. How has an oppressed class obtained so much protective legislation?

There is still abuse of individual women. Although MacKinnon's estimate that 38 percent of American women were sexually abused as children (p. 7) is probably a twofold exaggeration,[22] the lower figure is

---

p. A6. Margaret Atwood, Joyce Carol Oates, and Andrea Dworkin herself are among other woman writers whose depictions of brutal treatment of women might cause their works to be placed on the forbidden list.

21. Id.

22. *Sex and Reason* 399. Most of this is fondling rather than penetration, but it is nasty stuff and apparently can cause lasting psychological harm. Child pornography is already securely illegal; whether adult pornography plays any role in the sexual abuse of children is unknown.

still a shocker. Nevertheless her conception of American women as eternal victims, cowed, fearful, intimidated, and silenced—by pornography, yet—is clearly false, and, like many of the ideas of radical feminism, patronizing to boot. I do not know what has caused MacKinnon to become so obsessed with pornography, just as I do not know what has caused her to equate sexual intercourse with rape.[23] All I know is that her feelings on these subjects, like those of Patricia Williams on gender and race, discussed in the next chapter, have far outrun the facts.

23. "The major distinction between intercourse (normal) and rape (abnormal) is that the normal happens so often that one cannot get anyone to see anything wrong with it." MacKinnon, note 12 above, at 146. Imagine the grotesque consequences of taking MacKinnon seriously by substituting the word "rape" for the term "sexual intercourse" in every sentence in which the latter term appears.

The truth is that there are no races: there is nothing in the world that can do all we ask race to do for us.[1]

Nuance, Narrative, and Empathy in Critical Race Theory

The Alchemy of Race and Rights[2] describes its author, Patricia Williams, as a young black female law professor of contracts and commercial law whose abiding interest is the plight of the American black. Or plights, for she is particularly concerned with the lack of fit that her condition of being a black professional woman makes with the attitudes and expectations of the predominantly white community in which, as a professor in an academic field that has relatively few women, very few blacks, and therefore almost no black women, she mainly circulates. The lack of fit induces in her at times a sense of disorientation that is almost vertiginous. So it is a book about both "privileged" blacks like herself and her underprivileged coracialists at the bottom of the social totem pole.

The book offers a black feminist perspective on a variety of practices and institutions: law's pretense to objectivity and impersonality, surrogate motherhood, consumerism, constitutional protection of hate speech and condemnation of governmental efforts at affirmative action,

1. Kwame Anthony Appiah, *In My Father's House: Africa in the Philosophy of Culture* 45 (1992).
2. Patricia J. Williams, *The Alchemy of Race and Rights: Diary of a Law Professor* (1991).

the inept and insensitive behavior of well-meaning white liberal academics, and above all white racism in what she considers its hydra-headed manifestations. There is little that is new in the paraphrasable content of her criticisms. The novelty is the form, which can aptly be described as literary, in which Williams has cast her discussion of these legal and social issues. She is not unique in employing literary methods in legal scholarship; earlier and essentially isolated examples of this genre to one side, it is the methodological signature of critical race theory. But she is one of the most skillful practitioners of the genre.[3]

The subtitle of the book—"Diary of a Law Professor"—is a clue to her technique. The book is not literally a diary, although it contains some excerpts from the author's diary. But it is like a diary in presenting the author's analyses of legal and social issues in the form of reactions to her daily experiences, whether as consumer, law professor, television viewer, or daughter. The reader comes to understand that Williams's way of coping with the many stresses of her life is to write down her reactions to stressful or arresting events as soon after they occur as she can. Writing in a diary-like format is thus a form of therapy. But it also gives scope for her powerful gift for narration.

Her method is well illustrated by the chapter entitled "The Pain of Word Bondage." The title gives nothing away. The chapter opens with Williams and her friend Peter Gabel, a founder of critical legal studies, hunting for apartments in New York while preparing to teach a class on contract law together. "It turned out that Peter had handed over a $900 deposit in cash, with no lease, no exchange of keys, and no receipt, to strangers with whom he had no ties other than a few moments of pleasant conversation. He said he didn't need to sign a lease because it imposed too much formality. The handshake and the good vibes were for him indicators of trust more binding than a form contract" (p. 146). She in contrast "had friends who found me an apartment in a building they owned. In my rush to show good faith and trustworthiness, I signed a detailed, lengthily negotiated, finely printed lease firmly establishing me as the ideal arm's-length transactor." She reflects on the difference in approach between Peter Gabel and herself. Peter "appeared to be extremely self-conscious of his power potential (either real or imagistic) as white or male or lawyer authority

3. See Robin West, "Murdering the Spirit: Racism, Rights, and Commerce," 90 *Michigan Law Review* 1771, 1773 (1992).

figure. He therefore seemed to go to some lengths to overcome the wall that image might impose." For her, however, "raised to be acutely conscious of the likelihood that no matter what degree of professional I am, people will greet and dismiss my black femaleness as unreliable, untrustworthy, hostile, angry, powerless, irrational, and probably destitute," "to show that I can speak the language of lease is my way of enhancing trust of me in my business affairs" (p. 147).

We begin to understand that the difference in approach between Peter and her to the question of the apartment lease is emblematic of a difference between critical legal studies and critical race theory with respect to attitudes toward rights. A difference between friends over a personal matter mirrors a difference between friendly left-wing legal theories over a theoretical matter. Peter "would say that a lease or any other formal mechanism would introduce distrust into his relationship and he would suffer alienation, leading to the commodification of his being and the degradation of his person to property," while for her "the lack of formal relation to the other would leave me estranged" (p. 148). As a black "I have been given by this society a strong sense of myself as already too familiar, personal, subordinate to white people" (p. 147). "For blacks, then, the attainment of rights signifies the respectful behavior, the collective responsibility, properly owed by a society to one of its own" (p. 153). While thinking about this question she has been "studying something that may have been the contract of sale of my great-great-grandmother" (p. 156), and it brings home to her the fact that the black legacy in America includes a sense of always being "either owned or unowned, never the owner," the rights holder.[4]

Although this chapter is politically significant as an attempt within the Left to defend an important element of liberal jurisprudence against leftist criticism, it does not contain the most striking illustrations of Williams's narrative skills. We must go to another chapter for her remarkable description of a bizarre incident in which the Washington police arrested "one hundred parole violators who had been lured to a brunch with promises of free tickets to a Washington Redskins–Cincinnati Bengals football game" (p. 166). The television news, Williams reports,

> showed one hundred black men entering a hall dressed for a party, some in tuxedos, some with fresh shiny perms, some with flowers in their lapels,

---

4. A similar point, about women in general (irrespective of race), is made in Robin West, "Jurisprudence and Gender," 55 *University of Chicago Law Review* 1 (1988).

some clearly hungry and there for the promised food, some dressed in the outfits of anticipatory football spectators, in raccoon coats and duck-bill hats that said 'Redskins.' One hundred black men rolling up the escalators to the convention hall were greeted by smiling white (under-cover) masters of ceremony, popping flashbulbs, lots of cameras, and pretty white women in skimpy costumes. Everyone smiled and laughed, like children at a birthday party. Everyone looked as though they were about the business of having a good time together. We saw the one hundred black men being rounded up by a swarm of white men, white women (also undercover agents) dressed as cheerleaders bouncing up and down on the side, a policeman dressed as a chicken with an automatic hidden in the lining, a SWAT team dressed in guerrilla-warfare green bursting in with weapons drawn. (pp. 166–167)

At one level this is high comedy in the mode of Evelyn Waugh, Anthony Powell, or Tom Wolfe (on whom see Chapter 23). The deadpan style is highly effective, in particular the omission of a para-graph break or other transition between the arrival of the unsuspecting guests and their arrest, and the refusal to mark for the reader the most bizarre aspect of the entire episode, the policeman disguised as a chicken. But there is an undertone of pathos. Even though the one hundred black men are parole violators, criminals, we cannot help feeling that they have been cruelly tricked; perhaps we are even to read the episode as a metaphor for the plight of the black man in white America. Notice the subtle suggestiveness of describing the policemen as "*white* (undercover) *masters* of ceremony" (emphasis mine).

Another vignette is even closer to the manner of Tom Wolfe. A store near the campus of New York University sells, to "stylish coeds," "the slightly frumpy, punky, slummy clothes that go so well with bright red lipstick and ankle-high black bootlets." One day Williams notices a sign in the store window: "Sale! Two-dollar overcoats. No bums, no booze." Offended, she turns her head—and sees nearby "a black man dressed in the ancient remains of a Harris Tweed overcoat. His arms were spread-eagled as if to fly, though he was actually begging from cars in both directions. He was also drunk and crying and trying to keep his balance . . . So the sign was disenfranchising the very people who most needed two-dollar overcoats, the so-called bums" (p. 42).

The rhetorical highlight of the book, however, is the description of an episode at a Benetton clothing store. "Buzzers are big in New York City. Favored particularly by smaller stores and boutiques, merchants throughout the city have installed them as screening devices to reduce the incidence of robbery: if the face at the door looks desirable, the buzzer is pressed and the door is unlocked. If the face is that of an undesirable, the door stays locked. Predictably, the issue of undesirability has revealed itself to be a racial determination," as Williams discovers one Saturday afternoon when she

> was shopping in Soho and saw in a store window a sweater that I wanted to buy for my mother. I pressed my round brown face to the window and my finger to the buzzer, seeking admittance. A narrow-eyed, white teenager wearing running shoes and feasting on bubble gum glared out, evaluating me for signs that would pit me against the limits of his social understanding. After about five seconds, he mouthed "We're closed," and blew pink rubber at me. It was two Saturdays before Christmas, at one o'clock in the afternoon; there were several white people in the store who appeared to be shopping for things for *their* mothers. (pp. 44–45)

The power of this sketch lies in its compression, its vivid contrasting of the round brown face with the sales clerk's narrow eyes and pink bubble gum, its use of physical exclusion as a metaphor for social exclusion, its suggestion that the least significant of whites (this gum-chewing bubble-blowing teenage sales clerk) is utterly comfortable with exercising power over an older and more accomplished black, and its elegant summation of the clerk's reaction to her ("evaluating me for signs that would pit me against the limits of his social understanding"). Yet here at the very pinnacle of Williams's art the careful reader will begin to feel a sense of disquiet. Did Williams *really* press her face against the window—that is, did her face actually touch the glass? Or is she embroidering the facts for dramatic effect—making the insult to her seem even graver than it was because it shattered a childlike eagerness and innocence? Also, how does she *know* that the sales clerk refused to let her in the store because she's black? The only evidence she cites is that, since Christmas was approaching, it was unlikely that the store had closed, and that there were other shoppers in the store. The second point has no force. Stores normally stop admitting customers before all the customers already in the store have left—otherwise the store might never be able to close. The first point has greater force. Athough many stores close early on Saturday, the likelihood that a Benetton store in New York City during the Christmas shopping season would be one of them is slight. Yet Williams does not suggest that she has tried to find out whether the store was open. She does not suggest that she saw any customers admitted after she was turned away. The absence of a sign indicating that the store was closed would be some evidence that it was not, but she doesn't say anything about the presence or absence of a sign. Many stores list their hours on the front door. She makes no mention of this either. In all likelihood the store *was* open, but I am surprised that she—a lawyer—did not attempt to verify the point.

But of course the attempt might have been futile. And it is even possible, though I find no clues to this in the text, that her anger at the episode reflects in part a pervasive, debilitating uncertainty that confronts blacks in their encounters with whites. Not every disappointment that a black person encounters is a result of discrimination, and yet it may be impossible to determine which is and which is not. We like to know where we stand with other people, and this may be difficult for blacks in their dealings with whites.

Yet she had told us at the outset, in defense of doing legal scholarship in the form of story telling, "that one of the most important results of reconceptualizing from 'objective truth' to rhetorical event will be a more nuanced sense of legal and social responsibility" (p. 11). Unless "nuanced" is a euphemism for fictive, Williams has promised to get the particulars of an event or situation right, rather than submerging them in a generality, such as that whites hate blacks. That promise implies an effort to find out what *really* was going on in that white teenager's mind when he told her the store was closed. Maybe, as I said, it *was* closed; or maybe it wasn't but the clerk had his hands full with the customers inside. Maybe he was a disloyal employee who wanted to get his employer in trouble; maybe he was lazy, mischievous, rude, irresponsible, or just plain dumb.

The Alchemy of Race and Rights suppresses every perspective other than that of the suffering, oppressed black—except for that of the surrogate mother in the *Baby M* case[5] (Mary Beth Whitehead), whom Williams assimilates to an oppressed black by describing a contract of surrogate motherhood as a form of slavery. Williams does not mention Mrs. Stern, the wife of the man who made the surrogacy contract with Mrs. Whitehead, although Mrs. Stern was not only the coplaintiff in the *Baby M* case but sought to become the adoptive mother of her husband's child by Mrs. Whitehead.[6] Mrs. Stern wanted to have a child

---

5. In re Baby M, 537 A.2d 1227 (N.J. 1988).

6. Mrs. Stern was not a party to the surrogacy contract only because the Sterns were afraid

but was afraid to become pregnant because she had multiple sclerosis. So she and her husband decided to adopt a child. As an alternative to the interminable delays of conventional adoption the Sterns made a contract with Mrs. Whitehead, who already had several children, by which she agreed to be impregnated by Mr. Stern by means of artificial insemination and to give up the baby to the Sterns when it was born, in exchange for $10,000. There is a huge literature debating the pros and cons of surrogate motherhood, but both sides recognize that the wife of the father of the child is an interested party whose preferences should be given *some* weight. In Williams's rendition it is as if Mr. Stern, lacking either wife or girlfriend, decided (weirdly) to buy a child from Mrs. Whitehead. Mrs. Stern is made invisible.

This is a pattern. In discussing the case of Bernhard Goetz, who shot four black youths in a subway car and was acquitted of all but an illegal weapons charge even though he could not have been acting in *reasonable* self-defense, Williams disparages white fear of black crime by characterizing the criminal records of Goetz's victims as mere "allegations" (p. 77), by asking rhetorically how the community would have reacted to Goetz's action if he had been black and his victims white *and the crime had occurred in a department store rather than in the subway*—an added fictive touch that magnifies the malignant irrationality of Goetz's action—and by reciting irrelevant statistics showing that whites commit more crimes than blacks. What is omitted is that the prison population is almost half black,[7] although blacks are only 12 percent of the population, and that urban street (and subway) crime is committed mostly by blacks. Black criminality is a serious social problem. To pretend

---

that if she were made a party the contract might violate the state's law against the sale of babies. 537 A.2d at 1235. (The legal mind at work: Mr. Stern is not a baby buyer because he is the "natural" father; his wife would be because she is not the "natural" mother. Neither Williams nor Minow registers an objection to this "privileging" of biological relationships.) The contract did provide that in the event of Mr. Stern's dying, Mrs. Stern would have sole custody of the child.

7. Forty-seven percent in 1990. Computed from Louis W. Jankowski, *Correctional Populations in the United States, 1990* 83 (U.S. Dept. of Justice, Bureau of Justice Statistics, NCJ-134946, July 1992) (tab. 5.6). The white percentage that year was 48 percent. If imprisonment rates are taken to be adequate proxies for crime rates, these figures imply a black crime rate more than seven times the white crime rate. (The black male homicide rate is 7.7 times the white male homicide rate. U.S. Bureau of the Census, *Statistical Abstract of the United States 1993* 195 [113th ed.] [ser. 305].) Since most crime is intraracial, the disparity in crime rates implies that much "exploitation" of blacks is by other blacks. Over this delicate subject Williams draws a veil.

otherwise is an evasion.[8] AIDS, drug addiction, homophobia, neglect of children, anti-Semitism, and poor political leadership are other problems of the black community that Williams ignores.[9]

In a lengthy discussion of the Tawana Brawley episode, Williams manages to avoid mentioning that the charge that Brawley had been brutalized by white racists was fraudulent. It is an evasion to say that Brawley had been "the victim of an unspeakable crime . . . No matter who did it to her—and even if she did it to herself" (pp. 169–170). If she did it to herself, it was not a crime, at least not a crime against her. Williams's treatment of the episode further illustrates her blurring of the line between fiction and truth, to use a still serviceable though philosophically challenged distinction. "Tawana's terrible story has every black woman's worst fears and experiences wrapped into it. Few will believe a black woman who has been raped by a white man" (p. 174). Williams seems not to care whether the "terrible story" is true or not. This indifference suggests an unintended irony in one admirer's praise of Williams's work: "I believe Williams' stories the way I believe a good piece of literature."[10]

A white student at Stanford, unbelieving when a black student told him that Beethoven was a mulatto, put up a poster of Beethoven with his face blackened and his features Negrified. Williams is disturbed at the white student's incredulity that a genius could have a black ancestor. Of course the student may simply have been incredulous that *Beethoven* had a black ancestor, just as I would be incredulous to discover that my cat was Siamese, though I know that some cats are. The student may not have been a racist in any illuminating sense, although the defacing of the poster was, at the least, insensitive. What I find particularly striking in Williams's treatment of the episode is her uncritical assumption that Beethoven was in fact black. To begin with, it could not be a *fact;* it could only be a classificatory judgment. Beethoven passed as white; his parents and (and as we shall see) all his other known

8. For a work by a black legal scholar (not a conservative one, either) that does *not* pretend otherwise, see Regina Austin, "'The Black Community,' Its Lawbreakers, and a Politics of Identification," 65 *Southern California Law Review* 1769 (1992).

9. Of course to mention these problems is in some quarters to invite accusations of "libeling the Black poor" and "libeling the Black middle class." Robin D. Barnes, "Politics and Passion: Theoretically a Dangerous Liaison," 101 *Yale Law Journal* 1631, 1645–1646 (1992).

10. Kathryn Abrams, "Hearing the Call of Stories," 79 *California Law Review* 971, 1003 (1991).

ancestors were white; the idea that a person who is one-eighth or one-sixteenth or one-thirty-second or one-sixty-fourth black is in some interesting sense a member of the black race is sufficiently nonobvious to require examination. Williams misses the irony that what made it easy for the white student to Negrify the poster of Beethoven is that Beethoven was—white.

Was Beethoven a mulatto? Williams points us to no evidence that he was.[11] The standard biography of Beethoven carries his ancestry back to 1500, more than two and a half centuries before the composer's birth, and there is no reference to any blacks or other non-Europeans in the family tree.[12] Beethoven had a dark complexion and bristly hair, remarked by a number of his contemporaries and evident in some of the portraits; and there is an anecdote, not very well substantiated, that because of his appearance he was called "the Moor."[13] This proves nothing; nor the statement by the German anthropologist Friedrich Hertz that "one may easily trace in Beethoven slightly Negroid features."[14] Hertz was writing against Houston Stewart Chamberlain, who believed that there was a German racial type characterized by golden hair, blue eyes (*Himmelsaugen*—"Heaven's eyes"), and an elongated head, and that genius, including musical genius, is a function of race. Hertz pointed out that a number of German geniuses, including Goethe and Beethoven, were short and dark and had round heads, and in fact belonged to the "Alpine" racial type rather than the "Nordic," the latter being Chamberlain's idea of the Germanic. It was in this context that Hertz referred to Beethhoven's "slightly Negroid" features. He did not suggest that Beethoven *was* a Negro or had any Negro blood. He was merely underscoring Beethoven's remoteness from the Nordic type.

The "Moor" anecdote, the Hertz quotation, and similar rags and

11. She cites documents concerning the incident itself, including the university's "Final Report on Recent Incidents at Ujamaa House," *Campus Report,* Jan. 18, 1989, p. 15, but they do not attempt to substantiate the proposition that Beethoven was a mulatto; like her they take it for granted.

12. *Thayer's Life of Beethoven* 44 (Elliot Forbes rev. ed. 1967). The most complete scholarly study that I have found of black achievements lists the famous "whites" who had a black ancestor, such as Alexander Pushkin, but does not mention Beethoven, although his life falls within the period covered by the book and although the book appears to resolve all close questions in favor of classification as black. Ellen Irene Diggs, *Black Chronology: From 4000 B.C. to the Abolition of the Slave Trade* (1983).

13. *Thayer's Life of Beethoven,* note 12 above, at 72, 134, 646.

14. Hertz, *Race and Civilization* 123 (1928).

patches are assembled in J. A. Rogers's book *Sex and Race* in support of the remarkable proposition that "there is not a single shred of evidence to support the belief that he [Beethoven] was a white man."[15] Although Rogers's book is replete with interesting information, some of it documented, the book as a whole, which was printed privately and exhibits unmistakable signs of being the work of a crank, is uncritical and unreliable, and the evidence that Rogers marshals in support of his thesis about Beethoven's race is completely unpersuasive. In the most thorough examination of the issue that I have found, a black scholar has concluded that there is no factual basis for the claim that Beethoven was black.[16]

I anticipate the objection that it doesn't matter whether Beethoven was a mulatto or not and that only a racist—someone incredulous that a genius, and one so central to the cultural tradition of Europe, could be black—would doubt Williams's claim sufficiently to investigate the question. I agree that whites should not be distressed at the thought that Beethoven had a black ancestor. But it is legitimate to be concerned when a scholar is careless about facts.[17] Pragmatists may be dubious about truth with a capital T, but they respect those lowercase truths that we call facts.[18] Granted that issues of racial identity are ultimately issues of classification rather than of fact, the assertion that Beethoven was black or mulatto conveys an impression wildly at variance with the known facts about his ancestry. Williams ought either to be scrupulous about the facts or to acknowledge that she is writing fiction.

Earlier I mentioned black anti-Semitism. It seems that American blacks are on average (always an important qualification) more anti-Se-

---

15. Rogers, *Sex and Race*, vol. 3: *Why White and Black Mix in Spite of Opposition* 306 (1944).

16. "The Beethoven family appeared before 1500 and, continuing to 1917, was populated totally by the Flemish—no Spanish, no Belgians, no Dutch, no Africans." Dominique-René de Lerma, "Beethoven as a Black Composer," 10 *Black Music Research Journal* 118, 120 (1990).

17. As emphasized in Daniel A. Farber and Suzanna Sherry, "Telling Stories out of School: An Essay on Legal Narratives," 45 *Stanford Law Review* 807, 832–835 (1993), a critical survey of the "narratology" movement in contemporary legal scholarship.

18. As a leading pragmatist has remarked about Holocaust denial, "when it happens that the present shape of truth is compelling beyond a reasonable doubt, it is our moral obligation to act on it and not defer action in the name of an interpretative future that may never arrive." Stanley Fish, "There's No Such Thing as Free Speech, and It's a Good Thing, Too," in Fish, *There's No Such Thing as Free Speech* 102, 113 (1994).

mitic than whites and that the gap is widening.[19] The appearance may be misleading. It has been suggested that anti-Semitic blacks are anti-Semitic not because they have a special dislike of Jews but because they dislike whites, and virtually all Jews are white, so they dislike Jews; thus black anti-Semitism is growing simply because black dislike of whites is growing.[20] Still, whatever its significance, black anti-Semitism is an issue, and one that casts a shadow over still another shopping vignette in *The Alchemy of Race and Rights*. It is nearly closing time at an Au Coton store. This time Williams is not kept out. The staff is joking—about Jews. "'Speak of the devil,' said one of them as four other young people came into the store" (p. 126). Williams is perceived as "safe" by the staff and they let her overhear their anti-Semitic badinage. Although she strongly disapproves of anti-Semitism—had in fact, she tells us, had a quarrel with a friend who had made a mild anti-Semitic crack—she cannot completely repress the thrill of being an insider, complicit with the staff in its covert mocking of the Jews. Reflecting on the incident, she feels humiliated by it and concludes that "the hard work of a nonracist sensibility is the boundary crossing . . . the willingness to spoil a good party and break an encompassing circle, to travel from the safe to the unsafe" (p. 129).

She does not reveal the race of the sales clerks. Mark Tushnet charges that by this omission Williams avoids "engag[ing] in a sustained examination of antisemitism in the African-American community."[21] Had she identified the clerks' race she would have had to confront the sort of difficult question she regularly ducks. If the clerks were black, the issue is black anti-Semitism, itself emblematic of the pathologies, none of which she discusses, of black America. If they were white, the issue is reconciling the willingness of whites to treat a black as one of themselves in opposition to other whites with Williams's unrelievedly bleak view of American race relations.

Mention of black anti-Semitism brings me back to the question of Beethoven's color. That Beethoven was black is a typical and recurrent claim of the Afrocentrist movement, members of which have also

19. Gregory Martire and Ruth Clark, *Anti-Semitism in the United States: A Study of Prejudice in the 1980s* 42 (1982) (tab. 4.5); Jonathan Kaufman, *Broken Alliance: The Turbulent Times between Blacks and Jews in America* 273–274 (1988).

20. Ronald T. Tsukashima, *The Social and Psychological Correlates of Black Anti-Semitism*, ch. 10 (1978).

21. Tushnet, "The Degradation of Constitutional Discourse," 81 *Georgetown Law Journal* 251, 269 (1992).

asserted that melanin is positively correlated with intelligence, that the ancient Greeks stole philosophy from black Egyptians and, specifically, that Alexander the Great pillaged the library at Alexandria to steal Egyptian philosophical ideas for his old tutor, Aristotle (never mind that Alexander *founded* Alexandria and that the library was built long after his death), that Napoleon shot off the sphinx's nose so that no one would know that the sphinx had Negroid features, that not only Beethoven but also Haydn,[22] Cleopatra,[23] and Lincoln were black, that Beethoven's blackness is shown by (among other things) his confidence in his abilities, a confidence similar to that of Mohammed Ali,[24] that Dwight Eisenhower's mother was black, that America was first discovered by Africans, that AIDS was invented by whites to exterminate the black race, that the telephone and carbon steel were invented in Africa along with science, medicine, and mathematics, that "the [African] Blacks' conception of God was on a scale too grand to be acceptable to Western minds"[25]—and that Jews controlled the African slave trade and today are plotting with the Mafia the financial destruction of the black race.[26] Not all Afrocentrists are anti-Semitic; but irresponsible

22. This is one of Rogers's claims. Rogers, note 15 above, at 306–307. Its basis is that Haydn, like Beethoven, had a dark complexion.

23. Who was Greek, not Egyptian.

24. The "Mohammed Ali" referred to is of course the fighter, not the nineteenth-century Egyptian ruler Mohamed Ali, who was an Albanian.

25. Chancellor Williams, *The Destruction of Black Civilization: Great Issues of a Race from 4500 B.C. to 2000 A.D.* 246 (rev. ed. 1976).

26. On the claims of Afrocentrism, see, for example, Arthur M. Schlesinger, Jr., *The Disuniting of America: Reflections on a Multicultural Society* 64, 67–71, 79 (1991); Molefi Kete Asante, *Kemet, Afrocentricity and Knowledge* (1990); Rogers, note 15 above; Williams, note 25 above; Jerry Adler, "African Dreams," *Newsweek*, Sept. 23, 1991, p. 42; Alvin P. Sanoff, "Sorting out the African Legacy," *U.S. News & World Report*, March 16, 1992, p. 63; Edward Lucas, "Black Academic Blames Jews for His People's Ills," *The Independent*, Aug. 8, 1991, p. 6; Frank Phillips, "Wilkerson Says History Was Bleached," *Boston Globe*, Dec. 24, 1992, p. 16; Godfrey Hodgson, "The Smelting Nation," *The Independent*, Jan. 11, 1993, p. 23. The best substantiated of Afrocentrist claims are that the Western debt to ancient Egyptian thought has been underestimated and that many ancient Egyptians were black. See Martin Bernal, *Black Athena: The Afroasiatic Roots of Classical Civilization*, vol. 1: *The Fabrication of Ancient Greece 1785–1985* (1987). The second claim, however (see id. at 240–246; also pp. 248–262 of vol. 2 of *Black Athena, The Archaeological and Documentary Evidence* [1991], and Cheikh Anta Diop, *The African Origin of Civilization: Myth or Reality* [1974]), appears to be doubtful—see references in Schlesinger, above, at 76–78—although there certainly was intermarriage between blacks and Egyptians, as between blacks and Greeks and blacks and Romans. See Frank M. Snowden, Jr., *Blacks in Antiquity: Ethiopians in the Greco-Roman Experience* (1970). It should go without saying that much writing by blacks about the history of Africa and its people is sober historiography and is free from the

claims appear to be the hallmark of the movement, and I should have thought that Williams, as a lawyer and an academic, would have wanted to place as much distance as possible between herself and it rather than to embrace uncritically one of its representative wild claims.

Could it be—despite Martha Nussbaum's argument that imaginative literature in general and the novel in particular renders social reality with a degree of balance, nuance, and concreteness that provides a needed antidote to the partial visions furnished by abstract, generalizing social-scientific approaches, such as that of economics—that one-sidedness is an endemic risk of the literary depiction of reality, rather than a particular characteristic of Patricia Williams?[27] The belief that literature is edifying per se is akin to the belief, examined in Chapter 24, that rhetoric is edifying per se, making "evil rhetoric" an oxymoron. Unless one follows Tolstoy in building moral uplift into the very definition of great literature, one has to admit that much great literature is racist, misogynistic, anti-Semitic, sadistic, snobbish, homophobic, or anti-democratic. For that matter, much of it is not nuanced, particularistic, or judiciously balanced. Some of it is rule-bound, formalistic, abstract, symbolic, allegorical—one thinks for example of Kafka's great story "In the Penal Colony," which contains no proper names. Aristotle emphasized the typicality of literature—its striving to render the probable rather than the actual—in comparison to history, which in his view was the discipline that insisted on getting the gritty particulars right. In Chapter 23 we shall see that E. M. Forster's great novel *Howards End* is one-sided; Forster's imaginative resources were insufficient to render the commercial class, represented by Henry Wilcox and his son, from the inside. *Hard Times* is also one-sided, Dickens being incapable of an empathetic rendition of a utilitarian or economic outlook. Henry James could not "do" Jews, or Shakespeare members of the working class. Patricia Williams is not in bad company. But a writer who cannot see the problems of race relations in their full complexity because she cannot grasp the point of view of whites, although she has no difficulty reinterpreting *Pierson v. Post* from the perspective of the fox (p. 156),[28] is unlikely to be able to solve those problems.

---

irresponsible claims that I have been discussing. See, for example, Joseph H. Harris, *Africans and Their History* (rev. ed. 1987).

27. Martha C. Nussbaum, *Love's Knowledge: Essays on Philosophy and Literature* (1990).

28. Pierson v. Post, 3 Caines 175 (N.Y. Sup. Ct. 1805), held that to obtain a property right in a wild animal, such as a fox, you must reduce it to possession, as by killing it.

We accept one-sidedness in literature, moreover, because we make allowance for *autres temps, autres moeurs* and because factual accuracy and scholarly detachment are not rules of the literature game. But they are rules of the scholarly game, and Williams is writing as a scholar. If my criticisms of her in this chapter should turn out to be one-sided, misleading, and tendentious, she would not be impressed by my rejoining that mine is only one voice in an ongoing conversation and I can leave it to others to rectify any omissions or imbalance in my contribution.

If one-sidedness is the other side of literature's empathetic concreteness, empathetic awareness of strangers' pains and pleasures is the unexpected other side of the economist's Gradgrindian detachment. Consider rent control. The beneficiaries are plain to see: they are the tenants when the rent-control law is adopted. The victims are invisible: they are the future would-be tenants, who will face a restricted supply of rental housing because landowners will have a diminished incentive to build rental housing and owners of existing apartment buildings will prefer to sell rather than to rent the apartments in them. Economics brings these victims before the analyst's eye;[29] literature, and the type of legal scholarship that imitates literature, does not.

Maybe economic scholarship is not *really* empathetic. The economist does not enter imaginatively into the distress of the disappointed quester for rental housing; all he does is tote up some additional costs. But that may be a sounder way of doing policy than by cultivating empathy. A jurisprudence of empathy can foster short-sighted substantive justice because the power to enter imaginatively into another person's outlook, emotions, and experiences diminishes with physical, social, and temporal distance.[30] A more basic point is that the internal perspective—the putting oneself in the other person's shoes—that is achieved by the exercise of empathetic imagination lacks normative significance. Compare the maxims *tout comprendre c'est tout pardonner*

---

29. For a sample of the extensive economic literature on the (often hidden) costs of rent control, see Edgar O. Olsen, "An Econometric Analysis of Rent Control," 80 *Journal of Political Economy* 1081 (1972); Peter Linneman, "The Effect of Rent Control on the Distribution of Income among New York City Renters," 22 *Journal of Urban Economics* 14 (1987); Michael P. Murray et al., "Analyzing Rent Control: The Case of Los Angeles," 29 *Economic Inquiry* 601 (1991); Choon-Geol Moon and Janet G. Stotsky, "The Effect of Rent Control on Housing Quality Change: A Longitudinal Analysis," 101 *Journal of Political Economy* 1114 (1993).

30. *The Problems of Jurisprudence* 412–413.

and no man is a villain in his own eyes (an actor's adage). The second maxim should remind us that when we succeed in looking at the world through another's eyes, we lose the perspective necessary for judgment. We find ourselves in a stew of rationalization, warped perception, and overmastering emotion. (Any lawyer knows the risk of overidentification with his client.) The *tout comprendre* maxim expresses a different point: To understand another person completely is to understand the causality of his behavior, to see that behavior as the end of a chain of causes and thus as determined rather than responsible. It is to understand the person as completely as a scientist understands an animal, which is to say as a phenomenon of nature rather than as a free agent. If we understand a criminal's behavior as well as we understand a rattlesnake's behavior, we are unlikely to accord him much dignity and respect.

The project of empathetic jurisprudence invites us to choose between achieving a warped internal perspective and an inhumanly clinical detachment: between becoming too hot and too cold. The affective dimension of empathy leads to identification with the person whose fate or welfare is at stake; the intellectual dimension leads to embedding the person in a web of causes that transforms him from a free human being into (in Nietzsche's phrase) an irresponsible piece of fate. I take back nothing I said in discussing the German judges in Chapter 4 about the importance of remembering that other human beings are—human. That does not require us to be able to crawl into their minds. Indeed, a lively awareness that other people are in an important sense closed to us—that they have their own plans and perspectives, into which we can enter imperfectly if at all—is one of the planks of the liberal platform. It is a presupposition of individuality.

Another problem with Williams's method is a lack of clarity. Here is the ending of the chapter in which Williams stands up for rights against the critical legal studies movement: "Give [rights] to trees. Give them to cows. Give them to history. Give them to rivers and rocks. Give to all of society's objects and untouchables the rights of privacy, integrity, and self-assertion; give them distance and respect" (p. 165). What does it *mean* to give rights to history, or to entitle cows to privacy, integrity, and self-assertion? Is the reference to cows meant to put us in mind of Hindu doctrine regarding the sacredness of animals? Is Williams an animist, a "Green"? Is she the second coming of Walt Whitman? (More likely Carl Sandburg.) How can all this be squared with her being a fashion-conscious shopper?

What is a reader to make of the statement that "affirmative action is an affirmation; the affirmative act of hiring—or hearing—blacks is a recognition of individuality that includes blacks as a social presence" (p. 121)? Hiring a black applicant for a job could no doubt be thought an "affirmative" act compared to not hiring him, but that is not the normal sense in which the word is used in the expression "affirmative action." Affirmative action in the context of American race relations means, at a minimum, making special efforts to find jobs for blacks and at the most setting aside jobs for them for which whites are not permitted to compete. Williams does not make clear where on this spectrum she wants society to be or whether she wants it to be somewhere else entirely, as perhaps implied by the suggestion that simply hiring a black might count as affirmative action. I think she wants to be both on and off the spectrum, just as gay and lesbian advocates want homosexual orientation to be both an innate characteristic and not an innate characteristic. This is suggested by the distinction she draws on the same page between "programs like affirmative action" and "affirmative action as a socially and professionally pervasive concept" and by her endorsement of both.

Affirmative action in the common form in which it involves outright discrimination against whites invites just the sort of empathetic, nuanced attention that Williams tells us is promoted by her method of doing legal scholarship. Often it transfers wealth or opportunity from people who have not engaged in or benefited from discrimination to blacks who have not been much harmed by discrimination, and it tends to benefit the already most advantaged blacks at the expense of the least advantaged whites. As a result it may make little contribution even to equality of results and none to equality of opportunity. Consider affirmative action in college admissions. The black who gains admission through the relaxation of the normal admissions standard will not of course bounce the strongest white applicant; he will bounce a marginal applicant—in fact, an applicant much like himself, except for the difference in race.

Critical race theory proclaims "narratology" its distinctive contribution to the methods of legal scholarship. Narrative has two aspects, corresponding to Aristotle's contrast between history and literature.

Narrative in the sense of the telling of a story is the way we make sense of a sequence of events unfolding in history.[31] Black scholars like it because they believe that the current condition of the American black population cannot be understood without reference to the history of Negro slavery. But despite Williams's references to her great-great-grandmother, a slave, her book does not employ historical narration.

Narration is also a literary technique. To present an issue, such as the clash between critical legal studies and critical race theory, in the form of a story, such as the tale of Williams's and Gabel's experiences with signing a lease, is to reinforce or replace abstract argument with a portrait. Portraits, including the verbal portraits that we call literature—works that depict rather than overtly argue—can change minds. This role of verbal portraiture, as also of photographs, is especially valuable in situations in which we have difficulty *seeing* important aspects of a problem because it involves people whose experiences are remote from ours. In education and occupation Patricia Williams is like other establishment legal figures, but in race and all that that connotes in this country (at least when the race is black) she is not, and maybe one has to learn to see the world through her eyes as well as one's own before one can fully evaluate the arguments pro and con various racial policies. On this view the very one-sidedness of her presentation, however questionable by the conventional standards of scholarship and even by the professed standards of critical race theory (which promised us, remember, nuance), has value in providing insight into the psychology and rhetoric of many blacks. But if whites must acquire a stereoscopic biracial perspective in order to cope effectively with our society's racial problems, blacks must too.

31. Arthur C. Danto, *Narration and Knowledge* (1985), esp. ch. 15.

PART FIVE

Philosophical and Economic Perspectives

The great weakness of Pragmatism is that it ends by being of no use to anybody.[1]

chapter 19

So What *Has* Pragmatism to Offer Law?

I HAVE made pragmatic criticisms of legal thinkers while at the same time criticizing self-declared pragmatic legal thinkers, such as Horwitz and Minow, and denigrating legal realism—the manifestation of pragmatism in law. It is time that I said more about pragmatism and its relation to legal realism and to other currents of legal thought. Is it, after all, a useful term? Does it denote anything? Can we speak of a "new" pragmatism? What concretely has pragmatism to offer law? What is its place in philosophical and legal history?

Pragmatism and Law: A Brief History

In a nutshell: The pragmatic movement gave legal realism such intellectual shape and content as it had. Then pragmatism died (or merged into other philosophical movements and lost its separate identity), and legal realism died[2] (or was similarly absorbed and transcended). Lately pragmatism has revived, making one wonder whether a new jurispru-

1. T. S. Eliot, "Francis Herbert Bradley," in *Selected Prose of T. S. Eliot* 196, 204 (Frank Kermode ed. 1975).
2. Its death is beautifully described in Neil Duxbury, "The Reinvention of American Legal Realism," 12 *Legal Studies: Journal of the Society of Public Teachers of Law* 137 (1992).

dence is on the horizon that will bear the same relation to the new pragmatism as legal realism bore to the old. My answer is "no" on both counts. The new pragmatism, like the old, is not a distinct philosophical movement but an umbrella term for diverse tendencies in philosophical thought. What is more, it is a term for the same tendencies; the new pragmatism is not new. Some of the tendencies that go to make up the pragmatic tradition were fruitfully absorbed into legal realism, primarily through the writings of Holmes and Cardozo; others led, and still lead, nowhere. The tendencies that many years ago were fruitfully absorbed into legal realism can indeed help in the fashioning of a new approach to law, but it will be new largely in jettisoning the naive politics and other immaturities and excesses of legal realism. This refurbished, modernized realism will owe little or nothing, however, to the new pragmatism—if indeed there is such a thing, as I doubt.

Histories of pragmatism usually begin with Charles Sanders Peirce, although he himself, not without grounds, gave credit for the idea to a lawyer friend, Nicholas St. John Green,[3] and anticipations can be found much earlier—in Epicurus, for example.[4] From Peirce the baton is (in conventional accounts) handed to William James, then to John Dewey, George Mead, and (in England) F. S. C. Schiller. Parallel to and influenced by the pragmatists, legal realism comes on the scene, inspired by the work of Oliver Wendell Holmes, John Chipman Gray, and Benjamin Cardozo and realized in the work of Jerome Frank, William Douglas, Karl Llewellyn, Felix Cohen, Fred Rodell, Max Radin, Robert Hale, Fleming James, William Green, and others, most of them law professors at Yale or Columbia. Pragmatism and legal realism join in Dewey's essays on law.[5] But by the end of World War II both philosophical pragmatism and legal realism have expired (though traces of realism can be found as late as the 1970s in the work of Grant Gilmore and Arthur Leff): the first superseded by logical positivism and other "hard" analytic philosophy; the other absorbed into the legal mainstream and particularly into the legal-process school (see Chapter 1) that reaches its apogee in 1958 with Hart and Sacks's *The Legal Process*. Then, with the waning of logical positivism, pragma-

3. See Philip P. Wiener, *Evolution and the Founders of Pragmatism*, ch. 7 (1949).

4. Martha C. Nussbaum, "Therapeutic Arguments: Epicurus and Aristotle," in *The Norms of Nature: Studies in Hellenistic Ethics* 31 (Malcolm Schofield and Gisela Striker eds. 1986); see also id. at 41, 71–72.

5. Notably "Logical Method and Law," 10 *Cornell Law Quarterly* 17 (1924).

tism comes charging back in the person of Richard Rorty (and not only him, but also Richard Bernstein and Stanley Fish and Richard Poirier and many others), followed by critical legal studies—the radical son of legal realism—and later by more pragmatists (for example, Cornel West) and by a school of legal neopragmatists that includes William Eskridge, Daniel Farber, Philip Frickey, Thomas Grey, Frank Michelman, Martha Minow, Margaret Jane Radin, Cass Sunstein, and others. The others include myself, and perhaps also, as suggested by Rorty (see the Introduction), Ronald Dworkin—despite Dworkin's overt hostility to pragmatism—and even Roberto Unger. We have now been joined by Morton Horwitz (Chapter 11). The ideological diversity of this group is noteworthy.

In the account that I am reciting (not endorsing), pragmatism, whether of the paleo or neo varieties, stands for a progressively more emphatic rejection of Enlightenment dualisms such as subject and object, mind and body, perception and reality, form and substance; these dualisms being regarded as the props of a conservative social, political, and legal order. The triumphs of science, particularly Newtonian physics, in the seventeenth and eighteenth centuries persuaded most thinking people that the physical universe had a uniform structure accessible to human reason. It occurred to some that human nature and human social systems might have a similarly mechanical structure. The scientific outlook cast humankind in an observing mold. Through perception, measurement, and mathematics, the human mind would uncover the secrets of nature (including those of the mind itself, a part of nature) and the laws (natural, not legal) of social interaction—including laws decreeing balanced government, economic behavior in accordance with the principles of supply and demand, and moral and legal norms based on immutable principles of psychology and human behavior. The mind was a camera, recording activities both natural and social and alike determined by natural laws, and an adding machine.

Romantic poets and philosophers challenged this view, broadly scientific but flavored with a Platonic sense of a world of immutable order behind the chaos of sense impressions, emphasizing instead the plasticity of the world and the esemplastic power of the human imagination. "The Eye altering alters all," said William Blake in "The Mental Traveller." Institutional constraints the Romantics despised along with all other limits on human aspiration, as merely contingent. Even science they found dreary, as they strove for that sense of unlimited potential and of oneness with humankind, and indeed with the entire universe, that an infant feels. They were Platonists. "Be thou me, impetuous one!"—thus Shelley, addressing the autumn west wind. Even Keats's "Ode on a Grecian Urn," which begins in the celebration of art's permanence, soon becomes encumbered with images of thwarted desire, desolation, coldness, and loss.

The principal American representative of this school was Emerson, and he left traces of his thought on Peirce and Holmes alike. Emerson's European counterpart (and admirer) was Nietzsche. None of these was a "Romantic" in a precise sense, if there is such a sense. But like the Romantics they wanted to recast a passive, contemplative relation between an observing subject and an objective reality, whether natural or social, as an active, creative relation between striving human beings and the problems that beset them and that they seek to overcome. These thinkers deemed thought an exertion of will instrumental to some human desire (and we see here the link between pragmatism and utilitarianism). Social institutions—whether science, law, or religion—were the product of shifting human desires rather than of a reality external to those desires. Human beings had not only eyes but also hands.

This discussion can help us see why Truth has been a problematic concept for many pragmatists. The essential meaning of the word is observer independence, which the pragmatist is inclined to question or even deny. It is no surprise, therefore, that the pragmatists' stabs at defining truth—truth is what is fated to be believed, or what is good to believe, or what survives in the competition among ideas, or what the relevant community agrees on—are riven by paradox. The pragmatist's real interest is not in truth at all, but in the social grounds of belief ("warranted assertibility"). This change in direction does not necessarily make the pragmatist unfriendly to science (there is a deep division within pragmatism over what attitude to take toward science),[6] but it shifts the emphasis in thinking about science from the discovery of nature's eternal laws to the formulation of theories motivated by the desire of human beings to predict and control their natural and social

6. See Isaac Levi, "Escape From Boredom: Edification According to Rorty," 11 *Canadian Journal of Philosophy* 589 (1981); Paul Kurtz, *The New Skepticism: Inquiry and Reliable Knowledge* 66–72 (1992). The proscientific vein in pragmatism is well illustrated by Sidney Hook, "Scientific Knowledge and Philosophical 'Knowledge,'" in Hook, *The Quest for Being, and Other Studies in Naturalism and Humanism* 209 (1963).

environment. The implication, later made explicit by Thomas Kuhn, is that scientific theories are a function of human need and desire rather than of the way things are in nature, so that the succession of theories on a given topic need not bring us closer to "ultimate reality" (which is not to deny that scientific *knowledge* may be growing steadily, especially knowledge of how to do things, as distinct from abstract knowledge). But this is to get ahead of the story, because I want to pause in 1921 and examine the formulation of legal pragmatism that Benjamin Cardozo offered in his book published that year, *The Nature of the Judicial Process:* a clear and concise manifesto of legal pragmatism.

"The final cause of law," writes Cardozo, "is the welfare of society."[7] So much for the formalist idea, whose scientistic provenance and pretensions are evident, of law as a body of immutable principles. A straw man, this formalist? Hardly. How many modern liberals would describe racial or sexual equality as merely an expedient principle? How many originalists would describe originalism as merely an expedient principle?

Cardozo does not mean that judges "are free to substitute their own ideas of reason and justice for those of the men and women whom they serve. Their standard must be an objective one"—but objective in a pragmatic sense, which is not the sense of correspondence with an external reality. "In such matters, the thing that counts is not what I believe to be right. It is what I may reasonably believe that some other man of normal intellect and conscience might reasonably look upon as right" (pp. 88–89).

Legal rules should be viewed in instrumental terms. "Few rules in our time are so well established that they may not be called upon any day to justify their existence as means adapted to an end" (p. 98). The instrumental concept of law breaks with Aristotle's influential theory of corrective justice. The function of law as corrective justice is to restore an equilibrium, while in Cardozo's account "not the origin, but the goal, is the main thing. There can be no wisdom in the choice of a path unless we know where it will lead . . . The rule that functions well produces a title deed to recognition . . . The final principle of selection for judges . . . is one of fitness to an end" (pp. 102–103). The "title deed" sentence rebukes formalists who believe that for a law to be valid it must be shown to derive from an authoritative source.

Although the focus of *The Nature of the Judicial Process* is on the

7. Benjamin N. Cardozo, *The Nature of the Judicial Process* 66 (1921).

common law, Cardozo did not think the creative powers of the judicial imagination bound to wither when confronted by the challenge of textual interpretation. John Marshall "gave to the constitution of the United States the impress of his own mind; and the form of our constitutional law is what it is, because he moulded it while it was still plastic and malleable in the fire of his own intense convictions" (pp. 169–170).[8] An essay by the legal realist Max Radin clarifies and in so doing emphasizes the parity of statutes and the common law.[9] Judges are not to revise a statute, as they are free to do with a common law doctrine. But interpretation is a creative rather than a contemplative task—indeed, judges have as much freedom in deciding difficult statutory (and of course constitutional) cases as they have in deciding difficult common law cases.[10]

Yet despite realist effort to refocus legal scholarship from the common law to the emergent world of statute law, legislation proved a challenge to which the realist tradition, from Holmes to the petering out of legal realism in the 1940s and its supersession by the legal process school in the 1950s, was unable to rise. The trouble started with Holmes's well-known characterization of the judge as an interstitial legislator, which Cardozo echoes in *The Nature of the Judicial Process*. The characterization is useful in pointing to the legislative function of judges, but misleading in implying that judges and legislators are officials of the same stripe and merely different scope—guided and controlled by the same goals, values, incentives, and constraints. Were this true, the judicial role in regard to statutes would be greatly simplified; it would be primarily a matter of lending a helping hand to the legislature by filling in the unavoidable gaps in the legislature's

8. Holmes, we recall from the Introduction, had a more nuanced view of John Marshall's achievement.

9. "Statutory Interpretation," 43 *Harvard Law Review* 863 (1930); see also his later piece, "A Short Way with Statutes," 56 *Harvard Law Review* 388 (1942). Radin's views were strongly attacked in James M. Landis, "A Note on 'Statutory Interpretation,'" 43 *Harvard Law Review* 886 (1930). The attack, by one of the founders of the "legal process" school, amounts to saying that there are easy statutory cases as well as difficult ones—easy in the sense that the statute's meaning is clear on its face or can be clarified with judicious resort to legislative history. This is a reasonable qualification of Radin's skeptical approach.

10. "The 'plain meaning' of the statute offers us a large choice between a maximum and a minimum of extension. The 'intent of the legislature' is a futile bit of fiction. The 'purpose' requires a selection of one of many purposes. The 'consequences' involve prophecy for which the courts are not particularly prepared, and in which, by any calculus of probabilities, several choices of results are open." Radin, "Statutory Interpretation," note 9 above, at 881.

product. It is not true. The legislative process is buffeted by interest-group pressures to a greater extent than the judicial process is, and for this and other reasons statute law is much less informed by sound policy judgments than the realists in the heyday of the New Deal believed. It is no longer possible to imagine the good pragmatist judge as the happy partner of the legislature in the forging of sound public policy. The judge who acts on his conception of sound policy is apt to be working at cross-purposes with the legislature, just as in the old days when judges took the position that statutes "in derogation of the common law" should be narrowly construed. Fidelism to legislative purpose has become the hallmark of modern formalism—judges are to be faithful agents *despite* the perversity of the statutes they interpret.

A related shortcoming of legal realism was its naive enthusiasm for government, an enthusiasm that marked legal realism as a "liberal" movement (in the modern, not the nineteenth-century, sense) and is part of the legacy of legal realism to today's neopragmatism, which is so dominated by persons of liberal or radical persuasion as to make the movement itself seem, not least in their own eyes, a school of left-wing thought. Yet not only has pragmatism no inherent political valence; those pragmatists who attack the pieties of the Right while exhibiting a wholly uncritical devotion to the pieties of the Left (such as racial and sexual equality, the desirability of a more equal distribution of income and wealth, and the pervasiveness of oppression and injustice in modern Western societies) are not genuine pragmatists; they are dogmatists in pragmatists' clothing.

Another weakness of legal realism was its lack of method. The realists knew what to do—think things not words, trace the actual consequences of legal doctrines, balance competing policies—but not how to do any of these good things. It was not their fault. The tools of economics, statistics, and other pertinent sciences were insufficiently developed to enable a social-engineering approach to be taken to law. What *was* their fault—and is my last and I think best reason for wanting to avoid the term "legal realism" as a description of what *I* am trying to do—was a penchant for irresponsibility that the critical legal studies movement, which likes to think of itself as descended from legal realism, has inherited. There were first-rate legal scholars among the realists, such as Radin, Patterson, and Llewellyn at his best, but there were also *Law and the Modern Mind* and *Woe Unto You, Lawyers!*, the judicial performance of William Douglas, the empirical studies that went nowhere and in going nowhere discredited empiricism in law, the naive *dirigiste* political science and New Deal idolatry, the manifestos that were never fulfilled.

When *The Nature of the Judicial Process* appeared, John Dewey was the leading philosopher of pragmatism, and it is his version of pragmatism that is most in evidence in Cardozo's writings. Dewey continued to be productive for many years, but until the 1960s there was little that was new in pragmatism. Yet much that was happening in philosophy during this interval supported the pragmatic approach. Logical positivism, with its emphasis on verifiability and its consequent hostility to metaphysics, is pragmatic in demanding that theory make a difference in the empirical world. Popper's falsificationist philosophy of science is close to Peirce's philosophy of science; in both, doubt is the engine of progress and truth an ever-receding goal. The antifoundationalism, antimetaphysicality, and rejection of certitude that are leitmotifs of the later Wittgenstein and of Quine can be thought of as extensions of the ideas of James and Dewey. By the 1970s and 1980s the streams have merged to form contemporary pragmatism, represented by such figures as Davidson, Putnam, and Rorty in analytical philosophy, Habermas in political philosophy, Geertz in anthropology, Fish in literary criticism, and the academic lawyers whom I mentioned at the outset.

There is little to be gained, however, by calling this recrudescence of pragmatism the "new" pragmatism. That would imply that there were (at least) two schools of pragmatism, each of which could be described and then compared. Neither the old nor the new pragmatism is a school. The differences between a Peirce and a James, or between a James and a Dewey, are profound. The differences among current advocates of pragmatism are even more profound, making it possible to find greater affinities across than within the neo and paleo "schools"—Peirce has more in common with Putnam than Putnam with Rorty, and I have more in common (I think) with Peirce, James, and Dewey than I have with Cornel West or Stanley Fish. Pragmatists of my stripe—pro-science, classical-liberal pragmatists—are not rebels against the Enlightenment; nor are we Utopian dreamers. For us the significance of pragmatism in relation to the Enlightenment is in unmasking and challenging the Platonic, traditionalist, and theological vestiges in Enlightenment thinking.

What is more useful than to attempt to descry and compare old and new schools of pragmatism is to observe simply that the strengths of pragmatism are better appreciated today than they were thirty years ago and that this is due to the failure of alternative philosophies such as logical positivism to fulfill their promise and also to a growing recognition that the strengths of such alternatives lie in features shared with pragmatism. Prominent among these features are hostility to metaphysics and sympathy with the *methods* of science, as distinct from faith in the power of science to take religion's place as the deliverer of final truths.

The Uses of Pragmatism in Law

If both the old and the new pragmatisms are as heterogeneous as I have suggested, the question arises whether pragmatism has any common core, and if not what exactly is meant by wanting to make law more pragmatic. I said in the Introduction that I liked Cornel West's suggestion that the "common denominator" of pragmatism is "a future-oriented instrumentalism that tries to deploy thought as a weapon to enable more effective action."[11] Yet even this formulation is vague enough to embrace a multitude of philosophies that are inconsistent at the political or legal level, including a multitude of inconsistent jurisprudences. Recalling the quotation from T. S. Eliot that is the epigraph for this chapter, one may wonder whether pragmatism is definite enough to have any use in law—other than to knock ambitious legal theories, as I have been doing throughout this book.

Well, that is indeed one of its major uses. Another is to provide help in changing the character of the legal enterprise by nudging academic law a little closer to social science, and the judicial game a little closer to the scientific game. Pragmatism undermines a number of the objections to these projects, as we have seen. It may also have a few applications to specific issues in law. Consider the legal protection of free speech. If pragmatists are right and truth is not in the cards, this may seem to weaken the case for a high degree of legal protection of free inquiry, viewed as the only dependable path to truth. Actually it may strengthen the case. Plato believed in censorship. If, *contra* Plato, truth is unattainable, the censor, or the experts for whom he fronts, cannot

11. Cornel West, *The American Evasion of Philosophy: A Genealogy of Pragmatism* 5 (1989).

appeal to a higher truth as the ground for foreclosing further inquiry on a subject. The libertarian, in resisting censorship, can appeal to the demonstrated efficacy of free inquiry in enlarging knowledge. One can doubt that we shall ever attain "truth" but not that our fund of useful knowledge is growing steadily. Even if every scientific truth that we accept today is destined someday to be overthrown, our ability to cure tuberculosis and generate electrical power and build airplanes that fly will be unimpaired. The succession of scientific theories not only coexists with the growth of scientific knowledge but is the main engine of that growth. The point is not that the censor's beliefs are false in every case; they may well be true in many. It is that the practice of censorship, by curtailing competition in ideas, retards the growth of knowledge and the benefits that knowledge brings.

Yet despite the example of Holmes, whose influential defense of free speech in the *Abrams* dissent bears an unmistakable affinity to a famous essay by Peirce,[12] it would be a mistake to think that there is a pragmatic *doctrine* of free speech—that you can use pragmatism to tell a judge how to decide a particular free-speech case. If the pragmatist is alert to the benefits of hot rhetoric, he is also alert to its costs. Radical feminists argue that pornography does harm; critical race theorists that hate speech does harm. Nothing in pragmatism teaches that the harms caused by speech should be ignored; nothing justifies the privileging of freedom of speech over other social interests. For the pragmatist, the issues of pornography and hate speech are empirical: What are the harms caused by these things, and what would be the consequences— the benefits and the costs—of attempting to prevent those harms?

Cass Sunstein in his book *Democracy and the Problem of Free Speech* (1993) takes a recognizably pragmatic approach to freedom of speech. He points out that some restrictions on that freedom might actually increase the amount of speech (for example, if newspapers were forced to provide space for the critics of their editorial policies), and others (for example, restrictions on pornography) might confer nonexpressive benefits greater than the harms to speech—both points that a formalist defender of free speech would be reluctant even to consider. The result is a cautious, even an indecisive, book, but responsibly so, because the author is properly sensitive to the profound empirical uncertainty that

12. Compare Abrams v. United States, 250 U.S. 616, 630 (1919) (dissenting opinion), with Peirce, "The Fixation of Belief," in *Collected Papers of Charles Sanders Peirce* 223 (Charles Hartshorne and Paul Weiss eds. 1934).

fogs debate over the consequences of the various forms of speech and proposals for regulating speech.

It begins to seem as if the greatest value of pragmatism lies in preventing the premature closure of issues rather than in actually resolving them. It can, for example, help us maintain a properly critical stance toward certain entities that play a large role in many areas of law, particularly tort and criminal law, and that are pregnant with confusion. Such entities as mind, intent, free will, and causation are continually invoked in debates over civil and criminal liability, yet when tested by the pragmatic criterion of practical consequence they prove to be remarkably elusive. Judges and juries do not, as a precondition to finding that a killing was intentional, peek into the defendant's mind in search of the required intent. They look at the evidence of what the defendant did and try to infer from it whether there was advance planning or some other indication of a high probability of success, whether there was concealment of evidence or other indicia of likely escape, and whether the circumstances of the crime argue a likelihood of repetition—all being considerations that relate to dangerousness rather than to intent or free will. The principal social concern behind criminal punishment is a concern with dangerousness rather than with mental states, and the methods of litigation do not enable the factfinder to probe beneath dangerousness into mental or spiritual strata so elusive that they may not even exist.

Similarly, while concerned with effects and therefore with causes, the law does not make a fetish of "causation." It avoids the age-old philosophical controversies over the nature and existence of causation by basing judgments of liability on social rather than on philosophical considerations. People who have caused no harm at all because their plans were interrupted are regularly punished for attempt and conspiracy; people are sometimes held liable in tort law when their acts were not a necessary condition of the harm that ensued (as where two defendants, acting independently, simultaneously inflict a harm that would have ensued had only one acted); and a person whose act "caused" injury in an uncontroversial sense may be excused from liability because the harm was an unforeseeable consequence of the act. The conditions for legal liability to attach to a person's actions can be redescribed without reference to mind and causation.

My point is not that because intent and causation and the like do not exist in the sense in which brains or trucks can be said to exist they are not objective. Physical reality is not the touchstone of the pragmatist's idea of objectivity. Many things that cannot be touched or even located in books of account, such as "marginal cost" and imaginary numbers, are as objective as physical objects are, in the sense that statements about them can be adjudged true or false with as much confidence as statements about physical objects. That was my point in the Introduction about moves in chess. The valid complaint about law's imaginary entities is that they sometimes get in the way of thought rather than aiding it, making them "metaphysical" in the pejorative sense. Yet they have their use. The connected concepts of intention and free will, applied for example in the setting of criminal punishment, support the idea that people are different from other dangerous things, from rattlesnakes for example.[13] That idea is a useful antidote to the "friend-foe" mentality which disfigured German adjudication during the Hitler period and to the promiscuous invocation of dangerousness as a basis for preventive detention. Thus, although free will and intention have little if any place in the science game, they may have a place in the judicial game. So again we see pragmatism puncturing bad arguments (for example, that people have a "faculty" of "will" that determines their choices) rather than resolving practical issues, such as whether to continue employing the free will "fiction" in law.

There is nothing new about endeavors to puncture the law's so-called metaphysical balloons (which is just my point that there is nothing much new in neopragmatism). It was a favorite pursuit of the legal realists. But they did it with a left-wing slant. They were derisive about the proposition that a corporation had natural rights, since a corporation is just the name of a set of contracts. They were not derisive about the idea of corporate taxation, although since the corporation is not a person it cannot pay a tax. The payers of the corporate income tax are flesh-and-blood persons, by no means all wealthy, for among them are (or may be—the incidence of the corporate income tax is an issue much debated in economics) employees and consumers as well as shareholders. The legal realists also overlooked the possibility that the fiction of corporate personality may serve a useful economic function, just as the fiction of free will may serve a useful political function.

Pragmatism remains an antidote to formalism. The idea that legal questions can be answered by inquiry into the relation between con-

---

13. Cf. Sabina Lovibond, *Realism and Imagination in Ethics* 174 (1983).

cepts and hence without need for more than a superficial examination of their relation to the world of fact is as antipragmatic as it is anti-empirical. It does not ask, What works? It asks, What rules and outcomes form links in a logical chain to an authoritative source of law, such as the text of the Constitution or a common law doctrine that no one challenges?

The desire to sever knowledge from observation, which is the formalist's goal, is persistent and, to some extent, fruitful. Armed with the rules of arithmetic, one can drop a succession of balls into an urn and, if one has counted carefully, one will *know* how many balls there are in the urn without looking into it. Armed with the legal rule that there are no nonpossessory rights in wild animals, all you need to know to apply the rule is whether an animal is wild or domesticated. Legal rules economize on information, and that is a good thing. The danger comes when, for example, the rule about nonpossessory rights in wild animals is thought to generalize automatically to a rule that there are no such rights in *any* nonstationary natural resource. Then we can obtain the "correct" rule for property rights in oil and gas without having to delve into the economics of developing these resources, all right, but the risk that the resulting regime for oil and gas will be inefficient is very great. The pragmatic approach reverses the sequence. It asks: What is the right rule—the sensible, the socially apt, the reasonable, the efficient rule—for oil and gas? In the course of investigating this question the pragmatist will consult wild-animal law for what (little) light it may throw on the question, but the emphasis will be empirical from the start. There will be no inclination to allow existing rules to expand to their semantic limits, engrossing ever greater areas of experience by a process of verbal similitude. The formalist forces the practices of business and lay persons into the mold of existing legal concepts, viewed as immutable, such as "contract." The pragmatist thinks that concepts should be subservient to human need and therefore wants law always to consider the possibility of adjusting its categories to fit the practices of the nonlegal community.

This is where "metaphysical" entities engender confusion. There are voluntary actions; it does not follow that voluntariness is an attribute of actions. Some promises are contractual, meaning enforceable; it does not follow that they are enforceable because they are "contracts." We can speak of an act having been caused without positing an entity called "causation."

The current bastion of legal formalism is not the common law; it is statutory and constitutional interpretation. It is here that we find the most influential modern attempts to derive legal outcomes by methods superficially akin to deduction. The attempts will fail. The interpretation of texts is not a logical exercise, and the bounds of "interpretation" are so elastic (considering that among the verbal and other objects that are interpreted are dreams, texts in foreign languages, and, as we saw in Chapter 9, musical compositions) as to cast the utility of the concept into doubt. In approaching an issue that has been posed as one of statutory interpretation, pragmatists will ask which of the possible resolutions has the best consequences, all things that lawyers are or should be interested in considered, including the importance of preserving language as a medium of effective communication and of preserving the separation of powers by generally deferring to the legislature's policy choices.

A further complication for the theory of statutory interpretation is that we no longer think of statutes as typically, let alone invariably, the product of well-meaning efforts to promote the public interest by legislators who are devoted to that interest and who are the faithful representatives of constituents who share the same devotion. The theory of social choice has instructed us about the difficulties of aggregating preferences by the method of voting, while the interest-group theory of politics in the version revived by economists has taught us that the legislative process often caters to the redistributive desires of narrow coalitions and, in so doing, disserves any plausible conception of the public interest. Under pressure from both theories it becomes unclear where to locate statutory meaning, problematic to speak of judges discerning legislative intent, and uncertain why judges should seek to perfect through interpretation the decrees of the special-interest state. The main choices in interpretive theory that the new learning allows are either some version of strict construction or a pragmatic approach in which, recognizing the difficult and problematic nature of statutory interpretation, judges use consequences to guide their decisions, always bearing in mind that the relevant consequences include systemic ones such as the risk of debasing the currency of statutory language.

Mention of systemic concerns should help demolish the canard that legal pragmatism means rendering shortsighted substantive justice between the parties to the particular case. The relevant consequences to the pragmatist are long run as well as short run, systemic as well as individual, the importance of stability and predictability as well as of justice to the individual parties, the importance of maintaining language as a reliable method of communication as well as of interpreting statutes and constitutional provisions flexibly in order to make them speak intelligently to circumstances not envisaged by their drafters. It is true that considerations of piety, or of the organic ties between generations, or of a moral duty of consistency through time are unlikely to move the pragmatist judge. But it is always possible that some strand of formalist legal discourse—such as strict construction, free will, or rigorous adherence to precedent—might be justified on pragmatic grounds as the best guide to judicial decision-making. Strict constructionists, for example, when pressed to admit that their method cannot actually be justified by arguments of interpretive fidelity, sometimes respond that it is nevertheless justifiable on practical grounds as a way of limiting judicial discretion, increasing the predictability of statutory decisions, and disciplining the legislative process by forcing legislators to say what they mean. The pragmatist is obliged to consider the merits of such a response. We must be careful to distinguish pragmatic philosophizing from pragmatic adjudication and not to exaggerate the possibilities for using the former to underwrite the latter.

We must even, as I noted in the Introduction, consider the possibility that the pragmatic judge would think the pragmatic thing to be would be a formalist, just as a scientist might think the pragmatic thing to be would be a scientific realist. Yet although the discourse of judges has always been predominantly formalist, most American judges have been, at least when faced with difficult cases, practicing pragmatists, in part because the materials for decision in American law have always been so various and conflicting as to make formalism unworkable in most of the difficult cases and in part because judges are not so self-disciplined and intellectually sophisticated as academics like to imagine them. As Holmes pointed out in his dissent in *Lochner*—a decision usually denounced as an example of formalistic "liberty of contract" thinking—the majority was guilty not of formalistic decision-making but of basing decision on an economic theory (that of laissez-faire) that much of the nation did not accept.[14] To argue, against the suggestion that "pragmatism provides the best explanation of how judges actually decide

14. 198 U.S. at 75.

cases," that it "leaves unexplained one prominent feature of judicial practice—the attitude judges take toward statutes and precedents in hard cases—except on the awkward hypothesis that this practice is designed to deceive the public, in which case the public has not consented to it,"[15] is to infer judges' attitudes from the rhetoric of judicial opinions. Judges are often not candid and even more often not self-aware. It is easy to confuse one's strong policy preferences with the law. As for whether the public has consented to pragmatic judicial decision-making, a negative answer would not undermine the explanatory as distinct from the normative force of the pragmatic theory. The issue of public consent is in any event artificial. Judicial opinions are with rare exceptions written to be read by lawyers, not by lay people, and have in fact virtually no lay readership. Besides, the public seems not to have a coherent view of the appropriate balance between principle and result in judicial decisions.

It is true that after a bout of conspicuous judicial activism that lasted several decades (building through the 1950s, peaking in the 1960s, diminishing somewhat in the 1970s and greatly since), there is renewed interest in approaches that favor continuity with the past over social engineering of the future. These approaches are attractive to quondam judicial activists eager to conserve the Supreme Court's liberal decisions of the 1960s and 1970s against inroads by conservative judges, to many conservatives who believe that the judiciary remains committed to liberal policies, and most ingeniously to Dworkin, who argues that conservatives such as Bork are the real activists. There is renewed talk of tradition, of embodied but inarticulate wisdom (embodied in favored precedents, in professional training, in law's customary language), of the limitedness of individual reason and the danger of precipitate social change. The cautionary stance implicit in these approaches is congenial to the pragmatist, for whom the historical record of reform efforts is full of sobering lessons. But pragmatists are not content with a vague neotraditionalism. They know it will not do to tell judges to resolve all doubts against change and freeze law as it is, let alone to return to some past episode in what has been our permanent constitutional revolution (1950? 1850?). As the nation changes, judges, within the broad limits set by the legislators and by the constitution makers, must adapt the law to an altered social and political environment. No version

15. Ronald Dworkin, *Law's Empire* 161 (1986).

of traditionalism will tell them how to do this. They need to establish ends and to develop an awareness of how social change affects the appropriate means. They need the instrumental sense that is basic to pragmatism.

Dworkin's objection to pragmatism as a normative theory of law is that it is not his theory,[16] which he calls "integrity." About his theory I will say no more than that he attempts to justify it in terms that will not satisfy the pragmatist's insistence on a practical payoff. "Integrity," says Dworkin, "infuses political and private occasions each with the spirit of the other to the benefit of both," making "political obligation" the "protestant idea" of "fidelity to a scheme of principle each citizen has a responsibility to identify, ultimately for himself, as his community's scheme."[17] Law as integrity is, "finally, a fraternal attitude, an expression of how we are united in community though divided in project, interest, and conviction."[18] I get nothing out of such high-falutin' prose.

The relation between pragmatism and the most highly developed instrumental concept of law, the economic, warrants further examination. A recurrent criticism of efforts to defend the economic approach as a worthwhile guide for legal reform is that the defenders have failed to ground it securely in one of the great ethical traditions, such as the Kantian or the utilitarian. The criticism is sound as observation but not as criticism. The idea that law should attempt to promote and facilitate competitive markets and to simulate their results in situations in which market-transaction costs are prohibitive—the idea that I call "wealth maximization"—has affinities with both Kantian and utilitarian ethics: with the former, because the approach protects the autonomy of people who are productive or at least potentially so (which is most of us); with the latter, because of the empirical relation between free markets and human welfare. Although the economic approach is neither deducible from nor completely consistent with either system of ethics, this is not a decisive objection from a pragmatic standpoint. Pragmatists are unperturbed by a lack of foundations. We ask not whether the economic approach to law is adequately grounded in the ethics of Kant or Rawls or Bentham or Mill or Hayek or Nozick—and not whether any of those ethics is adequately grounded—but whether it is the best approach for

16. Id., ch. 5.
17. Id. at 190.
18. Id. at 413.

the contemporary American legal system to follow, given what we know about markets (and we are learning more about them every day from the economic and political changes that are taking place in foreign countries), about American legislatures, about American judges, and about the values of the American people.

We need not think of the norm of wealth maximization as one that borrows here from Bentham and Mill, there from Kant and Hayek, in an attempt to strike a compromise between rival comprehensive ethical doctrines. We can think of it rather in Rawls's sense of an "overlapping consensus."[19] People who subscribe to different comprehensive doctrines may nevertheless be brought to agree upon a political principle, such as wealth maximization, to govern a particular field of social interactions. So an egalitarian, a Millian liberal, an economic libertarian, and an aficionado of Aristotelian corrective justice might all be brought to agree that something like our present system of tort law, plausibly conceived as wealth-maximizing in its basic orientation, is the appropriate system for regulating most accidents.[20]

The economic approach cannot be the whole content of legal pragmatism. The libertarian character of the approach makes it unsuitable to govern areas in which redistributive values command a political or moral consensus; and because the approach works well only when there is at least moderate agreement on ends, it cannot be used to answer the question whether, for example, abortion should be restricted, although it can tell us something, maybe much, about the efficacy and consequences of the restrictions. Indeed one value of pragmatism is its recognition that there are areas of discourse where a lack of common ends precludes rational resolution;[21] and here the pragmatic counsel (or one pragmatic counsel) to the legal system is to muddle through, preserve avenues of change, not roil the political waters unnecessarily. On a pragmatic view the error of *Roe v. Wade* is not that it read the Constitution wrong—for there are plenty of well-regarded decisions that reflect an equally freewheeling approach to constitutional interpretation—but that it prematurely nationalized an issue better left to

---

19. John Rawls, *Political Liberalism* 39–40 and lect. 4 (1993); also Cass R. Sunstein, "On Legal Theory and Practice" (unpublished, University of Chicago Law School, 1993).

20. Cf. *The Problems of Jurisprudence* 387–391.

21. Compare Rawls, note 19 above, commending liberalism as the proper political philosophy for a society, such as ours, in which people have incommensurable values.

simmer at the state and local level until a consensus of some sort based on experience with a variety of approaches to abortion emerged.

With muddling through offered as a methodology of pragmatic jurisprudence, one may wonder whether that jurisprudence has progressed an inch beyond *The Nature of the Judicial Process*. Reviewing the items that I have listed as uses of pragmatism in law, we can see that Cardozo had a solid pragmatic grasp of the weakness of formalism and a good pragmatic theory of adjudication. But free speech was not an issue about which he was much concerned; the critique of intention and causation was less developed than it is today and certainly less salient in Cardozo's thinking; he was uninterested in interpretation and unrealistic about the legislative process; and he was innocent of the economic approach to law as a self-conscious methodology—it did not exist in 1921, or indeed until half a century later—though like most good common law judges he had intuitions of it.[22]

Although pragmatic jurisprudence embraces a richer set of ideas than can be found in *The Nature of the Judicial Process* or "The Path of the Law," one can hardly say that there has been much progress, and perhaps in the nature of pragmatism there cannot be. All that a pragmatic jurisprudence really connotes—and it connoted it in 1897 or 1921 as much as it does today—is a rejection of the idea that law is something grounded in permanent principles and realized in logical manipulations of those principles, and a determination to use law as an instrument for social ends. If it plants no trees, this pragmatic jurisprudence that I have been defending, at least it clears away a lot of underbrush. It signals an attitude, an orientation, at times a change in direction. That is something, and maybe a lot.

22. William Landes and I discuss an example—Cardozo's decision in Adams v. Bullock, 227 N.Y. 208, 125 N.E. 93 (1919)—in our book *The Economic Structure of Tort Law* 97–98 (1987).

Coase will never win the Nobel Prize for Economics.[1]

chapter 20

Ronald Coase and Methodology

W H E N the name Ronald Coase comes up in conversation, the economists and economically minded lawyers who follow his work are apt to say: He has written very little, but his percentage of hits is very high. In particular, he has written two great theoretical articles, published a quarter of a century apart but thematically continuous, which earned him the 1991 Nobel Memorial Prize in Economic Sciences. The articles are "The Nature of the Firm"[2] and "The Problem of Social Cost."[3] The latter, widely believed to be the most frequently cited article in all of economics, introduced (though it did not name) the Coase Theorem: If transaction costs are zero, the initial assignment of a property right—for example, whether to the polluter or to the victim of pollution—will not affect the efficiency with which resources are allocated. The major significance of the theorem has been to focus economists' attention on a neglected but very important facet of the economic system, the costs of market transacting. Restated as a hypothesis—if transaction costs are low, the law's assignment of rights and liabilities

1. Stewart Schwab, "Coase Defends Coase: Why Lawyers Listen and Economists Do Not," 87 *Michigan Law Review* 1171, 1190 n. 62 (1989).
2. 4 *Economica* (n.s.) 386 (1937).
3. 3 *Journal of Law and Economics* 1 (1960).

is unlikely to affect the allocation of resources significantly—the Coase Theorem has guided important empirical research, for example into the effects of no-fault divorce, which, consistent with the Theorem, has *not* increased the divorce rate.[4]

This impression of a lifetime's work compressed into two articles is not dispelled by the address that Coase gave upon receipt of the Nobel Prize.[5] For he discusses only those two articles, remarking modestly that he has "made no innovations in high theory" but adding quickly that he believes that the ideas in those articles, once they are absorbed into mainstream economic analysis, will "bring about a complete change in the structure of economic theory, at least in what is called price theory or microeconomics."[6] So they must be contributions to theory, and indeed fundamental ones: more than enough for a lifetime. Because the two articles were singled out by the Royal Swedish Academy of Sciences in its award of the Nobel Prize to Coase, it is natural that he should have made them the focus of his prize lecture. But it was not inevitable that they should be the only works that he discussed, and the impression of a life work's compressed into two articles that are really one is reinforced by his remarking that the "essentials" of his argument about the importance of transaction costs, which he regards as the point of both articles, had been presented in a lecture that he gave in 1932, when he was only 21 years old; "and it is a strange experience to be praised in my eighties for work I did in my twenties."[7] At the end of the Nobel lecture he explains that since the two articles demonstrate the centrality of transaction costs in the operation of markets, the next stage in research is to study contracts empirically because they are the method (more precisely, a method) by which business firms adjust to transaction costs.

If his work is destined to bring about "a complete change in the structure of economic theory," and to do this by the creation and study

4. See, for example, H. Elizabeth Peters, "Marriage and Divorce: Informational Constraints and Private Contracting," 76 *American Economic Review* 437 (1986). And recall the application of the Coase Theorem to the issue of "just cause" employment protection, discussed in Chapter 13.

5. R. H. Coase, "The Institutional Structure of Production," in Coase, *Essays on Economics and Economists* 3 (1994).

6. Id.

7. Id. at 8; see also Coase, "The Nature of the Firm: Origin," 4 *Journal of Law, Economics, and Organization* 1, 4–5 (1988).

of "large-scale collections of business contracts,"[8] Coase must believe that the dominant tendencies in modern economics are unsound. He does not say this in so many words in his Nobel lecture, but he has not been reticent on the subject elsewhere. He has repeatedly made clear his "dissatisfaction with what most economists have been doing . . . This dissatisfaction is not with the basic economic theory itself but with how it is used. The objection essentially is that the theory floats in the air. It is as if one studied the circulation of the blood without having a body."[9] "What have we been doing in the last 200 years? Our analysis has certainly become more sophisticated, but we display no greater insight into the working of the economic system and, in some ways, our approach is inferior to that of Adam Smith."[10]

Both the conventional impression of Coase's work and Coase's own "take" on his work, which reflects a methodological preoccupation ignored in the conventional appraisals, seem to me interestingly wrong. To begin with, it is not true that Coase has written only a few papers. His curriculum vitae lists six books or monographs and 75 papers. These works fall into three groups. One is theoretical and includes besides the two articles on transaction costs a series of very fine articles on public utility pricing[11] and an important article on the monopolization of durable goods.[12] The second group consists of a number of case studies of particular institutions, mostly public, such as the British Post Office, the British Broadcasting Company, and the Federal Communications Commission.[13] The third consists of articles dealing with the methodology of economics, often in the setting of a discussion of a particular economist, such as Adam Smith or Alfred Marshall. As the title of this chapter will have revealed already, this series of articles is the particular focus of my discussion. But one cannot understand the character or the limitations of Coase's overall economic position with-

8. Coase, note 5 above, at 14.

9. "The New Institutional Economics," 140 *Journal of Institutional and Theoretical Economics* 229, 230 (1984). See also Coase, *The Firm, the Market, and the Law: Essays on the Institutional Structure of Production* (1988) (esp. ch. 1), which reprints, with some additions, several of Coase's major articles. It is the best introduction to Coase's distinctive point of view.

10. "The Wealth of Nations," 15 *Economic Inquiry* 309, 325 (1977).

11. The principal article is "The Marginal Cost Controversy," 13 *Economica* (n.s.) 169 (1946).

12. "Durability and Monopoly," 15 *Journal of Law and Economics* 143 (1972).

13. See, for example, "The Federal Communications Commission," 2 *Journal of Law and Economics* 1 (1959), where the Coase Theorem was first adumbrated.

out viewing the body of his work as a whole. One cannot, for example, otherwise understand why he has declared war on modern economics.[14]

Coase's Contributions to Economics and Law

I begin with the series of papers on the marginal-cost controversy. Harold Hotelling and other high-powered economists had argued that if a service was produced under conditions of declining average cost— transportation over a bridge assumed to be in no danger of congestion was the standard example, although the analysis was assumed to be applicable to all services produced under conditions of declining average cost, such as gas, telephone, water, and electrical service—only a public entity could provide it efficiently. Only a public entity could charge a price equal to marginal cost even if marginal cost was zero yet stay in business by making up the deficit with taxation. A private firm would have to charge a price higher than marginal cost, and this would cause inefficient substitution away from the bridge. Coase pointed out that with price set equal to marginal cost there would be no way to discover whether the public actually valued the bridge more than it valued substitutes that, not being produced under conditions of declining average cost, would have to pay their way in the market without the help of a tax subsidy. The problem would disappear if government were omniscient, as implicitly assumed by Hotelling, but government is not omniscient,[15] and throughout his career Coase has insisted very sensibly that in evaluating the case for public intervention one must compare real markets with real government, rather than real markets with ideal government.

Hotelling was one of those innovators in "high theory" that Coase

14. Here are two representative quotations: "In my youth it was said that what was too silly to be said may be sung. In modern economics it may be put into mathematics." *The Firm, the Market, and the Law*, note 9 above, at 185. "When economists find that they are unable to analyze what is happening in the real world, they invent an imaginary world which they are capable of handling." Coase, "The Nature of the Firm: Meaning," 4 *Journal of Law, Economics, and Organization* 19, 24 (1988). See also "Marshall on Method," in Coase, note 5 above, at 167, 175. Coase believes that there will be a day for mathematical economics—but not yet. "Once we begin to uncover the real factors affecting the performance of the economic system, the complicated interrelations among them will clearly necessitate a mathematical treatment, as in the natural sciences, and economists like myself, who write in prose, will take their bow. May this period soon come." Coase, note 5 above, at 14.

15. If it were, moreover, as Coase also pointed out, it could charge the users of the bridge directly; there would be no reason for the taxpaying public as a whole to subsidize the project.

has told us *he* is not. Like so many economic theorists Hotelling was led by his theorizing to propose a socialist solution to an economic problem that, as Coase showed, could be handled (not perfectly of course) by private alternatives, such as two-part or multipart pricing,[16] once the false though analytically tractable assumption of omniscient government was dropped. Many years later Paul Samuelson would oppose pay television on the ground that it would make the price of television programs to the viewer exceed the programs' marginal cost, which was zero (the cost of adding one more viewer).[17]

The socialist pitfalls of high theory are a constant refrain in Coase's work.[18] For the first forty years of his professional life microeconomists were preoccupied with the problem of monopoly. They saw monopoly everywhere—"monopolistic competition" and "oligopolistic interdependence" were the theoretical constructs that extended the monopoly concept beyond classic single-firm monopolies and cartels—and they were quick to recommend government intervention by means of antitrust suits or other regulatory devices. They were apt for example to regard vertical integration as a monopolizing device, one that used "leverage" or "barriers to entry" to extend or protect monopoly power. "The Nature of the Firm" (note 2) had offered an alternative, nonmonopolistic explanation of vertical integration. Businessmen bring a part of the process of production within the firm, rather than arranging for it by contract with other producers, when the costs of coordinating the firm's inputs by market transactions exceed the costs of coordinating them hierarchically. The hierarchy is of course a contractual one. But employment contracts that entitle the employer to direct the employee's work are different from contracts with outside suppliers (independent contractors) for outputs specified as to price, quality, quantity, date of delivery, and the other dimensions of performance but with control over inputs left to the supplier.

Coase's hostility to monopoly explanations, a hostility that has been

16. For example, a price that has one component representing a share of the fixed costs of the service and another representing the marginal cost of serving a customer. So users of a bridge might pay a one-time fee calculated to defray the investment in the bridge plus a toll every time they used the bridge to defray the cost of the wear and tear caused by that use. See *Economic Analysis of Law* 354–356.

17. See the exchange among James Buchanan, Paul Samuelson, and Jora Minasian in volume 10 of the *Journal of Law and Economics* (1967).

18. There is a striking passage in "The Problem of Social Cost" in which Coase appears to be blaming all pollution on government. Coase, note 3 above, at 26.

vindicated by the waning of interest in antitrust law and policy in recent years, created a certain awkwardness for him when he wrote his appreciation of George Stigler upon the occasion of the latter's receipt of the Nobel Prize.[19] Much of Stigler's work had consisted of exploring monopoly problems, and in addition much of it was theoretical, even mathematical. Much consisted of regression analyses; and Coase is suspicious of econometrics,[20] just as he is of mathematical models in economics. It should come as no surprise, therefore, except for those who lump all economists employed by the University of Chicago into an undifferentiated "Chicago School," that the essay on Stigler is strained.

Coase begins by saying that Stigler is "seen at his best" in his work on the history of economic thought—a subject that has virtually ceased to exist in economics. A science tends to forget its founders: few physicists read Newton, or for that matter Einstein. But Coase does not believe that economics has made much progress since its founding; he regards Adam Smith as almost the only economist worth reading. This makes it natural for him to look with favor on studies in the history of economic thought; nevertheless it seems rather a backhanded compliment to declare Stigler's work in this marginal, esoteric, and declining field his best. Stigler's writings on monopoly are passed over quickly because "by concentrating on the problem of monopoly in dealing with an economic system which is, broadly speaking, competitive, economists have had their attention misdirected and as a consequence they have left unexplained many of the salient features of our economic system or have been content with very defective explanations."[21] He singles out for praise, as had the Swedish Academy in its Nobel citation of Stigler, Stigler's paper on the economics of information, because it offers a nonmonopolistic explanation for a variety of business arrangements, such as advertising and department stores. The Swedish Academy had also emphasized Stigler's theory of regulation, which Coase summarizes accurately as "treating political behavior as utility-maximizing [and] political parties as firms supplying regulation, with what is supplied being what is wanted by those groups (or coalitions) which

19. Coase, "George J. Stigler: An Appreciation," *Regulation*, Nov.–Dec. 1982, p. 21.

20. "If you torture the data enough, nature will always confess." Coase, *How Should Economists Choose?* 16 (American Enterprise Institute 1982). See also "Economists and Public Policy," in Coase, note 5 above, at 47, 58.

21. Coase, note 19 above, at 22.

are able to outbid others in the political market."[22] Coase is skeptical, because he doesn't believe that political behavior "is best described as rational utility-maximizing." Elsewhere he has described the standard economic assumption of man as a rational maximizer as "unnecessary and misleading" even when applied to market transactions,[23] and we shall see that he will have no truck with applying economics outside its conventional domain of explicit markets.

Besides the phenomena of declining average cost and of monopoly, externalities whether negative or positive are standard theoretical grounds for public intervention in markets (and both declining average cost and monopoly problems can be restated in terms of externalities). Coase took a bead on them in "The Problem of Social Cost" and in a later article, on lighthouses, where he showed that this classic (perhaps hackneyed would be a better term) example of a public good had in fact long been provided privately.[24] Although the lighthouse article is not one of Coase's better-known works, he reprinted it in *The Firm, the Market, and the Law*, no doubt because it makes one of his central antitheoretical points so effectively: that economic theorists use stock examples to illustrate their theories without bothering to inquire whether the examples are correct.

The anti-interventionist point of "The Problem of Social Cost" is not that the Coase Theorem (a term coined later, by George Stigler) shows that markets will internalize pollution and other negative externalities. Sometimes they will, but sometimes they won't. Coase believes that we live in a world of positive transaction costs—otherwise "The Nature of the Firm" would have had no subject. But intelligent decisions on public intervention often require more information than governments have or can acquire. Pigou's assumption that the way to deal

22. Id. at 24.

23. "The New Institutional Economics," note 9 above, at 231. "There is no reason to suppose that most human beings are engaged in maximizing anything unless it be unhappiness, and even this with incomplete success." *The Firm, the Market, and the Law*, note 9 above, at 4. Then why suppose that firms try to minimize transaction costs or that firms and individuals make advantageous trades if transaction costs permit? Because "for groups of human beings, in almost all circumstances, a higher (relative) price for anything will lead to a reduction in the amount demanded" (id.). But if people want to maximize their unhappiness, why don't they deplete their resources as rapidly as possible by buying more of a good when its relative price rises? Elsewhere Coarse has said that he would welcome the abandonment of the assumption in economics "that an individual's choices are consistent." "Duncan Black," in Coase, note 5 above, at 185, 190.

24. "The Lighthouse in Economics," 17 *Journal of Law and Economics* 357 (1974).

with a polluter is to tax or regulate him is, as Coase showed, superficial, because the victim of the pollution may be able to reduce or eliminate the cost of the pollution at a lower cost than the polluter. Pigou's approach can be patched up with the observation that in such a case the tax should be zero; then the polluter will not stop polluting and the victim will move away—the optimal result. But the need for the patch was not noticed until Coase's article on social cost.

The article suggests that English common law judges were quicker than economists to recognize the reciprocal character of pollution—the sense in which pollution is as much "caused" by the victim as by the polluter, although the better way to approach the question is to forget about causation and simply ask which party to a harmful interaction should be induced to change his behavior (of course it could be that both should be). This suggestion is, as we shall see, the germ of the positive economic theory of the common law—that common law judges have tried, whether consciously or not, to assign property rights and fashion liability rules in such a way as to minimize the misallocations caused by the presence of prohibitive transaction costs.

Hostility to public intervention in markets beyond what is defensible in strict wealth-maximization terms is a leitmotif of Coase's work. This hostility has fed Coase's doubts about modern economic theory. So many economic theorists in this century have been interventionist that economic theory itself has become dominated by concepts, such as "perfect competition" (the conditions for which are never found in the real world), "externality," "public good," "social welfare function," and "market failure," that sound like invitations to public intervention. These terms, and the vast bodies of formal theory that have grown up around them, assume the fragility of markets and the robustness of government, whereas Coase believes that careful observation of markets and government discloses the robustness of markets and the fragility of government. I think that his observation is basically correct but that in trying to explain the blindness (as it seems to him) of the interventionists he has got the causality backwards because he has the intellectual's propensity to assign intellectual rather than material or psychological causes to opinions. It is not that formal economic theory inherently favors public intervention; it is that economists inclined by temperament or life experience to favor big government will be inclined to formulate theories congenial to their preferences. Eventually their theories will collide with reality and be overthrown, as has now happened to a considerable extent with collectivist and interventionist economic theories. Even before it happened the bias in these theories had been exposed—notably by Coase himself in his attacks on the Pigouvian tradition.

The opposite danger is that economists inclined by temperament or life experience to favor a weak and passive government will overlook opportunities for fruitful government interventions. It is difficult to believe for example that the entire problem of pollution can be left to be sorted out by the market, or even by the market plus the common law of nuisance. And the role of regulation in creating markets, for example markets in pollution rights, must not be overlooked. Coase knows all this. He is not a doctrinaire adherent of laissez-faire. But, being skeptical about government, he insists that the costs of government intervention be compared with the benefits rather than assumed to be zero.

Coase's method of doing economics is similar to that of his idol, Adam Smith. Coase has explained that the "extremely difficult question" that Smith posed for himself was "how is the cooperation of these vast numbers of people in countries all over the world, which is necessary for even a modest standard of living, to be brought about?"[25] This sounds much like the question, How are the suppliers of inputs into a productive process to be coordinated? There are two possibilities—contracts with independent contractors (sometimes these contracts are standardized and pooled in formal markets) and contracts with employees—and whichever is cheaper will be the one adopted.[26] Thus, "there would be an optimum of planning since a firm, that little planned society, could only continue to exist if it performed its co-ordination function at a lower cost than would be incurred if it were achieved by means of market transactions and also at a lower cost than this same function could be performed by another firm."[27] So Coase predicted that if the conglomerate enterprise turned out not to be an efficient method of organizing production within a firm, these enterprises would spin off some of their divisions, with the result that less activity would

25. "The Wealth of Nations," note 10 above, at 313.
26. "We had a factor of production, management, whose function was to co-ordinate. Why was it needed if the pricing system provided all the co-ordination necessary?" Coase, note 5 above, at 7.
27. Id. at 8.

be coordinated by the firm and more by the market.[28] That is precisely what happened following waves of conglomerate mergers in the 1960s and 1980s.

When the costs of private coordination are prohibitive, the law may step in by specifying property rights or imposing liability, and again the analytic task according to Coase is simply to compare the costs of alternative methods of coping with transaction costs. The necessary comparisons are made by examining the operation of particular institutions through the lens of the case study, using interviews, judicial records, newspaper articles, and like sources of qualitative data; formal quantitative methods of empirical investigation—about which, as I have said, Coase is skeptical—are not essential. Coase had taken some law courses as an undergraduate, and in "The Problem of Social Cost" he examined several areas of the common law, particularly nuisance law, which he commended for *not* following Pigou's recipe of always placing liability on the injuring party. Summarizing, he said that

> in a world in which there are costs of rearranging the rights established by the legal system, the courts, in cases relating to nuisance, are, in effect, making a decision on the economic problem and determining how re- sources are to be employed . . . The courts are conscious of this and they often make, although not always in a very explicit fashion, a comparison between what would be gained and what lost by preventing actions which have harmful effects.[29]

Coase's Conception of Economics

One understands why Coase regards his Adam Smithian approach as fruitful. It *has* been, in his hands and those of like-minded economists, and it will continue to be. A lot can be done with simple economic theory combined with historical or even journalistic methods of em- pirical research, as distinct from methods that employ random sampling and statistical inference. But this only begins to explain the most unusual feature of Coase's writings, which is the *narrowness* of his conception of the domain and methods of economics. I have said that he considers his approach not only fruitful, but destined to transform

28. "Working Paper for the Task Force on Productivity and Competition: The Conglom- erate Merger," 115 *Congressional Record* 15938 (1969).
29. "The Problem of Social Cost," note 3 above, at 27–28.

economics, and that he thinks that the two centuries of economics since the publication of *The Wealth of Nations* have been largely wasted and we must begin to study large-scale collections of business records. He regards with complete insouciance one of his most signal achievements, the focus and thrust that "The Problem of Social Cost" imparted to the law and economics movement.[30] Many of the law's doctrines, procedures, and institutions can usefully be viewed as responses to the problem of transaction costs, being designed either to reduce those costs or, if they are incorrigibly prohibitive, to bring about the allocation of resources that would exist if they were zero. The law tries to make the market work and, failing that, tries to mimic the market. A sentence in the Nobel lecture epitomizes Coase's attitude toward the law and economics movement: "I will not say much here about its [the social-cost article's] influence on legal scholarship, which has been immense, but will mainly consider its influence on economics, which has not been immense, although I believe that in time it will be."[31] Between 1976 and 1990, more than a third of the citations to Coase's entire corpus, as recorded in the *Social Sciences Citation Index*, appeared in law journals rather than in economic journals,[32] and the fraction is growing.[33] Despite the Nobel Prize, Coase probably is an even bigger figure in law than in economics—an ordering with which he is not at all happy. It must quickly be added that as director of the law and economics program of the University of Chicago Law School and as editor of the *Journal of Law and Economics* Coase was immensely supportive of William Landes, myself, and other practitioners of economic analysis of law. This makes all the more puzzling his lack of interest in this movement that he has done so much to nurture.

The key to understanding Coase's methodological stance, in particular his hostility to formal theory, is, I suggest, his Englishness. Although

30. A movement described in Anthony T. Kronman, *The Lost Lawyer: Failing Ideals of the Legal Profession* 226 (1993), as "the most powerful current in American law teaching today. Law and economics now completely dominates some fields and is a significant presence in most others. No responsible law teacher, however sympathetic or mistrustful, can ignore it." Despite the important contribution to law and economics that Kronman made in his article "Mistake, Disclosure, Information, and the Law of Contracts," 7 *Journal of Legal Studies* 1 (1978), he is among the mistrustful. See *The Lost Lawyer*, above, at 226–240.

31. Coase, note 5 above, at 10.

32. William M. Landes and Richard A. Posner, "The Influence of Economics on Law: A Quantitative Study," 36 *Journal of Law and Economics* 385, 405 (1993) (tab. 6).

33. To 40 percent for the period 1986–1990. Id.

he has lived in the United States since the mid-1950s, he is as much an American as a nineteenth-century Englishman in the Indian Civil Service was an Indian. He claims not to have been significantly influenced by any American economist other than Frank Knight,[34] and he rarely writes about any American institution other than the Federal Communications Commission, the functions of which in regard to telephone companies and broadcasters have counterparts in English institutions studied by Coase before he came to the United States.

His Englishness expresses itself in a number of ways, one superficial: the wit, feline in its subtlety and sharpness, that he occasionally turns on his fellow economists is vintage English academic acid, as in: "The clumsiness of his [Adam Smith's] treatment and its lack of finish have been strongly criticized by some economists, so strongly, indeed, as to suggest that if only these writers had been around in 1776 Adam Smith would not have been necessary."[35] The other aspects of Coase's Englishness have a deeper significance. He writes in an English economics tradition shaped by Smith and Marshall, by Coase's teacher Arnold Plant, and by the nineteenth-century laissez-faire movement, and although he has written against Hotelling and other non-English economists, in particular Paul Samuelson, his major target remains Pigou.[36] The mathematical and statistical movement in economics, which is primarily American (or at least primarily non-English), has passed Coase by completely and indeed is an object of his scorn. He writes the limpid prose of the accomplished English essayist. Its self-conscious plainness, modesty, commonsensicality, and rejection of high theory make Coase the George Orwell of modern economics.

34. "The Fire of Truth: A Remembrance of Law and Economics at Chicago, 1932–1970" (Edmund W. Kitch ed.), 26 *Journal of Law and Economics* 163, 213–215 (1983) (remarks of Coase). Even about Knight, Coase says, "I have little doubt that in my later writings I have been greatly influenced by him, although in what ways it is not easy to say." "The Nature of the Firm: Meaning," note 14 above, at 20. Doubtless what he found congenial in Knight was Knight's belief that economics had made little progress since Adam Smith and his skepticism about the use of quantitative techniques to test economic propositions. Neil Duxbury, "Law and Economics in America" 44–46 and n. 172 (unpublished, University of Manchester Faculty of Law, 1994).

35. "The New Institutional Economics," note 9 above, at 317. And recall Coase's summary dismissal of mathematical economics and his dig at quantitative methods.

36. See index references to Pigou and Samuelson in *The Firm, the Market, and the Law,* note 9 above, at 216–217. It would be more precise to speak of the "British" rather than of the "English" economics tradition, since Adam Smith was Scottish, as was David Hume, a seminal figure in the broader "English" intellectual tradition that I touch on below.

Suspicion of theory is a bright thread in the tapestry of English thought. One has only to recall the antimetaphysicality of Samuel Johnson, Bentham, and Hume, and in this century of Moore, Ayer, and J. L. Austin—so different from the tradition of Continental philosophy—and the antitheoretical tradition of the common law, so different from the abstract, a priori, systematizing cast of Continental jurisprudence. Even within theory there are differences between Englishmen and others. Both Adam Smith's invisible-hand theory and Darwin's theory of natural selection, despite their generality and subtlety, are extremely simple, nonmathematical concepts that, once grasped, seem (though not to everyone) completely intuitive and obviously correct. (Compare Cournot with Smith, and Mendel with Darwin.) Coase's theory of transaction costs is in this tradition of simple theory, for after disclaiming "innovations in high theory" he explains in the next sentence of his Nobel lecture: "My contribution to economics has been to urge the inclusion in our analysis of features of the economic system so obvious that, like the postman in G. K. Chesterton's Father Brown tale, 'The Invisible Man,' they have tended to be overlooked."[37] But Coase's theory, not only the part that goes by the name of the Coase Theorem but also (and related) the part that questions whether liability should always follow causality, is not obvious, is in fact counterintuitive, and required an intelligence of a very high order, whether or not mathematically gifted, to discover (or create)—though it is true that, partly because of its simplicity, it is easy to understand, especially for people too young to have been brought up in the Pigouvian tradition. The Coase Theorem can be proved mathematically, but the elementary arithmetical "proofs" that Coase presents in "The Problem of Social Cost," using locomotive sparks and straying cattle, are completely adequate. Coase is living proof of Whitehead's dictum that "it requires a very unusual mind to undertake the analysis of the obvious."[38]

For Coase the significance of the Coase Theorem is "as a stepping stone on the way to an analysis of an economy with positive transaction costs,"[39] an analysis to be conducted without fancy tools either theoretical or empirical, but rather by means of case studies guided by "basic economic theory." The basic theory does not (or at least pretends not

37. Coase, note 5 above, at 3.
38. Alfred North Whitehead, *Science and the Modern World* 4 (1925).
39. Coase, note 5 above, at 11.

to) include the concept of maximization. It may not include the concept of equilibrium. In Coase's eyes one of the great strengths of Adam Smith's view of economics is that he "thought of competition . . . as rivalry, as a process, rather than as a condition defined by a high elasticity of demand, as would be true for most modern economists. I need not conceal from you my belief that ultimately the Smithian view of competition will prevail."[40] Coase is on perilous ground here. The idea of competition as a process, as rivalry, rather than as the condition of a market in which, because each seller faces a highly elastic demand for its product or service, no seller can obtain a supracompetitive profit by restricting his output (in other words, a market that is in competitive equilibrium), is a source of much of the unsound thinking about monopoly that Coase decries. If a market contains few firms, or if all the sellers of a product charge the same price, the naive see a weakness or absence of competition and begin talking about "oligopolistic interdependence" and "conscious parallelism." A firm might have at present no rivals at all yet charge a competitive price because of an imminent possibility of new entry into its market.

Why does Coase see himself locked in a life and death struggle with economic formalism, indeed with the whole of modern economics outside the pale of that small but gallant band of "new institutional economists" of which he is the guru?[41] It is mainly, I think, because of what I am describing as his English mistrust of abstraction. People are not in fact rational maximizers, prices do not in fact equal marginal cost, markets are never in equilibrium. The formal models of economics hold only as approximations. Coase is not interested in approximations. He is interested in observable reality. For him the value of Smith's "invisible hand" is that it directs our attention to visible phenomena, namely economic practices and institutions that can be observed, described, compared. Of course the "Chicago School" economists to

40. "The Wealth of Nations," note 10 above, at 318.

41. "Modern institutional economics should study man as he is, acting within the constraints imposed by real institutions. Modern institutional economics is economics as it ought to be." "The New Institutional Economics," note 9 above, at 231. Yet Coase has criticized the original institutionalists, John R. Commons and company, for their hostility to classical economic theory, because "without a theory they had nothing to pass on except a mass of descriptive material waiting for a theory, or a fire" (id. at 230) (the acid wit again). By "theory," Coase means Adam Smith's view of economics. The modern institutionalists to whom Coase is referring—the "new" institutionalists—include Thráinn Eggertsson, Victor Goldberg, Benjamin Klein, Douglass North, and Oliver Williamson. See the next chapter.

whom Coase is often but erroneously compared, economists such as Friedman, Becker, and Stigler, also believe that theory is valuable only insofar as it guides investigation of the visible world; that is a hallmark of the Chicago School. But they think that formal theory *is* valuable in that respect, whereas Coase believes that no theoretical apparatus more elaborate than that of Adam Smith is needed or even helpful—or even harmless. Yet the invisible hand is after all invisible—a part of the theory world, not of the real world—and mathematics can lend precision to theory, can uncover inconsistencies, can generate hypotheses, can enable concision and even promote intelligibility, and can sort out complex interactions,[42] while statistical analysis can organize and interpret voluminous data. It is unlikely that serious students of transaction costs will eschew the formal methods that Coase dislikes and be content with paging through business records. In fact the guiding theory for that study is, increasingly, game theory, a body of formal theory. Coase's influence in economics has been diminished by the fact that his articles do not speak the language of modern economics, which is mathematics, and by the fact that he has not attempted to develop a *theory* of transaction costs.

> Coase has been misunderstood because he did not make his argument as accessible as it might be, and because the operational content of transaction costs is obscure. Coase eschews geometry and mathematics . . . and instead uses ponderous arithmetic examples to explain his theories. Although this does not prevent Coase from recognizing and discussing the nuances present in those theories, many readers would benefit from having his arguments, once conceptualized, translated into a more formal language . . . Coase . . . makes no such efforts and does not acknowledge efforts at translations that have been done by others. A chronic problem with Coase's work has been that the concept of transaction costs is vague . . . Although Coase evidently acknowledges the need for operationalization, he has yet to address himself to this in a systematic way.[43]

Mention of mathematics raises a larger question, that of complexity versus simplicity in expression. Many people believe with Orwell that writing ought to be as clear as a windowpane, implying simple words and short sentences. For many purposes this is true. But it is not

42. As I tried to do, in a very modest way, in modeling the judicial utility function in Chapter 3; see also Chapters 24 and 26.

43. Oliver E. Williamson, Book Review, 77 *California Law Review* 223, 229 (1989) (footnotes omitted).

universally true. For one thing there is a question of audience. Nowhere is it written that every author shall try to reach as large an audience as possible. In many forms of writing the interested audience is unalterably small and in possession of a specialized vocabulary; there is no reason the author should avoid the use of that vocabulary. Before pronouncing a writer "unreadable," one should be sure that one is a member of his intended audience, rather than, as it were, a mere eavesdropper. More important, even if we don't agree with the Wittgensteinians that thought is impossible without language, it is apparent that limiting one's vocabulary can limit the range and depth of one's thought—ironically, a point stressed by Orwell himself, in *Nineteen Eighty-Four* (remember "Newspeak"?). A larger, richer vocabulary, even a more intricate syntax, may enable greater understanding. Modern-day economists may overdo the math, but it isn't true that mathematics is simply an obscurantist mode of communication.

I don't mean to endorse repetitiousness, deliberate obscurity, jargon whether for its own sake or intended to dazzle and confuse the reader, euphemistic concealments of unpleasant realities, peacock parades of erudition, the tortured circumlocutions of political correctness, mixed metaphors, labored attempts at humor, and other familiar vices of professional and academic writing. (Recall my strictures on postmodernist writing, in Chapter 14.) Indeed, the increasingly interdisciplinary character of scholarship should place a premium on clear, jargon-free prose—a *lingua franca* to enable communication with scholars in other fields. I mean only to insist that "good writing" and the plain style are not always synonymous. To muddy the waters further, I point out that not all clear thinkers are clear writers, that some bad writers are good writers—John Rawls, for example, is an undistinguished stylist with a genius for the striking, pregnant phrase ("original position," "veil of ignorance," "reflective equilibrium," "overlapping consensus")—and that some good writers are bad writers. George Stigler, the wittiest, most elegant writer among professional economists, accused himself of the "vice of brevity." He was right. His writing is so compressed that it often is unnecessarily difficult to understand. But I am straying from my point. It is simply to remind, by way of criticism of Ronald Coase's methodological stance, that simplicity has a price.

Hostility to theory is especially salient in Coase's discussions of what economics *is*. It is not, for him, a body of theory, approaches, or techniques. Least of all is it the science of rational choice. It is merely "a common subject matter," namely "the economic system," more specifically "the working of the social institutions which bind together the economic system: firms, markets for goods and services, labour markets, capital markets, the banking system, international trade, and so on. It is the common interest in these social institutions which distinguishes the economics profession."[44] We now can understand better Coase's skepticism about Stigler's application of the economic model to the political process and his lack of interest in the lawyers' appropriation of the Coase Theorem. Coase deprecates the efforts of economists such as Stigler, and Gary Becker—who is the greatest practitioner and exponent of nonmarket economics—to push economic theory into other disciplines, such as law, sociology, sociobiology, education, health, demography, and politics. The acid wit is much in evidence here. "The reason for this movement of economists into neighbouring fields is certainly not that we have solved the problems of the economic system; it would perhaps be more plausible to argue that economists are looking for fields in which they can have some success."[45] Coase allows that the generality of economic theory facilitates its application to other fields. But since in his view the binding force of a field is subject matter rather than theory, the practitioners of those other fields will learn the relevant bits of economic theory from the economists and, thus equipped, will enjoy a decisive advantage over them: knowledge of the particular subject matter of the field in question. He allows too that economics is the most advanced social science, but he attributes this not to any theoretical sophistication but to the happenstance that the economist has a convenient measuring rod— money—which enables him to make precise observations. That measuring rod is absent (or largely so) when economists move into disciplines that do not study explicit markets. In Coase's view the expansion of economics into other fields signifies the abandonment of economics. Theory—by its very power, its formalism, and its resulting generality, which tempts economists to seek easy victories over weak disciplines—is ruining economics.

There must be something wrong with this view. Sociologists, psychologists, Marxist political theorists, historians, anthropologists, and even classicists (such as the late M. I. Finley) also study the economic

44. Coase, "Economics and Contiguous Disciplines," 7 *Journal of Legal Studies* 201, 204, 206–207 (1978).
45. Id. at 203.

system, yet they are not economists. The root fallacy, reflecting a philosophical naiveté that philosophers of science have found to be characteristic of the methodological views of scientists, including economists,[46] is the tenacious belief that every word has a correct definition and that it is the task of understanding to find that definition and act in accordance with it. We have encountered this fallacy before; it is the essential false move of legal formalism. Nineteenth-century legal thinkers thought that the meaning of contract was a meeting of minds, and therefore if one posted a reward for finding one's lost cat the person who found and returned it but hadn't seen the notice wouldn't have a legal claim to the reward. This was an unhelpful way of approaching the question whether a finder should be allowed to claim a reward of which he had no knowledge. The answer ought to depend on practical considerations, such as the impact on finding and the costs of using the legal system to enforce rewards for casual finders, rather than on the definition of the word "contract." The question of what economists ought to be doing is likewise not profitably pursued by inquiry into the meaning of economics, especially given the circularity of defining economics in terms of the economic system.

When Coase predicts that economists will in the end fall flat on their faces in competing with practitioners of other disciplines, he is implicitly conceding that the boundaries of a discipline are set by practical considerations rather than by definitional ones. This is a step in the right direction—and incidentally one that might be illuminated by Coase's theory of the firm. But the reason he offers for thinking that these incursions will fail is that a discipline is defined by its subject matter rather than by its theories or methods, and this begs the question of what the subject matter of economics is. This view is inconsistent with his own powerfully argued view, similar to that of Kuhn, that within a science (including economics) the acceptance of a theory is determined by a competitive process rather than by the theory's conformity to some a priori criterion of theory soundness, such as predictive success.[47]

Even if Coase could be persuaded, in accordance with the economic concept of comparative advantage, to change his definition of economics to what economists do better than other people, this would help

46. See, for example, Daniel M. Hausman, *The Inexact and Separate Science of Economics* (1992); Hausman, *Essays on Philosophy and Economic Methodology* (1992).

47. This is the theme of Coase's American Enterprise Institute pamphlet, cited in note 20—in my opinion his finest essay on methodology.

only a little, because it would beg the question of who or what an economist is. Is a lawyer who studies law as a method of economic optimization, perhaps using economic techniques unknown to Coase, a lawyer or an economist, or both, or neither? Perhaps (though I greatly doubt it) economics departments will become exclusive preserves of "high theory," and the kind of economics that interests Coase will be done in business schools, law schools, public-policy schools, political-science departments, departments of sociology and of public health and of education, and so forth (Gary Becker has a joint appointment in economics and sociology), perhaps by people with two degrees. Why should anyone other than a university bureaucrat, which Coase emphatically is not, care? Should we be sorry that statistics broke off from mathematics, or that some universities have separate departments of pure and of applied mathematics? Michel Foucault made a greater contribution to our understanding of Greek and Roman sexuality than any classicist other than Kenneth Dover, but was not considered a classicist. Classics departments decide who shall be considered classicists, using criteria that include but are not limited to merit and influence. State regulatory authorities decide who shall be considered a lawyer. Disciplines differ in their flexibility. Classics is among the least flexible, economics and philosophy among the most because each is willing to count as a member in good standing of its field people who don't have the standard credentials, such as Herbert Simon and Gordon Tullock in economics and Ronald Dworkin in philosophy. So if the lawyers take over economic analysis of law completely, as Coase fears, probably they will be called economists. To whom are such things important?

Much of the exciting work done in economics, not least by Coase himself, over the last thirty years has been in areas usually thought to belong to the economics of nonmarket behavior, such as the economics of education, the political process, health, the family, and law.[48] (Because of the success of this work, many economists now think of these as areas of "market" behavior.) So if little or none of this work is really "economics" one can understand the disquiet with which Coase contemplates the present state of economic theory and the urgency with which he calls for "a complete change" in it. For maybe in economics

48. See Gary S. Becker, "Nobel Lecture: The Economic Way of Looking at Behavior," 101 *Journal of Political Economy* 385 (1993); also Jack Hirshleifer, "The Expanding Domain of Economics," 75 *American Economic Review* 53, 59 n. 24 (special anniversary issue, Dec. 1985), and other references in *The Problems of Jurisprudence* 370 n. 16.

proper as he would regard it the dominant movement *has* been toward greater formalization of economic theory rather than toward greater understanding of the economic system—though certainly not the only movement. Labor economics, which Coase acknowledges as part of economics, has made great strides in this period. Likewise the theory of finance, which deals with capital markets—markets that are a part of the domain of economics as Coase understands it. And the economics of regulation, as Coase has acknowledged;[49] and the economics of information, when applied to market phenomena, such as the dispersion of prices for the same good, rather than to (say) marital search, a subject that for Coase is outside economics. Even narrowly defined, economics has not stood still for thirty years, let alone for two hundred. But once one understands Coase's *very* narrow definition of the subject *and* his dislike of formalization, it becomes possible to understand how such an intelligent person can hold so questionable a view.

People have the weaknesses of their strengths. The eccentricity of genius, and the occasional cantankerousness that it breeds,[50] is another name for intellectual independence. It is a condition encouraged by a protracted and brooding intellectual isolation.

> Many of his main ideas were conceived very early in his life . . . He thought about these ideas and enriched his analysis by reading and observation for about thirty years. His life included long periods . . . in which he worked out his position completely alone, with little or no contact with others interested in economic questions . . . There can be no doubt that he enjoyed his own company and could work well on his own without requiring any stimulus from others.[51]

That is Coase, the greatest living English economist, writing about Adam Smith, his greatest predecessor. But it describes Coase equally well[52]—and not only because "The Problem of Social Cost" was published approximately thirty years after Coase began work in economics. We need not heed Coase's methodological prescriptions in order to realize that they have served him well.

---

49. Coase, note 20 above, at 19.

50. One review of *The Firm, the Market, and the Law* remarked the "querulous" tone of portions of it: "The message is 'I am misunderstood.'" Michael C. Munger, Book Review, 65 *Public Choice* 295, 296 (1990).

51. "The Wealth of Nations," note 10 above, at 310.

52. "Ronald is English to the tips of his fingers, [and] a natural recluse." George J. Stigler, *Memoirs of an Unregulated Economist* 159 (1988).

chapter 21

The New Institutional Economics
Meets Law and Economics

I QUOTED Coase in the preceding chapter as saying that the new (he called it the modern) institutional economics "is economics as it ought to be."[1] He is also one of the principal founders of the post-antitrust law and economics. So he can be said to stand at the intersection of these two movements, making it natural to suppose that there is considerable overlap between them—even, perhaps, that they are the same. There is an overlap, but not an identity, although the differences are ultimately rather unimportant because both fields are parts of economics and economics is increasingly a single field, utilizing a common paradigm in Kuhn's sense, and because many of the apparent differences are ones merely in emphasis and vocabulary.

What Is the "New Institutional Economics"?

The adjective "new" implies that there was a previous institutional economics, as of course there was,[2] and in fact still is.[3] The best known

1. For an introduction to the new institutional economics, see *Economics as a Process: Essays in the New Institutional Economics* (Richard N. Langlois ed. 1986).

2. For an excellent summary, see Terence W. Hutchison, "Institutionalist Economics Old and New," 140 *Journal of Institutional and Theoretical Economics* 20 (1984).

3. See, for example, Geoffrey M. Hodgson, *Economics and Institutions: A Manifesto for a*

of the original institutionalists, Thorstein Veblen and John R. Commons, flourished in the early decades of this century. The most famous of their living epigones is John Kenneth Galbraith; the leading practitioner is Allan Gruchy. Another member of the school is Willard Hurst, professor emeritus of law at the University of Wisconsin Law School. Ian Macneil of Northwestern University Law School can be placed in their camp too. (I shall return to Hurst and Macneil.) The leitmotif of the old institutional economics was (and is) the rejection of classical economic theory—in some versions of all theory—which invited Coase's dismissive characterization, quoted in the preceding chapter: "without a theory they had nothing to pass on except a mass of descriptive material waiting for a theory, or a fire."[4] I once tried to read Willard Hurst's magnum opus, a massive tome on the history of the lumber industry of Wisconsin,[5] but didn't get far. The book is a dense mass of description—lucid, intelligent, and I am sure scrupulously accurate, but so wanting in a theoretical framework—in a perceptible *point*—as to be unreadable, almost as if the author had forgotten to arrange his words into sentences.[6] It is a warning that the taste for fact that I would like to see developed in judges and law professors will turn to gall if unaccompanied by a taste for theory—not normative theory, so not what passes for theory in constitutional law, but positive theory, economic or otherwise, that guides the search for significant facts.

Modern Institutional Economics (1988)—which despite its title is highly critical of what I am calling the new institutional economics. The "old" institutional economics has its own society, the Association for Evolutionary Economics, and its own journal, the *Journal of Economic Issues*.

4. Of the (old) institutional school, George Stigler said, "The school died as completely as any school can die in the sense that it has no viable influence on even the successful schools and no current and important successors." "The Fire of Truth: A Remembrance of Law and Economics at Chicago, 1932–1970" (Edmund W. Kitch ed.), 26 *Journal of Law and Economics* 163, 170 (1983) (remarks of Professor Stigler). The antitheoretical character of the old institutionalism is acknowledged, indeed celebrated, in Jon D. Wisman and Joseph Rozansky, "The Methodology of Institutionalism Revisited," 25 *Journal of Economic Issues* 709 (1991).

5. James Willard Hurst, *Law and Economic Growth: The Legal History of the Lumber Industry in Wisconsin 1836–1915* (1964).

6. For more sympathetic evaluations, written from the perspective of critical legal studies, which likes the old institutionalists' politics and their hostility to neoclassical economic theory, see Robert W. Gordon, "Introduction: J. Willard Hurst and the Common Law Tradition in American Legal Historiography," 10 *Law and Society Review* 9, 44–45 (1975); Mark Tushnet, "Lumber and the Legal Process," 1972 *Wisconsin Law Review* 114.

The old institutional economists rejected classical economic theory, the theory of Adam Smith, thus endearing them to the practitioners of critical legal studies. The new institutional economics, in some versions anyway, rejects or at least severely questions neoclassical economic theory, as expounded for example by Paul Samuelson. The reasons for this rejection are both methodological and political. In order to facilitate mathematical formulation and exposition, neoclassical economic theory routinely adopts what appear to be, and often are, from both a physical and a psychological standpoint, highly unrealistic assumptions: that individuals and firms are rational maximizers, that information is costless, that the demand curves of individual firms are infinitely elastic, that inputs and outputs are infinitely divisible, that cost and revenue schedules are mathematically regular, and so forth. The unrealism of the assumptions sometimes drives a wedge between economic theory and the economic system that the theory is purporting to describe and explain. Since the reality does not fit the theory, it is natural, though surely not inevitable, for theoreticians to want to alter the reality. So—and here is where the political objection to neoclassical theory originates—because conditions in the real world never satisfy the theory's specifications for an efficient allocation of resources (price equal to marginal cost, no externalities, no second-best problems, markets complete, and so forth), neoclassical economic theory becomes a recipe for public interventions—antitrust laws, pollution-control laws, compulsory schooling, laws regulating employment, public utility and common carrier regulation, and much else besides. With every deviation from perfect competition labeled "market failure" and such deviations everywhere, it is hard to retain a robust faith in unregulated markets. This is disquieting to economic liberals (now more likely to be called conservatives), and it is no surprise therefore that they dominate the new institutional economics. (There is of course an influential strain in traditional conservativism of suspicion of all theory.)

The new institutional economists, however, are not against economic theory *tout court*. This is the vital difference between them and the old institutionalists. Some of them, like Coase, want to return to the earlier, simpler, looser, nonmathematical theory of Adam Smith. Being thus unworried about mathematical intractability, they are happy to relax the more austere assumptions of neoclassical theory. Others, like Oliver Williamson, have reservations about specific aspects of neoclassical theory but want to enrich rather than abandon it. Some new institutionalists do not want to change economic theory at all but merely want to see it applied across the full range of institutions in diverse cultures and epochs.[7]

Rejection of economic formalism, or of a certain version of that formalism, is the negative side of the new institutional economics. The positive side is the study of—institutions. It may be hard to see how an interest in institutions could distinguish the new institutional economics from all but the most abstruse mathematical economics. Below those dizzying heights *all* economists believe they are engaged in the study of institutions: the institutions of the economic system broadly or narrowly understood. Theorists of "perfect competition" think they are studying an institution called the price system or the market. The new institutionalists, like their predecessors the old institutionalists, think of institutions in a grittier sense. They study not "the market" but the concrete institutions that enable markets to work—for example, the rules of the Chicago Board of Trade, or long-term contracts in the uranium industry, or how public utilities set rates, or the terms on which diamonds are offered to dealers, or the common law system of property rights in animals, or the operation of restrictive covenants in a city without zoning laws, or the governance structure of conglomerate corporations, or how problems of trespassing animals are handled by ranchers in a particular county in California, or the emergence of the nation-state, or even the function of the engagement ring in the marriage "market."[8] Intensive scrutiny of particular institutions implies in turn a greater emphasis on the case study, based on histories and ethnographies, judicial opinions and other court records, newspaper and magazine accounts, and even interviews, than on studies of aggregated data analyzed in accordance with modern theories of statistical inference. So the impression is of a field that is skeptical not only about formal economic theory but also about econometrics.

Having been classified with the new institutional economists,[9] I must be very careful in my criticisms. I do not doubt for a moment that

7. For example, Thráinn Eggertsson, in his book *Economic Behavior and Institutions* (1990), is careful to distinguish his approach from that of those new institutionalists who question the rational-choice model. Id. at 6.

8. Margaret F. Brinig, "Rings and Promises," 6 *Journal of Law, Economics, and Organization* 203 (1990).

9. Kaushik Basu, Eric Jones, and Ekkehart Schlict, "The Growth and Decay of Custom: The Role of the New Institutional Economics in Economic History," 24 *Explorations in Economic History* 1, 2 n. 4 (1987).

there is a place in economics for case studies guided by informal theory—an apt description, in truth, of much of my own work—and therefore for the new institutional economics. But I reject any suggestion that the new institutional economics ought somehow to displace the rest of microeconomics. The view that it should is bound up with a dislike of abstraction, a sense that it falsifies reality. Abstraction does imply a departure from descriptive realism, but, as Milton Friedman has long argued, a theory is not necessarily false just because the assumptions on which it rests are unrealistic (that is, false in detail).[10] The idea that it is rests on a misunderstanding of the purpose of theory, which is not to describe the phenomena being investigated but to add to our useful knowledge, mainly of causal relations. For that purpose, an unrealistic theory may be quite serviceable—may in fact be essential. Suppose the question is whether imposing an excise tax on cigarettes will cause the price of cigarettes to rise and the number sold to fall. The answer, which is important to predicting both the health effects and the revenue effects of the tax, would not be obvious to a person innocent of economic theory; he might think that the cigarette producers would swallow the tax whole, leaving price and therefore output unaltered. One could model the problem by assuming that the cigarette industry is perfectly competitive, that its output is infinitely divisible, that the price of cigarettes is infinitely divisible, that consumers are perfectly informed, that prices can be changed instantaneously, and all the rest, and the model would predict that the excise tax would cause price to rise and output to fall. So if the excise tax were imposed and the effects were as predicted, we would have some reason to think that we had discovered a causal relation and that by further use of the model we might discover other causal relations.

The statistical counterpart to this observation is that it is possible to have a regression equation in which the coefficients of the independent variables are highly significant statistically even though the amount of variance explained by the equation is small.[11] This would mean that although the equation was not a complete or even adequate description, it had identified robust correlations. These correlations might well have causal significance and thus enable prediction and control.

10. Coase, however, rejects Friedman's methodological position. R. H. Coase, *How Should Economists Choose?* (American Enterprise Institute 1982).

11. Recall the brief discussion of this point in the Introduction, in the context of economic analysis of crime and punishment.

If, returning to the cigarette example, we wanted to know whether a cigarette excise tax would have a greater impact on purchases by educated than by uneducated people, we would need a more refined model. We might partition the full price of cigarettes into the nominal price and the perceived health costs and assume that the health costs and therefore the full price would be higher for educated consumers. There are several reasons for that assumption. The costs of bad health are greater the greater one's income is (there is more to lose if one is disabled by poor health); income and education are positively correlated; and the better educated have lower costs of information about health—so, among other things, the refined model would be relaxing the standard neoclassical assumption of complete, costless information. The refined model predicts that the demand of educated consumers for cigarettes will be less price-elastic than the demand of the uneducated because price is a smaller fraction of the full cost of cigarettes to the educated than to the uneducated, and therefore that the excise tax would have a smaller impact on purchases by the educated. If the prediction turned out to be correct,[12] we would have learned something about economic behavior, even though the refined model was still highly unrealistic because it assumed infinitely divisible prices and outputs, and so on. A model can be a useful tool of discovery even if it is unrealistic, just as Ptolemy's astronomical theory was a useful tool of navigation (and hence of "discovery" in another sense) even though its basic premise was false. Conversely, a full description, such as we find in Willard Hurst's book about lumber, can be useless.

We should be pragmatic about theory. It is a tool, rather than a glimpse of ultimate truth, and the criterion of a tool is its utility. One doubts how much research in pure mathematics there would be if mathematical discoveries seemingly of no utility when made (such as the discovery of non-Euclidean geometry in the nineteenth century) had not, time and again, been later found to have practical utility. For all I know, there is more truth in Hurst's book than in the entire economic literature on excise taxation. Only I cannot see the utility of Hurst's book.

Not only is it wrong to be against formal theory; it is wrong to suppose that formal economic theory is inherently interventionist.

12. For confirming evidence, see Gary S. Becker, Michael Grossman, and Kevin M. Murphy, "Rational Addiction and the Effect of Price on Consumption," 81 *American Economic Review* 237, 240 (Papers and Proceedings issue, May 1991).

Maybe *bad* formal theory is, but that's a different point. Neoclassical theorists used to be pretty casual about proposing the use of public funds to correct "market failures," because the theorists assumed that public funds could be obtained through income taxation with no important misallocative effects. In a *theoretical* paper—not a case study of the Internal Revenue Service—Milton Friedman showed that there was no reason in theory to expect the misallocative effects of an income tax to be any smaller than those of an excise tax.[13]

Coase's great papers on the firm, on the pricing of services produced under conditions of declining average cost, and on social cost may have grown out of his practically oriented education (his undergraduate degree was in commerce, not economics) and out of case studies, such as his study of the Federal Communications Commission, in which the Coase Theorem was first adumbrated. But they are theoretical papers. They correct neoclassical theory by adding transaction costs to the analytic framework (as George Stigler added information costs), by refuting Hotelling's case for public ownership of natural monopolies, and by showing that Pigou was wrong to suppose that the efficient way to correct a negative externality always is to tax or regulate the injurer. Coase has helped us to see that socialists deform economic theory in a socialist direction, requiring correction by economic liberals such as himself. It is a theoretical task.

And while it is right to distrust facile theorizing in economics as in other fields, we should not overlook the *efficiency* of theory. The tortoise doesn't always beat the hare. Milton Friedman is the world's most influential economic liberal. He conducted famous institutional studies of professionals' incomes and of the history of monetary policy in the United States, but those studies are peripheral to his significance for economic liberalism. That significance rests on his opposition to the progressive income tax, his insistence on the dependence of political liberty on economic liberty, his advocacy of the volunteer army and of a balanced-budget constitutional amendment, his criticisms of Keynesianism, his opposition to professional licensure and to paternalistic legislation such as the narcotics laws, and his proposals for education vouchers and for a negative income tax. It shows no disrespect to Friedman to point out that he has not conducted any detailed, painstaking case studies of the subject matter of his policy positions outside

13. Milton Friedman, *Price Theory*, ch. 3 (1976).

of the fiscal and monetary areas and (as noted in Chapter 1) professional licensure. He arrived at those positions as a matter of theory. Had he followed the case-study route his range would have been narrower and economics would be poorer as a result.

Here is another example of the fruitfulness of formal economic theory for the study of institutions. The household is an economic institution. It is as important to the economy as the firm is. It is also a nonstandard organizational form of the sort neoclassical theorists were apt to neglect. As they should not have done: The increased productivity of the household in recent decades as a result of the new labor-saving devices (not only kitchen appliances but also frozen dinners), improved methods of family planning, better communications, and technological advances in home entertainment has been instrumental in enabling increased female participation in the labor force, which is transforming the economies of the wealthy nations. The leading student of household production, Gary Becker, is a formidable theorist. His basic theoretical tool, which institutionalists old and new tend to deride, is the assumption that people are rational maximizers of their satisfactions. This assumption has guided fruitful empirical work by Becker and others, as well as bringing the household securely within the orbit of economic analysis. We need not regret the absence of economic case studies of individual families.

I have been purporting to describe the new institutional economics in gross, but in fact I have been describing the conception of the field held by Coase and those who identify closely with him. Oliver Williamson has a somewhat different conception—perhaps different emphasis would be a better word.[14] His approach is more eclectic than Coase's, both methodologically and politically. Williamson has no objection in principle to formal models or to econometric studies, and indeed rather than hankering for a return to the informal approach of Adam Smith he wants to build a new model of economic behavior that will incorporate not only certain insights of Smith and the "old institutionalists" but also the insights of modern psychology and organization theory.

---

14. See, for example, Oliver E. Williamson, "The Economics of Governance: Framework and Implications," 140 *Journal of Institutional and Theoretical Economics* 195 (1984), and "Reflections on the New Institutional Economics," 141 *Journal of Institutional and Theoretical Economics* 187 (1985). The fullest presentation of Williamson's approach can be found in his book *The Economic Institutions of Capitalism: Firms, Markets, Relational Contracting* (1985).

He wants to apply the enriched model primarily to vertical integration, corporate governance, and long-term contracts. He does not appear to be particularly interested in formal markets such as the securities and commodities exchanges, in property rights, in externalities, or in the critique of public regulation. Rather his focus is on types of contract, broadly understood, that are remote from spot contracts (where the conditions for perfect competition—many buyers and sellers, full knowledge, standardized goods, and so forth—are most likely to be satisfied, or at least approximated) and that instead are permeated by asymmetric information, bilateral monopoly, and uncertainty. Coase directed the attention of the economics profession to the importance of transaction costs. Williamson seeks to move down the research agenda implicit in Coase's work by exploring the sources of high transaction costs and the contractual and organizational devices that businessmen have devised to overcome such costs. Other votaries of the new institutional economics, such as Douglass North, comparing the state to a long-term contract, use transaction-cost economics to enrich the study of political institutions.[15]

But in the process of moderating Coase, Williamson has gone far toward collapsing the new institutional economics back into mainstream economics—which is fine with me. He believes that what he is doing is novel—that he is rejecting key assumptions of neoclassical economics, such as rational maximization, in favor of new concepts such as "bounded rationality," "asset specificity," "information impactedness," "dimensionalizing," and "opportunism"; that he is drawing new disciplines into economics, notably law and organization theory;[16] and that he is redirecting economists' attention to institutions previously ignored by them. The last point is correct, but it is unclear how much of Williamson's approach can be described as new theory and

15. See, for example, Douglass C. North, "Transaction Costs, Institutions, and Economic History," 140 *Journal of Institutional and Theoretical Economics* 7 (1984). North's work is linked—at the level of subject matter, not method—with the branch of the old institutional economics, illustrated by the work of Gunnar Myrdal, that emphasized institutional obstacles to the development of backward countries. See Christer Gunnarsson, "What Is New and What Is Institutional in the New Institutional Economics? An Essay on Old and New Institutionalism and the Role of the State in Developing Countries," 39 *Scandinavian Economic History Review* 43 (1991).

16. "The three interdisciplinary legs of NIE [New Institutional Economics] are law (especially contract law), economics (with a relentless emphasis on economizing), and organization theory (which is responsible for greater behavioral content)." "Reflections on the New Institutional Economics," note 14 above, at 190.

how much is the repackaging of old theory in a new vocabulary that is not necessarily an improvement, in point of clarity or precision, over the old one. Does "bounded rationality," for example, mean more than that economic actors have and must (rationally) act on less than full information? The costs both of producing and absorbing or processing information have been a part of mainline economic theory since Stigler's article on information costs, published in the early 1960s (see Chapter 20). They can be—they have been—incorporated into economic theory without the alteration of any fundamental assumptions, such as rational maximization; for rationality is not omniscience. Williamson argues that equating bounded rationality to positive information costs overlooks "the impossibility of thinking through complex but well-structured problems—such as describing the complete decision tree for chess."[17] But isn't that just an example of costly information processing?[18] Chess machines can process this particular class of problems at lower cost than most human beings. As for the "idea of mind as a scarce resource,"[19] does this mean anything more than that the mind has limited information-processing capabilities—in other words that not just the production, but the processing, of information is costly?

Williamson remarks people's "inability to correctly process low probability events."[20] Although this too sounds like a case in which the costs of processing information are high, Williamson is referring to a psychological literature that finds that human beings have systematic incapacities for accurately processing certain types of information, such as low-probability events, or information framed in particular ways.[21]

"Bounded rationality" could thus refer to (1) costs of acquiring information, (2) costs of processing information, (3) ineradicable uncertainties (if either type of cost is prohibitive) of the sort to which insurance is an institutional response, (4) distortions in information processing that result from the structure of the human brain, or (5)

17. Williamson, "Transaction Cost Economics Meets Posnerian Law and Economics," 149 *Journal of Institutional and Theoretical Economics* 99, 109 (1993).

18. It is so described by Williamson's guru, Herbert Simon. "Theories of Rationality," in Simon, *Models of Bounded Rationality,* vol. 2: *Behavioral Economics and Business Organization* 408, 416 (1982).

19. Williamson, note 17 above, at 110.

20. Id. at 109.

21. See, for example, *Decision Making: Descriptive, Normative, and Prescriptive Interactions* (David E. Bell, Howard Raiffa, and Amos Tversky eds. 1988).

some combination of the above.[22] It would be nice if Williamson would explain "bounded rationality" in these terms and indicate what he thinks the utility of the concept is.

Another of Williamson's favorite terms, "asset specificity," is at least clear; it refers to the existence of specialized resources and hence to the problem of bilateral monopoly. "Opportunism" is clear too. As used by Williamson and other economists, it means taking advantage— sometimes of a temporary monopoly, sometimes of superior information ("asymmetric information"); in other words it is self-interest in settings in which private incentives cannot be relied on to promote social welfare. These terms are happily free of the obscurities that surround "bounded rationality." But they are merely new words for old themes in economics. The increasing use of game theory to develop these themes comes out of—game theory, rather than out of anything special to the new institutional economics.

The novelty of Williamson's work lies not in identifying new sources of "market failure" and domesticating them for theory, or in formulating a theory of transaction costs; it lies in inviting economists' attention to a host of underexplored problems[23] and contributing to their solution by exploring the ways in which businessmen overcome transaction costs by a variety of devices in a variety of settings. Williamson has argued for example that the decentralized organization characteristic of conglomerate corporations economizes on the costs of information, compared to the traditional hierarchical structure, and by doing so enlarges the span of corporate management's control. And there is now a rich literature showing how firms adapt to the uncertainty, and the resulting bilateral monopoly problems and opportunistic temptations, of long-term contracts.[24]

But how much does this literature actually owe to the ideas of Williamson, or even for that matter of Coase? There is a clue in

22. For a useful discussion, see Kenneth E. Scott, "Bounded Rationality and Social Norms," 150 *Journal of Institutional and Theoretical Economics* 315 (1994).

23. It is greatly to Williamson's credit that he was willing to discuss important issues in economics, for example the behavior of the firm, before the theoretical tools for addressing the issues had been developed. Theory has now caught up.

24. See, for an example of this literature, Keith J. Crocker and Scott E. Masten, "Pretia ex Machina? Prices and Process in Long-Term Contracts," 34 *Journal of Law and Economics* 69 (1991). Benjamin Klein, a leader in this branch of the new institutional economics, provides a useful summary in his article "Self-Enforcing Contracts," 141 *Journal of Institutional and Theoretical Economics* 594 (1985).

Williamson's rather warped view (as it seems to me) of "the applied price tradition at Chicago."[25] He commends the Chicago School for "its insistence that nonstandard forms of organization be examined through the lens of price theory," but criticizes it for encouraging economists to "focus on monopoly features," such as price discrimination, as explanations for these nonstandard forms (tying arrangements, vertical integration, and so forth).[26] The criticism overlooks the central role of information costs not only in Stigler's article on the economics of information but also in his theory of cartels—where costs of information are one great theme and opportunism is the other.[27] The law and economics work at Chicago—work very much in the applied price tradition that Williamson properly associates with Friedman, Stigler, and their followers—is preoccupied with problems of uncertainty, bilateral monopoly, and opportunism and with how legal and economic institutions try to solve them.[28] None of this work is cited by Williamson even though law is one leg of the interdisciplinary tripod on which the new institutional economics is said by him to rest.

Twenty years ago one had a definite sense that economics was a field divided into rival schools—the Harvard School, the Chicago School, the MIT School, the Cambridge School, and so on. That is much less true today. The biggest difference today is between theoretical economics and applied economics. New institutional economics à la Williamson is a form of applied economics not easy to distinguish, save in vocabulary, from the other forms; and the only word in the new vocabulary that is genuinely useful is "opportunism."

Law and Economics

The roots of the law and economics movement are deep. Bentham applied economic theory to the behavior of criminals and the methods

25. "Reflections on the New Institutional Economics," note 14 above, at 189.
26. Id. at 189–190.
27. The relevant essays are in George J. Stigler, *The Organization of Industry* (1968).
28. For examples of papers in which those themes are particularly emphasized, see William M. Landes and Richard A. Posner, "The Independent Judiciary in an Interest-Group Perspective," 18 *Journal of Law and Economics* 875 (1975); Landes and Posner, "Salvors, Finders, Good Samaritans, and Other Rescuers: An Economic Study of Law and Altruism," 7 *Journal of Legal Studies* 83 (1978); Landes and Posner, "A Positive Economic Analysis of Products Liability Law," 14 *Journal of Legal Studies* 535 (1985); and Posner, "Gratuitous Promises in Economics and Law," 6 *Journal of Legal Studies* 411 (1977).

of criminal punishment. Holmes, Brandeis, Learned Hand, and Robert Hale prepared the ground for the reception of economics into American law. In the 1940s and 1950s, antitrust law, corporate law, public utility regulation, and federal taxation were brought under the scrutiny of economics; representative figures from that period include Aaron Director, Henry Simons, Donald Turner, and Henry Manne. In the following decade, papers by Coase, Becker, and Guido Calabresi ushered in the "new" law and economics, which emphasizes the application of economics to the central institutions of the legal system, including property, contracts, torts, criminal law, family law, civil and criminal procedure, damages and other remedies, admiralty, restitution, legislation, and common law rulemaking with its emphasis on decision according to precedent. The years since 1970 have witnessed an expanding torrent of scholarly writing across the full range of law and economics, old (where a significant area of development has been the economics of bankruptcy) as well as new.[29]

The law and economics movement differs from the new institutional economics in that it has no, or at least very few, aspirations to change economic theory or economists' empirical methodology. Partly because of the nature of its subject matter and partly because many of its practitioners have little formal training in economics or statistics, there is much reliance on informal theory and on case studies. But there is no hostility to mathematical modeling or econometric methodology, and the latest generation of law and economics scholars is deep into game theory. Nor, although some of the most prominent practitioners of law and economics are economic liberals in the tradition of Coase, Hayek, and Friedman, is there a political cast or agenda to law and economics, except insofar as any form of "bourgeois" economic analysis strikes left-wing radicals as political. The only thing that is distinctive

29. For a sense of the contemporary scope of the field, see *Economic Analysis of Law*. On the growing influence of the law and economics movement on law, see William M. Landes and Richard A. Posner, "The Influence of Economics on Law: A Quantitative Study," 36 *Journal of Law and Economics* 385 (1993); also Chapter 2 of the present book. There is a professional association, the American Law and Economics Association, and also a growing number of practitioners of law and economics in Europe, Japan, and Latin America. There is even a band of law and economics scholars in the line of descent from the old institutionalists. See *Law and Economics: An Institutional Perspective* (Warren J. Samuels and A. Allan Schmid eds. 1981); Nicholas Mercuro and Steven G. Medema, "Schools of Thought in Law and Economics: A Kuhnian Competition" 46–60 (Working Paper no. 12–93, Dept. of Economics and Finance, University of New Orleans, 1993).

about the movement, viewed as a movement in economics, is its subject matter; only viewed as a movement in law is it methodologically radical.

The subject matter of law and economics overlaps that of the new institutional economics at a number of points. Vertical integration, corporate governance, and long-term contracts are foci of law and economics just as they are foci of the new institutional economics. Students of those practices whom Oliver Williamson clasps to his bosom, such as Benjamin Klein, Victor Goldberg, and Paul Joskow, are also and equally and rightly considered practitioners of law and economics. Historically oriented new institutionalists such as Douglass North and Thráinn Eggertsson exhibit the same deep interest in property rights as law and economics scholars do.

The overlap between the two approaches is not total, and this leads to a difference not in theory but in theoretical emphasis. The preoccupation of the new institutional economists with transaction costs leads them away from price theory toward theoretical concepts tailor-made as it were for transaction-cost problems. (An exception is the concept of bilateral monopoly, which is part of traditional price theory.) The broader subject-matter domain of law and economics is conducive to a more eclectic theoretical approach. When the economist or economically minded lawyer studies even so recherché a subject (from a traditional economist's standpoint) as criminal law, he is likely to rely heavily on the tools of price theory, since while criminal punishments are not prices they have effects similar to those of prices. And likewise with studies of legal restrictions on the adoption market, or of the traffic in illegal drugs. But finance theory plays a large role in the economic analysis of corporation law, bankruptcy law, and other areas of commercial law, and public choice a large role in the economic analysis of statutes and constitutions. Human-capital theory also plays a large role in law and economics (we had a glimpse of that in Chapter 13), and may in fact explain some of the phenomena that particularly interest the institutionalists.

Still, there is much overlap between law and economics and the new institutional economics, and yet when Williamson speaks of law as one of the legs of the interdisciplinary tripod on which the new institutional economics rests he seems not to be referring to economic analysis of law, the defining activity of the law and economics movement. Organization theory is distinct from economic theory, so one could see the two theories as separate legs of an interdisciplinary trunk. But it is very difficult to see how the application of economic theory to law could be a third distinct leg. And then as I have said Williamson does not cite the "new" law and economics literature out of Chicago, although it deals directly with the very topics that interest him the most. He seems to think that legal theory somehow distinct from economic theory can contribute to the new institutional economics—can be a separate leg of the stool from economics—so naturally one of his favorite law professors is Ian Macneil, the noneconomic theorist of "relational" contracting.[30] Macneil believes that contract law has been too much concerned with spot contracts to the exclusion of contracts embedded in an ongoing relationship between the contracting parties.

This is music to Williamson's ears. But unfortunately—though all too commonly when one is speaking of legal "theories" that lack a foundation in economics—Macneil's theory of contracts has little content. He is in quest of "a *Grundnorm* recognizing the embeddedness of all exchange in relations."[31] If this means that we ought to think about the problems and opportunities that arise when parties have a continuing relation rather than merely meeting as strangers in a spot market, I agree. Such a relation may make contracts self-enforcing, because each party stands to lose if the relation terminates. Conversely it may create temptations to opportunistic breach—maybe one party's performance precedes the other's—or problems of bilateral monopoly, which can be acute in cases in which one party seeks modification of the contract, because the parties can deal only with each other. These are problems on which, as we saw in Chapter 13 with respect to employment contracts, economics has a strong grip. Neither Macneil nor any other "legal theorist" of contracts has anything to contribute to their solution.[32] If I am right that the new institutional economics and the law and economics movement are two sides of the same coin, Macneil's irrational hostility to the latter may explain his inability to make concrete contributions to the former. I do not think "irrational" is too strong a description of the following passage, which is representative: "The law-and-economics vision is one of two alternative

30. On Williamson's high regard for Macneil, see *The Economic Institutions of Capitalism*, note 14 above, at 68–73.

31. Ian R. Macneil, "Reflections on Relational Contract," 141 *Journal of Institutional and Theoretical Economics* 541, 542 (1985).

32. But the reader can judge for himself by reading Macneil's review article "Relational Contract: What We Do and Do Not Know," 1985 *Wisconsin Law Review* 483, esp. pp. 523–524.

visions of Hell in America. A realistic law-and-economics vision is simply a slightly milder, right-liberal mainstream Hell . . . An idealistic law-and-economics vision is a Hell of hedonistic markets governed, along with everything else in life, by private bureaucratic law unmitigated by any more due process than the private bureaucracies find it desirable to allow."[33]

So the law leg of Williamson's stool collapses; and as far as the organization-theory leg is concerned it adds, so far as I can see, nothing to economics that the literature on information costs had not added years earlier. I am therefore confirmed in my earlier suggestion that the new institutional economics, save in Coase's version, is just—economics; and I have said that the law and economics movement is just economics too. When the new institutionalists study long-term contracts and corporate governance and vertical integration and property rights and the like, they are doing the same thing that the law and economics scholars do when they study the same subjects. In that area of inquiry, at least, the convergence between the two approaches is complete. It is to be regretted that Oliver Williamson's taste for neologisms has made the convergence more difficult to recognize than it should be.

Rational Utility Maximization Revisited

The biggest gulf between the two movements arises from the new institutionalists' skeptical attitude toward rational utility maximization. Coase rejects this cornerstone of modern economic theory—he has called it "meaningless"[34]—yet at the same time says that his own approach is guided by the assumption that people prefer more to less.[35] So if I am offered a choice between 3 and 2 I will prefer 3. But what if I have another opportunity, worth 4? Then I will prefer it, because I prefer more to less. Well, but what if I have still another opportunity, worth 5? I will choose that. And so on—until I have maximized my

33. "Bureaucracy, Liberalism, and Community—American Style," 79 *Northwestern University Law Review* 900, 919 (1984).

34. Coase, "Coase on Posner on Coase," 149 *Journal of Institutional and Theoretical Economics* 96, 97 (1993).

35. "For groups of human beings, in almost all circumstances, a higher (relative) price for anything will lead to a reduction in the amount demanded. This does not only refer to a money price but to price in its widest sense." *The Firm, the Market, and the Law*, note 14 above, at 4.

utility. Not so, says Coase: Gary Becker's demonstration that "even if people are not rational, one would expect a higher price to lead to a reduction in the amount demanded" shows that it is an error to suppose that the fact "that a lower price leads to a greater amount demanded implies a rational maximizing of utility."[36]

Becker's argument is that since consumers have limited budgets, even irrational consumers will on average purchase less of a good when its price rises, because the consumers' resources will become depleted sooner. Becker did not suggest that he thinks that most or for that matter any consumers *are* irrational. Nor did he suggest that well-attested economic phenomena other than the downward-sloping market demand curve, such as the tendency of the prices of the same good to be equalized, can be explained without assuming rationality. But all this is an aside. Coase does not believe that people buy randomly. He thinks they prefer more to less. This implies that demand curves are negatively sloped because consumers are rational.

Could Coase believe that some cognitive or psychological defect prevents us from moving up the ladder of preferred alternatives in the manner that I described? That misfiring brain cells make us disregard opportunity costs or fail to disregard sunk costs? Unlikely. The concept of opportunity costs is fundamental to the Coase Theorem, and the distinction between sunk and avoidable costs is fundamental to the public utility pricing literature to which Coase has made distinguished contributions.

Williamson regards the very meaning of utility maximization as "obscure" if there are positive information costs.[37] What is the mystery? People array their opportunities and choose the one that is best; but the cost of identifying opportunities will limit the size of the array, so sometimes a person will make a different choice from the one he would have made had the costs of information been zero. When uncertainty is pervasive, people may fall back on simple rules of thumb, implying a disregard of information concerning the choice that would be optimal in the absence of the rule. It is even possible that an increase in uncertainty would cause people to admit *less* information into their decisional process, because the greater uncertainty might stem from a

36. Coase, note 34 above, at 97. The reference is to Becker's article on irrational behavior, which I cited in the Introduction.
37. Williamson, note 17 above, at 113.

greater unreliability of information; so we might find more rule-bound behavior in areas of greater uncertainty.[38] These complications place a strain on simple models of rational maximizing; they do not warrant discarding the concept.

38. Ronald A. Heiner, "The Origin of Predictable Behavior," 73 *American Economic Review* 560, 570–571 (1983).

chapter 22

What Are Philosophers Good For?

RICHARD RORTY, the best-known living philosopher of pragmatism, must be doing something right, because he's anathema to both Left and Right.[1] To the Left he is an apologist for "cold-war liberalism" and "bourgeois capitalist democracy," to the Right a philosophical termite gnawing at the foundations of Western civilization and a cheerleader for left-wing radicals such as Roberto Unger and Catharine MacKinnon. He is all these things in a sense, but his work is a unity, as I shall suggest, and an impressive one. It has a grave weakness, though: a deficient sense of fact, which is related to Rorty's lack of interest in science, and therefore in social science, and therefore in economics—and which is related, as well, to his belief in the plasticity of human nature. It is a weakness that calls into question the capacity of modern philosophy to contribute to the solution of concrete problems of law and of public policy generally. Not that Rorty is a typical philosopher; but the weakness of which I speak is typical of modern philosophy and helps to explain why philosophers have been less active in legal teaching and scholarship than economists have been. I have already expressed

---

1. As he charmingly acknowledges in Rorty, "Trotsky and the Wild Orchids," 2 *Common Knowledge* 140, 140–141 (1993).

some doubts about analytic philosophy,[2] and I shall amplify them in this chapter and extend them to other styles of philosophy, notably pragmatism itself.

Philosophy Today

Academic philosophers are people whose professional competence is centered on two activities. The first is the interpretation, elaboration, and criticism of philosophical texts—canonical older texts from Plato to Wittgenstein plus the books and articles being ground out at a frightening rate by members of present-day university departments of philosophy. The second activity is the use of the tools of logic and rhetoric to address problems set by the authors of the canonical texts— the problems of skepticism and free will and so on. It was not always thus. Plato and Aristotle were not primarily either exegetes or technical analysts. Nor for that matter Nietzsche, whom some analytic philosophers, however, would like to expel from the philosophical canon. Nor Wittgenstein.[3] But it is largely true today. And neither the canon, nor its modern elaboration, has much to say about any specific political, social, or economic problems. I except works of practical political theory by Aristotle, Mill, and others. But to me, more pertinently to Rorty, the philosophical canon is dominated by works (some of course by Aristotle and Mill) that explore such "fundamental," though some might think them more properly described as semantic and grammatical, problems as the nature of mind, will, and perception, the conditions of personal identity, the logic of mathematics, the reality of the external world, the warrants of true belief, the nature of rationality, the meaning of causation, the difference between things and concepts, the nature of science, and the objectivity of morals.

I do not mean to disparage the philosophical canon. It contains striking insights into human personality and the human dilemma. It challenges dogma by insisting that we try to justify even our deepest personal and professional beliefs. It is a powerful tool for dispelling linguistic confusions that muddy our thinking about things (or rather no-things) like "causation," "interpretation," and "free will." It has

2. See in particular the discussion of Dworkin and Rawls in the Introduction and in Chapter 5. Rorty himself is both an analytic philosopher and a critic of analytic philosophy.

3. Though exegesis plays a role, for example in *On Certainty*, which is in part a critique of G. E. Moore's argument against skepticism.

much to say about methodology in law and in social science, as we saw in discussing Ronald Coase's views. It offers examples—not limited to Socrates—of intellectual and moral courage of a high order. It is a source of many of our society's fundamental political and moral ideas, and of the leading ideas of several schools of jurisprudence. Forget legal realism's debt to pragmatism, or Langdellian formalism's debt to Plato: consider that behind Ackerman stands Habermas, behind Eskridge, Gadamer; behind Michelman, Rawls; behind Kronman, Aristotle; behind Cornell, Hegel; behind Kennedy, Sartre; behind Weinrib, Kant; behind Sunstein, Dewey; behind many of the law and economics buffs, Bentham and Popper. Pragmatism left its mark on the legal and judicial writings of Oliver Wendell Holmes and Benjamin Cardozo, and I have used philosophy throughout this book.

But none of these concessions—intended in no grudging spirit—to philosophy's importance implies that philosophical texts can fruitfully be mined for, or philosophers fruitfully consulted on, *specific* solutions to *specific* problems of social governance. The compartmentalization of knowledge—so conspicuous a feature of the modern world—may have condemned philosophy to irrelevance at the level of practice. Rorty knows this;[4] in fact said it long before I; but has yet to suit his actions to his words. For an implication of those words is that he should avoid making public pronouncements on practical issues—whether the economic policies of backward countries, or national health insurance, or subsidized day care, or legal restrictions on abortion—except when the experts on these questions try to bolster their positions with philosophical arguments. Philosophers are expert at batting down philosophical arguments, just as lawyers are expert at batting down legal arguments. Neither philosophers nor lawyers, however, have by virtue of their professional training and experience the ability to advise on issues of social policy.[5] Everyone has the right to have and express an opinion on such issues. But philosophers, as distinct from (depending on the

---

4. "Don't assume that because we are philosophers we can be of any special use, in our professional capacity, to struggles against imperialism, or racism." Rorty, "Truth and Freedom: A Reply to Thomas McCarthy," 16 *Critical Inquiry* 633, 641 (1990). This is not a new point. "To apply philosophical reasoning-procedures is one sort of work; working with them will not help us to determine whether, say, belief in Christianity helps men to live better lives, or whether blind men can estimate shapes accurately, or whether State patronage of the arts encourages mediocrity, or whether tragedy purges the emotions." John Passmore, *Philosophical Reasoning* 18 (1969).

5. Excluding, in the case of lawyers, subjects such as tort reform that are deeply entangled in legal technicalities, though even here the role of lawyers is limited.

issue) physicians, public health professionals, physicists, economists, engineers, military officers, social workers, architects, and other professionals having relevant expertise, have no greater right than Everyman. Rorty does not flaunt the title "philosopher" or claim that his knowledge of philosophy gives him insight into questions of public policy. But were he not a famous philosopher, he would have no market for his views on policy.

Some philosophers have had additional training, experience, or knowledge that enabled them to engage constructively with specific issues of public policy. Foucault, in preparation for writing his *History of Sexuality,* read deeply in the predominantly nonphilosophical literature on sexuality. Arthur Danto is a distinguished art critic as well as a distinguished philosopher, and a number of contemporary philosophers, including Stanley Cavell, Martha Nussbaum, and Rorty himself, can lay claim to distinction as literary critics (we shall consider a specimen of Rorty's criticism later). John Dewey's writings on education are an older example of a philosopher's contributing to practical life—and my children attended the school that he founded, the Laboratory School of the University of Chicago. William James was an important psychologist; Nietzsche too. But knowledge was less compartmentalized when Dewey and James wrote, and Foucault and Danto are exceptions that prove[6] the rule, since Foucault defines philosophy to include history, and Danto considers contemporary art to *be* philosophy. Ronald Dworkin is at once a distinguished philosopher and an influential commentator on legal questions, but he was trained as a lawyer.[7] Mill was an economist as well as a philosopher, Bentham a lawyer and an economist, and both predate the modern compartmentalization of knowledge. I shall note later the striking dearth of non-lawyer philosophers in the ranks of scholarly writers on law.

Rorty

In the central philosophical tradition of the West, a tradition in which the shaping hand of Plato is still visible, human reason is seen as engaged in an ever more successful quest to find the permanent, the

6. That is, probe. The notion that a rule is confirmed by showing that it has exceptions—the usual modern meaning of "exception that proves the rule"—is the purest nonsense.

7. The pitfalls in analyzing law with only a philosopher's understanding of it are described in George P. Fletcher, "Corrective Justice for Moderns," 106 *Harvard Law Review* 1658, 1661–66 (1993), reviewing Jules Coleman, *Risks and Wrongs* (1992).

ultimate, but fortunately the knowable truths that lie behind appearances—scientific truths, of course, but also moral and legal and political (and in some versions theological) ones, and perhaps even truth's aesthetic counterpart, beauty. In each area of inquiry the quest is seen as centripetal. The inquirers are believed to be converging on a uniform reality, which though hidden acts as a magnet to curious humans. That ultimate reality—God in some formulations, the physical universe in others, "the good" in others, the structure of human consciousness in still others—establishes an objective basis for our inquiries and thus enables us (in principle) to determine once and for all that the universe is billions rather than thousands of years old, that public school segregation violates the equal protection of the laws, that William Faulkner is a better writer than Margaret Mitchell, that peace usually is better than war, and that democracy is a better system of government than National Socialism. These are all things that most of us believe, and we would like to think that we believe them because they correspond to the way things are—that they are not just local prejudices, the product of our society and our upbringing.

Rorty disagrees.[8] He thinks we believe a thing because the belief fits our other beliefs. Two hundred years ago Negro slavery, though already controversial, nested comfortably in a system of beliefs having to do with the origins of and differences among races. We have other beliefs about these things today, with which slavery doesn't fit, and it has become anathema. Not because slavery "really" is wrong; there is no really about the matter if "really" is taken to point to something more "objective" than public opinion. Slavery just doesn't mesh with our current belief system, which includes a historically recent belief in racial equality that is held as dogmatically (though secretly doubted by many of its holders) as our ancestors held their belief in inequality. Rorty would I think be willing to take the next step and concede that this belief system was affected by the changing economic value of slavery and also that we continue to condone "slavery" by other names in a variety of settings including prisons and the nursery, as Akhil Amar argues (see Chapter 6). Similarly, until Copernicus's time and indeed somewhat later, the heliocentric conception of the universe had no

---

8. "I have always (well, not always, but for the last twenty years or so) been puzzled about what was supposed to count as a knockdown answer to Hitler." Rorty, note 4 above, at 637.

utility, so the issue of its truth didn't arise; some day that conception may again have no utility and be abandoned.

This is not the sort of free-range relativism that supposes that belief in slavery or the divine right of kings or the geocentric picture of the universe are current options for our belief system. It is a mistake to suppose that only proven or tautological propositions are held unshakably; in fact our most unshakable beliefs are intuitive, and often transient. But since there is no assurance that human inquiries will converge on some ultimate reality (because "ultimate reality" may not be accessible to human intelligence)—since, therefore, our thinking is relative to our position (nation, class, gender, race, and so forth)—progress, if one can call it that, does not come through either a parade-ground march on the boulevard of truth or sudden breakthroughs to truth. It comes from the accumulation of practical knowledge and from changes in the position from which we view the world. This is the kind of thing that happened when Copernicus decided to make the sun the center of the solar system in place of the earth or when Bentham proposed that animals had moral claims because they could experience pain.

The basic political task, in Rorty's view, is to create a social framework that, by the cultivation of tolerance and the legal protection of diversity and debate, encourages geniuses, like Copernicus and Bentham, Christ and Marx, Nietzsche and Freud, Dickens and Orwell, who are able through the deployment of powerful metaphors (such as "gravity," or "id," or "Scrooge," or "Big Brother") and other redescriptions to shatter our dogmas (though perhaps erecting new ones in their place), enrich our sense of possibility, add to our repertoire of techniques for controlling the physical and social environment, broaden our sympathies. The political system that places tolerance and diversity front and center is liberalism, because the liberal state is neutral about substantive values. It insists only on the procedural values, such as the protection of privacy and of freedom of belief and speech and of occupation, that are necessary to secure diversity of belief, expression, and ways of life. These values and their institutional safeguards constitute "epistemological democracy,"[9] which resembles but is distinct from the "deliberative democracy" that we encountered in the Introduction. It has nothing, or very little, to do with the popular will. It has everything to do with creating the conditions necessary for the intelli-

9. On which see Hilary Putnam, *Renewing Philosophy*, ch. 9 (1992).

gent discussion of every sort of question—personal, social, scientific, whatever.

All this seems to me basically sound. It is the generalization to the sphere of politics of the "fallibilist" vein in the philosophy of science. Fallibilists, such as Mill and Peirce, Dewey and Popper, emphasize scientific procedures and values rather than scientific truth—the process rather than the goal. The scientist is the inquirer who, disdainful of enlisting the power of the state to enforce agreement with his views—to obtain, in Justice Robert Jackson's striking phrase, the unanimity of the graveyard[10]—offers those views to a community of inquirers in a form that makes them refutable if they are false. The process of falsification results in a shifting of perspectives, each of which leaves a deposit in a growing repository of knowledge. The scientist's courage to be wrong provides a model for all inquirers. I grant that this is a somewhat idealized view of science, but those philosophers who can find no interesting methodological differences between science and literary criticism, or between science and magic, are looking through the wrong end of the telescope.

In emphasizing the process rather than the objects of science I do not mean to deny that science puts us in touch with things as they are, including some entities that although invisible to the naked eye—atoms and molecules and DNA and so forth—do exist, are not merely artifacts of theory. Yet the decision to slice up reality this way, into atoms, molecules, DNA, and so forth, is a human decision taken for expedient ends;[11] much technology evolves from trial and error rather than from applications of scientific theory; false theories, such as Ptolemy's theory of the universe, can yield true knowledge, for example how to navigate by the stars; and theories can never be shown to be true, but only to be false, or useful, or both. So the fallibilist approach to science does shift the emphasis away from the question whether scientific theory accurately represents the intrinsic nature of reality. And when the approach is applied to political, legal, and ethical questions, the sense in which inquiry can be said to teach us how things really stand becomes severely attenuated, and we can only hope that through the conflict and comparison and succession of theories we will become better, wiser,

10. West Virginia State Board of Education v. Barnette, 319 U.S. 624, 631 (1943).

11. So it is not *complete* nonsense to say that there were no dinosaurs until people discovered them; the idea of distinguishing these physical objects from the rest of the physical world—of recognizing a class of "dinosaurs"—was a human creation.

and happier. Discussing the dilemma of Sartre's imaginary "Pierre," who must decide whether to join the Resistance or take care of his aged mother, Hilary Putnam points out that whichever way Pierre chooses he may never know whether he chose right.[12] This sort of radical indeterminacy is common in law. The peculiar aptness of Rorty's brand of fallibilism and antifoundationalism to legal theory may explain why, according to a check of the LEXIS law review database, academic lawyers cite Rorty more often than they cite any other living philosophers except Rawls and Nozick (and Dworkin, but he's a special case).

Of course, as Rorty sometimes fails to remind us, experimentalism should not be fostered without any regard for its costs. The Nazi experiment in political theory taught us a lot, but one would have to be awfully curious to think the benefit worth the cost. No doubt we would learn a lot from reintroducing slavery, or adopting the Islamic system of criminal punishments, or breeding people as we do dogs. Challenging dogmas, including dogmas like freedom and humanity, is fine, but it is not a good of infinite value. It must be traded off against other valuable goods, such as life, liberty, happiness, and social stability.

The epistemological defense of liberalism, which incidentally resembles Holmes's defense of free speech, has been subjected to a variety of criticisms. The main ones are three. The first, which is made by philosophical realists and Catholics, among others, and which I shall not try to discuss because it belongs to the domain of indeterminate high theory, is that there *are* objective truths about science, morality, politics, and law, which we can find by the light of reason. The second criticism, made by Alasdair MacIntyre,[13] is that unless a society insists on some basic uniformity of outlook, disagreements will not be resolvable by reasoned debate akin to scientific inquiry because the disputants won't be standing on common ground. That is true, but it is not so ominous as MacIntyre believes. The hard core of fundamentalist anti-abortionists and the hard core of feminist supporters of abortion on demand do inhabit different moral universes, much as the abolitionists and slaveowners did. It is no accident that each side of the abortion debate uses abolitionist rhetoric and by doing so asserts an unbridgeable moral gulf between it and the other side. But neither side is politically dominant. So each in an effort to achieve dominance reaches

12. Putnam, note 9 above, at 194.
13. MacIntyre, "Moral Arguments and Social Contexts: A Response to Rorty," in *Hermeneutics and Praxis* 222 (Robert Hollinger ed. 1985).

out to the people who, occupying a patch of common ground with both extreme groups—feeling the weight of the objections to abortion on demand, on the one hand, and to the criminalization of abortion on the other—are able to make a reasoned or at least reasonable choice between them.[14] They are the uncommitted, like the members of a jury. Whatever their decision is, it will not satisfy the hard core on the losing side; the persons in that core will feel coerced, not convinced. Many losing litigants and defeated voting blocs feel that way, but such feelings are not inconsistent with social peace. A society need not spin apart for lack of normative consensus.

Third, Rorty's radical-feminist and other left-wing critics argue that liberalism is not really neutral. It biases debate: it allows some people to amass huge fortunes that they can use to manipulate public opinion, and consigns others to poverty and silence, as by forcing women into subordinate positions in household and market. There is nothing in liberalism to preclude tolerating such biases; but the particular empirical claim is false. Although the mass media in this country are owned mainly by giant corporations and wealthy individuals, not only their reporters and newscasters but even most of their editorial and feature writers are well to the left of center and vociferously criticize wealthy people, giant corporations, bourgeois liberalism, and conservative values. Spokesmen for women and formerly oppressed minorities have achieved positions of influence and high visibility in the universities, the media, and politics. Far from being silenced, they are courted by the most powerful communicative institutions in the nation, and they have succeeded in silencing a number of their timid critics in those institutions. (Who but I dares say "spokes*man*"?) The strongest, and loudest, criticisms of bourgeois democracy, liberal capitalism, free markets, consumerism, Western political and aesthetic values, patriarchy, heterosexism, the rich, the treatment of blacks and other minority persons, and everything else of which left-leaning radicals disapprove are heard not in the handful of countries that remain socialist in the wake of the

14. "Although there are many pro-choice and pro-life groups in the United States, and although these groups dominate the attention of the media, only a small percentage of the American population belongs to these highly partisan and highly polarized groups. The vast majority of the population is not polarized and does not hold starkly partisan attitudes. Most people fall between the two extremes and demonstrate considerable ambivalence of attitudes." Hyman Rodman, Betty Sarvis, and Joy Walker Bonar, *The Abortion Question* 143–144 (1987).

Soviet Union's collapse, but in the United States. Inequality of income and wealth does not, in fact, silence debate.

I have argued that two major criticisms of Rorty's position—that there isn't enough consensus in our society to permit a rational choice among competing moral or political perspectives and that liberalism silences its critics—are factually incorrect. One might have expected Rorty to say so. He hasn't, at least not clearly, for while on the one hand he does say things like, "I think our country—despite its past and present atrocities and vices, and despite its continuing eagerness to elect fools and knaves to high office—is a good example of the best kind of society so far invented," and, "People like me see nothing wrong . . . with the political and moral heritage of the Enlightenment," he balances such remarks with extraordinarily gloomy prophecies: "1973 may have been the beginning of the end"; "Sinclair Lewis' *It Can't Happen Here* may become an increasingly plausible scenario"; America "could slide into fascism at any time."[15] He finds in what he affectionately calls bourgeois democracy flaws so deep and wide as to bring him to the brink of despair, leading him to say, for example, that "if there is hope, it lies in the Third World."[16] I doubt that many people in the Third World would agree. Most of them would say that if there is hope for the Third World it lies in the speedy emulation of Western political and economic institutions—particularly capitalism and its institutional preconditions, namely property rights and the rule of law. The very term "Third World" may soon be an anachronism, even if isn't one already because the "Second World" (the Soviet empire) has vanished. As China and India and the nations of Latin America unburden their economies of state control (the nations of East Asia other than China itself having already, to a great extent, done so), "Third World" is on the way to becoming a synonym for Africa. Yet as late as 1988, with socialism already everywhere in shambles, we find Rorty hoping "that somewhere someday, the newly-elected government of a large industrialized society [such as Brazil would] decree that everybody would get the same income, regardless of occupation or disability."[17] This particular experiment, or at least a reasonable approximation to it (no one I

---

15. Rorty, note 1 above, at 141, 150–151. And all this in an article published in 1993!

16. "Unger, Castoriadis, and the Romance of a National Future," 82 *Northwestern University Law Review* 335, 340 (1988). Rorty has authorized me to say that he "now thinks this sentence 'dumb.'"

17. Id. at 349.

suppose has ever thought it feasible in its literal form), has already been tried repeatedly, in the Third World and elsewhere, beginning with the earliest period of Soviet Communism, and has always failed.[18] It is time to stop urging it on the very countries that would be most harmed by it. I remind the reader of my earlier point that social experimentation should not be thought costless, or always cost-justified. The deeper point is that a pragmatist ought to be interested in the results of previous experiments, and not just in more experimenting.

In 1991 we find Rorty expressing fear "that there are no initiatives which will save the Southern Hemisphere," possibly excepting "top-down techno-bureaucratic initiatives like the cruel Chinese only-one-child-per-family policy," and other, unspecified devices of "centralized planning."[19] Rorty's pessimism about the South is premature, when we consider the phenomenal economic growth in recent years of such major southern-hemisphere nations as Indonesia and Mexico. None of that growth is due to centralized planning; it is due to the dismantling of centralized planning to make way for free markets.

Four years before the dissolution of the Soviet Union, Rorty wrote that "time seems to be on the Soviet side," while denouncing as a "gang of thugs" "the shadowy millionaires manipulating Reagan."[20] Such statements put one in mind of the imaginary world inhabited by Rorty's left-wing critics, such as Jo Burrows, who in an essay published not in 1960 but in 1990 suggested that the international economic system may be unfairly stacked against the Soviet Union, who saw Sandinista Nicaragua as a locus of non-Marxist social and democratic reforms, who believed that poor countries could only "break into Northern monopolies" by "keeping skilled workers in the country" (the Berlin Wall?) and by "discouraging cash crops that may only benefit the rich" (discouraging exports?), who declared that liberal doctrine is "outdated" and that we need "an entirely new political system which accommodates East and West, North and South," and

18. See, for example, Peter J. Boetthe, "The Soviet Experiment with Pure Communism," 2 *Critical Review* 149 (1988). Other sites include China in the Cultural Revolution, Castro's Cuba, North Korea, and Republican Spain at the outset of the Spanish Civil War.

19. Rorty, "Love and Money," 1 *Common Knowledge* 12, 14–16 (1992).

20. "Thugs and Theorists: A Reply to Bernstein," 15 *Political Quarterly* 564, 566–567 (1987). Even more recently Rorty has written about "developments [in this country] reminiscent of Weimar," and asserted "that Republicans have spent 12 years looting the country, and that the blue-collar voters have apparently turned their backs on liberal Democrats once and for all." "The Feminist Saving Remnant," *New Leader,* June 1–15, 1992, pp. 9, 10.

who criticized Rorty for ignoring "pragmatic socialist alternatives which have been worked out in the Frankfurt critical studies movement."[21] This is the Left's clichéd dream world, and you don't awaken from it by reading Rorty's favorite writers, whether Nietzsche or Derrida, Sartre or Heidegger, Orwell or Nabokov. Some of these are great thinkers, but with the partial exception of Orwell[22] they have no more to contribute to solving the problems of the modern world than Praxiteles or Wagner does.

Rorty is not to be criticized for failing to foresee the imminent fall of communism; virtually no one else did, even among those who had made the study of communism their life's work. And despite the emotional pull which the dreams of the Left exert on him, he has shown far more sense than those who clung for so long to faith in communism, if not in the Soviet Union then in China, if not in China then in Cuba, if not in Cuba then in East Germany. His essay on intellectuals in politics is a courageous attack on the cult of political correctness and on the radical leftism of contemporary English departments.[23] And he has shown how we can save representatives of the "edifying" as distinct from the analytic tradition in philosophy such as Nietzsche and Heidegger from the charge of reactionary politics by reconceiving their projects as personal rather than as political or metaphysical—by seeing that, like Freud, they have valuable things to say about how we should live our personal lives, how (Nietzsche is particularly valuable here) we can take control of our lives. All of which is entirely compatible with, indeed enabled by, bourgeois liberalism, which, as Emerson and Mill saw, creates opportunities for individual experiments in living while the edifying thinkers are busy designing the experiments themselves.

What is missing in Rorty is the solid grasp of social science that is required not only to devise intelligent solutions to the problems of rich liberal countries, but even to recognize what those problems are—to distinguish them, in other words, from pseudoproblems. It is not clear, for example, that rich nations exploit poor ones, that either the federal

21. Burrows, "Conversational Politics: Rorty's Pragmatist Apology for Liberalism," in *Reading Rorty: Critical Responses to "Philosophy and the Mirror of Nature" (and Beyond)* 322, 337–338 nn. 27–28 (Alan R. Malachowski ed. 1990).

22. Partial because he never abandoned his faith in democratic socialism, a faith as half-baked as his criticism of communism was acute.

23. "Intellectuals in Politics: Too Far In? Too Far Out?" 38 *Dissent* 483 (1991).

budget deficit or Japanese competition is a truly grave problem for the United States (the latter is not a problem at all), that AIDS represents a social crisis for this country rather than an ugly, dangerous, but fairly easily controlled and only moderately expensive disease, that the total amount of money we are spending on health care is excessive although the allocation among patients may be distorted, that the shift of employment from manufacturing to services is a problem, that the savings and loan debacle is anything more than the predictable harvest of foolish New Deal banking regulations, that the problem of drug addiction is much more than an artifact of foolish efforts to solve it (like the alcohol problem during Prohibition), that income and wealth are too unequally distributed, that the American educational system taken as a whole is either markedly inferior to the educational systems of the other wealthy countries or starved for resources, or that our physical infrastructure is disintegrating. I do not think that we should regret the decline of labor unions any more than we should regret the decline of those other industrial dinosaurs, the Detroit automakers.

These assessments may be wrong. All I know for sure is that the so-called problems that I have just mentioned present difficult analytical and empirical issues that can no more be understood, let alone resolved, by the intuitions and analytic procedures of persons schooled only in the humanities than problems in high-energy physics or brain surgery can be understood and resolved by close study of the *Tractatus Logico-Philosophicus*. To Rorty, however, economic or other social-scientific theories that might be brought to bear on social problems are just—theory. And he is against social theory. But there are social theories and there are social theories. Just because deconstruction or neo-Austrian theories of anarcho-capitalism are useless for solving practical problems, it does not follow that no theories are useful for that purpose. Economics has no cogent theory of distributive justice, but it has a lot to say about the consequences of policies ostensibly designed to make the distribution of income and wealth more equal. A mountain of theoretical and empirical work on the consequences of rent control, price controls, the minimum wage, employment protection, public housing, the progressive income tax, health insurance, voucher systems, and the negative income tax provides the indispensable factual predicate for informed analysis of redistributive policies.[24]

24. Illustrative studies (not all negative!) are Finis Welch, *Minimum Wages: Issues and Evidence* (1978); *The Economics of Legal Minimum Wages* (Simon Rottenberg ed. 1981); Charles Brown, Curtis Gilroy, and Andrew Kohen, "The Effect of the Minimum Wage on

Rorty thinks that all we need to understand our social problems is a muckraking journalist's vocabulary that will equip us to talk about the rich ripping off the poor, the strong trampling on the weak, the excessive greed of the upper class, the selfish indifference of the middle class, and the control of government and the media by thugs and millionaires. For some purposes this vocabulary is adequate, as Orwell, a great journalist, proved. But it is an impoverished vocabulary for the description and solution of our social problems, which is why Orwell's advocacy of democratic socialism falls so flat today. Our social problems *may* be the consequence of string pulling or bad character or monopoly or concentrations of wealth—or they may be inherent features of modernity, or remediable or irremediable consequences of the friction between capitalism and democracy or even liberalism and democracy. These are studiable, empirical issues, as a body of important work in economics and political science, dealing with voting, interest groups, legislation, regulation, and other features of modern democratic government, attests. The necessary inquiry should not be short-circuited by a vocabulary that commits the inquirer in advance. Even if there are no deep, metaphysical realities of the sort that religious and philosophical thinkers in the central tradition of Western thought long believed, it does not follow that a shallow antinomianism is all we are left with. There are mid-level social scientific theories and empirical methodolo-

---

Employment and Unemployment," 20 *Journal of Economic Literature* 487 (1982); Edgar O. Olsen and David M. Barton, "The Benefits and Costs of Public Housing in New York City," 20 *Journal of Public Economics* 299 (1983); William A. Rabiega, Ta-Win Lin, and Linda M. Robinson, "The Property Value Impacts of Public Housing Projects in Low and Moderate Density Residential Neighborhoods," 60 *Land Economics* 174 (1984); Howard J. Sumka and Michael A. Stegman, "An Economic Analysis of Public Housing in Small Cities," 18 *Journal of Regional Science* 395 (1978); Robert A. Androkovich, Michael J. Daly, and Fadle M. Naqib, "The Impact of a Hybrid Personal Tax System on Capital Accumulation and Economic Welfare," 36 *European Economic Review* 801 (1992); James M. Snyder and Gerald H. Kramer, "Fairness, Self-Interest, and the Politics of the Progressive Income Tax," 36 *Journal of Public Economics* 197 (1988); Martin Feldstein, *Hospital Costs and Health Insurance*, pt. 2 (1981); Roger Feldman and Bryan Dowd, "A New Estimate of the Welfare Loss of Excess Health Insurance," 81 *American Economic Review* 297 (1991); Joseph Friedman and Daniel H. Weinberg, *The Economics of Housing Vouchers* (1982); E. Jay Howenstine, *Housing Vouchers: An International Analysis* (1986); Orley Ashenfelter and Mark W. Plant, "Nonparametric Estimates of the Labor-Supply Effects of Negative Income Tax Programs," 8 *Journal of Labor Economics* S396 (1990); John F. Cogan, "Labor Supply and Negative Income Taxation: New Evidence from the New Jersey–Pennsylvania Experiment," 4 *Economic Inquiry* 465 (1983); Allan H. Meltzer and Scott F. Richard, "A Positive Theory of In-Kind Transfers and the Negative Income Tax," in *Political Economy* 53 (Allan H. Meltzer, Alex Cukierman, and Scott F. Richard eds. 1991). On price controls, see Chapter 1; on employment protection, see Chapter 13; and on rent control, see Chapter 18.

gies whose utility is not undermined by their lack of metaphysical foundations.

I see no evidence that Rorty, or his critics on the left, have studied any of the political or social or economic problems about which they write, whether it is the foreign policy of the United States or the role of millionaires in the policies of the Reagan administration. Or that they even regard these as studiable problems, although the best example of this happens to be found not in work by or criticizing Rorty but rather in a book by Hilary Putnam, to whom I have already referred. Putnam is best known among philosophers for his work in mathematical logic and the philosophy of language, mind, mathematics, and physics. If there is anything more remote from, say, American policy toward South America than Derrida's *Of Grammatology* (to mention only Derrida's most lucid work), it is the highly technical branches of logic and philosophy in which Putnam has specialized. But like another Cambridge polymath, Noam Chomsky, Putnam has strong views on our policy toward Latin America. In a chapter originally delivered as a lecture in 1983 he denounces the imagined policy of Republican administrations of imposing dictatorships on Latin American nations.[25] Apparently it did not occur to him when recycling the lecture for publication in 1990 to examine the recent political history of the region. Had he done so he would have discovered that during the Reagan and Bush administrations every dictator or junta in Latin America, except of course Castro—whom I daresay Putnam at one time admired—had left or been kicked out by one means or another and been replaced by a reasonable simulacrum of democracy,[26] that one after another these nations had dropped their traditional resentment of the United States and were busy imitating its economic as well as its political institutions, and that this turn to free markets, free trade, private ownership of the means of production, and free elections, in short to the despised bourgeois liberal model, seemed to be bringing prosperity within reach of these impoverished nations. I do not suggest that the Republicans deserve credit for this, or that any U.S. government has ever made much effort to promote democracy and prosperity

25. *Realism with a Human Face*, ch. 12 (1990).

26. Since 1990 there has been backsliding to dictatorship in Haiti, Peru, and elsewhere, though I am not aware of anyone who blames the United States for these developments. For a balanced discussion of the democratization of Latin America during the 1980s, see Dietrich Rueschemeyer, Evelyne Huber Stephens, and John D. Stephens, *Capital Development and Democracy*, ch. 5 (1992).

in Latin America. I am merely questioning whether Putnam knows what happened there during the 1980s.

Putnam also says in his unintentionally self-referentially titled chapter ("How Not to Solve Ethical Problems") that he is not an economist, but he then goes on to opine on the problem of unemployment in the United States. Again the discussion is stale, as he is wringing his hands over the unemployment rate in 1982—10 percent, which is shocking enough but hasn't been seen since, as he neglects to inform the reader. Putnam apologizes for having twice in his life succumbed to the siren song of Marxism but is not sufficiently chastened by those experiences to withhold public comment on matters remote from his field of knowledge. He puts one in mind of another great logician who liked to express himself on quotidian political issues: Bertrand Russell.

Severely academic philosophers such as Rorty and Putnam are most profitably employed when making and refuting arguments based on the texts of which they are the expert students and critics. Rorty is operating well within the circle of his competence when he points out that demolishing the traditional philosophical foundations of liberalism does not demolish liberalism as a theory (no philosopher is going to have much success trying to demolish so successful a practice) because there is a perfectly good nonfoundational epistemological argument for liberalism, rooted in the nonfoundational philosophical analytics of Mill, of Peirce and Popper, and of James and Wittgenstein. But when Rorty prophesies the triumph of the Soviet Union or the coming of a Third World Messiah, he is talking about matters that he has never studied, matters for the study of which he has never attempted to obtain the necessary intellectual tools. Although he has praised scientists for their tradition of disinterested, systematic, fact-based inquiry, he has not approached political questions in a scientific spirit.

When Putnam writes, "Whenever we have given previously oppressed groups a chance to display their capacities, those capacities have surprised us,"[27] he is mouthing liberal pieties; if he investigated the matter he would quickly realize that his statement was false. When John Rawls denounces what he calls "market-strategic advertising, which is found in imperfect and oligopolistic markets dominated by relatively few firms,"[28] it is apparent that he is speaking at second hand. The giveaway is the phrase "oligopolistic markets dominated by relatively few firms":

27. Putnam, note 9 above, at 198.
28. Rawls, *Political Liberalism* 364–365 (1993).

dominated by relatively few firms is what oligopoly *means* in economics. He criticizes the advertising that such firms do because it seeks to influence consumers "through the use of slogans, eye-catching photographs, and so on"[29]—an equally apt description of the political advertising that he believes should be sacrosanct. Sacrosanct for some people, at any rate; for he is very critical of the Supreme Court's belief that it is unconstitutional for government to limit the amount of money that a political candidate can spend out of his own pocket. Rawls thinks that equality of basic liberties is denied if the rich can spend more on politicking than the poor, and that the Supreme Court's decisions allowing this are inconsistent with the Court's "one man one vote" rule in reapportionment cases. As I noted in Chapter 6, the actual effects of that rule are unclear; it is no clearer that rules limiting campaign expenditures promote democracy or the marketplace in ideas. Both sorts of restriction raise intricate theoretical and empirical questions,[30] none of which Rawls discusses.

When Elizabeth Anderson, another fine analytic philosopher, recommends the substitution of "workers' cooperatives" for capitalist firms, in part because "environmental protection tends to harmonize more with the interests as well as the ideals of worker-managed firms than with the interest of capitalist firms," since "workers, unlike capitalists, have to live in the communities where they work and so must live with the pollution they create,"[31] it is apparent that she, too, is writing at second hand. If "workers" include office workers as well as factory workers, or if a firm has several or many factories only some of which pollute, the majority of worker-owners may not be exposed to the firm's pollution. And even if they are, they have more to lose—their jobs—from pollution-control measures than shareholders would, because by raising the firm's costs such measures may make it less com-

---

29. Id. at 365.

30. See, for example, Alan I. Abramowitz, "Incumbency, Campaign Spending, and the Decline of Competition in U.S. House Elections," 53 *Journal of Politics* 34 (1991); Bruce Bender, "An Analysis of Congressional Voting on Legislation Limiting Congressional Campaign Expenditures," 96 *Journal of Political Economy* 1005 (1988); James B. Kau and Paul H. Rubin, *Congressmen, Constituents, and Contributors: Determinants of Roll Call Voting in the House of Representatives,* ch. 8 (1982). Even Cass Sunstein, as ardent a believer in political equality as Rawls, will go no further than to say that "the case for legal controls on campaign expenditures is plausible, but hardly clear-cut." Sunstein, *Democracy and the Problem of Free Speech* 99 (1993).

31. Anderson, *Value in Ethics and Economics* 213 (1993).

petitive and force the firm to curtail its ouput or even fold. Just a few pages earlier, moreover, Anderson had argued that workers undervalue workplace dangers.[32] Why should this not be true of worker-owners confronted with a choice between fewer jobs and less pollution? In fact the northwest plywood cooperatives, the principal "success story" of worker-owned firms in the industrial sector in the United States, have, according to an admirer of worker-owned firms whom Anderson cites, the same dirty, noisy, and dangerous working conditions as capitalist sawmills.[33]

She discusses none of these issues, fails to consider whether the rarity of successful worker-owned firms might tell us something about the feasibility of making over the entire economy in their image,[34] relies on an outdated literature based on the supposed success of Yugoslav worker-managed factories in the Tito era,[35] and ignores the extensive recent literature on the actual problems and performance of worker-owned firms.[36]

One last example of the unworldliness of philosophers. Rorty's discussion of Orwell's *Nineteen Eighty-Four*[37] is a first-rate piece of literary criticism, but it accepts as true the aspect of the novel that by 1989 history had falsified: its prediction about life in the 1980s. Rorty writes, "Sometimes things prove to be just as bad as they first looked. Orwell helps us to formulate a pessimistic description of the political situation which forty years of further experience have only confirmed."[38] What forty years actually showed was that Orwell had overestimated the power of government to brainwash a population. In 1989—the year the Berlin Wall was torn down and two years before the dissolution of

32. Id. at 195–203.

33. Christopher Eaton Gunn, *Workers' Self-Management in the United States* 130 (1984).

34. The kibbutz has been a fairly successful experiment in the socialist organization of production. But only a tiny and declining percentage of the Israeli work force has ever worked on kibbutzim. It would be perilous therefore to suppose that the kibbutz provides a model for the organization of an entire economy. It would be equally perilous to suppose that the American economy could feasibly be modeled on the plywood co-ops.

35. See Jaroslav Vanek, *The General Theory of Labor-Managed Market Economies* (1970).

36. For an excellent summary, see Henry Hansmann, "When Does Worker Ownership Work? ESOPs, Law Firms, Codetermination, and Economic Democracy," 99 *Yale Law Journal* 1749 (1990).

37. Rorty, *Contingency, Irony, and Solidarity,* ch. 8 (1989). Still another example is Margaret Jane Radin's philosophical defense of rent control, in her article "Residential Rent Control," 15 *Philosophy and Public Affairs* 350 (1986), which ignores the economic literature on rent control.

38. Rorty, note 37 above, at 182.

the Soviet Union—it should have been evident that decades of communist indoctrination had had only a superficial impact on the fundamental values and beliefs of the inhabitants of the communist states, including those who had been born—indeed whose parents had been born—under communism. When the lid was removed, the old loves, hates, prejudices, desires, and superstitions once again boiled over. The significance of television had turned out to be not, as Orwell had expected, as a medium of surveillance, but as a medium of worldwide communication that prevented the communist governments from shutting their people off from the essential truth about the West—that its inhabitants were freer, healthier, more prosperous. The only minds permanently bent by communism were those of intellectuals, because they were the only people with an investment in ideology.

Rorty knows all this but resists the implications because he believes—it is a false correlate of his rejection of foundationalism—that people are highly malleable by political and economic elites, perhaps highly malleable, period.[39] One does not have to subscribe to metaphysical notions about "human nature" of the sort that Rorty rightly derides[40] in order to construct from biology and social science a picture of human behavior and capacities that makes both Winston and O'Brien unrealistic creations. Average people (the Winstons of this world) are not as sheeplike as Orwell thought, nor members of political elites (the O'Briens) as efficient. "The people" are not the pliant tools of propaganda ministries, advertisers, or self-appointed religious or cultural elites. Not that people are incapable of great cruelty, violence, and stupidity, or immune to the appeal of political Pied Pipers, or possessed of a "faculty" of free will. *Pace* Bruce Ackerman (Chapter 7), I have no exalted view of the wisdom of the masses in democratic conclave assembled. But their minds cannot be bent by the modern state, or big business, or the media with the ease that Orwell and Rorty, the latter with less excuse because he has the experience of an additional four decades, have supposed. But it is natural that a teacher should believe in the feasibility of brainwashing.

The political Rorty has needlessly estranged the philosophical Rorty

---

39. In id. at 187, he offers the sexual instinct as an example of malleability. I find that odd. See Chapter 26 of this book.

40. "There is no such thing as human nature in the deep sense in which Plato and [Leo] Strauss use this term." Rorty, "Education, Socialization, and Individuation," *Liberal Education,* Sept./Oct. 1989, pp. 2, 5.

from parts of his audience—oddly enough on both ends of the political spectrum, but I am thinking particularly of people who, partly through the example of Rorty himself with his fulsome praise of Unger and MacKinnon, have succumbed to the fallacious view (which Rorty does not hold) that pragmatism is a left-wing philosophy formed to engender doubt about the foundations of the Western tradition in science, law, politics, and morality. Pragmatism is formed to engender doubt about all philosophical foundations, but not necessarily in order to upset the practices that appear to rest on them—rather to show that they do not rest on them, that their validity depends on the evaluation of their consequences rather than on their having foundations; that metaphors drawn from the building trades do not illuminate the justification of social institutions. It would be a *philosophical* mistake to support as a corollary of pragmatism Unger's illiberal enthusiasm for smashing, through such devices as a government department of destabilization, established practices that include such constitutive institutions of liberalism as property.

Pragmatism engages the clutch that disconnects the whirring machinery of philosophical abstraction from the practical business of governing our lives and our societies. It seeks to free us from preconceptions based on "philosophical" thinking. This important message is obscured when a leading philosopher of pragmatism offers us, however occasionally and offhandedly, tired clichés about the Third World and the Reagan millionaires, reflecting preconceptions as frail, arbitrary, and unexamined as any that support the edifice of conventional philosophizing.

Philosophy and Law

In tension with the argument of this chapter, Martha Nussbaum argues that philosophers have much to contribute to legal education and scholarship.[41] The role of the philosopher, in her view, is to ferret out the unexamined assumptions of practical people, such as lawyers and doctors and economists; to be in short like Socrates. I do not think that modern philosophers are much like Socrates, who risked, and ultimately sacrificed, his life because like Jesus Christ he insisted on

41. Martha C. Nussbaum, "The Use and Abuse of Philosophy in Legal Education," 45 *Stanford Law Review* 1627 (1993).

questioning beyond the limits of prudence the values and practices of the most powerful people in his community.[42] What is true is that many philosophers do ask deep and searching questions about the values of a community, though it is rarely their own community. An example is the questioning by philosophers of science of the practices of scientific communities, including the economics community. Nussbaum proposes several ways in which philosophers can play an analogous role in law. They can question the notion of rationality that is central to economic analysis of law. They can analyze, more rigorously than lawyers and judges can do, philosophical concepts such as justice, free will, and intent that crop up frequently in legal cases. They can straighten out the relation between "reason" and "emotion" in the law. She thinks the best way to get rigorous philosophizing into law is for law schools to hire philosophers on a half-time basis to teach regular law school courses that they would infuse with philosophical rigor. She is aware that many law professors bring philosophy into their courses and their writings already, but she worries that they do so amateurishly.

If philosophers have so much to contribute to law, the question arises why so few of them are employed by law schools. Is it *only* because law schools have (as they do) too confined a notion of law? Most law professors who do jurisprudence or bring philosophy into other areas of legal teaching and writing have an academic background in philosophy; some even have a doctorate in the subject. But virtually all of them also have a law degree, have never been a member of the faculty of a philosophy department, and have never published in philosophy journals. The counterpart situation in economics is different. Many contributors to economic analysis of law have not had law degrees, including Coase, Director, Landes, Polinsky, Shavell, and Simons; yet these economists (and others I could name) have been full-time members of law school faculties. A number of "pure" economists who have not had full-time, and sometimes have not had any, law school appointment have made direct contributions to legal thought; these include Alchian, Becker, Demsetz, Diamond, Ehrlich, Jensen, and Stigler. Although law professors have picked up all sorts of ideas from general philosophers, few such philosophers have discussed legal issues, whether doctrinal or

42. That is the most edifying interpretation of why Socrates got into trouble; another is that he was closely associated with the unpopular rulers of the oligarchy that preceded the restored democracy which condemned him. Karl Popper, *The Open Society and Its Enemies,* vol. 1: *The Spell of Plato* 192–193 (5th rev. ed. 1966).

institutional, in a significant way. Rawls and Rorty are illustrative of a number of general philosophers who mention law in passing; Jules Coleman (who has a full-time appointment at Yale Law School), Jeffrie Murphy, Judith Jarvis Thomson, and Nussbaum herself are illustrative of the small number of contemporary philosophers who have discussed legal issues more than casually without having had legal training. When one thinks of philosophers of law of the present day one thinks of such figures as Ronald Dworkin, Charles Fried, Peter Goodrich, Kent Greenawalt, Thomas Grey, H. L. A. Hart, Anthony Kronman, Frank Michelman, Michael Moore, Margaret Jane Radin, Joseph Raz, Donald Regan, Frederick Schauer, Brian Simpson, Cass Sunstein, Lloyd Weinreb, Ernest Weinrib, and Robin West—and they are all law professors.[43] Although Nussbaum believes that most philosophical writing in law journals is sophomoric, which she ascribes to the fact that "anything one picks up without years of relevant training and practice is likely to be badly done," while a philosopher with a half-time appointment in a law school could "learn, gradually, a great deal of law, by first taking law courses and then eventually teaching some of the regular first-year courses,"[44] it has been much more common for law professors to pick up enough philosophy to do jurisprudence than for philosophy professors to pick up enough law to do jurisprudence.

There are several reasons for this, and they make me pessimistic about Nussbaum's proposals. The first, mentioned earlier in this book, is that the techniques of analytic philosophy and of legal reasoning are similar. This has important career implications. A college student who has done well in philosophy and thinks he might like to apply philosophy to law has a reasonable expectation of doing well in law school, and a law degree is the only graduate degree he needs in order to become a law professor at twice the salary a philosophy professor can command or

43. In an effort to be a little more systematic about this comparison, I compared the professors listed under "jurisprudence" and under "law and economics" in Association of American Law Schools, *AALS Directory of Law Teachers 1992–1993* (1993), a directory (with brief biographies) of full-time faculty of American law schools. In a random sample of 184 of the 642 jurisprudence teachers, only 4 (2.2 percent) did not have a law degree, while out of the 118 law and economics teachers in the directory, 10 (8.5 percent) did not have law degrees. Incidentally, H. L. A. Hart doesn't quite fit my list. Although he was a barrister for a time, his undergraduate degree was in philosophy and his academic appointments were in philosophy until he was appointed Professor of Jurisprudence at Oxford. It was not customary at the time for British philosophers to get advanced degrees.

44. Nussbaum, note 41 above, at 1644.

to become a legal practitioner at several times the salary that either can command. Economic analysis, with its heavy reliance on mathematical and statistical techniques of modeling and empirical inquiry, is different from both legal and philosophical analysis. Mathematical and verbal skills are frequently uncorrelated, yet without verbal skills it is difficult to do well in law school because a conventional legal education places such heavy emphasis on reading and writing. So a college student who had a knack for economics and thought he might like to apply it to law would know on the one hand that if he studied law in law school he would not be learning analytical techniques that could be readily substituted for economic analysis and on the other hand that he would have no assurance of doing well in law school. He might therefore decide that he would be a net loser if he substituted law school for graduate training in economics. A related consideration is that a Ph.D. in economics has much greater market value than one in philosophy. Academic economists are paid more than philosophers, in part because economics Ph.D.s have good job opportunities outside the academy; and they can pick up extra money on the side from consulting. It is easy to understand why the budding economic analyst of law, unless he aspires to do doctrinal analysis, is more likely to go the economics Ph.D. route, forgoing a law degree, than the budding philosophical analyst of law is likely to go the philosophy Ph.D. route and forgo a law degree. The upshot is that philosophy is more likely to be applied to law by lawyers than by philosophers who have a joint appointment in law and in philosophy.

As I implied in my discussion of Coase's methodological views, it does not matter a great deal whether philosophy of law is done by people who call themselves law professors or by people who call themselves philosophers; that is primarily a matter of adjusting the boundaries between university departments. It matters a little because law schools lack some of the institutional characteristics that have proved important to the encouragement of sound scholarship in fields like philosophy. Yet it would be difficult to show that Ronald Dworkin would have been a better philosopher of law had he gotten a Ph.D. in philosophy as well as a law degree.

What matters a lot is that analytic philosophy has so many of the same drawbacks as legal reasoning. The razor-sharp logical and polemical skills that we associate with Anglo-American philosophy are great tools of criticism but do not get one very far toward the solution of practical legal problems, such as what to do about abortion or coerced confessions or capital punishment. Hilary Putnam remarks that "the standard methods of the philosopher—careful argument and drawing distinctions—are more successful in showing that a philosophical position is wrong than they are in establishing that any particular philosophical position is right."[45] *Philosophical* position—it must be even more difficult to use the standard methods of the philosopher to establish that a *non*philosophical position is right. To make significant progress toward the solution of practical problems of law and social policy you need to understand a lot about the particular legal or social practice in question. Most analytic philosophers are not comfortable on the plane of fact. (The nonanalytic philosophers of the Continental tradition are for the most part no different in this respect.) They prefer to show up the inconsistencies and other defects in the positions of people who have different intuitions from theirs about the practice in question than to try to justify their own intuitions. No wonder they have not played a larger role in the formation and critique of legal policy.

45. Putnam, note 9 above, at 134. Rorty wonders whether analytic philosophy can be saved "from a decadent scholasticism." Rorty, "Tales of Two Disciplines" (unpublished, University of Virginia Dept. of Philosophy, n.d.).

PART SIX

At the Frontier

chapter 23

Law and Literature Revisited

MY MAIN scholarly interest, since I began teaching law in 1968, has been the application of economics to law. But the focus of that interest has changed. In 1968 the principal fields of law to which economics was being applied were antitrust and the regulation of public utilities and common carriers; and those were the fields in which I began my scholarly work, having specialized in them while in government service from 1962 to 1968. As the years passed, however, I became more and more interested in the "new" law and economics, that is, the application of economics to fields of law seemingly unrelated or only peripherally related to competition, markets, prices, and other conventional economic phenomena. My interest in the application of economics to fields of law, and other areas of social practice, that are remote from the conventional domain of economics lies behind my reservations about Ronald Coase's methodological prescriptions, which construe the proper scope of economics so narrowly. It also explains the spilling over of my interest in law and economics into other interdisciplinary fields of law, such as feminist jurisprudence, critical legal studies, law and philosophy, law and political theory, and law and literature. Anyone who wants to explore the economics of surrogate motherhood, or of criminal responsibility, or of the efficiency of the common law, or of the redistributive effects of legislation, or of the behavior of judges, or of affirmative action, or of the legal institutions of societies known to us only or mainly through literary sources (such as the Homeric epics and the Icelandic sagas), is bound to rub up against the other interdisciplinary fields that I have mentioned and to become interested in what they have to contribute to our knowledge of law and the legal system whether in tandem or in competition with economics. The progressive dissolution of boundaries among fields of learning is an accelerating trend in scholarship generally. It is no longer easy to distinguish a sociologist from an anthropologist, or a classicist from either, or a literary theorist from a philosopher, or even an economist from an evolutionary biologist. This fraying of lines is as advanced in the academic study of law as anywhere, with the result that the very distinctions among the different fields of interdisciplinary legal study, such as law and economics and law and literature, are blurred, as I hope to show in the chapters of this last part of the book.

In 1988, when I published *Law and Literature: A Misunderstood Relation,* law and literature was a newish addition to the interdisciplinary study of law. I discussed it under four aspects. One—call it "law in literature"—was the depiction of law (broadly defined to include vengeance as a prelegal or extralegal system for maintaining social order) in works of literature; I examined such classics as *The Merchant of Venice, The Brothers Karamazov, L'Étranger, Billy Budd,* and *The Trial.*[1] Another aspect was the use of literary technique in legal documents; here my focus was on the rhetoric of judicial opinions.[2] Call this "law as literature." Third was the use of theories of literary interpretation to illuminate the perennial debate over proper methods of interpreting statutes and constitutions. Last ("literature in law") was the analysis of the four bodies of law that directly regulate the production

1. In *The Problems of Jurisprudence,* I supplemented this aspect of *Law and Literature* with a discussion of *King Lear* and of Manzoni's great novel (underappreciated in the United States) *The Betrothed* (*I Promessi Sposi*).

2. I discussed judicial rhetoric further in *Cardozo: A Study in Reputation* (1990), and intermittently in *The Problems of Jurisprudence* (see index references under "Rhetoric"). And recall the discussion in Chapter 1 of Herbert Wechsler's rhetoric, in Chapter 3 of the judge as a spectator of a play, in Chapter 9 of Robert Bork's rhetoric, in Chapter 14 of the Norse sagas, and in Chapter 18 of the use of narrative techniques by critical race theorists. And in the next chapter, which is devoted entirely to rhetoric, with special though not exclusive reference to legal rhetoric, I analyze a passage from the *Odyssey.*

and dissemination of literature: defamation law, privacy law, obscenity law, and copyright law.

The specific intersections of law and literature discussed in the present chapter are: (1) the *implicit* depiction of law in works of literature that do not seem to be "about" law at all, such as E. M. Forster's novel *Howards End* and the poetry of Wallace Stevens; (2) the depiction of law in popular literature, such as Tom Wolfe's novel *The Bonfire of the Vanities,* as distinct from classical literature; and (3) recent suggestions that the problems and usages of literary translation can be used to illuminate issues of constitutional interpretation. Items (1) and (2) are examples of law in literature; (3) illustrates the use of literary theory to guide legal interpretation.

The Implicit Literary Depiction of Law

E. M. Forster was not a lawyer, and although his most famous novel, *A Passage to India,* pivots on a criminal trial, no one to my knowledge has suggested that an earlier novel of his, *Howards End* (published in 1911), is a "legal" novel. Yet chapter 38 of *Howards End* presents a scene that ought to have a special resonance for the law-trained reader.

The novel revolves around a contrast in style and values between a pair of German-born but Anglicized sisters, Margaret and Helen Schlegel (Helen is the younger), cultured, sensitive, and high-minded, and the Wilcoxes, a thoroughly English family whose men, Henry and his son Charles, personify philistine middle-class commercial values, of which Forster disapproved. Margaret marries Henry after the death of the first Mrs. Wilcox, with whom Margaret had felt a spiritual kinship because of a shared love of the Wilcox home, Howards End—for which Henry and Charles of course care not a whit. Helen, who is unmarried, becomes pregnant by a pathetic young man of the working classes, Leonard Bast. Bast's wife had been Henry Wilcox's mistress at a time when he was married to his first wife. Wilcox had cast her aside ungenerously.

Chapter 38 opens with Henry's questioning Margaret in an effort to discover the identity of Helen's "seducer." He regards the pregnancy of his unmarried sister-in-law as a deep scandal—a reaction that for Forster epitomizes the hypocrisy of Victorian morality—to which only two responses are possible. If the seducer is unmarried, he must be forced to marry her; if he is married, he "must pay heavily for his misconduct, and be thrashed within an inch of his life" (p. 305).[3] (Subsequently Leonard Bast *is* thrashed, by Charles Wilcox—and, because he has a weak heart, dies, and Charles is sent to prison for manslaughter, breaking Henry's spirit.) Margaret doesn't want to reveal the seducer's name to Henry (and doesn't—he discovers it later from someone else), so she changes the subject. She asks him whether Helen may stay at Howards End, as she wants very much to do, this last night before she goes off to Munich to have the baby in seclusion. Henry is appalled at the suggestion. Although he begins his response mildly enough by questioning Helen's reasons for wanting to stay at Howards End, he gets nowhere—Margaret insists that the only important thing is that she does want to stay—and quickly changes his tack. "If she wants to sleep one night, she may want to sleep two. We shall never get her out of the house, perhaps" (p. 306). A lawyer's ears should prick up because Henry is resorting to a familiar lawyer's gambit—the "slippery slope" (what nonlawyers call the "thin edge of the wedge" or "the camel's nose under the tent"). It is a variant of Herbert Wechsler's concept of "neutral principles." If you accept claim *a*, you must consider whether that commits you to accept *b, c . . . n* on the ground that there is no principled distinction among the claims, hence no logical stopping point; and then you must consider the consequences of the entire set of claims. To suppose that this principle of logical argument obliterates the distinction between a visit of one night and a visit of indefinite length is absurd; and we may begin to wonder whether Henry Wilcox isn't an inflexible, dichotomizing, rule-obsessed, in short *legalistic* reasoner, and whether his insistence that the only possible responses to Helen's pregnancy are a shotgun marriage or a criminal assault on the seducer isn't of a piece with his "slippery slope" argument in point of obtuse rigidity. As further evidence of this we learn elsewhere in the novel that Mrs. Wilcox, the legal owner of Howards End, had wanted to leave the house to Margaret but had expressed her intention in a note that did not comply with the formalities required of an effective will—so Henry, standing on his legal rights, had torn up the note, perpetrating an injustice in the name of legal justice.

The sense of his obtuseness is reinforced when he fails to catch the meaning of Margaret's remark, "Will you forgive her—as you hope to

3. Page references are to the Vintage Books edition (1954) of *Howards End*.

be forgiven, and as you have actually been forgiven?" (p. 307). The reference is to Henry's relationship, which Margaret had forgiven, with the woman who is now Leonard Bast's wife. But the remark has a further significance, as an appeal to mercy over against strict legal justice; and as such it further identifies Henry as a legalistic thinker when he rejects it saying, "I know how one thing leads to another." When he fails to react to her further remark, "May I mention Mrs. Bast?" (p. 308), Margaret becomes enraged. "Margaret rushed at him and seized both his hands. She was transfigured. 'Not any more of this!' she cried. 'You shall see the connection if it kills you, Henry! You have had a mistress—I forgave you. My sister has a lover—you drive her from the house . . . Only say to yourself: "What Helen has done, I've done."'" Yet even this sally has no effect. Committed as he is to the fundamental precept of legal justice that like cases must be treated alike, Henry insists that "the two cases are different." But not being a clear thinker he is unable to identify the difference, so again he changes tack: he accuses Margaret of trying to blackmail him, thus placing her words in a legal category with which to offset his own wrongful conduct. The charge of blackmail is false. Margaret has not, expressly or by implication, threatened Henry that unless he lets Helen stay the night at Howards End she will expose his relationship with Mrs. Bast. Henry is a very poor legal reasoner, but the interesting thing is that a novelistic setting remote from a trial or any other identifiably legal scene resounds with the unmistakable echo of legal rhetoric and reasoning.

It is apparent that Forster associates the legal style of thinking with the failure to connect heart and mind. ("Only connect . . ." is the famous epigraph of *Howards End* and in effect Forster's motto.) To Forster the human tragedy is that people become enmeshed in structures of thought that prevent them from leading emotionally satisfying lives. He was no doubt thinking primarily of the strand of Victorian sexual morality that by its rejection of homosexuality had contributed to making his own personal life miserable, but in *Howards End* this rejection is displaced onto Henry's rejection of Helen for her lesser violation of the Victorian code. The code itself Forster associates with the legal mentality (and at the time he wrote, only a decade after the trial and conviction of Oscar Wilde, homosexual sex was not only immoral but criminal), which he imagines to be rigidly committed to inflexible dichotomies and abstractions that are insensitive to the complexities of human emotion and as a result inflict needless suffering. A common literary reaction to law,[4] it undervalues rule and abstraction as methods of bringing order out of the chaos of social interactions. But my main point is simply that a lawyer's insights may be helpful in uncovering layers of meaning in works of literature ostensibly unconcerned with law.

Wallace Stevens, unlike E. M. Forster, was a lawyer. But until Thomas Grey wrote a book on Stevens no one had supposed that his poetry had anything to do with his "day job" as a lawyer-executive for an insurance company.[5] Grey's book is particularly relevant to my concerns because he is a pragmatist and argues that Stevens's poetry supports the pragmatic outlook on law. Grey believes that legal thought oscillates between unrealistic extremes—the "official" position that legal conclusions follow deductively from sound general principles and the "opposition" line that law is really just politics—and that Stevens in his poetry can be seen "as a kind of therapist for the habitual and institutional rigidities of binary thought" that generate this oscillation (pp. 6–7). I agree with the first point, that it is silly to suppose that the issue in jurisprudence is whether law is all logic or all politics, and with Grey's further point that those "law and lit" types who believe that the choice is between conceiving of the judge as a poet (their preference) and conceiving of him as an economist are embracing a precious and irrelevant aestheticism.[6] I am also persuaded by his suggestion that to the extent that Stevens is a "philosophical" poet the philosophy is pragmatism; and this enables Grey to draw some interesting parallels with Holmes. But I don't agree that Stevens's poetry is a useful corrective for the type of unpragmatic dichotomizing which we encountered in Chapter 1 and of which Grey rightly accuses major schools and figures in jurisprudence.

As Exhibit A for his thesis, Grey offers "The Motive for Metaphor,"[7] where Stevens contrasts the world of metaphor ("The obscure moon lighting an obscure world/ Of things that would never be quite expressed") with what we today would call the "real" world: "Steel against intimation . . ./ The vital, arrogant, fatal, dominant X." The algebraic symbol is an effective metaphor for the nonmetaphoric, de-

---

4. See *Law and Literature*, ch. 2.

5. Thomas C. Grey, *The Wallace Stevens Case: Law and the Practice of Poetry* (1991).

6. "Strategically, to accept the separation of heart and head and align with the heart in the ensuing party struggle [with, for example, the law and economics movement] is to relegate oneself to marginal, weekend, after-hours status—and to losing" (p. 89).

7. *The Collected Poems of Wallace Stevens* 288 (1955).

personalized, efficient, Gradgrindian, "bottom line" orientation that characterizes the world of "primary noon,/ The A B C of being,/ The ruddy temper, the hammer/ Of red and blue, the hard sound." Grey sees Stevens as contrasting the poet's world of metaphor and delicate shadings with the world of the hard-headed, practical, decisive lawyer who disdains ambiguity and metaphor and, in Holmes's famous words, "thinks things, not words" (and we might also recall here Holmes's aphorism that law is the calling of thinkers, not of poets). So read, the poem "cleanly separates—as Stevens did in his life, and as Judge Posner tells us [in *Law and Literature*] we should do in our legal scholarship— the realms of poetry and law" (p. 59).[8] But Grey thinks that, read more closely, the poem can be seen to be blurring the dichotomy between the metaphoric and real worlds. He notes for example that while spring, a transitional season, is an apt metaphor for the nuanced, tentative, elusive (and allusive) world of poetry or metaphor, Stevens chose as his symbol for the clear-eyed world of quotidian reality not summer, as the reader is expecting, but a moment—noon—that lasts but an instant and occurs in every season. The contrast between the world of metaphor and the world of action is further blurred by the fact that the poem's opening lines ("You like it under the trees in autumn,/ Because everything is half dead"), while describing the world of metaphor, are uncharacteristically flat, clear, and literal for Stevens. So, Grey concludes, Stevens is insisting that the metaphoric world is not all a dreamy mist and the real world is not all hard-edged masculine clarity (life according to Henry Wilcox). Both worlds are a mixture of hard and soft, clear and blurred, masculine and feminine. "The primary reading [of the poem] has 'The Motive for Metaphor' warning of the dangers of lawyers' locating their subject too much in literature's obscure world of rustling leaves and melting clouds, too little in the harsh smithy of noonday sweat and violence. The secondary reading, the other side that Stevens brings us to hear after resisting our intelligence almost successfully, warns of an opposed jurisprudential danger" (p. 64).

I don't see this. I think that what the poem is about is—the motive for metaphor, rather than anything to do with law.[9] Grey's association

---

8. I don't accept this characterization of my position, but let that pass.

9. "The motive for metaphor, according to Wallace Stevens, is a desire to associate, and finally to identify, the human mind with what goes on outside it, because the only genuine joy you can have is in those rare moments when you feel that although we may know in part, as Paul says, we are also a part of what we know." Northrop Frye, *The Educated Imagination* 33 (1964).

of the world of "primary noon," "the ruddy temper," "steel against intimation," "X," and so forth with law is arbitrary. We lack in Stevens's poem the kind of pointers that enabled us to read Henry Wilcox's argument against Helen's being permitted to stay overnight at Howards End as legalistic and the scene in which he makes them as a criticism of the legal sensibility. When Grey says for example that "'Steel against intimation' then juxtaposes two aspects of law: its sharp rigidity . . . and its flexibility before the imagination" (p. 67), I worry that he is in the grip of a preconception rather than responding to what could reasonably be thought to be "in" the poetry. Grey reminds us that Stevens was, after all, a lawyer. But even on its own terms this resort to biography is unconvincing because of Stevens's separation of his legal from his poetic practice (more on this shortly). And it will bother those of us who think that textual interpretations must have *some* support in the text to be convincing, that a literary text is not merely an aid to biography any more than a statutory text is merely an aid in the interpretation of legislative history (committee reports and the like). Since, moreover, poetry is a metaphoric medium, any "statement" that it makes about the "real" world will perforce be couched in metaphoric terms. And since a fresh metaphor implies the yoking of dissimilar terms it is easily taken ironically, as the New Critics, who considered irony a pervasive feature of poetry, used to emphasize; but this tells us more about poetry than about law. Some of the specific examples that Grey uses to demonstrate the inescapably metaphoric character of daily reality are unconvincing. An example is the substitution of noon for summer (or winter) to signify that reality. The word "summer" has complex associations, whereas "noon" brings straight to mind the sun's brightness[10] and thus complements the "harsh sound" and "sharp flash" with which Stevens extends the image of the real world in the next stanza.

The deeper problem with Grey's approach is the implausibility of supposing that "The Motive for Metaphor" can nudge judges, lawyers, or law students even a little distance toward a sensibility or frame of mind to which "binary thought" in jurisprudence would be uncongenial. Stevens himself, as Grey explains in the first three chapters of his book, though a great poet, succeeded almost completely in

---

10. That is why the title of Arthur Koestler's best-known novel—*Darkness at Noon*—is so arresting.

dichotomizing the practice of law and the writing of poetry;[11] should we expect Stevens's *readers* to be less successful in this regard? Grey underestimates the extent to which modern man lives a compartmentalized life[12] in which the reading of poetry might be thought a relief from practicing or writing about law rather than a source of guidance for the lawyer-reader's professional endeavors.

Grey uses Stevens to make the further point that the scientific quest for orderly and even elegant patterns in the chaos of sense experience, a quest to which Grey finds the legal counterpart in Langdell's version of formalism, is motivated by the *pleasure* that such a quest yields. Repose, order, certitude, closure, completeness, perfection—these are hedonistic goals. "The proponents of Strict Law are not the ascetic servants of their own legend, but hedonists of another kind" (p. 96), drawn, in Stevens's words, to a vision of "Total grandeur of a total edifice,/ Chosen by an inquisitor of structures/ For himself."[13] Grey thinks that this passage can help us understand why formalism has such a grip on the legal imagination. At the same time he insists that change, which he associates with equity over against strict law, has its own delights and hence that the changelessness of logical and mathematical truths is not only a source of but also a limitation on the pleasure that formalism can yield. Quoting Stevens, he reminds us that "Death is the mother of beauty" because death is inseparable from the change of seasons. "Is there no change of death in paradise?" "Does ripe fruit never fall?"[14]

Again I am troubled by the lack of any legal references, express or implied. Stevens is saying that scientific or other systematic thought is a source of pleasure to its practitioners but that other activities should

11. This conclusion is questioned, however, in David A. Skeel, Jr., "Notes toward an Aesthetics of Legal Pragmatism," 78 *Cornell Law Review* 84, 94–104 (1992).

12. See Erving Goffman, *The Presentation of Self in Everyday Life* (1959). I return to this point in Chapter 25.

13. "To an Old Philosopher in Rome [Santayana]," in *Collected Poems*, note 7 above, at 510–511. Stevens may intend us to associate "inquisitor" with Dostoevsky's Grand Inquisitor, that ostensibly self-denying creator of a "total edifice."

14. These quotations are from "Sunday Morning," in *Collected Poems,* note 7 above, at 69. "Death is the mother of beauty" may remind us once again (see Chapter 19) of Shelley's ode to the autumn west wind, which he addresses as "Destroyer and Preserver"—"O thou/ Who chariotest to their dark wintry bed/ The wingèd seeds, where they lie cold and low,/ Each like a corpse within its grave, until/ Thine azure sister of the Spring shall blow/ Her clarion o'er the dreaming earth, and fill/ (Driving sweet buds like flocks to feed in air)/ With living hues and odours plain and hill."

be recognized as yielding their own pleasures and indeed as pointing up certain hedonistic limitations of purely intellectual pursuits. True enough; and at this level of abstraction, there doubtless are possible applications to legal theory. But to approach the formalist-realist debate through Wallace Stevens is to begin awfully far away from one's object.

Lawyers might be able to derive some professional utility from studying the poetry of Wallace Stevens simply because his poetry is dense and difficult, which tempts the reader (which tempted Grey) to seek aids to understanding in the poet's biography. In this his poetry resembles many legal texts, the difficulty of which invites the reader to seek illumination from extrinsic sources, such as the legislative history of a statute, corresponding to a poet's intentions as revealed in his biography, letters, or critical writings (to all of which sources Grey has recourse). Reading a poem by Wallace Stevens requires the reader not only to attend carefully to every word but also to consider to what extent he can appropriately seek guidance to meaning from sources outside the text itself, as well as requiring the linguistic and cultural competence that Stevens would have expected his readers to bring to their reading of his poetry. One of the most important characteristics of a good lawyer is being a careful and resourceful reader, and immersion in poetry and other difficult imaginative literature is therefore not the worst preparation for the study of law.

As part of a general hostility to the so-called "canons of construction" by which judges pretend to be able to find "the" meaning of contracts, statutes, wills, constitutional provisions, and other legal rules and instruments, I have long criticized as manifestly unrealistic the principle that the reader of a statute or contract or other legal rule or instrument should assume that every meaning was placed there for a purpose—that there is no surplusage, inconsistency, mistake, or irrelevance. I now see with the aid of my own interpretive struggles with the poems of Wallace Stevens discussed by Grey that there is another and more favorable light in which to regard this principle. It is an antidote to hasty, careless, lazy reading. If we assume that every word is there for a purpose, we are made to read and ponder—every word, as we would surely be led to do by a good teacher of poetry. It is only when that principle of interpretation is transformed from a discipline to an algorithm that it is aptly criticized as unrealistic and misleading. At some level, then, law and literature—even when the literature half is the poetry of Wallace Stevens, a lawyer who kept his "day job," his "primary noon" work, separate from his writing of poetry—do converge.

Law in Popular Literature

The law and literature movement has tended to focus on masterpieces of world literature that take law for their theme, such as *The Merchant of Venice* and *The Trial*.[15] But anyone who has even a nodding acquaintance with modern American popular culture realizes that it is suffused, even preoccupied, with legal themes.[16] I must however leave to others the analysis of the presentation of law in movies and in television dramas, limiting myself to literature, with special reference to Tom Wolfe's best-selling novel, *The Bonfire of the Vanities* (1987).

The novel depicts the progressive enmeshment of the protagonist, Sherman McCoy, in the coarse, dingy, and sordid operation that is (according to Wolfe) the Bronx criminal justice system today. McCoy is investigated, questioned, arrested, indicted, and, after the first indictment is dismissed because of false testimony before the grand jury, reindicted. An epilogue briefly recounts his first trial, which ends in a hung jury; when the novel ends he is about to be retried. (The epilogue also alludes briefly to a tort action against McCoy.) The offense he is charged with is reckless endangerment, which blossoms into vehicular manslaughter when the victim dies. McCoy had picked up his mistress, Maria Ruskin, at Kennedy Airport in his sports car and on the way back to Manhattan had gotten lost in the South Bronx. A pair of teenagers—one a drug dealer ("The Crack King of Evergreen Avenue")—had thrown a tire in front of McCoy's car and when he got out to move the tire had approached him in a fashion that McCoy rightly interpreted as menacing. A scuffle ensued. Maria took the wheel. McCoy jumped back into the car, and as it pulled away it hit the other teenager (not the Crack King). Maria didn't stop and neither she nor McCoy reported the incident to the police. The prosecutors, abetted by self-appointed black leaders, knee-jerk liberals and radicals (such as the "Gay Fist Strike Force Against Racism"), and a scandal-mongering press,

---

15. In *Law and Literature* I did discuss, though very briefly, one work of popular fiction, E. L. Doctorow's novel *Ragtime*, but only for its borrowings from Heinrich von Kleist's classic novella, *Michael Kohlhaas. Law and Literature* 46.

16. See *Symposium on Law in Popular Culture*, 98 *Yale Law Journal* 1545 (1989).

portray the victim to a credulous public as the honor student that he is not.

The novel is attentive to the criminal process and its personnel. Larry Kramer, the assistant D.A. who prosecutes McCoy, is one of the principal supporting characters in the novel, along with Judge Kovitsky, the judge assigned to the case. The novel's gallery of minor characters includes the publicity-seeking D.A. himself, other lawyers, other defendants, court officers, and a juror, "the Girl with Brown Lipstick," whom Kramer pursues with a comic ineptness that culminates in scandal when he tries to rent for their trysts the "love nest" (rent-controlled, of course) in which McCoy and Maria Ruskin had held *their* trysts. In addition to the proceedings directly involving McCoy, Wolfe treats us to an extended episode of plea bargaining and to a portion of a homicide trial.

It does not follow that because *The Bonfire of the Vanities* has a legal plot, legal characters, and legal scenes, it is "about" law in a rich and interesting sense. A work of literature, to flourish in a different culture from the one in which it was conceived—to *be* literature, in other words—must not be too local, too topical, in its themes, and therefore we should not expect a work of literature to depict law in a form calculated to engage a lawyer's or a law professor's professional interests.[17] Even less should we expect this of a work of popular fiction, at least one as popular as *The Bonfire of the Vanities.* A book does not sell hundreds of thousands of copies in a short period by appealing to narrowly professional or academic concerns. The pertinent difference between classical and popular literature is thus that the former accretes its vast audience over decades, centuries, even millennia, and the latter in a much shorter period and sometimes all at once.

It does not follow that all popular books, any more than all classics, are predestined never to have anything interesting to say about law. Lawyers' professional concerns do not exhaust the social interest of law; nor do the arcane investigations conducted by students of jurisprudence. It is true that many works ostensibly about law, notably Kafka's *Trial,* use law as a metaphor for other dimensions of human experience and are therefore misunderstood when read literally. But such classics as *Eumenides, The Merchant of Venice, I Promessi Sposi,* and *Billy Budd*

---

17. *Law and Literature,* ch. 2, especially pp. 71–79. Works of literature may contain local themes—consider whaling in *Moby-Dick* or twelve-tone music in Mann's *Doctor Faustus*—but to endure as literature must transcend them.

have much to say about law at the jurisprudential level if not at that of legal practice. And Dickens's great legal novels, *Pickwick Papers* and *Bleak House* (not to mention *David Copperfield* and *Great Expectations,* both of which have notable lawyer characters), not only have jurisprudential interest but were significant contemporary criticisms of the English legal system. And a popular contemporary novel about law may afford a better glimpse of how lay people regard law than would a public opinion poll.

When I first read *The Bonfire of the Vanities*[18] I did not think it significant at any of these levels. This was not because I thought it a bad book—I considered (and consider) it a good and even excellent one, with descriptions of rich people's fatuous dinner parties that can bear comparison with such descriptions in Proust. It just didn't strike me as the sort of book that has anything interesting to say about law or any other institution. I had no doubt that with his enormous journalistic skills and impressive narrative ability Wolfe could write a penetrating fictionalized critique of the American legal system. I noted Dickensian touches in the grotesquerie of *The Bonfire of the Vanities* but remarked that it was not a book that aspired to be another *Bleak House* or *Pickwick Papers.* I said that with strain one could find elements in the book that had jurisprudential significance: the danger of misusing the legal process for political ends; the radicalizing effect (on McCoy) of being prosecuted (as the old saw goes, if a conservative is a liberal who has been mugged a liberal is a conservative who has been arrested); the capacity of a public arrest to inflict profound, life-altering humiliation, making the actual outcome of the criminal process almost a side issue; the effect of racial hostility on the rule of law; the difficulty of doing justice across large social-class differences; even the difficulty of reconstructing history by the methods of litigation. But I said that these things were in, not of, the book because the author had not treated them in a fashion that altered our understanding of them.

I now consider that estimate of the book ungenerous and unperceptive. *The Bonfire of the Vanities* has turned out to be a book that I think about a lot, in part because it describes with such vividness what Wolfe with prophetic insight (the sort of thing we attribute to Kafka) identified as emerging problems of the American legal system. The book

18. And wrote the review essay on which this part of the chapter is based and which in part I now recant: "The Depiction of Law in *The Bonfire of the Vanities,*" 98 *Yale Law Journal* 1653 (1989).

was written before Michael Milken was convicted and Clark Clifford indicted; before investment bankers and securities brokers were dragged, crying, in handcuffs from their offices on charges of criminal fraud that often turned out to be unsubstantiated; before courthouses became scenes of violence; before the Tawana Brawley fraud; before the trials of the police who beat up Rodney King; before the Los Angeles riots that followed the acquittal in the first of those trials; before the trial of the rioters; before the indictment of O. J. Simpson. American legal justice today seems often to be found at a bizarre intersection of race, money, and violence, an intersection nowhere better depicted than in *The Bonfire of the Vanities* even though the book was written before the intersection had come into view.

I will not try to elaborate these points, save one. The mistreatment by the American criminal justice system of persons charged but not yet convicted of crime is an international scandal. Persons accused of white-collar crimes are arrested in the most public and shaming manner possible and led in handcuffs to jail to be booked, but are then released on bond. Persons accused of crimes of violence are generally though not always drawn from social strata in which a public arrest is not a conspicuous badge of shame, but they are thrown into jail to languish, sometimes for many months, sometimes in horrible conditions, while awaiting trial. It is curious to reflect that the arrest of Joseph K in the first chapter of *The Trial* is immensely more *civilized* than any arrest would be likely to be in the land of freedom at the threshold of the twenty-first century.

All this is not to say that *The Bonfire of the Vanities* is primarily about law. The legal theme develops naturally out of the author's main aim, which is to satirize the diverse social classes and ethnic groupings that coexist uneasily in New York City and to a lesser extent in other American big cities. The book exploits to the hilt New York City's most arresting feature, now even more pronounced than when Wolfe wrote the book. This is the juxtaposition of grotesque extremes of opulence[19] and squalor, the former symbolized by McCoy and his Park Avenue/Wall Street set, the latter by the Bronx County Criminal Court with its crummy and overcrowded facilities, its clientele of black and Hispanic criminals, and its harried, underpaid, precariously middle-class

---

19. Yet even Wolfe could not imagine someone—Michael Milken, in fact—who earned $500 million in salary one year.

judicial and law-enforcement personnel. Shuttling between the extremes is a rich cast of hustlers, social climbers, toadies, hangers-on, and con men, seeking to share in the opulence and avoid sinking into the squalor. There is an *egregious* quality about New York City that provides a field day for a sharp-eyed and sharp-tongued social satirist.[20] (Wolfe has a particularly keen eye for prices and for how people dress.) This is not to say that Wolfe describes New York City and its institutions with complete fidelity. He exaggerates the sordidness of New York, less by misdescribing—I am told on good authority that his portrayal of the Bronx County Criminal Court is essentially accurate, although its environs aren't *quite* so hellish as he describes, and indeed that the whole book is a *roman à clef* populated by institutions and characters instantly recognizable to knowledgeable New Yorkers—than by suppressing complexity. But that is the satirist's privilege.

For Wolfe is in the tradition of Bosch and Swift in portraying humanity at its worst, and it is therefore part of his technique to present a one-sided view of his subject. His target is not only the individual but also the group to which the individual belongs. This is a salient but not endearing feature of the novel, for one can acknowledge, without embracing "hate speech" codes, that group libel raises hackles and can cause pain. Among the groups (of varying sensitivity, to be sure) that Wolfe ridicules are blacks, Jews, WASPs, Englishmen, homosexuals, Yuppies, liberals, politicians, women, the rich, and people who serve the rich. So encompassing is the denigration of human types that it would be misleading to describe Wolfe as a bigot, for a bigot divides the world into us and them. Although Wolfe appears to dislike blacks and disserves the cause of racial friendship by studiously neglecting any positive black character types, it hardly seems that he likes whites. He does seem to have a soft spot for the Irish, but Irish readers will wince with the rest, since it appears that Wolfe admires the Irish *only* for what he describes as their invincible stupidity—the source in his view of their physical courage, the only virtue he acknowledges in them. One of Wolfe's Jewish characters, Judge Kovitsky ("a Jewish warrior, a son of the Masada," as Larry Kramer muses, p. 111),[21] is presented in a generally favorable light (as a tough guy, naturally, because it is tough guys that Wolfe, a southerner—so now I'm indulging in some stereo-

20. In Chapter 18 we saw the same skill deployed by another acute observer of the New York scene, Patricia Williams.

21. Page references are to the 1988 paperback edition of Wolfe's novel.

typing—admires). But this is balanced by the sharply antipathetic depiction of other Jews, such as Kramer, who is unethical, envious, vain, lecherous, ugly, and in the end ridiculous; Lopwitz, the Wall Street *parvenu;* the tabloid publisher nicknamed the "Dead Mouse"; and Maria's husband, the cuckold Ruskin who operates a charter service for pilgrims to Mecca. On the other hand, the English journalist Fallow—a lush, sponge, and anti-Semite—is the single most despicable character in the book, and if I had to guess which if any of the satirized groups Wolfe *actually* dislikes, it would be the English (which of course would be consistent with his fondness for the Irish). I am tempted to say that Wolfe is like Nietzsche, of whom it is difficult to say whether he dislikes Jews or anti-Semites more, but of course Wolfe may hate no group, and may simply wield a wicked pen.

The ecumenical character of the satire saves it from being vicious. And, vicious or not, it is redeemed, for me anyway, by a handful of brilliant scenes: "the wagon-train recess" at the Bronx County Criminal Court;[22] the trading floor at McCoy's brokerage firm; the society dinner at the Bavardages,[23] with its "bouquets" of guests, its "Social X-Rays" (the anorectic middle-aged society women) and "Lemon Tarts" (the mistresses or young wives of rich old men); the logistics of getting to a party a few blocks from one's home (a limousine is *de rigueur*); the restaurant death scene that I mentioned; Fallow's improbable journalistic coup in uncovering the details of McCoy's "crime"; and my favorite scene of all—arguably Dantesque but at least worthy of Dickens, and certainly of Kafka—enacted when in the course of an investigation Kramer asks to use the phone in a police station and is directed to a room in which he finds three black men, each sitting at a desk:

> Kramer thought of how unusual it was to come across an entire bureau made up of black detectives. The one at the desk nearest the door wore a black thermal vest and sleeveless black T-shirt that showed off his powerful arms.
>
> Kramer reached toward the telephone on his desk and said, "Use your phone?"
>
> "Hey, what the fuck, man!"

22. The judges and other court personnel park their cars a few blocks from the courthouse but are afraid to walk into the parking lot after dark. So if it appears that court will run late, they interrupt the proceedings for what they call a "wagon-train recess," in which all court personnel go and get their cars from the lot and park them outside the court. The recess is signaled by one of the bailiffs chanting "Yo-ohhhhhhh" (p. 178).

23. The French word for to chatter or gossip is *bavarder.*

Kramer pulled his hand back.

"How long I gotta sit here chained up like a fucking animal?"

With that, the man raised his powerful left arm with a terrific clattering. There was a manacle on his wrist, and from the manacle a chain. The other end of the chain was manacled to the leg of the desk. Now the other two, at the other desks, had their arms up in the air, clattering and yammering. All three of them were chained to the desks.

"All I did was *see* the motherfucker whack that sucker, and he was the motherfucker that *whacked* that sucker, and I'm the one you got chained up like a fucking animal, and that motherfucker"—another terrific clatter as he gestured toward a room in the rear with his left hand—"he's sitting back there watching fucking TV and eating ribs."

Kramer looked to the back of the room, and sure enough, back there in a locker room was a figure sitting on the edge of a chair lit by the hectic flash of the television set and eating a length of barbecued rib of pork. And he was indeed leaning forward daintily. The sleeve of his jacket was tailored to show a lot of white cuff and gleaming cuff link.

Now all three were yammering. *Fucking ribs . . . fucking chains! . . . fucking TV!*

But of course! The witnesses. Once Kramer realized that, everything, chains and all, fell into place. (pp. 223–224)

The Bonfire of the Vanities is not a "great" novel, if one's benchmark is Dickens or Dostoevsky. Its plot and characters are merely threads connecting a series of tableaux such as the one above. Its prose is pedestrian; "lit by the hectic flush of the television set" is the only memorable phrase in the tableau of the witnesses, and it's not as good as the best of Patricia Williams. The characters are shallow—this may be related to Wolfe's misanthropy—and are revealed by the rather too simplistic device of making the reader privy to their thoughts. And about two-thirds of the way through the novel the author's energy flags; so inferior is the novel's last third to its first two-thirds that it is as if Wolfe had died and left the book to be completed by a hack. Satire increasingly gives way to broad and eventually tedious burlesque. The scene in which a courtroom mob attacks Judge Kovitsky for dismissing the indictment against McCoy is overdone and implausible; the halo around Kovitsky's head at this point shines too brightly. And the hints of redemption for McCoy that Wolfe starts to drop are maudlin. The book peters out; Wolfe seems to have had no idea how to end it.

But this is the only criticism that counts. The fact that the novel lacks rich plot and multidimensional characters and distinguished prose merely identifies it as a certain type of novel; for the same observations could be made about *Nineteen Eighty-Four*. The "novel" is not a closed genre. The satirical or political novel (*The Bonfire of the Vanities* is both) should not be judged by its resemblance to novels of a psychological or philosophical character.

Or to novels deeply concerned with law or justice. Wolfe is interested neither in law reform in the sense that interested Dickens nor in human and divine justice in the sense that engaged Sophocles and Dostoevsky. The depiction of the criminal process in *The Brothers Karamazov* is designed not to provide local color or narrative suspense, or to be a caricature or an exposé, but to contrast rational inquiry, exemplified by the criminal justice system, with religious insight—to the disadvantage of the former.[24] The only religions in *The Bonfire of the Vanities* are Reverend Bacon's extortion racket and the Wall Streeters' worship of Mammon. The law for Wolfe is simply another setting—no different in any material respect from a dinner party on Park Avenue, or a dinner at a fancy restaurant, or the "ant colony" where Larry Kramer lives with his wife, infant, and au pair on his meager civil servant's salary—in which to observe the comic pratfalls of trivial people. Although the politicization of prosecutors' offices and the assembly-line character of criminal justice in the nation's big cities are genuine social problems that the novel vividly depicts, there is no suggestion that any of these problems might be alleviated, let alone solved. On the contrary, the reader is led to believe that the present criminal justice system of the Bronx will soon give way to one dominated by the minority that is already a majority in the Bronx and that *that* system will be even worse than the present one, for there will be no Kovitskys in it. To stimulate social reform (other than through proposing some "invisible hand" mechanism that will turn private greed into social benefit) an author must convey the impression that he believes that there are at least some good people in the society. If there are none, not only is reform unlikely to succeed but there is no reason we should *want* it to succeed—the people do not deserve a better life. New Yorkers, as depicted by Tom Wolfe, are mostly freaks and monsters who neither deserve a better system nor would profit from it, save in the mercenary sense.

We might expect the popular literature about law to tell us a great deal about how lay people view law. But we learn nothing from *The*

24. *Law and Literature* 166–171.

Bonfire of the Vanities on this score that the classical legal novels, such as *The Brothers Karamazov* and *Pickwick Papers,* had not taught us already: that lay people expect technicalities to matter (and it is on a technicality that the first indictment against McCoy is dismissed); that they are not surprised when miscarriages of justice occur (McCoy, remember, is innocent of the charges against him, and the real culprits are used as false witnesses by the prosecution); that they expect legal proceedings to be interminable and excruciatingly expensive; and that they have no illusions about the moral and intellectual shortcomings of judges, lawyers, jurors, and other participants in the machinery of legal justice, and about the corrosion of that machinery by political and personal ambitions and fears. Judge Kovitsky does get to make a Law Day speech to Larry Kramer: "What makes you think you can come before the bench waving the banner of community pressure? The law is not a creature of the few or of the many. The court is not swayed by your threats" (p. 676). But Kovitsky is duly punished for his independence: he is denied renomination.

The public is more cynical about law than the profession is, and it is useful for legal professionals to be reminded of this from time to time even if we should have known it all before from other and greater works of literature or from everyday observation, common sense, and the news media. I said in Chapter 9 that one of the things that derailed Robert Bork's appointment to the Supreme Court was that he and his supporters did not understand what the public expects from judges: did not understand—understandably—that it expects, in fact, incompatible things. Maybe we cannot learn a great deal from popular culture about how the public actually views the law, but we—we legal professionals—can learn something, and to our profit.

The Bonfire of the Vanities is a fine novel with limited relevance to the deep issues of jurisprudence. An obscure short story of no literary merit that I can discern,[25] H. B. Whyte's "Non sub Homine,"[26] has unlimited relevance to them. The story is set in the future. The federal courthouse in Foley Square (New York again) houses the largest computer ever

---

25. Of course I may simply be repeating my mistake of underrating *The Bonfire of the Vanities.*

26. Which can be found in *Dark Sins, Dark Dreams: Crime in Science Fiction* 121 (Barry N. Malzberg and Bill Pronzini eds. 1978). "H. B. Whyte" is the pseudonym of a New York lawyer. The story was first published in 1975 in a science-fiction magazine. My page references are to the version in *Dark Sins.*

built. Programmed with every legal decision ever made, every statute ever passed, every regulation, and so forth, the computer uses its huge library of decisions and other legal materials to answer legal questions. It does such a good job that it has displaced the courts, which have been relegated to ceremonial functions. And by thus "taking law out of the hands of man" the computer has "generated a new respect for law" (p. 123).[27]

But now a crisis has occurred. A seemingly routine case involving the assignability of a lease has been submitted to the computer, and the computer has failed to render a decision. The computer's operator, a man named Cook, discovers that the problem is not a mechanical malfunction; it is that after examining all the pertinent authorities the computer had "concluded that there was nothing to choose between either result. It had, in fact, even printed out two separate neatly worded and closely reasoned opinions, each reaching opposite conclusions." Cook and his assistant Jane read the two opinions and realize that "there was nothing to either that was not completely justified. It was clear that either opinion would fully satisfy the litigants who were still waiting in the Hall of Questions below them" (p. 124).

Cook is appalled. "The 2–10 [the name of the computer] is infallible," Cook finds himself saying. "It cannot be permitted to fail." Jane remarks, "With you, the machine could never fail. People, relationships, meaning, all of that, that didn't matter at all just as long as the damned machine—." This reminds Cook "that at some time in the past he had or had not loved the girl; it didn't matter . . . The system was being threatened" (pp. 124–125). Randomly choosing between the two decisions that the computer has prepared, Cook picks the one in which the plaintiff wins and tells Jane to process it. Then with Jane's aid he reprograms the machine so that from now on it will choose a winner at random whenever it cannot make a reasoned choice between the litigants. "The impartiality of the machine could never be questioned, nor its authority." The only rub is that Jane knows what he has done. On her way out she remarks to Cook, rather gratuitously as it seems

27. Life imitates art: "A new computer service called QuickCourt gives do-it-yourselfers practically all the information needed to file uncontested divorces, make small claims, collect judgments and settle landlord/tenant disputes without hiring a lawyer. And here's the kicker—it's free. The talking, bilingual computer (currently online in the Maricopa County Superior Court law library . . .), dispenses court information, defines common legal terms and calculates child support payments." "Simplifying Legal Work," *Arizona Republic,* June 25, 1993, p. A20.

to me, "You're a cold person." Cook mulls this over. She is wrong, he decides. "I'm not cold at all. I have feelings . . . for the 2–10" (p. 125). He decides to electrocute her to protect the secret of how the computer decides indeterminate cases. End of four-page story.

It is not a story likely to win a literary prize. The characters are wooden, the plot perfunctory, the prose pedestrian, the premises absurd (most absurd is the premise that the machine had not from the start been programmed with an algorithm for deciding evenly balanced cases). But as a parable of jurisprudence it is immensely suggestive. It shows us the traditional "rule of law" ideology carried to its logical extreme, with the displacement of human by mechanical judgment. It shows us the psychology of people who want to empty the law of emotion, and how such a psychology is compatible with destructive fury. Anticipating feminist jurisprudence, it presents us with a contrasting vision of legal judgment and embodies it in a woman. It shows us the helplessness of mechanical judgment confronted by uncertainty.

Above all, the story makes us think about the ineradicable element of creativity in legal judgment. The computer has been programmed with all decided cases. It is supposed to decide new cases by reference to them. But many of those decided cases (all that were not mere replays of earlier cases) were once new cases. How is a new case to be decided when the only materials for decision are old cases that by definition are different from it? A computer needs more in its memory bank than this computer has been given; needs as much, in fact, as fallible humans have in their memory banks.

Further reflection on this thin but suggestive science-fiction parable will lead us to see, what might at first glance seem puzzling, why the decision of even the closest case by the flipping of a coin is considered grave judicial misconduct.[28] The reason—or at least the reason I want to consider, because there are others, including judicial reluctance to acknowledge the element of indeterminacy in the adjudicative process—is that such a decision adds no insight or information to the stock of existing cases. This would not matter if a judge's only function were to decide cases in accordance with existing rules. For then the entire content of the law would reside in the rules, and the judge would be strictly a resolver of disputes (like a baseball umpire)—and flipping a

28. A judge in New York City was removed from office some years ago in part for admitting that he flipped a coin to decide closely balanced cases; and recall the trial of Justice Bridlegoose, on the charge of using dice to decide cases, in *Gargantua and Pantagruel*.

coin is not the worst way of resolving a dispute if it is irremediably uncertain which disputant is in the right. But suppose the judge is a rule applier only when the rules and their application are clear, and a rule*maker* otherwise, as I suggested in Chapter 3. Suppose, then, that what we want from judges is not an umpireal decision in all cases but an umpireal decision in most cases and a legislative judgment in the remainder. The judge who flips a coin in the indeterminate case fails in his duty to make a legislative judgment in that case.

The point is not that if only the judge would think harder about the case he would come to the right result, so that the stricture against coin-flipping is necessary to prevent judges from becoming lazy. If the case is indeterminate, as many cases are, there is no right result, and then the coin flip produces as right a result from the litigants' standpoint as any other method of dispute resolution. In the indeterminate case we don't ask that the judge get it right—an unattainable demand— but that he use the occasion to create law. We now can see that among its other limitations Cook's computer would be deciding cases under ever staler and more obsolete rules, because the only information on which it could base its decisions would be the human judgments that had been programmed into it when it was built. Every year it would do a worse job, even if no one were the wiser about how Cook had jiggered it to solve the problem of the indeterminate case.

Translation as Interpretation

That literature presents interpretive problems which might illuminate the interpretive problems presented by the Constitution is not a new idea. That the problems of translating a work of literature from one language to another might illuminate constitutional interpretation is a new idea.[29] The proposal is literary in two senses. It borrows from the scholarship on literary translation and from examples of such translation; and it is itself metaphoric, since we do not "translate" the Constitution in the sense of rendering it into a different language. There are literal problems of translation in law: the use of interpreters by witnesses who don't speak English, or the translation into English of statutes, treaties, contracts, trial exhibits, and other legally relevant

---

29. James Boyd White, *Justice as Translation: An Essay in Cultural and Legal Criticism* (1990); Lawrence Lessig, "Fidelity in Translation," 71 *Texas Law Review* 1165 (1993).

documents written in a foreign language. But such problems do not interest the "interpretation as translation" school.

The argument comes in two forms, which are problematic in different ways. James Boyd White argues that since "no sentence can be translated into another language without change," translation can only be "the composition of a particular text by one individual mind in response to another text,"[30] and a judicial opinion interpreting a provision of the Constitution should be viewed in the same light. The premise is overstated. Some sentences can be translated into another language without any loss of meaning: instructions for assembling a kitchen table, for example. The provision of the Constitution that the President must be at least 35 years old, or the provision that each state is entitled to two senators, can be "translated" from eighteenth-century linguistic, political, and social understandings into those of the twentieth century without loss of meaning, even though longevity has increased and the method of choosing senators has changed.

This is more than a quibble. It shows that literal translation is not an oxymoron. And by doing so it also shows that translation involves making choices none of which need be either "right" or "wrong." Take Agamemnon's usual sobriquet in the *Iliad: anax andrōn*. A literal translation might be "supreme leader of the warriors," but that is stilted. If we wanted to make the *Iliad* sound modern we could translate the term as "Supreme Allied Commander" or even "Chief Honcho" (this would be like playing Shakespeare in modern dress). Or if we wanted to preserve the sense of antiquity, of cultural distance, we could leave the term untranslated, as in "Kaiser Wilhelm" (versus "Emperor William"). We might compromise with "Lord Agamemnon," as some translations of the *Iliad* do, but this sounds a bit British Imperial. The choice among these myriad possibilities, none clearly satisfactory, none clearly right or clearly wrong, has to do with the effects the translator is aiming at and the intended use of the translation and hence the intended audience for it. Although White expects reflection on the difficulties of literary translation to engender humility in the judge faced with the task of "translating" an eighteenth-century document into the culture of today, an alternative inference to be drawn from the practice of literary translation is the translator's free-

---

30. White, note 29 above, at 250, 254.

dom. If a translator can choose between a literal and a free translation, why not a judge between a literal and a free interpretation?

So one is not surprised that where White finds an injunction to humility, Lawrence Lessig finds a license for judicial creativity. Building on the strong lawyerly intuition that constitutional and statutory interpretation must, to be legitimate, be faithful to the constitutional or statutory text, and adding that translation aims at preserving the meaning of the original text, Lessig argues that faithful translation cannot be literal, because the cultural significance of words changes. "Lord" may be an adequate literal translation of *anax andrōn,* but it means something so different to modern Americans (Lord Peter Wimsey? Lord Haw-Haw? Lord Acton?) that to affix it to "Agamemnon" alters Homer's meaning for American readers. To preserve meaning in an altered social context we might have to choose a literal *mis*translation. This shows that "the translator is empowered to *change text.*"[31] The same ought to be true, Lessig argues, for judicial interpretation of the Constitution.

It is a powerful argument, informed by a deep study of the theory and practice of translation.[32] But it does not answer the fundamental question, which is whether a modernizing translation of constitutional commands is a good thing. Lessig says yes, because otherwise we are not being faithful to the constitutional meaning. He acknowledges that fidelity is only one criterion of a good translation. The point I would emphasize is that it is an *ambiguous* criterion of a good translation. A translation is faithful in one sense if it sticks to the denotations of the words translated, even though the result will be stilted, even misleading. A loose translation that conveys a better sense of how the author might have expressed himself had he been a modern American will for some purposes be a better translation. But it is not more "faithful to the original"; it is merely faithful to the original in a different sense. The choice between fidelities will depend upon such considerations as the intended or potential audience, the character of existing translations, the translator's talents, and the author's preferences (if he is alive and controls translation rights).

Remember *Hitler's Justice: The Courts of the Third Reich* (Chapter 4)? The German title is *Furchtbare Juristen: Die unbewältigte Ver-*

---

31. Lessig, note 29 above, at 1191.
32. See id. at 1189–1211.

gangenheit unserer Justiz, which means approximately "Dreadful Lawyers [or possibly 'Despicable Jurists']: The Refusal to Confront the History of Our Courts."[33] The English translation of the title was thus very free indeed. But this can probably be justified by the difference between the audiences for the German and the English edition. A literal translation would make the American reader suppose the book was about American courts. More important, the German title is intended for readers likely to think highly of the German court system, and it warns those readers that the book is going to challenge their preconceptions.[34] American readers are not likely to be shocked by any criticism of any German institution during the Hitler period, so they would find Müller's title, if translated literally, misleadingly sensationalistic— promising surprises that (to an American audience) it does not deliver. So far the example supports Lessig. Yet the literal translation of the title of Müller's book could hardly be called a *mis*translation. It might be jarring to an American, yet it would convey the character of the book in a way that the loose translation does not. The loose translation makes the book seem more scholarly and dispassionate than it is; the literal translation alerts the reader to the fact that the book has a polemical intent and may therefore have a problem of balance, as we saw in Chapter 4 that it does. A literal translation of the title would have reduced the sales of the book in America, but the loose translation may have caused some readers to misread the book.

A translator is empowered to change text, but whether he is right to do so in a particular instance depends on a host of contextual factors— and in the legal setting they are factors remote from those that bear on the question how best to translate Müller's title. The theory and practice of translation undermine the inevitability of strict construction, but they will not help lawyers and judges to choose between strict and loose construction in particular areas of law.[35]

Suppose we asked what the best translation of some work of literature or philosophy would be if the only objective were to convey its meaning clearly, without regard for readability or emotional impact. The answer would probably be a literal translation with numerous footnotes ex-

---

33. *Bewältigung der Vergangenheit* is the term used to denote confronting and acknowledging, as opposed to denying, rationalizing, or covering up, the Nazi past.

34. Walter Otto Weyrauch, "Limits of Perception: Reader Response to Hitler's Justice," 40 *American Journal of Comparative Law* 237, 240–241 (1992).

35. Lessig acknowledges this possibility. Lessig, note 29 above, at 1268.

plaining the ways in which the translation might mislead. Untranslatable words and phrases (such as *anax andrōn* or *Bewältigung der Vergangenheit*) might be left in the original, and their meaning explained by bracketed paraphrases. Anachronisms, false cognates, conventions, changes in the cultural, linguistic, and historical context—all would be patiently explained. The result would be charmless and copious, but the loss of meaning would be minimal. The problem of translation would be "solved." And this helps us see what that problem really is: it is the problem of striking a compromise between the desire to preserve the original meaning of the original text and the desire to inveigle, attract, please, delight, or even just economize on the time of, some target contemporary audience. No doubt the problem of constitutional interpretation could be seen as analogous, but the analogy would be too distant to be illuminating.

In urging that we think of interpretation as translation, both White and Lessig are making an argument in the form of a metaphor. The problem with argument by metaphor, like argument by analogy which it closely resembles, is that it requires—translation. Literary translation and constitutional interpretation do have things in common, but there are also differences, and the differences may dominate the similarities. Translation in its conventional rather than extended sense is concerned with the specific problem of equivalence in different languages and has different aims from constitutional interpretation, and nothing in the theory or practice of translation supports a general preference for strict over loose translation, or the reverse. The utility of "translation" as a touchstone of sound constitutional interpretation is rhetorical rather than analytical. In the hands of a skillful rhetorician like Lessig, it furnishes an idiom with which the activist judge can turn the tables on the strict-constructionist judge by accusing the latter of infidelity to the constitutional text and, because Lessig conceives of fidelity in translation as a blend of creativity with humility, of lack of humility as well![36] Ronald Dworkin plays a similar table-turning trick by defining law so broadly that it includes all of political morality. This definition enables him to call judges who are unwilling to make constitutional law a branch of political and moral philosophy not only timid, crabbed, and unfeeling, but also—lawless. Amar and Widawsky's tactic—activism in the guise of originalism—is similar (Chapter 6), and Lessig has been

36. See *The Problems of Jurisprudence* 22.

admiringly bracketed with Amar as new-style liberal originalists who have hoisted Bork with his own petard.[37]

The dazzling accusation that the self-announced fidelists are unfaithful must ultimately fail. Literal translations, like musical performances using authentic instruments (Chapter 9), are "faithful" in a perfectly intelligible sense. By the same token, a translation is not bad or even unfaithful by virtue of being loose, so that even if the activist judge cannot claim the exclusive mantle of legitimacy for his method, he can fend off accusations that it is illegitimate because deficient in fidelity, without denying that legitimacy depends on fidelity. But am I unreasonable to wish that the rhetorical bandwagon had never gotten started in the first place? That the activist judges of the Warren era had not pretended to be originalists? That conservatives in the 1980s—Bork and Meese and the rest—had not pretended to be originalists? And that the current defenders of the Warren era's decisions and general approach would not pretend to be originalists? Could not the merit of such decisions as *Brown, Griswold, Roe, DeShaney,* and *Hardwick* be examined without the pretentious and ultimately useless rhetorics of interpretative methodology? Or—to introduce the next chapter—am I being too hard on rhetoric?

37. "Jeffrey Rosen Replies," in "'Life's Dominion': An Exchange," *New Republic,* Sept. 6, 1993, pp. 44, 45.

chapter 24

Rhetoric, Legal Advocacy, and Legal Reasoning

O NE of the principal jobs of lawyers is advocacy, often derided as making the worse appear the better cause. Legal advocacy illustrates the practice of "rhetoric" in the sense of persuasive speech; and ever since Protagoras it has been understood that one use of rhetoric is, indeed, to make the weaker appear the stronger argument.[1] Protagoras and Gorgias are the best-known of the sophists, who flourished in the fifth and fourth centuries B.C. and who are often considered the inventors of rhetorical theory, although it has been argued that the real inventors were Plato and Aristotle—that before them the distinction between the unadorned idea or message and the different verbal or otherwise expressive forms in which it can be encoded in order to maximize its persuasive force was not understood.[2]

The modern connotation of "sophist" and "sophistic" is a clue to the ambivalent repute in which the art of rhetoric is held in our culture.

---

1. G. B. Kerferd, *The Sophistic Movement* 101 (1981). Protagoras may have been misunderstood slightly. He may have meant that rhetoric could be used to make an undeservedly weak argument somewhat stronger. Edward Schiappa, *Protagoras and Logos: A Study in Greek Philosophy and Rhetoric*, ch. 6 (1991).

2. This is the theme of Thomas Cole, *The Origins of Rhetoric in Ancient Greece* (1991).

The word "rhetoric" itself has for most of us the negative connotation of deceptive or overelaborate speech—the opposite of speaking to the point. One of the issues on which Plato and Aristotle famously differed is whether rhetoric is mainly bad (Plato) or mainly good (Aristotle). We can make progress toward the resolution of this dispute, I shall argue, by attending to the economics of persuasive speech. Rhetoric is not just expression, however; for Aristotle, as for many of his modern followers, it is also a method of reasoning. So viewed, it is closely allied to casuistry in moral reasoning and to the case method in legal reasoning. I shall be examining the cognitive as well as the persuasive conception of rhetoric, and also the relation, thought by some to be intimate, between rhetoric and pragmatism.

I shall not of course be writing on a clean slate. But although the literature on rhetoric is enormous, it is of limited variety and low average quality compared to the literature of its traditional rival, philosophy. The *chef d'oeuvre* remains Aristotle's *Rhetoric,* beyond which more than two millennia's worth of subsequent literature has made few advances.[3]

Some Economics of Persuasive Speech

Persuasion means trying to bring someone around to your opinion on a matter without paying or coercing him. One method of persuasion is to convey information, but persuading and informing are different. Persuasion may be effected without conveying information, and not only if information is defined (rather too restrictively) as being always "true." And true information may not persuade, either because it is not believed or because, although believed, it gives the recipient no incentive to act in accordance with the persuader's desire. Persuasion can supply reasons for acting through the communication of either true or false information that induces belief and desire, or it can bypass reason altogether and make a base appeal to the emotions, which is Catharine

3. The best modern introduction to the field appears to be Brian Vickers, *In Defence of Rhetoric* (1988). On casuistry, see Albert R. Jonsen and Stephen Toulmin, *The Abuse of Casuistry: A History of Moral Reasoning* (1988). The *economic* literature on rhetoric, and on communication more broadly, is meager. See the references to *The Economics of Justice* in note 10 below; also William M. Landes and Richard A. Posner, "Trademark Law: An Economic Perspective," 30 *Journal of Law and Economics* 265, 271–273 (1987) (discussing the economics of language). Economists have discussed closely related problems, however, under such rubrics as information costs, statistical discrimination, and signaling.

MacKinnon's conception of how pornography works. But we shall see that it would be a mistake to suppose that reason and emotion are always in conflict.

Rhetoric can be given an economic cast by making the plausible assumption that people generally make choices on the basis of the balance of benefits and costs as it appears to them—benefits and costs that need not be pecuniary and need not be compared by an explicit process of calculation—and that beliefs are inputs into a person's estimation of benefits and costs. Thus, the persuader can try to work his listener around to his views in one of two ways. He can seek to influence the listener's beliefs, or he can seek to influence or bypass the (normally implicit) balancing process that the listener uses to make choices, so that the listener is led to make a decision that he would not have deemed cost-justified had his decisional process been left alone.

I shall concentrate on efforts to influence beliefs. A speaker can influence the beliefs of his audience in two ways. One way is by supplying information, broadly understood to include false as well as true information and also deductions and inferences and other logical or inductive manipulations of "fact" that furnish evidence or proof to the rational mind, as well as the underlying data that are manipulated. The other way to influence an audience's beliefs is by using signals of one sort or another to enhance the credibility of the speaker's arguments—such signals as speaking with great self-assurance or furnishing particulars about oneself that make one seem a credible person. This way is temporally first, because the speaker must place his audience in a receptive mood before he can hope to change its beliefs through information.[4] The creation of this receptive mood was called in classical rhetoric the "ethical appeal."

The persuader whose goal is fixed will choose that mixture of rhetorical devices—including true information, lies, signals, and emotional appeals—that, at least cost to himself, will maximize the likelihood of achieving that goal. The qualification "whose goal is fixed" is important. Often the persuader will have a range of goals, ranked from the most to the least desired, and he may not aim at the most desired

---

4. Much advertising is of this character—the most striking example that of the advertiser who pays for expensive television programming in the hope of inducing television viewers to watch his commercials. Advertising is an important modern arena of rhetoric, in which the classic devices of rhetoric, such as the ethical appeal, are well understood. See Larry Percy and John R. Rossiter, *Advertising Strategy: A Communication Theory Approach* 75–92 (1980).

because the cost of persuading the audience to accept it may be prohibitive. The variables that determine this cost we may call "distance" and "tenacity." The cost of persuading an audience to believe X will be lower, other things being equal, the shorter the distance between X and Y,[5] where Y is the audience's prior belief concerning the subject matter of the speech. The shorter the distance, the less perturbation to the audience's existing web of beliefs will be caused by the adoption of belief X. People are rationally reluctant to make fundamental changes in their belief systems and are therefore more likely to adopt a new belief if it does not require them to abandon many of their existing beliefs.

Reference to "fundamental changes" brings to the fore the second variable, tenacity. People hold their beliefs with varying strength. The more strongly a belief is held, the more reluctant a person will be to give it up, even if to an outsider the change in beliefs that is being urged seems a small one. The history of religious controversy is rich in examples.

The tenacity of the audience's beliefs is likely to affect the speaker's choice of rhetorical ends, distance his choice of rhetorical means as well. The skillful rhetorician will be careful to build bridges between the audience's existing beliefs and the belief that he wishes to induce the audience to adopt. Hence the importance of analogy as a rhetorical device.

An important factor in a speaker's choice of rhetorical methods is the cost to the audience of acquiring and processing (call these things together "absorbing") information. Normally a speaker wants to be understood, so it would not make sense for him to speak a different language from his audience's. But there is much more to the costs of absorbing information. Aristotle explained that the function of rhetoric is to induce belief in circumstances in which apodictic demonstration is impossible. The significance of this point can be demonstrated with the help of (naturally) an analogy: that of "selling" an idea to selling a good. A good has some probability (p) of failure, and the consumer's choice whether to buy it can therefore be modeled as

$$EU_j = (1 - p)B_j - pL_j,$$

5. Akira Yokoyama, "An Economic Theory of Persuasion," 71 *Public Choice* 101, 103 (1991); cf. Percy and Rossiter, note 4 above, at 162.

where EU_j is the expected utility of good j, B is the benefit to the buyer if the good works, and L is the loss if it fails. The "good" might be an idea, and then p would be the probability that it was a false or bad idea. Suppose the idea is that God exists. It is an example of an idea that cannot be proved or disproved by the methods of science or logic. Pascal famously argued that since the benefit of accepting this particular idea if it is true is so enormous (eternal salvation) relative to the loss if it is false, you should if rational believe in God even if you think the probability of His existence small. That is, EU_j may be positive even if p is large, provided that B_j is sufficiently greater than L_j. (To be precise, EU_j will be positive if the ratio of B_j to L_j exceeds the ratio of p to $1 - p$.) It was an argument that, whatever its flaws (belief is not entirely voluntary, God might be unimpressed by so opportunistic a worshipper, and a choice of the wrong sect might be as fatal as remaining an agnostic), implicitly recognized the economic structure of the problem of persuasion.

Economists distinguish between "inspection" goods, whose quality can be determined at the time of sale (for example, the ripeness of a cantaloupe, by squeezing it) and "credence" goods, which have to be taken on faith (for example, the durability of a refrigerator). The consumer's costs of information are much higher in the latter case. The ideas that a speaker tries to "sell" to his audience often are credence goods, and the significance of the ethical appeal is that it increases the audience's willingness to repose faith in the speaker.

The significance of the costs of information to the rhetorician's audience is overlooked by some present-day pragmatists, such as Richard Rorty and Donald McCloskey, in this respect the heirs of Nietzsche, who argue that *all* efforts to induce belief are rhetoric. The argument is not always intended as a compliment to rhetoric,[6] even when the list of rhetorical devices is extended to include every conceivable method of rational inquiry or demonstration, so that we read for example that among the "figures of argument" is "prolepsis (anticipating and discounting possible objections)."[7] We should resist that extension. For if all the devices of reason, including the syllogism and statistical infer-

---

6. Peter Goodrich puts it nicely: "Rhetoric, in other words, takes its revenge upon rationalism, not by reasserting any intrinsic merit or value to the rhetorical discipline but by claiming that rationalism too is ill of a figurative virus." Goodrich, *Legal Discourse: Studies in Linguistics, Rhetoric and Legal Analysis* 110 (1987).

7. Peter Goodrich, *Reading the Law: A Critical Introduction to Legal Method and Techniques* 193 (1986).

ence, are "figures of argument," the term "rhetoric" loses its distinctness and utility:

> The discipline [of rhetoric] is aggrandized virtually beyond recognition in the work of those neorhetoricians—Kenneth Burke and Chaim Perelmann, for example—who wish to turn it into an art of practical reasoning concerned not simply with mastering, as need arises, premises drawn from ethics, politics, psychology, or wherever, but making significant additions on its own to the total store of such wisdom. To proceed in this fashion is, as Aristotle says (*Rhet.* 1.4 1359b12), to claim for rhetoric what belongs to a different art.[8]

The average scientific paper is less "rhetorical," in a perfectly intelligible sense of that word, than the average political address or the average closing argument to a jury. The reason is that the cost of information is much lower to a scientific audience for a scientific paper than, for example, to the lay audience of a politician's speech on macroeconomics or foreign policy. The higher an audience's cost of absorbing information, the more a speaker will rely on forms of persuasion that avoid taxing the audience's absorptive capacity and thus minimize that cost. It is easier for an audience to understand that a scientist is reputable than to understand the details of his theory, and therefore we can expect a scientist addressing a lay audience to take pains to establish his reputability. Preference for representative over direct democracy rests in part on the insight that it is cheaper for the voting population to determine the competence and integrity of a politician than to evaluate competing policy proposals.

The high costs of information may explain the emphasis in law and politics on adversarial procedure. We need not buy into the lawyers' mystical faith in the production of truth by contests of liars—contests more likely to produce dizziness than knowledge—to accept that the prospect of rebuttal is a deterrent to dishonest rhetoric because it reduces the likelihood that the audience will be deceived. Since the benefits of dishonesty are reduced, the competing speakers are more likely to confine themselves to valid or at least colorable points. We expect less reliance on adversary procedures where the audience is expert and therefore less manipulable; it would be foolish to propose that scientists model their procedures on those of lawyers.[9]

8. Cole, note 2 above, at 20.
9. Though such proposals are occasionally made. For discussion, see Richard H. Gaskins, *Burdens of Proof in Modern Discourse*, chs. 1, 5 (1992).

The economic approach to rhetoric implies that a speaker will appeal to his listener's self-interest, but it need not be a crass appeal, or self-interest narrowly conceived. I shall illustrate with an example from Homer. Its antiquity should not surprise. We expect ancient and primitive societies to have highly developed rhetorical techniques,[10] because these techniques do not depend on the possession of modern scientific or technological knowledge and because they are especially valuable in settings where information costs are high. By the same token we should not be surprised that rhetoric, which flourished in ancient Greece and Rome, the Middle Ages, and the Renaissance, has since lost ground in competition with other disciplines. Outside of specialized areas of discourse and inquiry, information costs have declined with the spread of literacy, universal education, better communications, increased knowledge, the emergence of information specialists, the growing prestige of scientific and other rational methods of inquiry, and the development of institutions ranging from schools and universities to product warranties, department stores, and representative (as distinct from direct) democracy, for economizing on information costs. All these are alternatives to rhetoric and have contracted its domain.

In Book VI of the *Odyssey*, Odysseus is shipwrecked on his way home to Ithaca after a twenty-year absence, and is washed ashore near the mouth of a river on the island kingdom of Scheria—naked, filthy, exhausted, and alone. He encounters the princess of the island, Nausicaa, who had come down to the river with her attendants to wash clothes. The attendants flee when they see this repulsive apparition, but Nausicaa stands her ground. Odysseus addresses her.[11] He wants clothing and eventually assistance in getting home. He has no way of proving who he is. How is he to persuade Nausicaa to help him?

He begins with a heavy dose of flattery, by asking her whether she is a goddess or a mortal; if the latter, then, so fair is she, "triply happy are your father and your honored mother, and triply happy your brethren," and "he will be happiest of all who succeeds with his gifts of courtship and leads you to his home. For my eyes have never seen a

10. For some evidence, see my book *The Economics of Justice* 172–173, 276–277 (1981); also *Law and Literature* 278, where I analyze the rhetoric of another Homeric passage. I do not claim that Homer had a *theory* of rhetoric; and Cole, note 2 above, ch. 2, points to a number of limitations of the rhetorical *practice* revealed by the Homeric epics.

11. *Odyssey*, vol. 1, bk. vi, pp. 216–219, lines 149–185 (A. T. Murray trans. 1919, reprinted 1974 in the Loeb Classical Library). I have taken the liberty of modernizing Murray's diction.

mortal such as you, whether man or woman." After twenty lines of laying it on thick in this way, Odysseus finally mentions his plight: "heavy suffering has come upon me." He explains briefly that he was shipwrecked, adding, "I do not think my troubles are over yet." Only then—twenty-six lines into a speech of only thirty-seven lines—does Odysseus ask Nausicaa to take pity on him, pointing out that among other things he knows no one on the island. And all he asks for is that, assuming that the pile of clothes she and her attendants brought to the river to wash were wrapped in something, she give him the wrapper to cover his nakedness, and that she show him where the city is. The request is stated briefly and Odysseus then changes the subject from himself to her. "As for you, may the gods grant you all that your heart desires," specifically including a husband and a home. He continues in this vein for a few more lines, and the speech is over.

Since Odysseus cannot pay Nausicaa for helping him, he must place her in a donative mood. The economic theory of altruism teaches that an altruistic transfer is likelier the greater the disparity in wealth between donor and donee. People usually set a much higher value on their own welfare than on that of a stranger. But given diminishing marginal utility of money, even weak altruism may bring about a situation in which a transfer of wealth will increase the donee's utility by more than it diminishes the donor's. Suppose D_r derives 100 utiles (an arbitrary measure of subjective utility) from his first dollar, but because he is very wealthy derives only 1 utile from his last dollar. D_e, being very poor, would derive 100 utiles from receiving one more dollar. Suppose further that D_r, being moderately altruistic, derives 2 utiles of satisfaction from every 100 utiles that D_e obtains. Then by transferring a dollar to D_e, D_r will increase his own utility by 1 utile $(2 - 1)$, making the transfer a utility-maximizing act for D_r. To induce the transfer, D_e will want to remind D_r of how wealthy D_r is and how poor he, D_e, is.

That is how Odysseus proceeds. The first part of his speech is primarily devoted to establishing how wealthy Nausicaa is prospectively, since her loveliness will enable her to obtain a wealthy husband (one who will outdo her other suitors in giving her fine bridal gifts). Odysseus doesn't have to spend much time persuading Nausicaa of his present poverty; that is evident from his appearance. Having established the disparity in their wealth, he emphasizes how slight the cost of the gift he is asking for (a rag and a bit of information) is to her, because the smaller that cost the more likely the gift is to bring about a net increase in the donor's utility. Nevertheless he offers some compensation for the modest gifts that he is asking for by ending his speech with wishes for Nausicaa's happiness. Good wishes are worth little, but a small benefit can offset a small cost.

The first part of Odysseus's speech has the additional function of reassuring Nausicaa concerning the speaker's character. By pretending to be unsure whether Nausicaa is mortal or divine, Odysseus is seeking to allay any fear of this dirty and naked man that might cause Nausicaa, like her attendants, to flee from his presence; for a mortal, like himself, would be unlikely to attack a divinity. And by heaping praise on Nausicaa, Odysseus shows himself to be at once courteous, respectful, and articulate. He uses civilized words to offset his uncivilized physical appearance. By doing so he signals, moreover, that he may not be what he seems—he may be, as in fact he is, a powerful man temporarily down on his luck, hence someone who might one day be in a position to repay Nausicaa's kindness to him. So there is the hint of the possibility of reciprocal altruism.

Odysseus's speech thus is highly rational even though it conveys little information of a conventional sort. The appearance of paradox in this statement (highly rational, but little information) comes from the familiar but false antithesis between reason and emotion.[12] Emotions direct, focus, and concentrate attention (as in Samuel Johnson's quip that the prospect of being hanged concentrates the mind wonderfully), reinforce commitments, furnish motivation, and foster empathetic knowledge (and otherwise stimulate the imagination), while reason in turn furnishes triggers to and disciplines, directs, and constrains emotion. Generosity is an emotion, but the economic analysis of altruism teaches that it is an emotion activated by perceived disparities in wealth and by the size of the prospective transfer, and it therefore depends on knowledge.

Plato versus Aristotle

If I am correct so far, we should not despise rhetoric as irrational, even when it employs persuasive methods far removed from the scientific. This should make us feel a little more comfortable about legal advo-

12. An antithesis criticized in Ronald de Sousa, *The Rationality of Emotion* (1987), and Martha C. Nussbaum, *Need and Recognition: A Theory of the Emotions* (Gifford Lectures 1992/93, unpublished).

cacy—it need not equate to making the worse appear the better cause even if it is (as it is) heavily rhetorical. But before accepting a conclusion so comforting to the legal profession we should examine Plato's famous attack on rhetoric in the *Gorgias*. It is a dialogue heavy with irony. In it Socrates suggests that were he ever to be put on trial in Athens he might well be condemned to death because he would not employ the rhetorical arts to win an acquittal. In so saying he is anticipating his own death, for the dialogue was written after Socrates' trial and condemnation.

Rhetoricians, like Gorgias, were frequently hired to write speeches for litigants. They thus occupied, in a society that lacked a legal profession, a role akin to that of trial and appellate lawyers in our society. Socrates presses Gorgias on the social value of rhetoric, inducing him to accept Socrates' formulation that "rhetoric produces persuasion. Its entire business is persuasion."[13] Gorgias further concedes that, when used in law courts, rhetoric is the kind of persuasion that produces belief about justice and injustice without instilling knowledge of these things, rather than belief with knowledge, because the rhetorician "could never instruct so large a gathering on such weighty matters in a short time" (p. 14; 455). Gorgias is led to boast that in a debate between a rhetorician and a physician over who should be elected public physician, the rhetorician would win and be elected. Socrates describes this as "a case of the ignorant being more persuasive than the expert in the company of the ignorant" (p. 18; 459).

Socrates traps Gorgias into agreeing that just as a doctor must learn medicine to practice it, so a rhetorician must learn justice to discourse on it. Hence—Gorgias is further willing to concede, here buying into an aspect of Socratic ethical theory at once fundamental and dubious— a good rhetorician must be a just man, because in that theory people do bad things only out of ignorance. And a just man would not speak

---

13. *Gorgias* 11 (W. C. Helmbold trans. 1952) (p. 453 of the Stephanus Greek edition). (I shall use both page references: hence "p. 11; 453." Terence Irwin's 1979 translation of the *Gorgias* is more scholarly, but for my purposes Helmbold's more idiomatic translation is preferable.) Plato's attack on rhetoric in the *Gorgias* is exhaustively criticized in Vickers, note 3 above, at 84–120, which draws heavily on earlier criticisms by E. R. Dodds and especially by Irwin. Plato discussed rhetoric in several other dialogues, but I have no need to go beyond the *Gorgias*. Incidentally, Plato's Gorgias is, whether intentionally or not, a caricature of the historical Gorgias, a considerable figure in the psychology of communication. Charles P. Segal, "Gorgias and the Psychology of the Logos," 66 *Harvard Studies in Classical Philology* 99 (1962).

unjustly. Yet Gorgias had already conceded that rhetoricians sometimes abused their talent by arguing the unjust side of a case. So rhetoricians must not know what justice is, and Gorgias seems to have no idea even of what rhetoric is. Pressed for his own definition of rhetoric, Socrates calls it a knack (in the sense that the possessor cannot explain how or why it works) of people who are skillful in dealing with other people. A knack akin to cookery and composed mainly of flattery, rhetoric is to justice as cosmetics are to gymnastics and as cookery is to medicine. The cook "pretends she knows which foods are best for the body; so that if a cook and a physician had to dispute their claims before a group of boys . . . the physician would starve to death" (p. 25; 464). And Socrates himself, if he is ever tried, will "be like a physician tried before a jury of children on the accusation of a cook" (p. 100; 521).

Callicles, another participant in the dialogue, rebukes Socrates for failing to understand that the only principle of justice is that "the stronger shall rule and have the advantage over his inferior" (p. 52; 483). If this is right, Socrates is foolish to worry that the art of rhetoric does not conduce to a deep understanding of the just. But Socrates rejects the principle of might makes right. He argues that "doing wrong must be avoided more sedulously than suffering it" (p. 106; 527), because the accounts will be adjusted in the afterlife. The souls of the dead will "all be judged in nakedness, for judgment must not be passed till they are dead. The judge also must be naked and dead in order that the judgment shall be just, his very soul contemplating the naked soul of each man who has died" (p. 103; 523). The man who is adjudged just will proceed to the Islands of the Blessed, the unjust to Tartarus, "a prisonhouse of retribution and judgment" (p. 102; 523).

There are obvious difficulties with the case that Plato (through Socrates) mounts against rhetoric. First but least, Plato lacks, it might seem, the courage of his convictions. The Platonic dialogue, including the *Gorgias,* is a highly rhetorical form of discourse. I have mentioned the use of irony. Plato also relies heavily on analogy, as when he compares rhetoric to cosmetics and to cookery. And there is the use of myth or fantasy (the tale about judgment in the afterlife), and the dialogue format in which real historical figures are given speeches to utter that probably are largely fictitious.

This is not a serious difficulty with Plato's case against rhetoric; one can fight fire with fire yet still think fire on balance a bad thing, though the *Phaedrus* suggests that Plato distinguished between rhetorical methods that were good because their purpose was good and the bad methods of the sophists. What is a serious difficulty is that Plato's reassuring emphasis on perfect justice in the afterlife distracts from the practical problem of how to prevent the conviction of the just, for example Socrates himself. He might well have escaped condemnation at his trial had he used rhetorical arts or hired a skilled rhetorician to write his speech to the jury, for a substantial minority of the jurors voted to acquit him anyway; his case wasn't hopeless. Indifference to the here and now has never been a viable principle of social order, though it made Socrates a secular saint.

Aristotle had an altogether friendlier view of rhetoric. His treatise[14] begins by implicitly brushing aside Plato's criticisms, explaining that previous writers on rhetoric have dealt "mainly with non-essentials," namely "the arousing of prejudice, pity, anger, and similar emotions" (p. 2152; 1354a). Emotional appeals should be—in well-regulated states, he says, they are—forbidden, rendering rhetoricians whose stock in trade is the making of such appeals speechless. With these abuses of rhetoric out of the way, rhetoric can be seen to be "useful because things that are true and things that are just have a natural tendency to prevail over their opposites, so that if the decisions of judges are not what they ought to be, the defeat must be due to the speakers themselves, and they must be blamed accordingly" (p. 2154; 1355a).

Aristotle makes a threefold division of methods of persuasion. The first is the ethical appeal. The second, which is closely related, consists of putting the audience in a receptive frame of mind. The third is the argument of the speech. Here Aristotle emphasizes the enthymeme, which in modern logic is a syllogism in which one of the premises is unstated because it is a matter of common knowledge. So one might say that Socrates is human and therefore must die, in place of the cumbersome syllogism all humans must die, Socrates is a human, therefore Socrates must die. It is doubtful that Aristotle used the term in so limited a sense; he may have meant by it merely a claim backed by reason, as when a conclusion probably but not certainly follows from the premises, rather than certainly as in the case of a syllogism,[15] or

14. Aristotle, *Rhetoric* (W. Rhys Roberts trans.), in *The Complete Works of Aristotle: The Revised Oxford Translation*, vol. 2, p. 2153 (Jonathan Barnes ed. 1984). Again I shall cite to the page (and column) number in the standard Greek edition (Bekker) as well as to the page number in the translation.

15. M. F. Burnyeat, "Enthymeme: Aristotle on the Logic of Persuasion," in *Aristotle's "Rhetoric"—Philosophical Essays* 3 (David J. Furley and Alexander Nehamas eds. 1994).

when the premises are probably rather than certainly true.[16] In any event, by placing the enthymeme (rather than, say, the speaker's voice or gestures) at the center of the rhetorical stage, Aristotle is asserting the rationality of rhetoric. This in turn shows, as he explains, that it is absurd to argue that a person should be allowed to defend himself by force but not by words, for the use of rational speech to get one's way is more distinctively human than the use of force. Aristotle adds that just as the enthymeme is (in some not wholly clear sense) the rhetorical counterpart of the syllogism, so the example is the rhetorical counterpart of induction.

Not only the method of argument but also the empirical base is more informal in rhetoric than in logic, mathematics, or science. "Before some audiences not even the possession of the exactest knowledge will make it easy for what we say to produce conviction," because the uninstructed cannot be persuaded by argument based on knowledge, since knowledge implies previous instruction. So the rhetorician must use "notions possessed by everybody" (p. 2154; 1355a). We thus have a picture (elaborated in the remainder of the treatise) of the rhetorician who, having established his credibility with the audience and induced an attentive, receptive attitude, proceeds to make his case with informal logic, plus evidence that he relates to the audience's prior structure of beliefs by appealing to common knowledge.

There are several objections to this picture. The first is that it assumes that the bad sorts of emotional appeal can be kept out of the rhetorician's bag of tricks. It is true that in a modern trial the grosser forms of appeal to emotion—such as placing the defendant's character rather than his act on trial by a recitation of his past misdeeds, horrifying the jury with graphic photographs of the defendant's bloody victim, and appealing to racial or religious hostility—can be kept out by rules of evidence. But subtler yet perhaps equally misleading forms of emotional appeal cannot be. There is little if anything that a judicial system can do to prevent a lawyer from dressing in a manner designed to convey to the jury that he is an ordinary person like themselves,[17] or from taking acting lessons so that he can convey a more credible impression of sincerity, or from picking expert witnesses for their winning personalities, or from flattering jurors and judges, or from using intona-

---

16. Cole, note 2 above, at 154–156.
17. More on "dressing for [forensic] success" below.

tion, facial expressions, and bodily gestures to convey misleading impressions.[18]

We can deflect this objection to Aristotle's defense of rhetoric a little, however, by recalling that emotion can clarify as well as fog the understanding. If for example an advocate's appeal to the emotions induces in the judge or juror an empathetic understanding of a victim's or an accused wrongdoer's motives, drives, and beliefs, the appeal may enable the tribunal to form a more accurate impression of essential facts and so render a more just judgment.[19] Rhetoric can be a "means for making truth sound like truth—the only means, on many occasions, that are available."[20]

The second objection to Aristotle's position is that he misunderstands "distance" and "tenacity"—what might together be called "persuadability"—by making the reference point truth rather than the audience's existing beliefs. Bayes's theorem teaches that a rational person's priors (that is, the beliefs he has before he is exposed to a new argument or evidence) will influence the belief that he forms on the basis of the new argument or evidence. If two astronomers had debated in the year 1250 A.D. the question whether the earth revolves around the sun or the sun around the earth, the astronomer who took the first position would have had a much harder time persuading the audience than the astronomer who took the second position, even though the first astronomer's position would have been much closer to the truth.[21]

Third, even when there is no tension between what is true and what the audience believes (the audience may have no belief that would be upset by adopting either belief urged by the contending speakers), if the speakers are of unequal skill the one who is in the wrong may nevertheless prevail.[22] This is true even if all emotional factors are banished, since people differ greatly in their intellectual skills as well as in their skills at arousing emotion. The inequality of advocates is ig-

18. It might be possible to prevent lawyers from coaching witnesses. European legal systems try with some success to do so; the American legal system does not.

19. Martha C. Nussbaum, "Equity and Mercy," 22 *Philosophy and Public Affairs* 83 (1993).

20. Cole, note 2 above, at 140.

21. The truth is that the earth and the sun both revolve around an imaginary point that is near the sun.

22. Stated differently, successful rhetoric depends on the speaker (his skills, etc.) and the audience (its receptivity, etc.), just as successful medicine depends on both the doctor and the patient. Cole, note 2 above, at 87–88.

nored in James Boyd White's attempted refutation of Plato's denunciation of rhetoric.[23] White further loads the dice against Plato by comparing the ideal practice of law with the practices denounced in the *Gorgias* without indicating how we are to get from the real to the ideal, and also by claiming that "the law converts the raw materials of human nature and conflict into another form of life and language, into argument about justice."[24] This treats "justice" as a universal concept, implying that a Nazi lawyer's appeal to justice would have, if not the identical content as an American lawyer's, still an inextinguishable edifying core. This is the lawyer's faith that people become good by talking. It is only by ignoring the realities of the legal process that one can erase all tension between rhetoric and rationality, as in the extraordinary statement by Jonsen and Toulmin that in law "the 'rhetoric' of any case—how it can be presented *most persuasively*—in no way conflicts with its 'merits'—that is, the *rational strength* of the relevant arguments. In practical enterprises such as civil law, that is, the role of 'theory' is, at one and the same time, *both rational and rhetorical.*"[25]

When Aristotle gets beyond generalities and begins to discuss the details of rhetorical performance, we find ourselves in that amoral lawyer's world in which for every argument, however sound, there is a plausible counterargument by which the lawyer can indeed hope to make the worse appear the better cause.[26] The ability to generate opposing arguments is known in the lexicon of rhetoric as "invention," and it is just the sort of thing that troubles people about rhetoric. Aristotle has a marvelous discussion of how to argue either side of a contract case. After listing a number of arguments in favor of enforcing a contract, such as that "a contract is a law, though of a special and limited kind . . . and that the law itself as a whole is a sort of contract, so that anyone who disregards or repudiates any contract is repudiating the law itself," and "most business relations—those, namely, that are voluntary—are regulated by contracts, and if these lose their binding force, human intercourse ceases," he trots out the counterarguments: "The duty of the judge as umpire is to decide what is just, and therefore

---

23. "Plato's *Gorgias* and the Modern Lawyer: A Dialogue on the Ethics of Argument," in White, *Heracles' Bow: Essays on the Rhetoric and Poetics of the Law* 215 (1985).

24. Id. at 232.

25. Jonsen and Toulmin, note 3 above, at 298.

26. For a modern catalog of forensic thrusts and parries, see Pierre Schlag and David Skover, *Tactics of Legal Reasoning* (1986).

he must ask where justice lies, and not what this or that document means." And "we must see if the contract . . . contradicts any other previous or subsequent contract; arguing that the subsequent is a binding contract, or else that the previous one was right and the subsequent one fraudulent—whichever way suits us" (p. 2192; 1376b). It's that phrase "whichever way suits us" that sticks in the nonlawyer's craw.

If both Plato's attack on rhetoric and Aristotle's defense of it are deeply flawed, where are we? To answer this question we must consider *why* Plato and Aristotle differed on the social value of rhetoric. The main reasons are that they had different conceptions of rational inquiry and different assessments of the nature and capacities of the rhetorician's audience. Plato thought that scientific and ethical inquiry consisted of clearing away the mental debris that interfered with people's ability to *see* truth and goodness, and that the rough-and-tumble of legal and political oratory merely piled up more debris. Aristotle believed (surely correctly) that truth was often hidden, that probabilistic approximations were in many cases all that were feasible, and that these were facilitated by the rhetorical techniques that he catalogued.

As for the difference between Plato and Aristotle in the evaluation of the audience for rhetoric, although Aristotle is emphatic that the audience frequently is uninstructed and therefore irreducibly obtuse, he does not consider it contemptible. One reason he does not is that, as he explains, he is more interested in political than in forensic rhetoric, and he believes that an audience is more attentive to a political debate because such a debate involves matters important to themselves, whereas when they are jurors judging a case, the outcome of the debate usually is of no importance to themselves (but only to the litigants) and they are therefore less attentive.[27] In a tiny embattled direct democracy, such as that of Athens, as distinct from a huge secure representative democracy, such as that of the United States, the personal benefit from voting correctly and hence following political debates carefully is indeed likely to exceed the benefit from voting correctly and listening carefully as a juror. The theoretical point is that we can expect rhetoric to be less responsible the less the individual member of the audience has to gain from making the right choice.

27. Notice the parallel between the suggestion that disinterest is positively correlated with lack of attention (one might say that disinterest fosters uninterest) and my discussion in Chapter 3 of how efforts to ensure judicial disinterest foster judicial laziness.

Plato in the *Gorgias* is more interested in forensic rhetoric, and he regards the audience for such rhetoric—the large Athenian juries, which were not permitted to deliberate but simply voted their verdict at the conclusion of the trial—as no better than children. Plato was an aristocrat, so this dismissive evaluation of the capacity of his fellow citizens came naturally to him. Aristotle was also critical of the Athenian jury, but, as I have said, emphasized political rather than forensic rhetoric. Both ignored the possibility that if the jury could be persuaded that it was playing a judicial "game" that depended on adherence to certain rules of attentiveness and disinterest, it might behave as responsibly as it would if some other, more obvious form of self-interest were engaged.

The contrast between Plato's and Aristotle's assessment of rhetoric suggests that the social as distinct from the private value of rhetoric is likely to be lower, the greater the audience's cost of absorbing information. But the relation between the two variables is actually more complex. If information cost is zero, rhetoric has no value; it is harmless, but also useless. And if the cost is very high, rhetoric may be indispensable—but also so dangerous that the power of decision should be taken away from the ignorant, manipulable audience. For rhetoric must not be confused with education, which "proposes to put before us the arguments on both sides of the question in their true light, giving each its proper degree of influence, and has it in view to persuade no farther than the arguments themselves appear convincing," while rhetoric "endeavors by all means to persuade us; and for this purpose it magnifies all the arguments on the one side and diminishes or conceals those that might be brought on the [other] side."[28]

The cost to an audience of absorbing information is related positively to the complexity of the subject matter of the contest and negatively to the audience's familiarity with (or specialized knowledge of) that subject matter, to its general education, and to its intelligence and rationality. The less intelligent and knowledgeable the audience, and the intrinsically more complex the subject matter of the contest, the further the audience's prior beliefs are likely to lie from the truth. The higher therefore will be the costs to it of absorbing information, and thus the more likely are the speakers to resort to base emotional appeals (the kind that blur rather than sharpen insight), misleading signals, and

28. Adam Smith, *Lectures on Rhetoric and Belles Lettres* 62 (J. C. Bryce ed. 1983).

false information and the more likely is the audience to form, as a result of the speakers' efforts, another false belief. Plato doubtless thought that the accusation against Socrates, that he had corrupted the youth of Athens, not recognized the gods of the city, and introduced new gods, required a complex evaluation of which the jury at Socrates' trial had been incapable; and since the dramatic focus of the *Gorgias* is the trial of Socrates (though never mentioned directly in it, and indeed lying outside the temporal frame of the dialogue), it is not surprising that the implied verdict passed on rhetoric is a negative one. The verdict would be meaningless were there no conceivable alternative to the form of trial to which Socrates was subjected; then the only sensible criticism would be of Socrates, for failing to hire a rhetorician to assist him. But it is possible through rules of evidence and other procedural or institutional innovations to reduce the use of rhetorical methods to resolve legal disputes; and the higher the costs of information to the tribunal, the more attractive such innovations are.

Aristotle, in contrast to Plato, emphasizes[29] a somewhat idealized situation in which the audience for a debate, although lacking expert knowledge of the subject matter, is intelligent, attentive, and fair-minded and in which the competing speakers are prevented from exceeding the bounds of reasonable argument. Here the costs of absorbing information, while positive, are not so high as to invite or reward the most deceitful rhetorical methods; and the range of those methods is restricted by at least rudimentary procedural norms.

One can see why democrats tend to be friendly to rhetoric and suspicious of science. Rhetoric takes seriously the opinions of the ordinary person—taken to an extreme, rhetoric could be said to make public opinion the arbiter of truth—while science vests authority in experts. Plato in the *Republic* wanted philosophers to rule by force and deception,[30] and would probably have favored the type of professional, largely juryless judiciaries that we find on the Continent today; while Protagoras, with his doctrine that sound judgment requires listening to every man's opinion, has been called the "first reasoned defender"

29. Not exclusively, for there is a fair amount of discussion in the *Rhetoric* of emotional appeals, the book being a manual of practical rhetoric as well as a theoretical treatment of the subject.

30. On the political implications of Aristotle's differences with Plato over rhetoric, see Mary P. Nichols, "Aristotle's Defense of Rhetoric," 49 *Journal of Politics* 657 (1987).

of democracy.[31] But there is such a thing as too much democracy. The absence of institutional controls over the Athenian jury (there were no professional judges and no right of appeal) is frightening to anyone who values rights. The Athenian legal system gave too much scope for inflammatory rhetoric and placed the nonconformist free-thinking intellectual, such as Socrates, at great risk. Democracy and rhetoric line up on one side of a divide, individualism on the other; liberalism straddles the divide uneasily. Or, emphasizing the inroads that unconstrained democracy can make on the freedom of the marketplace of political ideas, we might say that too much democracy in the short run can lead to too little democracy in the long run.

Comparison of Plato's and Aristotle's views on rhetoric suggests above all that one should not try to place a normative evaluation on legal (or other) advocacy in gross. (The efforts of the defenders of rhetoric to do so may be one reason for the low esteem in which the discipline is held. Poor rhetoricians they, they overargue their case.) The critical issue is the intellectual competence and emotional maturity of the tribunal in relation to the complexity of the questions in the case. If through a combination of the rules of evidence and the jury's emotional and intellectual development the advocates are led to confine themselves to the rhetorical methods commended by Aristotle, all of which are pertinent to rational inquiry in those circumstances of radical uncertainty that are so common in litigation that goes to trial,[32] their efforts will be conducive to rational results.

This discussion suggests an answer to a question raised in Chapter 1—whether an actor hired to read the lawyer's closing argument should be deemed engaged in the practice of law and therefore barred unless he is a lawyer himself. It is hardly feasible to forbid lawyers to take acting lessons, but it is feasible to forbid them to hire actors to read their arguments. The effect of such a bar is to reduce the investment in courtroom theatrics that are as likely to deceive as to inform the jury. The time costs to a lawyer of taking enough acting lessons to have a prospect of becoming a proficient actor are high, while the likely value to the lawyer-actor in improved effectiveness with juries probably is low because skill at acting is more the result of native ability than of training—otherwise the very high incomes of successful actors would

31. Schiappa, note 1 above, at 184.
32. The law employs devices such as summary judgment for keeping from the jury cases in which there is no fair doubt, by resolving such cases before trial.

be difficult to explain. So a rule against hiring actors to read closing arguments is not likely to be evaded wholesale by lawyers' becoming (better) actors themselves, although I know one very successful trial lawyer in Chicago who has taken acting lessons.

It is notable that in England until well into this century, barristers (that is, advocates—trial and appellate lawyers) generally did not take their university degree in law and indeed received little formal instruction in it but were recommended to study the Greek orators instead. The solicitors were expected to do the legal research and analysis and the barristers to be eloquent, skillful at repartee, verbally resourceful—in a word rhetorical. It is also notable that our most intellectual judge, Holmes, who though himself a master rhetorician thought law the calling of thinkers rather than of poets and hoped to see law eventually placed on a scientific footing, defined law as the prediction of what judges do. To define law so is to define it from the counselor's rather than the advocate's perspective, and the counselor's role is primarily analytical while the advocate's is heavily rhetorical.

"When I became America's first wardrobe engineer, my initial clients were courtroom lawyers . . . Good courtroom lawyers are super salesmen and consummate actors, and they well realize that nonverbal forms of communication are frequently just as important (and sometimes more so) as the facts of a case."[33] Mr. Malloy may be exaggerating, but there is a kernel of good sense in what he writes, although I am properly startled to read that "if you have an equal number of lower-middle-class whites and middle-class blacks on a suburban jury, dress for the blacks. The prejudice of the whites against gray will be less than the prejudice of the blacks against blue."[34] I don't know whether this is true but I am sure that it is something a conscientious trial lawyer should ponder. To acknowledge this is to acknowledge the remoteness of forensic rhetoric from scientific procedures of inquiry and proof.

Rhetoric as Reasoning

I anticipate the objection (*prolepsis*) that I am treating rhetoric as a collection of devices for persuading and that by doing so I am overlooking the fact that it is also a kind of thinking,[35] maybe the only kind

33. John T. Malloy, *New Dress for Success* 295 (1988).
34. Id. at 299.
35. See, for example, Jonsen and Toulmin, note 3 above, at 72.

that it is feasible for lawyers and judges to engage in—perhaps for *anyone* to engage in. This issue will occupy us for the rest of the chapter.

Analogy. I begin with Cass Sunstein's defense of analogical reasoning in law.[36] One might have thought that analogy, like metaphor or anecdote, was strictly a device for stimulating the imagination or making an argument vivid and had nothing really to do with thinking. Sunstein, however, argues that analogy enables rational legal outcomes to be achieved when, because either critical information or agreement on premises is lacking, there is no overarching theory from which the "right" outcome could be deduced with the aid of some factfinding. If employers are forbidden to fire employees for refusing to perjure themselves on the employers' behalf, a court can treat this as a reason to believe—reasoning by analogy—that employers should also be forbidden to fire employees for filing workers' compensation claims. This "reasoning" seems to work, Sunstein argues, even if the court has no fully worked out theory of when employers should be forbidden to fire employees at will (see Chapter 13). It looks, then, as if reasoning by analogy enables the reasoner to move from one particular (a case, for example) to another without having a theory or general law of which both are instances.

I don't get it. I don't see how one can reach a rational conclusion in the employment case without discovering or positing a *reason* why employers are forbidden to fire employees for refusing to commit perjury. The reason presumably is to discourage perjury; and then we might consider whether there is equal reason to encourage the filing of workers' compensation claims and whether any consideration weighs against such encouragement that might not have been present in the perjury case. One can call this reasoning by analogy if one likes, but what is really involved is querying (or quarrying) the earlier case for policies that may be applicable to the later one and then deciding the later one by reference to those policies.[37] This is further evidence that

36. "On Analogical Reasoning," 106 *Harvard Law Review* 741 (1993). The editors of the *Harvard Law Review* label this important article "Commentary" and place it between the student-written "Notes" and the student-written "Book Notes," while "Articles" appear at the front of the issue, ahead of the "Notes." Apparently the editors felt that Sunstein's article, being a mere 50 pages long, couldn't be considered a full-fledged legal article. Prolixity must certainly be one of the principal rhetorical devices employed by lawyers.

37. Compare G. E. R. Lloyd, *Polarity and Analogy: Two Types of Argumentation in Early Greek Thought* 412–413 (1966), which after describing passages in the *Rhetoric* that suggest "how Aristotle might have attempted to justify many of his analogies, namely on the grounds

law is best regarded as a policy science—though maybe a primitive one, given its curious dependence on those policy considerations that can be culled from published judicial opinions—rather than as some special branch of reasoning. It is no surprise that "real" reasoning by analogy—going from an old to a new case on the basis of some felt "similarity"—has been a source of many pernicious judicial doctrines, including many traditional, and now largely discarded, antitrust doctrines. An example is the "leverage" doctrine, which is based on a crude and misleading analogy between the use of leverage to lift a heavier body and the incentive of a monopolist of one good or service (for example, machinery for making salt) to monopolize complementary goods or services as well (such as the salt).[38]

Both the appeal and the pitfalls of reasoning by analogy arise from its formalistic character. Although Sunstein is against formalism and regards reasoning by analogy as the triumph of practical reason over the deductive methods favored by legal formalists, the use lawyers make of the technique is in fact formalistic. If they have a case involving the appropriate system of property rights for a new natural resource, say petroleum, they examine decided cases dealing with "similar" resources, say water or rabbits. They do not go out and talk to petroleum engineers, ecologists, or natural-resources economists. They treat the issue as one *internal* to legal materials, an issue of the relations between legal concepts. They do this because the lawyer's dream is to be able to decide new cases purely by reference to old ones, that is, without knowing anything outside "the law."

I do not wish to bad-mouth analogy, which I relied on heavily in Chapter 3, comparing judges to theatrical spectators and to participants in games for fun, and earlier in this chapter, comparing persuasion to the sale of goods. Analogies can be suggestive, even illuminating. But when lawyers and judges reason analogically from old cases to new, it usually means that they are limiting their analysis of the present case to what can be found in prior cases; and as in the example of using

---

that the cases he compares are each instances of the same general laws," points out that "the fact remains that the form which his reasoning takes, on these occasions, does not conform to what the theory . . . would seem to demand. It does not consist of (1) a careful induction to establish the general rule, and (2) a deduction applying the rule to a further particular case, but rather of a direct comparison between one particular case and another."

38. For other criticisms of reasoning by analogy in law, see *The Problems of Jurisprudence* 86–100. On the "leverage" theory, see *Economic Analysis of Law* 311–312.

wild-animal cases to frame a regime for oil and gas, the prior cases often constitute an impoverished repository of fact and policy for the decision of the present one.

Analogy does have one thoroughly worthwhile function in law that goes beyond the suggestive or metaphoric: fixing the boundaries of a legal rule or doctrine. This is a critical rather than a creative use of analogy. The focus is on differences rather than on similarities, and the effect is to curtail rather than to expand rules. Suppose once again that the rule is that fugitive resources (anything that can move around) cannot be owned until they are reduced to possession, and is illustrated by cases involving rabbits and other wild animals ("ferae naturae"). Then the Socratic questioner—for the critical use of analogy is the mainstay of the Socratic law school classroom—might ask: does this mean that oil and gas cannot be owned until they are reduced to possession? The intelligent answer is "No." Oil and gas are much more valuable than rabbits and most other wild animals, therefore at greater risk of being depleted prematurely, therefore more likely to justify the cost of establishing nonpossessory rights; and forbidding such rights will impair incentives to conserve.[39] The misleading analogy of oil and gas to rabbits thus shows that the rule was defined too broadly.[40]

One of the most important skills of lawyers is determining the scope of legal rules,[41] for the typical question that a client puts to a lawyer is whether a proposed course of action would violate a legal rule. Because of the vagueness of language, the verbal statement of a rule is often not a reliable guide to its actual scope. To determine that scope one puts hypothetical cases that are within the outer semantic bounds of the rule and one asks whether these cases, which are "like" enough as a semantic matter to count as applications of the rule, fit its scope as defined by reference to the rule's purpose and to other relevant sources of policy guidance.

---

39. Cf. Harold Demsetz, "Toward a Theory of Property Rights," 57 *American Economic Review* 347 (Papers and Proceedings issue, May 1967).

40. Do not think this an esoteric example. "The use of the wild animal analogy was sufficiently frequent that oil and gas have been classified as wild minerals or minerals ferae naturae. Because of the large volume of oil and gas litigation, one receives the impression that there are more oil and gas cases in which reference is made to the law of wild animals than there are wild animal cases." Eugene Kuntz, *Treatise on the Law of Oil and Gas,* vol. 1, § 4.1, pp. 112–113 (1987) (footnote omitted).

41. This point helps explain why, as I pointed out in Chapter 22, brilliant mathematicians and scientists, should they happen to lack good verbal skills, do not make brilliant lawyers.

This procedure resembles the hypothetico-deductive model of scientific inquiry. In that model, which though now understood to be an inaccurate description captures important features of the scientific process, the scientist proposes a theory and deduces from it empirical hypotheses that he then tests. If the hypothesis flunks the test the theory is falsified and must be altered or abandoned. Similarly, we might have a "rule" that all political speech is constitutionally protected, which implies that a threat to kill the President because he has violated Montesquieu's conception of the separation of powers is privileged. But we know the death threat is not privileged, and this means that our rule is unsound in the broad terms in which we stated it and must be restated. The use of hypothetical cases viewed as potentially misleading analogies to cases within the core of a rule or doctrine is the counterpart to the hypotheses that the scientist confronts with experimental or observational data. The rule that only possessory rights may be obtained in fugitive resources had to be altered when confronted with the example of oil and gas. In both the hypothetico-deductive model and its moral and legal counterparts, the goal is consistency or coherence—between theory and observation in the scientific realm, between a moral theory and unshakable moral intuitions in the moral realm, and in the legal realm between a legal theory and immovably established legal decisions.

This use of analogy to establish consistency between our theories and the cases that we accept as fixed features of our legal landscape is different from its "creative" use, in which the vague notion of "likeness" serves to identify theories that may be usable as resources for deciding novel cases. When oil and gas first became valuable resources and lawyers cast about for legal theories that might be used to regulate them, intuitions of likeness pointed the lawyers—misleadingly—to the regulatory regime for rabbits and foxes. Analogy brings candidates for legal governance forward for our consideration, and this is a valuable function, akin to that of emotions like fear and desire in directing our thoughts along one channel rather than another. But we must refer to policy, purpose, and consequence to pick the analogy that shall govern the new case. To say for example that forbidding abortion is like permitting slavery invites us to consider why we dislike slavery and whether the reason or reasons are applicable to abortion. The analogy gets us only to the threshold of analysis, and we may have difficulty crossing the threshold if the only places in which we look for information about policies, purposes, and consequences is the body of judicial opinions. Since the law is to a great extent a collection of cases that once were genuinely new, the fact that lawyers are masters of reasoning by analogy will not excuse their failure to develop a more receptive attitude toward the methods of inquiry used by other disciplines.

Casuistry. Reasoning by analogy as lawyers use the term is similar, perhaps identical, to the casuistic method of moral and religious reasoning. In both types of reasoning one moves from case (real or hypothetical) to case rather than from theory to case; "casuistry" *means* case-based reasoning. Jonsen and Toulmin in their defense of casuistry (note 3) point out that we often have to make choices without the aid of a comprehensive theory; that we often are more confident about the proper outcome of a case, whether a law case or a moral dilemma, than we are about any theory from which that outcome might be deduced; that we can often agree on cases more readily than on theories; that general rules, norms, or maxims often require adjustment to fit particular cases; that (the same point) there is a role for equity, Aristotle's *epieikeia,* in the application of general rules to specific cases; that, in short, circumstances alter cases; that good judgment, therefore, is as important as analytical power. I agree with these points but don't see how they identify a distinctive style of reasoning. Cases to the lawyer or moralist are like data to a natural scientist. The scientist who ignores the fit between his theory and the data is doing a bad job; and so too the judge or lawyer who does not understand that exceptions to rules are often necessary to make the rules "fit" the cases that the rules are supposed to govern. Both examples illustrate the importance of empirical sensitivity in different realms of human thought. But it is a shame that the lawyer's and the judge's database is so often limited to judicial opinions.

Jonsen and Toulmin tell the fascinating story of the evolution of Catholic doctrine on usury.[42] Over a period of centuries, Catholic theologians, reasoning cautiously from case to case, turned the doctrine virtually on its head—changed it from being an absolute prohibition against lending at interest to a prohibition only against lending at interest to a person in distress. In the course of this doctrinal (r)evolution, which was stimulated by commercial expansion and resulting

---

42. Jonsen and Toulmin, note 3 above, ch. 9. See also John T. Noonan, Jr., *The Scholastic Analysis of Usury* (1957).

pressure from merchants and bankers to be permitted to obtain and to make business loans, the theologians stumbled on the concept of opportunity cost: a person who lent money incurred a real cost, measured by the benefit that he could have obtained from an alternative use of the money. If economics had been a well-developed science at the time, an economist could have explained to the theologians in a few minutes why interest was compensation rather than theft; but there were no economists, so the theologians had to find their way to this insight without the aid of theory. What they were doing, in difficult circumstances, *was* economics; it was not some special thing that lawyers and theologians do particularly well.

Where "rhetoric" in a useful sense of the word entered the controversy over usury was in the theologians' efforts, which have obvious counterparts in law, to maintain an appearance of continuity with a tradition that included (literally) sacred texts. The theologians had two persuasive tasks. One was to persuade the clerical community that business loans were not sinful.[43] The other was to persuade the lay community that Catholic doctrine was consistent and intelligent, rather than discontinuous and (formerly) mistaken. Similarly, judges want both to persuade of the correctness of their decisions and to persuade that their decisions are consistent or at least continuous with the decisions of their predecessors. But we should not confuse a rhetoric of continuity with a moral obligation to adhere to precedent.

Metaphor. Earlier I mentioned "leverage." It illustrates the law's use of metaphor. Metaphor plays a useful cognitive role in jolting a person out of his existing frame of reference by getting him to look at something in a fresh, and perhaps a more illuminating, way. So even if one agrees, as I would be inclined to do, that a metaphor has no meaning beyond the literal, implying that most metaphors are false, or, more precisely, that their truth value is irrelevant,[44] we can see that, as Cass

43. Compare the invention of double-entry bookkeeping, which has been ascribed to the rhetorical aim of making commercial transactions, including lending at interest, seem nonexploitive: "It [the double-entry account] demonstrates that for every profit made there has been a set of equal and corresponding debts incurred." James A. Aho, "Rhetoric and the Invention of Double Entry Bookkeeping," *Rhetorica*, Winter 1985, pp. 21, 34.

44. "Patent falsity is the usual case with metaphor, but on occasion patent truth will do as well. 'Business is business' [or 'no man is an island'] is too obvious in its literal meaning to be taken as having been uttered to convey information, so we look for another use . . . The ordinary meaning in the context of use is odd enough to prompt us to disregard the question of literal truth." "What Metaphors Mean," in Donald Davidson, *Inquiries into Truth and Interpretation* 245, 258 (1984).

Sunstein, James Boyd White, and others insist, there is a sense in which rhetoric is a way of thinking and not just a way of persuading an audience to believe what the speaker has already fully thought out. From Heraclitus's river and Plato's cave to Neurath's boat, Wittgenstein's language games, Ryle's ghost in the machine, Goodman's grue, and Rawls's reflective equilibrium and veil of ignorance, metaphor has lain close to the heart (to speak metaphorically) of the most rigorous philosophizing.

A way of thinking, metaphor, yes, but often of an undisciplined and misleading character. Recall the passages that I quoted from Aristotle's discussion of how to argue a contract case. If one may judge from his discussion, Athenian contract law of the fourth century B.C. had very little structure,[45] so that it was indeed possible to argue equally for and against the enforcement of almost any contract. Legal rules narrow the field for forensic rhetoric and that is one of their virtues, which "law is rhetoric" buffs are apt to overlook. Modern contract law has a great deal of structure, enforcing agreement on premises, ruling out a variety of arguments, silencing, in the vast range of contract cases, the glibbest advocate of the worse cause. Uncertainty of legal rights and duties is neither a constant of nature nor a thing to be prized because it maximizes the role of rhetoric.

Rhetoric and science. When conceived as the residual set of methods of reasoning and persuasion employed *faute de mieux* where because of lack of information, lack of agreement on premises, absence of a ruling paradigm, irremediable vagueness, or incommensurability of values, the usual processes of scientific or quasi-scientific inquiry—processes of logic and empirical verification—are unavailable, rhetoric is neither a good thing nor a bad thing. It is merely an indispensable thing in those areas, which still bulk large in law though they do not pervade it to the extent that the practitioners of critical legal studies believe, in which more definitive methods of resolving disagreement are unavailable.

Rhetoric's most impassioned defenders will not accept my attempt to distinguish between rhetorical and scientific reasoning. We can examine the issue further with the help of Herbert Wechsler's article on neutral principles in constitutional law, discussed in Chapter 1. This

45. This was a general characteristic of Athenian law of the period, as emphasized in David Cohen, "Rhetoric, Morals, and the Rule of Law in Classical Athens" (forthcoming in *Zeitschrift der Savigny-Stiftung für Rechtsgeschichte*).

heavily rhetorical article celebrates rhetoric's conventional antithesis, reason. A parallel example is the *Gorgias,* which while denouncing rhetoric and exalting reason makes its case by rhetorical rather than analytical means. To select as one's theme the celebration of reason can have the side effect of making one's rhetoric invisible. We tend to take people at their face value. If they proclaim their allegiance to reason we are dulled to the possibility that their argument on behalf of a reasoned approach to their subject is not itself an appeal to reason. A weak science may therefore trumpet its scientific character, its disdain for rhetoric, to mask its weakness. By doing so, however, it gives hostages to the "everything [including science] is rhetoric" school.

The deceitful potential of scientific rhetoric may seem especially great in areas of economics, including the economic analysis of law, in which efforts to test economic hypotheses with empirical data rigorously analyzed in accordance with the best statistical methods are rare and the results inconclusive. Science, including social science—including economic science, and not only in its applications to law—does not, as actually practiced, quite fit the most influential models of scientific methodology, such as the hypothetico-deductive model mentioned earlier. As Coase and McCloskey have emphasized in the spirit of Kuhn, economic theories are not in fact held to the high standards implied by the influential discussions of scientific and economic methodology by Carnap, Popper, Friedman, Stigler, and others;[46] those standards are aspirational rather than operational. McCloskey exaggerates, as when he treats the result of a natural experiment (such as a rise in price that leads to a fall in demand, or queuing following the imposition of price controls, or the benefits that economists correctly predicted from deregulation)[47] as a narrative, or "human capital" as a metaphor. He is too much an "everything is rhetoric" person for my taste, and is particularly unconvincing when arguing that economics would improve if only economists would recognize that they are really rhetoricians.[48] But he has identified a number of unedifying rhetorical devices of

46. R. H. Coase, *How Economists Should Choose* (American Enterprise Institute 1982); Donald N. McCloskey, *The Rhetoric of Economics* (1985).

47. Clifford Winston, "Economic Deregulation: Days of Reckoning for Microeconomists," 31 *Journal of Economic Literature* 1263 (1993).

48. Donald N. McCloskey, "The Consequences of Rhetoric," in *The Consequences of Economic Rhetoric* 280 (Arjo Kramer, Donald N. McCloskey, and Robert M. Solow eds. 1988). For criticism, see Stanley Fish, "Comments from outside Economics," in id. at 21; Robert M. Solow, "Comments from inside Economics," in id. at 31.

academic economists, including misleading uses of statistical inference.[49] I acknowledge the existence of a scientistic rhetoric that the classical rhetoricians overlooked because they wrote when scientific method was in its infancy and that the connotation of "rhetoric" as ornamental speech obscures.[50] Maybe there is no "neutral" language, no prose as transparent as a windowpane. While Wechsler offered tokens of personal certitude to enhance the credibility of his arguments, an opposite tactic not necessarily less rhetorical is to pretend to be speaking impersonal truths—to be in effect an oracle. (So the Greeks had the idea after all.) To suppress the authorial "I" can be as misleading as to induce your listener to infer certainty from your certitude. Scientists seek to bolster their authority by affectations of mathematical rigor, by use of an intimidating jargon, by suppressing doubts, and by concealing the personal, judgmental factor in the evaluation of experimental, statistical, or observational results. Some analytic philosophers, like legal formalists in the tradition of Langdell, "geometrize" their subject.[51]

The pragmatist is less likely to overlook these rhetorics of reason than the nonpragmatist. The foundationalist—a Plato or a Bentham, say, or a modern scientific realist—is impatient with rhetoric because he thinks he can establish through logic or mathematics or reflection or whatever a pipeline to the truth, and no one supposes that rhetoric is an apt tool for constructing such a pipeline. He doesn't like the metaphor of "conversation" as a characterization of inquiry. For him, inquiry is individual rather than social; his favorite organ is the eye, with its penetrating gaze into the heart of things, not the ear, alert to human chatter. Rhetoric belongs to the shadow world (as it seems to a Platonist) of approximations and probabilities and opinions and at best warranted beliefs, a world of talk but not of clear vision and ultimate truths.

49. See also Coase, note 46 above, at 14–17.

50. For an illustrative rhetorical analysis of a well-known scientific paper (Watson and Crick's two-page paper in *Nature* announcing the discovery of the double-helix structure of the DNA molecule), see Lawrence J. Prelli, *A Rhetoric of Science: Inventing Scientific Discourse* 236–256 (1989). Of particular relevance to my discussion are McCloskey, note 46 above, and the essays in *The Rhetoric of the Human Sciences: Language and Argument in Scholarship and Public Affairs* (John S. Nelson, Allan Megill, and Donald N. McCloskey eds. 1987). See also Jeff Mason, *Philosophical Rhetoric: The Function of Indirection in Philosophical Writing* 68–72 (1989), discussing the rhetoric of A. J. Ayer's manifesto for logical positivism, *Language, Truth, and Logic.*

51. Martin Warner, *Philosophical Finesse: Studies in the Art of Rational Persuasion*, ch. 1 (1989).

But if you think that the twittering shadow world is our world, including the part investigated (or constructed) by science, then you are apt to think that Protagoras, Gorgias, and the other sophists were on the right as well as the pragmatic track when they merged fact and opinion, notably in Protagoras's slogan that "man is the measure of all things."[52] If science doesn't put us in correspondence with what is really "out there," how different is it from a judicial decision that purports to state what the law is, or for that matter what the facts are? Recall that Gorgias admitted under Socrates' prodding that although he made speeches about justice he didn't know what it was. That should not have bothered Gorgias. He didn't think there was anything *to* know; it was all opinion. The merging of fact and opinion gives forensic advocacy its purchase and therefore invites the pragmatist, who is sympathetic to such a merger, to think of science on the model of law, rather than the reverse as Langdell and other legal formalists had tried to do. Hence the paradox that Richard Rorty admires the ethics of scientific inquiry because he thinks it a model of reasonable, fair-minded, and democratic intellectual activity, but does not much admire science, which he thinks destined to fail in its stated quest for an accurate description of the way things are.

Yet even if pragmatism has succeeded in dethroning science from its position as the successor to monotheism in the role of deliverer of final truths, this does not mean that science has been shown to be on the same level with propaganda, censorship, picketing—and casuistry and legal reasoning—as methods of resolving disagreement. We should ask whether there isn't a *big* difference in degree between the rationality of economic and other scientific and social-scientific inquiry on the one hand, and on the other the rationality of the much more rhetorical methods of inquiry and argument that are commonly used in law.[53] We should remind ourselves that differences of degree can be important, that there is a useful distinction between fiction and fact, and that a work like Patricia Williams's *Alchemy of Race and Rights* is closer to the fiction end of the spectrum than a comparably distinguished work of science would be.

---

52. Interpreted in Schiappa, note 1 above, ch. 7, to mean that all judgments are relative to a frame of reference.

53. "It would be a mistake . . . to replace an arrogant scientism with a rampant rhetoricism." J. E. McGuire and Trevor Melia, "Some Cautionary Strictures on the Writing of the Rhetoric of Science," *Rhetorica*, Winter 1989, pp. 87, 88.

Above all we should reject the argument of naive humanists that the very distance of rhetoric from science makes rhetoric intrinsically edifying and humane. On this construal, rhetoric becomes synonymous not only with both reason and expression, but also with the good, and thus emerges as the master discipline, subsuming everything from math to ethics. This deprives the term of utility; it is better to confine it to the nonlogical, nonscientific, nonempirical methods of persuasion. Then at least rhetoric has a subject, rather than being a name for everything. When rhetoric is moralized, rhetorical analysis of judicial opinions turns into the old lawyers' game of congratulating the judges who agree with you; and it becomes impossible to remark the rhetorical prowess of a Hitler.[54] He exemplified the two principal ways in which rhetoric can be pernicious. The first consists of conveying information to an audience about how to exploit or despoil some other group. (This is the light in which some feminists regard pornography.) The second consists of throwing monkey wrenches into the audience's cognitive apparatus (also an element of the feminist case against pornography defined as the graphic or explicit, hence likely to be sexually arousing, representation of sex). Great shrieking orators like Hitler convey meaning without sense and win agreement without comprehension.[55]

Granted, the fact that rhetoric can be used for evil purposes does not distinguish it from science. It is the other differences that explain why "rhetoric" has retained its ambivalent valence despite the strenuous efforts of the neorhetoricians to rehabilitate it. The least important is the ready-made quality of rhetoric, the fact that it does not produce knowledge. Typified by the English barrister, who is briefed by the solicitor and doesn't even meet his client, the rhetorician works with the materials he is given. He is not a discoverer. Manuals of rhetoric do not teach the reader how to construct scientific theories or conduct empirical research or do experiments. And the rhetorician doesn't stick his neck out. No Socrates, he is respectful of public opinion, or less politely the prejudices of his audience. That is one reason why the literature of rhetoric is duller than that of science or philosophy. Rhetoric comes into its own not, as Aristotle thought, when there is radical

54. See Roderick P. Hart, *Modern Rhetorical Criticism* 357–362 (1990), for an acknowledgment, rare in the literature of rhetoric, that Hitler was indeed a distinguished practitioner of the art. Cf. Vickers, note 3 above, at 414.

55. The master satire of such oratory is the episode of Mynheer Peeperkorn at the waterfall, in Thomas Mann, *The Magic Mountain* 620–621 (H. T. Lowe-Porter trans. 1961).

uncertainty but when the facts are known and the question is how to bring an audience to understand and be moved by them. That was the situation that confronted Lincoln, a highly successful trial and appellate lawyer and possibly the greatest master of rhetoric in U.S. history. But by invoking Lincoln I mean to show that I am not *criticizing* rhetoric in remarking its lack of originality. *That* difference between rhetoric and science is just the difference between marketing and production, and an economist is unlikely to assign primacy to the latter—realistically, marketing is a phase of production.

Two differences between rhetoric and science do have normative significance, however. First, much of rhetoric is mutually offsetting—the parrying of an opponent's rhetorical thrusts. This is not a characteristic of science, although there is a certain amount of duplication of effort arising from the competitive character of the scientific enterprise.[56] Second, science (which for present purposes can be understood as including mathematics and logic) tends to falsify false propositions, and thus to promote truth, whereas rhetoric has no such tendency.[57] Consider a set of propositions that are candidates for belief. They can be either true or false, and either believed or disbelieved, making a fourfold division: propositions that are true and believed, those that are true and disbelieved, those that are false and believed, and those that are false and disbelieved. In general, belief in true propositions yields greater utility than belief in false ones, and disbelief in false propositions yields greater utility than belief in false ones. That is,

$$U_1(t, b) - U_2(t, d) = Z_1 > 0,$$

$$U_3(f, d) - U_4(f, b) = Z_2 > 0.$$

Let $Z \equiv Z_1 + Z_2$ represent the utility of believing what is true and disbelieving what is false. To achieve this state, however, is not costless, and let us denote the costs of achieving it by c. Only if $Z > c$ will the state be achieved. Rhetoric operates on c—but it can raise or lower it. It can make truth sound like truth, but it can also make falsehood sound like truth and thus induce a false belief, and it can make truth sound like falsehood and thus induce a false disbelief. Even when it is

56. It is a pronounced characteristic of technology; consider trade secrets, and races to patent commercially valuable inventions.

57. For further examples, see *Law and Literature*, ch. 6, esp. pp. 279–281.

free from falsehood—and often it is not—rhetoric tends to alter (or confirm) beliefs whether they are true or false.

These are not reasons for trying to outlaw rhetoric, any more than for trying to outlaw advertising and litigation, which have similar attributes—which can in fact be regarded as departments of rhetoric. But they can help us understand why rhetoric is held in lower esteem than science.

chapter 25

The Legal Protection of the Face
We Present to the World

AN INTRICATE complex of interrelated laws, judge-made and statutory, protects this interest that has no name, the interest I am calling
"the face we present to the world." Economics, with a bit of simple
game theory (remember Chapter 14) and some help from philosophy,
can help us thread this maze, uncover the law's unity, think concretely
about problems often obscured by sonorous talk of "privacy," and
incidentally provide a bridge between the discussion of rhetoric as
signaling in the preceding chapter and the discussion of sexuality in the
next one. I have discussed this subject at length elsewhere,[1] which

---

1. See in particular my book *The Economics of Justice*, pt. 3 (1981), and my article
"Blackmail, Privacy, and Freedom of Contract," 141 *University of Pennsylvania Law Review*
1817 (1993). For other economic analyses of the subject matter of this chapter, see *Conference
on the Law and Economics of Privacy*, 9 *Journal of Legal Studies* 621 (1980); Stephen M. Renas
et al., "Toward an Economic Theory of Defamation, Liability, and the Press," 50 *Southern
Economic Journal* 451 (1983); C. J. Hartmann and S. M. Renas, "Anglo-American Privacy
Law: An Economic Analysis," 5 *International Review of Law and Economics* 133 (1985);
Douglas H. Ginsburg and Paul Schectman, "Blackmail: An Economic Analysis of the Law,"
141 *University of Pennsylvania Law Review* 1849 (1993); Steven Shavell, "An Economic
Analysis of Threats and Their Illegality: Blackmail, Extortion, and Robbery," 141 *University
of Pennsylvania Law Review* 1877 (1993).

allows me to be brief here; but what I shall be presenting is an extension rather than merely a summary of previous work, and also a reply to a major critic of that work.

Privacy, Reputation, and the Self

We construct—not always consciously of course—the self that we present to the outside world. We construct it by what we do, what we wear (recall the discussion of dressing as sexual signaling in Chapter 16), what we say, and what we don't say; by cosmetics and sometimes by cosmetic surgery. We make representations and misrepresentations, and also conceal a lot, about our character, wealth, history, physique, health, and intentions. In short, we self-present or self-advertise,[2] as a step toward the self-fashioning that is the core of the concept of individualism defended by George Kateb (see the Introduction) but that has instrumental as well as intrinsic utility. Some people "sell" their constructed public self in almost a literal sense, as when a celebrity demands a high fee to lend his name or face to a commercial advertisement, paying careful attention, too, to the likely impact of the particular advertisement on other opportunities to exploit his public self.[3] The rest of us "sell" our constructed public self in the figurative sense of using it to make advantageous transactions in employment and marriage markets and, more generally, in the market for human relationships whether of a personal or of a commercial character. The reader of this book will have become accustomed by now to divorcing the concept of "market" from pecuniary transactions.

A heterogeneous body of civil and criminal law protects the constructed public self. The law of defamation (libel and slander), and a closely related part of the tort law of invasion of privacy, the part that provides a remedy for casting a person in a "false light," prevent people from impairing the constructed public self through untruths. The most problematic aspect of the tort law of privacy is its occasional use to prevent people from impairing the constructed public self through truths, a use reinforced by the criminal law of blackmail, which forbids the sale of silence to the person whose secret the blackmailer has discovered.

2. See Erving Goffman's classic, *The Presentation of Self in Everyday Life* (1959); also Roger Ingham, "Privacy and Psychology," in *Privacy* 35 (John B. Young ed. 1978).
    3. Cf. *Douglass v. Hustler Magazine, Inc.*, 769 F.2d 1128 (7th Cir. 1985).

The least problematic—though also least related to privacy—aspect of the tort of invasion of privacy, the "right of publicity," gives a person the right to prevent the use of his name or face in advertising without his consent. The right is invoked most frequently by celebrities who are not shy but merely want to control the marketing of the right to use their name or face in advertising in order to maximize their income; hence its name. The right of privacy has still other aspects that are unrelated or only tenuously related to the constructed public self. The Fourth Amendment's prohibition of unreasonable searches and seizures, originally understood to protect property rights, broadly conceived, is nowadays more often seen as protecting privacy in a sense distinct from property. (Wiretapping invades privacy of communications, but does not trespass on property rights.) Intrusive surveillance, as by the photographer Ron Gallela who used to follow Jacqueline Onassis around, infringes the tort right of privacy. There are state and federal privacy statutes, concerned with the accuracy of government records of people. And "right of privacy" is the reigning judicial euphemism for the right of abortion and other legally protected aspects of sexual or reproductive autonomy. I am not interested in any aspects of privacy law here except the legal protections of the public self.[4]

Defamation and the false-light privacy tort are parallel not only to each other but also and illuminatingly to the false disparagement of a product or service. There is no mystery about why the law should give a remedy to a seller whose competitor tells the public falsely that the seller's products are defective. But we who are not manufacturers or merchants also "sell" ourselves to others, whether they be employers, employees, readers, friends, family members. If someone falsely disparages us, and the falsity is believed, we lose valuable transactions—and so do the people with whom we would have transacted. X might be Y's most valuable employee; if, because someone has falsely accused X of being dishonest, Y fires him, both are losers.

The other side of the coin, however, is that accurate, truthful disparagement of people as of goods and services improves the operation of the market in personal and commercial human relationships. If X is dishonest and Y would fire him if he knew, then revealing X's dishonesty to Y will improve the operation of the labor market. If

4. For excellent discussions of the legal aspects of privacy, see Julie C. Inness, *Privacy, Intimacy, and Isolation* (1992); Robert C. Post, "The Social Foundations of Privacy: Community and Self in the Common Law Tort," 77 *California Law Review* 957 (1989).

one's constructed public self misleads people with whom one deals, the destruction of the construct removes a barrier to informed transacting.

It might seem that the very idea of "constructing" a public self would connote falsity. But what is artificial is not necessarily false. Advertising is artificial but often true. If a person dresses soberly in order to project a sober image, he is not advertising himself falsely if in fact he is serious, conscientious, and self-controlled. Often, moreover, the only method of constructing a public self that a person need employ in order to create the public self that he wants is to behave well in his job or his personal life; his public self will then be constructed by people who know him or know of him and who draw inferences about his character and qualities from his behavior or from what others have told them about him. He will in short acquire a reputation, which is different from his own efforts at signaling the possession of particular traits but is closely related as effect to (partial) cause. There is an analogy to the "ethical appeal" in rhetoric, discussed in the preceding chapter.

A deeper point is that the idea of the self, the inner, private, "real" self, the "real me," is itself a construct. What we say and do in public, when we are speaking and acting deliberately, is a selection from a vast array of possible words and deeds that consciousness brings before our imagination for evaluation and choice. We may if self-aware realize that were it not for constraints—the costs and benefits that our interactions with other people generate—we would say and do quite differently; and we may consider our unconstrained, because secret, impulses and beliefs the more authentic, the more disinterested, because uninfluenced by costs and benefits. But on reflection it is odd that we should think our private fantasy life more "real" than our public life. This would imply, perversely, that most speech consists of lies, since we "conceal" in our public utterances and even our most private conversations a myriad of hostile, lustful, angry, and contemptuous feelings that whirl about the "inner" recesses of thought. Only someone who thought (on insufficient evidence, as it seems to me) that the fantasy life is indeed more authentic than the public self should think it a source of mendacity that the latter is not a simple conduit for the former. In terms of communication or signaling theory, the construction of a public self enables us to eliminate "noise" or "cross-talk" from our communications, which would retard rather than facilitate comprehension of our intentions and behavior.[5] The "inner" self, the fantasy self, may provide interesting clues to our presocial desires, as we shall see in the next chapter; but it is not on that account more authentic than our public self.

Or rather public selves; people have multiple public selves, corresponding to the multiple "markets" in which they "sell" themselves.[6] We construct one self for our spouse, another for our parents, another for our employer, and so forth, the constructs corresponding to different brands, designed for different markets, of the same basic product. Erving Goffman calls these different public selves roles. The theatrical analogy is apt (recall that I used it in Chapter 3 in discussing judges), but a little misleading because we distinguish between an actor and his roles and regard the former as the more authentic self, yet I am denying that our many selves should be viewed as projections of an "inner" self. I shall not try to solve the mystery of who this "we" is who "constructs" our various public selves.

I have associated the public self with signaling and reputation, corresponding to speaker and audience in rhetoric. We signal our intentions, our competence, and so forth by words and deeds, endeavoring to shape the reputation that the public will bestow on us on the basis of its interpretation of those signals.[7] It is no accident that we often speak more freely to strangers whom we do not expect ever to encounter again than to our intimates,[8] or that old people, whose transactional future is truncated, tend to speak less guardedly about themselves than younger people do.

Despite the transactional function of reputation, the common anal-

5. Both the parol-evidence rule, which operates primarily to limit the use in interpreting a contract of evidence of what the parties said during precontractual negotiations, and the hostility of some judges to the use of legislative history in the interpretation of statutes, can be viewed as efforts to facilitate communication by suppressing noise.

6. See Goffman, note 2 above; Ingham, note 2 above. This point is also emphasized in one of the most interesting of the philosophical articles on privacy: James Rachels's article "Why Privacy Is Important," in *Philosophical Dimensions of Privacy: An Anthology* 290 (Ferdinand David Schoeman ed. 1984).

7. The economic function of reputation is the subject of a substantial economic and game-theoretic literature illustrated by Arnoud W. A. Boot, Stuart I. Greenbaum, and Anjan V. Thakor, "Reputation and Discretion in Financial Contracting," 83 *American Economic Review* 1165 (1993).

8. Not just a local American phenomenon. See Georg Simmel, "The Stranger," in *The Sociology of Georg Simmel* 402, 404 (Kurt H. Wolff ed. 1950).

ogy of reputation to money, as when one speaks of "earning" a "golden" reputation, is misleading. It was after all a moralist of dubious reliability (Iago in *Othello*) who said, "Who steals my purse steals trash . . ./ But he that filches from me my good name/ Robs me of that which not enriches him,/ And makes me poor indeed." We don't *own* our reputation, the way we own the money in our pockets; it is the opinion held of us by others, and it can be withdrawn by them without compensation. And he who strips away another person's undeserved reputation "enriches" those who might transact with the person.

Emphasis on the instrumental function of privacy and reputation is an important corrective to the uncritical approbation so frequently bestowed on these goods. We imagine the sense of privacy to be one of our distinctions as humans, and yet the "lower" animals have a sense of privacy too; for them, too, "one of the functions of privacy is the withholding of information that otherwise might provide an opponent with a competitive advantage."[9] Privacy is costly to achieve, so, being a good with a very high private value because of its utility in advancing people's plans and projects, we should not be surprised that it is what economists call a superior good—demand for it is not only a negative function of price, but also a positive function of income. Modern people have vastly more privacy than their ancestors not because the cost of obtaining privacy has fallen but because modern people are much more wealthy than their ancestors. Privacy is a private good of great value, but sometimes a social bad. A high level of privacy is a source not only of the rich sense of individuality that Kateb celebrates but also of potentially acute dangers to the social order. Crime, subversion, and fraud are all facilitated by privacy, so it is natural and not reprehensible that society has fought the trend toward greater privacy with such devices as wiretapping and computerized databases of personal information.

The transactional function of the public self can help to explain some otherwise puzzling distinctions in the laws that protect that self. One involves the survival of some but not all rights to that protection after the death of the holder of the right. The right to sue for invasions of privacy that take the form of publicizing intimate personal facts, and (with unimportant exceptions) the right to sue for defamation, are

9. Peter H. Klopfer and Daniel I. Rubenstein, "The Concept *Privacy* and Its Biological Basis," 33 *Journal of Social Issues*, no. 3, 51, 60 (1977).

extinguished with the death of the plaintiff. But, increasingly, the right to publicity is heritable. The explanation is simple, once an economic view of these rights is taken. When one dies, one ceases transacting, and the rights that facilitate one's transacting cease to have any value. (So it is only an apparent exception to the nonsurvivability of the right to sue for defamation that the right survives the death of the defamed person if the defamatory statement is that he had a heritable disease.) But a celebrity's name or likeness that has advertising value after the celebrity's death remains a marketable commodity; and in general and in this instance as well the efficiency with which resources are allocated is maximized when valuable commodities are ownable. If everyone can use Elvis Presley's likeness in advertising, the advertising value of the likeness may fall to zero. A real economic value, however tawdry it may appear to highbrows, will therefore be wiped out by overuse due to absence of property rights, just as a commons may be overgrazed because the owner of each grazing animal does not consider the cost to the other owners resulting from his animal's grazing.[10]

A Note on the "Actual Malice" Rule in Defamation

It is easy to see why the law protects truthful reputation, and it may seem, but it is not, equally easy to see why that protection is limited (by the "actual malice" rule[11] of *New York Times Co. v. Sullivan* and other rules that the Supreme Court has created in the name of the First Amendment) when the reputation is that of a public figure and the assailant is a publisher or television station. The economic argument for the limitation is straightforward but incomplete. The activity of discovering and disseminating the truth about public figures, especially but not only officials, has great social value. But it is impossible for the discoverer-disseminator to transform the whole of that social value into private value, that is, income; and the prospect of income is usually a condition of undertaking a costly activity. Property rights in information are incomplete. Because the copyright laws protect only the form in which a journalist or other writer expresses himself and not the substance, which can be copied freely, the threat of tort liability for

10. With heavy grazing, each animal has to graze more in order to obtain his fill of food, resulting in a weight loss that diminishes his sale value.

11. The defamer must either know that the defamatory statement is false or be recklessly indifferent to whether it is true or false.

defamation can exert a disproportionate deterrent to investigative newsgathering. By diminishing that threat, the law can actually bring about a closer alignment of social and private value. In economic jargon, the law may permit certain costs to be externalized (the costs to the defamed person, costs that the defamer could be made to bear only through liability)[12] in order to make it more likely that certain benefits, being external, will be conferred—the benefits to readers of other articles or books, which copied the defamer's theme, ideas, and techniques but not his words.

This argument overlooks, however, another rule of defamation law, the rule that makes a publisher liable even if he merely repeats a defamatory statement made by another, without vouching for its accuracy. If the derivative defamer were immune from liability it would be difficult to induce any publisher to take the first step, that is, to make an arguably defamatory statement about a public figure. For he would bear all the expected liability costs, offset only by the publicity value of a "scoop." But if the copiers take as it were the bad with the good—the expected cost of being sued for defamation as well as the benefit of publishing an exciting report—the negative effect on the incentive for investigative reporting of the incomplete system of property rights in ideas is diminished. The benefits are externalized, but so are the costs—for anyone who copies the first publisher's report assumes, as well, a share of the expected liability for defamation, because he may be sued as well as the original defamer.

Another reason to doubt whether the actual-malice rule is efficient is that it protects the second and subsequent publishers more completely than it protects the first, because they are unlikely to know or even strongly suspect that the defamatory statement is false and hence are unlikely to be held liable for repeating it, at least if it was first published or broadcast by a reputable company. So there will still be a deterrent to being first with the story.

Another name for a public figure is a newsworthy figure. As newsworthiness, a proxy for the social value of information about a person, diminishes, so, appropriately, does the legal protection of the publisher. But I have been arguing that the actual-malice rule may give publishers more protection than they need in order to have adequate incentives to obtain and publish news even about public figures.

---

12. Or, as we shall see, through punishment for the crime of blackmail.

The Tort of Publicizing Intimate Facts

It is easy to see why the law, even if it is not much impressed by high-falutin' rhetoric, Iago's or anyone else's, about reputation, provides remedies for *false* attacks on people's reputations; those attacks reduce the information value of the constructed public self. A deep puzzle about the legal protection of the constructed public self is why the law sometimes furnishes remedies against *truthful* assaults on the construct. It does this through the part of the tort law of privacy that imposes liability for the public disclosure of true but private, personal, usually intimate facts, and through the criminal law of blackmail, which punishes people who threaten to dislose true facts about a person unless he pays them for their silence.[13]

We should distinguish between two sorts of true but private facts that people don't want publicized. One is the sort that impairs reputation and by doing so reduces one's opportunities for favorable transactions; call this *discrediting* publicity. The other is the sort that causes embarrassment by revealing aspects of a person that while not necessarily or even typically discreditable are not part of one's constructed public self, that are concealed. Let us call this *embarrassing* publicity. The first category is illustrated by disclosure that one has a criminal record, or has had a sex-change operation, or is suffering from a fatal disease, or has a history of mental illness, or is bisexual. These are all facts about a person that may cause others to shun him, whether rightly or wrongly. Embarrassing but not discrediting publicity is illustrated by a newspaper photograph of a person bathing or defecating or of his scar from an operation, or a newspaper report that his daughter was raped and murdered.

People's desire to conceal things that would not cause the people they want to transact with to refuse to do so or to charge a higher price (pecuniary or nonpecuniary) for doing so does not fit comfortably with the economist's idea of rational man. Furtiveness or secretiveness about things that do not affect our fitness for the social interactions we desire is, in the present state of knowledge about human psychology, a mysterious, brute fact about that psychology. But a brute fact it is, like the preference for some foods over others even when they do not differ in

---

13. Blackmail based on false facts about a person is criminal also, but it is a close criminal analogue to defamation.

nutritional value or price; and this is important in an economic analysis even if the economist can't (at least qua economist) understand it. The law protects the things that we value, provided it can do so without imposing disproportionate costs on others, without inquiring too closely into why we value them. It would be presumptuous as well as illiberal to do otherwise.

Parallel to the mystery of why we want to conceal "embarrassing" personal facts is the mystery of why there is a market for learning these facts about complete strangers, since knowledge of these facts serves no instrumental end. But this is another brute fact that the economist is obliged to consider, like the taste for pornography which it somewhat resembles. It shows that there are costs to suppressing this market as well as costs in allowing it to operate. The competing costs have to be balanced. The tort law of privacy does this, obliquely but unmistakably, by comparing the offensiveness of the disclosure to its newsworthiness. Comparison is facilitated by the inverse relation between these competing costs or values. The more offensive a disclosure, the less newsworthy it is apt to be; and the more newsworthy it is, the less offensive it is apt to be. No matter how private or squeamish we are, we realize that unusual circumstances can thrust even the most private, intimate details of our lives into the public domain; our privacy is qualified, much as our property rights are qualified by the government's power of eminent domain. Even a nonelected public official, who may have none of the exhibitionism that many politicians exhibit, knows and if sensible accepts that his private life is subject to greater scrutiny than that of a private individual; and a private individual knows that should he have the misfortune to be the victim of a crime or some natural disaster or even the good fortune to be wealthy or gifted the intimate details of his life may engage a legitimate public curiosity.[14] Conversely, even those of voyeuristic bent understand that others are deeply affronted by the revelation of intimate details that titillate but do not convey useful information, and also that the bent can be indulged without invading another person's privacy.

A brace of cases will illustrate these points. In the first, the *New Yorker* had published a "where is he now" article about a man who had been a math prodigy as a child but in adulthood had turned into an eccentric recluse.[15] Since he had minimal transactions with other peo-

14. As in Kelley v. Post Publishing Co., 98 N.E.2d 286 (Mass. 1951).
15. Sidis v. F-R Publishing Corp., 113 F.2d 806 (2d Cir. 1940). The article was written by the humorist James Thurber, under a pseudonym.

ple, the article could not be defended as unmasking a reputation that he was using to obtain undeserved advantages in dealing with other people. But there is abiding curiosity, not prurient or tittering, about the phenomenon of the child prodigy and about genius more broadly, which made the article newsworthy, as Sidis himself could probably have been brought to understand. The court held that the publication of the article was not tortious. In the second case,[16] a newspaper published a photograph of a woman in a fun house taken just as a jet of air blew her dress up around her waist. She obtained damages, not because the publication of the photograph was likely to impair her transactional opportunities but because the invasion of privacy was at once offensive and gratuitous (related points, remember); even in 1964, people who wanted to look at pictures of women's legs had plenty of opportunities to do so without invading anybody's privacy. I worry a little about the value judgment implicit in ranking curiosity about child prodigies higher than curiosity about a woman's legs. But I think it can be avoided by emphasizing that the latter curiosity is more easily satisfied without having to embarrass someone.

An altogether more questionable victory for a privacy plaintiff was *Melvin v. Reid*.[17] Mrs. Melvin was a former prostitute, who had been prosecuted for murder but acquitted. After the acquittal she abandoned prostitution, married, and (she alleged) had for seven years lived a blameless respectable life in a community in which her lurid past was unknown—when all was revealed in a movie about the murder case, *The Red Kimono*, which used her maiden name. The movie had not misrepresented the facts about her. It had revealed facts that were likely to make people shun her. The court held that the allegations of the complaint stated a claim of tortious invasion of privacy. The decision is surprising from a legal as well as from an economic standpoint because in effect it abrogates the defense of truth to a charge of defamation. The movie did not reveal the intimate details of the plaintiff's sex life or show nude photographs of her; it merely reported the sorts of events in a person's past life which people use to construct the person's reputation, good or bad. The judges may have felt that people would give too much weight to the plaintiff's past in predicting her future behavior—would be too reluctant to credit her avowals of complete reformation. But that is just the kind of paternalistic, and in the cir-

16. Daily Times Democrat v. Graham, 162 So. 2d 474 (Ala. 1964).
17. 297 Pac. 91 (Cal. App. 1931).

cumstances none too plausible, attitude toward market behavior ("market" including the market in personal relationships) that the economist generally thinks an inappropriate basis for government regulation. It is not surprising that, although followed in a few cases, *Melvin v. Reid* has generally been rejected.[18]

The case generally thought to have written finis to *Melvin v. Reid* is *Cox Broadcasting Corp. v. Cohn*.[19] A Georgia statute forbade the publication of names of rape victims. A television station obtained the name of a woman who had been raped and murdered from the indictment of her assailants and broadcast it in defiance of the statute. The woman's father brought a tort suit against the broadcaster, claiming that the broadcast had violated his right of privacy. The broadcaster argued that the name of the woman was a matter of public concern, but the Georgia supreme court held that the statute established the contrary, and affirmed a finding of liability. The U.S. Supreme Court reversed, holding that the statute violated the First Amendment. The Court did not say that the publication of truthful information can never be the basis of a suit for invasion of privacy. But it held that the First Amendment creates a privilege to publish matters contained in public records even if publication would offend the sensibilities of a reasonable person.

It is a strange case from the standpoint of both the plaintiff and the defendant. The invasion of privacy was tenuous. Remember who was suing—not the rape victim, who was dead, but her father. The fact that one's child has been raped and murdered is ugly and painful, but it is not the kind of intimate personal fact that most people want to conceal. On the contrary, the families of crime victims often participate actively in the investigation and prosecution of the criminal and sometimes try to publicize the crime in order to stimulate more vigorous and effective efforts at preventing and punishing such crimes. At the same time the newsworthiness of the rape-murder victim's *name* is very difficult to understand. Her friends and acquaintances would find out what had happened to her even if her name was not broadcast on television, and strangers would not be enlightened on any matter of public concern

18. See, for example, Rawlins v. Hutchinson Publishing Co., 543 P.2d 988, 993–996 (Kan. 1975); Romaine v. Kallinger, 537 A.2d 284, 294–295 (N.J. 1988); cf. Forsher v. Bugliosi, 163 Cal. Rptr. 628, 639 (Cal. 1980); Street v. National Broadcasting Co., 645 F.2d 1227 (6th Cir. 1981).

19. 420 U.S. 469 (1975). See also Florida Star v. B.J.F., 491 U.S. 524 (1989).

by knowing what her name was. The Court's idea that the public has a right to know what is in public records is question-begging; the Georgia statute made a part of every rape indictment, namely the rape victim's name, a nonpublic record.

A case like *Cox* but stronger for the defense is *Haynes v. Alfred A. Knopf, Inc.*[20] The defendants were the publisher and the author of a best-selling book about the migration of rural southern blacks to northern cities that had begun in the 1940s.[21] Although the book is a serious social history, the author is a journalist and the book is journalistic rather than social-scientific in its approach, focusing on specific individuals, both blacks involved in the migration and white politicians involved in the antipoverty programs of the 1960s. The central figure in the narrative, and a principal source of the author's information about the lives of blacks involved in the migration, is a woman named Ruby Daniels, who after being a cotton picker on a southern plantation moved to Chicago, had the common experiences (poverty, welfare, life in the "projects," children out of wedlock who in turn had their own children out of wedlock, and so forth) of the "ghetto" black, and in her old age moved back to her hometown in Mississippi. While in Chicago, she had lived with, had had four children by, had eventually married, and had ultimately divorced another migrant from rural Mississippi, Luther Haynes, the plaintiff (along with his wife) in the suit. The book contains descriptions of Luther Haynes's philandering and drinking and his neglect of Ruby Daniels and their children. But in the early 1970s Haynes had remarried and begun to straighten out his life. By the time *The Promised Land* was published in 1991, Haynes was a sober, employed, respected member of his community—a deacon of his church—enjoying with his wife a middle-class income and style of life. He argued to the court, although unsuccessfully, that he like Mrs. Melvin should be allowed to bury a past that did not do justice to his current character and would merely humiliate him and his wife.

To the economist the proper balancing of a person's past and present conduct with a view toward a realistic assessment of his character and so of his fitness for future transactions is something for potential transactors, not courts, to do. In addition, the story of Luther Haynes is highly newsworthy. The plight of blacks in the inner city is a subject

20. 8 F.3d 1222 (7th Cir. 1993). I admit to bias as the author of the court's opinion.
21. Nicholas Lemann, *The Promised Land: The Great Black Migration and How It Changed America* (1991).

of transcendent public significance, and a case study of individual blacks, while not the only and perhaps not the best method of illuminating the subject, is a valid method. It is no answer that the author could have used a pseudonym for Luther Haynes. Protecting Haynes's privacy securely would have required other changes of name as well— for example, changing Ruby Daniels's name—and perhaps changes in other details about him. Such changes would have converted the book from investigative journalism to sociological fiction, a worthy genre illustrated by *The Bonfire of the Vanities* (Chapter 23) but not the only worthwhile alternative to aggregative, impersonal social-science approaches to social history. And a fictionalized Luther Haynes might well be denounced as a degrading stereotype of black men.

The Promised Land has been widely praised by scholars, including distinguished black scholars.[22] Yet its publication would have been far more costly, and perhaps infeasible, if the black persons (by no means limited to Luther Haynes) whose past histories of discreditable conduct the book recounts had a right to obtain damages for the injury to their reputation, or at the least to force changes that would reduce the credibility and marketability of the book. It might seem that if the book in its uncensored state were *that* good it would have been profitable to publish even if the publisher had had to make good the Haynes's damages. But the publisher could not hope to capture the entire social value of the book in the price he charged for it, since other writers can use the ideas in it without having to pay for them—and can avoid liability for invasion of privacy simply by not mentioning the Hayneses.

The case might well have been decided differently if the book had disclosed intimate details of Luther Haynes's relationship with Ruby Daniels or his wife or other women. Such details would not have been germane to the book's theme or to Haynes's reputation. They would be neither newsworthy nor of value to potential transactors with Haynes, and their public disclosure would have been far more offensive, in part because of the gratuitousness of such disclosure. The book's treatment of Haynes is not titillating or voyeuristic.

A curious feature of all these privacy cases is that the decision to sue is an abandonment of the plaintiff's privacy, since facts reported in court records are, quite apart from the questionable but authoritative

---

22. Two cited in this book: Henry Louis Gates Jr. (Chapter 2) and Patricia Williams (Chapter 18).

holding in the *Cox* case, normally public. Readers of this book who happen not to have read the opinions in *Sidis, Cox, Melvin,* and *Haynes* have been made privy to the facts that the plaintiffs in these cases wanted concealed. To obtain an effective remedy, therefore, the successful plaintiff in a privacy case ought to be able to recover not only the primary damages inflicted by the publication but also the secondary damages resulting from the publicity that the case itself received or is likely in the future to receive. I am not aware of this point's having been noticed before, and the oversight may explain why there are so few privacy cases.

Kim Lane Scheppele has taken issue with an earlier version of my analysis of the privacy cases.[23] She thinks that as positive analysis—an attempt to explain the pattern of judicial decisions—it founders on *Melvin v. Reid* and the cases that follow it. But she cites only three cases that follow it. Two were decided under California law[24] in the wake of *Melvin* and are of equivalently doubtful validity after *Cox.* The third was a case in which a magazine published a photograph of a woman in a hospital bed. She had a rare disease that caused her to have an enormous appetite yet lose weight. The title of the accompanying article was "Starving Glutton."[25] The title was defamatory, since "gluttony" (one of the seven deadly sins) implies a character flaw rather than a disease. Furthermore, the name of the patient was irrelevant because the article was about the disease, not about her. In this respect the case was different from *Haynes* or, as Scheppele acknowledges, *Sidis.* And the article was not intended or likely to alert, say, an insurance company to which the woman might have applied for a life or health insurance policy without disclosing her affliction.

Scheppele argues that I have got the law exactly backwards, because courts award damages for the public disclosure of discreditable information about people *(Melvin)* but not for nondiscreditable information. But *Melvin* is, at best, a minority position in the law of privacy. And the only cases she cites for the proposition that courts do not award damages for the public disclosure of nondiscreditable informa-

23. Scheppele, *Legal Secrets: Equality and Efficiency in the Common Law* (1988), esp. ch. 13.

24. She is mistaken in saying (id. at 249) that Virgil v. Time, Inc., 527 F.2d 1122 (9th Cir. 1975), was not. A case brought in federal court under the diversity jurisdiction, the tort issues in it were governed by California law.

25. Barber v. Time, Inc., 159 S.W.2d 291 (Mo. 1942).

tion are cases in which, unlike the *Graham* case, the information was not embarrassing, so its disclosure would not have been highly offensive to the average person—for example, truthful information about pay raises that the plaintiff had received.[26]

She argues that a rule which strips people of legal protection of the secrecy of their newsworthy personal attributes or of their discreditable personal histories will cause people to expend additional resources on concealment, substituting self-help for legal remedies against invasions of their privacy. Those additional resources, which might be devoted to such things as changing one's name or place of residence or even undergoing cosmetic surgery, would be wasted from a social standpoint, as they would serve only to conceal newsworthy information and foster uninformed transacting. Evaluating this argument requires distinguishing between two types of case. In the first the individual has not done anything that he would have expected to evoke public curiosity. Sidis would not have expected to be written up in the *New Yorker*, or Haynes to be treated by the author of a best-selling book as a representative figure in the great black migration from South to North, or Cohn to be the father of a woman who was raped and murdered. Since such people do not expect to be publicized whatever the state of privacy law, they are unlikely to expend resources on securing their privacy more effectively. In the second type of case, well illustrated by *Melvin v. Reid*, a person has done just the sort of thing that evokes public curiosity; but the more she tries to conceal it, the better a "story" she creates. Mrs. Melvin would not have been remarkable had she not tried to conceal her past behind the mask of a virtuous housewife.

Blackmail

The most difficult question about the tort law of privacy is how to integrate it with the criminal law of blackmail; and blackmail is full of puzzles of its own. If Nicholas Lemann had gone to Luther Haynes and offered not to use his name in *The Promised Land* in exchange for $1,000, Lemann would have been guilty of the crime of blackmail. What sense does criminalizing such conduct make? An economic answer is that the suppression of the name would reduce the social value

26. Scheppele, note 23 above, at 250.

of the book. It might seem that the author would take that into account in setting his price for changing the blackmail victim's name. This would be true if the author could capture the full social value of the book in his royalties from its sale. But we have seen that he could not. Once *The Promised Land* is published, other students of the nation's racial problems can use its ideas and research without compensating the author. Allowing blackmail would reduce the social benefits of publication.

This analysis is fine as far as it goes but is incomplete, as it ignores the regulatory aspect of blackmail.[27] The payment of blackmail is often much like a fine, only paid to a private law enforcer (the blackmailer) rather than to the state. The analogy is particularly close when, as is common, the blackmailer is threatening to report a crime committed by the blackmail victim. But this is only a subset of blackmail cases. Haynes may have been subject to blackmail, but not because he was guilty of any conduct for which he might (thirty-odd years after the event) be prosecuted. In the case of the blackmailing of homosexuals, the conduct, whether or not nominally criminal, is, as we shall see in the next chapter, the manifestation of an involuntary condition,[28] which would not be altered by permitting blackmail. A person does not choose to be homosexual and would not unchoose even if there were no legal protection against being blackmailed. Of course people who blackmail homosexuals, or would do so if blackmail were legal, are rarely publishers, so the social cost of this blackmail does not consist in a reduction in newsworthy information. It consists in the expenditure of resources that have no social value because all they do is transfer wealth from one person (the blackmail victim) to another (the blackmailer). If blackmail were legal, homosexuals would devote increased resources to concealing their condition, would be more miserable, might even engage in forms of concealment that could be highly costly to third parties, such as (in the age of AIDS) heterosexual marriage; yet if I am correct that homosexual preference or orientation is innate, the number of homosexuals would not be reduced.[29] The misery and the efforts at concealment induced by blackmail would have no social

27. An explicit theme in Eric Ambler's thriller, *A Coffin for Dimitrios* (1939).

28. I am speaking of persons of homosexual orientation or preference, as distinct from "opportunistic" homosexuals; the distinction is explained in the next chapter. Both sorts might be blackmailed, of course.

29. All this is subject to the distinction in the previous footnote.

product. The blackmailing of criminals may conceivably reduce the crime rate; not so the blackmailing of people who have an involuntary condition.[30]

Regulatory blackmail is best illustrated by cases in which the blackmailer threatens to report his victim's crime to the police, who would be quite likely to prosecute the victim if they had the information which the blackmailer has threatened to turn over to them, but not otherwise. In such a case the blackmailer is a kind of supplemental law enforcer, and the payment of blackmail may be the only punishment for his victim's crime. So if blackmail were legal the crime rate might fall.

There is no completely adequate economic explanation for why such blackmail is illegal. It has been argued that legalizing blackmail might result in too much criminal law enforcement. But this could happen only if the blackmailer were permitted to prosecute, as well as to inform on, his victim if the latter refused to pay up. As long as the public prosecutor retains the authority not to prosecute, he not only controls the amount of law enforcement but can indirectly regulate the amount of blackmail, since the less likely a prosecution is the less a blackmail victim will be willing to pay his blackmailer and therefore the less blackmail there will be.

Another possible explanation for the illegality of regulatory blackmail is that legalizing it would raise the price that the public law enforcement authorities would have to pay for information. They would be competing with the blackmail victim; in effect the blackmailer would be auctioning off the incriminating information that he collected to the highest bidder. Police rely heavily on paid informants, who would charge more if they had an alternative market for their information. But against this must be weighed the expansion in the resources devoted to gathering information about criminals if blackmail were legal. The increase in the price of incriminating information would stimulate an expansion in supply, and the law enforcement authorities might be better off even if they had to pay a higher price per item of information.

Blackmail may be an example—uncongenial to either an economic or a pragmatic approach to law—of the law's developing through uncritical reasoning by analogy. The term "blackmail" originally referred to the use of threats of force to obtain money or other value.

---

30. Another example would be blackmailing a man who was impotent. Allowing such blackmailing would hardly be likely to reduce the incidence of impotence.

Blackmailing was thus a synonym for extortion. The prohibition of extortion is unproblematic. Not because the extortionist's victim yields to the threat "involuntarily"—a person who tenders his money in response to the robber's demand "your money or your life" is making a deliberate choice with full knowledge of the alternatives—but because most of us would prefer to live in a world in which we would not be subject to such demands. When however the threat is to do something that the threatener has a perfect right to do, such as reporting a crime, the case for prohibition is more problematic. In the subset of cases in which the threat has no regulatory potential—when its only purpose and effect are to transfer wealth from the victim to the threatener—the case for prohibition can again be made. In fact it resembles the case against simple extortion. Both are cases of sterile, in the sense of unproductive, wealth transfers, producing a net social loss measured by the value of the resources used to make and defend against such transfers.

But when the blackmailer is threatening to expose criminal or other misconduct for which the victim has not been punished, there is an additional and possibly beneficial consequence which the analogy to threats of force obscures. Suppose, to return to the example of the dishonest employee, that X is embezzling money from his employer, Y, and Z knows it. Z demands that X pay blackmail. If blackmail is legal, Z may be able to extract from X something very close to X's full profit from embezzlement. If so, embezzlement may be deterred. Of course it is possible that if blackmail is illegal Z will report X to Y; he may even try to charge Y for the information, which would be a legal transaction. Then again he may not. It is difficult to determine a priori whether allowing blackmail in such situations will make embezzlement less or more common. The law's insistence that a threat's a threat has retarded investigation of the likely consequences of authorizing blackmail as a supplement to public law enforcement.

A remarkable feature of blackmail as of privacy is that there are so few cases. I have been able to find only 124 reported American blackmail cases in the last century.[31] I am sure I have missed some and of course many successful prosecutions are never reported because there is no appeal, but when one considers that the total number of reported American cases in this period is in the millions, the paucity of my count

31. "Blackmail, Privacy, and Freedom of Contract," note 1 above, at 1841–1843.

is remarkable. My conjecture is that blackmail between strangers is rare, and blackmail between acquaintances common but largely undetectable. The latter point is the simpler. Blackmail, because illegal, is clandestine, informal, and unorganized. This makes it difficult for a blackmailer to obtain information about a stranger that the latter for obvious reasons will take pains to keep secret. Most blackmailers therefore are acquaintances of their victims, and in many of these cases the blackmailer and his victim have an ongoing relationship. In such a case the tacit communication of a blackmail demand is feasible, and the blackmail payment itself can take the form of a subtle, and often a nonpecuniary, adjustment in the terms of the relationship. Wives who know their husbands' guilty secrets are, I predict, better treated by their husbands; and this is, functionally but not legally, blackmail.

In the case of strangers, the transaction costs of blackmail are high because of its criminality. By making a blackmail demand, the blackmailer arms the victim with all the information the latter needs to report the blackmailer to the police. The victim knows, moreover, that should he do this the blackmailer probably will not carry out his threat to spill the beans, because if he does, the police, prosecutor, jury, and judge will regard this as an aggravating circumstance. The victim also knows that since blackmail is illegal and therefore clandestine, the blackmailer is unlikely to think that paying the added penalty for carrying out his threat is a worthwhile investment in developing a credible reputation as a blackmailer. If the victim is reasonably confident that the blackmailer will think through this sequence of moves correctly and decide not to retaliate if his bluff is called, the victim will call his bluff—though a complicating factor is that *after* the blackmailer has served his punishment there is nothing to prevent him from spilling the beans in revenge; this could be prevented only by attaching a postsentence condition prohibiting the blackmailer from ever doing so, on pain of further punishment. (A further impediment to blackmail is that in the absence of legal enforcement of blackmail contracts, the victim cannot be sure what exactly he is buying. His uncertainty will reduce the amount he is willing to pay and hence the frequency of blackmail.)

We should not expect this strategy to work in the rare case where the blackmailer has evidence not of some relatively minor peccadillo but of a major crime that the police are unlikely to ignore in their zeal to punish blackmailing. In such a case the victim's counterthreat to report the blackmail attempt to the police will not be credible. At the other extreme, blackmail is least likely to be attempted or succeed in the very case in which it is most objectionable from an economic standpoint because it has no potential regulatory function. That would be the case where the information possessed by the blackmailer is embarrassing rather than discreditable or, even if the latter, still is not likely to be altered by the possibility of blackmail. Although homosexuals have long feared blackmail and undoubtedly have been more frequent blackmail victims than heterosexuals, if my economic analysis is correct the amount of successful blackmailing of homosexuals is slight (or what is analytically similar, the average blackmail payment by homosexuals is low). The reason is that a homosexual who reports a blackmail attempt to the police is not in danger of being prosecuted for a crime. Knowing this, the blackmailer will also know that his blackmail attempt is quite likely to be reported, especially because once it is reported the blackmailer dare not carry out his threat to disclose his victim's secret, since if he does he will be punished more severely.

This discussion brings out an important qualification to the discussion of victimless crimes in Chapter 17. While such crimes are often very costly to control, this is not true when committing the crime requires a complex transaction. Although resources are devoted to enforcing the prohibition of blackmail, the delicacy of the negotiations required to effect a blackmail transaction as well as the difficulty the blackmailer has in selling a credible promise of silence apparently are enough to assure a low incidence of the crime provided only that the activity is driven underground by being criminalized. In much the same way, a law against cartels must greatly reduce the amount of price fixing even if enforcement of the law against secret price-fixing conspiracies is lackluster, since the making of effective price-fixing contracts, like the making of effective blackmail contracts, is difficult without legal protection.[32]

32. George J. Stigler, "The Economic Effects of the Antitrust Laws," in Stigler, *The Organization of Industry* 259, 269–270 (1968).

chapter 26

Economics and the Social Construction of Homosexuality

THERE is no more troubled field of law today than the regulation of sexual behavior, broadly understood. Whether the issue is abortion, gay rights, pornography, sexual harassment in the workplace, rape, the sexual abuse of children, surrogate motherhood, the treatment of transsexual prison inmates, or the legal response to AIDS and to births out of wedlock, not only are the courts deeply involved but, as I have argued in *Sex and Reason,* they have very little idea of what they are doing. Conventional legal reasoning carries them nowhere in this area, and the emotional and taboo character of the underlying phenomena makes common sense an unreliable guide.

What better area, then, in which to demonstrate the utility of a pragmatic, scientific, economic approach to law? To that task I dedicate this final chapter, in which I refine and extend the economic analysis of homosexuality presented in *Sex and Reason*[1] and relate that analysis to the debate between essentialist and social-constructionist theories of homosexuality.

1. See index references to "Homosexuality" and "Homosexuals." In the book, as in this chapter, I use the word "homosexuals" without pejorative intent, though I realize that most male homosexuals prefer to be called "gays."

The Approach Described and Applied

Homosexual preference and behavior. The basic assumption of economics, or at least of the brand of economics that I peddle, is instrumental rationality: the individual chooses the means that are most suitable, as a matter of both costs and benefits, to his ends, the latter usually being assumed to be given to him rather than freely chosen by him.[2] The choice of means need not be and often is not conscious, so there is no paradox in referring to rational choice by animals. Since emotion and reason are not necessarily antagonistic, there is also no paradox in supposing that sexual behavior, despite the intense emotions that precede and accompany it, may fruitfully be modeled as rational.

It is helpful to distinguish between sexual desire, comprehending both appetite and preference, and sexual behavior. Sexual desire consists of both drive (desire in the "push" sense) and attraction (desire in the "pull" sense), and determines ends in the means-ends sense. Sexual behavior is the menu of means. The more intense a person's sexual *appetite* is, the more he will value sexual activity in the sense of being willing to give up more of some other good in order to engage in it, while his sexual *preference* structure will affect the value he attaches to different forms and objects of sexual activity and also to variety in sexual partners. Appetite or drive thus primarily affects substitutability between sexual and nonsexual activities, while preference primarily affects substitutability among different sexual activities and partners. I assume that in general though not in every case men have a stronger sex drive than women and a greater taste for variety of sexual partners, by which I mean not a taste for bisexuality (though that may be true also) but a taste for multiple partners of the preferred sex. The empirical support for these assumptions, controversial though they are in feminist circles, is considerable, and there is a respectable although not conclusive biological theory that explains the empirical data.[3]

The difference between sexual desire and sexual behavior exposes an ambiguity in the concept of homosexuality. The concept could refer to

2. I do not suggest that instrumental rationality is the only tenable conception of rationality. See Robert Nozick, *The Nature of Rationality*, ch. 5 (1993).

3. On both points, see *Sex and Reason*, ch. 2; Richard Green, *Sexual Science and the Law* (1992); Simon LeVay, *The Sexual Brain* (1993); David M. Buss and David P. Schmitt, "Sexual Strategies Theory: An Evolutionary Perspective on Human Mating," 100 *Psychological Review* 204 (1993), esp. 210–212.

a preference, strong or weak, for same-sex relations, or alternatively to the fact of engaging in same-sex relations (whether often or seldom), or even to some combination of preference and behavior—maybe the only "real" homosexual is one who both prefers same-sex relations and acts on his preference.[4] There is no reason to insist on a single meaning for the word; the important thing is to make clear what one means by it in particular uses or contexts. For now, it is enough to note that in ordinary American English a "homosexual" is anyone who, other things being equal, prefers someone of the same sex as a sexual partner to someone of the opposite sex. In the language of economics, this "preference homosexual" will buy more same-sex than other-sex activity if the full price (comprehending nonpecuniary as well as pecuniary factors) is the same. The perfect bisexual would then be one who will buy the same amount of each type of sex if the full price is the same. When I use the term "homosexual" I shall mean a preference homosexual unless I indicate otherwise.

Emphasis on the distinction between homosexual *preference* and homosexual *behavior* may seem misplaced in an economic analysis. Economists are known for their distrust of people's declared motives and their consequent insistence on inferring preferences from behavior ("revealed preference," or putting one's money where one's mouth is). But my approach is consistent with the revealed-preference tradition.[5] Homosexual preference in my analysis is inferred not from what a person says about his sexual preferences but from the behavioral choices that he makes *when confronting an equal price for heterosexual and homosexual relations*. The empirical measurement of homosexual preference so defined is very difficult, but the conceptual focus on preference-revealing behavior is reasonably clear, though not perfectly so for reasons that should be obvious from the discussion of the "real self" in the preceding chapter.

4. Advocates of homosexual rights prefer the term "orientation" to "preference" because they think the latter connotes choice or mutability; and while many of them are made anxious by biological theories of homosexuality (recall Martha Ertman's reaction, discussed in Chapter 16) they deny that one chooses to be homosexual as one might choose to be a lawyer or a Methodist. I agree that homosexuality is not chosen, but as economists tend to take preferences as given rather than chosen (and to focus on choices given preferences), "preference" and "orientation" have similar connotations in an economic analysis of homosexuality.

5. Some economists believe that revealed-preference theory enables economics to dispense with the concepts of utility and utility maximizing. I do not think so, for reasons powerfully marshaled by Amartya Sen, in "Internal Consistency of Choice," 61 *Econometrica* 495 (1993), but the issue is not important to my analysis.

Homosexual preference as I am defining it is not uniform. Some people have a strong aversion to engaging in homosexual behavior; in my terms, they will avoid it even if it is much cheaper than heterosexual behavior. Other people have a strong aversion to engaging in heterosexual behavior. Kinsey devised a scale of zero to six to represent the range of homosexual preferences. A zero has only heterosexual preference, a six only homosexual preference. A three is a perfect bisexual, indifferent to the sex of his partner. Kinsey proxied preference by "fantasy": what kind of sexual relations do we (day)dream of having? Our fantasies reveal preferences that have a certain (though not the only or even primary) authenticity because they are not affected by costs and benefits stemming from our interactions with other people. They are in a rough sense presocial, biological preferences.

The preference spectrum probably is bimodal, in much the same way that "handedness" is bimodal. The vast majority of people are right-handed, a small minority are left-handed, and a tiny minority are ambidextrous, yet some right-handed people can write with their left hand without too much difficulty while some left-handed people can write with their right hand without much difficulty. If there is strong social pressure to write with the right hand, most left-handed people can learn to do so, but they will never be comfortable. Similarly, the vast majority of people appear to have a strong heterosexual preference, although some of them regard a homosexual relationship as somewhat substitutable for a heterosexual one. A small minority, probably no more than 4 percent of males and 2 percent of females (and possibly smaller),[6] have a strong homosexual preference but again some of these

6. *Sex and Reason* 294–295. Even lower estimates are suggested by recent large-scale sex surveys in England and France, summarized in ACSF Investigators, "AIDS and Sexual Behaviour in France," 360 *Nature* 407 (1992), and Anne M. Johnson et al., "Sexual Lifestyles and HIV Risk," 360 *Nature* 410 (1992); by a substantial new survey of American men, John O. G. Billy et al., "The Sexual Behavior of Men in the United States," 25 *Family Planning Perspectives* 52, 59–60 (1993); and by preliminary data from a large sex survey being conducted by a group at the University of Chicago headed by Edward Laumann of the sociology department. A comprehensive review of the data from sex surveys concludes that "only about 2–3% of sexually active men and 1–2% of sexually active women are currently homosexual." Tom W. Smith, "American Sexual Behavior: Trends, Socio-Demographic Differences, and Risk Behavior," p. 6 (National Opinion Research Center, University of Chicago, GSS Topical Rep. 25, Version 1.2, Oct. 18, 1993); see also id. at 33 (tab. 8). The usual objection to inferring the percentage of homosexuals from surveys is that "closeted" homosexuals will conceal their sexual preference from however skilled an interviewer. If so, this would imply that the more tolerant the society, the larger the percentage of homosexuals that would be revealed by surveys. There is no such relation. In fact, surveys of sexual practices in the

consider a heterosexual relationship substitutable although inferior. The number of people who are bisexual in the sense of regarding male and female sexual partners as being of essentially the same desirability, or even closely substitutable, apparently is very small.

In an economic analysis, the values, shaped in part by location on the Kinsey scale, that people place on the various ends of sex, such as pleasure, cementing a relationship, disguising one's sexual preference, establishing, expressing, or reinforcing dominance, and producing children, determine, along with the different costs of the different kinds of sexual behavior, the amount and kinds of that behavior that people engage in. Obviously a man who has a strong homosexual preference will set a high value on homosexual relations. But if threat of punishment, religious scruples, fear of disease or of social ostracism, or desire for children causes the expected cost of such relations to exceed the expected benefit, he may, despite his preference, substitute heterosexual for homosexual relations. Or he may decide to forgo all sexual relations.

Imagine a society which is intolerant of homosexuals and in which AIDS is rampant. (Some might think this an accurate description of our society.) A man who had a strong homosexual desire might nonetheless engage in a certain amount of heterosexual intercourse because he wanted children, because he wanted to pose as a heterosexual in order to avoid the social stigma and occupational and other economic discrimination that might be visited on a known homosexual, because AIDS made his preferred form of homosexual intercourse (for example, anal intercourse without condoms) too costly, or because repression made it costly for him to find other homosexuals with whom to have a relationship. Yet even in such a society a person of strong *hetero*sexual preference might sometimes engage in *homo*sexual behavior if he had a strong sex drive (implying a preference for another sexual activity, rather than a nonsexual activity, as a substitute for a most-preferred sexual activity that is unavailable) and if the cost of heterosexual intercourse were very high, as it might be if he were confined to a sexually segregated institution such as a naval ship or a prison.

Scandinavian countries, which are more tolerant of homosexuality than the United States is, reveal a lesser frequency of homosexual behavior than the U.S. survey data do. The Scandinavian data are summarized in Mads Melbye and Robert J. Biggar, "Interactions between Persons at Risk for AIDS and the General Population in Denmark," 135 *American Journal of Epidemiology* 593, 600 (1992).

Formally, a homosexual act will be chosen over a heterosexual one if

$$(B_1 - C_1) > 0, \quad (B_1 - C_1) > (B_2 - C_2), \tag{1}$$

where B_1 and B_2 are the benefits of the homosexual and the heterosexual act, respectively, to a particular person and C_1 and C_2 are the respective costs to him. The reason for the first condition is that if the net benefit of the homosexual act, though greater than that of the heterosexual act, is zero or negative, the person will choose abstinence (the no-sexual-costs, no-sexual-benefits alternative) instead.

The second condition in (1) can be rewritten as

$$(B_1 - B_2) > (C_1 - C_2). \tag{2}$$

This helps us see that even if a person prefers, say, a homosexual to a heterosexual act, if the cost of the former is greater (perhaps because of threat of punishment or because he wants to have children) he may substitute the heterosexual act unless his aversion to it is very great. For example, let B_1 and B_2 be 10 and 5 respectively, and C_1 and C_2 9 and 1 respectively. Then even though the person prefers the homosexual act both to abstinence (because $(B_1 - C_1) > 0$) and to the heterosexual act (because $B_1 > B_2$), he will engage in the heterosexual act because $B_1 - B_2 = 5$ is less than $C_1 - C_2 = 8$, or equivalently, from inequality (1), because the net benefit of the homosexual act, $B_1 - C_1 = 1$, is less than that of the heterosexual act, $B_2 - C_2 = 4$.

The economic approach to homosexuality yields interesting, testable, and to some extent supported hypotheses about homosexual behavior. The most dramatic is the well-substantiated substitution of safe sex for unsafe sex by male homosexuals in the wake of the AIDS epidemic.[7] The cost of unsafe sex having risen, there was substitution toward safe sex—a greater use of condoms in anal intercourse, a reduction in the average number of sexual partners per male homosexual, a tendency to substitute relatively safe activities such as oral intercourse and mutual masturbation for anal intercourse, which (if unshielded) is much more likely to transmit the AIDS virus. Safe sex is not a perfect substitute

---

7. For discussion and references, see Tomas J. Philipson and Richard A. Posner, *Private Choices and Public Health: The AIDS Epidemic in an Economic Perspective*, ch. 2 (1993).

for unsafe sex even when it is perfectly safe. If it were, we would expect not only complete rather than partial substitution of safe for unsafe sex, but also that the substitution would have occurred *before* the AIDS epidemic, since other sexually transmitted diseases were already rampant among homosexuals. Since safe sex must therefore be perceived by homosexuals as costly, we should expect that AIDS has caused not only some substitution toward safe sex but also some reduction in the amount of homosexual sex, though not as great a reduction as would occur if safe sex were not an option. One alternative to homosexual sex is abstinence and another is heterosexual sex (see inequality [1]), so the more costly homosexual sex becomes, the more abstinence and heterosexual sex we should expect.

A major determinant of rational homosexual behavior is sexual search cost, the cost of matching up with a suitable sexual partner. It is not just an information cost. If it were, it would be zero rather than, in my use of the term, infinite if a person were confined in a place where he knew there were no potential sexual partners for him.

The concept of sexual search cost is helpful in explaining why homosexuals are concentrated in cities, and not all cities but usually just one or several per country, depending on the size.[8] If homosexuals were distributed proportionately equally rather than concentrated in a small number of locales, the cost of search would be very high because the fraction of the total population that is homosexual is so small. To take an extreme example, a man might be the only homosexual in his village, so that to find a sexual partner of his preferred type he would have to incur substantial time and travel costs. These costs are greatly reduced if homosexuals cluster in a few places where, because of their concentration, there is a large homosexual population to search over.

Maybe the example is too simple. For if the village has two homosexuals, would not each be as well off as he would be in a city that had a large homosexual population? Although he would have many more potential sexual partners to choose from in the city, he would face much greater competition there for the sexual partner of his choice. This assumes, however, what is always perilous in dealing with male sexuality, indifference to variety in sexual partners. (And we should therefore expect less geographic concentration of lesbians than of gay men, since

8. For empirical evidence, see ACSF Investigators, note 6 above, at 408; Johnson et al., note 6 above, at 411.

women, including lesbians, have on average less taste for variety of sexual partners.)[9] A more important point is that experience with the dating, cohabiting, and marriage markets suggests that a satisfactory matching of sexual partners requires search across a large sample of possible partners because of the highly idiosyncratic character of persons when viewed as candidates for an intimate relationship. If so, the effect of a concentrated population of homosexuals in reducing search costs is likely to dominate the costs of increased competition. Of course much homosexual (also heterosexual) sex is of the "spot market" kind—the anonymous encounter in the restroom, or with a prostitute—and here the relational aspect is minimized. But anonymous sex implies a large number of potential sexual partners, for which a large concentration of the relevant population is necessary.

Suppose, however, that as a consequence of low search costs in cities in which homosexuals are concentrated the homosexuals in those cities pair off in couples, leaving few unattached homosexuals for newcomers to date. Then the opportunities for the newcomers might not be much better than in the small towns from which they had come. But because men have a greater desire for variety of sexual partners than women do, male homosexual couples tend to be less stable than heterosexual (or lesbian) couples.[10] This may be changing as a result of AIDS, which has raised the cost, especially to (male) homosexuals, of having multiple sexual partners. We might therefore expect that large cities would be losing some of their attractiveness to homosexuals. Another benefit of city life for homosexuals is that it is easier to escape detection in a big city. So we can expect that tolerant societies have less geographic imbalance in their homosexual population than intolerant ones do, since the benefits of concealing homosexual preference are smaller in tolerant societies.

The concept of sexual search costs may help explain why many homosexuals have an "effeminate" manner—a gait, posture, speech, mannerisms, or style of dressing recognizably distinct from the corresponding ensemble for the "straight" man. Women are easily distinguishable from men even in casual encounters because of gross physical differences especially of shape and voice. But homosexuals are not easy to distinguish from their heterosexual counterparts, so the adoption of

9. See note 3 above; also Chapter 16 and *Sex and Reason* 91–92.
10. See *Sex and Reason* 305–307.

a distinctive manner[11] enables sexual preference to be signaled (as in a memorable passage in Proust, describing the first meeting between Charlus and Jupien), thus reducing the costs of homosexual search. The signal is not entirely clear, because some heterosexual men are effeminate.[12] But the unclarity may actually be valuable to homosexuals in a repressive society, because then "straights" cannot be certain that an effeminate man is a homosexual. This point suggests the possibility that there might be less, rather than (as one might expect) more, effeminacy in a tolerant society than in an intolerant one.

The substitutability of sexual practices is often ignored in discussions of public policy, for example policy toward AIDS. Conservatives, observing that homosexuals and bisexuals are a major source for transmission of the disease in the United States and other Western nations, suppose that measures to repress homosexuality would reduce the spread of the disease. That is not clear. One effect of such repression would be to increase the benefits of (heterosexual) marriage to persons of homosexual preference, since such marriage both facilitates the concealment of homosexual preference and provides an alternative sexual outlet that is more desirable the more costly the preferred alternative of homosexual relations is made. Consistent with this hypothesis, it appears that homosexuals are in fact more likely to marry in repressive than in tolerant societies.[13] A married homosexual may engage in homosexual relations on the side, contract AIDS, and transmit it to his wife—especially since his proposing that they have safe sex could be a tip-off to his double life. From the standpoint of controlling AIDS, therefore, it might make sense to legalize homosexual marriage, which by lowering the cost of durable homosexual pairing off would reduce homosexual promiscuity, a factor in the rapid spread of AIDS in the homosexual community.

A related point is that a reduction in the social stigma of homosexuality would reduce the incentive of homosexuals to cluster in cities, where they can form their own insulated communities. The concentration of a potentially infective population, unless the concentration

11. Not necessarily an effeminate one. Other methods of signaling homosexual preference have become as or more common, such as leather clothes and bandanas. See, for example, "Clothing," 1 *Encyclopedia of Homosexuality* 246 (Wayne R. Dynes ed. 1990).

12. Which suggests, by the way, that having an effeminate manner is not entirely voluntary.

13. Michael W. Ross, *The Married Homosexual Man: A Psychological Study* 110–111 and tab. 11.1 (1983).

results from or has the effect of quarantining that population, can accelerate the spread of a disease by increasing the number of persons exposed to it. Concentrating the homosexual population reduces the search cost of homosexuals who desire sex with multiple sex partners, a recognized risk factor for AIDS; encouraging that population to disperse (encouragement that homosexual marriage might provide) would therefore reduce homosexual promiscuity and with it the spread of the epidemic.

Some conservatives who are concerned about the AIDS epidemic support the laws, found in about half the states of the United States, criminalizing sodomy. They believe that these laws reduce the number of homosexual acts. Economics can help us see that a more realistic goal of policy would be to forbid only those homosexual acts that are likely to transmit AIDS. Although historically "sodomy" meant anal intercourse, most American sodomy statutes explicitly forbid oral as well as anal intercourse and impose the same penalty on both practices. (Hardwick of *Bowers v. Hardwick* fame had been caught engaging in oral, not anal, intercourse and charged with sodomy.) This is a mistake. Homosexuals should be encouraged to substitute oral for anal intercourse, because it is very difficult to transmit the AIDS virus by oral sex. For the same reason they should be encouraged to substitute anal intercourse with condoms for anal intercourse without—yet both are punishable with equal severity under the existing sodomy laws.

Although if sodomy laws are to be retained they should be confined to unshielded anal intercourse, in order, as I have said, to channel homosexual behavior into safer forms, the economic case for their retention is very weak. As with other consensual crimes, the costs of enforcement are very high—so high that the sodomy laws are virtually unenforced. And cost is not the only factor; public support for criminalizing voluntary sexual relations between adults, even when the relations are homosexual, is weak. The benefits of an unenforced law are low, and here probably negative; the sodomy laws contribute to an atmosphere of hostility toward homosexuals that undermines efforts to contain the AIDS epidemic, for the reasons noted above.

Were sodomy laws enforced, they would impose heavy costs on homosexuals, much as forbidding vaginal intercourse would with respect to heterosexuals. Because of AIDS and other serious sexually transmitted diseases, characteristic homosexual practices such as unshielded anal intercourse impose external costs, by increasing the risk of disease to future sexual partners (and to *their* future sexual partners) of a person who might become infected through such practices. Hence an act of homosexual intercourse, even when between fully competent and consenting adults, cannot be considered Pareto-superior to the no-intercourse case because it does not make at least one person in the world better off *and* no one worse off. But since sexually transmitted diseases are preventable at moderate cost by safe sex, it is unlikely that a policy of banning homosexual intercourse, even if such a policy were enforceable at reasonable cost, would increase social welfare in the economic sense, which emphasizes the satisfaction of preferences. A more direct way of dealing with the externality problem, and a method now employed by a number of states, is to criminalize the knowing exposure of one's sexual partners to the AIDS virus.

Opportunistic homosexuality. I noted that persons of predominantly heterosexual preference may nevertheless engage in homosexual behavior when the cost of heterosexual behavior is prohibitive. We should not be surprised, therefore, that preference heterosexuals in prisons, navies and merchant marines, monasteries, boarding schools, and other sexually segregated institutions frequently resort to homosexual acts because their heterosexual opportunities are highly limited or even nonexistent. Preferring as they do heterosexual to homosexual sex, these "opportunistic" homosexuals like to play the insertive role in oral and anal intercourse because that is closer to the male role in heterosexual sex, and they prefer teenage boys to grown men because the former are physically more like women, being, typically, smaller and more delicate than grown men and having less body hair, softer skin, and higher-pitched voices. In other words these men seek, in good economizing fashion, the closest possible substitute that they can find for their preferred, but prohibitively costly, sexual activity.

We should distinguish among sexually segregated institutions along the dimension of voluntariness. Imprisonment is involuntary.[14] Becoming a priest is voluntary. (Service on naval ships is sometimes involuntary, more often voluntary.) We should therefore expect a higher fraction of priests than of prisoners to be persons of predominantly homosexual preference. The cost of being denied heterosexual oppor-

14. Well, not entirely, because a person who chooses a criminal over a legitimate career may be said to assume the risk of imprisonment.

tunities is lower for such persons than it is for persons of predominantly heterosexual preference, so the former are more likely to self-select into a career in which heterosexual opportunities are reduced. It is true that in medieval Europe, boys were frequently steered into the priesthood, and girls into nunneries, by their parents, rather than choosing freely. Yet the selection bias described above might still operate. Suppose, as was common among medieval families from which priests and nuns were recruited, that dowries were demanded in marriage. Then fathers of teenage girls would tend to steer the less marriageable girls into nunneries, because such girls would require larger dowries; and among these less marriageable girls lesbians would probably be overrepresented, since some lesbians have a "masculinate" manner that is unattractive to men. Likewise, fathers of boys would tend to steer their less marriageable sons into the priesthood, because these boys, among whom homosexuals would tend to be overrepresented, would not do well in competing for brides with large dowries.

Since, however, homosexual acts are more disapproved within the clerical community than within the prison subculture, the frequency of homosexual acts may be greater in prisons than among priests at the same time that the fraction of persons with a predominantly homosexual preference is larger among the latter. This point illustrates the difference between homosexual preference and homosexual behavior—indeed, in this example the two phenomena are correlated negatively.

Signaling is important to an understanding of homosexuality in the American Catholic priesthood today. Because priests are not permitted to marry, the priesthood is a good place for a homosexual to "hide"; his status as a bachelor is less likely to be taken as evidence of homosexuality than if he were permitted to marry. Many bachelors, of course, are heterosexual. But because the fraction of bachelors who are homosexual is higher than the fraction of married men who are homosexual, bachelorhood is often considered evidence of possible homosexuality. (Notice that as the marriage rate declines in a society, this signal becomes weaker.) As a society becomes more tolerant of homosexuality, so that the benefit of the closet declines, the percentage of homosexual priests will decline; likewise, of course, if the priesthood were opened to married men.

The sexually segregated institution is one illustration of the proposition that the prevalence of homosexual behavior is an inverse function of the sexual availability of women to men. Here is another. There is more competition for women in a polygamous society[15] than in a monogamous one. In a polygamous society, men are not limited to a single wife. The result is a scarcity of women, particularly for younger men, who on average have fewer resources with which to obtain a wife. We should therefore expect opportunistic homosexuality to be greater, other things being equal, in a polygamous than in a monogamous society and to take the form primarily of pederasty, that is, a sexual relationship between a man and a boy. That is the form of homosexual behavior preferred by persons of predominantly heterosexual preference because, as I said, boys are more like women than grown men are. Moreover, we expect the pederasts in the polygamous society to be found primarily among young rather than older men, because it is the former who cannot afford wives.

Female prostitution, it is true, would be an alternative to pederasty as a way of meeting the sexual demands of bachelors. But in a polygamous society women are costly because of their scarcity relative to the demand, so prostitution is likely to be expensive. In an economic sense, the cost of prostitution includes the opportunity that the woman gives up by being a prostitute. The more she is in demand as a wife, the more she gives up by becoming a prostitute, so the higher is the compensation she will demand for becoming one. Of course if there is slavery the price of prostitutes may plummet; female slaves are a close substitute for prostitutes.

Even a monogamous society may have an imbalance in favor of women that, by driving up the price of heterosexual (including marital) sex, increases the demand for what I am calling opportunistic homosexuality. In ancient Athens the widespread practice of female infanticide and the sequestration of nubile girls in order to satisfy the demand for virgin brides limited the access of young bachelors of the citizen class to sexual partners of the same class but opposite sex. One is therefore not surprised that pederasty (as celebrated for example in Plato's dialogues on love) appears to have been common in the citizen class.[16] But perhaps one *should* be surprised, because prostitution was

---

15. Technically, in a polygynous society, that is, one in which men are permitted to have more than one wife but women are not permitted to have more than one husband. The vast majority of polygamous societies are polygynous.

16. See *Sex and Reason* 38–45 and the references cited there—especially K. J. Dover, *Greek Homosexuality* (2d ed. 1989).

also common, making the situation unlike that of a polygamous society, a prison, a naval vessel, and other familiar sites of opportunistic homosexuality, where access to women is prohibitively costly. There were also many female slaves. Prostitutes and slaves, however, were foreign or lower-class women and so could not fully satisfy the romantic longings of the young men of the citizen class; consistent with this point, Platonic and other ancient Greek pederastic literature emphasizes the mental and spiritual aspect of the pederastic relationships rather than the physical, though this emphasis may contain a large measure of rationalization. And while many men today, and doubtless in ancient Athens as well, would not consider any sort of boy a substitute for any sort of woman, we have no reason to suppose that pederasty was universal among the citizen class in Athens or even that it was a dominant social practice—only that it was more common than it is in a society such as ours in which girls are not killed at birth or sequestered until marriage. A further point is that in the citizen class of ancient Athens marriage was characteristically a relationship between radically unequal persons—an older man, educated, active in the world, and a young woman (often a teenage girl), uneducated and home-bound— and that this inequality, exemplified by the fact that Athenian husbands and wives were not expected to take any of their meals together and that child tending was considered a task for male slaves rather than for the child's mother, must have reduced the affective value of marriage and may thereby have shifted the focus of romantic theorizing to socially more equal relationships. One of these was the relationship between a young bachelor and his *gymnasium* boy lover.

Yet with all these points granted, the puzzle of widespread pederasty in a society in which prostitutes were plentiful and cheap persists. If a *companionate* relation sealed by sex was sought (for which a relationship with a prostitute would not be a close substitute), why didn't the young bachelors pair up with each other, rather than chase boys?[17] One can easily imagine opportunistic homosexuality between men of the same age and status emerging in a society, such as that of ancient Athens, in which men were considered superior to women. From such a premise it would be natural to infer that relationships among men are superior to relationships between men and women (and *a fortiori*

---

17. I consider and reject a possible noneconomic answer to that question at the end of this chapter.

between women and women—the Greeks thought lesbianism unnatural) and that the relationship could be completed, sealed, perfected by physical intimacy, like the exchange of blood in a "blood brotherhood." There is a demand for companionate relationships; and sex, as I argue in *Sex and Reason,* can cement such a relationship. If companionship with women is infeasible, men will substitute companionship with men and may cement it with sex. Endowed as they are with a superfluity of procreative capacity, many men are sufficiently sexually indiscriminate to incur little cost from the eroticization of the male bond. On this interpretation the very absence of companionate marriage and other forms of companionate relationships with women increases male bonding, and male bonding is incipiently or potentially homoerotic because of the function of sex in sealing relationships.

This analysis points to homosexual relations between men of the same age, not to pederasty. Yet the latter appears to have been the dominant form of opportunistic homosexuality in the ancient Greek world. If same-sex relations are more pleasurable for a heterosexual man when the sexual object is boyish and therefore more like a woman, he will trade off this benefit of pederasty against the companionate benefit of a more equal relation and may therefore choose the former. Plato's *Symposium* suggests, however, that for some men in ancient Greece the companionate benefit of equal-age same-sex relationships exceeded the sexual cost.[18]

Another causal factor in Athenian pederasty may have been male rivalrousness.[19] Men compete for women, both to spread their seed and to establish a hierarchy of power. Competitive masculinity is a dimension of sexuality different from companionship but also missing from relations with prostitutes. Athenian-style pederasty provided an outlet for this aspect of male sexual desire, as does homosexual activity among normally homophobic black inmates of modern American prisons. Competitive homosexuality is a theory of Athenian pederasty distinct from that of reproducing social hierarchy, which I discuss later. The focus here is not the relative position of man (lover) and boy (beloved)—the *erastes* and the *eromenos*—but the relative position of the competing men.

18. Achilles and Patroclus, in the *Iliad,* may illustrate this kind of homoerotic relationship. Eva Cantarella, *Bisexuality in the Ancient World* 10–11 (1992).

19. The competitive aspect of Greek sexuality is emphasized in John J. Winkler, *The Constraints of Desire: The Anthropology of Sex and Gender in Ancient Greece,* chs. 2–3 (1990).

Given the salience of pederasty in Athenian culture, or at least in elite circles of that culture, it may seem curious that the ancient Greeks lacked a distinct idea of homosexuality in the modern American sense, that is, as a strong preference for same-sex over opposite-sex relations. (Similarly, men in "macho" societies will frequently deny that there are *any* homosexuals in their society.) There are two reasons for the difference; both support the economic approach. First, the more common opportunistic homosexuality is, the less likely people are to be aware of the existence of homosexual preference. Opportunistic homosexuals, remember, are persons of heterosexual rather than homosexual preference. Since preference homosexuals appear to be a small minority in all societies, homosexual behavior in a society in which opportunistic homosexuality is common will tend to be dominated by persons of heterosexual rather than of homosexual preference, making the latter inconspicuous. Second, the emotional distance in the average Athenian marriage would have reduced the cost to preference homosexuals of marrying, since they could fulfill their (meager) marital duties at low cost to themselves.[20] With homosexuals able to fit smoothly into the basic institution of the society, their homosexual preference lacked social significance—was unremarkable and therefore unremarked, much like left-handedness today.

With the rise of companionate marriage, conceived of as marriage between at least approximate equals, homosexuals found it more costly to marry; marriage now involved a degree of intimacy difficult to achieve without a bond of mutual sexual desire. Companionate marriage tends to extrude what I am calling preference homosexuals from a basic social institution, namely marriage, making them more conspicuous and thus for the first time riveting public attention on the existence of a class of persons whose sexual preferences differ from those of the majority. A further point is that adultery is a more serious offense in a regime of companionate marriage, and homosexual activity by a married man is a form of adultery.

It may seem odd that until almost the end of the Victorian era, men whom we today would call homosexuals tended to be thought of as normal men of unbridled appetite. But in a society that placed a high premium on virginity and hence tended to the sequestration and sexual

20. See, for example, Cantarella, note 18 above, at 90. Most homosexual men are capable of having full intercourse with women (that is, are capable of penetration and ejaculation), even if they don't enjoy it. *Sex and Reason* 100–101.

anesthetization of marriageable (and married) women, many men of strong sexual appetite would lack adequate heterosexual outlets and some of them would turn to homosexual sex (others of course to female prostitutes). These men would differ from ordinary heterosexuals only in tending to have more intense sexual appetites and—a closely related point—to lack "self-control" (because the stronger an impulse is, the costlier it is to repress it). Because Victorian like ancient Athenian marriages were often deficient in intimacy, men of homosexual preference like Oscar Wilde could have successful or at least unremarkable marriages. Once again, awareness that there was a class of men of distinctly homosexual preference was muted. The salient category was sodomites, not homosexuals.

I have been discussing the demand of the opportunistic homosexual for a woman substitute, but one must also consider the demand of the preference homosexual for male sex partners whether or not themselves preference homosexuals. I conjecture that a handsome heterosexual man will have, on average, more homosexual experience (opportunistic on his side) than a heterosexual man who is not handsome. Men, whether heterosexual or homosexual, attach more value to good looks in a sexual partner than women do. So a handsome man will have more of a competitive advantage over homely men in the homosexual than in the heterosexual sex market.

Lesbianism. I have thus far focused almost entirely on *male* homosexuals. I shall not apologize for failing to give equal time to both sexes, and not only because I have discussed lesbianism already, in Chapter 16. Male homosexual activity and preference as well appear to be far more common than female homosexual activity and preference and have far more often been the subject of punishment. Moreover, male homosexuality has been made socially problematic by the AIDS epidemic in a way that lesbianism has not—lesbian relations do not transmit the AIDS virus. But economics does have something to say about lesbianism. As with male homosexuality, we should expect the relative costs of heterosexual and homosexual behavior to affect the relative prevalence of these behaviors among women of homosexual preference. Since prostitutes have difficulty forming durable, emotionally adequate relationships with men, it is no surprise that lesbianism is common among prostitutes.[21] Whether, overall, opportunistic homosexuality is

---

21. See *Sex and Reason* 179.

likely to be more common among women than among men is difficult to say. On the one hand, since the demand for sex appears to be on average weaker among women than among men, women are less likely to encounter the problem of unavailability of preferred sexual outlets and therefore are less likely to substitute a less preferred outlet. On the other hand, precisely because the demand for sex is on average weaker among women than among men, we can expect women to be readier to substitute toward same-sex relations if there are nonsexual reasons to do so. Together these two points suggest the following pair of testable hypotheses: the "sexual revolution" of the 1960s and 1970s, by expanding the heterosexual opportunities of women (in part by reducing the cost of sex to women—the contraceptive pill being the key factor in this cost reduction), reduced the amount of opportunistic lesbianism; the feminist movement of the 1970s and 1980s (and continuing into the 1990s), by fostering female hostility toward men, has increased the amount of opportunistic lesbianism.

Normative analysis. Although I have now broadened my canvas to take in lesbianism, the focus has remained on positive rather than normative economic analysis—on explaining phenomena rather than on changing public policy, though I veered into the latter subject when I was discussing AIDS-actuated public policies toward male homosexuality. Economics has value in the normative as well as the positive analysis of sex. Although I have already discussed homosexual marriage, I want to add that an economic analyst, at least one of free-market bent, is unlikely to place much emphasis on expanding so heavily regulated an institution as marriage. It is true that modern marriage is a matter of free choice and is dissoluble almost as easily as a contract of partnership. But the contracting parties' freedom is constrained because the married couple is not permitted to make a legally enforceable agreement on all the terms, including duration and the consequences of dissolution, of their "contract." There is an economic argument for deregulating marriage, thereby transforming it in the direction of cohabitation contracts, where the parties choose their own terms. The strong statement of commitment implicit in a decision to marry under the present legal regime for marriage would yield to an equally strong, if not indeed stronger, commitment implicit in a decision to marry, or (if one wants to reserve the term "marriage" for the familiar, regulated institution) cohabit, under a contract terminable only by death, serious wrongdoing, or other dramatic change of circumstance. There would have to be protective provisions for children in any potentially procreative union. But with that important proviso (of limited but, because of the possibility of adoption and of artificial insemination, not negligible applicability to homosexual unions as well as heterosexual ones), I would be unworried by an evolution from status to contract,[22] resulting in an essentially uniform treatment for homosexual and heterosexual relationships.

Other important issues of public policy toward homosexuality include job discrimination, with specific reference to the exclusion of homosexuals from the military; child custody; and age of consent (in this country invariably higher for homosexual than for heterosexual relations, in those states that do not forbid homosexual intercourse). Again the economic perspective is helpful but, even more clearly than before, not decisive. I have already discussed, in reference to AIDS, the issue of retaining the sodomy laws. I shall further illustrate normative economic analysis of homosexuality with the ban on homosexuals in the armed forces,[23] leaving the other topics to the discussion in *Sex and Reason*.

Apart from symbolic issues and (what is closely related) the implications for the self-esteem and social acceptance of homosexuals generally, there are two obvious costs of the ban. First, to the extent enforced it reduces the field of selection, thus forcing the government to pay higher wages or other compensation to military personnel because there is less competition for positions; in other words, the ban reduces the supply of applicants for military jobs, although, in part because the ban was porous even before the recent modification, probably not by much. More important are the costs of enforcing the ban; they are not trivial. There is, however, a potentially offsetting benefit: to the extent that heterosexuals do not want to serve beside homosexuals, the removal of the ban would increase military personnel costs; the government would have to pay higher wages to hire and retain heterosexual personnel. This effect, which need not be completely offset by the greater supply of potential recruits from the homosexual population,

22. To economize on transaction costs, couples might be offered a menu of fixed contracts to choose among, much as people choose among health or retirement plans. Presumably a couple could customize one of the forms to its particular needs, if none of the forms seemed quite right for it and it was prepared to bear the additional transaction costs.

23. The ban has been modified. The extent to which the modification signifies a real change in military policy toward homosexuals and lesbians is unclear, and I will not speculate on the question.

implies that even if the leadership of the Department of Defense had no hostile feelings toward homosexuals, and indeed believed (as it well may) that they make just as good soldiers as heterosexuals do, it might continue the ban in order to minimize overall personnel costs, in just the same way that were it not for the laws forbidding racial discrimination in employment, a nonbigoted employer might refuse to hire blacks because his white workers would demand a wage premium for incurring the perceived disutility of working in proximity to blacks. The very symmetry between these hypothetical arguments for racial discrimination and for discrimination against homosexuals will for many people condemn the latter form of discrimination without regard to economic considerations. But I wish to abstract from other considerations.[24]

Which means that I also want to abstract from the question whether the relaxation of the ban against homosexuals in the military would reduce operational effectiveness by impairing the morale of heterosexuals. That is an issue, in the first instance at least, of military science rather than of economics, and I will not try to address it here. I have merely pointed out that even if the issue were ignored, there would be an economic argument for retaining the ban although other arguments might outweigh it. I conclude that economic analysis does not tell us whether, on balance, the ban on homosexuals in the military should be retained or abolished.

This is a general point about the economic analysis of sexual practices. Suppose it is the case—it is the case in this country today—that there is a large reservoir of apparently unreasoning fear of and hostility toward homosexuals, so that many people would derive utility from measures to repress homosexual activity. Should that utility be weighed equally with the utility that homosexuals derive from homosexual activity, in deciding whether repressive measures are efficient? The answer to that question is "no" for those who, like John Stuart Mill or Ronald Dworkin, reject, as illegitimate sources of public policy, what Mill called preferences with regard to the "self-regarding" conduct of other people and Dworkin calls "external preferences." That is my position too, but to defend it, as I tried to do in *Sex and Reason*, would carry me outside

24. I take a broader view of the issue in *Sex and Reason* 314–323. For background to the debate over homosexuals in the armed services, see Jeffrey S. Davis, "Military Policy toward Homosexuals: Scientific, Historical, and Legal Perspectives," 131 *Military Law Review* 55 (1991).

the boundaries of economics as they are generally, even generously, understood today.

Economics and the Social Construction of Sexuality

I promised to relate the economic analysis of homosexuality to the debate between essentialists and social constructionists over the nature of homosexuality. There are two arenas of debate. The first and less important concerns whether homosexual preference is more or less fixed or innate, on the one hand, or a matter of choice on the other. There is increasing evidence that the strong homosexual preference that marks a person in our society as a homosexual or a lesbian is probably genetic, if not genetic congenital, if neither then the product of physical or psychological factors impinging on persons in their infancy.[25] It is of no importance to my economic analysis which it is. The analysis would be affected if homosexual preference, like homosexual behavior, were chosen. But that now seems extraordinarily unlikely.

Although many homosexual-rights advocates resist, primarily it seems on political grounds,[26] genetic and other biological theories of homosexuality, few of them claim that homosexual preference is something one adopts or cultivates, as one might cultivate a taste for classical music

25. Besides evidence cited in *Sex and Reason,* see Green, note 3 above, at 63–84; LeVay, note 3 above; J. Michael Bailey et al., "Heritable Factors Influence Sexual Orientation in Women," 50 *Archives of General Psychiatry* 217 (1993) (and studies cited there); Dean H. Hamer et al., "A Linkage between DNA Markers on the X Chromosome and Male Sexual Orientation," 261 *Science* 321 (1993). For a good popular summary of the evidence, see Chandler Burr, "Homosexuality and Biology," *Atlantic Monthly,* March 1993, p. 47; and for a skeptical view of it, William Byrne and Bruce Parsons, "Human Sexual Orientation: The Biologic Theories Reappraised," 50 *Archives of General Psychiatry* 228 (1993), and Janet Halley, "Sexual Orientation and the Politics of Biology: A Critique of the Argument from Motibility," 46 *Stanford Law Review* 503 (1994). The evidence consists of studies of identical twins, comparisons of the brains of homosexual and heterosexual men who died from AIDS, the lack of any authenticated "cures" for homosexual preference, the fact that homosexual preference appears to be found in all human societies despite enormous differences in sexual mores and methods of child rearing, the existence of homosexuality in many animal species, the self-reported experience of homosexuals of having been aware of their sexual preference from the earliest period of their sexual awareness, and, most recently, indirect evidence that there is a gene predisposing to male homosexuality, transmitted through the maternal line. See Hamer et al., above. Each piece of evidence is contestable, but the cumulative force is great.

26. The political economy of the homosexual-rights movement raises fascinating issues, which I shall not discuss here. See Philipson and Posner, note 7 above, ch. 8, for some conjectures based on the economic theory of interest groups.

or fine wines. If they thought this, they would be playing into the hands of the religious right, which believes that homosexuality could be extirpated if potential homosexuals were prevented from engaging in homosexual behavior and thereby acquiring a taste for it, and could even be "cured" if society induced homosexuals to confine themselves to heterosexual behavior until they developed a taste for that. In support of this position a rabbi has argued that the fact that many homosexuals have dated or even had intercourse with women shows that homosexual preference is not biologically determined.[27] The idea that preferences follow behavior, Pavlov-fashion, is reminiscent of the argument that Hamlet makes to his mother—that if she refrains from sexual relations with her husband one night it will strengthen her will to refrain the next night, and the next, and eventually every night.

One could believe that sexual preference, even if not chosen, is unstable. Robin West confesses: "I am no clearer now than I was twenty years ago in what direction my sexual orientation lies . . . I have no idea whether I'm a 'Kinsey one' or a 'Kinsey three' or a 'Kinsey six.' I think the same is true of most of the people I know well, and I suspect that it is also true to some degree of most people I do not know well who are in some way 'like me' in class, age, and cultural awareness."[28] I am floored by this statement. A Kinsey six is a person with an *exclusively* homosexual orientation, and it is difficult to believe that over a period of twenty years of adulthood (for West was not a child twenty years ago) one could have "no idea" whether one was exclusively attracted to members of one's own sex or almost exclusively attracted to members of the opposite sex (a Kinsey one).

The central debate over the social construction of sexuality is not about the innateness or mutability[29] of *individual* sexual preference over the course of a lifetime, however. It is about the mutability of what one might have supposed to be strongly biologically determined, hence in a useful sense *fundamental,* human nature. A representative thesis

27. Dennis Prager, "Homosexuality, the Bible, and Us," *Public Interest,* Summer 1993, pp. 60, 73–75. Prager fails to distinguish between opportunistic and preference homosexuality, and refers to none of the biological evidence concerning the latter.

28. West, "Sex, Reason, and a Taste for the Absurd," 81 *Georgetown Law Journal* 2413, 2433 (1993) (footnote omitted). See also Janet E. Halley, "The Politics of the Closet: Towards Equal Protection for Gay, Lesbian, and Bisexual Identity," 36 *UCLA Law Review* 915, 934–946 (1989).

29. Not the same thing. A taste, once acquired, might be immutable; this is true of some addictions. It would not be an argument against preventive efforts.

of radical social constructionism, in which the influence of Foucault is palpable, is that homosexuality was invented in the nineteenth century by European psychiatrists, so that when we speak of the "homosexuality" of the ancient Athenians we are necessarily speaking of a different phenomenon from twentieth-century American homosexuality—further evidence being that the effeminacy that some believe to be a "natural" characteristic of homosexuality was not a feature of Greek homosexuality.[30]

If by "homosexuality" we mean not a particular class of preferences or a particular class of acts but a concept or definition prevailing in a particular society at a particular time, ancient Greek homosexuality is indeed a different phenomenon from modern American homosexuality. Greek homosexuality was dominated by the practice of pederasty by opportunistic homosexuals (that is, heterosexuals by preference), while American homosexuality is dominated by the practices of persons who have a strong homosexual preference. Effeminacy is associated with preference homosexuals rather than with opportunistic homosexuals; indeed it is likely to be consciously adopted as a signaling strategy by preference homosexuals who, especially in a society intolerant of homosexuality, may have difficulty identifying each other and may use the ambiguous signal of effeminacy to reduce sexual search costs without giving themselves away to the "straights." So it is not surprising that effeminacy is not associated in ancient Greek thought with homosexual behavior.

If any social constructionists believe that no men or women had strong preferences for same-sex over different-sex relations until the word "homosexuality" was coined in the second half of the nineteenth century,[31] they are putting the linguistic cart before the emotional horse. A person can have a feeling, an impulse, a desire, an aversion without being able to name it. Infants have feelings before they can speak, and animals have feelings; the second example is particularly pertinent given the considerable overlap between human and animal sexuality—given that we *are* animals. You can't have a desire for a pizza

30. David M. Halperin, "One Hundred Years of Homosexuality," in Halperin, *One Hundred Years of Homosexuality and Other Essays on Greek Love* 15 (1990).
31. Cf. id. at 30. For criticism of the radical constructionist view of homosexuality by a homosexual philosopher, see Richard D. Mohr, *Gay Ideas: Outing and Other Controversies,* ch. 7 (1992). Although I have used the term "radical constructionist" and would describe myself as a "moderate constructionist," it is common to equate social constructionism with radical constructionism, just as it is common to equate feminism with radical feminism.

before the pizza is invented, but you could be hungry before then.[32] Sexual orientation is more like hunger than it is like desire for an invented product like a pizza. If all—and it is not a little—that social constructionism is taken to entail is that the expression or concealment of homosexual preference in particular sexual practices and mannerisms, the geographic dispersion or concentration of homosexuals, the amount of homosexual behavior, and the culturally dominant concept of homosexuality are different across societies and epochs and that many societies lack a distinct concept of homosexual preference (for which the word "homosexuality" was coined) because the practice of homosexuality in those societies is dominated by heterosexuals, I agree against anyone who suggests that Plato and Freud were talking about the same thing when they discussed the sexual desire of males for males. In between these positions is Martha Nussbaum's suggestion that the social conditions in ancient Athens increased not only the demand for pederasty but also the desire for it.[33] In my analysis, sexual preference is a constant, and changes in social conditions alter behavior merely by changing the costs and benefits associated with different forms of sexual behavior. So scarcity of women might induce pederasty, or savage punishments for sodomy induce homosexuals to marry, without any effect on preference (disposition, inclination).

I similarly do not believe, as might a more convinced social constructionist, that the preference of Athenian bachelors for boys over each other reflected an inability, in a society in which heterosexual relations were relations between unequals (a dominant male and a subordinate female), to visualize sexual relations between equals, such as two adult males of the citizen class. If that were true, we would expect opportunistic male homosexuality to be less pederastic the more sexually egalitarian the society was. I do not believe that this pattern holds. So here is a case in which economic analysis and radical constructionism generate incompatible—and testable—hypotheses.

And not the only case. I believe that not only the gender of the preferred sexual partner, but also preferences for frequency of sexual intercourse and for variety in sexual partners, are largely innate rather than constructed. I am therefore skeptical that either discrimination

32. Cf. Hilary Putnam, *Renewing Philosophy* 111–114 (1992), pointing out that it is one thing to say that we made the Big Dipper, another to say that we made the stars.
33. Martha C. Nussbaum, "Constructing Love, Desire, and Care" (unpublished paper, Department of Philosophy, Brown University, 1993).

against homosexuals (including the refusal to recognize homosexual marriage) or patriarchal ideology is a major factor in the instability of male homosexual unions; for why then are lesbian unions more stable? Even noncompanionate marriage, with its "double standard" that reflects in part the different innate preferences of men and women, can be stable. A monogamous relationship between two men is much less likely to be, and this wholly apart from the absence of children, a traditional cement of marriage. When neither partner has a taste for monogamy, the relationship is likely to be ruptured by sexual jealousy. Or so at least I predict; for this is another area for fruitful empirical study. If the social constructionists are right, we should expect stable monogamous male homosexual relations in societies that are tolerant of homosexuality and are not dominated by the traditional "patriarchal" values.

My prediction depends on the belief that apart from sexual orientation, homosexual men are like other men, not like women. If they or some of them *are* like women—if as used to be believed homosexuals form a "third sex"—the prospects for durable monogamous relationships between homosexual men would be improved. But I doubt that any social constructionists will challenge my assumption that homosexual men are like other men other than in the preferred gender of their sexual partners, merely in order to save their optimism about homosexual monogamy. For it is fundamental to the constructionist project that all of us basically are alike, that socially significant differences seemingly attributable to the genes really are social constructs.

William Eskridge invokes Foucault to support a less radical version of the social construction of human sexuality than I have been considering so far, yet a version that Eskridge considers antithetical to pragmatism.[34] (So what better place to end this book?) I proposed in *Sex and Reason* that the ban on homosexuals in the military be relaxed rather than eliminated, and while urging that homosexuals be permitted to form domestic partnerships, I stopped short of advocating that homosexual marriage be recognized. My position strikes Eskridge as pragmatic in taking existing attitudes and institutions for granted as a baseline from which to make strictly incremental changes. A social constructionist perspective, he believes, would demonstrate the insta-

---

34. William N. Eskridge, Jr., "A Social Constructionist Critique of Posner's *Sex and Reason:* Steps toward a Gaylegal Agenda," 102 *Yale Law Journal* 333 (1990).

bility of the baseline—that there is nothing natural about hostility to homosexuals or about heterosexual marriage, that these are social constructs which will change as fast as society changes.

The suggestion that pragmatism and social constructionism are opposed is at first glance puzzling. Is not the rejection of traditional baselines the very essence of pragmatism, as Cass Sunstein never tires of stressing? Is it not the pragmatic project "to refloat the world, to make it less stationary and more transitional, to make descriptions of it correspondingly looser, less technical, more uncertain"?[35] What better description of social contructionism could be imagined?

The difference is this. Social constructionists, when they turn normative, tend to be Utopian. Sensing the fluidity of all social arrangements, they believe that a slight nudge might bring about a social revolution. Pragmatism does not entail incrementalism or encourage veneration of the status quo, but neither does it teach that the rejection of foundationalism entails a denial of the stubbornness of attitudes or the inertia of institutions. A pragmatic reformer is concerned with what works and therefore cannot ignore public opinion or political realities just because the things he wants to change are not rooted in nature but instead are "mere" social constructs. (So here is another example of the recurrent point that pragmatism provides few guides to concrete action.) I agree that hostility to homosexuals and limits on who may marry are social constructs, that they do not have the weight of nature or the moral law behind them. Hostility to homosexuals is not a feature of all human societies and therefore is unlikely to have a biological basis; and while heterosexual marriage is closely connected to human biology, the recognition of marriage between homosexuals would not violate any biological imperative. What the authors of the Bible thought about homosexuality is not likely to move the pragmatist, who sees nothing in principle to prevent the overthrow of established attitudes and institutions and knows plenty of cases in which fears of the consequences of radical changes—such changes as allowing religious or political freedom or dismantling the laws segregating the races or admitting women into the legal profession—proved to be unfounded.[36] But hostility to homosexuals in American society today is no less a brute fact for not having a credible biological or supernatural basis, and it is a fact that

35. Richard Poirier, *Poetry and Pragmatism* 40 (1992).
36. Recall from Chapter 10 James Fitzjames Stephen's ominous prophecy concerning the consequences of female emancipation.

any responsible policy maker must take into account in considering proposals for reform. It is not the case that attitudes that do not have a biological basis are always easy to change. We must not ride Blake and Emerson and Nietzsche to the conclusion that every feature of the social landscape is no stronger than the facades of a Potemkin village, no more stable than the turn of a kaleidoscope. Ethnic and religious hatred are examples of tenacious though irrational beliefs that the serious political reformer must treat as hard social facts though not accept as permanent realities; and they happen to be examples that hatred of homosexuals resembles. The immediate establishment by legal fiat of complete equality between homosexuals and heterosexuals may be as unrealistic in the contemporary American setting as complete racial and sexual equality would have been in 1850. Social constructionism has not abolished reality, pragmatically defined as the domain of the—temporarily—unalterable.

Credits · Index

Credits

Portions of the following articles are reprinted with the permission of the copyright holders: "Legal Scholarship Today," 45 *Stanford Law Review* 1647 (1993), and "Bork and Beethoven," 42 *Stanford Law Review* 1365 (1990), both copyrighted © by the Board of Trustees of the Leland Stanford Junior University; "The Deprofessionalization of Legal Teaching and Scholarship," 91 *Michigan Law Review* 1921 (1993), and "Medieval Iceland and Modern Scholarship," 90 *Michigan Law Review* 1495 (1992), both copyrighted by The Michigan Law Review Association; "Duncan Kennedy on Affirmative Action," 1990 *Duke Law Journal* 1155, copyrighted © by Duke Law Journal; "Legal Reasoning from the Top Down and from the Bottom Up: The Question of Unenumerated Constitutional Rights," 59 *University of Chicago Law Review* 433 (1992), and "Foreword," in James Fitzjames Stephen, *Liberty, Equality, Fraternity* 7 (1992), both copyrighted © by The University of Chicago; "Democracy and Dualism," *Transition*, summer 1992, p. 68, copyrighted © by Oxford University Press; "Democracy and Distrust Revisited," 77 *University of Virginia Law Review* 641 (1991), copyrighted © by Virginia Law Review Association; "Law as Politics: Horwitz on American Law, 1870–1960," 6 *Critical Review* 559 (1992), and "Richard Rorty's Politics," 7 *Critical Review* 1 (1993), both copyrighted © by the Center for Independent Thought; "Ms. Aristotle," 70 *University of Texas Law Review* 1013 (1992), copyrighted © by Texas Law Review Association; "The Radical Feminist Critique of Sex and Reason," 25 *Connecticut Law Review* 515 (1993), copyrighted © by the

Index